U.S. BATTLESHIPS

U.S. BATTLESHIPS

AN ILLUSTRATED DESIGN HISTORY

By Norman Friedman

Ship Plans by Alan Raven and A. D. Baker III

Naval Institute Press
Annapolis, Maryland

Copyright © 1985
by the United States Naval Institute
Annapolis, Maryland

All photographs are official U.S. Navy.

Library of Congress Cataloging in Publication Data

Friedman, Norman, 1946–
  U.S. battleships.

  Bibliography: p.
  Includes index.
  1. Battleships—United States.   I. Title.
V815.3.F74   1985   623.8′252′0973   85-13769
ISBN 0-87021-715-1

Printed in the United States of America on acid-free paper ⊗

10 9 8 7 6

Contents

Acknowledgments

This book could not have been written without the assistance of many friends over a period of about thirteen years. I particularly appreciate the assistance of Mildred Grissom, Kit Ryan, George Kerr, Philip Sims, and Charles Wiseman in helping me gain access to many BuShips files still under Navy control. Mrs. Lorna Anderson of Opnav located files of the former Ship Characteristics Board. Harry Schwartz, now retired, and Elaine Everly guided me through the former Navy files now in the National Archives; many others helped make available to me the wartime BuShips files at Suitland under National Archives auspices; the Navy-controlled files at the Federal Record Center; and the former C&R plan files now at Alexandria, Virginia. For assistance at the Naval Historical Center, I am grateful to Dr. Dean Allard and his staff, especially Cal Cavalcante, Gerri Judkins, Kathy Lloyd, and Martha Crowley. Mrs. S. M. Edwards of Navsea, now retired, provided many plans on microfilm.

Alan Raven and Arthur D. Baker III helped illustrate the text, and the latter doubled as technical editor, catching many errors and making valuable suggestions. He also provided many of the photographs.

Other good friends deserve thanks for generous assistance: Charles Haberlein, David Lyon, Norman Polmar, Larry Sowinski, Thomas Hone, Christopher Beilstein, Robert Sumrall, Wayne Arny III, and Christopher C. Wright. They supplied me with significant material from their own collections as well as invaluable comments and corrections. The errors remaining are, of course, my own responsibility.

Special thanks go to my wife, Rhea, for her supportive and inspirational presence.

Key to Battleship Drawings

ADM	Admiral's Cabin	GAS	Gasoline
ADS	Air Defense Station	GYRO	Gyro Room
AR	Auxiliary Room	HANG	Hangar
AUX CIC	Auxiliary CIC	HR	Handling Room
BLO	Battle Look-Out	IC	Interior Communications Room
BR	Boiler Room	LR	Loading Room
BRS	Battle Radio Station	MACH	Machinery (combined Engine and Boiler) Space
BULL	Bull Ring		
CAPT	Captain's Cabin	MAG	Magazine
CAT	Catapult	MR	Motor Room
CB	Crew Berthing	NAV	Navigating Bridge
CEN	Central (Fire Control) Station	OG	Officers' Galley
CG	Crew's Galley	PH	Pilot House
CH	Chart House	PLOT	Plotting Room
CM	Crew's Mess	PM	Powder Magazine
CONN	Conning Station	PR	Pump Room
CR	Control Room	RAD	Radio
CT	Conning Tower (or ship control section of conning tower)	RC	Radio Central
		RP	Radar Plot
DF	(Radio) Direction Finder	SC	Secondary Conn
DG	Diesel Generator	SLO	Surface Look-Out
EH	Engine Room Hatch	SR	Shell Room
ER	Engine Room	SSG	Ship Service Generators
EVAP	Evaporator	ST	Stores
FCS	Fire Control Station	TB	Trash Burner
FCT	Flag Conning Station (Tower)	TR	Torpedo Room
FLAG	Force Command Station	USR	Underwater Sound Room
FND	Foundary	VEG	Vegetable Stowage
FP	Flag Plot	VENT	Ventilating Trunk
FR	Flag Radio	WARD	Wardroom
FW	Fresh Water		

Note: In cross-sections, "lb" or pounds indicates plating thickness, where 40 lbs is 1 inch; this is weight per square foot.

U.S. BATTLESHIPS

Introduction

For more than half a century, the battleship was the primary instrument of sea power and was, therefore, the fundamental strategic weapon of such navies as those of the United States and Great Britain. It excited the kind of high-level interest that today is associated with strategic missiles; in 1904 and again in 1908 the president of the United States himself examined the plans for the new American battleships. The battleship was also a political symbol, the single most expensive weapon system of its time. That was why the agreements to limit battleship construction, signed in 1921, 1930, and 1936, seemed so significant at the time. It was also why the U.S. decision to resume battleship construction in 1937, and then to invoke the escalator clause in tonnage the following year, was so painful. A few years later the battleship was again attacked as a symbol, this time in the political struggle for the primacy of air power: thus the pejorative implication of "battleship admiral."

Battleships still retain their evocative power and considerable glamor. When the *New Jersey* was recommissioned, amid much debate, there was no lack of volunteers to man her. With their heavy guns, battleships are far more *visibly* powerful than the aircraft carriers and submarines which have eclipsed them. Visually, the *New Jersey* and her sister ships are surely the most elegant of all U.S. battleships and much more graceful than the aircraft carriers.

The battleship was unique among the warships of its day in that it balanced the greatest offensive power with an equivalent defensive power: the first rule of battleship design was that the ship be protected against fire up to the strength of her own guns. In theory, then, a battleship could sink any other type of ship, but only the guns of another battleship could usually sink her. Lesser warships, such as cruisers, might survive an encounter with battleships, but only by fleeing.

A single battleship had only limited value. It was more a national symbol than a military force. Effective sea power required an integrated combination of battleships and supporting warships, a *battle fleet* that trained and operated as a unit. For the United States, the development of such a fleet called for much more than the construction of a requisite number of modern battleships. The Navy had to change its system of deployments, from the dispersed "stations" of the nineteenth century to the concentrated fleets of the twentieth. In this sense, the creation of the U.S. battle fleet was the beginning of the modern, global, U.S. Navy. In turn, the concentration of the sixteen active battleships into President Theodore Roosevelt's Great White Fleet was the culmination of a naval revival that had its origins in the U.S. steel cruisers first built nearly a century ago.

The battle fleet was the basis of Captain Alfred Thayer Mahan's concept of sea power through command of the sea. The dominant battle fleet could sweep any enemy fleet from the sea, and by so doing it could protect friendly shipping. Although an enemy might try to slip commerce raiders out onto the ocean, the battle fleet blockading his coast would surely catch most of them. Given its shielding strength against enemy battleships, much weaker but more numerous convoy escorts could protect seaborne trade against the necessarily flimsier raiders. Similarly, any power faced with seaborne attack would find it easier, and ultimately less expensive, to deal with that attack at its source rather than to build up defenses all along its coast. That reasoning underlay the initial U.S. decision, made in 1889, to build a battle fleet.

Both heavy guns and protection were extremely costly, increasingly so as the guns grew in size and power. Smaller navies gradually abandoned their hopes of maintaining battle fleets through the latter years of the nineteenth century and the early years of the twentieth and, instead, turned their efforts to buying equalizers—relatively inexpensive weapons that could be carried by inexpensive craft yet capable of sinking the most powerful battleship. Much the same hope underlies the vogue for fast missile-firing attack boats in Third World navies today.

The battleship at the peak of its development. The graceful newly completed USS *Missouri* lies at anchor, 1944. At this writing, she is being refitted for service which may last out the remainder of this century. Note the long narrow bow, characteristic of the four *Iowas*, the fastest U.S. battleships.

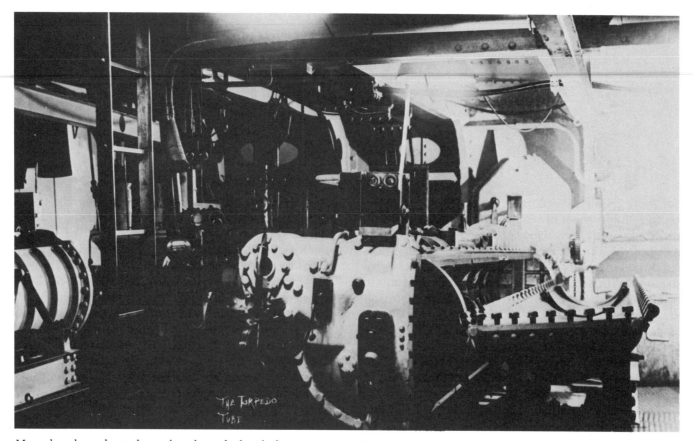

THE TORPEDO
TUBE

Most dreadnought and pre-dreadnought battleships were armed with torpedo tubes as well as with guns. In dry dock on 9 October 1916, the *Florida* (*facing page*) shows the bar that guided torpedoes as they emerged from her hull (it is the girder, with circular holes cut in it, protruding from her side below the line of workmen on scaffolds). The bar supported the torpedo as it emerged. Otherwise the passing stream of water would have broken it or knocked it off course. The above photograph shows a side-loading torpedo tube aboard the slightly earlier battleship *Delaware*, as it was photographed about 1918. Torpedoes were transported along the monorail above the tube and then lowered into it. Orders to the crew to fire were delivered through the speaking tube. It was generally conceded that torpedoes were an extremely effective weapon but that their underwater tubes were a hazard because they constituted weak points in systems of bulkheads protecting against underwater hits. For a time, therefore, U.S. designers and planners expected to move the tubes topside— where they presented a fire and explosion hazard. They were, therefore, omitted from the ships reconstructed in the interwar period.

The torpedo, the antiship missile of its day, was the major example of such an equalizer. Self-propelled, it at first demanded little of the platform launching it, yet its heavy warhead could open the bottom of a large ship. Much the same might be said of current antiship missiles, such as the French Exocet. Torpedoes were carried by battleships themselves, by coastal craft, by fleet destroyers, and later by aircraft. With the exception of battleships, all torpedo launchers were built in great numbers, and torpedoes sank battleships even before World War One. Yet the battleship did not die off. Its designers and operators had four countermeasures available.

First, through nearly all of the battleship era, heavy guns outranged the torpedo. That is why early torpedo-carrying destroyers were intended to attack only at night, when poor visibility would overcome the advantages of the gun. It is also why searchlights (for

torpedo defense) were so important in battleship design. Much of the impetus for longer battle ranges (which led in turn to the development of the all-big-gun ship) can be traced to a desire to keep ships out of torpedo range.

Second, the sheer size of the battleship made it possible for her designers to provide some measure of protection against underwater explosion, particularly after about 1905. Such armor always had its limits, but its existence forced up the size of torpedo warheads and thus the size of the torpedoes themselves and the size and cost of their carriers.

Third, battleship designers could provide weapons specifically intended to deal with torpedo-carrying craft. The more powerful the defensive weapons, the higher the price which could be exacted, and the less economical the apparently inexpensive torpedo became. The same logic applied both to anti-

10/9/16

destroyer guns and to antiaircraft guns. Fire control was a major issue: the better the fire control, the more effective the defensive battery. Before World War Two, the Royal Navy concluded that it had provided such heavy antiaircraft batteries that enemy aircraft would avoid dealing with its battleships. It was proven wrong when the *Repulse* and *Prince of Wales* were sunk off Malaya in 1941. Less than a year later, however, the new U.S. battleship *South Dakota* was able to beat off a heavier attack at Santa Cruz, thanks in large part to superior fire control.

Fourth, because of its sheer size, a battleship could generally outrun substantially smaller craft in any considerable sea. Well out to sea, then, battle fleets were largely immune to surface torpedo attack except when such attacks were part of gunnery actions. Prenuclear submarines did not complicate matters very much because they had only limited underwater mobility. Moving at higher speed on the surface, they could be detected by screening ships or aircraft and forced to dive—thereby losing their mobility. Maneuverability itself was a major form of protection, since the torpedo was not very much faster than its target.

Aircraft were the great and terrible exception to these rules. At first they could not carry weapons powerful enough to deal with sophisticated systems of underwater protection. Even during World War Two, only three modern battleships were sunk by aerial torpedoes: the British *Prince of Wales* and the Japanese *Yamato* and *Musashi*. In the latter two cases, bombers had to destroy large antiaircraft batteries before they could deliver coordinated torpedo attacks. Even at that, ten or more torpedoes were needed to sink a ship.

As for aircraft bombs, they generally would have had to be dropped from very high altitudes to achieve enough velocity to penetrate heavy deck armor. While they were falling, a maneuvering ship would easily evade them. The problem was really solved only when the Germans introduced guidance, the first battleship victim of guidance being the Italian *Roma*, in September 1943. Her sinking, much more than Pearl Harbor or the loss of the *Prince of Wales*, marks the end of the battleship era.

Perhaps more important, carrier aircraft could strike targets far inland, transforming the role of sea power itself. Although aircraft carriers were physically far more vulnerable than battleships, they could fight at greater ranges and could (in theory) evade any battleship long before it approached. Even so, there was a transitional period during which carriers were vulnerable to massive surface attack, as during the Battle off Samar in October 1944, when Japanese battleships and heavy cruisers came close to wiping out the American escort carriers covering the Leyte landings. American doctrine before and during World War Two envisaged a combination of fast carriers for long-range strikes and battleships to protect against surface attack by other battleships. The Japanese actually planned several such surface strikes but were unable to carry them out, and the fast battleships served more as heavy antiaircraft escorts.

The contrast between with the battleship and the aircraft carrier, in theory her successor, was dramatic. While a battleship could, it was thought, be sunk only by another battleship, a carrier could be disabled and sunk by another of her kind as well as by shellfire from cruisers or battleships. Carrier design was always characterized by attempts to mitigate great perceived vulnerabilities, far beyond anything the battleship designers encountered.* The enormous effort required to sink the Japanese super battleships *Yamato* and *Musashi* suggests, moreover, that single carriers were only marginally capable, even in 1945, of sinking battleships.† It is sometimes suggested that the abortive strike cruiser (CSGN) or the Soviet *Kirov* is a functional successor to the battleship because each emphasizes antiship firepower. Battleships, however, combined offensive firepower with defensive protection. The strike cruiser, though, was not even as well protected as a World War Two heavy cruiser. It could not possibly expect to absorb a single major-calibre (for example, a Soviet cruise missile) hit without serious dislocation. Battleships were designed to survive numerous hits by the most powerful projectiles of their time, major-calibre shells.

For the United States, the decision to build battleships marked a radical shift in naval strategy and, indeed, in the national attitude toward the role of naval forces. At the beginning of the modern U.S. fleet in 1883, U.S. naval thinking had three distinct focal points. First, the major potential enemy, Britain (or, perhaps, some other Continental power), in some new version of the War of 1812, might seek to seize territory in the New World or to subjugate the United States by attacking coastal cities. Second, the United States tended to consider itself the master of the New World, even though several South American navies were more powerful than her own. The position of Spain in Cuba combined both the first and second concerns. Finally, the United States had important interests throughout the world, and naval forces were needed to show the flag and to promote

---

* See this author's *Carrier Air Power* (Greenwich, England: Conway Maritime Press, 1981) and *U.S. Aircraft Carriers: An Illustrated Design History* (Annapolis, Md.: U.S. Naval Institute Press, 1983) for examples.

† As late as the 1950s, the Royal Navy considered air attacks on modern Soviet cruisers difficult in the absence of specialized antiship stand-off weapons. This attitude explains British interest in new battleship designs as late as 1945. The U.S. Navy, blessed with larger numbers of new battleships, had no need for further construction but even so expected to complete the suspended *Kentucky* as a special antiaircraft screening ship.

commerce. The Perry expedition to Japan in 1853, and the Korean expedition of 1871 fall in this category. This latter mission required cruisers (steam sloops and frigates) rather than capital ships. Although the United States had built a few sailing line-of-battle ships before the Civil War, until almost the turn of the present century she spent most of her naval money on what would today be considered cruisers.*

Battleships began as ironclads or armored ships in the period just after the Crimean War. The United States built some of the earliest ones, such as the revolutionary *Monitor*, and the Civil War saw the first instance of ironclad-on-ironclad combat. Apart from the armored frigate *New Ironsides*, however, the Civil War ironclads were riverine or coastal craft. The oceangoing ships of the large Civil War building program were cruisers intended to hunt down Confederate commerce raiders. As is common after wartime mobilizations, the products of mobilization determined the direction of postwar operatons. Such products were primarily cruisers, both in service and under construction. Several oceangoing monitors had also been laid down, but only one, the USS *Dictator*, was completed during the Civil War and work on five others ceased soon afterwards, primarily because they were irrelevant to U.S. naval requirements as they were then understood. The other monitors were coastal or riverine craft and could only be considered defensive in any war with European or South American powers.

The naval strategy for a war with England combined coast defense (by forts and by monitors of Civil War type) with cruiser warfare against British commerce, as in 1812. When seagoing armored ships were advocated, they were conceived as a seaward extension of the coast-defense system or as a counterweight to the growing strength of the South American navies. Even after the United States almost came to blows with Spain in 1873, over the seizure of the gun-running steamer *Virginius* and the execution of most of her crew, there was no attempt to build oceangoing ironclads. Instead, a few cruisers and five coast-defense monitors were authorized, the latter (for political reasons) as "reconstructions" of existing craft.

The naval revival that began about a century ago initially envisaged the construction of a new and more efficient fleet of commerce-raiding cruisers; through 1889 most of the ships authorized were of that type. Congress believed that proponents of a battle fleet were also proponents of an outward-looking foreign policy and that the decision to build even a few capital ships would carry immense implications. Cap-tain Alfred Thayer Mahan's achievement was to change this mindset. He convinced Secretary of the Navy Benjamin Tracy that the surest means of coast defense was the destruction of the enemy's fleet, as far away as possible, to seize control of the sea and thus to deny the enemy the highway it represented, which alone was the means of assaulting the New World. This forward strategy has been implicit in U.S. thinking ever since. Tracy convened a Policy Board in July 1889, apparently with the express purpose of reaching such a conclusion, and proposed the creation of a large battle fleet in his annual report to the Congress that November.

The Policy Board report was initially derided, but from 1890 onwards an oceangoing battle fleet was steadily built up. Seizure of the Philippines, Hawaii, and Puerto Rico in 1898 made the United States a global power. The new responsibilities imposed by the possessions justified large naval programs. There were so many battleships in 1906, in fact, that under President Theodore Roosevelt the United States had the second largest (and perhaps the most modern) battle fleet in the world. With the appearance of the all-big-gun (dreadnought) battleship, however, it became obsolete, and Congress only reluctantly provided further new ships. As a result, the United States fell to third place by 1914, after Britain and Germany. Even at that, progress had been remarkable— in only three decades, the U.S. Navy moved up from a position below that of Peru to near the very top.

As a disciple of Mahan, President Roosevelt wanted naval power, not merely numbers of ships on scattered foreign stations. Power necessitated a concentrated battle fleet to deal with a number of distant potential enemies. This concentration defined U.S. naval strategy through 1941. The two main war scenarios were seizure of the Phillipines by Japan and a descent on the New World by Germany. In neither case would the U.S. fleet begin the war anywhere near the ultimate battle area. For example, the German attack was predicted to begin with the seizure of a base in Central America or farther south. The U.S. fleet would have to steam several thousand miles to meet its adversary. Its steaming endurance and reliability, then, would be critical. These considerations explain, for example, why the U.S. Navy hesitated before adopting steam turbines (which were relatively uneconomical in fuel) for its battleships. Later, the need for very long range was a major factor in the U.S. adoption of high-pressure, high-temperature steam machinery.

After World War One, the Pacific strategy was further complicated by Japanese control (through League of Nations mandates) of the chains of Pacific islands formerly owned by Imperial Germany. Steaming through them en route to the western Pacific, the U.S. fleet would be subject to attack by Japanese

---

* See this author's *U.S. Cruisers: An Illustrated Design History* (Annapolis, Md.: U.S. Naval Institute Press, 1984) for the evolution of the "New Navy" cruisers.

submarines and naval aircraft. Its survival would depend, in large measure, on underwater armor—which in turn could be provided only in proportion to total ship size. That in turn was limited by treaty from 1922 onwards. When Britain proposed further reductions in battleship size, U.S. negotiators vetoed them on the ground that torpedoes and bombs, the weapons the fleet would face in the Mandates, would not (indeed, could not) be limited.

The political decision to build a U.S. battle fleet raised the question of ultimate fleet size: which foreign navy would the United States have to match? Great Britain was the traditional prospective enemy (and indeed the subject of one of the earliest war plans of the New Navy), but her fleet was so large that no early advocate of U.S. naval revival could imagine matching it. Congress would have shrunk from the expense involved. Even so, the 1889 long-term plan envisaged a fleet second only to that of Britain—which was one reason why it was derided. By 1897 Theodore Roosevelt, who was then assistant secretary of the navy, was calling for parity with Germany, which he described as a rising power quite capable of seeking colonies in the New World. The post–Spanish-American War long-range fleet plans appear to have been predicated on the German navy laws for fleet expansion.

Only during World War One did the General Board, the senior naval council, espouse parity with the leading naval power, Great Britain. The board argued that the next war would be the inevitable result of competition for world markets and that the United States alone would have to face the victor in Europe. Remarkably, its analysis, carried out after the bloodletting of 1914–15, denied the possibility that all of the combatants would be exhausted. The doctrine of parity survived U.S. entry into the war in 1917, and it was achieved as a result of the Washington Naval Arms Conference of 1921. The Washington Treaty set the ratio of capital ship tonnage between Britain, the United States, and Japan as 5:5:3. From then until 1936, the size of the U.S. battle fleet was set, not by strategy, but by treaty.

Perhaps the most striking feature of U.S. battleship development was the paucity of actual experience, particularly in combat, upon which so massive an investment was made. Between the end of the Civil War in 1865 and the decision to resume battleship construction in 1886, naval technology evolved radically, as indeed it continued to do for another twenty years. The only available real-life testing occurred in a series of minor naval wars in what would now be called the Third World. Although every major navy conducted extensive proving-ground tests of guns and armor, critical factors such as fire control appear to have been neglected almost until the turn of the century. Moreover, major experiments to ascertain the effect of shellfire on real ships were conducted only during the first decade of this century. The Royal Navy, which conducted such experiments at much the same time as the U.S. Navy, derived radically different lessons, so that constructors in the two countries, drawing on much the same technology, produced very different ships. U.S. files reveal little comprehension of British reasoning in this regard.

Moreover, when ships did enter battle, their fates were generally determined by details that would never have been considered in their designs. For example, the Royal Navy appears to have lost three battle cruisers at Jutland not because their armor was too thin (weight having been traded for speed), but because their flash-protection (which consumed virtually no weight) was defective. There is also evidence that their powder was extremely unstable. Similarly, the U.S. battleship *Arizona* appears to have been lost because a small black powder magazine (containing catapult charges) exploded, touching off her forward magazines. Survivability analysis would not have touched on such minute details.

This bears on any comparison between designs, either within the United States or between the United States and foreign designs. So few U.S. battleships experienced major battle damage that virtually none of the designs can be described as combat-tested. Typically judgment of the merit of a ship is based on her seagoing performance or upon the reliability of her power plant. Both are clearly important, but, particularly in the case of a battleship, they can hardly tell anything approaching the full story. Even in terms of firepower, much depended on fire control, which again is hardly the province of the overall designer of the ship.

In his extensive studies of British capital ships, Dr. Jon Sumida discovered that a small fire control computer, the Pollen (Argo) "clock," enormously improved the hitting ability of several British World War One capital ships. Dr. Sumida believes that much of the fire control failure at Jutland can be explained as a failure of the Dreyer "table," a simple computer chosen instead of the Argo clock. The U.S. Navy adopted a Pollen-like system, the Ford clock, in 1916. Its success in very long-range fire control, particularly in the decade after World War One, had profound effects both on tactics and on ship design. In fact, it now appears that battleship and cruiser torpedo tubes were abandoned by the U.S. Navy because of a rising faith in long-range fire. Even so, it is important to be aware that such fire control considerations usually entered only obliquely into the overall design of the ships.

This situation bears comparison with that which has obtained since 1945. Again, technology has evolved very rapidly, and, again, there is little operational experience. Small wars such as that in the Falklands thus gain enormous significance, probably out of all proportion to the nature of the lessons learned. Again, too, there is very little real understanding of the effects of naval weapons and very little interest in the reasoning adopted by rival naval constructors. Finally, little attention is paid to combat systems, as compared with weapons and their launchers, in evaluations of alternative designs and in ship-to-ship assessments. In some ways the situation is even worse than it was during the battleship era, in that little note seems to be taken of the clear arcs and commands of the various radars, whereas the height (hence the optical range) of range-finders and directors was an important issue in battleship design.

Previous books in this series have described the U.S. design organization in some detail; the notes which follow will, therefore, be brief. Throughout the period of U.S. battleship design, the Navy was divided into a seagoing (line) organization and a shore establishment. The latter consisted of a number of independent bureaus, each responsible only to the civilian secretary of the navy. Until 1915 there was no statutory senior naval officer. All operational orders were, at least in theory, signed by the secretary of the navy, following the American tradition of civilian control over the military. Thus the two primary organizational issues for the U.S. Navy were the coordination of the bureaus and the gradual increase in the power of the professional officer corps, culminating in the current extremely powerful Office of the Chief of Naval Operations (OpNav), which actually does control the successors of the old bureaus.

In 1883, at the dawn of the New Navy, the matériel bureaus were Construction and Repair (C&R), responsible for hull design; Steam Engineering (later Engineering, or BuEng), responsible for machinery; Ordnance (BuOrd), responsible for armor and weapons; and Equipment. The latter was abolished in 1909, its responsibilities split between C&R and BuEng. The role of the bureau can be seen in old ship structural weight breakdown listings, in which, before 1909, generators and other electrical systems were listed as equipment rather than as machinery (that is, a BuEng responsibility). In 1940 C&R and BuEng merged as the Bureau of Ships (BuShips). The standard structure of U.S. weight breakdowns also shows a division in responsibility for protective material, with BuOrd assigned heavy side armor and C&R relatively thin splinter plating and deck armor. There was also a Bureau of Navigation, responsible for personnel assignments and for the day-to-day operation of the navy. Within the bureau system, it represented the views of the seagoing side of the navy, and until 1912 its chief was the principal professional advisor to the secretary. Later it became the Bureau of Naval Personnel.

The recurring nightmare was that hulls would be designed with insufficient internal volume for their machinery or with insufficient space or weight to carry their designed batteries. To avoid such a situation, the secretary of the navy formed a Board on Construction, consisting of the bureau chiefs and the director of naval intelligence, in 1889. The minutes of its meetings show just how sharp the conflict between different ship characteristics could be. Even so, by about 1904 there was a widespread perception that the board did not reflect the views of the seagoing arm of the service. It was considered innately conservative; the technical bureaus generally tried to avoid major changes in design. Many believed that this conservatism was particularly evident in the controversy over construction of an all-big-gun (dreadnought) battleship.

The secretary of the navy convened a second board, the General Board, in 1900, as a result of the Spanish-American War. It descended directly from the Strategy Board, which had helped plan wartime operations. Although the board was initially concerned primarily with war planning, inevitably it was drawn into questions of fleet composition and thus of warship characteristics. The great reform of 1908, following the Newport Conference (see Chapter 4), was the elimination of the Board on Construction and the assignment to the General Board of future ship characteristics. In effect, the board coordinated the bureaus by reviewing the sketch designs which C&R produced. The *Nevada* was the first major General Board product; the *Iowa* fiasco of 1938 (see Chapter 13) illustrated its inability to enforce day-to-day coordination. In theory, from 1908 to beyond the end of U.S. battleship construction, the General Board, which consisted of senior admirals, was the principal source of advice on ship characteristics.

That this was advice, not determination, was very significant; the civilian secretary of the navy had the final say. From 1913 onwards, for example, Secretary Josephus Daniels resisted the board's attempt to increase the size of U.S. battleships. The chief of naval operations served as acting secretary in the absence of the secretary of the navy. That was particularly important during the Roosevelt Administration, when the secretary was frequently incapacitated, and it explains the fate of the *North Carolina* design (see Chapter 11). In a more general sense, from the end of World War One on, the General Board and the chief of naval operations competed for control of ship design. The CNO ultimately won, but only after the end of the U.S. era of battleship design, that is, in 1941.

The following account concentrates on one phase of battleship design—Preliminary Design, during which the overall configuration of the ship is chosen. In U.S. practice, during most of the period under review, ships were designed in three phases: Preliminary, Contract, and Detail. Preliminary Design was carried out by a specialist group within the Bureau

The battleship *West Virginia* (*above and facing*), the last U.S. battleship of the dreadnought era, is shown under refit at Puget Sound Navy Yard, 21 August 1933. The small circular platforms on her foremast had been erected for her Mark 19 antiaircraft directors, which were connected to the unusual antiaircraft range-finder shown. This range-finder could be turned both vertically and horizontally. The Mark 19s had previously been mounted at a lower level. During this refit 12-foot armored range-finders were mounted in their previous locations, to serve the secondary battery. Note the wire connecting the Mark 19 to the 12-foot armored range-finder one level down. About 1940, Mark 19s in the fleet were enclosed in small armored boxes and provided with stereoscopic range-finders. It is these enclosed directors that appear in photographs of the battleships at Pearl Harbor. Note also the wiring connecting the roof of the 20-foot range-finder atop the pilot house to the foremast itself, with its range "clock" (concentration dial), for communicating the range to other ships. A similar clock was mounted on the mainmast. Both could be rotated so that they could be visible to ships not exactly in line ahead. The structure atop each mast contained, from top to bottom, the main battery director, the main battery spotters and fire controls, and a pair of secondary battery directors, which obtained their ranges from the small armored range-finder below the Mark 19 platform. By this time part of the signal platform, below the navigating bridge, had been enclosed and the platform itself extended to provide space for machine guns forward of the conning tower. As a result, although a searchlight was mounted on this level, the 12-foot flag range-finder formerly there had to be removed. Another machine gun was mounted atop this enclosed space, which included the navigator's chart house. The chart house under the pilot house became the flag plot. The emergency level below consisted largely of the two massive vertical vents and passageways, with captain's and admiral's emergency cabins in its forward part. The object split off from the forward face of the signal bridge is another 0.50-calibre machine gun. Visible on the bridge wing are a pelorus, a small signaling light, and a 24-inch signaling searchlight, with the flag lockers at the rear. Note also the roof of the conning tower, with its array of periscopes. Internally, the front of the conning tower was allocated for ship control. The rear half was an armored fire control tower, served by special spotting glasses. At the time of this photograph, U.S. battleships were just being fitted with eight 0.50-calibre water-cooled machine guns each, as an antistrafing measure. Note the large *E*s, for engineering and presumably for tactical excellence, on the ship's after funnel and on the signal bridge side abeam the machine guns, and the ship's number (48) atop her No. 2 turret, in white.

of Construction and Repair (from 1940, the Bureau of Ships). Its product was generally termed a "Spring Style" by analogy with the spring line of women's fashions. This sketch design was approved by the General Board and the secretary of the navy. Then a much more elaborate Contract Design was developed from it. Major changes were possible at this stage, although generally the tenor of the Preliminary Design survived. Shipyards bid on the basis of the contract plans, and it was their responsibility to

develop them further into working drawings, from which the ships were actually built. Typically a lead yard was selected to prepare working drawings for an entire class. In a few cases, the yards made important changes, as in the machinery and underwater protection of the *Iowa* class and in the hull form of the *Cleveland*-class light cruisers.

One peculiarity of the bureau system was that, although contract plans were quite detailed, the machinery spaces were left blank. That was the responsibility, until 1940, of the Bureau of Engineering and its contractors. Gibbs & Cox, for example, became famous as the machinery designer for destroyers.

Battleships were generally denoted by the *fiscal year* (FY) of their authorization. During the battleship era the U.S. fiscal year ran from 1 July of the previous *calendar year* to 30 June of the next year, for example, fiscal 1911 ran from 1 July 1910 through 30 June 1911. Battleship 1939 was the FY39 battleship, the *South Dakota*.

Some technical notes are in order. First, much more than most warship types, battleships were *weight-critical*, in that key components—guns and armor—were extremely dense. By way of contrast, modern designers generally find their ships *volume-critical*: their hulls can easily carry the necessary weights, but finding space for essential components is more difficult. Weight estimates were the first stage of battleship design, and breakdowns of the weights of hull, armor, armament, and so forth have been given in the text wherever possible. Compared on a class-by-class basis, they give a fair approximation of the alternative trade-offs available to the designer. Very approximately, 60 percent of the design (normal) displacement of a battleship could be divided among armor (including decks), weapons, and machinery.

Weight issues were particularly important during the treaty period, when displacements were set by international agreement. Designers had to use every available ton without risking overweight, and the reader will note the attention lavished on attempts to save as little as a fraction of 1 percent during the early design period of a ship. Such figures were almost irrelevant, given the random over- and underweights of actual construction. Their prominence came from the fact that absolute displacement limits had been set.*

In the weight tables, the "hull weight" includes not merely hull structure but also the weight of protective decks. Wherever possible, deck weights are given separately, and "bare hull" denotes hull weights excluding decks and bulkheads for torpedo protection. Hull weights also include miscellaneous splinter protection (thin armor), which could be extensive. The "protection" weight grouping includes not only side armor but also the weights of barbettes *and turrets*, both of which could be substantial. Thus the listing for battery includes only the guns and their mountings. These weight groupings *do not* correspond to those used by other navies, such as the Royal Navy, and direct comparison between U.S. and foreign designs is, therefore, difficult.

Perhaps the most striking feature of these tables is the steady growth of deck protection, as reflected in hull weight and in the declining percentage of displacement devoted to "protection," that is, to vertical armor. Since vertical armor defined *minimum* battle range whereas deck armor defined a *maximum* battle range, this evolution corresponded in part to increases in expected effective gunnery range. Also, machinery weights (at least after 1909) included electric plant weight, which increased rapidly during the immediate pre–World War Two period.

The design, or normal, displacement of a ship could be defined in various ways, depending on the fractions of the full capacity of "variable loads" such as fuel and ammunition counted in the design figure. The choice of artificially low fractions would make the ship appear to be relatively small, which might be attractive for political reasons. Since the design displacement was also the displacement at which the ship ran her trials, artificially low figures might make for better trial speed performance and, therefore, for bonuses for the builders. On the other hand, the location of belt armor and the designed freeboard were both predicated on the design waterline and thus on the designed displacement and draft. Here artificiality in design might equate to poor seakeeping and insufficient protection in reality. That was exactly the problem with the *Indiana* class, the first true oceangoing U.S. battleships, whose nominal coal supply was only 400 tons but which rarely operated with less than 1,200 on board.

Prior to the Newport Conference (1907) the standard for the U.S. Navy was two-thirds fuel, reserve feed water, stores, and ammunition. After the conference, the ammunition figure was increased to full load. Early in World War Two, the fuel and stores figures were again increased, to full load, a change which in itself accounts for part of the growth in U.S. displacements at this time. Even the standard displacement carefully defined at Washington in 1922 was subject to considerable variation (see especially Chapters 12 and 13, on the U.S. treaty battleships).†

Note that plating thicknesses were often specified in pounds rather than inches. This measurement was based on the weight of a square foot of plating, at

---

* This is still a problem—from time to time ships are built under displacement limits chosen to hold down cost. The *Perry*-class frigate is a recent example. One naval architect commented that the *actual* displacement of a ship varies by several percentage points as she moves through waves, so that such absolute limits have little meaning. A carefully developed paper-saving of one or two percent vanishes in the noise.

† For some comparisons with foreign practice, see this author's *Battleship Design and Development, 1905–1945* (Greenwich, England: Conway Maritime Press, 1978) and A. L. Raven and J. Roberts, *British Battleships of World War Two* (London: Arms and Armour Press, 1978). In the U.S. case, the adoption of torpedo-protection systems incorporating large empty (void) spaces further complicated matters, as in an emergency these spaces could be filled with fuel oil, for extra steaming range.

about 40 pounds to the inch, and was generally used for up to 5 or 6 inches.

Battleship armor had to protect five distinct targets: her waterline (that is, her buoyancy and stability); her vitals (machinery and magazines, typically below the waterline); her weapons; her hull structure supporting weapons and other stuctures; and controls (conning tower and fire controls). The nature of the threat against each target depended on developments in gun design and on effective battle range. For example, the danger to the waterline was numerous hits, causing flooding. On the other hand, a single penetrating hit in the vitals might be disabling or even (if in a magazine) totally destructive. Early battleships faced only slow-firing heavy guns, hence only small numbers of potentially dangerous hits. By the late 1890s, even relatively heavy guns fired rapidly, and ships faced numerous hits. As battle ranges increased from about 1905 onwards, however, the number of hits to be expected in battle decreased rapidly. For example, during World War One, five percent hitting was considered good shooting at 15,000 yards. Under such conditions the single devastating hit would be the major threat. Even so, the standard U.S. design criteria throughout the battleship era included protection of enough of the waterline so that a ship could survive riddling of her unprotected ends. By way of contrast, in the *Nelsons* the British took the position that belt, or waterline, armor was primarily protection against a few hits penetrating to the ship's vitals. In consequence, the British could save weight by using a short belt covering only the vitals rather than a belt that would cover a fixed percentage of the waterline itself.

Alternatively, a ship fighting at short range (as in night battles before the perfection of radar) might be disabled by large numbers of hits on her necessarily unarmored superstructure, as was the case with the Japanese battle cruiser *Hiei* in November 1942. Pre-dreadnoughts, which had to be able to fight at very short ranges, were protected against such hits, as were many of the World War One-era dreadnoughts. When ships were designed to fight at much longer ranges, however, plunging hits on decks became more and more important. Because they covered large areas, decks were extremely heavy per unit thickness, and they absorbed the weight previously available for light superstructure protection.

Battleships had to resist two very different types of shell, high explosive (HE) and armor piercing (AP). Early AP shells were practically solid, achieving their effect by smashing the internal structure of a ship. From about 1900 onwards, however, AP shells had a substantial explosive content, detonated by delayed action fuzes that functioned only after the shell passed through substantial armor; they would pass through light plating or light armor without bursting. Light armor could protect against the resulting fragments, or "splinters." The U.S. Navy used the characteristics of such shells in two ways. In its early dreadnoughts, thin armor was sometimes used to cause AP shells to burst before they could reach vital spaces; light splinter armor stopped the resulting fragments. In later "all or nothing" ships such as the *Nevada*, all available weight was devoted to the heaviest armor, on the theory that unarmored areas (such as the secondary battery) would be essentially immune.

By way of contrast, HE shells would burst approximately on contact and would destroy light plating. Medium armor, which would burst AP shells without stopping them, would resist HE. Much of the difference between British and U.S. dreadnought design practice was due to British concentration on resisting HE rather than AP rounds, reflecting experiments carried out early in this century.*

Armor design practice was based on expected battle ranges. Until about 1910, expected battle ranges were considerably less than 10,000 yards, and shell trajectories were very nearly horizontal; shells would strike the side of the ship, or they would hit the deck at a shallow grazing angle. Direct penetration of the deck armor, however thin, would be unlikely. Nor would shells strike underwater. Direct protection of the vitals, then, could be limited to a belt which would cover the area below the waterline likely to be uncovered by waves or by rolling and pitching. The deck, at or near the waterline, protected the vitals from splinters created as shells hit armor above the waterline or from debris created by the destruction of less heavily armored structures above the main belt.

With the *Nevada* class of 1911, much greater battle ranges were accepted. Shells might strike the deck at steep enough angles to penetrate it, and a separate splinter deck was provided beneath the armor deck to protect the vitals from resulting splinters. The deck itself was moved up to form, with the wider belt, an armored box protecting the vitals.†

Even the concept of protection changed. For many years, the criterion had been the *minimum* safe battle range at which the belt armor would defeat some standard shell (often the shell the ship fired). Deck armor defined a *maximum* range at which the ship

---

* See D.K. Brown, "Attack and Defense" Part 5, in *Warship* No. 33 (1985). The British fired large HE-filled (lyddite) shells at the old ironclad *Belleisle* and were much impressed by the combination of heavy smoke (blinding gun-layers), smashing effect (on unarmored parts of the ship), and small splinters, which traveled great distances to cut vital cables. They believed that similar damage had been decisive in The Russo-Japanese War. British practice in combat was to use lyddite or common (HE) shell at ranges at which AP would not be expected to penetrate.

†Again, the British view was that too many "vital services" of the ship would be vulnerable to HE attack, that the big shells, even in small numbers, would flood the ends of the ship.

would be protected: at greater ranges, shells fell more steeply and therefore penetrated a greater and greater thickness of armor. This outer range limit had been academic for many years, but it became more and more realistic as fire control improved. BuOrd argued that the only reasonable description of protection was the *immune zone* defined by the belt and deck performance (inner and outer edges). The General Board accepted it as the standard for new ship characteristics in 1929, in connection with the *New Orleans*-class heavy cruisers. Given an immune zone of fixed total width, for example, it was possible to measure the tonnage effects of moving the whole zone in or out.

U.S. battleship development coincided with three revolutions in naval gunnery: the rapid-firing (RF, or, in foreign parlance, QF) medium-calibre gun; the faster-firing, medium-range heavy gun; and truly long-range heavy gunnery.

Where the heavy guns of the late 1880s and 1890s fired once every few minutes, RF weapons of about 5- or 6- inch calibre could, it was claimed, fire up to ten or twelve HE rounds per minute. At first RF performance appeared to be achievable only through the use of brass cartridge cases, which at the time were a considerable industrial achievement. Once the virtues of rapid fire had been appreciated, however, earlier slow-firing weapons, which carried their powder in bags, were modified for much faster rates of fire. Moreover, with the development of smokeless powder, heavy guns could fire much more rapidly. Unlike previous powders, smokeless guns left no residue in the barrel, which required clearing after each round. In 1897, for example, the average U.S. 13-inch gun required 320 seconds, over five minutes, between rounds; a decade later, the standard interval was 40 seconds. Similar results obtained for the lighter weapons: the 6 inch of 1897 fired once every 90 seconds, compared with once every 8.2 seconds in 1907. This improvement overshadowed the difference in rate of fire, which had been so important, between "bag" and fixed-ammunition guns, as the interval for fixed-ammunition RF 6 inch was 7.9 seconds in 1907. In 1897 it had been 40, with something closer to 10 promised by BuOrd.

Smokeless powder also made for higher velocities and hence flatter trajectories and greater accuracy at long range. Gunnery experts such as Admiral William S. Sims in the United States began to achieve high hitting rates at ranges beyond the effective reach of the lighter weapons, 6,000 to 10,000 yards. At long ranges the 6-inch RF guns were ineffective, and clearly the time would come when the 8 inch would also lose its value. Hence the radical shift to all-big-guns. For the United States it was an ironic one; the great wave of U.S. pre-dreadnought construction, between 1901 and 1907, coincided with the series of gunnery advances that made these ships obsolete.

The *Texas* and *Maine* were designed in 1886, just before the advent of medium-calibre RF guns. They were, therefore, designed with limited areas of extremely heavy armor, to resist relatively small numbers of heavy-calibre hits. By way of contrast, large volumes of medium-calibre HE fire could smash the unprotected upper works of these ships, threatening the foundations of their protected guns. Although HE fire could not sink a ship, it could certainly disable one. The designs proposed in 1889 by the Policy Board (see Chapter 1) provided protection against this threat. The obvious solution was to spread medium armor over the sides of ships, at the cost of increased total armor weight, hence an increase in the size (and cost) of ships. This increase was mitigated by a drastic improvement in armor quality, which reduced the thickness (hence weight) of main belt armor.

Although AP shells would penetrate the new medium armor, they would have only a local effect. Without armor, HE shells would smash large areas of plating; with even relatively thin armor, their explosions would be negated. Typically medium armor was applied as an upper belt, which protected the structural integrity of the ship and its seaworthiness. A thin flat deck at the waterline separated it from the lower belt, with its very different function. A variation on this system employed a deck sloping down at the sides to the *lower* rather than the *upper* edge of the main belt. Shells penetrating the main belt had to pass through the deck slope as well. On the other hand, flooding in the volume between deck slope and belt might cause serious loss of buoyancy and stability, which could be averted by subdivision and by filling this space with water-excluding material. In many ships light armor was extended to the ends of the ship to protect buoyancy, stability, and freeboard.

The RF battery itself presented a good target for RF fire. Prior to the development of such weapons, the battery of medium-calibre guns, if it was mounted at all, could be considered essentially immune to heavy shellfire. The low rate of fire of the heavy guns guaranteed that their shots would not be wasted on a secondary battery, in which any single hit might, at best, disable only one of many guns—indeed, in which a single hit might well pass through without hitting any of the guns. With the advent of RF guns in large numbers, however, "casemate" armor had to be spread over them.

The mixed-calibre battleship designs of the turn of the century were quite logical, given slowly firing heavy guns whose limited accuracy demanded short battle ranges, RF guns that fired HE shells, and machine guns and machine cannon that were effective at the then-prevailing short battle ranges. The heaviest guns would try for hits of individually devastating effect on belt or on main battery. The lighter weapons would attack area targets, those less well-protected areas vulnerable only to great numbers of hits. As heavy guns became more efficient, navies introduced a third element, a semi-heavy gun (8 inch in U.S. practice) intended to defeat the thickened side armor which had itself been introduced to counter 6-inch RF fire.

About the turn of the century the heaviest shells changed character. Where formerly armor-piercing shells had carried no explosive charge, after 1902 U.S. AP shells were designed to penetrate heavy armor and *then* burst. The thin upper belts provided against light high-explosive shells would, then, tend to *cause* bursts rather than shield against them.

Much of the extension of armor areas would have been impractical had it not been for radical improvements in armor material itself. In the 1880s side armor was usually a compound—mild steel bonded to a wrought iron back. The steel face would break up projectiles. Any that penetrated were stopped by the wrought iron backing, which absorbed the energy of the projectile by yielding under stress. Later the wrought iron was replaced by mild steel, with each layer assigned a figure of merit of about 0.6.* Nickel steel, introduced about 1889, had a figure of merit of about 0.67 and was the first modern steel alloy armor. It remained in use for relatively thin deck armor after it had been replaced for vertical plating. Modern armor—Harvey nickel steel and then Krupp Cemented—appeared about 1893. It had a revolutionary impact, since its figure of merit might vary from 0.9 to 1.2. These steels were face-hardened, to break up projectiles striking them.

All of these steels had about the same density, each square foot of 1-inch thick plate weighing about 40 pounds. Every improvement, then, translated directly into a saving in weight. For example, 10 inches of the mild steel that protected the *Texas* was equivalent to only 6 inches of Harvey or Krupp plate used about 1900; for every 10 tons of armor in the earlier ship, a similar ship built a decade later would require only 6 tons.

The second gunnery revolution was the advent of the all-big-gun ship, which would fight at 6,000 to 10,000 yards, where only 12- or 14-inch guns would be effective. There was no longer much point in defending against medium-calibre weapons. Trajectories, however, were still flat. The U.S. solution was to thicken the upper armor belt, so that, like the main belt, it woud resist heavy shells. Any shells that penetrated would burst above the watertight, splinterproof deck at the waterline. Thick armor could not

be placed higher in the ship, as it would entail too much topweight. To protect the uptakes and the secondary (antidestroyer) guns, then, the designers used a combination of thin "casemate" armor on the side and splinter protection inboard.

The second revolution lasted only a few years. When practicable battle ranges exceeded about 10,000 yards, plunging shellfire had to be taken into account. This was the origin of the *Nevada* armor design (see Chapter 5), in which medium armor was abandoned altogether, providing sufficient weight for a heavy protective deck and also for a much thicker belt.

The only later major development was the use of armor patches to protect against underwater hits, which were a growing concern. At the longer ranges attainable by the 1920s, shells would often strike the water short, at angles so steep that the shells would keep travelling underwater and hit the ship well below the waterline. Special armor patches were applied to the *North Carolina* to resist such hits, and the armor designs of the *South Dakota*, *Iowa*, and *Montana* clases were all designed to resist underwater shell hits. Apparently unknown to the U.S. designers, the Japanese actually designed their shells to follow stable underwater trajectories, with special long-delay fuzes (see the account of damage to the *South Dakota* in Chapter 12).

The gunnery revolutions corresponded to the major divisions in battleship design from pre-dreadnought to dreadnought to super- or post-dreadnoughts. The term is derived from the revolutionary HMS *Dreadnought* of 1906, the first all-big-gun ship. Pre-dreadnoughts were generally armed with a mixture of weapons, including four (in a very few ships, six) heavy guns. For example, U.S. pre-dreadnoughts of the *Connecticut* class were armed with four 12-inch guns as well as eight 8 inch, twelve 7 inch, and twenty 3 inch, plus machine guns. The 8-inch and 7-inch guns *as well as* the 12 inch were intended to attack other battleships. They formed a secondary battery. The 3-inch guns, on the other hand, were intended to defend the ship against torpedo attack by destroyers and torpedo boats.

The concept behind the all-big-gun ship was to sweep away the secondary battery, leaving a ship only with the heaviest guns (to deal with other battleships) and with antidestroyer (then called "antitorpedo") weapons. These latter were soon termed a secondary battery, and their calibre increased as destroyers became larger and as their torpedoes gained range. At first all dreadnoughts were armed with 11- or 12-inch main battery guns. When calibres increased, to 13.5 inches in the Royal Navy and 14 inches in the U.S. and Japanese navies, the ships were termed "super-dreadnoughts." Similarly, ships designed for longer-range battle—beyond about 10,000 yards and hence with increased deck armor— were distinguished from the original dreadnoughts

---

* This figure compares the stopping power of the armor with that of a plate of modern Krupp steel. It would take 12/0.6, or 20, inches of such plate to equal the performance of a plate with a figure of merit of 1.0. Similarly, it would take only 10 inches of plate with a figure of merit of 1.2 to achieve the same performance. See N. Okun, "Armor and its Application to Warships, Part 1," *Warship International* XIII, 114-22 (1976).

The battleship *Arkansas* (*above and facing*), shown on 1 January 1945 at San Pedro after a refit, is the classic illustration of U.S. battleship durability. Commissioned in 1912, she survived *in active service* for thirty-three years, before being sunk at Bikini in 1946. The unusual turreted directors atop her bridge and atop her stub mainmast are Mark 50s, for her 3in/50 antiaircraft battery. The main battery was controlled by a prewar type masthead director, connected to the Mark 3 radar on her foretop. Her 5-inch secondary battery was controlled from the level beneath it, a platform relocated when her cage foremast was removed in 1942. The open bridge was characteristic of U.S. warships rebuilt or designed during World War Two, being adopted because of early British and U.S. experience of air attacks.

as "post-Jutland" (post-1916) ships, although the U.S. Navy had adopted such design policies as early as 1911. In any case, it seems wise to distinguish the later U.S. ships, from the *Nevada* onwards, from their dreadnought predecessors. The fast battleships of the 1930s form yet another distinct group.

The development of the first U.S. battle fleet, the Great White Fleet, coincided with the development of the modern understanding of ship propulsion, that is, the amount of power needed to drive a given hull at a given speed. Although Froude in England began tank testing as early as 1879, the concepts he espoused were not fully accepted (at least in the United States) for another two decades, and the *Virginia* class, authorized in 1899, was the first to enjoy the full benefits of tank testing. For the purpose of this book,

the single most important hydrodynamic fact is that, for a given displacement and a speed range typical of most battleships, the longer the ship, the less power it needs to reach a given speed. Thus, any weight saving achieved by shortening a ship would have to be balanced against the weight *increase* necessary to provide more power. The difference between the *North Carolina* and the *South Dakota*, an increase of 9,000SHP to balance a reduction in waterline length from 714 to 666 feet, is a case in point.

Waterline, rather than overall, length is the key figure, and except as indicated, it is the *length* in design tables.

Power is expressed either as EHP (*effective* horse power), IHP (*indicated* horse power), or SHP (*shaft* horse power). EHP is the power actually transmitted into the water, and the ratio between it and the power

applied to the propeller shaft is the propulsive efficiency, typically about 50 percent. IHP is the standard power measurement for reciprocating engines, SHP for steam turbines. Propellers are most efficient when they rotate at relatively low speeds, which is why the early reciprocating plants were far more efficient than the faster-turning turbines. Much effort, therefore, went into means of coupling high-speed turbines to slow propellers. The United States adopted a turboelectric drive during World War One, abandoning it between wars only because its weight was an unacceptable burden when ships were limited in overall displacement by treaty. The alternative was reduction gearing, first used in destroyers and cruisers (and the British battle cruiser *Hood*) during World War One.

Note, finally, that guns began to be described by a combination of their calibre (for example, 12 inch) and their length *in calibres*, so that a 12in/50 or 12-inch 50-calibre gun is 50-feet long from breech face to muzzle. The longer the gun, the longer the period of acceleration of the shell, hence the higher the velocity. The development of the U.S. pre-dreadnoughts coincided with improvements that slowed the rate of burning of powder, so that this added distance could be used more effectively. Hence the increase, both in muzzle velocity and in gun length, between the *Indiana* and *Iowa* of the 1890s and the *Connecticut*s of about 1905.

Higher velocity made for better penetration, as the pentrating energy of a shell was proportional to the square of its velocity (but only directly proportional to the weight of the shell itself). As a result, navies tended to abandon larger-calibre guns in favor of smaller ones firing higher-velocity shells. The most extreme case in U.S. service was the adoption of an 8in/45 in some armored cruisers that were apparently conceived as fast battleships. Higher velocity was also attractive because it made for a flatter trajectory and, thus, for easier fire control, at least at medium ranges. However, it also made for rapid barrel wear. In 1905, for example, BuOrd had to de-rate existing 12in/40 guns from a rated velocity of 3,000 ft/sec to 2,400 ft/sec; the former figure would not be reached again until the advent of the 12in/50 five years later. From about 1908 onwards, however, it became obvious that the limit of 12-inch gun development had been reached with the 12in/50, and calibres began to increase once more, first to 14 and then to 16 inches.

Similar considerations applied to secondary weapons. For example, the 5in/51 was prized for many years for its very flat trajectory. Long barrels made guns difficult to maneuver, particularly by hand, however, and antiaircraft weapons were generally shorter, the great example being the 5in/25. The famous 5in/38 of World War Two was *dual-purpose*, compromising between a higher velocity (for better shooting against surface targets) and a short and easily maneuvered barrel for shooting against fast-moving air targets.

Wherever possible, the detailed changes in light antiaircraft battery and in radar and director equipment during and after World War Two have been described, so that the reader has a full picture of ship equipment at various times. Note that BuOrd equipment, including fire control radars, was always described by Mark numbers; search radars had letter designations, such as SC or SG.

1

Beginnings:
The Pre-dreadnoughts

Congress authorized the first U.S. battleship, the small *Texas*, in 1886. Two decades later the United States was the second strongest naval power, measured in battle line strength. Most of this growth occurred in two bursts: from 1890 to 1896, when four classes displacing 10,000 to 11,000 tons were designed; and from 1900 to 1902, with the planning of two large classes of 14,000 to 16,000 tons. Within each group, class followed class much too quickly to incorporate operating experience. Moreover, the technology of warship construction and armament advanced very rapidly, so that the weapons of the Spanish-American War of 1898 were obsolescent at the time. Nevertheless, this war shaped the three classes, the *Virginia*, the *Connecticut*, and the *Idaho* designed after it. As of 1904 the United States had twelve first-line battleships in service, twelve more in various stages of construction, and a thirteenth authorized but not laid down, as well as eight large armored cruisers under construction.

With little operational experience in hand, theoretical analysis of fleet tactics and of new battleship types, conducted primarily at the Naval War College at Newport, was extremely influential. Perennial topics discussed at the War College–General Board summer conferences between 1903 and 1910 included the ideal composition of the future U.S. fleet (that is, the future building program); the relative values of speed and protection; the possible utility of a large cruiser with battleship armor but with limited firepower; and the possible utility of a bat-

tleship armed primarily with torpedoes. Tactical issues included the maximum number of battleships that could operate as a single tactical unit, a question affecting possible fleet composition. The War College also evaluated the potential of the all-big-gun battleship and compared U.S. with foreign designs.

No less important was the pace at which the United States developed into a major industrial power. The *Texas* of 1886, for example, had to be built to an imported design, and delays in obtaining material, principally armor, from domestic manufacturers held back her completion until 1895. In contrast, the *Indiana*, of about 70 percent greater displacement, was authorized in 1890 and commissioned five years later. Almost from the first, it was U.S. policy to employ only materials and equipment made in the United States. Thus, the limitations of U.S. industry, such as the early inability to produce satisfactory large-calibre rapid-fire (RF) guns, had their own impact on U.S. designs.

The history of the modern U.S. Navy begins with the Naval Advisory Board convened by Secretary of the Navy William H. Hunt in June 1881. At that time, battleships, seagoing capital ships, were anathema. The classic U.S. naval strategy, as practiced in the Revolutionary War and in the War of 1812, was commerce raiding. The United States tacitly admitted it could not hope to challenge any major European fleet. At best, it could hope to wear down an enemy by gradually destroying his merchant fleet. Such a strategy also reflected U.S. isolationism, its lack of

The U.S. Navy combined bold innovation with some bureaucratic confusion, as typified by the superposed 8 inch-13 inch turret of the *Kentucky*. Because the guns and turret armor were designed by the Bureau of Ordnance, and the turret structure by the Bureau of Construction and Repair, the 13-inch guns were mounted relatively far back in the turret. Their ports were, therefore, relatively large. As a young officer on the Asiatic Station, William S. Sims claimed that a lighted match thrown through the ports would land on the floor of the magazine below and, therefore, that the guns might easily be disabled by shells passing through their open ports. A reformist, he charged that these ships were "the greatest crime ever perpetrated against the white race." Note the recoil cylinders above the 13-inch guns, visible through the gun ports and the fighting tops on the mainmast, with their small-calibre rapid-firing weapons. The lens has somewhat distorted the distance between 13-inch and 8-inch turrets. (Library of Congress)

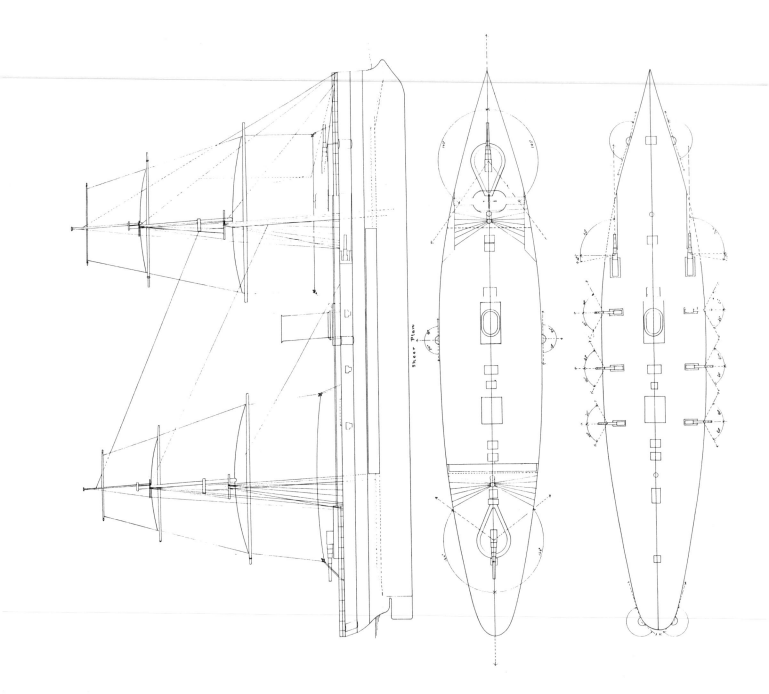

Sheer Plan

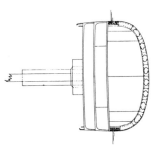

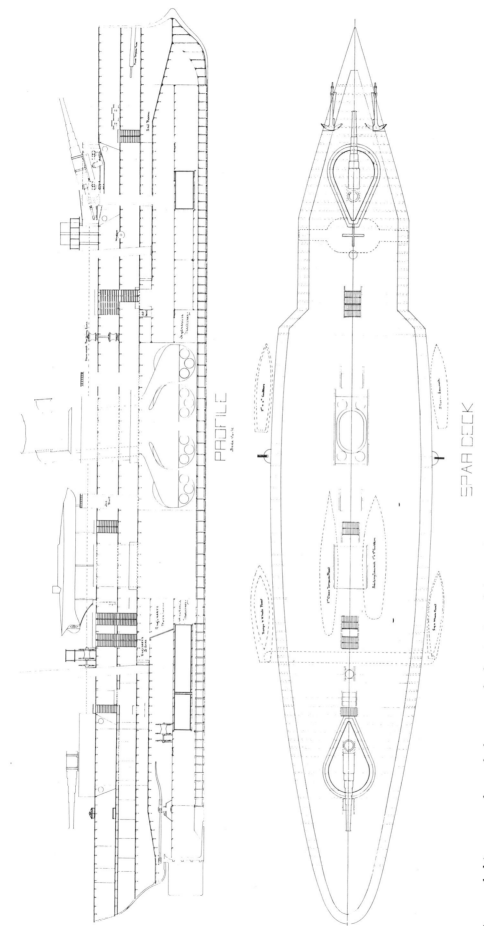

PROFILE

SPAR DECK

Armored ships were planned almost at the beginning of the modern U.S. Navy. This is the 1885 Bureau of Construction and Repair design for a 5,000-ton armored cruiser (300 feet × 62 feet × 21 feet 9 inches, 5,250IHP for 15 knots) with two 10-inch guns. The accompanying battleship design appears to have been lost. Although neither design was proceeded with, their characteristics determined those of the *Maine* and the *Texas*, which were built. (U.S. National Archives)

interest in seeking confrontations with foreign nations. Battleships represented a means of projecting naval force abroad and, as such, were initially shunned by the 1881 advisory board, which, while not ruling out their construction, was careful to avoid including battleships in its plan for naval reconstruction.

The counterargument was that commerce raiding could not deal with the threat of enemy battleships attacking the U.S. coast. As this argument gained currency, interest in more powerful units grew. During the debate on the abortive 1884 authorization bill, for example, one senator refused to vote for more unarmored cruisers but expressed himself as willing to vote $50 million for battleships. At the same time, the Naval Advisory Board was designing a U.S. battleship, albeit a small one.

In its last (November 1884) report, the board noted that, in order to be able to enter all principal American ports, such a ship could not draw more than 23 feet of water; the dry docks at Boston and Norfolk would fix its beam at 58 feet; and only the dry dock then under construction at Mare Island on the Pacific coast could take a modern 10,000-ton battleship. Hence if length were set at about 300 feet (draft at 23), the ship could not much exceed 7,000 tons. Such a small, short-ranged armored ship might not have been at a complete disadvantage in confronting European battleships, few of which had the range to reach the New World without making considerable sacrifices that might have made them vulnerable to the American ships. That was just what the Russian Baltic Fleet discovered at Tsushima in 1905.

Although these specific restrictions would pass as the shore establishment was built up, they represent a type of limit which appears again and again in U.S. practice and, indeed, in the development of all navies. In particular, the 23-foot limit on battleship draft was to return twelve years later.

The advisory board was part of the Republican Administration of Chester A. Arthur. The sheer prominence of its naval reconstruction program made it a target for an extremely partisan press, and the vehemence of attacks made at the time obscures the merits of the situation. The incoming Democratic secretary of the navy, John H. Whitney, continued the program but rejected the detailed work of the board, as noted in the companion book in this series on cruisers. Whitney argued that U.S. designers and technologists were backward, that it was essential to buy the best European (that is, British) designs as models. Both in cruisers and in the new armored ships, his policy was to build competitive U.S. and foreign designs.

The Bureau of Construction and Repair (C&R) developed two parallel designs, one for a 7,500-ton battleship with four 10-inch guns and one for a 5,000-ton "belted cruiser" or armored cruiser with two 10-inch guns; details are given in Table 1-1. Both preliminary plans were complete by October 1885. In both designs, all 10-inch guns were mounted singly on the upper or spar deck, two on the centerline, the superstructure being cut away to allow the bow mounting to fire 50 degrees abaft abeam, and the stern mounting 50 degrees forward of abeam. In the battleship design two other 10-inch guns were mounted on the broadsides, each with a 180 degree arc of fire. The 6-inch guns were mounted on the gun or main deck below, on the broadside, two firing forward, two astern, and the others on the broadside, in 3-inch shields.

Table 1-1. C&R Battleship Designs, 1885

	Battleship	Armored Cruiser
Displacement	7500	5000 tons
Length	320	305 feet
Beam	64	57 feet
Draft	24	21.75 feet
Main Battery	4	2 10-inch
	6	8 6-inch
Secondary Battery	14	14 Hotchkiss
Belt	10-7	10 inches
Belt Width	8	5.5 feet
Bulkheads	9	
Deck (ends)	2(3)	2(3) inches
Main Barbettes	8	
Rig	Brig	Signaling Only
Power	8500	8500 IHP
Speed	16.5	17.5 knots
Coal	1200	1000 tons

Note: Both battleships and armored cruisers were to carry a "full complement" of torpedoes, for discharge both above and below water. The cruiser would also carry machine guns in her fighting tops.

Armor would consist of a waterline belt covered by an armor deck, over the machinery and magazines. Each ship would also have a ram bow. The battleship, but not the cruiser, would have sail power.

On paper, the battleship corresponded approximately to the British "armored cruiser" or second-class battleship Warspite, and the cruiser to the new British *Orlando*. The British, French, and Russian navies had all built second-class capital ships of very long range to serve on foreign or colonial stations, and roughly similar ships had been sold to a number of second-rate navies, such as that of Brazil. The contemporary U.S. naval literature made much of the fact that the Brazilians had two such ships and the United States, none; might not the Brazilians raid the U.S. coast with impunity? It is difficult to say whether this imbalance had much effect on the decision finally to build a U.S. capital ship. The almost universally held view that, to be taken seriously, a navy had to have battleships probably sufficed within the service, and the supposed threat of the Brazilians made a useful public talking point.*

Whitney chose to average out the two designs, asking Congress for two armored vessels, each of about 6,000 tons, capable of at least 16 knots. They were authorized on 3 August 1886, marking the United States's first departure from the pure coast defense–commerce raiding strategy.

It appears to have been Whitney's intention to build one ship to a C&R design, while having the other designed privately, probably abroad. He therefore announced a design competition for two ships, one to be an armored cruiser, the other a battleship. Circulars were issued on 21 August 1886. They were somewhat vague (for example, coal endurance was to be "large") but they included main batteries of four 10-inch guns for the cruiser, and two 12 inch for the battleship, in each case with six 6-inch guns, four 6pdr Hotchkiss guns, four (six in the battleship) 3pdr Hotchkiss, two 1pdr Hotchkiss, four 47mm revolving cannon, four 37mm revolving cannon, and four Gatling guns, as well as six torpedo tubes (two at the ends and at least two of the broadside tubes underwater). Minimum waterline armor was to be 11 (12 in the battleship) inches, with 10.5 (12) inches over the heavy guns. Maximum speed was to be 17 knots. The armored cruiser was to have sail power, for long cruising range. It was to be limited, however, to "two-thirds" of full sail power, that is, somewhat limited in sail area. Full sail power was based on the tonnage and immersed cross section of a ship. Maximum draft was to be 22 (23 for the battleship) feet. Designs were due on 7 March 1887.

Both winning designs had their big guns mounted off the centerline, an echelon, an outcome dictated by the demand for heavy end-on fire. The cruiser, which became the USS *Maine* and was later redesignated a second-class battleship, was a C&R design. It was loosely patterned on the Brazilian *Riachuelo*. The battleship competition, however, was won by a British constructor, William John, general manager of the Barrow Shipbuilding Company, later the Naval Armament and Construction Company, Ltd., and then the Vickers Barrow-in-Furness yard.

Both ships were built in navy yards and both were greatly delayed in construction, partly because of the very late delivery of their armor. By the time they

were completed in 1895, U.S. naval policy had changed radically, and both were obsolete in terms of mission and technology. Thus, neither had much impact on later American efforts. For example, the battleship, the USS *Texas*, was completed with gun turrets that could load at only two angles of train: along the centerline and directly abeam. Such fixed-train loading was common in battleships designed before about 1890 but largely disappeared within a few years. Indeed, the *Maine* had turrets capable of loading at any angle of train.

The design of the USS *Texas* is interesting mainly as an expression of the contemporary—albeit momentary—state of the art. She was protected only against the heaviest guns, with no light armor against smaller-calibre high-explosive (HE) shells. The short 12-inch waterline belt was covered by a 3-inch deck, the latter sloping down forward and aft of the belt. Above the armor deck, the bases of the turrets were connected by a heavy armored redoubt extending diagonally across the ship, enclosing the conning tower as well. Since there was no light armor either at the ends or above the main belt, *Texas* was extremely vulnerable to rapid-fire (RF) guns firing HE shells, a threat not very important at the time of her conception yet extremely significant within a few years.

End-on fire was considered important because these ships were conceived in the context of single-ship actions involving ramming, which in turn would require a direct approach to an enemy ship. It is difficult to imagine successful ramming even in 1886. Although battleships retained their ram bows for another two decades, end-on fire was not important in any U.S. battleship after the *Texas*. The en echelon arrangement lost favor abroad late in the 1880s, as it became evident that blast effects on ships' hulls made end-on fire essentially impossible.

Even as much as five years before the *Texas* was completed at Norfolk Navy Yard, her design was clearly obsolete. In February 1890 the then-new Board on Construction proposed a total redesign of the *Texas* in which the two 12-inch guns would be mounted in separate turrets and the heavy redoubt eliminated. The board hoped that the guns might be relocated to the centerline or even mounted together in one twin turret. But construction was well advanced, and Secretary of the Navy Benjamin Tracy, who had entered office in 1889, ordered the heavy redoubt retained and limited the board to detail improvements.

The armored cruiser, or second-class battleship, became the *Maine*, which was blown up in 1898 in Havana harbor. Her construction had been delayed by a fire in the drafting room of the New York Navy Yard and also by the late delivery of her armor. By the time she was ready, the concept of the armored cruiser had moved beyond her. In 1886, an armored cruiser was a small battleship for service far over-

---

* This situation nicely illustrates the central problem of the naval reformers of the 1880s. They wanted to build up a modern fleet, and the only real threat was the one presented by the great powers of Europe. However, to emphasize this threat would also be to frighten Congress by its magnitude. Congress could not be expected to accept naval reconstruction if that entailed rapid build-up of a battle fleet comparable to, say, that of France. Similarly, even after a considerable U.S. fleet had been built up, the explicit goal was always parity with the *second* naval power. Only the events of World War One made parity with the greatest navy in the world, the Royal Navy, possible (see Chapters 7 and 8).

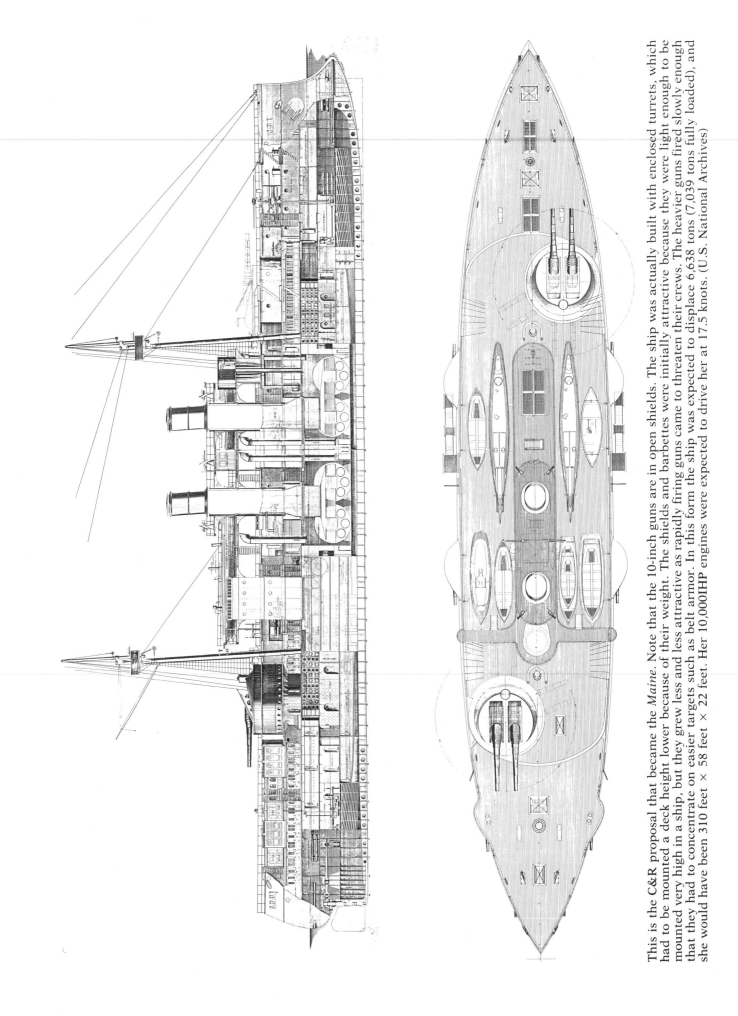

This is the C&R proposal that became the *Maine*. Note that the 10-inch guns are in open shields. The ship was actually built with enclosed turrets, which had to be mounted a deck height lower because of their weight. The shields and barbettes were initially attractive because they were light enough to be mounted very high in a ship, but they grew less and less attractive as rapidly firing guns came to threaten their crews. The heavier guns fired slowly enough that they had to concentrate on easier targets such as belt armor. In this form the ship was expected to displace 6,638 tons (7,039 tons fully loaded), and she would have been 310 feet × 58 feet × 22 feet. Her 10,000IHP engines were expected to drive her at 17.5 knots. (U.S. National Archives)

seas, with a relatively heavy armored belt. A decade later, she was a fast, long-range commerce-destroyer with limited protection. The transformation was largely due to the advent of lightweight armors such as Harvey steel.

Whitney asked for two more armored ships in 1887, the year following Congress's authorization of the *Maine* and the *Texas*. One ship was to be built under contract and one in a navy yard, together with three fast cruisers. Congress refused, however, and only in 1888 authorized a third armored ship, intended essentially as a somewhat enlarged *Maine* or *Texas*. Of this ship, no final design was prepared. In February 1889, the Board on Construction was still trying to reduce tonnage from an unacceptable 8,300 or 8,400 tons to about 7,500 tons, to remain within congressional cost limits. At this time her main battery was set at two 12-inch guns in a barbette forward on the centerline, one 10-inch gun aft in a barbette on the centerline, and six 4-inch RF guns in the superstructure, with 11-inch side armor. In August, the Board on Construction proposed a redesign in which four 11-inch guns (a calibre not developed for the U.S. Navy) would replace the mixture of 12- and 10-inch weapons. This design was never advertised for bids, however. Such a ship no longer coincided with U.S. naval policy.

Even before the Policy Board had reported, Secretary of the Navy Benjamin Tracy was resolved to end the policy of building small, substandard capital ships. He agreed with Mahan: the United States must have a battle fleet capable of dealing with the European powers. Smaller armored ships would be a hindrance. On the other hand, lightly armored long-range cruisers would be valuable as commerce raiders. Secretary Tracy ordered the 1888 ship built as a fast cruiser; it became the *New York*. The only other armored ship authorized under the Whitney administration was the coast-defense ship *Monterey*, built under a special harbor and coast-defense appropriation described in Appendix A.

The end of Whitney's administration was marked by a rather unusual authorization. Congressman B. R. Thomas of Ohio, a lame duck member of the House Naval Committee, caused Congress to authorize what he called an "armored cruising monitor" of his own design, on 2 March 1889, just before the change of administration—which also radically changed U.S. naval strategy. Thomas apparently hoped to minimize capital ship cost by building up from a monitor. The usual problem of armor weight would be solved by limiting the ship to deck armor, reducing target area by filling special tanks before battle. Thomas expected his craft to make 17 knots, a high speed for the time, on 7,500 IHP at a displacement of only 3,130 tons. The curved deck was to be 3-inches thick on the flat and 4.5 at its sides. Armament was to have

been a pair of 10-inch guns in a turret forward, a single 6-inch gun in a shield aft, and a 15-inch pneumatic dynamite gun in the bows.

The latter was a radical attempt to make big HE shells practical by substituting the steady pressure of compressed air for the sharp kick of contemporary powders. There was considerable interest in this type of weapon, and three of them were actually mounted in the special cruiser *Vesuvius* before improvements in gun propellant made it obsolete.

The cruising monitor is significant as a demonstration of the enormous power of the Congress. Although elaborate descriptions appeared in the secretary's *Annual Report* for 1889, the Board on Construction considered her design impractical and reported that she would have to be lengthened by 30 feet to carry sufficient weights. Secretary Tracy later testified before the House Naval Affairs Committee (which no longer included Thomas) that he considered such redesign impossible under the authorization. The issue was not trivial as Congress had, after all, appropriated $1.5 million. On the other hand, Tracy wanted to build oceangoing battleships, and the Thomas ship was at best a distraction. He therefore interpreted the authorizing law as narrowly as possible and killed the project, after several attempts at redesign by the Board on Construction between August 1889 and January 1890 foundered on the limited size and capability achievable on the appropriated sum.

At this juncture Secretary of the Navy Tracy convened a new Policy Board. Much impressed by the ideas of Captain Alfred Thayer Mahan, he sought a new U.S. naval strategy, a conscious attempt to achieve command of the sea by building a long-range fleet capable of engaging enemy battle fleets in their own home waters. The new board, ordered into existence on 16 July 1889, reported the following 20 January. As early as November 1889, however, the secretary proposed a large battle fleet in his *Annual Report*—twelve seagoing battleships for the Atlantic and the Gulf of Mexico, and another eight for the Pacific, plus twenty coast-defense ships.

At this time only three seagoing armored ships had been authorized (of which two, the *Maine* and *Texas*, were under construction), plus eight coast-defense ships (five monitors laid down in 1874-75, *Monterey*, the cruising monitor, and a new ram which would become the *Katahdin*). Secretary Tracy requested eight new battleships, the maximum number he believed could be built simultaneously. He argued that the lead time required to build a navy was so long that the country could not wait until an emergency; so much of the industry and wealth of the country was concentrated on its coasts that sea power was an absolute necessity. Congress, however, refused to contemplate anything so ambitious.

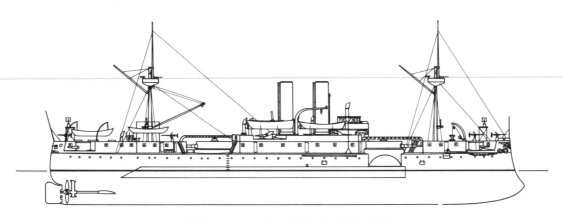

Maine as completed. (A. D. Baker III)

The Policy Board assumed that any serious foreign attack would come in two phases: first, the capture of a fleet operating base, probably in the Caribbean; and, then, operations off the East Coast, which offered many attractive targets. The operating base would be essential if the enemy fleet were to spend any time at all in the target area. Indeed, the *denial* of possible operating bases was a fixed feature of U.S. naval exercises down to World War One. The board assumed that a battleship could operate effectively at a distance equal to about one-third of its coal endurance. Thus, to attack the United States *without* a nearby base, battleships based in European ports would require an endurance of about 10,000 or 12,000 miles. Of twenty modern British battleships, for example, only seven could hope to operate against the United States from their home bases, but another ten with similar capabilities were under construction. On the other hand, using Western Hemisphere bases, the British could operate fifteen of their twenty modern ships (that is, those with an endurance of 5,000 miles or more at 10 knots). Britain was unique among the major European powers in possessing such bases.

The board argued that this circumstance could change relatively rapidly, through some shift of European alliances, whereas it would take many years to build up an effective battle fleet. Perhaps the most worrying imminent change was the planned construction of a Panama Canal by a French company. Once completed, the canal might well become a French base, and France the dominant naval power of the Western Hemisphere—unless the United States built up a sufficiently powerful navy of her own.

The Policy Board envisaged two fleets: one consisting of ten fast (17-knot) long-endurance battleships (10,800nm at 10 knots, 13,000 at economical speed, remarkable figures for the time), to carry war to enemy waters. Such ships were justified, in part,

as a "fleet in being" that would compel an enemy to retain powerful forces in home waters. The second fleet, built around twenty-five shorter-range ships, would dominate the western Atlantic and eastern Pacific. They would break any blockade and would be responsible for the destruction of an enemy fleet operating base. Draft would be limited to 23.5 feet so that ships could pass over the bars at the mouths of the Southern ports.

The home defense fleet would operate inside a line 1,000 miles off the Atlantic coast, from the mouth of the St. Lawrence River south to the Windward Islands in the Caribbean and to Panama. Its units would require good seakeeping qualities, and a range of about 3,000nm. In contrast to ships of great endurance, they would require a speed of only about 15 knots (a trial speed of 15.75 was specified). Coal endurance was set above the minimum, at 4,600nm at 10 knots and at 5,200nm at economical speed.

Probably for reasons of economy, the board called for three categories of short-range ships: first class (eight ships of 8,000 tons with four 13-inch guns); second class (ten of 7,100 tons with four 12-inch guns); and third class (five of 6,000 tons with two 12-inch and two 10-inch guns). The three armored ships already authorized fit only into the third class. The total program also included substantial numbers of rams, cruisers, and torpedo craft for local defense; the estimated cost was $281.5 million, a huge sum for the time.

Congress was shocked by the Policy Board report. Senator Eugene Hale of Maine, one of Tracy's chief supporters, feared that no money at all would be approved. Tracy had hoped to reveal this large program only gradually, but the Policy Board leaked it instead. The House did approve three 8,500-ton battleships in April 1890, and Tracy helped cool tempers by claiming that the three ships (The *Indiana*s) were so powerful that twelve, rather than the twenty

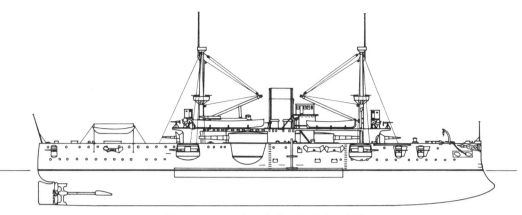

Texas as completed. (A. D. Baker III)

planned in 1889, would suffice. At the same time he was able to cut costs by retiring the surviving Civil War monitors to state militia duty.

Congress, then, approved three coast-defense (that is, short-range) battleships, a cruiser, and a torpedo boat. Perhaps as significantly, the last of the small armored ships, which became the *New York*, was redesigned as a long-range armored cruiser. Henceforth, the United States would build only first-class battleships. It is conventional to describe the designation "coast-defense battleship" applied to the three *Indiana*s as a sop to congressional fears of overseas warfare, but a reading of the Policy Board report (which, after all, was used to justify these three ships) makes it clear that they were the first installment of a rational fleet plan. That plan differed from the board's largely in its stretched-out time scale, a situation common to many later multiyear programs.

The most powerful available gun was the 13in/35, at this time still in the design stage; during 1890 forgings for the prototype would be ordered. Weight would have to be saved in some ships, so the planners would mount a new 12in/35. BuOrd promised a 5-inch RF weapon, which it considered "the largest calibre admitting of reasonably convenient fixed ammunition and well adapted to the attack of unarmored or lightly protected sides." An unusual feature of the long-range design was provision for two engines on each shaft, either of which could be used for cruising while the other was shut down to prolong engine life. This ingenious solution to the problem of reciprocating engine endurance was expected to cost only 6 or 7 percent more (in weight) than conventional power plants.

Having in mind the new dangers of HE shells and RF guns, the board rejected thick side armor for its long-range ships, favoring a curved protective deck and thin side armor (which would protect against medium shells fired by RF guns). Barbettes for four

heavy guns would rise directly from the heavy deck, and the sides above it would be filled with water-excluding material. In theory, large-calibre AP shells penetrating the 5-inch belt would destroy little of the water-excluding material, whereas explosive RF shells would not pass through even 5 inches of armor. There was, however, some fear that, if the 5-inch belt were too high, an AP shell entering on one side and glancing off the deck might strike the off-side belt and carry out a large portion of that side of the ship. This problem was not so severe for guns mounted along the side of the ship in casemates, since it seemed likely that AP shells hitting so high above the armor deck would pass cleanly through both sides of the ship. The board believed that this unusual solution would be about 1,200-tons lighter than a more conventional heavy belt.

The board was much more conservative in its proposals for the coast-defense ships, calling (in the first-class ship) for a 17-inch main belt extending over 72.5 percent of the waterline length, covered by a flat 2.75-inch deck and a 4-inch upper belt (casemate); above this four 5-inch guns were set in individual gunhouses on the weather deck. The second- and third-class ships were to have their belts reduced in proportion to their displacement, to 15 and 12.5 inches, respectively. The report admitted that this armor scheme was a compromise in accordance with foreign practice. It would appear that this was the design the board expected to see developed into a real ship and that it was wariest of radical ideas for that reason. Certainly the *Indiana* bears a close resemblance to it.

All of the Policy Board designs seem relatively small for their expected gun batteries and performance, and the ships actually built to meet the board's requirements were considerably larger. The *Indiana*s, which corresponded to the first-class short-range design were about 25 percent heavier, although its di-

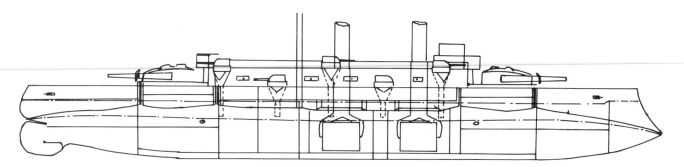

The Policy Board's proposed first-class, long-range battleship, armed with four 12in/35, ten 5-inch RF guns, twelve 6pdr, six lpdr, two 37 mm revolver cannon, and six underwater torpedo tubes. It would have displaced 10,000 tons fully loaded (326 feet 6 inches PP × 71 feet 6 inches extreme; 69 feet 9¾ inches on the waterline × 25 feet 4½ inches), and its 11,000IHP engines would have driven it at 17 knots. The belt armor, only 5 inches thick, is indicated by broken lines; the shape of the 3-inch armor deck is indicated by solid lines. The guns were in circular turrets in British-style elliptical barbettes, loading only when on the centerline. Note that the turrets slope down at the front and therefore that their ports extend into their roofs, protected by 3-inch plates fixed to the guns. All-round loading still lay in the future. There are tandem engine rooms, for two engines per propeller shaft.

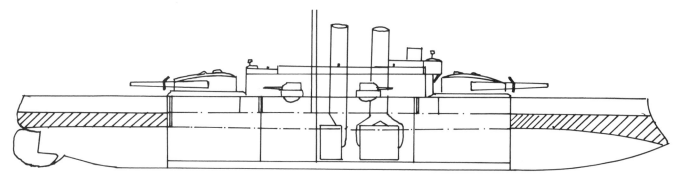

The Policy Board's first-class, short-range battleship, almost certainly the starting point for the *Indiana* design. Broken lines indicate the upper and lower edges of the belt, and the shaded areas at the ends are filled with water-excluding material, a common feature of battleships of this period. Armament was four 13 inch/35, four 5-inch RF, six 6pdr, four 1pdr, two 37 mm revolver cannon, and six torpedo tubes. The ship would have displaced 8,000 tons loaded (296 feet PP × 67 feet 9½ inch extreme × 23 feet 3 inch) and was expected to achieve 15.8 knots on 7,500IHP. The belt was 17-inch armor on 2-inch backing, closed at the ends by 14-inch armor bulkheads and above by a 2.75-inch armor deck; the ends were protected by a 3-inch underwater deck and by 6-foot thick belts of water-excluding material, as shown.

mensions and other characteristics (see Table 1-2) were fairly close to those of the ships actually built. It seems likely that the board intentionally understated displacements to gain political acceptance.

Three "coast-defense battleships" were duly authorized on 30 June 1890, to displace about 8,500 tons and to have a coal endurance of about 5,000nm. As designed, they showed two major changes: thicker belt armor (18 inches rather than 17 inches) and a mixed secondary battery (four 8in/35 and four 6in/40 in shields) rather than the uniform 5-inch RF battery previously specified. The latter change was the more significant, as it represented a clear break from contemporary foreign practice.

The United States could not, as yet, manufacture even 5-inch rapid-fire guns, whereas foreign battleships were armed with, and armored against, 6-inch weapons of this type. The difference of an inch in calibre might seem trivial, but the weight of a shell rises at least as the cube of the calibre, so that a ratio of 1.2 in calibre equates to a ratio in shell weight of

about 1.7. Since all of these shells were explosive, it was shell weight that counted.

In effect, the United States was an underdeveloped country attempting to improve its technology and match foreign weapons of a more sophisticated type. The solution was to use a heavier if slower-firing weapon, the 8-inch gun. Its shell would be about four times the weight of that of the 5 inch, or 2.3 times the weight of a 6-inch gun either RF or conventional. Moreover, 8-inch shells would defeat armor designed to resist the 6 inch.

This was not a happy choice. Eight-inch guns were heavy and cumbersome. In a short ship built on a limited displacement, blast interference would be severe. For a given total of guns and ammunition, a 6-inch battery could devote more weight to ammunition and so probably develop a far better rate of fire. Such arguments were actually made when the 8-inch gun was temporarily abandoned in 1896.

In 1890, however, that was not a feasible alternative. No reason was ever publicly given for the

The first modern U.S. battleship, the *Indiana*, is shown as (very slightly) modernized, fitted with a cage mainmast but still retaining her original bridge structure. This photograph must have been taken very soon after the modification—she was still wearing her old white-and-buff color scheme. Note her extremely low freeboard. The deficiencies of the original design were aggravated by overloads of coal and ammunition. Because the ship had no mainmast as completed, installation of the cage mast was relatively simple.

adoption of the 8-inch gun; battleships mounting it were merely described as far more powerful than their foreign counterparts. However, the reasoning given here accords both with contemporary accounts of difficulties in U.S. RF gun development and with later claims for the virtues of the 8-inch weapon. In some ways this design decision resembles a series of choices made by another underdeveloped country striving for military adequacy, the Soviet Union. Modern Soviet naval strategy is based on the use of heavy antiship missiles, which can be described, often, as somewhat inferior equivalents of naval aircraft, bought by a fleet which could not afford carriers. Many Westerners have seen these weapons in a far more impressive light, mainly because Western navies would adopt missiles only if they were intrinsically superior to aircraft already available. Some parallels can be found in published contemporary British reactions to the *Indiana*s.

Standard U.S. Navy contacts of this period allowed builders to propose alternatives to the official design. William Cramp and Sons suggested that the ship be lengthened 12 feet to accommodate twin 8-inch turrets (for a total of eight guns) as well as more powerful engines. Cramp received a contract for two ships, *Indiana* and *Massachusetts*. Congress specified that the third ship be built on the West Coast: Cramp's design was used by the Union Iron Works for the *Oregon*. Displacement rose to 10,300 tons, and length increased to 350 feet 11 inches. Although the contract design called for seven above-water torpedo tubes, the ships were completed with five (four in the *Indiana*). During construction the design was further

modified, the truncated cone-shaped turrets initially proposed being replaced by conventional cylindrical ones. BuOrd argued that the cones would be too crowded. This modification was made to several U.S. designs of this vintage. In addition, Harvey armor was substituted for some of the nickel steel originally specified, pointing the way toward lighter but still effective armor suits. At the time it was claimed that 16-inch Harvey would have been equivalent to the 18-inch nickel steel belt specified and that the change would have saved 60 tons. It was rejected solely in order to avoid delay.

The three *Indiana*s were not particularly successful. Although designed with substantial *maximum* bunker capacity, their armor was so placed as to be ineffective if they carried more than 400 tons. Unfortunately they usually operated fully loaded, so that an already low freeboard was only made worse, and contemporary writers derided them as extremely wet. Even though the hulls had been lengthened in order to take, first, 8-inch guns and then 8-inch turrets, they suffered badly from blast interference. Later writers would suggest that they were overgunned, but that seems unfair in view of the problems the designers faced.

For example, in 1896 the Walker Board on battleship design, which was responsible for what became the *Illinois* class, criticized the *Indiana*s as cramped and undermanned. Only nine line officers were assigned to each ship, which meant none for the torpedoes, the main deck battery, or the secondary battery, and no margin for officers killed in action. The board considered the complement listed more suited

Anatomy of an Indiana-Class Battleship, Circa 1898

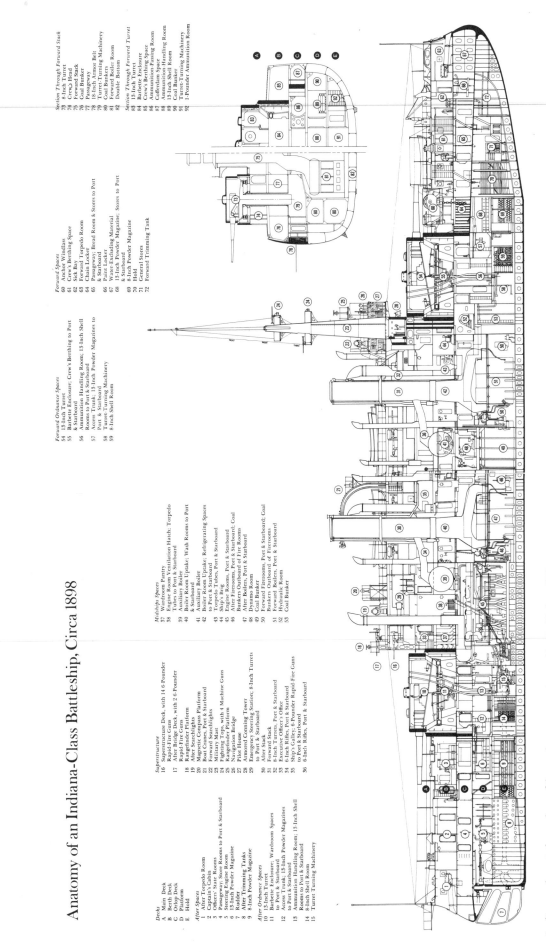

Decks

A Main Deck
B Berth Deck
C Orlop Deck
D Platform
E Hold

After Spaces

1 After Torpedo Room
2 Captain's Cabin
3 Officers' State Rooms
4 Passageway; Store Rooms to Port & Starboard
5 Steering Engine Room
6 13-Inch Powder Magazine
7 Rudder
8 After Trimming Tanks
9 8-Inch Powder Magazine

After Ordnance Spaces

10 13-Inch Turret
11 Barbette Enclosure; Wardroom Spaces to Port & Starboard
12 Access Trunk; 13-Inch Powder Magazines to Port & Starboard
13 Ammunition Handling Room; 13-Inch Shell Rooms to Port & Starboard
14 8-Inch Shell Room
15 Turret Turning Machinery

Superstructure

16 Superstructure Deck, with 14 6-Pounder Rapid-Fire Guns
17 After Bridge Deck, with 2 6-Pounder Rapid-Fire Guns
18 Rangefinder Platform
19 After Searchlights
20 Magnetic Compass Platform
21 Boat Cranes, Port & Starboard
22 Military Mast
23 Forward Searchlights
24 Fighting Tops, with 4 Machine Guns
25 Rangefinder Platform
26 Navigation Bridge
27 Pilot House
28 Armored Conning Tower
29 Emergency Steering Station; 8-Inch Turrets to Port & Starboard
30 After Stack
31 Forward Stack
32 8-Inch Turrets, Port & Starboard
33 Executive Officer's Office
34 6-Inch Rifles, Port & Starboard
35 Ship's Galley; 6-Pounder Rapid-Fire Guns to Port & Starboard
36 6-Inch Rifles, Port & Starboard

Midships Spaces

37 Wardroom Pantry
38 Engine Room Ventilation Hatch; Torpedo Tubes to Port & Starboard
39 Auxiliary Boiler
40 Boiler Room Uptake; Wash Rooms to Port & Starboard
41 Auxiliary Boiler
43 Boiler Room Uptake; Refrigerating Spaces to Port & Starboard
44 Torpedo Tubes, Port & Starboard
45 Engine Rooms, Port & Starboard
46 After Firerooms, Port & Starboard; Coal Bunkers Outboard of Fire Rooms
47 After Boilers, Port & Starboard
48 Dynamo Room
49 Coal Bunker
50 Forward Firerooms, Port & Starboard; Coal Bunkers Outboard of Firerooms
51 Forward Boilers, Port & Starboard
52 Hydraulic Room
53 Coal Bunker

Forward Ordnance Spaces

54 13-Inch Turret
55 Barbette Enclosure; Crew's Berthing to Port & Starboard
56 Ammunition Handling Room; 13-Inch Shell Rooms to Port & Starboard
57 Access Trunk; 13-Inch Powder Magazines to Port & Starboard
58 Turret-Turning Machinery
59 8-Inch Shell Room

Forward Spaces

60 Anchor Windlass
61 Crew's Berthing Space
62 Sick Bay
63 Forward Torpedo Room
64 Chain Locker
65 Passageway; Bread Room & Stores to Port & Starboard
66 Paint Locker
67 Water Excluding Material
68 13-Inch Powder Magazine; Stores to Port & Starboard
69 8-Inch Powder Magazine
70 Hold
71 General Stores
72 Forward Trimming Tank

Section Through Forward Stack

73 8-Inch Turret
74 Crew's Head
75 Forward Stack
76 Coal Bunker
77 Passageway
78 18-Inch Armor Belt
79 Turret-Turning Machinery
80 Coal Bunkers
81 Forward Boiler Room
82 Double Bottom

Section Through Forward Turret

83 13-Inch Turret
84 Barbette Enclosure
85 Crew's Berthing Space
86 Ammunition-Passing Room
87 Cofferdam Space
88 Ammunition-Handling Room
89 13-Inch Shell Room
90 Coal Bunker
91 Turret-Turning Machinery
92 1-Pounder Ammunition Room

Indiana-class inboard profile and cross sections. (A. D. Baker III)

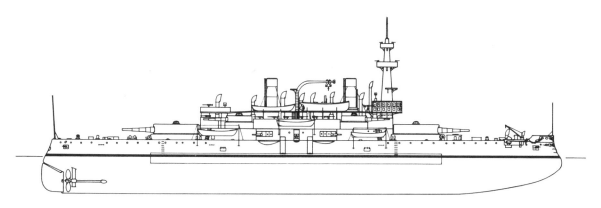

Indiana as completed. (A. D. Baker III)

to a cruiser than to a battleship, but even carrying so few officers and men the ship was badly cramped.

Table 1-2. Battleships of the Policy Board, 1890

Design	A	B	C	D
Displacement	10,000	8,000	7,100	6,000 tons
Length (OA)	349-2	314-0	308-0	298-0 ft-in
Length(PP)	326-6	296-0	290-0	280-0 ft-in
Beam (EXT)	71-6	67-9.5	64-6	61-6 ft-in
Hull Depth	38-4.5	33-9	32-10	31-2 ft-in
Draft	25-4.5	23-3	22-6	21-0 ft in
Guns				
13in/35	---	4	---	---
12in/35	4	---	4	2
10in/35	---	---	---	2(Barbette)
5-inch RF	10	4	4	4
6-PDR RF	12	6	4	4
1-PDR RF	6	4	10	10
37mm R.C.	2	2	2	2
Torpedo Tubes	6	6	6	6
Belt (Length)	5	17-(164)	16-(160)	15(155) in(ft)
(Above Water)	4-9	2-10	2-8	2-6 ft-in
(Below Water)	5-0	4-6	4-6	4-6 ft-in
Deck	3	2.75	2.675	2.5 in
Turret	16	17	16	15 in
Power	11,000	7500	6750	6500 IHP
Speed	17	15.8	15.8	15.8 knots
Coal	675	300	265	230 tons
Endurance	5400/10	2770/10	2650/10	2550/10 NM/KTS
GM(EST)	5-0(2-6)*	5-0	4-6	4-0.8 ft

*Figure in parentheses refers to riddled condition.

The board considered the nominal draft of 24 feet (with 400 tons of coal) unrepresentative, since the ships would always go to sea with much greater loads aboard. The *Indiana*, for example, had an ammunition allowance of 400 tons and a coal allowance of 400, although her full coal capacity was 1,600 tons. When inspected upon completion, she had only 120 tons of ammunition and 400 of coal on board, but in service, with 100 tons of ammunition and 1,200 of coal, she drew 25 feet 8 inches (compared with a design draft of 24 feet). With full loads of coal and ammunition, she would draw about 27 feet. "This increased immersion reduces her speed and freeboard, affects her tactical qualities, and alters the position of the armor belt. At her maximum draft the belt would be entirely submerged."

The board was outraged. In the future, battleships would be designed for a normal load including not less than two-thirds of full capacity of ammunition, stores, and coal. That was in 1896, after two more classes, *Iowa* and *Kearsage*, had been designed.

Even so, the *Indiana*s made a great impression on foreign observers. Their designers apparently had solved the problem of cramming an enormous weight of ordnance, far more than in contemporary British ships, into a very compact hull. For some reason the issue of the 6-inch RF gun was never mentioned, although it could easily have been deduced from statements made in contemporary Navy Department *Annual Reports*. Indeed, this point—that it was easier to build large conventional guns than large-calibre RF weapons—appears not to have been widely understood even within the U.S. service.

It remained to build the prototype seagoing, or long-endurance, ship. The Democrats gained control of the House of Representatives in November 1890, and no battleship was authorized in 1891. Senate conferences, however, restored a ship after the House deleted it the following year, and on 19 July 1892 Congress approved a "seagoing coastline battleship" (as opposed to a "coastline battleship") of about 9,000 tons, which became the *Iowa*. The Policy Board had

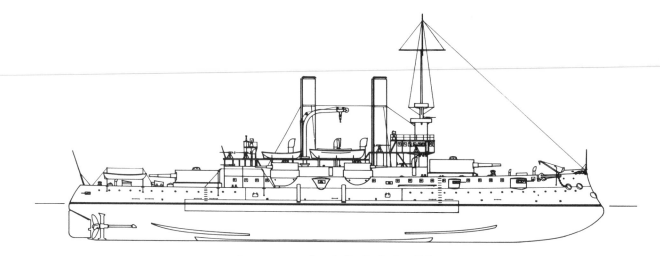

Iowa as completed. (A. D. Baker III)

planned to trade protection for long endurance, but C&R preferred to save weight in the main and secondary batteries (12-inch vs. 13-inch guns, on the ground that the smaller-calibre gun was now extremely effective; and 4-inch RF instead of the earlier 6-inch BLR) and belt armor (14-inch Harvey, more effective than the 18-inch nickel steel of the earlier class). Elimination of the 6-inch guns made the 8-inch guns, if anything, more necessary, since apart from the 12-inch guns they were the only real punch available against light armor.

What made the *Iowa* a seagoing battleship was her long forecastle, extending aft to the after 8-inch turrets. Associated with it was a longer hull and a somewhat greater displacement than the *Indiana*s, 11,410 rather than 10,288 tons. The 8-inch turrets were set further apart, and seakeeping was much improved. Coal capacity, most importantly at normal displacement, was much increased. It seems coincidental that the displacement of this ship was close to that which the Policy Board predicted for a conventionally protected long-endurance ship, 11,200 tons. The *Iowa* was the last design to follow the Policy Board pattern even in overall concept.

Externally, the *Iowa* was most noticeable for her very tall funnels, adopted to improve the draught to her boilers. In her tumble-home and her funnels she corresponded to the contemporary armored-cruiser *Brooklyn*. She made a greater impression as a much better seaboat than the *Indiana*s. As late as 1898, when later battleships were still under construction, the Board on Construction could call for an "improved *Iowa*"—meaning a long-forecastle seaboat—as its choice for future construction.

Although C&R continued work on further battleship designs, none was authorized in 1893 or in 1894. Tracy was out of office, and government funds were scarce because of a depression in 1893. Secretary of the Navy Hilary A. Herbert had opposed Tracy's bat-

tleships in 1890, but in 1893 he had been converted to Mahan's views, calling for at least one battleship in his 1893 report, and then for three the following year (FY95). Two were authorized on 2 March 1895, the *Kearsage* and *Kentucky*.

They were a distinct departure, with its double-decked turret, in which two heavy and two medium guns were combined to take maximum advantage of each centerline position. The *Kearsage* was unique among American battleships in not being named after a state. Instead, she memorialized a Civil War steam sloop, just lost, which had defeated the Confederate raider *Alabama* in a famous battle in 1864. Although the authorizing act required that one ship be built on the Pacific coast, both were built by Newport News.

C&R circulated four sketch designs late in March. Their hull was a compromise, with 3 feet more freeboard than the *Indiana* but without the forecastle of the *Iowa*. Nominal coal capacity was also a compromise: 500 tons, compared with 400 for the *Indiana* and 625 for the *Iowa*. The C&R paper made no distinction between home and distant fleets; in five years the Policy Board concepts had sunk without trace.

Side armor was increased to 15 inches and, in a new departure, the armor deck sloped down towards the ends from the top of the main belt, to increase the protected hull volume. By this time BuOrd actually had a 5-inch RF gun, and the designs all showed a long 6 inch-armored casemate carrying fourteen of them amidships. To provide space for it, the 8-inch turrets of earlier designs had to be pushed out toward the ends of the ship. Mounting some or all of the 8-inch guns on the centerline would, therefore, maximize broadside firepower even if the number of 8-inch guns had to be reduced.

Gunhouses had been considered for the 5-inch battery, but they were rejected on grounds of weight, complexity, difficulty of control, and problems of

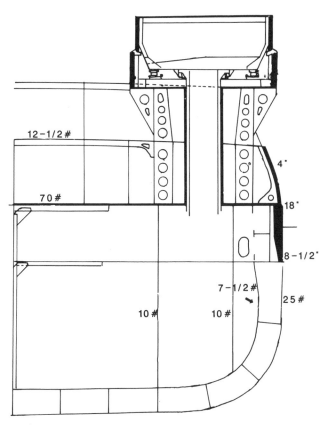

Indiana cross section

Cross sections of the *Indiana* and *Iowa* are shown for comparison. The *Indiana*-class cross section was taken from a plan dated 1893. It shows (in dashed outline) the 8-inch turret as originally planned, with sloped sides. Virtually all U.S. warships of this period were designed with cone-sided turrets, but in 1892 the Bureau of Ordnance had this policy reversed, arguing that such turrets were too cramped. Note also the very short barbette of the 8-inch turret in the *Indiana*, compared with the much broader barbette of the *Iowa*. Rapid-firing guns might have been able to collapse the *Indiana*'s turret by undermining the relatively unprotected structure below it; see the light armor protecting the side above the *Iowa*'s belt.

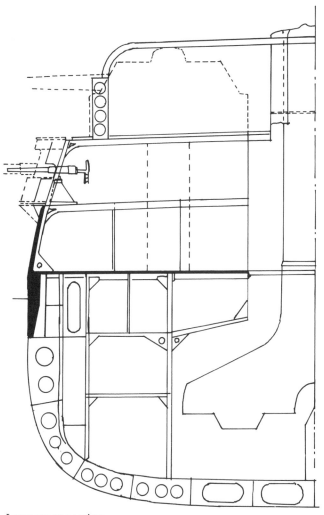

Iowa cross section

ammunition supply. The 6-inch casemate would be proof against the 6-inch shellfire of foreign battleships at 1,000 yards. At the same time the 8-inch gun was justified for its ability to penetrate just such armor at a similar range. It could, in turn, be defeated by 10-inch armor, but it appeared that such heavy protection would be impractical even on the greater displacements of foreign ships.

The main battery was to repeat the 12-inch gun of the *Iowa*, on the theory that, even within a decade, few if any ships would be proof against it, while the heavier 13-inch gun could not fire nearly as rapidly.

As for the 8-inch battery, the C&R alternatives were (A) with four turrets arranged lozenge-fashion (two on the centerline, two in the waist); (B) with two 8-inch turrets on the beam forward, and one superfiring aft; (C) with two 8-inch turrets on the centerline, both superfiring; and (D) in which the same pair of turrets was mounted in the waist, so that the broadside was reduced to two 8-inch guns. In all of the superfiring designs, the heavy 12-inch turrets were to have been protected from 8-inch blast by 1-inch plates spaced two feet above them. Even so, it seemed unlikely that the superfiring guns would be able to fire near the centerline without injuring the crews of the heavy guns.

C&R favored design (A), which provided the heaviest 8-inch broadside, at the least risk of losing firepower in the event of battle damage; clearly the 8-inch turrets could not be so well protected as the heavier ones. BuOrd liked none of the designs. An ensign in the bureau who would later become its chief, Joseph Strauss, devised the double-story turret as a solution. He argued that, of all the C&R plans, only (C) could be considered a real improvement, but that even it was too subject to blast and that it unduly constricted the superstructure (that is, the casemate). Strauss also argued that the crews of the forward 5-inch guns would be subject to blast when the forward 8-inch turret was trained abaft the beam.

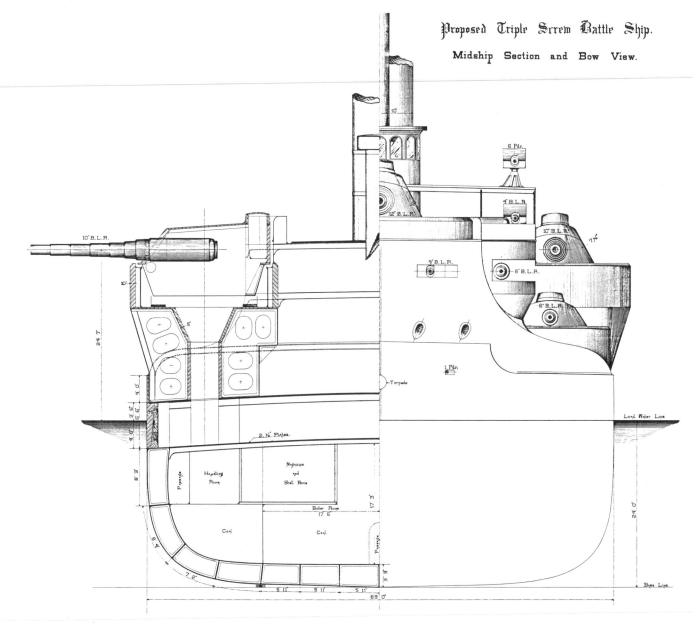

Proposed Triple Screw Battle Ship.
Midship Section and Bow View.

Although no battleships were authorized after the *Iowa* (*above and following pages*), U.S. constructors continued to develop new designs. This proposed triple-screw battleship of 1892–93 clearly reflects French and German ideas of the time, with its single-gun turrets and its fat military masts. An official model of the cruiser *New York* shows similar masts, which were abandoned before the ship was completed. The triple screws show the influence of George Melville, the long-time chief of the Bureau of Engineering. Although far from later U.S. practice, this was not a flight of fancy; it was signed by Philip Hichborn, in 1893 chief constructor. Presumably the design originated in the expectation that the Republicans, and Benjamin Tracy with them, would survive the 1892 election.

Hence he offered his design (E), in which an 8-inch turret was rigidly fixed to each of the 12-inch turrets. Strauss argued that the 8-inch turret would actually gain considerably in protection, since its barbette would be the barbette of the lower turret.

Weight would actually be saved. Because of advances in turret design the 13in/8in mount ultimately adopted weighed less than the twin 13-inch turret of the *Indiana*, 947 rather than 987 tons (without ammunition).

It could be argued that under many circumstances it might be desirable for the 8-inch guns to fire at some part of an enemy ship other than that at which the 12-inch guns would fire, to which Strauss replied that in practice even a large ship was a small target at any realistic battle range, so that all guns would generally be pointed at her middle. At shorter ranges, since the 8-inch guns fired two or three times while the heavier ones loaded, the double turret could train back and forth to allow them to engage their own

Proposed Triple Screw Battle Ship.

Principal Dimensions.

Length over All _____ 393'.0'
Length on Water Line _ 387'.0'
Breadth on Water Line 69.0'
Draught (Mean) _____ 24.0'
Displacement _____ 11000. Tons.
I.H.P. (Forced Draft) 14000.
Speed _____ 18. Knots.
I.H.P. (Assisted Draft) 10900.
Speed _____ 17. Knots.

Armament.

2.12'. B.L.R.
2.10'. B.L.R.
8. 8'. B.L.R.
8. 4'. B.L.R.
8. 8. Pdr. R.F.G.
4. 3. Pdr. R.F.G.
8. 1. Pdr. R.F.G.
9. Machine Guns.
6. Torpedo Tubes.

Armor Thickness.

Complete Belt or Side Armor.
Thickness. 14'. 12'. 10'. 6' And 4'.
12'. B.L.R. Barbette _____ 12'.
12'. B.L.R. Turret _____ 8'.
10'. B.L.R. Barbette _____ 10'.
10'. B.L.R. Turret _____ 7½' And 8'.
6'. B.L.R. Barbette And Turret. 6'.
Protective Deck _____ 3'.
Conning Tower And Tube _____ 10' And 7'.

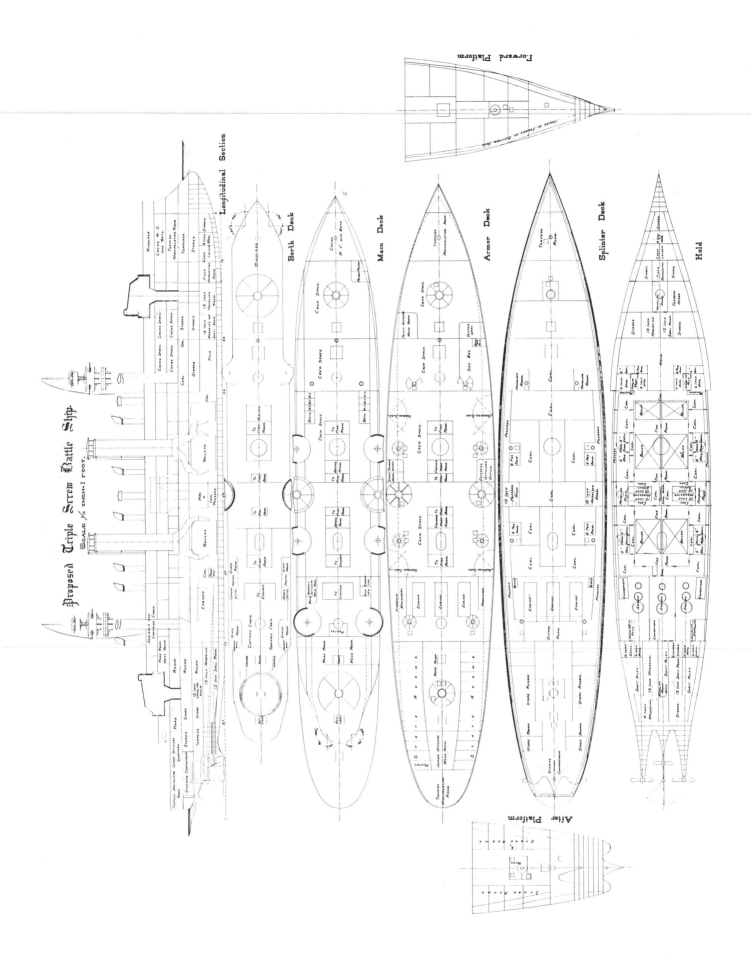

Proposed Triple Screw Battle Ship.
Scale 1/16 inch-1 foot.

Longitudinal Section

Berth Deck

Main Deck

Armor Deck

Splinter Deck

Hold

Forward Platform

After Platform

Photographed at Boston in October 1916, the *Kearsage* shows standard modifications to U.S. pre-dreadnoughts carried out after the world cruise of the "Great White Fleet." Her bridgework has been drastically cut down, and the canvas covering the rail above her conning tower indicates her conning position. A wheel, located within her cage foremast, has been covered by an awning within the mast proper. Small unarmored range-finders have been mounted above her two turrets. Note her very low freeboard, a major defect of several U.S. battleship classes. (Ted Stone)

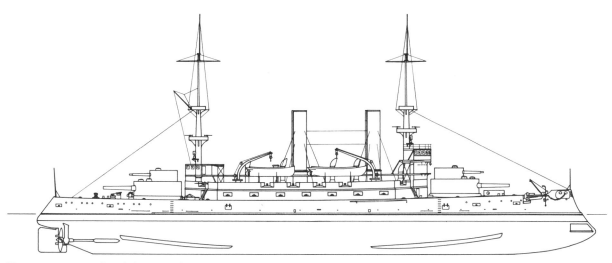

The *Kearsage* as completed (A. D. Baker III)

targets. Strauss estimated, for example, that it would take only thirty seconds to train such a turret from one side to the other, so that "a heavy fire could be maintained against a weak enemy to port while the [heavy] guns were being prepared for delivering their blows against a stronger enemy to starboard. . . ."

Strauss particularly emphasized the elimination of blast interference within the heavy gun battery, noting that it was a major problem abroad. For ex-

ample, in the French *Brennus* "a system of bugle calls has been adopted by which one or more guns' crews must desert their guns and seek cover from the blast of some heavy gun that is about to be fired."

BuOrd also challenged the move back to the 12-inch gun. It considered the 13 inch to be 30 percent more powerful and noted that 15-inch plate would stand up to 12-inch fire even at 1,000 yards; at that range 14-inch armor (as in the *Iowa*) would keep out

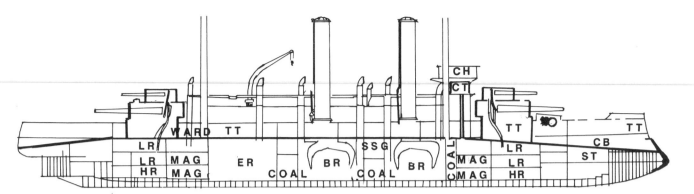

Inboard profile of *Kearsage* as completed.

90 percent of such shells. To keep out the 13-inch shell, however, the plate would need 40 percent more resistance. No could BuOrd see why the 13-inch gun should fire materially more slowly than the 12 inch, since similar power-loading equipment was being provided for both. Here it appears that C&R had in mind the adoption of handloading for greater simplicity.

BuOrd also questioned the proposed ammunition load. A 12- or 13-inch gun could be expected to fire once in five minutes, an 8 inch once in two, and a 5 inch, three times per minute. Sixty-five shells per heavy gun were specified, which BuOrd equated to 162 per 8 inch and 487 per 5 inch; the figures actually adopted were 75 and 100. Even allowing for the greater difficulty in refilling major-calibre magazines, this seemed ludicrous, and the bureau proposed 50 rounds per heavy gun, 125 per 8 inch, and 250 per 5 inch.

C&R protested, but BuOrd won, both in configuration and in the question of the 13-inch gun. The crucial test was a proving-ground experiment against a target representing the side armor of the *Iowa*: at 1,500 yards the 13-inch gun penetrated easily but the 12 inch did not.

The ships were built with improved protection. The belt was thickened to 16.5 inches, and, although its width remained at 7 feet 6 inches, the belt as a whole was raised 6 inches, so that 3 feet 6 inches was carried above water at normal displacement. BuOrd had argued for a full foot rise, but C&R had maintained that it was relatively unimportant whether the belt was submerged. Far worse for its lower edge to be *exposed* to shellfire; hits above the belt would tear up the side of the ship, and flooding could be controlled by water-excluding material. Atop the belt was a 2.75-inch deck (70-pound armor atop two 20-pound layers) under which (at the armor shelf level) was a 25-pound (10 over boilers) splinter deck. Fore and aft of the machinery spaces the belt tapered to 10.5 inches, but behind it the armor deck sloped (covered now by 80- rather than 70-pound armor) to the lower edge of the belt, so that the *effective* thickness remained the same. Armor bulkheads fore (10 inch)

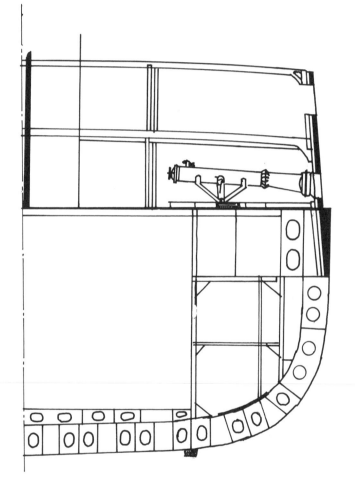

Cross section of *Kearsage* as completed, at her engine room. Note the trainable above-water torpedo tube, about the same size as a secondary battery gun.

and aft (12 inch) closed the space between side belt and sloping deck at the ends of the machinery spaces. Aft of the main belt the armor deck sloped down to the waterline. Its armor covering increased to 160 pounds to protect shafts and steering gear from plunging hits. The casemate or upper belt was 6 inches thick (5-inch armor on two half-inch layers), closed by 4-inch bulkheads extending to the barbette armor.

The sloping magazine protection was an innovation; another was 4-inch bow armor to protect seaworthiness from waterline hits forward. The corresponding after extension would not come until the *Virginia* class.

Neither ship was commissioned before 1900, so that two more classes were laid down before any lessons of actual operation could be learned. Gunnery trials were successful, so that at the least the Strauss concept could be considered technically, if not tactically, proven. By that time, however, progress in gunpower had been so swift as to make both 8-inch and 13-inch guns obsolete.

As might be imagined, the *Kearsage* design was controversial. Some foreign observers considered it a most efficient concentration of offensive power, although no foreign navy moved to duplicate it. Others considered it yet another example of American overgunning. To some extent the question of the basic design was obscured by detail problems. For example, defects in the design of the 13-inch mountings made it necessary to mount these weapons so far back in the turrets that very large gun ports were required, and these in turn appeared to negate much of the value of the turrets' proper. In addition, the large 5-inch casemate, the first of its kind in U.S. practice, was not broken up by splinter bulkheads. A single hit might wipe out the entire battery.

Perhaps partly in view of controversy surrounding the *Kearsage*s, the secretary of the navy convened a board on future battleship design under Rear Admiral J. G. Walker on 25 March 1896. As of this date exactly one modern U.S. battleship, the *Indiana*, was in commission, and there was very little experience in her performance. The *Iowa* and the *Kearsage* were on the way. The Walker Board could choose either to duplicate one of the three or to suggest something new.

The board rejected the entire concept of the coastal battleship. The primary issue in a naval war would be the defeat of an enemy battle fleet attempting to establish a base in the New World. Moreover, given the paucity of coaling stations south of the Chesapeake, it seemed likely that U.S. battleships operating in or near the West Indies might actually be farther from their coaling stations than their enemies. The West Indies, already important, would become the most probable theatre of war if, as appeared likely, a Panama Canal were built. Finally, "we have long stretches of inhospitable coast and much bad weather. Our battleships, even if strictly 'coastline' in their sphere of operations, have greater need to be strictly 'seagoing' than vessels of their class operating in the Mediterranean, or in the narrow seas of northern Europe."

At the same time, the Naval War College recommended that draft be limited to 23 feet on the basis of war games envisaging naval combat on the South Atlantic and Gulf coasts. U.S. ships so designed would be able to enter harbor whereas deeper-draft European battleships would have to stay outside the bars. This was very much a counsel of weakness, since a strong U.S. battle fleet would have had no need to flee into its harbors.

A combination of beam limited by docks and restricted draft implied that displacement could not rise much above that of the previous classes. Seakeeping would require an *Iowa*-type forecastle, hence a reduction in weights (such as guns) high in the ship. The board was unwilling, however, to revert to the 12-inch gun, considering the smashing effect of the heaviest gun well worth its slower rate of fire. The double-turret was rejected, particularly as it had not been tried in practice. The *Iowa* arrangement might have been preferable, if not for its unacceptable weight. Moreover, the board wanted to simplify armament, with only a single calibre between the heaviest weapons and the torpedo-defense battery. It did endorse the armor belt arrangement adopted in the *Kearsage*.

Fortunately BuOrd had a new rapid-firing 6-inch gun to offer which, it expected, would fire three to five times as often as an 8-inch gun in a turret. The gun itself weighed so much less that about twice as many could be carried, so that, weight for weight, a 6-inch battery could provide six to ten times as many rounds per minute as an 8-inch battery. The board estimated an effective superiority of seven to one in number of shots per unit time, which amounted to 700 vs. 250 pounds of shell. The higher rate of fire derived not only from the lighter weight of the 6-inch shell but also from the assumed superiority of guns mounted on an open deck (if behind armor), a point that would be important in the debates over the *Virginia* and *Connecticut* classes.

The Walker Board also questioned the value of the 8-inch gun as an armor penetrator. True, it could put an AP shell through the 6-inch armor of foreign secondary batteries. It could not, however, put explosives behind even such armor. On the other hand, a single 13-inch common (HE) shell could probably put most of an enemy casemate out of action. This should have been no great surprise: the 8-inch gun was at best a compromise in the absence of a satisfactory American rapid-firing medium-calibre gun.

Congress authorized three ships, the *Illinois*, *Alabama*, and *Wisconsin* on 10 June 1896. C&R worked particularly fast: the circular for bidders was ready only twelve days later, and contract plans on 28 August, only fifty-eight working days from the start of design work. The Walker Board itself had reported only on 10 May.

The design had two characteristic features: a new balanced 13-inch turret with a sloped face; and funnels abreast rather than in tandem, the boilers being

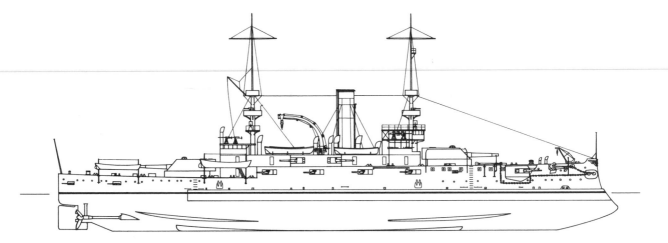

The *Illinois* as completed. (A. D. Baker III)

set athwartships rather than fore and aft. They were the last fire tube boilers in U.S. warships. As for the turrets, they had an overhang at the rear, and the new face plate made it possible to mount the trunnions closer, so that the ports were considerably smaller. Balancing eliminated the lists experienced in the *Indiana*s when their guns were trained on the beam. The two turrets were placed as close together as possible to reduce heavy weight near the bow, which would cause pitching. Fourteen 6-inch guns were mounted between them, four of them in an upper level. The system of protection followed that developed for the *Kearsage* class.

No new battleships were authorized in 1897. Although the Republican platform of 1896 had supported further naval expansion, neither President McKinley nor his secretary of the navy, John D. Long, seems to have had much interest in the issue. Moreover, with five ships under construction (and not due for completion until 1899 or later), there was little pressure for new construction to keep yards busy. Completion of the authorized ships was being delayed by a dispute over the cost of their armor, which was considered excessive. This problem would delay the construction of several classes of U.S. battleships of this period. Long went so far as to recommend only a single battleship (for FY98) in his 1897 *Annual Report* to Congress, on the grounds that U.S. naval power, having doubled over the last few years, would suffice for almost any emergency. The destruction of the *Maine* radically changed the situation.

On 25 April 1898 the United States declared war on Spain, and a week later, on 4 May, Congress authorized a large naval program, including three battleships, one of which was to be named after the destroyed second-class battleship *Maine*. The form these ships would take was by no means obvious. The Board on Construction initially called for an improved *Iowa*, that is, a good seaboat, with 13-inch,

8-inch, and 6-inch guns. When it came to a vote, though, the choice was between duplicating the previous (*Illinois*) class or buying an improved *Iowa* in which the 12-inch gun would be replaced by a 13-inch, and the 4-inch by a more powerful 5-inch weapon. The 8-inch gun was clearly still popular, but the discussion brought out the advantages of simplifying ammunition supply by supressing it. Moreover, it seemed unlikely that 8-inch guns could be accommodated on the available displacement. Duplicating the existing *Illinois* design, which had no 8-inch guns, would moreover save construction time.

This decision did not quite stand, since the new ships, which became the *Maine* (BB 12) class, were modified to incorporate several major advances in technology. First, with the success of smokeless powder, heavy gun development turned back to smaller calibres coupled with higher velocities. The first product of this trend was a new 12in/40. Second, Krupp Cemented armor became widely available, so that belt thickness could be reduced. On 8 October 1898 the Navy Department officially approved substitution of both 12-inch belt armor for the previous 16.5 inch and the 12in/40 for the earlier 13in/35 gun. Finally, water-tube boilers had become sufficiently reliable to warrant their use in battleships. Although Chief Engineer George Melville wanted both water-tube boilers and five-cylinder quadruple- (rather than triple-) expansion engines from the first, the Board on Construction resisted any substantial change in design. Although Melville's proposals would have increased efficiency and saved weight, they would not have increased speed.

On 17 May 1898 the U.S. naval attache in Paris(!), however, reported that a battleship being built by Cramp (in Philadelphia!) for Russia would be capable of 18 knots, 2 knots more than the new battleships as then designed, on a similar displacement, thanks to her Niclausse water-tube boilers. Secretary

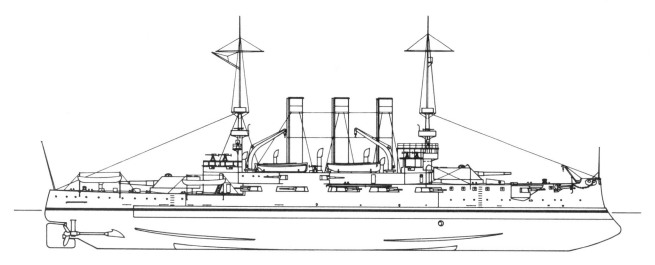

The *Missouri* as completed. (A. D. Baker III)

The *Maine* (BB 10) was one of a group of six U.S. pre-dreadnoughts roughly analogous to contemporary foreign practice, hence lacking the intermediate 8-inch battery. She is shown as modernized with cage masts and with minimal bridge structure. There are unarmored long-base range-finders atop her turrets. Unlike the later dreadnoughts, she retained a substantial chart house at the base of her cage foremast. The canvas screen above it protected a "conning platform" inside the mast, on which stood a wheel and a pelorus. The larger canvas screen defined an open, or "flying," bridge from which the ship was conned. In later designs it was provided with long removable wings. Note that several 6-inch secondary guns have been removed, and the wet forward gun port plated over. During and after World War One the searchlights on most U.S. battleships were concentrated on one level on each mast, with a control position below them, and the canvas screens were replaced by metal windscreens. The *Maine* was not so thoroughly modernized, but a canvas windscreen was erected to protect the flying bridge. It connected the canvas of the bridge with the canvas of the conning platform and had windows in it. This photograph is undated but was probably taken about 1917. (U.S. National Archives)

of the Navy Long proposed that the date of closing bids be set back so that the ships could be redesigned for higher speed, but the Board on Construction dissented on the ground that none of Melville's proposed changes would be satisfactory. Melville was able to inform the bidders, however, that, all things being equal, speed would be an important consideration in the contract award.

Cramp now offered to lengthen the ship by 15 feet, using Niclausse boilers to achieve 18 knots. Newport News wanted to add almost 20 feet to achieve 18 knots at about 12,500 tons. This bid incorporated

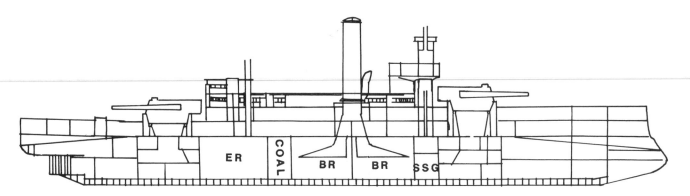

Inboard profile of *Illinois* as completed.

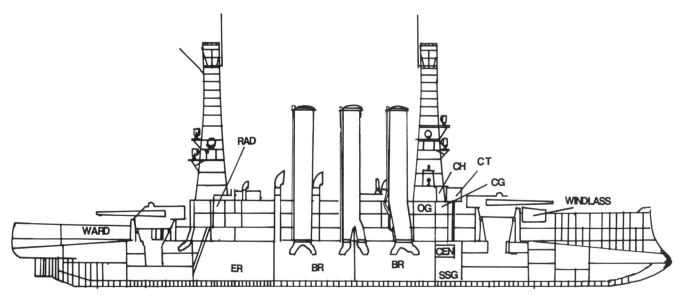

Inboard profile of *Maine* (BB 10) as modernized with cage masts. Note the installation of a central (fire control) station, which the U.S. Navy considered the key to long-range gunnery.

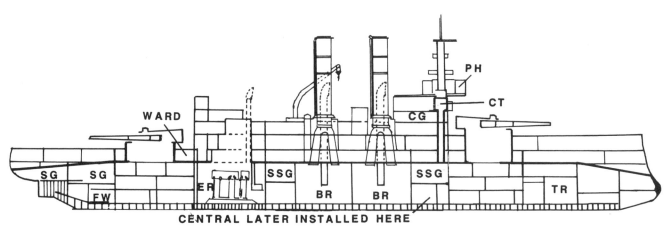

Inboard profile of *Idaho,* a *Maine*-sized battleship designed about five years later.

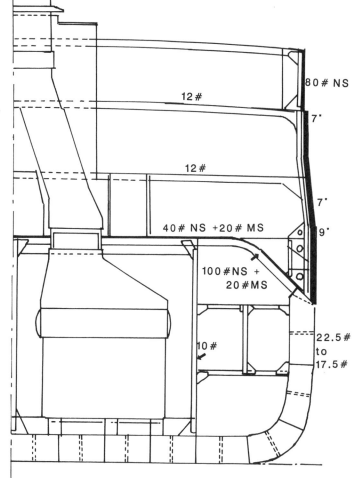

Cross section of *Idaho*.

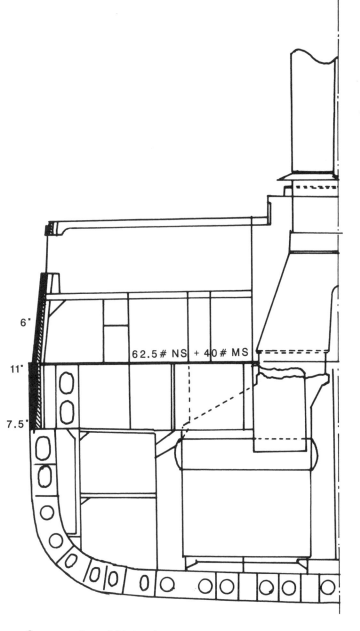

Cross section of *Maine* (BB 10).

Melville's proposed modifications, and it was his design which was built. A 60 percent increase in horsepower (to 16,000) was accompanied by the addition of two 6-inch guns to the broadside battery. The weapons were 50 rather than 40 calibres long. Another innovation was the submerged torpedo tube, which replaced the more vulnerable above-water type.

The outward indication of a major change in engineering plant was a shift to three funnels in tandem, associated with twelve Thornycroft boilers rather than with the previous eight. The *Maine* differed from her two sisters in having twenty-four Niclausse boilers.

The *Maine*s were the last of their generation. As their design progressed, the United States became a world power through victory over Spain. In addition, the U.S. Navy received its first modern combat experience, testing the *Texas*, *Indiana*, and *Iowa* designs. Ironically, that experience enhanced the prestige of the discredited 8-inch gun. In the major naval battle, Santiago, the 13-inch guns made no hits at all, whereas the 8-inch made thirteen (which was still a poor showing, as 319 rounds had been fired). Moreover, officers present at this and other battles had been very favorably impressed by the range and flat trajectory of the weapon and probably also by its relatively good rate of fire. It should have been no great surprise that the slow-firing 6-inch guns in use at this time made much less of an impression.

It seems remarkable in retrospect that no one analyzing this experience commented that the weapons in combat were at least a full generation *behind* weapons planned for ships then under construction. Throughout the history of modern warships, however, combat experience, no matter how objectively irrelevant, has had enormous impact. For example, the British found 4.5-inch guns essential as a means of supporting troops landing in the Falklands. It is by no means clear that such force support will be needed again, particularly in the context of the NATO scenario which, in theory, defines British naval requirements. Yet future British ASW frigates will all be armed with 4.5-inch guns.

The strategic effect of the victory was to end the argument over coast defense. From now on, the United States would operate an ocean fleet. Congress was willing to accept ships about 2,000 tons larger than their predecessors, according to the language of the first postwar appropriation act, passed on 3 March 1899 and under which the *Virginia*, *Nebraska*, and *Georgia* were built. Even more tonnage proved necessary, and more money was added as part of the Act of 7 June 1900, which resulted in the *New Jersey* and *Rhode Island*. The 13,500-ton figure had been proposed by the Board on Construction in a 12 July 1898 memorandum on the 1899 program for Secretary Long.

The memorandum envisaged an improved *Maine*, armed with four 12-inch guns, sixteen 6-inch, ten 12 pdr(3-inch) antidestroyer guns, twelve 6 pdr, and six machine guns. Belt armor would be 12-inch Krupp, and speed 18.5 knots. This was a compromise. Chief Constructor Hichborn and the chief of BuOrd and president of the board, Captain Charles O'Neill, wanted 13,000 tons, against the chiefs of Equipment, Captain R. B. Bradford, and Steam Engineering, George W. Melville, both of whom preferred 14,000 tons. Hichborn also preferred a mixed battery, including eight 8-inch in turrets and about twelve 5-inch, the side armor corresponding in extent to that of the *Alabama* but reduced from 16.5 to 13.5 inches.

The board did not return to considering the new battleship until October 1899. The *Kearsage* arrangement was clearly the most efficient way of combining 8-inch and 12-inch guns, but it had yet to be tested. Several on the board feared the consequences of entrusting four guns to a single man and to a single gun-training engine. Captain O'Neill favored the superposed turret, and believed that on 13,500 tons he could have a combination of two superposed 8-inch and two 8-inch turrets in the waist, plus four 12-inch guns, twelve 6-inch RF, and sixteen 3-inch antidestroyer weapons. The battery would total 1,441 tons, about 10.6 percent of the displacement, a practicable figure. The chief constructor disagreed. He was willing to vote for separate 12- and 8-inch guns but argued that it would not be long before both were replaced by 10-inch weapons. Melville still disliked the complexity of three major calibres. Bradford settled the issue: the 8 inch was superior to the 6 inch because it could penetrate the 6-inch armor that shielded the secondary batteries of foreign battleships.

Speed was controversial. Bradford was willing to accept 18.5 knots, but O'Neill considered that insufficient. He wanted 20. The board compromised by requiring at least 19 knots.

The two major alternative designs both incorporated the new 8in/45: (A) with four 8-inch turrets arranged as in the *Indiana* and *Iowa*, and (B) with two double (*Kearsage*-type) turrets and two more 8-inch turrets in the waist, for a broadside of four 12-inch and six 8-inch guns. Both were high-freeboard flush-deckers, for good seakeeping. Design A had sixteen 6in/50 on her gun deck, B, twelve. The pace of design and construction had been so hectic that the *Kearsage* turret, three classes back, had not yet been tested.

The Board on Construction now included three seagoing officers in its makeup. In May 1899, the board favored Design A, but one of the seagoing officers dissented so strongly that the secretary of the navy called a second board to reconsider the matter. Eight line officers were added to the Board on Construction; it seems noteworthy that the chief of BuOrd was not included.

The larger group favored the superposed turrets, seven to four, although one member, Rear Admiral Albert S. Barker, voted to build three battleships of Design A and two of Design B. Twelve of the thirteen members of the new board actually approved this rather grotesque proposal, which stood for a time. The lone dissenter was David W. Taylor, representing the chief constructor. He argued that surely one plan or the other must be the better, and that the matter was far too important to compromise. Moreover, uniformity in design would be a major advantage. "To divide these vessels between two types is to definitely advertise to the world that although we have completed two superposed turret vessels [the *Kearsage*s] we do not know whether or not they are better than if they had been built with separate turrets. . . ."

Although the secretary of the navy approved the majority report, six months later BuOrd came out in favor of uniformity of design, proposing that the two waist turrets of Design B be replaced by four additional 6-inch guns. Although bids had already been received and contracts awarded, the secretary now called yet another board into session. It consisted of the Board on Construction plus two rear admirals and five captains, a total of twelve. In a final vote, ten favored design B. It was later claimed, however, that several had actually preferred design A but had voted for B to defeat the new BuOrd design.

Thus the design built as the *Virginia* was fixed only on 5 February 1901, almost two years after authorization. As Taylor had foreseen, the effect of this delay was to destroy confidence in the judgment of the Navy. The new appropriation act of 3 March 1901

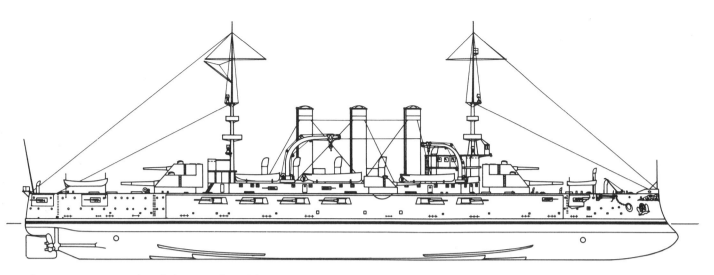

The *Georgia* as completed. (A. D. Baker III)

required that the secretary of the navy provide a detailed rationale for the design of the next battleships and armored cruisers. Two battleships were, however, authorized on 1 July 1901.

As for the *Virginia*s, gunnery improvement was their downfall. According to Rear Admiral Seaton Schroeder, who commanded the *Virginia*,

> by a strange paradox, the great increase in the rapidity of fire of our heavy guns from, say, one shot in three minutes to three shots in one minute, virtually neutralized the advantage of having 8-inch guns where they could be fired without interfering with the 12-inch. Whenever a gun is fired in a turret there is a certain amount of concussion which precludes firing another for a few seconds; and, even with smokeless powder, the heated gasses linger for an appreciable time in front after each discharge, making it impossible to point for the next shot until they have been wafted away. With the two 12 inch in a turret firing alternately, and each able to fire every twenty seconds, there would be only about ten seconds between 12-inch shots; and if the 8 inch were to 'butt in,' they would probably interfere with the next 12in shot—the last thing to be thought of. As that problem gradually developed, and the rapidity of fire increased, each ship tried different combinations of fire to obtain maximum opportunities for fire—single-barrelled salvos, double-barrelled salvos, double-barrelled 8-inch salvos combined with single-barrelled 12 inch, and so on. But the ultimate conclusion was that rapidity of fire had knocked out the superposed turret.

Even worse, by the time the new superposed-turret battleships were complete, HMS *Dreadnought* had appeared, to make them entirely obsolete.

For all that, they were fine ships. An increase of 3,000IHP over the *Maine*s, coupled with a much longer hull, guaranteed 19 knots, which was good for a pre-dreadnought and certainly up to foreign standards.

Maximum belt armor was again reduced, this time to 11 inches, and the protective deck sloped down at the sides to meet the lower edge of the belt and so to reinforce it. Great metacentric height made them very lively even in a light seaway. Battleships given antitorpedo "blisters" in the 1920s would behave similarly.

Even before they had been laid down, the *Virginia*s were succeeded by a larger and more powerful class of strikingly different design, the *Connecticut*s. On 6 March 1901, the secretary of the navy asked the Board on Construction for yet another study of future battleship designs. As before, the technical members of the board disliked the superposed turret, and some argued that weapons mounted singly in casemates could fire much faster than guns in turrets (and single enclosed guns, more rapidly than multiple enclosed guns). On 13 June, for example, the chief constructor, Admiral F. T. Bowles, noted that despite the weight saving entailed in multiple turrets, the French had tried hard to keep to single mountings.

BuOrd introduced a new weapon, a high-powered 7-inch gun, the most powerful whose shell could be handled by a single man.* It was, then, the most powerful weapon that could operate without loading machinery. It could achieve a high rate of fire even though, unlike the 6 inch it would replace, it employed bagged powder charges. The prototype was test-fired in August 1901.

Inspired by the new weapon, the board initially favored a BuOrd proposal in which both 8-inch and 6-inch guns would be replaced by twenty-four 7 inch. There would also be twenty-four 3-inch antitorpedo

---

* The shell weighed 165 pounds, compared with about 100 pounds for a 6 inch and about 250 pounds for an 8 inch, which had to be handled either by power or by several men. The 7-inch gun was, therefore, the largest capable of really rapid fire in the context of existing technology.

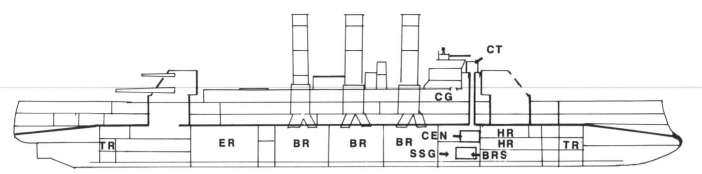

Inboard profile of *Nebraska*, 1919. Cranes and masts have been omitted for clarity. Note the central station and battle radio station, both installed during modernization.

boat weapons. In view of the increasing threat of HE shellfire, the main armor was further spread out and, therefore, thinner than in the preceding class. The belt would be 10 inches thick over the machinery, 9 inches over magazines, and 4 inches to the ends, covered by a 6-inch upper belt and a 7-inch casemate. The protective deck would be flat over the machinery spaces, to allow for fore and aft ammunition passages, and sloped elsewhere. It appeared that a slight increase in power, in a longer hull with finer ends, would maintain speed at 19 knots. Displacement would rise to 15,560 tons.

C&R proposed instead a modified *Virginia* armed with sixteen 8-inch guns: twelve in turrets (four superposed) and four in casemates. The casemate weapons were later eliminated, so that the minority report by the board showed twelve 8 inch on 15,860 tons. There would also be twelve 6 inch and eight 3 inch. The majority rejected so great a reduction in the torpedo defense battery.

As in the case of the *Virginia*s, this split report did not end the argument; in November the entire board managed to agree on a third design mounting eight 8-inch guns (in four waist turrets) as well as twelve 7 inch on the broadside. This combination was not really so strange as it appeared at the time. Although the 7-inch and 8-inch guns differed in calibre by only an inch, the 7-inch shell weighed 165 pounds, the 8 inch, 250, and the guns were quite far apart in capability. The board justified its retention of the 8-inch gun as necessary to pierce the medium armor which covered much of the upperworks of contemporary battleships. It considered the 7 inch the best possible rapid-fire weapon, capable of penetrating 7 inches of armor at 3,000 yards, that is, at battle range.

Compared with the original majority design, this one had thicker (11-inch) belt and casemate (7 inch vs. 6 inch), adopted in view of recent increases in gun power. On 25 July 1902, the Board on Construction approved a reduction of deck slope armor from 3.5 to 3 inches (as in the *Virginia*s). The barbettes were also reduced below the gun deck, where they were already protected by a transverse bulkhead and

side armor (10 inch front and 7.5 inch rear were cut to 6 inches).

Two ships of this type, the *Connecticut* and *Louisiana*, were authorized on 1 July 1902. Three more were added the following year (3 March 1903: the *Vermont*, *Kansas*, and *Minnesota*) and, finally, the *New Hampshire* on 27 April 1904. In the last four ships the upper side belt was thickened from 6 to 7 inches, to resist the increasingly powerful intermediate batteries of foreign battleships; the main side belt was made uniform (9 inches) between the end turrets as weight compensation. The protective deck was sloped amidships to increase the effective thickness of side armor.

The last ship, the *New Hampshire*, incorporated further detail improvements. Her main transverse bulkheads were unpierced by doors, for better watertight integrity in the event of damage, and her berth and gun decks were rearranged amidships to add about 200 tons of coal capacity. Her magazines were rearranged to stow 20 percent more 12-inch and 7-inch projectiles in wartime, although her peacetime ammunition allowance matched that of her sisters. Her armor scheme was also modified, her side armor being shortened but the decks over her magazines being doubled (80- rather than 40-pound plate). Coal bunkers were modified so that coal could go directly from the upper bunkers to the boilers, leaving coal in lower bunkers to serve as torpedo protection in battle. Externally, she could be distinguished by the number of her hawsepipes, two rather than four, associated with the adoption of simpler and lighter windlasses.

These ships were designed for 18 rather than 19 knots, their greater length permitting a considerable reduction in power compared with the *Virginia*s. As completed, the six *Connecticut*s might be considered the peak of American pre-dreadnought battleship development. But as all were completed *after* HMS *Dreadnought*, they have to be considered obsolete from birth.

The other two U.S. pre-dreadnoughts, the *Idaho* and *Mississippi*, were the first of several attempts to

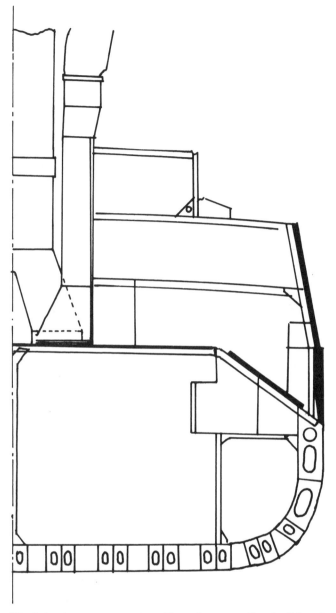

Virginia-class cross section. Note the centerline bulkhead through the boiler rooms, a common pre-dreadnought feature. It was later abandoned, at least in the U.S. Navy, because underwater damage on one side could flood so large a compartment that the ship could capsize. It was considered better to allow a ship to flood across her entire beam, if the torpedo defeated her underwater protection.

prune back the growth of battleship size and cost. U.S. battleships showed several bursts of growth, one of the most spectacular surely being the jump from the *Maine* of 1898 to the *Virginia* and then to the *Connecticut*. Until the latter class, the constructors had consistently exceeded the nominal displacement figures written into the authorizing acts (for example, 15,000 rather than 13,500 tons for the *Virginia*s). The reaction should have been no great surprise. It was led by George Dewey, Admiral of the Navy and

chairman of the General Board. He saw no reason for what he, as a nontechnologist, considered excessive growth. Like many successors, he preferred numbers of ships to individual size, an argument which would soon be prominent among enemies of the new dreadnoughts.

The program submitted to Congress in the spring of 1903 initially called for three *Connecticut*s. However, Dewey and then-Captain Alfred Thayer Mahan argued forcefully for smaller ships, and the Senate bill provided for four 12,000-ton battleships (and two armored cruisers). The Board on Construction well understood the sacrifice a 4,000-ton (25 percent) cut would entail; supported by President Theodore Roosevelt, it fought back. In the end, a compromise act bought both the three *Connecticut*s and two 13,000-ton battleships, at the cost of the armored cruisers originally requested.

The question now was what would be sacrificed to save 3,000 tons. On 27 May 1903 the chief constructor submitted five sketch designs. He had three alternative approaches. The new ships could be scaled down from the *Connecticut*s, or up from the *Maine*, or they could be built to a fresh design altogether. In the first concept, speed (loss of 1.5 knots), coal capacity (loss of 500 tons out of 2,000), armor (2 inches of belt), and weapons (two 7 inch and eight 3 inch) would have to be pared down. Seakeeping would also suffer, as the main deck would have to be cut down aft, and there would be no mainmast. Alternatively, the *Maine* could be scaled up, fourteen 7 inch replacing the sixteen 6 inch of the earlier ship. Hull depth would be increased to provide additional head room in the battery, and armor would be improved (deck sloped throughout and belt extended aft).

Because the two ships would have to be misfits, the chief constructor considered two radical options. One was a fast battleship, combining battleship armor with the main battery of the large armored-cruiser *Tennessee*. Since the latter displaced 1,500 tons more, this was not really practicable. Or, it would be possible to mount an all-big-gun battery, twelve 10 inch (see Chapter 2).

None of these alternatives was particularly attractive. On 10 June 1903 the cut-down *Connecticut* was chosen, although one board member, Admiral Bradford, objected to the loss of speed and thus preferred the improved *Maine*, capable of 18 knots. The chief constructor countered that 1 knot would cost a large fraction of the battery, and that nine existing ships were limited to 16 or 17 knots. The controversy continued through the fall of 1903, and opinions from the fleet were requested. Line officers uniformly expressed their disappointment at what could be attained on 13,000 tons. However, the board had never suggested that 13,000 equalled 16,000; it was merely trying to do its best on a congressionally limited

Virginia is shown after post–world cruise modifications. Note the range-finder atop her foremast and the bridge constructed on the roof of her conning tower. The funnel bands indicated her division and her position within that division: Third Battle Division, fourth ship. All bands were black. Of this class, only the *Virginia* and *New Jersey* had searchlight positions between their funnels, and only the *Virginia*, *Nebraska*, and *Rhode Island* had round rather than rectangular main tops.

Experimentally camouflaged during World War One, the *New Jersey* illustrates standard wartime modifications. Three of her six broadside 6-inch guns have been removed, and her bridge greatly enlarged, surmounted by a long-base range-finder. Her torpedo-defense (fire control) platforms have been plated in and fitted with vee-form wind baffles. They are also shielded from the light of the searchlights they control, which are mounted directly above, as in contemporary British ships. The British considered director control of searchlights an enormous advance. Without it, the searchlight operators were blinded by their lights, and the lights functioned as little more than beacons for destroyer attack. Note the armored range-finder atop the after 8 inch-12 inch turret. The camouflage scheme was a MacKay "disruptive low-visibility pattern" being tested against range-finders.

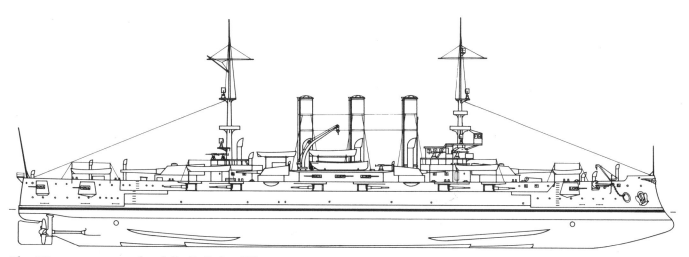

The *Minnesota* as completed (A. D. Baker III)

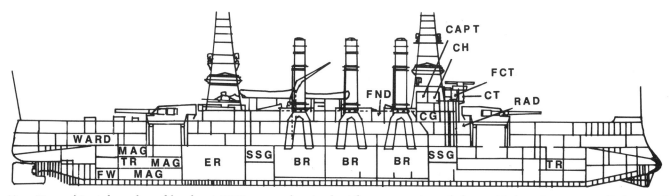

New Hampshire inboard profile about 1918, as modernized with cage masts and then with long-base range-finders and vee-form torpedo defense tops.

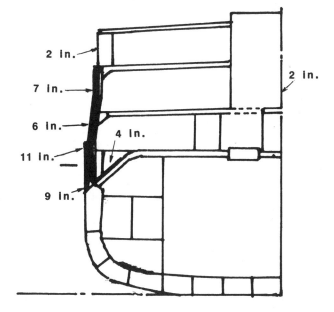

Connecticut-class cross section. The thickened area on the inner bottom at the turn of the bilge is not armor. It is wooden decking for coal passers. Similar features have been omitted from the other cross sections for clarity.

displacement. At a 7 October meeting Bowles displayed two sketch designs showing what 18 knots might cost: all armor above the main deck, some of the battery, and 250 tons of coal. Bradford replied that "there is not a single foreign ship building that is less than 18 knots . . . . We always prided ourselves on having a little smarter ships. . . . " However, the decision went in favor of the cut-down *Connecticut*, and contracts were signed in December.

It was not surprising that the two *Mississippis* were not very successful. Completed in 1909, they were placed in reserve as early as 1912. Two years later they were sold to Greece, the proceeds paying for a new dreadnought battleship.

The history of U.S. pre-dreadnoughts began with the 1890 Policy Board, which tried to specify the ultimate size of the battle fleet. In 1898 Germany instituted a Navy Law which not only set the size of the fleet but also required replacement as ships aged. The General Board suggested a similar plan for the United States in September 1901. It assumed that each ship would take four years to build and that ships would pass to the second line eighteen years

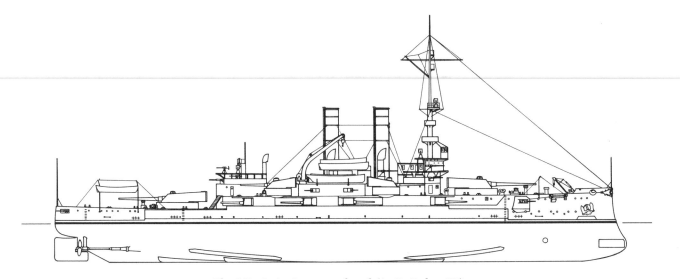

The *Mississippi* as completed (A. D. Baker III)

after commissioning. Two ships would be laid down each year, building up to a fleet of thirty-six first-class battleships in 1927. By this time the board assumed that the two most likely future naval enemies were Germany and Japan, an assumption that would remain constant until the end of World War One. Although other European powers could find themselves in conflict with the United States, the General Board tended to reason that public opinion in such democracies as France and England would prevent war. In Germany and Japan, on the other hand, public opinion could easily be controlled by the ruling government, which was known to be militaristic.

In theory, then, the United States would have to maintain both Atlantic and Pacific fleets, each equal to the possible enemy in that ocean. Matters were further complicated by German possession of many South Pacific islands, which could serve her as fleet bases in wartime. Germany could, therefore, in theory attack in either the Atlantic or the Pacific. In practice, the board seems to have assumed that Germany and Japan would not act together. If the U.S. fleet could deal quickly and decisively with the stronger of the two enemy fleets, it thought that the other would be deterred. If, however, the fleet were only barely equal to, or slightly superior to, one of the two enemies, then, as a War College report suggested, "it is likely that, in the event of hostilities, the other, without declaring war against the United States, will try to filch from us, as did France during our civil war." The basis for U.S. fleet size was therefore the projected size of the German fleet.

On 21 September 1903, the secretary of the navy asked the General Board to design a long-range building program, to begin with the next session of Congress. The board now called once more for two new ships per year, from 1904 through 1915. That would give the United States forty-eight battleships

in 1919. No figures were given for programs beyond 1915, and the board no longer assumed that ships would be reduced to second rank after eighteen years. If downgrading were taken into account, nine of the forty-eight ships in service in 1919 would be counted as second-class.

The origins of the forty-eight-ship figure are by no means clear. In September 1904, for example, the Newport Summer Conference called for a total of fifty modern battleships (excluding the three *Indiana*s) by 1914. Such figures were generally based on the estimated future German strength on the basis of the Navy Law. The Atlantic fleet would match the German fleet; another fleet, 50 percent as large, would have to be maintained in the Pacific, so that the total U.S. force had to be one-and-one-half times as large as the German fleet. The fifty-ship program, for example, called for six ships in FY06, four each in FY06-FY09, and three each in FY10 and FY11, for a total of twenty-eight new ships. It seems likely that the rather more conservative figures produced by the General Board reflected a more realistic view of what Congress would provide.

Later reports by the Newport Summer Conference indicate the reasoning involved. In 1904, with both Russia and Japan about to be made prostrate by the Russo-Japanese War, Germany was the most probable future enemy. She planned to have thirty-eight first-class battleships by 1920. With the Panama Canal in U.S. hands, the 50 percent superiority would no longer be needed, and the Summer Conference called for a battle line strength of thirty-eight ships by 1914. Ships would pass to the second-class twenty years after launching.

In 1909, the Summer Conference reported that the German program called for a total of forty-two battleships and twenty-one armored cruisers in service by 1917. Japan would have twenty battleships and twenty armored cruisers in 1915. The U.S. Navy, then, should base its strength on the forty-two German battleships; using the Panama Canal, it could bring the same ships into action against Japan. It was assumed, too, that about 25 percent of all U.S. ships would be refitting at any given time, hence that the United States would need at least a 25 percent superiority over Germany. Battleships would be organized in squadrons of nine ships (in three divisions), the fleet consisting of six such squadrons, fifty-four ships.

Another calculation, also dated 1909, called for an active fleet equal to the combined *existing* fleets of Germany and Japan. At this time the German High Seas Fleet consisted of seventeen battleships; and the Japanese were expected to have fourteen by 1911. If U.S. ships operated in squadrons of nine, the 2nd and 4th Committees of the Summer Conference called for two active squadrons and two reserve divisions in the Atlantic (twenty-four ships) supported by a squadron of armored cruisers and a squadron of scouts; and two squadrons (eighteen) in the Pacific, supported by at least one squadron of armored cruisers. That made for forty-two battleships, not counting future construction by either potential enemy.

On 17 October 1903 the General Board reported its forty-eight-ship program, each battleship to be armed with four 12-inch and eight 8-inch guns and "as many 6 inch and lighter calibres as practicable, depending upon displacement." The board also wanted at least one, preferably two, underwater torpedo tubes on each side. It appears that the board had in mind an upgraded *Maine* rather than a repeat *Connecticut*. Armor protection equal to that of the earlier ship was specified, and freeboard was to be high forward. Key characteristics were a sustained sea speed of 16 knots to Culebra (Panama) and back, and a maximum steaming radius of 6,000nm.

The General Board appears to have been unaware

of just how expensive sustained speed and long range could be. It hoped to achieve its requirements on a *full load* displacement of 16,000 tons, which was very different from the *normal load* of 16,000 tons assigned the *Connecticut*s. The *Connecticut*s were limited to a sustained sea speed of about 15 knots, and their radius was about 5,500 miles, yet their full load displacement was 17,665 tons. The weight saving due to reversion to the 6-inch gun would be more than balanced by the cost of underwater torpedo tubes. As recounted in the companion book in this series on U.S. cruisers, the board encountered similar difficulties in its attempt to specify cruiser characteristics.

The exercise illustrated the tension between the strategic problems appreciated by the General Board and the technology and resources of the time. It is also characteristic that the seagoing officers of the General Board did not at all appreciate the considerable displacement and cost increases associated with what they regarded as relatively small demands for additional speed and range. For example, the board did not at first realize that "sustained sea speed" was a most exacting criterion. In December, it retreated to specifying trial speed (18 knots). However, the board then reiterated its demand for minimum displacement, thinking its battleship would displace no more than 14,500 tons (normal displacement).

A conference committee of the Board on Construction and the General Board fixed on a 16,000-ton battleship armored like the *Vermont*, but with 6-inch guns (23 January 1904). Two battleships and two armored cruisers were requested, but Congress authorized only one of the battleships, which actually duplicated the *Vermont*.

Perhaps the most important effect of the exercise was to inject the General Board into the process of drawing up the annual program and, as importantly, the characteristics to be required of its ships.

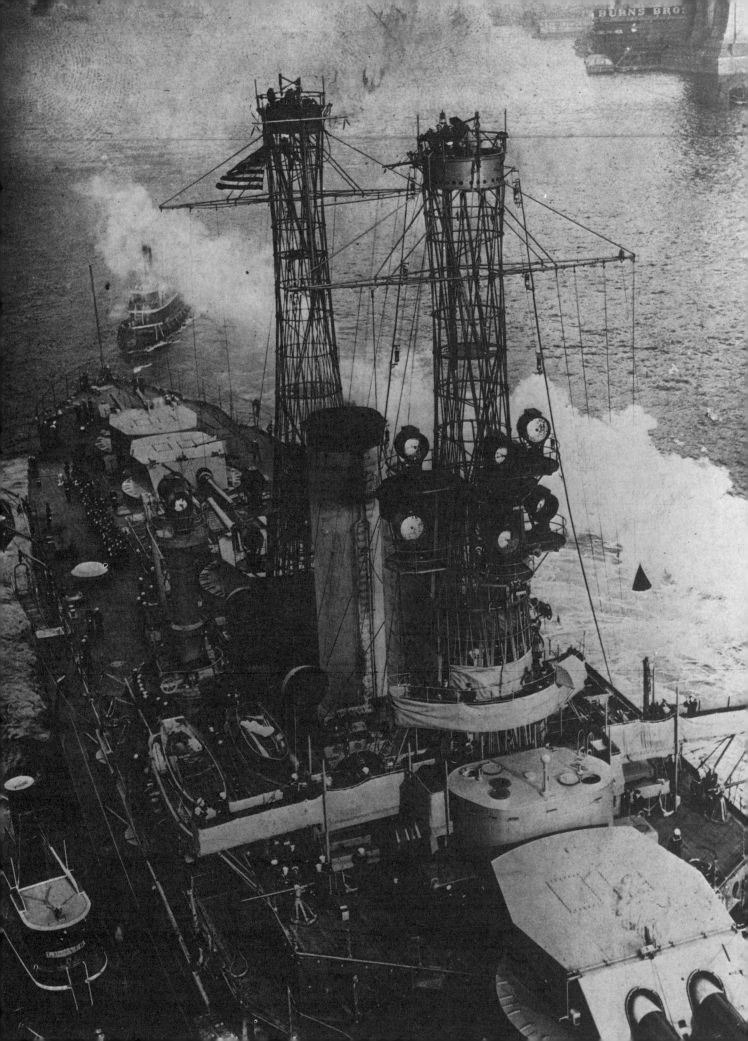

2

The All-Big-Gun Ship

Early in this century, several navies simultaneously decided to shift to a main battery composed entirely of the heaviest guns. The first and most famous product of this innovation was the HMS *Dreadnought*, which gave her name to a generation of all-big-gun battleships. Parallel to but independent of her conception was the American *South Carolina*, in many ways an equally revolutionary design. She introduced a superfiring main battery, a design economy which gave her a better-protected broadside equal to that of her British contemporary on about 3,000 tons less displacement.

The American path toward the single-calibre capital ship can be traced to 1901, although the earlier insistence on a powerful "secondary" battery of 8-inch guns may also have been significant. When the 8-inch guns were seen to be inadequate in penetrating heavier foreign armor at greater battle ranges, it was natural to replace them with more powerful weapons, the only limit being the calibre of the main battery itself. Several U.S officers seem to have reached this conclusion nearly at the same time. For example, the March 1902 *Proceedings* of the U.S Naval Institute published an article by Lieutenant Matt H. Signor advocating a battleship armed with two triple 12-inch turrets at the ends and with two triple 10-inch turrets in the waist, with a secondary battery of 5-inch high-velocity guns (60-calibres long). He theorized that one large gun would be more valuable than two 8 inchers. Signor's paper had no direct effect, but it is significant as a sign of a way of thinking

within the Navy. It was taken seriously enough for the *Proceedings* to publish comments in its next (June 1902) issue by the Navy's leading gunnery expert, Professor P. R. Alger, as well as by David W. Taylor, a future chief constructor, already becoming known for his work on ship propulsion. Both considered the proposed design impractical in detail but felt that it compelled attention for its bold attack upon problems of battleship design only then becoming apparent. Although Alger objected to the triple turret proposed by Signor, he favored a main battery of eight 12-inch guns, in what must be one of the earliest serious proposals for a homogeneous big-gun battery. Taylor wanted to power the battleship of the future with steam turbines, overcoming their low fuel economy at cruising speed by using variable-pitch propellers.

Signor's ideas were not altogether futuristic. One of C&R's proposals, the unsuccessful Scheme 5, submitted in May 1902 for what became the *Mississippi* design, was a 16.5- or 17-knot flush-decker armed with twelve 10-inch guns in twin turrets: two at the ends and four in the wings. This configuration was quite popular with designers of all-big-gun ships before 1905, although in the end only German and Japanese ships were actually built to it. Almost certainly the configuration was an extrapolation from mixed-calibre types with medium-calibre guns in wing turrets.

The bureau may also have sketched a larger all-big-gun ship at this time. In 1904, trying to discour-

The *Florida* passes under the Brooklyn bridge about 1911. She typifies the austerity of the American dreadnoughts, her bridge almost nonexistent and deliberately exposed to the weather. The long bridge wings were erected only to enter or leave harbor. Saluting guns are visible beneath them. Note, too, that her topmasts have been lowered to pass under the bridge. The New York Navy Yard was so important that the free height under the Brooklyn Bridge, like the locks of the Panama Canal, was a major design limitation on U.S. warship development. The canvas wrapped around the cage mast protects a helmsman on a permanent platform *within* the mast. Below him was a chart house, which could be taken down before battle. Officers on the navigating bridge wrapped around the mast had a covered chart table, visible on the right. The ship was designed to be steered primarily from the conning tower. Note its lozenge (assymmetrical) shape and the periscopes protruding beside the two open hatches. The tall structure emerging from the conning tower appears to be a pelorus, with a magnetic compass, for the use of the bridge officers. The *Utah* was completed with a different type of conning tower, supporting a cylindrical fire control tower.

age criticism of its slow progress on what ultimately became the *South Carolina*, C&R claimed that "almost two years before" it had submitted a homogeneous battery sketch to the Board on Construction, only to have it rejected. Later attempts by historians to find such a sketch failed, but it may have been an alternative design for the *Connecticut*.

As in the Royal Navy, an important incentive for adopting larger guns was that only they would be effective at the greater battle range possible because of improved gunnery. Yet another incentive was that larger guns were necessary to continue to outrange torpedoes fired by hostile battleships. In 1903, the General Board argued that torpedoes then entering service could hit at the then-expected battle range of 3,000 yards, which seemed to imply that the torpedo and not the gun would be the primary weapon of the future. As a result, the Naval War College studied a battleship armed primarily with underwater torpedo tubes.

The gunners, however, soon won this battle by increasing effective gun range. With every extension of range, the heavy guns gained in effect compared with medium guns. The lighter shells lost velocity and, therefore, penetrating power faster than the heavier ones. That left the lighter guns only the advantage of a higher rate of fire, but that counted for little if the shells could not penetrate. Moreover, at long range gunners had to "spot" the fall of shot to correct their aim. That in itself reduced the effective rate of fire, as a succeeding round could not be fired before the previous one struck. The longer the range, the lower the *maximum theoretical* rate of spotted fire.

Advocates of the lesser weapons might claim that in an actual battle ships would ultimately close to ranges at which the smothering effect of rapid fire would tell, but by 1904 the gunnery of the largest weapons had improved to the point where decisive hits would be made at the greatest ranges. This conclusion was confirmed by battle experience in the Russo-Japanese War, but serious planning for all-big-gun ships came considerably earlier in the major navies, based on peacetime gunnery experiments. The crucial decisions were all made before the end of the Russo-Japanese war. Ironically, war experience was later used by such detractors of the new type of battleship as Admiral Mahan, the great strategist.

The U.S. ships can be traced directly back to studies conducted from 1901 onwards by Lieutenant Commander H. C. Poundstone, who submitted a paper arguing the case for much larger battleships to President Roosevelt in December 1902. In an appendix he argued, as had Signor, that there was little point in retaining the 8-inch gun. Better to replace the existing mix of 12- and 8-inch guns with 11 and 9 inch; better, too, to save weight and gain numbers by using the smallest possible heavy-calibre weapon. Poundstone's paper was not published by the *Proceedings* until the June and September 1903 issues. By that time he had decided that a uniform battery of 11-inch guns would be much more effective. The leading Italian naval constructor, Colonel Vittorio Cuniberti, published his concept of an all-big-gun battleship in *Jane's Fighting Ships* (as "An Ideal Battleship for the British Navy") in October 1903. The following year Poundstone cited the claimed popu-

Table 2-1. Poundstone's Battleship Designs

Name	Feasible	Probable	Possible
Displacement	17,850	18,550	19,330 tons
Length	480	480	500 ft
Beam	78.5	80	81 ft
Draft	25	25	25 ft
Freeboard (Amidships)	22	22	20 ft
Main Battery	4-11in/50	4-11in/50	12-11in/50
Intermediate Battery	8-9in/50	14-9in/50	---
Secondary Battery	12-7in/50	---	---
Anti-Torpedo	16-3in/50	20-3in/50	40-3in/50
Torpedo Tubes	3	3	6
Belt Armor	9-7-5	10-8-6-4	10-8-6-4 in
Casemate	8	9*	9* in
Turrets	11	11	11 in
Intermediate Turrets	9	9	--- in
Secondary Turrets	7	---	--- in
Upper Armor Deck	1.5	---	--- in
Armor Deck	1.5/3	1.5/3	1.5/3 in
Speed	18	18	18 kts
Coal	1000/2200	900/2300	900/2700 tons

Note: Where it is marked by an asterisk, the casemate is an auxiliary (upper) belt, as in U.S. practice a few years later.

larity of the idea in Europe to support it in the United States. He argued that an 11in/50 could penetrate Cuniberti's ship at 6,000 yards, which he considered the maximum effective battle range, and therefore that it would be the ideal weapon.

By this time the General Board was aware of Poundstone's ideas, which it discussed at the annual Newport Summer Conference in 1903. War game studies begun that July showed that a battleship armed with twelve 11- or 12-inch guns hexagonally arranged would be equal to three of the more conventional type. After the 1903 Summer Conference, the college staff prepared a memorandum on an all-big-gun ship for the War College president. It reported considerable informal discussion of such a ship, "which found a guarded expression of approval in the report of one committee on the composition of the fleet." The central argument was that effective torpedo range, then 3,000 yards, set effective gun range, and that at 3,000 yards the 8-inch and 7-inch guns of the intermediate battery could not penetrate the armor covering them. Moreover, gun ranges would surely rise, since a 4,000-yard torpedo was in prospect. BuOrd had, in fact, just contracted for a 21-inch torpedo which would run 4,000 yards at 25 knots, and 3,000 at 29 knots.

If it was accepted that the two functions of battleship armament were to destroy other battleships and to beat off torpedo attacks, then there was no logical role for the intermediate battery. The first required the heaviest weapons behind the heaviest armor, the second the lightest weapons (of sufficient calibre) behind little or no armor. Nothing in between would be effective in either role.

No one could decide, according to the War College staff, what might be achieved with the weight saved by eliminating the secondary weapons. Given this barrier to further discussion, the conference much favored a ship armed only with the heaviest guns and with 3-inch antidestroyer weapons.

The latter might well not have to be used during fleet engagements. "Many officers do not believe that torpedo craft can, or will, cruise with the fleet and they do believe that battleship engagements will be fought by battleships alone. This belief has perhaps more reason in our own case than in that of European nations, owing to our distance from probable enemies.

"On this theory, the light guns of the proposed battleship will not be manned during fleet actions or battleship duels, but their crews would be kept in reserve in comparative safety behind armor. These light guns would be terribly knocked about without armor; but it is a fair question whether they would be more injured if behind armor that heavy projectiles would be sure to pierce, probably to burst within the ship. The intermediate battery of the present bat-

tleship in action is sure to be the scene of wreck and carnage; in the proposed battleship the wreckage will also occur, but the crew will not see it, nor be exposed to carnage with the attendant loss of morale."

The sense of the Summer Conference, then, was that C&R should try to design a ship armed with twelve 12-inch guns and as many 3-inch as could be accommodated. The General Board was impressed, and in October 1903 it formally asked C&R for a feasibility study. The board did not include the all-big-gun ship in its 1904 long-range construction program only because the study had not yet been completed. The board was interested enough that on 26 January 1904 it renewed its request. The potential ship was to be armed with at least four 12-inch and eight other heavy guns of at least 10-inch calibre; and the only other guns were to be 3 inchers for torpedo defense. High speed and special armor protection for the uptakes were also demanded. The retreat from a homogeneous heavy battery seems to have reflected doubts that the heaviest guns could be mounted on the broadside.

C&R did nothing with this request. Later it claimed that its draftsmen and constructors had been required for the higher priority project of designing the ships authorized in 1904, which included the *New Hampshire*. The bureau also observed sarcastically that quite competent authorities had been happy enough with a mixed battery only a short time before, that is, when the General Board had produced its long-range plan. In fact, C&R did not begin work on a design with four 12-inch and eight 10-inch guns until September 1904.

The 1904 Summer Conference compared this design, under the name *South Carolina*, with its 1903 ship and with the *Connecticut*. As the War College staff had argued the previous year, the conference considered the minimum gunnery range, set by the effective range of the torpedo, to be 3,000 yards. At that distance the 8-inch and 7-inch guns could, respectively, penetrate only 8-inch and 6.5-inch thicknesses of Krupp armor and, therefore, were incapable of doing fatal damage. Even the 10-inch gun would penetrate only 12 inches of Krupp armor, and then only if its shell struck perpendicular (normal) to the belt, an unlikely circumstance. Only the 12-inch gun itself, then, could be satisfactory, quite apart from its advantages in fire control and in simplified ammunition stowage and supply. At the same time, the conference was asked to consider the effects on battleship tactics of longer-range (7,000 to 8,000 yard) torpedoes, which would strengthen its arguments in favor of the all-big-gun ship.

Although speed was clearly important, conference after conference concluded that relatively small advantages in speed might not be very important. One calculation, for example, showed that even a speed

The *Michigan* is shown in her original form. Note her prominent chart house, forming the base of her cage foremast, and the very small size of her conning tower. A wheel and pelorus were mounted inside the cage mast, above the chart house, and below the forward searchlight platform. Her funnel bands show that she was the third ship of the Fourth Battle Division.

advantage of 3 knots (18 vs. 15 knots) would be insufficient to permit the faster fleet to "cross the T" of the slower; the slower fleet could always turn to evade. The principal exception to this argument was that, in defending an objective, the slower fleet might be at a fatal disadvantage, since the faster could evade it and still reach the objective. This case was particularly important to the U.S. Navy, with its fear that a foreign power might try to secure a base in the New World, and it accounts for U.S. interest in building battle cruisers (see the companion book on cruisers in this series).

A 1910 analysis concluded that, even to gain the weather or sun gauge (that is, to steam with the sun shining into the eyes of opposing gun-layers) a fleet would need a superiority of at least 3 knots. Even then it was not clear that such a position would be so great an advantage, as darkened-sight telescopes and glasses might well overcome sun glare. As for altering or maintaining the battle range, a 10 degree arc of fire equated to a 4-knot speed advantage: 4 knots would allow a fleet to alter the range by 1,000 yards in fifteen minutes, whereas with equal speeds, the fleet with a 10 degree advantage in arcs of train could alter the range by a similar amount while keeping sights on the enemy in thirteen minutes. Such arguments had considerable bearing on future U.S. interest in higher-speed ships.

At this remove it seems remarkable that it was only in 1904 that the Summer Conference recommended the abandonment of the ram bow in U.S.

battleships, as gunnery range had been well beyond point-blank range for some decades. This change was expected to save about 40 tons.

Given the conclusions reached at Newport, and the reluctance of C&R to develop a corresponding design, it was very important that Poundstone worked out detailed all-big-gun designs. In June 1904, he presented three designs to the General Board and the Bureau of Navigation that illustrated "the strong probability that intermediate guns will soon have so increased in calibre as to render possible the adoption of a homogeneous big-gun battery." Poundstone's ultimate ship, the USS *Possible*, mounted twelve 11-inch guns on 19,330 tons.

At this time, Poundstone's close associate, Lieutenant Commander W. S. Sims, was revolutionizing American naval gunnery and thus was a natural advocate of the all-big-gun ship. The president turned to him for advice when the issue came up in the fall of 1904. The Board on Construction had claimed that the mixed-battery *New Hampshire* was superior to any other battleship in the world, that a uniform battery was impractical, that in action lighter guns would be decisive. Sims was able to rebut these arguments by citing the gunnery results attained in the 1904 fleet target practice and by displaying a viable all-big-gun design, Poundstone's project of the previous summer.

President Roosevelt's interest in the project ended C&R's procrastination, but it was still not clear whether the new ship should mount the 10-inch gun.

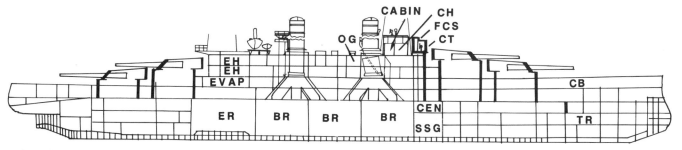

Inboard profile of the *South Carolina*, 1918. Her large mast-base chart house has been removed and her conning tower enlarged, with a small fire control section ("tower") at its rear end. These ships had the bases of their mainmasts covered in canvas through most of their careers. These bases covered the engine room hatches.

In view of later accounts of the origin of the *Dreadnought*,* it is interesting that the possibility of gunnery confusion due to two calibres as close as 10 and 12 inches was never raised. For example, Sims and Poundstone stressed the advantages of homogeneity in terms of ammunition supply and of the transfer of crews from disengaged guns to replace wounded gunners. In October 1904, W. L. Rodgers of the Naval War College wrote a long and detailed memorandum on this question, pointing out that as ranges became longer the difference in accuracy and hitting power between even 10- and 12-inch guns became enormous. It was not much later that a British naval observer of the Russo-Japanese War would remark that at battle ranges only the 12-inch guns were noticeable, the 10-inch shells being barely felt and anything smaller not felt at all. The Americans, however, never saw that report.

Rodgers went on to argue that an adequate single-calibre ship would have to be considerably larger than the current *Connecticut*; he estimated that ten 12 inchers would require 18,300 tons, twelve 12 inchers, 21,100. Thus he failed to appreciate congressional reluctance to relax the new 16,000-ton limit it had just set. C&R's achievement, then, ultimately required ingenuity on an order of magnitude beyond that exhibited by Poundstone and the Naval War College analysts. Its first sketch designs were pedestrian; twin 10-inch or single 12-inch guns replaced the twin 8-inch wing turrets of earlier battleships. The extra weight represented by these more powerful weapons increased stress on the hull. In addition their barbettes cut great holes in the upper deck, which formed the upper flange of the ship strength girder. In October 1904, the bureau complained that it was too hard-pressed to handle these unprecedented structural problems immediately but expected to resolve them within the next three months. The conclusion seems to have been that the heavy

wing turrets were impractical on a 16,000-ton ship, at least without some drastic compromise of strength or protection.

Meanwhile Congress authorized two new battleships, to be called *South Carolina* and *Michigan*, on 3 March 1905. With no Navy proposal to guide them, the legislators renewed the 16,000-ton limit. It expressed their feeling that battleships had grown too fast and that the *Connecticut*s were excessively large, but it ignored foreign developments: British and Japanese ships were already approaching 18,000 tons. The disparity was actually even greater, because the U.S. rules required that a much larger fraction of the total fuel capacity be included in the normal displacement. All of the single-calibre designs before the General Board called for far greater displacements, yet the board did not consider asking for more displacement until much later.

The chief constructor, Washington L. Capps, turned to a radical solution. He began with the observation that the primary objective of battleship design was broadside fire. Most of his contemporaries appear to have thought in terms of single ship actions, which involved a great deal of ahead and astern fire; hence, for example, the wasteful use of two wing turrets abreast in the HMS *Dreadnought*. Capps was far more sophisticated. He saw the individual ship only as an element of the larger fleet. In all navies fleet action was synonymous with the line of battle, that is, with broadside fire.

So developed the superfiring main battery, which eventually became the international standard. All guns must be on the centerline if all were to fire broadside; on a limited displacement it would have been criminal to waste the weight of even a single 12-inch emplacement. Superfiring was essential if length and volume were to be conserved—and on 16,000 tons the hull would have to be little larger than that of the previous class. In the absence of experiments, Capps could not be at all sure that the superfiring guns could fire close to dead ahead or astern. But he knew that was not the point—there was no blast problem on the broadside.

* The ballistics of the two guns would differ considerably. Yet their splashes might be confused, so that spotters would try to apply corrections based on 10-inch fire to the 12-inch guns and vice versa.

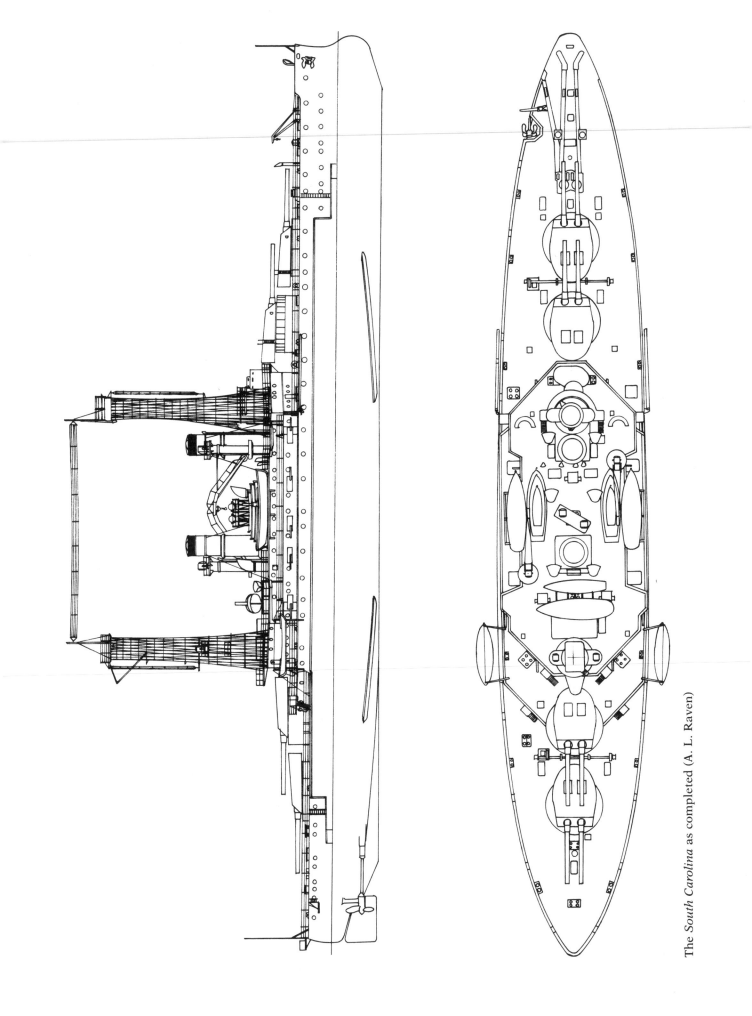

The *South Carolina* as completed (A. L. Raven)

The *Michigan*, as modified early in World War One, is shown in 1916 or 1917. Note the large range-finders atop her two superfiring turrets and the smaller one atop her enlarged conning tower. The canvas above it protects a navigating bridge near the steering platform inside her cage mast. The original mast-base chart house has been removed. The significance of her two-tone paint job is unknown. (O. W. Waterman)

The centerline arrangement consumed much of the volume within the ship, so that Capps had to economize in many ways. For example, most of the officers had to be moved from their traditional quarters aft to a position amidships in the superstructure. Volume problems aft were aggravated by the need to cut the ship down a deck level there in order to save weight. Machinery would have to shrink to fit the space between the two sets of magazines fore and aft, each of them larger than before. The boiler rooms were also squeezed from each side to provide torpedo protection spaces outboard of them. The motive for greater gunnery ranges was, after all, supplied largely by the torpedo. Moreover, on the limited displacement available there could be no increase in power, and even to maintain the power of earlier ships would be a struggle. Capps advocated steps as radical as cutting the number of boilers by a third, but ultimately all BuEng could give him was more compact boiler rooms, achieved by eliminating centerline bulkheads. As visible evidence of this economy, the *South Carolina*s had two small funnels in place of three larger ones in the *Connecticut*. Thus, unlike the *Dreadnought*, the first American all-big-gun ship achieved no great increase in speed over its predecessors. Later, because they were so much slower than the later turbine-engined ships, the *South Carolina*s would even be combined tactically with the pre-dreadnoughts. That was beside the point—their

revolutionary contribution to the U.S. Navy was in their main battery.

Capps had to provide not merely more big guns but also more shells for sustained firing. Previous designs had been based on a tacit assumption that most damage would be done by rapidly firing light and medium guns, hence the prevalence of armor well under 10 inches, even in belts. Hence also the allowance of only sixty rounds per 12 inch gun. At the low rate of fire envisaged, a battle would be over before that much could be used up. Instead, the new design provided one hundred rounds per 12-inch gun, for rapid and well-coordinated fire. That figure became the standard for subsequent U.S. dreadnought designs; it was substantially increased only for the designs of the 1930s. In this case it required more magazine volume, all of it on the centerline, competing with the machinery for space.

This was Scheme S. It appears to have been number nineteen in a sequence of all-big-gun designs since the index card of a blueprint of Schemes A through R has survived. A search of the C&R plans collection of the National Archives, however, has failed to locate it. The superfiring idea may have been accepted as early as April 1905, when Capps asked BuEng to shrink engineering spaces "to increase the main battery," that is, to give him more centerline space at the ends. We do know that Capps was able to report that previous studies had come out heavy, but that

At the Philadelphia Navy Yard in 1919, the *Michigan* shows typical World War One modifications: vee-faced screens around her torpedo-defense platforms; searchlights mounted above them for director control; and a bridge better protected from the weather. Like many other U.S. dreadnoughts, she mounts a pair of 3-inch antiaircraft guns atop her two boat cranes. Note the closed shutters of her broadside 3-inch antidestroyer guns and the removal of her long-base range-finders.

such calculations as he had already made indicated that the new design was properly balanced as early as 26 June 1905.

The *South Carolina* introduced an entirely new type of gun sight, the hyposcope, to American service. Rigidly connected to the gun trunnion, it was set into the side of the turret. Previous sights, in turret roof hoods and connected to the guns via elaborate linkages, had been subject to "lost motion" and therefore sometimes did not correspond precisely to gun elevation. This correspondence in turn became more important at increased range, particularly when firing salvoes. With the hyposcope, a range transmitted to all guns would result in identical true elevations set by the pointers at all the guns, hence a closely bunched salvo. Each gun was "pointed" (elevated) separately, but a single sight-setter in the turret was responsible for setting the range on both hyposcope sights. A third sight, for the gun-mount trainer, projected through the turret roof.

It is often suggested that the U.S. Navy adopted its characteristic turret-side sights in order to be able to fire its superfiring guns dead ahead without disabling the gunners of the turrets below. That seems unlikely. Capps appears neither to have feared trouble from blast nor to have considered end-on fire important. The ships did still retain a trainer's sight in the turret roof, and BuOrd considered roof sights

again for the next battleship class, in March 1907. The hyposcope was attractive for its simplicity, its reliability, and, incidentally, its greater efficiency in the use of available light.

Even so, the question of end fire had to be settled. If blast were found to be a serious problem, measures would have to be taken to blank off the dangerous firing arcs, as was done in many foreign ships at this time. Accordingly the monitor *Florida* was modified to represent a ship with superfiring turrets. A 12-inch gun was removed from her turret and mounted in her superstructure, in such a way that the turret could be trained to simulate various conditions. A wooden gun was mounted in its place to simulate the closure and air space present in a service turret. It was expected that the muzzle pressure of the supercharged 12in/40 used would actually exceed that to be expected of the longer 12in/45, and in general conditions were arranged to give greater blast than might be expected in service. The turret itself was modified to represent that of the *South Carolina* (no sight hoods in the roof, but sights cut into the sides) except that the sights were mounted slightly farther aft to be closer to the muzzle of the superfiring gun.

The Board on Construction attended the tests, held on 6 March 1907, ultimately occupying the turret. Capps himself stood at the sights while a full charge was fired. In a second series of tests on 15 March,

The *Michigan* is shown entering Honolulu harbor with the U.S. Fleet, 7 March 1920. She has just been fitted with range clocks (at the level of her mast searchlights) and her turrets had been painted with deflection scales, so that ships accompanying her could tell at what range and at what bearing she was firing. The base of her mainmast was covered with canvas throughout her career. This ship was no longer than a pre-dreadnought, but her superstructure had to be much shorter, to accommodate two turrets rather than one at each end. She and her sister therefore were unusual in carrying some of their boats athwartship, as shown here. Note, too, the absence of the broadside 3-inch guns. Their shutters have been opened.

the turret was trained to bring the superfiring gun directly over the sights, which Capps once more manned. According to the official report of the test, "the shock felt was trifling, and the officer at the sight felt no jar, nor was his vision of the horizon interrupted otherwise than by the smoke of discharge." Capps was vindicated; the only change made in subsequent turrets as a result of these tests was a slight thickening of the turret roof.

The other outstanding gunnery aspect of the design was the cage mast. As early as 1904 experimental long-range firing showed that the heavy guns could hit any target a spotter could keep in view. The fleet that could hit first, that is, at a greater range, would gain an enormous advantage. The higher the observer, the farther he could see. However, the higher the observer, the larger the target represented by the mast supporting him. The cage mast was designed to place spotters as high as possible above the deck on what amounted to an invulnerable mast. Armor was out of the question because of topweight. Instead the mast was built up from many redundant members, each them too light to detonate a shell. Shells

would merely snip a few without destroying the whole mast or blasting the fire control top.

This solution was unique to the United States, the Royal Navy preferring a heavy tripod.* Perhaps the problem was not nearly as urgent as the U.S. experts believed. The British, for instance, never lost a tripod in battle, although one was damaged at the Falklands in 1914. The other European navies appear not to have been interested enough in very long-range fire to have considered fire control masts seriously. The Germans, for example, appear to have expected short ranges in the low-average visibility of the North Sea.

Capps himself made no reference to fire control. He wanted only to avoid top hamper, fearing that masts would tend to burst shells and hence destroy bridgework. His solution was to keep the masts away from the bridge, placing them between the funnels, on either beam. The same masts, whose primary roles included signaling and the support of radio anten-

* Several Czarist Russian battleships had lattice masts, rather more compact than the U.S. cage. Two Argentine battleships, the *Moreno* and *Rivadavia*, designed by the U.S. Fore River Yard, each had a cage foremast.

nas, would serve as the kingposts of boat cranes. Similar logic governed the placement of the single big tripod on the HMS *Dreadnought*.

Meanwhile, in December 1905, the Board on Fire Control called for each ship to have a raised spotting platform, perhaps on a lattice mast. The board's report was not finally approved by the Navy Department until well into 1906, and the next June BuOrd proposed a light "fire control bridge" between the two masts. It would be only 64 feet above the waterline, below the funnel tops and, hence, nearly smoke free; to raise it far enough above those tall funnels to regain freedom from smoke would be impractical. That, in turn, condemned the ships to what was now perceived as short-range gunnery. *If* spotters could operate as much as 100 feet above water, hits might be made at ranges as great as 10,000 yards.

The Bureau of Navigation therefore proposed that the low bridge be replaced by a pair of lattice masts. BuOrd and the Board on Construction resisted on the ground that any change at this stage would be expensive. The technical bureaus considered the existing type of military mast, 4 feet in diameter at its base, unlikely to fall in battle. Senior fleet officers, however, disagreed. Fire control was too important to entrust to a structure that could be brought down by a single hit and would suffer splinter damage over its entire length. It was essential, obviously, to protect not only the guns but also the fire control system upon which they depended.

That fall, the Atlantic Fleet battle practice showed just how valuable the aloft platform could be. Ships could fight at 10,000 yards, provided that at least two fire control station's 100 feet above water were available, so that at least one would be free of smoke at all times. Positions 75 feet up were frequently shut out, not by funnel smoke but by the smoke of the heavy guns themselves, an effect that would be increased in a ship with eight rather than four such weapons.

Now, the secretary of the navy decided on the lattice mast. Developed by C&R Design Branch, under Naval Constructor R. H. Robinson, it consisted of strands of wire in the form of a hyperboloid of revolution, with circular bands reinforcing it every few feet. In theory several elements within a sector, that is, between two bands, could be cut without bringing down the mast. Any one element could be cut in several places, as long as they were in different sectors.

To test it, a model was built, loaded, and attacked with wire clippers. Then a full-scale mast, 125 feet high and inclined at an angle of 10 degrees, was mounted on the monitor *Florida* and attacked with live ammunition. It carried an extra weight of 4 tons to simulate loads which might be applied by a rolling ship. On 27 May 1908, four 4-inch and one 12-inch shell were fired at it, but the mast stood even with five elements in one sector cut (by the heavy shell). Two officers went up to the simulated fire control top and tried but failed to set it swaying: the voice and electrical connections within the mast, which were essential to its purpose, were uninjured. In a later test on the former battleship *San Marcos* (ex *Texas*) a similar mast withstood thirteen 12-inch shells fired at point-blank range. BuOrd now enthusiastically supported the new mast, and the decision to adopt it soon followed.

In the summer of 1908 most of the fleet was cruising around the world, but the two small *Mississippi*s were just being completed. *Idaho* became the first ship with a cage mainmast. Ships under construction were redesigned; in the *South Carolina*s the pole masts were cut down to become kingposts and searchlight platforms, cage masts occupying the traditional centerline positions. The returning ships of the Great White Fleet received first one, and then two cage masts as the new masts became available from 1909 onwards. Masthead height was limited to 125 feet by a requirement to clear the Brooklyn Bridge, 135 feet above mean high water at its center, for access to the New York Navy Yard. This limit was an important though little-known determinant of U.S. warship design for many years. Even as late as the 1950s, attack carriers were designed to fold down their radar masts so as to be able to enter one of the Navy's most important yards.

In the *South Carolina*s, the armored deck (2 inches over magazines, 1.5 inches over machinery) was flat, and it met the main belt at its upper rather than its lower edge. This made sense because it was less likely that AP shells would penetrate the thicker belt, so that the armored deck became a shield against splinters and debris due to penetration of the casemate (that is, of the upper belt), which extended up to the forecastle deck, and covered most of the length of the armored deck. Unlike the *Connecticut*, the new design lacked an "upper casemate," since there were no medium guns for it to protect; there was also no bow or stern armor. The belt and casemate were closed fore and aft by bulkheads of comparable thickness, and the main belt was backed by coal bunkers. Foreshadowing the reasoning employed in the *Nevada* design, Capps observed that "it would be better for a large projectile to go right through than to have the armor thick enough to explode it." He did spread some 1.5-inch nickel steel (splinter armor) over the ends, but this plating was probably intended only to keep large shells from peeling away the side armor as they hit. Flooding forward was to be restricted by a watertight underwater armored deck 1.5-inches thick, and aft a curved 3-inch deck covered the steering gear.

The *Michigan* is shown at the end of her career, awaiting the breakers, at the Philadelphia Navy Yard, 26 October 1923. Details of her bridge and upper deck are clear. Note the small chart house at the base of her mast and the flimsiness of the weather protection around her flying bridge. Many photographs of this type were taken to prove that the United States was complying with the terms of the Washington Treaty by breaking up its ships.

This system—a thick belt covered by a thin flat deck with a thick "casemate" or upper belt above—was standard in American dreadnoughts down to the *Nevada* class, which introduced a radically different scheme.

The main belt, 8 feet wide, was somewhat narrower than that of the previous *New Hampshire*, but it was thicker, 10 inches at the waterline (tapering to 8 inches at the bottom) rather than a uniform (and shorter) 9 inch belt in the earlier ship. Moreover, over most of its length it was thicker; 12 to 10 inches over magazines and 9 to 11 inches over the machinery spaces in between. The casemate tapered from 10 inches where it met the upper edge of the main belt to 8 inches at the top; it had originally been planned as 7 to 9 inches (compared with 7 inches in the *New Hampshire*) but was increased when the light armor at the ends was eliminated. It was backed by coal bunkers. On the other hand, the barbettes had to be somewhat thinner (partly because a much greater total area had to be protected, consisting of two double-height barbettes as well as two of standard height). They were reduced from the usual uniform 11-inch thickness to 10 inches and to only 8 inches where one barbette shielded another. The turrets were unchanged in thickness, but they were more compact, which reduced net armor weight.

Capps was particularly proud of the underwater protection he had been able to work into the design. Two additional longitudinal bulkheads were run through the boiler spaces. Although they had to be pierced for coal to be passed, in battle the outer bulkheads could be closed up, coal being passed either from the upper bunkers or from the inner wing bunkers. It was not yet understood that the shock of an underwater explosion would spring the scuttles open, invalidating an advanced design concept. This system of coal protection to the vitals bcame standard in subsequent U.S. designs. It required no great use of armor, and foreign writers saw that as a weight saver required by the displacement limit; the U.S. Navy saw no great point in underwater armor until much later, with the introduction of the "Davis torpedo" (see Chapter 5). Coal protection made for a beamy ship, which in turn provided the extra inherent stability required to balance the topweight of superfiring guns. In the new design, magazines were surrounded by storerooms to buffer against underwater hits.

The ships were less innovative in their machinery, which duplicated the reciprocating type of earlier ships and thus did not match the turbines of the new *Dreadnought*. Although Capps made provision for turbine propulsion in the design, he later stated that he preferred to try out the turbine in a scout, not in a valuable battleship. "It must be shown," he wrote, "that we are getting something we know to be better, and that we cannot say." The Bureau of Engineering did convince the Board on Construction to allow builders to propose turbine propulsion for the new ships, and when the bids came in that June, the bureau was all for building two competitive sisters. The Navy, however, was bound to accept the lowest bids compatible with military efficiency, that is, the bids for two reciprocating-engined ships. Capps himself was unwilling to accept turbines unless they were offered at lower prices.

C&R worked out detailed plans between July and November, formally submitting them to the department on 10 November. The Board on Construction approved the plans on 23 November 1905, and the secretary assented on 15 December, ten days after the British *Dreadnought* was laid down. Thus the U.S. Navy certainly went to the single-calibre ship before the British plans became public knowledge; similarly, the British project was well under way before final plans of the American ship had been drawn.

The 1905 Newport Summer Conference strongly endorsed the *South Carolina* design, considering its turret arrangement "superior to any . . . yet devised, at home or abroad." Even if the superfiring guns could not be fired over small arcs on the centerline, that would be a small price. However, the conference considered the 3-inch gun too small for effective antitorpedo work; available data were insufficient to show whether the 4- or 5-inch gun should be adopted in its place.

A conference committee specially studied the antitorpedo gun issue. It argued that the gun would have to disable the torpedo boat or destroyer or kill enough of its crew before it approached within an effective range defined by the performance of the latest torpedo, 4,000 yards at 28 knots. Destroyers generally had boilers in two or more compartments, protected by 2-inch steel. Hitting would require a

very flat trajectory, hence a high-velocity gun. The gun would have to be powerful enough to have a considerable smashing effect, yet light enough to be handled easily and to fire rapidly. The committee noted that antitorpedo gun calibre had risen steadily from the 6pdr (57 mm) once accepted, and that both the Russians and the Japanese appeared to have concluded from their recent combat experience that 4.7 inches was best.

The committee therefore compared the U.S. 3-, 4-, and 5-inch RF guns for their ability to penetrate 2-inch Krupp steel at 3,000 and at 4,000 yards. The 3-inch gun would be effective only at 1,000 yards and could therefore be dismissed. The 4-inch gun could barely penetrate 2-inch armor at 4,000 yards even when hitting perpendicular to the plating, which would be unlikely in battle. That left either the 5-inch gun or some improved 4-inch weapon. The committee preferred the latter, since it was lighter (and therefore could be carried in greater numbers), and since it fired more rapidly (typically about 9.6 shots per gun per minute, compared with 7.8 for the 5 inch). With its flatter trajectory, the 5-inch enjoyed an advantage in hitting rate at 4,000 and 5,000 yards. BuOrd was developing an improved 4-inch gun, but the next (*Delaware*) class was fitted instead with the existing 5in/50.

As for armor, the conference condemned what it considered insufficient protection for the steering gear. Nor did it accept an armor deck applied as three layers of mild and nickel steel; one layer of armor steel would be much better. The requisite weight might be saved, for example, by reducing the heavy bow bulkhead closing off the end of the belt, on the theory that bow-on action was unlikely.

Considering later U.S. interest in armoring the uptakes, it is notable that the conference argued *against* such protection. Even if the smoke pipes were riddled, blowers could surely make up for the loss of draught to the boilers.

Given the 1904 recommendation to abandon the ram bow, the 1905 conference thought retention of such a bow in the new ship a major flaw. It considered the ram a menace, in that collisions seemed likely in wartime, particularly in fleet actions. The forepart should be designed instead for dryness at high speed, with a flared bow and overhang. The latter might even reduce the effects of collision. At least in later ships, what appeared to be a ram bow was actually a bulbous bow that increased speed. Wetness continued to be a problem until after World War One (see Chapter 5), and many seagoing officers would later argue that C&R had developed hull forms better adapted to high speed in smooth water than to high seagoing speed.

Perhaps most important of all, the conference considered the *South Carolina* too small. Firepower and armor and machinery already consumed all of the available displacement, yet it was clear that underwater protection would have to be improved dramatically. Unless some unacceptable sacrifice were to be made, that would require a larger ship.

The General Board shared this view. On 30 September 1905 it suggested that the Navy Department petition Congress for relaxation of the tonnage limit to 18,000 tons, to gain twelve 12 inchers and higher speed. It would appear that the board did not realize that on even that displacement the increased armament would have to be mounted hexagonally, so that there would be no gain in broadside. Even then 18,000 tons might have been optimistic: the German *Nassau*, with 11-inch guns, was larger. On 28 October the board retreated to a requirement that all future battleships mount at least ten 12-inch guns. A month later the Board on Construction formally rejected the call for a larger ship for 1905.

Building progress was slow, in distinct contrast to the case of the *Dreadnought*. Specifications for bidders were not issued until 21 March 1906, and the Board on Construction was still debating turbine vs. reciprocating engines as late as June 1906. The authorizing act of March 1905 required that construction begin during FY06, which ended on 30 June 1906, but the two ships were not laid down until December 1906, after the completion of HMS *Dreadnought*. By the time they were complete, the Royal Navy had four dreadnought battleships and three battle cruisers in service.

The outstanding seagoing characteristic of the *South Carolina*s appears to have been heavy rolling. For example, the captain of the *Michigan* reported that she rolled and pitched more than other battleships under similar circumstances. She was less steady than either the *Kearsage* or the *Illinois*, in both of which he had served. The roll was quick but easy and without a jerk at its end. It would appear that the culprit was the inertia associated with the superimposed turrets, which would make it relatively difficult to stop any roll once started. The increased inertia would also somewhat ease the rolling motion of the ship, hence the comment that the rolls did not end with a jerk. The short period could be attributed to the great metacentric height, adopted in these ships to make them more survivable in the face of underwater attack. The *Virginia*s, with their superposed turrets (also representing great weights far from the rolling axis of the ship), behaved similarly. Capps could not have known that in the spring and summer of 1905, as the *Virginia*s, two classes back, were then still under construction.

It appears that the United States was not alone in underestimating the effect of inertia. In Germany the *Nassau* class presented very unwelcome rolling characteristics, as a result of the inertia associated with

their heavy wing turrets. In fact, the inertia changed the period of roll to the point where it coincided with the period of North Sea waves. Rolling could, therefore, build to the point of danger. The Germans had to install larger bilge keels, which cut speed, to damp them out.

By 1906 even foreign ships under construction with mixed-calibre batteries exceeded the congressional tonnage limit. Thus the next authorizing act of 29 June 1906 called for a battleship "carrying as heavy armor and as powerful armament as any known vessel of its class, to have the highest practicable speed and the greatest practicable radius of action." The only limit imposed on this super ship was cost. Hull and machinery could not exceed $6 million, compared with $4.4 million for the previous class. HMS *Dreadnought* had just been launched, and such meagre particulars as had been published suggested—incorrectly, as it turned out—that she far outclassed the *South Carolina*s authorized the previous year and not yet even laid down.

The General Board view was that C&R should now meet the characteristics it had laid down in 1904, except that all twelve heavy guns should be 12 inches, and that the secondaries should be 5 inches rather than 3 inches, given the "improved range of the modern torpedo and the greater offensive qualities of the latest torpedo boat destroyers." Chief Constructor Capps sketched both ten- and twelve-gun designs. A quirk of the authorizing act required the Navy to solicit competing designs from private naval architects. Since there could be no evaluation until late 1906, the ship would not be laid down until late in 1907. The low quality of the private designs ensured that all subsequent U.S. battleships would be C&R products. The new ship would ultimately be built to the ten-gun design as the USS *Delaware*, the first U.S. battleship to combine the all-big-gun battery with turbine propulsion for high speed.

Capps reported both alternative designs well in hand by July 1906. He estimated that on 20,500 tons he could provide ten 12 inchers, twelve to sixteen 5 inchers (with 200 to 250 rounds per gun), and engines like those of the *Virginia*, for a speed of 20 knots. Additional tonnage, about 3,500 more tons, would buy two more 12 inchers and heavier engines such as those of the armored cruiser *Pennsylvania*, for 21 knots. Capps and the rest of the Board on Construction regarded this return as far too small. The ship could be cut down to 22,000 tons by omitting some armor, but even then it was not well liked. Sheer size was part of the problem. Congress might be willing to give up explicit limitation, but even ten guns (a 25 percent increase in battery) would cost a 25 percent increase in tonnage, hence in cost (which actually rose more rapidly, by about a third). Congress would not again impose a tonnage limit (except for

Running trials, the *North Dakota* shows the low forward casemate gun fitted only very briefly. Even in very smooth water, as here, it was nearly drenched.

The *North Dakota* is shown as modified, the forward gun moved up into the superstructure, on the 01 level. Her funnel bands proclaim her the second ship of the First Battle Division. Note the rearrangement of her searchlights, now paired atop her derrick posts. The towers alongside her funnels have been discarded. This class could be distinguished from the similar *Florida*s by the positions of funnels and masts. The second funnel was *abaft* the mainmast.

the later treaty limits), but in 1912 one of its leaders would ask where the rapid increase in tonnage could be expected to lead.

The central design problem was that heavy twin turrets had to be spread along much of the length of the hull, stressing it. The closer the heavy weights to the ends of the ship (that is, the greater the number of turrets), the greater the stress. Worse, high speed

required fine (and therefore not too buoyant) ends, and also that a great portion of the length amidships be devoted to machinery, which in turn would push the turrets towards the ends. On the other hand, without a displacement limit Capps could reduce stresses by deepening the hull. He restored the full deck height aft, and added a forecastle forward, for better seakeeping and to add space for officers' quarters. On the other hand, he kept the secondaries at gun-deck level, as in the *Connecticut*s—including two guns a full deck level below the forecastle right forward. Trials photographs show that not only were these guns very wet even in calm weather, but also that their sponsons broke up the smooth flow of the bow wave and hence wasted power.

As for armament distribution, Capps hit upon the solution of interposing the engines between Nos. 3 and 4 turrets. No. 3, superfiring, represented the greatest weight because of its taller barbette. It would be supported by the greatest underwater volume— the greatest buoyancy—closest to amidships. Some distance aft, Nos. 4 and 5 were level and back to back. This arrangement had two serious vices. The No. 3 turret could not really fire right aft with No. 4 trained forward, in view of blast effects on the sights of No. 4. Thus fire dead astern was only two 12-inchers, where it might have been four had No. 4 turret been raised. In addition, the arrangement of engine and boiler rooms required that steam lines surround the magazine of No. 3 turret. Only later would it be seen that such hot lines could easily heat the powder within, degrading its ballistics. It is only fair to Capps to point out that many of his contemporaries, including Watts, the designer of the British dreadnoughts, committed the same sin, which they considered inescapable on structural grounds.

At about this time, the General Board changed its attitude toward the secondary gun, as did Rear Admiral N. E. Mason of BuOrd on the Board on Construction. A study of 3- 4- and 5-inch guns showed the 5in/50 best, at least twelve being desirable. Capps was able to supply fourteen: two right forward, ten in a casemate amidships, and two aft abeam No. 5 turret. The two forward guns were moved into the superstructure after sea trials.

BuOrd also wanted six underwater torpedo tubes, angled out fore and aft and dead abeam, but internal volume was largely consumed by machinery and magazines, and only two could be accommodated.

Protection largely followed that of the *South Carolina*s, with the improvements increased displacement could confer. Thus the main belt was uniform in section from end to end, 11-inches thick at its top and 9 inches at its bottom, covering more than three-quarters of the waterline, and 8-feet wide. It was covered by a 1.5-inch armor deck (2 inches over magazines). Atop this was a 7 foot 3 inch wide "lower casemate," 10 inches at its lower edge and 8 inches at its upper. This side armor, closed at its ends by 9-inch and 10-inch bulkheads, was well in advance of contemporary foreign practice, although that was not appreciated at the time. The steering gear was protected by 1.5-inch nickel steel spread over the hull aft. It may well have been intended to burst shells, the splinters of which would be caught by a 3-inch

sloping deck aft of the belt. As in the previous class, the ends were soft, the belt covering so much of the waterline that, according to Capps, "changes in trim by reason of the compartments forward and abaft the bulkhead armor having been riddled . . . [would be] so small as not to interfere with the maneuvering of the vessel."

Above, Capps fitted a 5-inch upper casemate with 5-inch bulkheads diagonal to Nos. 2 and 3 barbettes. Since the hull itself was 1⅛-inches thick, the total casemate armor was really about 6 inches. However, BuOrd had recommended against any light armor at all, on the theory that it would burst AP shells which would otherwise pass through without exploding. Guns and crews that might otherwise have survived anything but a direct hit would be destroyed. Capps replied that the casemate armor was part of the structural strength of the ship; it helped preserve the ship girder from shellfire that might otherwise tear up the side plating. In 1906 battle ranges were still expected to be so short that numerous hits by light rapidly firing guns had to be expected; the casemate would protect against them. In addition it would protect the uptakes by acting as a burster. Only incidentally was it to be considered protection for the secondary guns. Much later the *Nevada* would show a very different solution to this problem.

As compared with the *South Carolina*, the turret armor eventually (in 1907) showed only a thickening of the crown to 3 inches, as a result of the *Florida* experiments.

Underwater protection was by a layer of coal with an empty space outboard, as in earlier designs. There were no centerline bulkheads, and special arrangements were made for counterflooding.

The twelve-gun C&R design was similar, but only 5,356 tons were available for armor, compared with 5,009 for the ten-gun ship. Out of this had to come an additional turret and barbette, so that savings in the side armor were necessary. Although the ship herself was 40 feet longer, the belt could not be lengthened to match, and even so its width had to be reduced. Its soft ends therefore represented a real vulnerability.

In these designs, C&R was influenced by the Russo-Japanese War. Captains accustomed to conning their ships from open bridges refused to retreat into their cramped conning towers in battle. But that conning tower could itself burst incoming shells, showering bridges with splinters and killing entire staffs at a blow. C&R therefore tried to do away with permanent bridges, on the theory that officers should be forced in peacetime to operate under wartime conditions, in their conning towers. For navigation in confined waters, they were provided with a steering position enclosed within the base of the mast. This battle between the ship operators, who wanted open

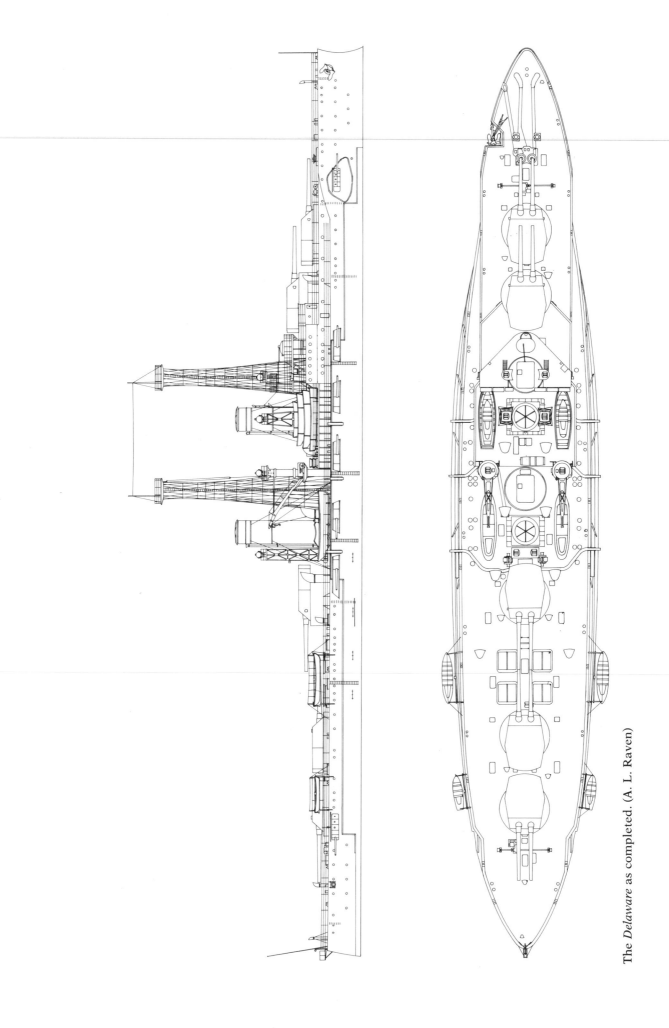

The *Delaware* as completed. (A. L. Raven)

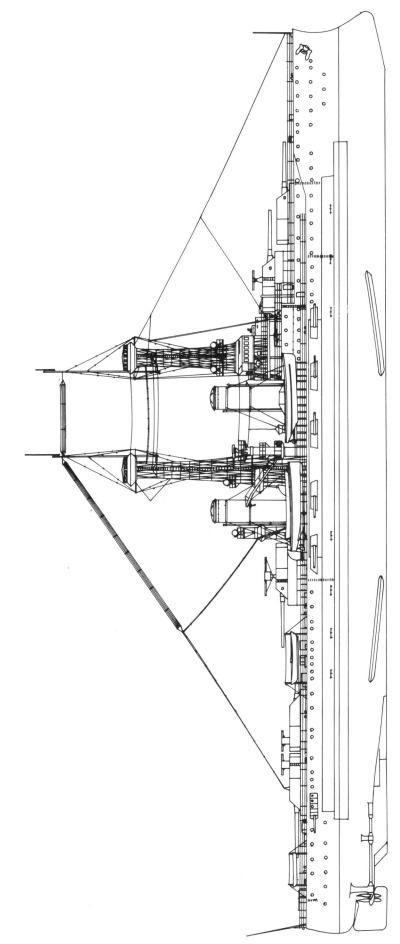

The *Delaware* about 1921. (A. L. Raven)

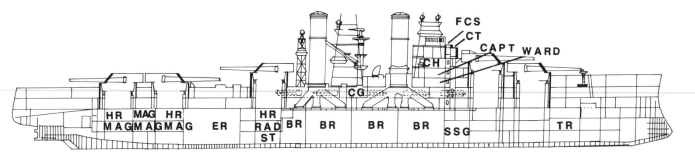

Inboard profile of the *Delaware*, 1921. Note the broadside guns, shown as dashed lines.

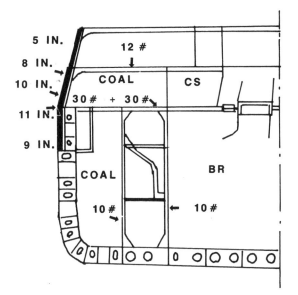

Cross section of the *Delaware*.

bridges, and the designers (and, later, the General Board), who emphasized the use of the conning tower, continued through to World War Two. It explains the austere appearance of the early American dreadnoughts.

These *Delaware*-class ships were designed before the advent of the cage mast, and C&R planned to provide them with a fire control bridge slung between two military masts athwartships. The funnels were, therefore, set well apart, to minimize smoke interference, the after one being as far aft as possible. As in the *South Carolinas*, when the ships were actually built, the military masts were reduced to kingposts and searchlight platforms, and cage masts were erected on the centerline. However, the effect of the earlier version survived in the unusual arrangement of the case masts. With no space between the after funnel and No. 3 turret, the mainmast had to go between the funnels, with a small searchlight tower being placed aft.

Six private designs were submitted. All but one were so incomplete as to be nearly useless, and they tended to be both obsolete in concept and unimaginative, with mixed batteries, inefficient armament disposition, and poor protection. Only a design by the Fore River Shipbuilding Company was deemed worthy of serious consideration. It makes an interesting contrast to the C&R designs (see Table 2-2).

Often private builders, supposedly unconstrained by bureaucracy, produce ships far more heavily armed for their size than their naval counterparts—a very well known case in 1906 was the British Admiralty vs. Elswick in cruiser design. The Fore River design was another example of a very heavily armed ship, carrying fourteen 12 inchers, twenty 4 inchers, and four torpedo tubes at 21 knots on 22,000 tons. Its lower casemate was uniform 11-inch armor, and side armor covered a slightly greater length than did that of the C&R twelve-gun design. The heavy guns were arranged as in the C&R ship except that two wing turrets replaced No. 3 turret aft. As in many British ships of this period, the secondary guns were entirely unprotected.

Those two extra 12-inch guns and the lower casemate armor had hidden costs, an example of the truism that on paper, *but not in practice*, the Navy designs often looked worse than flashier commercial ones. In this case the barbettes were reduced to narrow tubes extending through the protective deck. The structural support represented by the barbettes in more conventional designs was entirely absent. In addition the wing turrets weakened the upper deck. The designers had tried to balance this by extending the forecastle deck aft, but that was not nearly enough. The weight of three turrets immediately abaft the break of the forecastle made that discontinuity in the ship girder a major stress concentration. The wing turrets would be too close to the beam to be adequately protected against underwater attack. Overarming would also cram the hull with magazines, which in turn would be too close to the sides—and which even so would hold only eighty rounds per gun, where C&R provided a hundred. Nor did it appear that blast effects of the ship's own guns had been taken into account.

On 19 November 1906 the special board, convened under Assistant Secretary of the Navy Truman R. Newberry, found in favor of the C&R ten-gun design.

Table 2-2. Designs for the Newberry Board, 1906

Design	Fore River	C&R	C&R
Displacement	22,000	20,000	22,000
Length(WL)	540	510	554-7.5
Beam	88-5	85-2.6	85-2.8
Draft	25	27	27-3
Speed	21	21	21 kts
12in Guns	14(7X2)(80)	10(5X2)(100)	12(6X2)(100)
5in/50 Guns	---	14(240)	16(270)
4in Guns	20	---	---
Torpedo Tubes	4	2	2
Main Belt	11-9	11-9	11-9
Casemate	11	10-8	10-8
Upper Casemate	---	5	5
Barbettes	10	10	10
Turrets	12/8/8(rear)	12/8/8	12/8/8
Weights:			
Protection	6066	5009	5356
Ordnance	1970	1482	1773
Machinery	2200	1935	2345
Coal	3000	2300	2500
Oil	---	340	340

Note: Ordnance weights include ammunition. Number of rounds *per gun* is in parentheses. Turret-top thickness is not given.

The twelve-gun type was insufficiently armored, a defect curable only by exceeding the cost limit, in which case it would be "distinctly superior to any battleship now existing or known to be contemplated." The twelve-gun C&R design became the *Wyoming* of 1908–09, 4,000-tons heavier than the 1906 design.

As for Fore River, it sold two very large battleships to Argentina in 1910. They bore a strong family resemblance to the 1906 proposal, but exceeded 27,000 tons, even with one fewer centerline turret aft and with many other changes. The resulting class was not nearly so flashy, and in fact received considerable attention for its underwater protection. Their design was frequently compared with the *Wyoming*.

The contest winner was duplicated by another ship authorized on 2 March 1907. The *Delaware* and *North Dakota*, battleships 28 and 29, were laid down within a month of each other in the late fall of 1907. The American naval press termed them the first U.S. dreadnoughts—ten 12 inchers, 20 knots or more—ignoring the dreadnought status of the *South Carolina*s. Much later some antimilitary writers were to suggest that the motive for this designation was to raise the tempo of American construction by exaggerating the inferiority of the American fleet.

In 1907, many believed the steam turbine, which appeared to promise sustained high-speed steaming, to be the power plant of the future. The previous standard prime mover, the reciprocating engine, was generally denigrated because it tended to shake itself to pieces if run at full power for very long. On the

other hand, it promised much greater fuel economy, which was important to a Navy expecting to cross the Pacific en route to a decisive battle against Japan. The problem was aggravated by a combination of relatively slow U.S. construction and rapidly changing battleship technology. By the time the two 1907 ships had been completed and tested, three more classes had been designed. All were to have been turbine-powered, but in fact three of the six ships had reciprocating engines instead, largely as a result of the disappointing trials of the turbine-engined *North Dakota*.

The two ships were built as competitive sisters, their design providing enough volume for either conventional reciprocating engines (*Delaware*) or for the American-designed Curtis turbine (*North Dakota*). The alternative British Parsons turbine would have required much longer engine room spaces. Since the two ships did not run trials until 1909–10 they could not provide experience to guide the Navy in its choice of machinery for some time. However, Capps predicted as early as July 1907, on the basis of tank tests and the known performance of steam turbines, that the *North Dakota* would have a 25 percent shorter radius at 16 knots, and 45 percent shorter at 14 knots—in a Navy expecting to have to steam across the Pacific to fight Japan. His estimate was borne out on trials. Meanwhile, the *Delaware* proved capable of steaming at full speed for more than twenty-four hours without needing repairs. The key to this endurance was forced lubrication of the engine bearings. The conclusion was that, at least at 21 knots, reversion

The *North Dakota* is shown at sea during post–World War One gunnery practice. Note the searchlight control platform under the searchlights abaft her after funnel and the 3-inch guns atop her derrick posts. The small raised range-finder platform atop the conning tower was unique to this class. The large object on her stern is a battle practice target. A concentration dial is visible on her foremast, and the two superfiring turrets show deflection markings. The pattern of spray shows that the hull secondary weapons could be drenched even in relatively calm weather. Her thick black smoke was characteristic of coal-burners. Note also the large armored range-finder (probably of 20-foot base) atop her No. 3 turret and the much smaller one (probably of 5-foot base) atop No. 4, with a spreader for radio antennas atop No. 5.

The *Delaware* is shown at Guantanamo in January 1920, her broadside 5-inch battery removed and the screen to her flying bridge and conning platform very visible. At its top, it has been merged with the square searchlight control platform, which projects from the vee-faced bridge.

The *North Dakota*, shown about 1920. Note the screen protecting her helmsman (on her conning platform, as distinct from her conning tower). Compared with her original appearance, she now has a much larger flat-topped (rather than domed) conning tower, and a long-base range-finder mounted on the roof of No. 2 turret. World War One experience also shows in the sharp reduction in her boat complement. Life rafts are mounted all over her turrets and even on the side of her hull. They were relatively rugged, whereas boats would soon be destroyed by shells exploding as they struck. Boats were soon restored as a peacetime necessity. Much the same thing happened during and after World War Two.

to reciprocating engines seemed to carry no real penalty. That was not entirely borne out by later experience; the reciprocating-engine battleships performed poorly in the Pacific in the late 1930s.

On 13 May 1908 Congress authorized two more battleships, "similar in all essential characteristics" to the two just laid down. They became the *Florida* and *Utah*. C&R planned to rearrange the machinery spaces to permit installation of "any suitable type of turbine machinery," the contest between Curtis and Parsons remaining very much an open one; and a new secondary gun, the 5in/51, was introduced. A new splinter armor, STS (Special Treatment Steel), replaced the earlier nickel steel.

The engine room had to be lengthened to accommodate the long Parsons turbines. To do that, the after boiler room had to be eliminated, and hence

the remaining rooms (which were somewhat more cramped than in the previous class) had to be widened by about 4 feet. To maintain the width of the coal and void torpedo protection abeam the boilers, the ships were made 3 feet beamier than their predecessors. This rearrangement showed in closer funnel spacing. The greater beam increased metacentric height, a quantity in which the *Delaware*s were notably deficient, and this increase more than made up for the topweight added by more powerful secondary weapons. The closeness of the funnels precluded the unusual masting arrangement of the earlier ships. Pole masts were initially proposed, but quite soon the Navy switched to cages, fore and aft of the funnels.

As for the secondaries, C&R wanted a 6-inch gun, covered by 6.5-inch casemate armor, the latter the

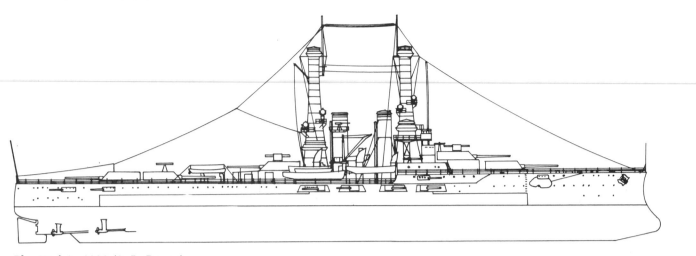

The *Utah* in 1923 (A. L. Raven)

only change in armor thickness from the *Delaware*s. Capps conceded that there was no need for a heavier antidestroyer weapon; the Japanese Navy was mounting 6-inch guns. Capps argued that the gun would have to deal with cruisers and also damage the unprotected parts of enemy capital ships. The latter argument suggests that Capps did not fully understand the fire control aspects of all-big-gun battleship design. The Board on Construction approved the 6-inch battery on 25 May 1908, but that was not to stand. In view of the considerable fleet criticism of both the *Delaware* and *Florida* designs, the department, under presidential order, called a battleship design conference at the Naval War College (see Chapter 3).

This Newport Conference of 1908 particularly criticized the lack of heavy splinter protection for the uptakes and for the secondary battery. Any solution would add weight, and as compensation the ship would have to be armed with 5- rather than 6-inch guns. The conference sought a compromise in the form of a new higher-velocity 5-inch gun, the 5in/51 which replaced the earlier 5in/50, and became standard in later U.S. dreadnoughts. Sixteen were mounted

in the *Florida*s—eight in the casemate, two directly above, two in the forecastle, and four aft. Thus the gun deck mounting forward was already recognized, in the summer of 1908, as pointless, yet the *Delaware*s would run their trials with just that arrangement more than a year later.

The *Utah* was fitted with an armored revolving fire control tower atop her conning tower, as proposed by BuOrd in November 1909, while both ships were already well under construction. The bureau wanted an enormous structure carrying the main range-finder, but it was forced to retreat, since the conning tower would have had to be enlarged to barbette size, with attendant weight and structural problems. A variety of types was proposed for installation in the *Wyoming* through *Nevada* classes. The prototype was installed in the *Utah*. However, her sister ship, *Florida*, only had her conning tower enlarged with a view to later installation. Towers were also installed in the *Wyoming* and *New York* classes. All were relatively light structures of splinter armor. By 1911 a much heavier type was once more being proposed, this time for the *Nevada*. It was rejected, partly in view of the success of the roomy

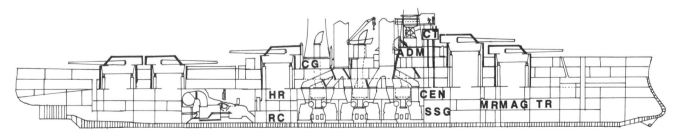

Utah inboard profile, 1923. The engines, boilers, and the coal-passing scuttles in the bulkhead behind the boilers have been drawn in. The location of the scuttles makes it clear that no coal-burning battleship could really be safe from underwater hits, as the scuttle doors, however secured, could spring open.

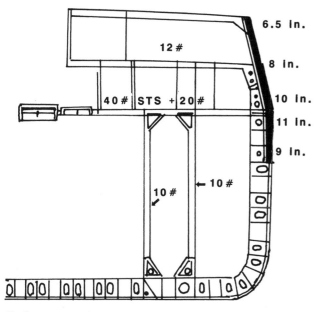

Utah cross section.

conning tower of the *Florida*, which housed both ship and fire control parties under armor. Also, newer ships had little need for a special revolving armored range-finder because range-finders were built into superfiring turrets, starting with the *New York* class.

Somewhat paradoxically, some of these same ships were fitted with entirely unprotected long-base range-finders on turret tops. These instruments appear to have been intended only to obtain an initial range, after which corrections would be by spotting—by the party in the protected conning tower, and by men in the tops, who could not be protected in any case. This made particularly good sense if the battle were to be fought at such long range that there would be relatively few hits. In such a case an AP hit on light armor would have destructive effect over a wide area, whereas it would be unlikely to hit an exposed range-finder. This argument, already well understood by 1906, had become the basis of U.S. armoring doctrine by 1911.

3

Theodore Roosevelt's Fighting Machine, 1907–09

Between 1890 and 1908 American constructors designed thirty-one battleships, largely on the basis of theory and foreign practice. U.S. Navy battleships took relatively long to build and for quite some time did not operate together in permanent formations of any great size. As a result, although on paper the United States possessed a strong battleship force, in fact its Navy had little war-fighting power and the small squadrons continued to operate as in the pre-steel Navy. Their primary role was to exert U.S. influence in various areas of what would now be called the Third World. That was the paramount peacetime naval role, valid only so long as the United States faced no enemy with a strong *and* concentrated battle fleet.

President Theodore Roosevelt saw that sea power should be used very differently. He considered his battle fleet his single most powerful instrument of foreign influence. The greater its war-fighting power, the greater its efficacy as a diplomatic instrument. That in turn required the president to concentrate the fleet, even though such concentration would leave many areas of importance uncovered. This was a Mahanian view: the guarantor of sea power anywhere in the world was a concentrated battle fleet superior to that of any rival.

Thus, the local squadrons were abolished, and the sixteen active battleships were formed into an Atlantic Fleet, which was welded together by the 'Round the World Cruise of 1907–09, the cruise of the Great White Fleet. The cruise was intended to demonstrate the efficacy of the new policy: U.S. battleships might be withdrawn from the Far East, for example, but the entire fleet would still be able to enforce the writ of the United States anywhere in the world.

Roosevelt's views may have been strengthened by the experience of the Russo-Japanese War. The U.S. naval observer attached to the Russians, Lieutenant W. S. McCully, considered the division of the Russian battle fleet between the Baltic and the Far East criminal. It would have been better for the Russians to have concentrated all of their ships in a single fleet, even if on the outbreak of war all had been located 10,000 miles from the theatre of operations. Separation made it easier for the Japanese to defeat the Russians in detail. From a U.S. point of view, the cruise of the Russian Baltic Fleet from Kronstadt to defeat at Tsushima had to seem analogous to a prospective U.S. fleet cruise to the Far East to deal with a Japanese fleet which had, for example, destroyed local U.S. forces in the Philippines.

The world cruise tested the seagoing (and, to some extent, war-fighting) characteristics of the new classes of U.S. battleships, and as such had a profound effect on subsequent designs. Even before the cruise, critics such as then-Captain W. S. Sims (who had the president's ear) had charged that the existing organization for warship design was far too conservative and hence unlikely to bring the fleet to anything like the required level of efficiency. The cruise tended to confirm these charges. President Roosevelt, therefore, convened the Newport Conference of 1908, at which the General Board finally became responsible for the characteristics of U.S. battleship design. The line officers and the planners, rather than the technicians of the material bureaus (as in the Board on Construction) now took control, a pattern that has persisted ever since. From 1909 to the end of the battleship era, U.S. battleships were designed to meet General Board characteristics.

The cage mast, seen here aboard a U.S. pre-dreadnought, was the single most visible symbol of the revolution in fire control led by reformers such as William S. Sims. Their success led them on to attack the bureau system itself and thus to precipitate the Newport Conference. This is a mainmast. Note the mesh platforms within the mast, and the ladders projecting up through it, leading to the circular fire control platform at the top.

The world cruise was primarily intended to demonstrate that the United States could project naval power across the Pacific to meet the growing power of Japan. Tension between Japan and the United States grew in large part from the position in the Orient that this country won in 1898 by its seizure of the Philippines. One might go so far as to say that the main issue between the two countries was always the Japanese drive for hegemony in the Far East. In 1906 the United States opposed that drive by mediating the Russo-Japanese War on terms the Japanese considered unfair. Discrimination against Japanese living on the West Coast was also a major source of Japanese resentment against the United States.

In 1906, the likely scenario for war would have begun with Japanese seizure of the Philippines. The three-battleship squadron had just been withdrawn as part of the fleet reorganization. Japan was much too powerful to be countered by local forces. At least from this time on, the U.S. strategy for Pacific warfare envisaged little more than a holding action in the Philippines. The main effort would be represented by an American fleet fighting its way across the Pacific to relieve or recover the Philippines. The difficulties of such an operation had just been demonstrated by the unfortunate cruise of the Russian Baltic fleet halfway around the world to disaster at Tsushima. The world cruise was intended to demonstrate that the United States would present Japan with a much more serious challenge.

U.S. battleship designs reflected this strategy. Alone among the major sea powers the United States contemplated serious naval operations halfway across the world from its bases. For the next forty years it would deliberately design its capital ships to operate at enormous distances and would consciously sacrifice many qualities other navies deemed essential. The cruise, then, was a test of exactly those qualities of *strategic* mobility most important to U.S. planners.

Congress was by no means clearly in favor of so provocative a move as a fleet cruise to Japanese waters. Suppose Japan chose to attack the fleet? President Roosevelt chose to announce the cruise in stages, beginning with a run from Hampton Roads to San Francisco (2 July 1907). Even this limited step was widely interpreted as a signal to Japan of American concern with Pacific affairs. Some observers suggested that Japan might react by declaring war. Once the fleet was on the West Coast, Roosevelt sent it across the Pacific, and then home to Norfolk via the Atlantic, but this plan was announced only gradually.

The cruise was the first real test of the new battleships which had been designed and built so rapidly under President Roosevelt's administration. Although they were already obsolescent (in view of the big-gun revolution), their behavior at sea furnished many lessons for future construction. A senior naval constructor, R. H. Robinson, accompanied the fleet, and both he and the C-in-C, Rear Admiral Robley D. Evans, submitted extensive reports, the latter reflecting those of the individual captains under his command.

Apart from coal, the fleet turned out to be largely self-sustaining, surprisingly so in an era of delicate reciprocating engines. Robinson concluded that the radius of future U.S. ships at an economical speed of 10 to 12 knots should be at least 6,000nm. In order to achieve such low-speed performance, both he and Admiral Evans were willing to forgo turbines, which at the time were considered the only means of achieving sustained high cruising speed. Few outside the U.S. Navy appreciated just how important long endurance could be, and most contemporary observers considered the United States backward in not passing to turbine propulsion when the Royal Navy did in HMS *Dreadnought*. As a whole, the fleet was good for an economical speed of 8 knots, "excluding the *Maine*, which has no economical speed and burns over 30 tons of coal a day in port."

Both Robinson and Evans emphasized the need for tactical homogeneity, but that was a point well appreciated already, as witness the construction of five *Virginia*s and six *Connecticut*s of very similar qualities, followed by two *Michigan*s deliberately designed for tactical homogeneity with the *Connecticut*s. Such requirements were read by the naval constructors to mean that there would be no fewer than four ships, that is, one battle division, of each class. Tactical homogeneity would also require that the smaller battleships through the *Maine*s, or at least through the *Alabama*s, be laid up in reserve as incompatible with the later ships.

The largest of the ships, the *Virginia*s and *Connecticut*s, had all been designed before any seagoing experience had been accumulated with their predecessors, the *Alabama*s and the *Maine*s. This inexperience showed in the wetness of all the ships. Robinson, for example, reported that all took water aboard forward in any but the smoothest sea, although generally that did not put turrets out of action. His proposed remedies included flare at the bow, the omission of such spray-creating projections as bill-boards (for anchors) and gun sponsons, and increased freeboard forward. These improvements would be essential in future fast battleships. Similarly, low quarterdecks (as in the *Maine* class) were often flooded by a quartering sea, although, again, they were not so wet as to put after turrets out of action.

These observations applied to moderate (trade belt) weather and to a fleet speed of 10 knots or less. The new all-big-gun ships would cruise at 15 knots or more, and the fleet's problems suggested that firing at such a speed (or at 10 to 12 knots in heavier weather)

The Newport Conference was too late to modify the *Utah*, seen here as newly completed, with a prominent cylindrical fire control tower atop her armored conning tower.

might be difficult. Future ships, then, would need more freeboard, and their turret guns would have to be higher. That in turn would require more beam (to maintain stability) and greater size.

Secondary and tertiary guns, generally mounted one deck below the main deck on the gun deck, fared much worse. Robinson reported that the forward 3-inch guns on the *Connecticut* class were useless at any speed in practically any sea. Further aft, the broadside 7-inch guns on the weather side were generally useless at speed in trade wind conditions or worse. Even if relatively little water got through the gun port, it made the deck slippery and sighting difficult. Admiral Evans agreed that at 10 knots with an ordinary trade wind anywhere forward of the beam, the weather guns had been shuttered. They could have been fired, but only at the risk of flooding. Given the natural roll of the ship, water would have risen over the coamings of the shell hoists and would have reached the powder, ruining it. The admiral estimated that guns could not have been fired at all, or the shutters cleared, at 15 knots. The guns on the weather side were important because a commander could be expected to prefer them to the guns on the lee (sheltered) side, since the latter weapons would suffer from errors due to refraction of light through firing gases.

Future battleships would not have 7-inch gun deck batteries, but they would require antidestroyer (torpedo-defense) guns, and those weapons would have

to be served at high speed. Robinson concluded that at least some of the torpedo-defense weapons should, in future, be mounted much higher in the ship. In theory, destroyers would attack after a gunnery engagement, to finish off crippled ships. The guns, therefore, would have to be armored, as otherwise they would be destroyed during the heavy-gun action. That would conflict with the problem of wetness, however. Robinson's suggested compromise, which reflected practice in several contemporary foreign designs, was to split the battery between a protected gun deck and exposed mountings on turret tops or elsewhere.

The *Utah* design had already been completed, so the first class affected by the experience of the world cruise was the *Wyoming*, which did have high secondaries. The *Nevada*, the next design, carried her secondary weapons higher yet. The last bow casemates in U.S. service were the gun deck mounts forward on the *Delaware* and *North Dakota*, both designed much earlier. It was not understood until much later, however, that *any* casemate set into the side of the hull would be wet. The solution was to move guns into the superstructure, set back from the side, as in the *New Mexico*s of 1914 (see Chapter 5).

The other great seagoing question was the proper width and placement of the side armor. One surprise of the cruise was that, even fully loaded and in smooth to moderate seas, ships often exposed the lower edge of their belt armor, so that shells might easily pass

The *Florida, Utah*'s sister ship, is shown at the Naval Review of October 1912. Note that she lacked her sister's fire control tower and that she had already been fitted with unarmored range-finders atop her superfiring turrets.

under it to reach magazines and machinery. To some extent this was because of the profile of crests and troughs made by the ship's bow wave. Belt design was also complicated by the range of displacements that had to be accommodated; Admiral Evans considered the standard 8-foot-wide belt inadequate.

Moreover, although local flooding by hits above the belt could generally be disregarded, flooding at the bow could have serious consequences. Even at 10 knots, the bow wave rose 2 or 3 feet above the bow armor, and even 5-inch or 6-inch shells could open the hull plating. The bow would fill as the ship pitched, and she would go down by the head, bringing her screws and rudder out of the water. Admiral Evans therefore endorsed a suggestion that the waterline belt curve up at the bows and that the bows be covered with 2-inch or 3-inch armor as far aft as Frame 17. Robinson wanted to extend belt armor as far down as possible and to have bow and stern armor follow the expected wave profiles—which was not actually done until the *South Dakota* class of the 1930s.

He emphasized protection for the steering gear, noting that in the Russo-Japanese War several ships were either lost or severely damaged because of steering-gear damage.

All of these suggestions required much more armor, that is, much more weight. In a balanced design, that meant much larger ships. In 1908, the Navy was beginning to build them.

The pre-dreadnoughts were very cluttered topside, not merely because of their extensive minor batteries but also because of the mass of bridges and boats deemed necessary. Experience in the Russo-Japanese War suggested that unncessary structure tended to burst shells so that their splinters would kill personnel standing in exposed positions. The solution was evidently both to eliminate potential shell-bursters and to enlarge armored positions so that the ships could be fought from them. It was not clear whether such positions could ever be entirely satisfactory for peacetime ship-handling. That was not the point: both Evans and Robinson pressed, successfully, for simpler superstructures. Ships would be steered from their conning towers, in peace as in war, and the only bridge would be a simple structure at the level of the floor of the conning tower.

The conning tower would have to be large enough to accommodate the captain, navigator, and three or four other men at the wheel, instruments, and voice tubes. Access would be primarily from below, that is, under armor, although the usual door would be retained so that an officer on the bridge could control a helmsman inside. A flagship, then, would require a larger conning tower; it followed that flagships should be so designated at the time of construction. The issue was not living space but rather the size of the heavily armored conning tower. Given this requirement, it would be impractical to follow existing practice and make all battleships flagships.

To encourage officers to use the conning tower, Admiral Evans wanted to make it the only steering station protected from the weather. Ships would be conned from outside only when entering harbor or going alongside a dock. Thus the flying bridge could be eliminated, although portable bridge wings could

The *Florida* is shown in 1918, with 3-inch antiaircraft guns atop her derrick posts, deflection scales on her turrets, and large (probably 20-foot) range-finders atop her superfiring turrets. A smaller range-finder (5-foot) surmounts No. 4 turret. Note that her protected bridge wings are at the level of her conning tower roof, with a much higher vee-faced top protecting her conning platform.

be fitted, to be unrigged when clearing for action. The conning tower would be directly above the central (fire control) station which, Admiral Evans proposed, should contain duplicate ship control devices (wheel, compass, helm indicator, and so on) as an emergency secondary conning position.

These views prevailed, both in future U.S. designs, and in the reconstruction of the fleet after its return from the world cruise. For example, the existing small conning towers were replaced by considerably larger ones and most bridgework eliminated—only to be replaced during and after World War One, as the fleet again discovered how important vision could be during high-speed bad-weather steaming.

Finally, there was fire control. In 1907 the United States had just adopted the system of control by spotters, who required positions very high above water. High and nearly indestructible cage masts were an important feature of the new battleships, but in 1907 the entire issue was still very much open. Evans criticized the existing pole masts: they vibrated excessively and were vulnerable to single hits. He also wanted fire control telephone leads protected, arguing on the basis of reports of British experiments with the old ironclad *Hero*.

These cruise reports were compiled early in the exercise, Robinson's being dated 4 March 1908. Admiral Evans was replaced by Admiral Charles S. Sperry at San Francisco. The two reports, however, appear to have represented the lessons of the cruise, which ended only on 22 February 1909, 45,000 miles after the departure from Hampton Roads.

Meanwhile, another important set of conclusions had been reached in Newport, at the Naval War College, as a result of the reform movement within the Navy. Promotion was virtually entirely by seniority, and it was very slow, even though the fleet was growing in size. Many within the junior officer corps argued that it was so slow that officers gained high command much too late in their careers. For example, Evans had had to leave his fleet command because, just as he had gained sufficient experience of his command, he passed retirement age. A number of the younger officers, notably William S. Sims and Bradley Fiske, enjoyed the president's active support as they sought radical reform. Most of the radicals were gunnery specialists who could, rightly, consider themselves leaders in the all-big-gun ship revolution. It appeared to them that the independent bureaus, each jealous of its prerogatives, were unwilling to work toward the common good of furthering the ongoing naval revolution in technology and tactics. Sims had made his name by reforming U.S. naval gunnery, enormously increasing the effective rate of fire and the rate of hitting per round by methods BuOrd often considered impractical. His great supporter had been President Roosevelt, who was so concerned with warreadiness.

To the radicals, the issue was whether operational effectiveness could ever gain priority over technical convenience. Their solution was to advocate a naval General Staff. Congress had rejected just such a plan in 1904, fearing a loss of its power over the Navy. The rebels considered President Roosevelt their nat-

The *Florida* is shown off New York City on 23 April 1919. She still lacks a peacetime complement of boats and is equipped largely with life rafts. Note that the forward range-finder has been armored. Two of her broadside 5-inch guns have been landed.

ural ally, and they feared that they would have little chance of success once he departed. They became more and more frustrated as his second (probably, in their view, last) term continued without any approach to the basic reform they wanted. They therefore resorted to the press. At their suggestion, Henry Reuterdahl, the American contributor to *Jane's Fighting Ships*, published an article, "The Needs of Our Navy," in *McClure's Magazine* (January 1908) (some historians have suggested that Sims himself was the actual author). Reuterdahl's charges included insufficient freeboard, excessive immersion of the main armor belt, and unsafe turrets, the latter unmodified despite two serious turret explosions as recently as 1903–04.

At this time, the U.S. Navy used a single-stage hoist from magazine to turret. In contrast, the Royal Navy used two stages, which were much safer; for an explosion in the turret could, at least in theory, ignite the magazine via a direct hoist. Indeed, a 1904 explosion aboard the *Missouri* had very nearly done so. Single-stage hoists were also unable to keep up with the rates of fire Sims and his colleagues had made possible. This meant that shells had to be stowed *in* the turrets, again a dangerous arrangement.

The chief constructor and the head of the Board on Construction attempted to answer these criticisms in a Senate hearing. Their defenses of the belt location and freeboard seem reasonable in retrospect, when viewed only in their technical context. However, at face value many of their statements appeared self-serving.

To the disappointment of the reformers, the hearings, which were largely defensive in tone, hardly touched their main target, the bureau system as such. The reformers were driven to a desperate measure, a letter from Commander Albert Key to the secretary of the navy. Key commented on the new *North Dakota*, which he had seen fitting out as he awaited completion of his new ship, the scout cruiser *Salem*. Sims sent a copy to the president, the result being the Newport Conference.

The Navy Department called a conference on 2 July 1908, ostensibly to inquire into defects in the *North Dakota* and their possible rectification in the *Utah* design but actually as an inquiry into the general problem of battleship design and into the *process* of battleship design. Those present included the General Board, Commanders Sims and Key, and such naval architects as David Taylor (a future chief con-

The *Utah* is shown on 27 December 1918. Note that, compared with the *Florida*, she has a substantial bridge structure built around her flying bridge and conning platform.

structor) and Robert Stocker (who would be responsible for U.S. underwater protection systems about a decade later).

Key worded his attack very strongly so as to gain attention. His main points were as follows:

—Grossly inadequate protection for 5 inch guns and uptakes. Key suggested that as light armor (as in the existing ships) would only serve to burst AP shells it would be better to do away with such protection altogether.

—The torpedo-defense battery would be too wet. Key suggested that the 5-inch guns be mounted in the open atop the turrets, unarmored.

—The upper belt should be eliminated as a waste of armor weight; rapid 12-inch fire would destroy it in any case.

—No. 3 turret should not be located between engines and boiler rooms, to avoid passing hot-steam lines through its magazine.

—The U.S. 12-inch gun was not as powerful as those of England, France, and Germany.

—Designed drafts were unrealistic in that they did not follow the ⅔ loading suggested by the Walker Board.

"This [Walker Board] recommendation, the most important part of the report of a board of sea-going officers, approved by the Secretary of the Navy, is consistently and deliberately ignored, with the result that the vessels of the Atlantic Fleet are over draft as measured by the rule of the Walker Board . . . the two of the *Kentucky*

class 27 inches, the three of the *Alabama* class 20 inches, the three of the *Ohio* class 20 inches, the five of the *Virginia* class 24 inches, the two of the *Louisiana* and three of the *Kansas* class 17 inches."Key argued that armor belts were not *sufficiently* immersed, that the usual 5 feet of armor below water was not enough. He then claimed insufficient *above*-water protection.

At Newport the General Board was joined by the staff of the Naval War College and by other officers. President Roosevelt spoke on 22 July, and he presided over several sessions. Before he left he ordered that all resolutions before the conference be voted upon and that the votes *by name* be reported to the Navy Department.

The conference chose to thicken the protection of the secondary battery. In the *Utah*, a weight equivalent to an 8-inch casemate (obtained by trading the proposed 6-inch battery for 5-inch guns) was to be used for a combination of side armor and fore and aft splinter bulkheads protecting the uptakes, the latter not less than 1½ inches thick, and intended to isolate the gun positions, so that bursts on one gun would not destroy all. The conference also called for higher, drier, gun positions. It condemned the 5-inch battery of the *North Dakota* as wet even in trade wind conditions. Nor did it like the location of the No. 3 turret, although that was recognized as possibly inescapable. The conference hoped that the *Utah* design could be modified, with No. 4 turret raised and No. 3 lowered, and additional protection applied to

The *Utah* is shown in her final configuration before reconstruction. Although this photograph was dated October 1924, it was probably taken much earlier, since it shows deflection markings on her superfiring turrets. The short cylinders of Vickers-type secondary battery directors are visible abeam her cage foremast (on the 01 level) and abeam No. 3 barbette, on the main deck level. The larger range-finders are 20-foot units. The smaller, 5-foot units are for the secondary battery. Note that No. 2 turret carries both. Of the secondary battery guns, only the foremost weapon on each side has been landed.

the steering gear, at a cost of no more than a sixty day delay.

Generally, the conference redefined design displacement to include ⅔ supply of fuel and full ammunition, one of Key's most emphatic points.

The other important results of the conference also related to future designs. Thus, one resolution called for tests to determine "the actual effects of gun fire upon armor at battle ranges." Another called for the removal of the conning tower of a ship and its replacement by wooden towers of various shapes, to determine the most effective. Advocates of tactical homogeneity obtained a resolution to build future ships in groups of four.

Finally, "the conference recommends that for the battleships subsequent to the four whose characteristics are indicated in the above report . . . several designs, representing different schools of thought for each projected type, be prepared and at the proper time be submitted to a special board of officers, not to exceed 13 in number, considered best qualified for the duty of criticizing and modifying the designs presented, and finally of recommending to the Department the design believed by a majority of the board to embody all the qualities, military and otherwise, best adapted to the needs of the United States Navy at the time of the board's report."

In practice, this meant that new designs were submitted to the General Board, which wrote the "characteristics" to which ships were designed. The Board on Construction was dissolved. This shift was prob-

ably by far the single most important result of the Newport Conference.

Both the world cruise and the Newport Conference reflected a more general determination, largely on the part of President Roosevelt, that the fleet be brought closer to war-readiness. Thus, on its return, the pre-dreadnought fleet was extensively modernized in 1909–11. Perhaps the most striking indication of the new priorities was that the ships were repainted in wartime gray rather than in peacetime white and buff. This change had already been effected for ships in home waters. In addition, peacetime bridgework was largely eliminated, as Admiral Evans had proposed. Conning towers were considerably enlarged, cage masts (and modern fire controls) installed, and secondary batteries somewhat redistributed.

The change in color seems superficial in comparison to the others, but it must have had profound psychological effects, in that it must have reminded personnel throughout the fleet of the potential for war. It is not clear whether this was intentional or whether experiments during the world cruise suggested that gray paint was valuable as camouflage.

In all but the oldest ships (the *Oregon* and *Iowa* classes), elaborate bridges were replaced by minimal platforms and enlarged conning towers. Cage foremasts, with searchlight platforms and spotting platforms on top, were fitted. Cage mainmasts were easier to install, since much less structure had to be cleared away and no conning tower had to be added.

The *Florida* is shown at Guantanamo Bay, January 1920. She differs slightly from her sister. Note that her forward secondary range-finder is carried atop her navigating (flying) bridge and that her searchlight control platform is a flat-sided, windowed enclosure. Both ships were unusual in that their foremast searchlights were carried on two levels. Note the absence of lower-deck broadside guns, which were reinstalled soon afterwards.

That is probably why the first four pre-dreadnoughts received only cage mainmasts: The *Massachusetts* in 1909, *Indiana* and *Oregon* in 1910/11, and *Iowa* in 1911. Similarly, the new battleships *Mississippi* and *Idaho*, fitting out when the Great White Fleet returned from its cruise, were almost immediately fitted with cage mainmasts, where previously they had had no mainmasts at all. They had to wait until the end of the reconstruction program in 1911 for new bridgework, conning towers, and foremasts.

In other classes the foremast and bridgework were replaced first, on what appears to have been an emergency basis. Thus in 1909 the *Missouri, Ohio, Illinois, Wisconsin, Virginia, Rhode Island, Nebraska,* and *Minnesota* all had cage foremasts. The others received the full two-mast refit at one time, and by 1910 only the *New Hampshire* lacked cage masts. By 1911 all of the post-*Iowa* battleships had two cage masts and new conning towers.

Lighter batteries were also redistributed and altered. By 1911 the slow-firing secondary batteries of the early battleships were clearly obsolete. All 6 inchers were removed from the *Indiana*s and replaced by a total of twelve 3-inch antitorpedo boat weapons: four on top of the deckhouse amidships, one on each

8-inch turret, two on each 13-inch turret. Two hull 4-inchers were removed from the *Iowa* and a single 4 incher mounted atop each of six turrets, for a final total of ten.

The world cruise proved that the bow 3-inch casemates of the newest pre-dreadnoughts were so wet as to be useless and they were removed. In the two *Idaho*s they were relocated to the tops of the forward 8-inch turrets, and in the *Mississippi* a pair of 3 inchers were also moved to the bridge wings, a modification impractical in her sister ship because of the enlarged conning tower fitted to her. By way of contrast, the forward (6-inch) casemates of the *Illinois* and *Maine* classes were not removed at this time. In the two *Kearsage*s, four open 5 inchers were added atop the casemate. The gun deck secondary weapons, which had proven too wet in all ships so fitted, were *not* removed at this time.

Modern two-stage shell and powder hoists replaced the earlier single-stage system, a modification attributable to the gunnery critics.

The magnitude of the program can be gauged from the cost of modernizing a *Kearsage*, about $675,000. By way of comparison, the new battleship *Utah* cost $8,954,076 in 1908 dollars.

4

The *Wyoming* and *New York* Classes, 1910–11

The Newport Conference of 1908 resulted in a new series of battleships, the earliest to survive through the Second World War. In a single step, displacement (hence cost) rose by almost a third. From now on, American battleships would be the largest in the world.

The new ships also marked the end of the Board on Construction, and the beginning of the power of the General Board over ship characteristics. Previously there had been no detailed design requirements. The chief constructor, sitting on the Board on Construction, had proposed designs and the board had passed on them. The General Board merely suggested the number of ships to be built and made general remarks as to their characteristics. The Newport Conference erected what amounted to an adversary procedure in place of this informal one. Henceforth characteristics would begin with the General Board planners. The bureaus would try to satisfy them, and the board would choose among their proposals.

The *Wyoming* and *New York* classes represented a transitional stage in this process. The *Wyoming* was designed by the Board on Construction in response to very general directives resulting from the Newport Conference. The following year, although the General Board was responsible for design characteristics, it had too little time to frame new requirements and produce a new design to satisfy them, so that the *New York*s were also essentially Board on Construction ships. Experience with their design, however, did enable the board to frame its first set of characteristics, for what became the *Nevada* class, in mid-1910.

The pressure for a wholly new design came from a general belief that the international standard of battleship calibre would soon rise above 12 inches. It was known that the Royal Navy had under construction a 13.5-inch weapon, and Germany appeared ready to abandon her 11-inch gun, which many considered already equivalent to the 12-inch of other fleets. The Newport Conference favored a heavily armored ten 14-inch type for future construction, and some officers maintained that the *Utah*s should have eight 14-inch rather than ten 12-inch.

A 1.5 or 2-inch increase in calibre might seem small, but it would entail an entirely new standard of destructiveness. Existing 12-inch ships, upon which enormous sums had been and were being spent, would be (at best) obsolescent. Moreover, it would take a considerable jump in displacement to buy protection *against* the new guns. Hence the general reluctance to take the step up.

The larger-calibre gun would be more effective because its shell would be heavier in proportion to its frontal area. Since shell weight was proportional to the *cube* of the calibre, whereas area was proportional to the square. A one-sixth increase in calibre was equivalent to a 70 percent increase in weight, from 850 to 1400 pounds. The shell with greater weight per unit area would lose velocity to air resistance more slowly, that is, it would retain more of its initial velocity longer. Hence a 14-inch shell fired at a lower muzzle velocity would have a higher striking velocity at long range—and improvements in fire control were increasing battle ranges. These considerations led the Royal Navy to abandon its high-velocity 12in/50 in favor of the 13.5-inch gun and, a few years later,

The *New York* seen from a kite balloon, while making 17 knots, 1919. Before the advent of reliable spotting airplanes, kite balloons were an effective means of seeing beyond the ship's horizon. As such they were widely employed within the British Grand Fleet, to which the *New York* was attached. Note the contrast between the long 5in/51 secondary battery guns on the 01 level just abaft No. 2 turret and the 3in/50 antiaircraft guns on her derrick-post tops.

Newly completed, the *Wyoming*, then one of the largest battleships in the world, steams on trials. Note the wetness of her foremost 5-inch gun and the simplicity of her bridge arrangements: bare (and temporary) bridge wings at conning tower level; and a canvas-protected flying bridge and conning platform higher up, with a torpedo-defense platform surmounting them.

to abandon that gun for a relatively low-velocity 15in/42.

Adoption of a new gun would be risky and expensive. If experience with high-powered 12-inch weapons was a guide, a major jump in gun performance would carry its own technical problems, unpredictable in advance. Any navy planning the surprise introduction of a new gun would have to rush it into production without a lengthy testing program and, furthermore, would have to build the ships at the same time as the gun. Any failure would force the navy to substitute lighter weapons, destroying the balance of the design and probably losing considerable ground in the international naval arms race. Such considerations have often been cited in connection with Winston Churchill's 1911 decision in favor of the 15-inch gun in the *Queen Elizabeth* class.* They afflicted the U.S. Navy no less in 1908–10.

BuOrd estimated that gun-mount work would begin upon authorization of the new ships, which would probably be in March 1909. In December 1908, the bureau estimated that drawings for the mountings would take six months, with another eighteen months for actual construction. Thus, the project might be completed by June 1911. A new and longer (higher-velocity) 12-inch gun would entail a similar delay,

but to retain the old 12in/45 would save the six months. As for the guns, a 12in/50 was already under construction at Bethlehem Steel, for delivery about 15 July 1909. It would probably be finished and proved by October, seven months after authorization of the ships. The 14-inch would probably require another two months, and in either case about eighteen months more would be required for manufacture, so that the choice of 14 inches over 12in/45 would delay the ships by about nine months, with guns ready in July 1911 rather than in October 1910, and their mounts in June 1911 rather than in January.

The Newport Conference had not imagined any of the problems that might befall a new gun not yet even designed. It suggested this nonexistent weapon as the future U.S. standard, and on 26 August 1908 the Secretary of the Navy Victor H. Metcalf implemented the conference's decision by asking C&R to sketch eight and ten-gun 14-inch ships, with the heaviest practicable armor, and speeds of 20 knots or more, for delivery of these sketch designs the following January. Meanwhile BuOrd was to compare the existing 12in/45 and the projected gun. C&R, less optimistic than the seagoing officers at Newport, decided on its own initiative to develop a twelve 12-inch design as a hedge against rejection of the new gun, basing it on the unsuccessful 1906 study.

The General Board shared this skepticism, emphasizing the high cost of a 14-inch gun ship and noting that even though Britain had a 13.5-inch gun under construction, she was still mounting the 12in/50 aboard her new battleships.

---

* Churchill decided to order five ships before the new 15-inch gun arming them had been tested. Had the gun failed, the ships would have been limited to the very inferior battery of eight 13.5-inch guns rather that the ten mounted in contemporary British ships. He switched from coal to oil fuel at the same time.

The *Arkansas* is shown at the New York Naval Review of October 1912. Note the bow blister intended to protect her forward 5-inch gun.

President Theodore Roosevelt took a personal interest, inquiring about the new designs as early as 15 September 1908. Two days later Secretary of the Navy Metcalf was able to report that the eight-gun ship would displace about 24,000 tons, the ten-gun ship 27,000 (at Newport the estimates had been 21,500 and, at worst, 25,000) tons. The indicated jump in displacement, even for the smaller ship, was impressive. In 1908 there were no dry docks in the country large enough to accommodate the larger alternative. Roosevelt leaned toward the eight-gun ship.

BuOrd claimed that the current battle range, then estimated at 8,000 to 8,500 yards, was unlikely to increase much further. At such ranges the existing 12-inch gun could penetrate all armor, so there was little point in developing a more powerful gun. The bureau's conclusion appears to have been derived from incorrect notions about spotting, since only about two years later ships were firing experimentally at 12,000 yards, at which range existing armor certainly could defeat the existing 12-inch gun.

BuOrd weighed three factors in comparing the proposed 14in/45, with a muzzle velocity of 2,600 ft/sec, to the existing 12in/45 (2,800 ft/sec): rate of fire; destructive effect; and accuracy. Bore erosion would probably limit both guns to a life of about 150 rounds, although later the bureau would suggest that any difference would likely favor the larger weapon. Presumably the greater bulk of the new shell would slow fire, roughly in the ratio of shell dimensions (that is, calibre). The flatter-trajectory 12-inch would be more accurate, its larger danger space equating to greater tolerance for error in range estimation. At a battle

range of about 8,000 yards, experts estimated that the 14-inch would make about 10 percent fewer hits. Destructive effect was difficult to estimate precisely, but the ratio of shell weights, 3 to 5 in favor of the larger shell, could be used as a measure. Multiplying through, the ratio of values might be taken as 7 x 10 x 3 divided by 6 x 9 x 5, or 7 to 9 in favor of the larger gun. Then the alternatives could be compared:

	Value of Battery	Displacement	Value/ Displacement
Utah	70	21,500	3.2 per thousand tons
Twelve 12in	84	26,000	3.2
Eight 14in	72	25,000	2.9
Ten 14in	90	27,000	3.3

The last column might be equated, roughly, to firepower per unit *constuction* cost. It does not take into account costs, both monetary and tactical, which favored the concentration of weapons in a few larger ships. The eight-gun design was in trouble from the beginning.

BuOrd also argued that the probability of hitting was roughly proportional not only to the danger space (the tolerance for errors in range), but also to the number of rounds per salvo, that is, to the number of turrets, since practice at the time was to fire one gun turret in each salvo. Salvos were, at least in theory, centrally aimed, so that fire control errors should have been common to all shells of a salvo. These considerations heavily favored the 12-inch gun,

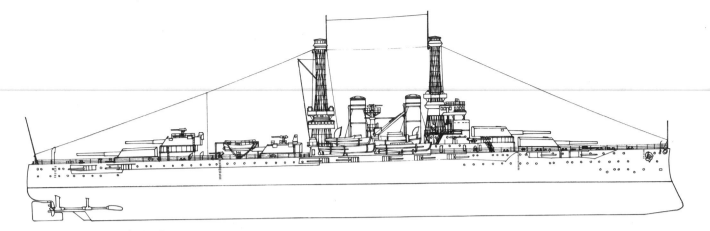

The *Texas* in 1918. (A. L. Raven)

since it had a larger danger space (roughly in the ratio 10 to 9) and since there would be more 12-inch guns on a given displacement. Finally, the bureau feared adoption of a gun not yet even tested in prototype form. It suggested that a 12in/50, a straightforward refinement of the existing 12in/45, be developed in parallel with the new 14-inch gun.

C&R prepared three alternative designs: 404(four turrets, 14-inch); 502(five turrets, 14-inch); and 601(six turrets, 12-inch). The leap in size was breathtaking. In December 1908, the largest U.S. warships *in commission* were 16,000-ton pre-dreadnoughts. Ships of 20,000 tons, themselves considered outsize only two years before, were under construction, and two slightly larger ships were to be laid down early the next year. Even the smallest of the proposed ships would displace at least 25,000 tons—probably more as completed. And the figure definitely favored the two larger proposals. With such large ships, drydocking was an important issue. Design 502 could be docked only at Puget Sound and at Pearl Harbor; at New York only if the dock there were lengthened 5 feet, which was considered difficult at best. By contrast, 601 could dock on both coasts, and 404 presented no problem at all.

Fearing delays associated with a wholly new gun, the General Board chose Design 601 on 30 December 1908. It argued for twelve guns to match the batteries of the new Russian battleships, the *Gangut*s. Moreover, the new ships had to be tactically compatible with the 14-inch ships that must appear in the end. Hence the choice of 601 over some improved ten-12-inch design. At the same time the longer 12-inch gun and a prototype 14-inch gun were approved.

On 3 March 1909 Congress authorized Battleships 32 and 33. As in the previous year, President Roosevelt fought hard for four battleships, but Congress granted him only two, partly in view of the great expense they represented. The act specified that the new ships were to be "similar, in all essential characteristics to the battleship authorized. . . for the fiscal year ending June 30, 1908," that is, to the *North Dakota*. Similar language had appeared the previous year in the appropriation for the two *Utah*s, which had matched the previous year's design, as they had been modified *North Dakota*s. Members of the House and Senate naval committees had long been aware of the change contemplated in the new ships, and some of them, particularly Senator B. R. Tillman of South Carolina, had been outraged— at 26,000 tons the new ships would be the largest in the world.

The new 12-inch gun weighed about 3 tons more than its predecessor. Its increase of 100 feet per second of muzzle velocity bought 0.4 inches more penetration at 9,000 yards. The more important gain was in hitting probability, the danger zone increasing by about 8 percent. The turrets were redesigned for all-elevation loading, which required a larger, hence heavier, barbette. The longer, heavier gun had to be balanced by a longer turret overhang, in which twenty-six shells were stored. Additional balancing weight was provided by a 12-inch armor plate across the rear of the turret. The total cost of the modified main battery was 347 tons, which was paid for by eliminating proposed torpedo nets (73 tons), and STS internal armor (88 tons), by some detail savings, and by a reduction in the design margin, the insurance against weight increases, almost to zero. Every U.S. battleship design of this period began with provision for torpedo nets and ended up without them, whereas foreign battleships all had them. They were abandoned abroad only after battle experience in World War One showed that they could easily be dislodged and damaged during a gunnery action, threatening to wrap themselves around the propellers. Thus it was fortunate that the U.S. Navy never installed them.

Torpedo nets were only one symptom of a wider problem, the increasing power of destroyer torpedo attack. Behind their screen of destroyers, the battleships had their own secondary batteries and whatever underwater protection their designers could provide. Since the destroyers were generally expected to attack on the night following a daylight gunnery battle, effective searchlights were considered nearly as important as the guns themselves, much effort being devoted to their proper siting and use. This was, moreover, the first class to be designed in light of the experience of the world cruise; the secondary guns had to be high enough to be dry.

The obvious solution would have been to place the secondary battery in the forecastle, as indeed was done in the 1912 ships. However, the break of the forecastle itself would have been a point of strain, a break in the continuity of the ship girder. The designers chose instead to employ a flush deck with sheer sloping aft from bow to stern, thereby gaining both strength (greater depth of ship girder) and about 4 feet in height of secondary guns above water. This type of hull was unique among battleships built at the time. Foreign designers generally preferred to avoid sheer, gaining deck height (if at all) by adding deck levels.

Many at the Newport Conference had voted for unprotected secondary weapons in the superstructure or even on the turret tops—anywhere, so long as they might have a good command and minimal interference from spray. This was the practice in the Royal Navy, but it used a much lighter 4-inch gun, not the big 5in/51 favored by the United States. The designers of 601 chose a middle course, in which ten of the twenty-two 5in/51 were in an armored casemate amidships. Two bow and four stern guns on the gun deck were unarmored. There were also a pair on the upper deck aft, another on the superstructure deck forward, and yet another on the bridge deck forward, all entirely in the open.

The problem was to preserve the guns during the daylight gunnery action, yet have them ready at night with the widest possible command, that is, as high above water as possible. It was already known that casemate armor would tend to burst AP shell, so that heavy shell hits amidships would probably wipe out the ten 5-inch there. On the other hand, HE shells fired by enemy secondary guns or even by his destroyers might wipe out unprotected guns, the plating around which would not detonate AP. In addition, the casemate was required as a burster to protect the uptakes.

Several radical features were tried. The designers proposed that secondary guns be mounted on the sides of the superfiring turrets fore and aft, but this idea, the closest the Navy came to Key's turret tops, was rejected in November 1908. These guns were mobile only because of the turning of the turrets; the guns could be supplied with ammunition only very

slowly; and they could be wiped out by shells bursting against the turret sides. As submitted, Design 601 actually had two guns mounted on the weather deck aft, recessed into the deck so that the turrets could fire over them. This concept was abandoned only in March 1909, and the two guns replaced by a single weapon mounted at the extreme stern on the gun deck immediately beneath the upper, or weather, deck.

The Navy did not expect its guns to stop all the destroyers. From the first it sought passive underwater protection, generally in the form of coal between the vitals and outboard void compartments. In Battleship 1910 it added underwater armor, partly to counter a new weapon, the Davis torpedo-gun, proposed by Lieutenant Commander Cleland Davis, USN, in August 1907. His torpedo warhead would fire an HE shell through the hole made as the torpedo struck. Since all armor was predicated on the assumption that shells striking the water would soon lose their energy, the main protection of the vitals was side and overhead armor. If successful, the Davis device would require underwater *armor* as well.

First tests, in January 1908, were impressive. A simulated torpedo-gun fired its shell right through a caisson, and Davis was permitted to fit short 8-inch guns to two torpedoes. The chief of ordnance was skeptical. He did not believe that, after passing through coal-filled compartments, shells would really be more destructive than the usual 200 pounds of guncotton. However, he approved a full-scale experiment against the monitor *Florida*, and the need for some kind of internal armor became widely accepted within the service. C&R provided 1.5-inch STS bulkheads extending from the torpedo room forward to the after turret and extending from the inner bottom up to the armor deck in all three of its designs. It was hoped that the shell, slowed by its passage between outer bottom and bulkhead, would be stopped by this thin armor. The bulkhead might also serve as a flooding and blast boundary against conventional torpedoes. Many foreign battleships already had such protection, but this was the first torpedo-protection bulkhead in U.S. practice. Tests a few years later (see Chapter 5) would show that the Davis gun was far less effective than a conventional torpedo.* Worse, the external armor which would defeat it would actually *enhance* the effect of an underwater explosion. Ironically, that was not true of C&R's halfway measure, the torpedo bulkhead, which actually would

---

* However, there is evidence that both the United States and Britain were still experimenting with torpedo-guns as late as 1919. The British director of naval construction (DNC) went so far as to urge that British tests be suspended for fear that foreign navies might be inspired to develop a weapon effective against the existing type of protection, which had been evolved during World War One against conventional (high-explosive) torpedoes.

improve protection against torpedoes with conventional warheads.

Before any tests could be made, the 14-inch main battery gun was specified, and the Board on Construction had to save weight to compensate. Elimination of the torpedo bulkhead abeam the engine rooms saved 88 tons, and it was justified on the ground that the engine rooms were already protected by wide coal bunkers. This was an implicit vote of no confidence in the Davis-gun. In April 1909, however, two 8-inch shells fired at the proving ground at velocities like those of the torpedo-gun easily penetrated 1.5-inch STS, even at a 45 degree angle. The chief constructor argued that the torpedo bulkhead would still suffice, that proving ground tests tended to be weighted in favor of the shell.

The great increase in displacement bought much better protection in all three designs. Compared with the defective 1906 twelve-gun design, Design 601 had another inch of side and barbette armor. The side armor was uniform in cross section from end to end, tapering from 11 inches at the top to 9 inches at the lower edge (and 8 feet wide), covered by a flat 1.5-inch to 2-inch deck and then by a "lower casemate" 9-feet wide, tapering down to 9 inches at its upper edge. Above it the amidships secondary guns were protected by a 6.5-inch "upper casemate." The main belt was closed fore and aft by 11-inch and 9-inch bulkheads, angled to meet the end barbettes, and the ends of the ship were unprotected. Behind the casemate armor and the 5in/51 guns were longitudinal splinter bulkheads protecting the uptakes and the off-side secondaries. There were also the usual curved deck over the shafts and steering gear aft and a 5-inch aft continuation of the main belt.

This epitomized U.S. battleship protection in the period before "all or nothing." It was designed to deal with two kinds of damage: (1) to buoyancy and stability, by hits near the waterline; and (2) to vitals, by shallow plunging fire plus splinter damage due to AP shells bursting within the ship.

The main belt was intended to defeat the first threat. Hits on the side well above the waterline would not damage a ship's stability or buoyancy, but their bursts

The *Arkansas* (*above and facing*) is shown as modified shortly after World War One, with octagonal tops for torpedo defense and for searchlight control. The after one was mounted low down to avoid smoke interference. Note the hull blister forward under the plated-in forward casemate, and the blister for her starboard hawsepipe. The stern view shows the plated-in position of her after-most 5-inch gun, as well as the pair of 3-inch antiaircraft guns atop her No. 3 and No. 5 turrets, both of which also carried range-finders. A third pair topped her derrick posts, and the fourth sat abeam the No. 5 barbette.

would create splinters which might destroy machinery, magazines, guns, and crew. Side armor was intended to burst AP shells striking above the waterline in places where they would do minimum harm, their fragments stopped by splinter armor (STS). Thus the "lower casemate" was both a burster and a means of stopping lighter HE shells; the flat watertight deck was internal fragment protection. It also sealed the top of the belt, most of the latter being underwater to resist hits made as rolling, swells, and the ship's bow wave exposed the side below the waterline. As ships grew larger, the "lower casemate," which began as rather thin armor, approached the main belt in thickness, as in the 1908 ships.

Russo-Japanese War experience demonstrated that severe damage to the uptakes would fill the inside of a ship with smoke. Some form of protection was required, but there could be no hope of using very heavy armor, for weight reasons. From 1904 onwards splinter armor had been provided. The 1908 ships had a new system of uptake protection. The upper casemate would burst shells approaching the uptakes, and their splinter armor would protect them against the resulting fragments. The same burster would protect against AP shells plunging (at shallow angles) over the side armor to strike directly at the

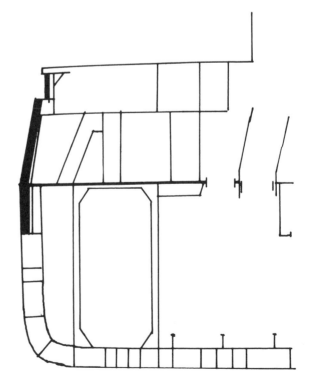

Wyoming cross section. The *New York* was similar, albeit with somewhat heavier side armor.

The *Wyoming* is shown shortly after World War One, probably about 1920, in Puget Sound. She has the 1920 octagonal tops, but carries only two (rather than eight) 3-inch antiaircraft guns. Note the Vickers-type 5-inch director abeam the base of her mainmast, between her boats and a ventilator.

The *Texas* at Hampton Roads, December 1916. Note her *E* for Engineering Excellence, on her second funnel, her unarmored range-finders, atop Nos. 2, 3, and 4 turrets, and the two 3-inch antiaircraft guns, the first aboard a U.S. battleship, atop her derrick posts. The last dreadnought-era battleship in the world, the *Texas* has been preserved by her name state.

STS armored deck below, as well as against shells which might otherwise burst in the unengaged side of the antitorpedo battery. However, the problem of steeply plunging shells had not as yet received much consideration, because they would occur only at ranges beyond those envisaged in 1908. Shells passing over the belt ouside the central casemate could still strike the flat deck directly. Far more important, they could penetrate the thin parts of the barbettes, where they were masked—from flat- or shallow-trajectory fire only—by the lower casemate.

On the theory that a ship's armor should match her guns, 11-inch - 9-inch armor was considered appropriate for ships armed with 12-inch guns. The two 14-inch gun designs showed better protection, with 13-inch belts (the lower 4 feet tapered to 9 inches), 12-inch - 8 inch lower casemates, and 12-inch barbettes so tapered that the total of side and barbette armor would always be at least 13 inches. This standard would not actually be reached until Battleship 1912, the *Nevada*.

About the time Congress approved Battleship 1910, the *Wyoming*, the General Board began to consider Battleship 1911, and by 21 April 1909 it had decided in favor of two more ships of about the same size—but the question of calibre remained. The Royal Navy was adopting a 13.5-inch gun BuOrd had described as only a hedge the year before. The board asked C&R for improved versions of both Design 502 and the *Wyoming*; the eight-gun ship was no longer worth considering, given the approval of the large twelve-gun design. Should the prototype 14-inch gun succeed, the modified 502 would be favored. The board specified only that her speed should rise to 21 knots, the weight of the extra machinery to come from a reduction in armor to the standard of the *Wyoming*s. A third possibility, a 28,000-ton ship with twelve 14 inch and twenty-six 5 inch, was briefly considered but rejected early in 1910, although it would have had more firepower per ton than the modified 502, Design 506.

Early in January 1910 the prototype 14-inch gun was fired very successfully, the shots being "remarkable for the uniformity of results." The modified *Wyoming* design, 602, was doomed, although the General Board would not make that formal until 29 March. Battleships 34 and 35, the *New York* and *Texas*, were not authorized until 24 June 1910. Aside from the adoption of a new gun, gunnery improvements in this *New York* design were relatively subtle.

The revolution in long-range gunnery was symbolized by the provision, for the first time, of an armored central station (plotting room) below decks. It was essentially an afterthought, and hence had to be placed *atop* the protective deck, for the magazines and machinery spaces monopolized protected hull volume. The central station was enclosed in a thin box of splinter armor, which would protect it against shallow-trajectory shells, shells which would be burst by the surrounding lower casemate side armor. However, the plotting room itself was part of a move toward much greater gunnery range. At such longer ranges, beyond 10,000 yards, shells would plunge steeply, and many would strike the thin deck, and the thinly protected plotting room, directly. In this sense the *New York* design was fundamentally contradictory.

The modified design did solve a major problem. Power (hence the volume of engine and boiler rooms) had to be increased by about 14 percent (28,000 to 32,000SHP to achieve 21 knots) without any increase in armored length. To compensate, magazine volume was reduced, each accommodating no more than seventy-five or eighty shells and charges, the remainder being carried within the turrets and handling rooms. Plans were developed for both two-shaft (Curtis) and four-shaft (Parsons) turbine plants.

The design was circulated through the fleet in March 1910. The questions raised are interesting principally for their effect on the General Board, then working on Battleship 1912, the *Nevada*. Both the C-in-C Atlantic Fleet, Vice Admiral Seaton Schroeder, and the inspector of target practice, Commander L. C. Patman, objected to the main battery arrangement which obstructed some of the arcs of No. 3 turret. Steam lines passed around its magazine. Yet to move No. 3 aft would be to strain the hull dangerously. This turret and its problems could be eliminated entirely if a triple turret were to be adopted. Admiral Schroeder also found the turret armor too thin, preferring 5-inch roofs and 10-inch rear plates. That improvement was rejected because it would have added 110 tons very high in the ship, reducing stability.

The fleet was well aware, too, of the flaw in the location and protection of the central station (and, for that matter, of the thinly protected barbette bases). The remedy to plunging fire would be additional burster armor *above* the thin STS structures (barbette bases, central station), that is, an armor deck atop the "lower casemate." The new armor deck would not stop many shells; rather, it would burst them and thin splinter armor would stop the resulting splinters. Thus a splinter deck would have to be provided below it, to protect magazines and machinery. As for the side armor, the "lower casemate" had reached the thickness of the waterline belt. Why not consolidate the two "belts" into one? The new belt could be a single strake of armor, less likely to break up under the impact of shells than the former combination of belt and casemate. These ideas were the basis of the Battleship 1912 (*Nevada*) design, which introduced the revolutionary "all or nothing" armor. Redesign of Battleship 1911 (*New York*) to accom-

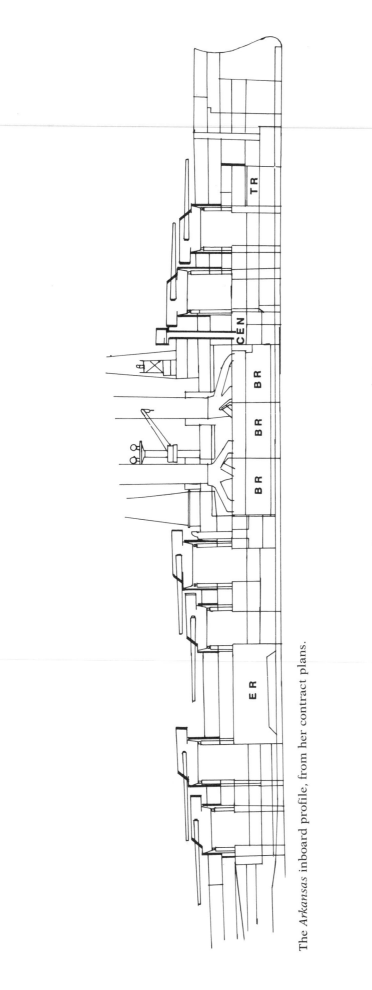

The *Arkansas* inboard profile, from her contract plans.

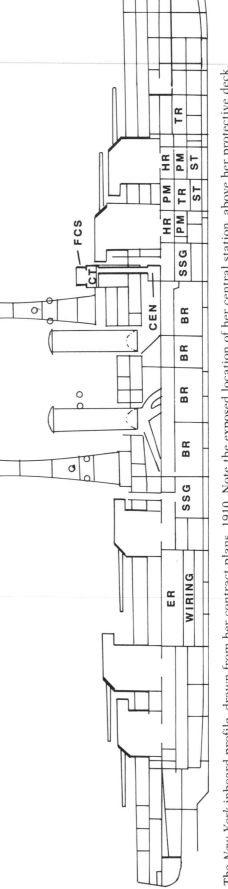

The *New York* inboard profile, drawn from her contract plans, 1910. Note the exposed location of her central station, above her protective deck.

The *New York* is shown off Brest, having convoyed President Wilson to France for the Versailles talks, in December 1918. Her steam launch was in the water; note the bare skids on which it rested and the rigged boat boom. The splinter mattresses surrounding her conning platform are clearly visible under the forward searchlight control platform. Her bridge wings have been rigged. She had not yet been fitted with range clocks at this time, but deflection markings are barely visible on No. 1 turret.

plish these radical changes was rejected at the time in view of the delay it would entail.

Another perceived defect was insufficient protection for the steering gear, a 5-inch extension of the waterline belt. American battleships tended to pitch sufficiently to expose the lower edge of this armored strip, making the steering gear vulnerable. Surely something more substantial could be provided. Beyond these questions was the problem of a ship designed to face 12-inch guns but forced in practice to face the new 13.5. The belt armor would probably suffice, but no one knew whether the 6.5-inch upper casemate would burst the new shells.

Advocates of turret-top antitorpedo guns proposed that the six amidships casemate guns be relocated in pairs to Nos. 2, 3, and 4 turrets. C&R argued that the turret top guns would add too much topweight, both directly and indirectly, by requiring additional conning tower height, so that officers inside could see over the turret top guns.

Torpedo experts suggested that the usual provision for two underwater tubes should be doubled in view of advances in torpedo performance. The two extra torpedo tubes would have interrupted the continuity of the torpedo bulkhead. Their torpedoes represented too valuable an offensive power to reject, however, and the standard battery for U.S. battleships was revised to four underwater tubes. That applied only to the *New York* and *Nevada* classes; it had to be abandoned in the *Pennsylvania* class (see Chapter 5).

By this time the United States had her first dreadnoughts at sea. They showed disappointing seagoing performance. The General Board attributed their wetness forward to the lack of flare in their ram bows, actually plough (almost bulbous) bows designed to reduce resistance, hence increase speed—

in smooth water. The board preferred a flared or clipper bow. C&R pointed out that, were waterline length and displacement kept constant, the straight stem would cost about 0.2 knots, and the clipper about 0.25. To retain the present speed would require, respectively, 8 and 14 more feet on the waterline and correspondingly greater weights devoted to the hull rather than to more useful purposes. Later R. H. Robinson of C&R would cite the General Board's interest in such detailed questions of naval architecture as typical of its interfering attitude.

Advertisements for bids were issued for one ship, the USS *Texas*, on 27 September 1910. Her sister, the *New York*, would be built at the New York Navy Yard. The conditions for bids included a provision that, although turbines were favored, a reciprocating engine plant of superior performance might be chosen. Such a provision had been standard for some years. The entire process, which culminated in the opening of bids on 1 December, was delayed somewhat by the adoption of the new 14-inch gun.

These ships represented a triumph for then Secretary of the Navy George von L. Meyer. President Taft had demanded that the fiscal year 1911 Navy budget be cut by $10 million. Senator Eugene Hale of the Naval Affairs Commitee was skeptical; the usual annual increases would eat up such a sum. Meyer had actually cut the budget by *$24 million*, after which he had added back $14 million for two large battleships, as well as a repair ship (or the equivalent in destroyers) and 3,000 men. Hale had suggested that he save $5 to $10 million by cutting the size of the battleship that year, but Secretary Meyer had stood firm for size and firepower.

C&R managed to improve protection in the course of detail design. On its forward and outboard sides the fire control station could be protected by 6-inch

The *New York* is shown off Brest, having convoyed President Wilson to France for the Versailles talks, in December 1918. Her steam launch was in the water; note the bare skids on which it rested and the rigged boat boom. The splinter mattresses surrounding her conning platform are clearly visible under the forward searchlight control platform. Her bridge wings have been rigged. She had not yet been fitted with range clocks at this time, but deflection markings are barely visible on No. 1 turret.

armor rather than by 1.5-inch (60-pound) STS, but nothing could be done about its roof. Another inch was added to the waterline belt, so that it was now 12 inch - 10 inch, with a 6-inch extension aft. This was possible largely because the main belt was very close to the level of the center of gravity, so that added weight would have little effect on stability, hence needed no weight or moment compensation elsewhere.

The greatest change at this time was in propulsion. In January 1910 the United States had as yet no dreadnoughts in service, although four were nearly ready, three more had been laid down and one more would soon be. Entirely on the basis of experience with pre-dreadnoughts, observation of foreign practice, and theory, the Navy had passed through four distinct battleship classes and was about to order a fifth while designing a sixth (Battleship 1912). The entire program might be considered a gamble, an outstanding feature of which was faith in the turbine as the engine of the future. Alone among the great navies, the U.S. Navy required great range in its capital ships. But poor fuel economy was the one great defect of early turbines.

Trials of the turbine prototype *North Dakota* during 1910 made this point. At cruising power, she was nearly 30 percent less economical than her reciprocating-engine sister. For Battleship 35, it was estimated that reciprocating engines would confer a radius of 7,060nm at 12 knots, Curtis turbines only 5,606. In the latter case the ship would be unable, for example, to reach Manila from the West Coast, even though one of the two central scenarios for U.S. naval strategy was war with Japan in the Far East.

By this time the development of forced lubrication had made the piston engine much more reliable at full power. The reciprocating engine might have little potential for future development, but that was not the question. The battle fleet must not be an experiment, it must be a reliable instrument for the projection of power over great distances. The General Board had to opt for the reciprocating-engined ship proposed by the Newport News Shipbuilding and Dry Dock Company.

Ironically, the greater propulsive efficiency of the piston engine permitted a reduction in installed power, so that in the end the *New York* required only 28,100IHP to make 21 knots, whereas a major factor

Steaming off Brest with the Sixth Battle Squadron late in 1918, the *Texas* shows how close water could come to the broadside secondary mounts in even a moderately rough sea. Both of her superfiring turrets carry flying-off platforms, the first in U.S. service. She would not actually launch an airplane until the following year. Note, too, her vee-fronted enclosed navigating bridge, with a range-finder on top. She would retain it throughout her long career, and it would always distinguish her from the *New York*.

At Puget Sound in July 1921, the *New York* shows her flatter-sided navigating bridge and octagonal tops for secondary battery and searchlight control. Her wettest (furthest forward) 5-inch guns have been removed and their ports plated in. She has been fitted with the usual complement of four Vickers-type 5-inch directors: two on the 02 level forward; and two near No. 3 turret, aft. At this time she had only two 3-inch antiaircraft guns but was scheduled to be fitted with six more.

in the design had been the allowance for 32,000. At least at first, the reciprocating engines seem to have been quite successful. However, they were a constant cause of complaint during the interwar period. In the early 1920s, one U.S. officer went so far as to suggest that the *Texas*, at that time the best gunnery ship in the fleet, would soon have to be re-engined with turbines. That was never done, however.

The *New York* joined the British Grand Fleet as the flagship of Rear Admiral Hugh Rodman in December of 1917. As such, she was subject to extensive examination by British officers and naval constructors, and one constructor's comments show the contrast between contemporary U.S. and British practice. They are undated and unsigned but were probably prepared by E. L. Attwood, a senior constructor, soon after the *New York* arrived in British waters:

> The bridges are much complained of; there is no shelter on the bridge and they have had to improvise a shelter which, however, has to be dismantled in action as it fouls the sight from conning tower.

It is understood that Admiral Rodman will ask to have bridges, tops, etc. fitted on the lines of the British practice, but if any weights are to be placed on the foremast at all approaching the fittings in British ships, I think that the cage masts will have to be removed and tripods fitted. The Admiral says that the after mast might be removed from the ship.

There is a boat crane each side for lifting the heavy boats and the Officers express great satisfaction, but they make the ship very conspicuous. The boats are badly stowed on the Weather Deck forward each side, and some were lost on the passage across.

The oil fired galleys are found to be perfectly satisfactory and no alternative for coal burning has been provided as has been insisted upon in the case of the *Hood*.

The electric bakery is also very satisfactory and the bread is beautifully baked.

. . . the guns in 'tween decks cannot be used in a seaway; [they] are not provided with any spray shields. It is understood that it is intended to remove these guns and to place some on and above the weather deck. . . . The Admiral stated that he had only two guns fit for use for anti-destroyer purposes and even these guns are difficult to sight in a heavy sea.

It was noticed all over the ship that many sloping ladders had been provided, the original vertical rung ladders still being retained, the idea being to make getting about as convenient as possible.

In the cabins running water is provided and the drain is into a large jug immediately below the washbasin.

The cabin fitments were of steel and somewhat elaborate as compared with British practice. Folding desks, etc., are provided of very neat construction, but appear very expensive and as an example, in these desks there is a small cupboard with a combination lock.

The cabin arrangements are very extensive and accommodation is provided for the lowest grade of Officer "ensigns," some of them sleep 2 in a cabin. The Commander has a large day cabin, sleeping cabin, bath room, WC, and shower bath.

A gauge for measuring the draft inside the ship is fitted both forward and aft.

The Torpedo Room is very large with two torpedo tubes each side. The tubes are side loaded. The Officers express great dissatisfaction as regards the methods for clearing the tube of water which are very meagre. Admiral Rodman [considered] the torpedo armament very inefficient.

The arrangements for convenience and comfort of the crew are very much in excess of what is provided in British ships, e.g., there is a large Barber's Shop with 8 of the "dentist" type of chair and all up-to-date fittings for such a Barber's Shop.

A dentist is carried on board and is fully occupied in his own office in attending to the crew.

The mess decks are very clear as compared with British practice and the "general mess" system is adopted. The stools and tables are short and light and stored overhead except at meal time.

The apartments for Admiral, Captain, Chief of Staff are all very large, and the Admiral expressed the opinion that they should be considerably cut down and the space used for some more useful purpose, e.g., mounting of smaller guns.

Attwood clearly had little interest in the U.S. concept of armor protection. By 1917 the *New York* had, after all, long been superseded by the "all or nothing" ships of the *Nevada* and later classes. They did not serve with the Grand Fleet but were examined at length by Attwood's colleague, Stanley Goodall (later director of naval construction during World War Two) in the United States.

Attwood was concerned with immediate improvements that could be made to the ship to make her battleworthy. His remarks are interesting because they show the extent to which details, far below the level of the concerns expressed during preliminary design, could determine a ship's survival in combat. Attwood's suggestions reflect three years of seagoing and battle experience in the Grand Fleet:

[T]here are far too many WT doors, especially at the ends of the ship. These doors are closed at sea but in the event of damage they would inevitably leak if the bulkheads were strained, and the watertightness of the ship would be seriously jeopardized. For example, on the level of the Platform Deck in a steering gear compartment, I was able to walk through on the same level through a series of WT[watertight] doors right up to the Engine Room. [Doors] that could be dispensed with should be removed and the holes in bulkheads permanently plated over.

In the midship part of the ship there are WT doors between mess spaces purely for convenience, and such doors also I think should be removed and the holes plated up.

The Boiler Rooms are provided with a trunk which ends on (our) Upper Deck [U.S. first deck, just below the weather deck] with a shallow coaming and a non WT cover. This hatch is on the outboard side of the splinter bulkhead and immediately near to the gunport. If the retention of this escape trunk is considered necessary. . .[it] should be plated to the Weather Deck and provided with a WT door with a good height of sill above the deck.

Certain guns in the 'tween decks had been removed and the [non-WT] shutters still remain. . .if the guns are permanently removed the side should be closed in by a riveted structure.

The ventilation is in large units with large trunks going through the ship, and one case was noticed on (our) Main Deck [U.S. first deck] forward where a non-WT ventilation trunk about 15×12in went through a WT bulkhead immediately alongside a WT door. On either side of the bulkhead small pipes for ventilating the lower compartments were led; it is understood that some of these pipes have been blanked off...the drawings [of the ventilation system] should be closely examined to see how far the watertightness of the ship could be more adequately preserved, but I am afraid that to do this at all effectively would [require that the ship be laid up] for some time.

The [air] supplies to the fans forward and aft are

Six 3-inch antiaircraft guns were added in 1922; pairs were mounted atop Nos. 3 and 4 turrets, both of which retained their long-base range-finders. Note the seaplane perched on *New York*'s fantail, to be handled by an extemporized crane.

obtained from large mushrooms on the Weather Deck forward and the Weather Deck aft; it would be better [to use] smaller [mushrooms as] now adopted in the Royal Navy and, at any rate in the case of the after Weather Deck, [the ventilators should be] provided with WT slide valves.

The shell is stowed in shell rooms on the same level as the magazine in addition to that stowed in the turntable, . . .taken out of the shell room in to the handling room and thence to the hoist by means of an overhead rail with a portable piece through the WT door.

In case of emergency, it would take some time to disconnect the portable piece and close the door, but I am afraid nothing is possible in this case to improve matters.

There are many glass lights in the Weather Decks to light cabins, mess spaces; I think these ought to be permanently removed and the holes plated over as they would be broken in action.

A number of WT doors have glass bulls-eyes; I think these should all be removed and permanently plated over.

There is a dredger hoist at the rear of each [secondary] gun with a WT door and a shallow coaming, if possible. It is thought that this coaming should be made higher as some [water] would come in and go right down below.

Attwood's paper was passed on to the U.S. Navy, but it is not clear how many of his suggestions were followed. Certainly later British critics repeated the theme of excess "luxury" and complication in U.S. designs (see Chapters 5 and 8).

Attwood's main criticisms applied to two separate issues. One was the ability to operate freely in heavy weather, with seas washing freely over the exposed weather deck. The pre-1914 U.S. Navy thought of itself as a heavy-weather Navy, but the extensive modifications made during and after World War One suggest that the North Sea weather was substantially worse than what the U.S. Navy had experienced in the past.

The second problem was survivability, particularly in the event of battle damage. The Grand Fleet had had extensive experience with shock, that is, with shattered glass and sprung watertight doors. The problem of the doors would surface again in World War Two, and in its war-built ships the U.S. Navy would go to considerable lengths to seal all bulkheads below a "damage control deck." Attwood's critique may have affected the details of the last U.S. dreadnoughts, in that British constructors who visited them did not comment on excessive faith in watertight doors.

5

The Standard Type: Battleships, 1912–17

With the *Nevada* class, Battleship 1912, the U.S. Navy developed a basic design that it continued to build to the end of the dreadnought period. Its essentials were oil fuel, "all or nothing" armor, and a compact arrangement of the main battery in four turrets, triple or twin. Even size remained almost constant from the second such design, the *Pennsylvania* (Battleship 1913) onwards, so that the first major departure was the *South Dakota* class of FY18, and that was no more than an enlarged version of the earlier designs.

These standard battleships continued and then leveled off the trend of steady growth in size and cost begun with the *Delaware*s. They attracted their share of political controversy. In 1903 the General Board had assumed tacitly that the United States would, in future, maintain a steady pace of two battleships a year. In 1904, however, Congress approved only one ship (for FY05), so the General Board asked for three ships in 1905. From 1907 through 1914 it asked for four each year to make up for lost ground. A reluctant Congress saw ships grow larger and larger, more and more expensive. It balked, approving only one ship in FY07 and FY08 and, again, in FY13 and FY14. The provision of two ships in fiscal year 1911 (the *New York*s) had amounted to a personal triumph on the part of Secretary of the Navy Meyer.

Although President Taft announced that he wished to continue President Theodore Roosevelt's policy of two battleships per year (1910 and 1911 for FY11 and FY12), the Democrats gained control of the House of Representatives in 1910, and their caucus rejected any battleships at all. The Senate voted two, and the compromise was only a single ship in FY13, the *Pennsylvania*. In December 1912 Taft urged that the lame-duck Congress approve three ships to restore the pace. As Senator Tillman's letters show (see Chapter 6),

however, Congress was much concerned with the rapid increase in battleship size and cost, and it rejected Taft's argument.

Taft's successor, Woodrow Wilson, was a much less enthusiastic supporter of military expenditure. His secretary of the navy, Josephus Daniels, finally ended the growth of U.S. battleships by rejecting a series of General Board proposals. On the other hand, Daniels also rejected the Democratic party's successes in holding the Navy to only one battleship in each of fiscal years 1913 and 1914. In his first *Annual Report* to Congress, he pared the General Board's request from four to two ships, but on the ground of insufficient revenue rather than insufficient justification. Daniels strongly supported the two-ships-a-year program and arranged for the sale of the two obsolete pre-dreadnoughts *Idaho* and *Mississippi* to Greece to pay for a third FY15 ship, which partly redressed the gap left by two single-ship years. By that time war had broken out in Europe, and political conditions in the United States had changed radically to favor increased naval construction.

The logic of "all or nothing" protection was that at very long ranges, ships would be attacked primarily with AP shells since hits might be anywhere on a ship, and HE would be useless against thick belt or deck armor. In consequence only the heaviest armor (or no armor at all) was worth using: anything in between would serve only as a burster. By way of contrast, the Royal Navy concluded at about this time that heavy HE shells would be extremely effective against unarmored portions of ships, and used considerable amounts of medium armor, which could resist HE fire, in its dreadnoughts. Only after World War One did the Royal Navy adopt "all or nothing" protection, in the abortive 1921 battleships and bat-

The fleet flagship *New Mexico* leads the U.S. battle line in the Pacific, 13 April 1919. The next two ships astern are the first of what became the standard type of U.S. battleships, the *Oklahoma* and *Nevada*. A flying-off platform had just been installed atop her No. 2 turret. When in use, it would be extended over the three guns, portable sections connecting with the rings visible on them. Note, too, that her forward 5-inch guns have not been mounted, their casemates plated over. The chains in the water at her bow were for paravanes, a World War One device to protect ships from minefields.

tle cruisers, and in the *Nelson*s, all of which were expected to fight at longer ranges than those envisaged for the earlier British dreadnoughts. To the extent that the U.S. battleships, then, were designed specifically to fight at extreme ranges, they were well ahead of their time. For example, the protection of U.S. battleships was not significantly revised in view of the lessons of the Battle of Jutland, although other navies distinguished their pre- and post-Jutland designs.

The most important such distinction was in deck protection against plunging fire. From the *Nevada* onwards, two decks totaling 4.5 to 5 inches of deck armor were provided throughout the length of the citadel. Their cost, in terms of weight, was minimized by reducing armored length, that is, by reducing the number of turrets, which in turn meant accepting triple mounts. Length was also reduced by the adoption of oil fuel and, in the *Nevada*s, acceptance of a lower speed. The decision to armor the uptakes on the scale used for barbettes also cost considerable weight, high in the ship. What is remarkable is that, although the *Nevada* evolved in something of a haphazard manner, all of its features interlocked perfectly, optimized for gunnery combat at very long range.

The General Board originally specified triple turrets only because of its disgust with the awkward five- and six-turret arrangements of the previous two classes. As for the use of uniformly heavy armor, it was not adopted until well into the design, although the principle of abandoning light armor had been accepted as early as 1908. Even then, the only medium armor in the *Arkansas* had been the upper casemate, which the designers saw primarily as a burster to protect the uptakes. The development of the new armor scheme began with the new deck arrangement, intended to counter plunging shells. This deck arrangement inspired the amalgamation of lower casemate and belt, the joint between them being eliminated. The new belt was ultimately tapered in thickness only below the waterline, where the water around the ship provided considerable protection. The armor deck was set above this wider belt, and a second, unarmored (but watertight) deck lay at the waterline, curving down at the edge to meet the bottom of the belt. The General Board initially assumed that a belt as thick as that of the previous class— 11 inches—would suffice to keep shells out of the space below the armored deck. At this point there seems to have been little interest in protecting the vitals of the ship from splinters formed by shells which did manage to penetrate the belt armor.

The effect of the new armor concept is shown in Table 5-1, in which the *Wyoming*, *New York*, and *Nevada* protection weights are compared. Note the much greater emphasis on deck protection in the *Nevada*.

Table 5-1. Redistribution of Armor

	Wyoming	*New York*	*Nevada*
LWL	554	565	575 ft
Protected Length			400 ft
Upper Casemate	223.06	261.67	--- tons
Lower Casemate	1704.04	1680.33	--- tons
Belt	1373.94	1549.16	3788.0 tons
Bulkheads	103.49	127.42	331.9 tons
Uptakes	---	---	342.6 tons
Armor Deck	---	---	2037.0 tons
Splinter Deck	1219.55	1322.11	1254.0 tons
Barbettes	2190.62	2085.39	2080.0 tons
Turrets	958.87	856.11	914.8 tons
Conning Tower	225.61	238.42	413.8 tons
Total Side Armor	3301.04	3491.17	3788.0 tons
Total Protection	7999.18	8120.62	11162.1 tons

These ideas circulated informally within the bureaus. In May 1910, C&R sketched a modified *New York* (A in Table 5-2). No. 4 turret was eliminated and the remaining four turrets tripled, for a twelve-gun battery; No. 3 was raised to fire over the former No. 5. Thus the engine room was still between two turrets, as in previous U.S. designs, and steam pipes still passed around a magazine. The arrangement was reminiscent of that of the British battlecruiser *Tiger*. The motive may have been to avoid an excessive concentration of weight aft, which would have required far greater weight devoted to hull strength, that is, subtracted from the useful load. As for side armor, the belt tapered from 11 inches to 9 inches below the waterline and was covered by an armor deck similar in thickness to that of the *New York*. The upper casemate was eliminated. The only side armor above the protective deck was 2-in STS around the uptakes. As in the final *New York* design, there were four underwater torpedo tubes, at the ends of the belt. Only seventeen 5-inch antitorpedo guns were provided, but with far better command, for the most part: one each atop Nos. 2 and 3 turrets, six in the superstructure, four forward, and five aft in the hull. None was armored, BuOrd policy calling for the abandonment of such protection to avoid bursting AP shells. C&R estimated that on 27,500 tons such a ship could attain as much as 23 knots on 37,000SHP. Like the *New York*, she was a flush-decked coal-burner.

The next month the General Board issued formal characteristics, calling for twelve 14-inch guns, 21 knots, and the new protective scheme, with special attention paid to protection of the uptakes. C&R commented that in its new position the armor deck would contribute substantially to girder strength, but it feared a loss of protection. The 12in/50 could penetrate 11-inch armor beyond 15,000 yards; the

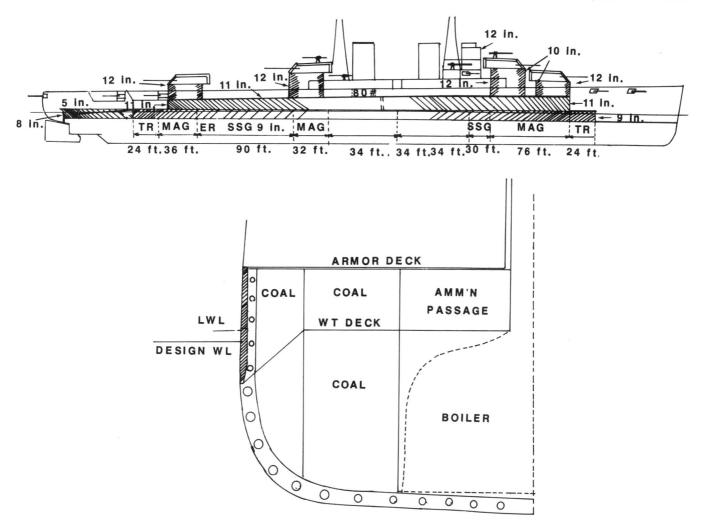

The original Preliminary Design sketch of *Nevada*, dated May 1910. As shown here, the upper belt was a uniform 11 inches in thickness, the lower tapering from 11 inches at its upper edge to 9 inches at its lower. Uptake protection was limited to 80-pound splinter plating. The thickness of the protective deck was not given on the original sketch. Note, however, that in the cross section the armor deck (atop the belt) was distinguished from the watertight deck meeting the lower edge of the belt. The upper of the two waterlines shown was the load waterline, the lower, the designer's waterline. A speed of 22.75 to 23 knots was expected on 27,000 horsepower, generated by 16 boilers in four boiler rooms. Note that the seventeen 5-inch guns of the secondary battery included single guns atop the superfiring turrets and a single gun right aft.

new 14 inch would be even more powerful. To be impenetrable at battle ranges, the belt would have to be 14-inches or even 16-inches thick. Otherwise shells passing through it would burst in the vitals, since there would be no armor deck to stop them. In response the General Board proposed to armor the slopes of the lower (watertight) deck with 1.5-inch STS, and to connect the knuckle of this deck, 20-feet inboard, to the 2-inch upper armor deck with a 1.5-inch STS longitudinal bulkhead. This thin plating, much like the protection of the contemporary Russian *Gangut*, was expected to trap and stop the splinters of shells burst by the belt armor. The 20 feet was to provide sufficient space to be certain that the AP shells would explode before penetrating the internal STS bulkhead.

The size of the ships was set, virtually by default, at this time. Even though they had no approved design in hand, the technical bureaus had to make cost estimates for the 1912 program. Estimates based on the design of Battleship 1911, the *New York*, therefore appeared in the secretary's *Annual Report*, issued in the fall of 1910; they in turn formed the basis of the authorizing act, which limited hull and machinery to $6 million. That implied a tonnage limit of about 27,000, too little to meet the full characteristics as they developed.

In the fall of 1910 the General Board and the bureaus began to receive reports of a year of sea experience with the first quartet of dreadnoughts actually in service. In September *Delaware* reported that the magazine cooling equipment was a failure; No. 3

Table 5-2. Origin of the Nevada Class (1911)

Design	A	B	C	D	E
Date	May, 1910	11 Jan	4 March	9 March	11 March
Displacement	27,500	29,000	27,000	27,000	27,000
Length	600	600	565	565	565
Beam	90	96.5	95	95	95
Draft	28.5	28.5	28.5	28.5	28.5
14in Guns	12	12	8	10	10
Belt	11-9	12-6.5	14-12	13-8	14-8
Above Water			9	7-6	7-6
Below Water			7	8-6	8-6
Armor Deck		80		40+20	40+20
Splinter Deck		None	Yes	40+20/60+20	40+20/60+20
Power	37,000		28,100	28,100	24,800
Speed	22.75-23		21	21	20.5
Radius			8000	8000	8000
Hull	10,280	10,650	10,640	10,663	10,565
Fittings	1170	1262	1300	1300	1300
Protection	6550	8549	7940	9600	8150
Machinery	2700	2071	1985	1985	1752
RFW	247	193	187	187	165
Battery	1561	1584	1199	1357	1357
Ammunition	1301	1380	1036	1195	1195
Equipment	400	435	403	403	403
Outfit	650	696	643	643	643
Fuel Oil	2267	1600	1667	1667	1470
Margin	374	580			

NOTE: Design designations are the author's. They do not appear in the original documents. Except for Scheme A, all date from 1911. The 11 March version was adopted on 31 March 1911. Scheme A had the earlier type of belt, 8-feet wide, with an 11-foot wide lower casemate. Similarly, Scheme B had an 8-inch lower casemate and 6.5-inch upper casemate. It was abandoned because of its excessive size, and a 588 foot, 28,000 ton design (details of which have not survived) was submitted instead on 13 February. Scheme A had seventeen 5-inch guns; Schemes C through H had twenty-one 5-inch guns and four 21-inch torpedo tubes. They had twelve boilers and were all powered by twin screw reciprocating engines. Note that Scheme A, turbine-powered with sixteen boilers, was unique in being coal-fuelled, with 2,000 tons of coal and only 267 of oil. Armor for Scheme A included 12inch-10inch barbettes, and turrets had 14-inch faces with 8-inch sides and 4-inch roofs. By way of contrast, Schemes C through H had 14-inch uptakes, and their turrets had 16-inch faces, 10-inch and 9-inch sides with 9-inch backs and 4.5-inch roofs, on 13-inch barbettes. In Scheme F, the belt had a double taper. For 2 feet on either side of the waterline it is 14 inches thick, tapering to 11 inches at its upper edge and to 8 inches at its lower edge. Alternatively, it could be a single-taper belt as in the other designs, in this case 13 inches thick down to 2 feet below the waterline, then tapering to 9.4 inches at its lower edge. In this design, all but No. 4 turrets (twin) were triples. Schemes J and K traded off half a knot of speed for additional armor, including (in J) 18-inch turret face, 11-inch and 10-inch turret sides and rear, and 15-inch barbettes; in K, 16-inch turret face, 10-inch and 9-inch turret sides, and 14-inch barbettes. They had 17-inch conning towers.

magazine could not be kept cool enough. As a result, the guns of No. 3 turret did not match those of the other turrets in ballistics (because of differences in powder temperature), and the ship's salvos were too widely dispersed. She could not hit as well as expected at long range. The structural design of the ship, which required that the turrets be relatively evenly distributed along her length, limited her fighting power. Because it stiffened the hull, the new higher armored deck would solve this problem. The two after turrets could be concentrated abaft the engines, and steam lines would not have to pass around any of the magazines.

This was also the occasion for the U.S. Navy to shift from coal to oil fuel. By 1910 the United States was already a major oil producer, possessing a large part of the known world-oil reserves. Oil fuel was, therefore, attractive from an economic point of view.

It had been advocated for some years for ships on the Pacific Coast, which was rich in oil but not in coal. The *Delaware*s were the first U.S. battleships to mix oil and coal burning.

Experience with the *Delaware* showed the advantages of adopting oil as the sole fuel, rather than (as in many navies) as a supplement to coal. Oil had several well-known advantages. Its greater thermal content, compared with coal, would yield a far greater steaming radius for a given weight of fuel, a peculiarly American concern, given the problems of Pacific warfare. Refueling at sea would be far easier and more rapid; *Delaware* tested a jury rig for this purpose. In addition, coaling had always required gunnery equipment such as telescopes to be covered over to avoid damage from coal dust, so that a ship coaling at sea was effectively out of commission for an extended period. The boiler-room crew, tradi-

F	G	H	J	K
17 March	21 March	21 March	28 March	28 March
27,500	27,700	27,000	27,500	27,500 tons
570	575	575	565	565 ft
95	96.5	96.5	96	96 ft
28.5	28.5	28.5	28.5	28.5 ft
11	12	10	9	8
14-8	13-9.4	13-8	16-6	15-6 in
7-6	7-6	7-6	7-6	7-6 in
8-6	8-6	8-6	8-8	8-8 in
Deck Armor as Scheme D			4	4 lbs.
			60/80	60/80 lbs.
	24,750	24,800	23,000	23,000 IHP
	20.5	20.5	20	20 kts
7000	6000	7000	6000	6000 nm/k
10,900	11,025	10,730	11,934	12,050 tons
1346	1362	1317	1314	1314 tons
8270	8350	8150	8050	8050 tons
1766	1748	1752	1625	1625 tons
166	165	165	153	153 tons
1436	1515	1357	1230	1199 tons
1296	1383	1195	1121	1036 tons
406	408	403	406	406 tons
644	644	643	644	644 tons
1270	1100	1288	1023	1023 tons
				tons

tionally the worst source of indiscipline at sea, would be drastically reduced; the *Delaware*'s engineer estimated that 100 firemen and 112 coal passers might be replaced by a total of 24 men. The elimination of the corresponding quarters would save space and weight, as would the elimination of coal-handling space around the boilers. In all, 12 feet 6 inches would be saved on the length of the boiler rooms, that is, on the volume of large floodable compartments and also on the length of the portion of the ship which had to be protected by heavy armor. Operationally, it would be far easier to raise steam, no fuel would be wasted "burning down fires" in port, and forced draft and sealed fire rooms, with their attendant gas hazards, would no longer be needed. Forced draft also drained auxiliary power and required a multitude of ventilators. Oil fuel reduced top hamper and, hence, target area. Unlike coal, oil left no solid residue. A coal-burner running at high speed had to slow to clean her boiler grates every few hours or they would become useless. In contrast, oil promised sustained full speed as long as fuel held out.

Rear Admiral Schroeder, commanding the Atlantic Fleet, and BuEng both enthusiastically endorsed all-oil fuel. For example, the oil-burning equivalent of the *New York* would have devoted 500 rather than 691 tons to boilers and would have required only a single funnel, hence would have suffered far less from topside crowding. Steam production per pound of fuel (that is, steaming endurance) would rise about 55 percent. Per square foot of grate, it would rise by a quarter.

C&R demurred. The fuel would now be distributed below the waterline, and fairly uniformly along the length of the ship. The former would lower the center of gravity, increase GM, and make the ship less steady. The latter would increase weight at the ends of the ship, pulling down the ends of the ship girder. With the loss of coal would come the loss of coal protection, and weight would have to be allocated for more extensive internal armor. Ironically, a few years later oil would be considered an important protective material against underwater damage.

At the end of November 1910, the General Board chose oil as the sole fuel of future American battleships. Two years later Britain followed suit with the *Queen Elizabeth* class. In her case, the choice was much riskier, since Britain had large domestic supplies of steaming coal but had to import oil from the Middle East. When U-boats nearly shut the Mediterranean shipping lanes in 1917, British oil reserves were badly depleted. One consequence was that, at least for some considerable time after the United States entered World War One, the most modern U.S. battleships, all of which were oil-burners, could not be assigned to British waters.

As for underwater protection, the General Board proposed a 5-inch lower side belt 4 feet wide, con-

The *Nevada*, the prototype "all or nothing" battleship, lies at anchor, newly completed. She was the first of twelve such ships, another seven being cancelled before completion. Note the temporarily rigged bridged wings and the amidships 5-inch guns sealed into their ports by shutters.

tinued to the turn of the bilge by 2-inch STS (as an outer skin) to resist Davis-gun torpedoes and shells falling slightly short but retaining enough energy to do damage. Experiments later showed that when a conventional torpedo was exploded against it, *external* underwater armor tended to form splinters which could tear apart the interior of a ship. The heavier the armor, the worse the splinters. This was unknown, however, in 1910.

BuOrd argued that it would be far better to widen the main belt by 2 feet than to introduce a point of weakness in the juncture between main and lower belt. Armor tapered down by more than 5 inches could not be face-hardened, so the belt itself could not taper to less than 6.5 inches or 7 inches. There could not even be a smooth transition between the two belts. As for the 2-inch STS, in the absence of experimental data the General Board retreated to a more conventional arrangement, a complete 1.5-inch torpedo bulkhead set well inboard.

Even though all of these issues had been settled by November 1910, C&R kept pushing for the new ship to be a slightly modified *New York*. It argued that the proposed 1912 characteristics would cost time and, moreover, would require an increase in displacement of 1,000 to 3,000 tons, more likely the latter, an increase expressly prohibited by the cost

limit passed by Congress. Had not the board itself approved the *New York* as recently as June 1910? The General Board replied tartly that it was too bad that it had not been able to intervene earlier in the *New York* design and that the 1912 characteristics had been drawn directly from an examination of the defects of the earlier design.

Meanwhile the General Board had decided to move back to reciprocating engines for the coal-burning *New York*s. Oil fuel was so much more efficient (in thermal content per pound), that even the inefficient turbines would yield sufficient steaming radius. The *Nevada* was, therefore, powered by Curtis turbines, although reciprocating engines were retained for her sister *Oklahoma*. In both, oil fuel allowed a considerable weight economy.

On 13 February 1911, C&R produced its interpretation of the General Board characteristics (B in Table 5-2). It followed the General Board armor concept, including the 5-inch belt, but there was also an upper casemate to protect the uptakes. Additional uptake protection included 1-inch STS to the upper deck, and 8 feet of 1.5-inch STS in the smokepipe. The designers attempted to keep the secondaries dry by mounting them in a long forecastle. Of twenty-one 5in/51, fourteen were in the forecastle (ten behind armor amidships), five aft as in previous ships, and two more high in the superstructure. Reciprocating engines were now specified, but C&R noted that the compartments could accommodate two-stage Curtis turbines as well, although a Parsons installation would require redesign. At 588 feet overall, Battleship 1912 would be the longest American warship yet designed. Only four dry docks as yet incomplete, at New York, Norfolk, Puget Sound, and Pearl Harbor, could accommodate it.

This design was rejected. In order to concentrate on heavy armor, the designers shortened the hull and eliminated both upper casemate and lower (5-inch) belt. The result was the famous "all or nothing" type in which only the heaviest armor remained. Variations with speeds of 20, 20.5, and 21 knots and main batteries of eight, nine, ten, eleven, and twelve 14in/45 were tried. On 30 March 1911, the General Board selected a ten-gun, 20.5-knot design (E in Table 7-1). In this type, the weight saved was used to provide 13-inch armor over the uptakes and to bulge the belt out to 14 inches for 4 feet around the waterline. A complex series of tapers reduced this to 11 inches at its upper edge and 8 inches at its lower. The 1.5-inch upper and lower armor decks (the latter with 2-inch slope) enclosed a 16-foot-wide belt and were connected inboard by a 1.5-inch splinter bulkhead. Only 24,800IHP were required, and it was estimated that 1,470 tons of oil fuel would suffice for the required endurance of 8,000nm at 10 knots. A similar ship would require 28,100IHP to make 21 knots, at a cost in machinery and reserve feed water of 255 tons— nearly the equivalent of an inch of belt armor or more than 1 1/2 feet of belt width. Compared with a 21-knot, ten-gun design (D of Table 5-2), the lower speed bought an inch of belt armor and 3 inches on the conning tower.

C&R considered the upper armor deck too thin and proposed to gain 500 tons of displacement by lengthening the ship 10 feet, to 575 feet. Very little of that would go into hull structure (that is, into the congressionally limited cost of hull and machinery). Rather, the extra length would improve the speed-length ratio enough to balance off the extra tonnage (so no more power would be needed), and there would be enough extra weight for a 3-inch upper armor deck.

In June BuOrd pointed out that single plates with the complex taper specified could not be manufactured. Instead, the belt would have to be constructed in two strakes with a horizontal joint running its length, a weak point the designers had been at pains to avoid. The solution was a simpler 13-inch belt tapering only once, to 8 inches at its lower edge. In July C&R proposed the elimination of the 1.5-inch splinter bulkhead, in favor of an extra half-inch of belt armor, whence the 13.5 inch - 8 inch belt that would characterize all later American dreadnoughts.

Shortly before this the designers had increased belt width to 17 feet 4 5/8 inches, which added about 150 tons. This figure, too, was characteristic of U.S. battleships to the end of the dreadnought era.

The triple turret was basic to this design. It alone provided the weight and length savings that allowed much heavier side armor which made the "all or nothing" concept practicable. In addition, the adoption of the triple turret eliminated such design flaws as steam lines around magazines and the inefficient placement of the heavy guns.

Turrets with more than two guns were no novelty to the U.S. Navy of the time. There were already in service seven pre-dreadnoughts with superposed quadruple turrets. Although they were not well liked, these turrets did provide some experience with complex ammunition supply problems. In 1901 Lieutenant Signor had proposed a triple turret (see Chapter 2), and in 1905 C&R briefly considered a "semisuperposed" turret mounting three 12-inch guns for the South Carolina, presumably as an alternative to the superfiring design actually adopted. In March 1910, calculations for a triple 12 inch were made in connection with the New York design, although there is no evidence that such a mounting was ever a serious possibility. C&R recommended that three-gun trials be carried out on the old battleship Indiana, but nothing was done. That May, however, estimates for a triple 14 inch for Battleship 1912, the Nevada, were ordered.

The three 14-inch guns were rigidly connected, two trunnions sufficing for all three, to save weight, space, and personnel. In U.S. gunnery practice at this time, each gun was elevated by a pointer beside it, the turret being turned by a single trainer. In a triple turret, it was not clear where the pointer of the middle gun would stand. The problem was solved by having one pointer per turret. In any case no premium was then assigned to independent elevation of the guns. Many were, however, concerned that a blow disabling any one gun would knock out the entire turret. It also seemed overoptimistic to assume that the linked guns would retain their alignment as the ship rolled and pitched in heavy seas, yet there was no provision for fine adjustment. Finally, the designers were apprehensive of the effect of cutting three, rather than two, large holes in the turret face plate, and adopted very heavy armor, initially 20 inches, later reduced to 18 inches, to strengthen it.

An experimental turret was authorized on 31 January 1911, and on 31 March the basic Nevada design, incorporating it, was approved by the secretary of the navy. On 11 June BuOrd reported that the turret would not be ready before April 1912, more than three months *after* the contracts to build the ship would have to be signed. If the turret failed, the

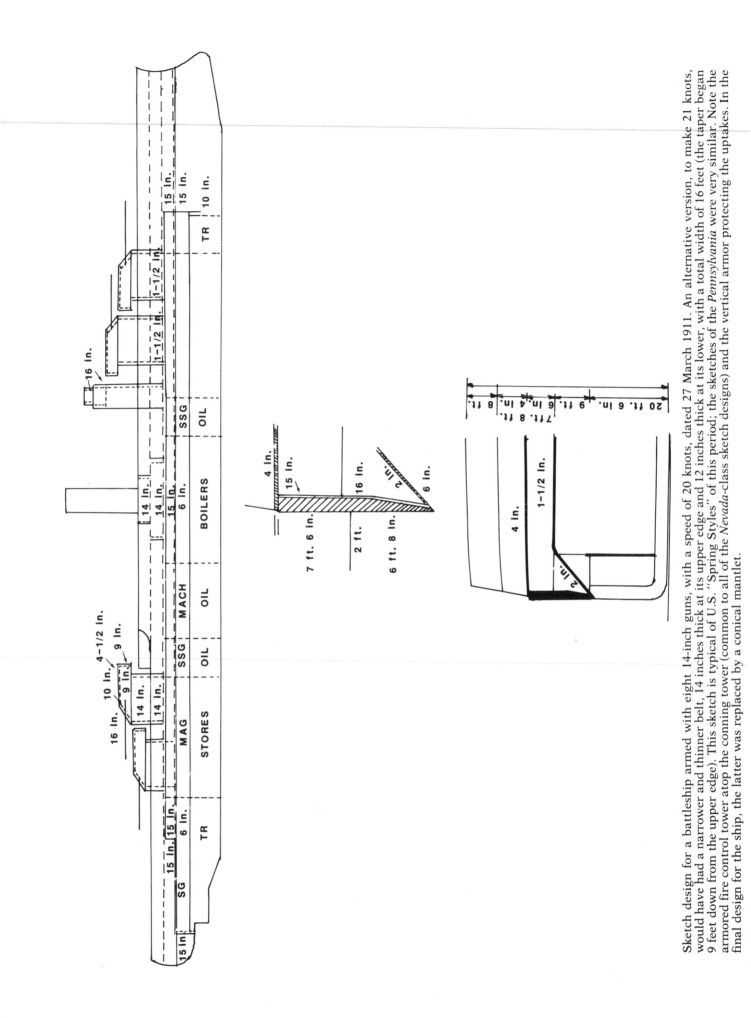

Sketch design for a battleship armed with eight 14-inch guns, with a speed of 20 knots, dated 27 March 1911. An alternative version, to make 21 knots, would have had a narrower and thinner belt, 14 inches thick at its upper edge and 12 inches thick at its lower, with a total width of 16 feet (the taper began 9 feet down from the upper edge). This sketch is typical of U.S. "Spring Styles" of this period; the sketches of the *Pennsylvania* were very similar. Note the armored fire control tower atop the conning tower (common to all of the *Nevada*-class sketch designs) and the vertical armor protecting the uptakes. In the final design for the ship, the latter was replaced by a conical mantlet.

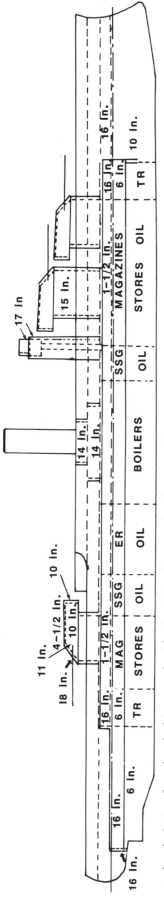

A sketch design for a battleship armed with nine 14-inch guns, dated 27 March 1911. This one was designed for 20 knots.

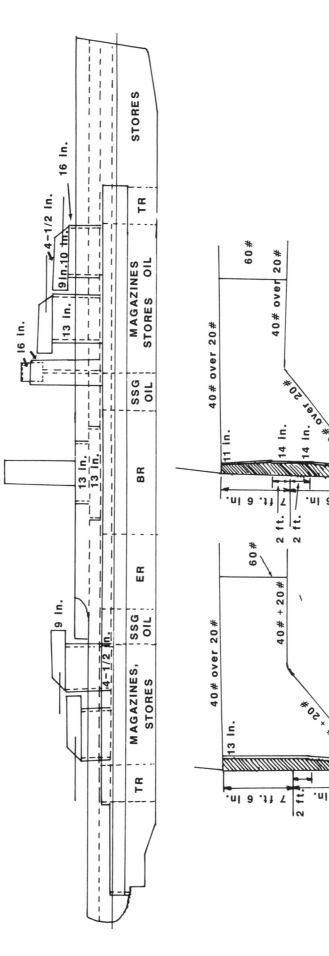

A sketch design (for what became the *Nevada*) of a battleship armed with ten 14-inch guns, with a speed of 20.5 knots. The two cross sections show the two alternative belt designs proposed. That on the left is essentially the design adopted, 13 inches thick at its upper edge, tapering below the waterline to 8 inches. That on the right is the earlier design, 11 inches thick at the upper edge, tapering to 14 inches, and then, below water, from 14 inches back down to 8 inches. In each case, the belt as a whole extended 7 feet 6 inches above water and 8 feet 8 inches below water, and the area of maximum thickness extended 2 feet below the waterline. In the earlier version, the 14-inch section extended for 2 feet on either side of the waterline, as shown. Both versions showed a 60-pound splinter bulkhead inboard, which was eliminated in the final design. Notes on the original drawing indicated that 136 tons would be added for every extra foot of main belt width below water, or 270 tons for every added inch of thickness of main belt armor. However, 283 tons could be saved if steaming radius were reduced from 8,000 to 7,000nm. Note that some of the designs in this series, such as the 8-14-inch ship, had endurances of only 6,000nm. Alternative four-turret designs included one with twelve guns and one with eleven guns (both forward turrets were triples).

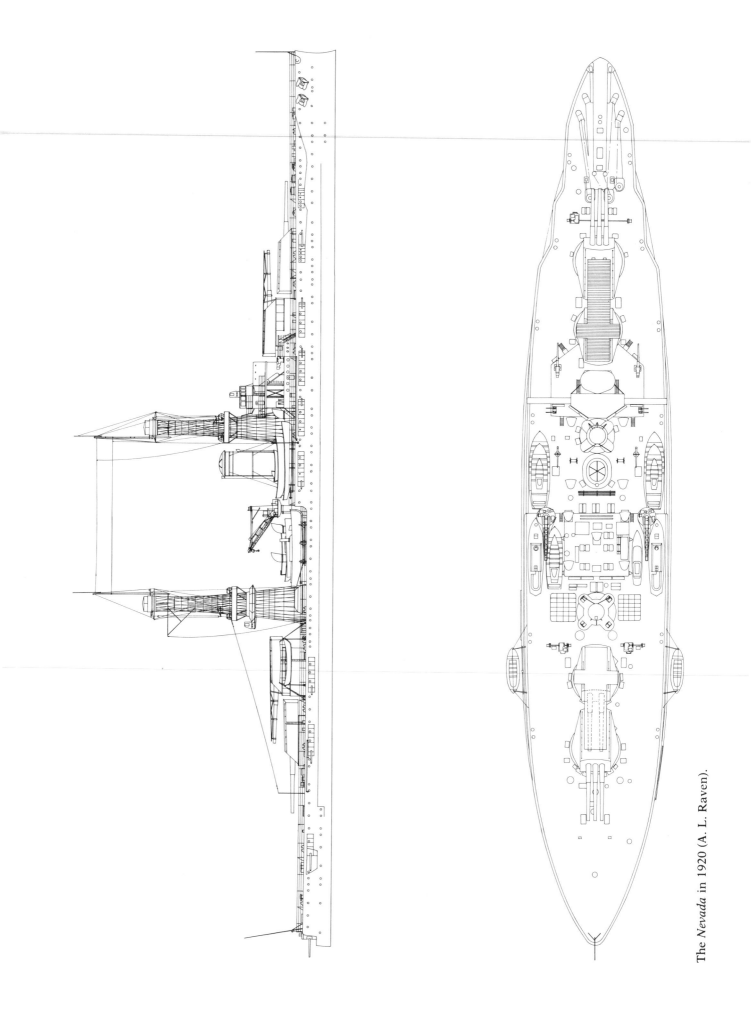

The *Nevada* in 1920 (A. L. Raven).

builders would be able to sue the Navy for large damages. C&R, ever cautious, counselled the department to abandon the triple turret for the present, but on 19 June the secretary of the navy formally refused. A 17 June Office of Naval Intelligence (ONI) report of foreign triple turret projects may have had some effect on this decision. Nonetheless, it was a courageous gamble, equivalent perhaps to the British decision to adopt the 15-inch gun in the *Queen Elizabeth* class the following January.

The experimental turret was not actually ready until August 1912, by which time another class mounting it, the *Pennsylvania*s, had been approved. It was quite successful, the chief problem being interference between the center and side guns. The cure turned out to be a short interval between firings, so that projectiles would leave the guns at least 75 feet apart. An ironic twist was that the two wing guns, fired simultaneously, interfered, even though they were farther apart than were twin guns actually in service. It was concluded that such interference was probably the cause of salvo dispersion then being experienced in the fleet, the practice being to fire both guns of a turret simultaneously. No previous interference experiments had been made.

In August 1911, BuOrd proposed to eliminate the revolving fire control tower designed into U.S. battleships from the *Utah*s onwards. There had always been suspicions that so light a structure could be jammed or destroyed in battle. Moreover, it isolated the fire control party from the captain in the conning tower. With the separate fire control tower abolished, fire control instruments went into after part of the conning tower, where a separate fire control position was screened off from the ship control section by a 1.5-inch division plate and furnished with periscopes for observation. This practice persisted to the end of the dreadnought era. The battleships designed in the 1930s, however, had separate (upper) conning tower levels devoted to fire control.

Armored range-finders were installed in the roofs of Nos. 2 and 3 turrets. Later, additional range-finders were mounted in the open, on the same "all or nothing" principle as were the secondary guns: in the absence of heavy armor, better to avoid light armor, which would serve only to burst AP shells.

Even as the new design was being completed, the old *Texas* was being sunk as the target ship *San Marcos*. Modern AP shells were, if anything, more destructive than had been imagined. The *Nevada* design file shows a notation favoring a 17-inch belt, to be paid for by reducing speed (to 20 knots), endurance (to 6,000nm), and firepower. The test firing also demonstrated the value of the waterline splinter deck.

Two ships, Battleships 36 and 37, the *Nevada* and *Oklahoma*, were authorized by an act of Congress on 4 March 1911, and contracts were signed on 22 January 1912 for completion in three years. Both were actually delayed for more than a year.

This design was circulated through the Atlantic Fleet in the fall of 1911. Most disliked the single-slide turret, and many hoped that by substituting a straight or clipper bow for the existing ram type the ship would be made dryer in rough weather. The strongest comments were reserved for the location of the secondary battery. Existing ships, designed essentially to pre-dreadnought standards, were, understandably, quite wet. Thus the captain of the *Florida* reported in April 1912 that broadside guns "will be practically useless on the weather side in much weather in which torpedo boats could live and make an attack. Even in moderate weather, and sometimes in a sea hardly worthy of so serious a designation as moderate, the *Florida*'s gundeck guns are covered with spray...Ships of the present great displacement do not ride the seas, they go through head seas, and beam seas break on them." Captain Hood of the *Delaware*, soon to join the General Board, reported that only the two guns in the superstructure would be available in any weather. Guns mounted in the cliff-like side of a large ship, however high, would almost always be wet, yet destroyers could already attack in almost any weather, and they were rapidly growing in size and in seaworthiness.

Hood wanted the *Nevada*s altered to overcome this defect, but the General Board was lukewarm. Torpedoes were gaining range so rapidly that it was no longer clear that conventional secondary guns could disable them in time. It might, then, be wiser to eliminate the secondary weapons altogether, devoting the weight gained to underwater armor. The actual destruction of attacking destroyers would be relegated to the fleet's destroyer screen, possibly assisted by shrapnel or cannister shot fired by the main battery guns.

The existing system of searchlights and 5-inch guns had been designed to defeat night torpedo attacks delivered within 2,000 yards. Beyond that the searchlights could not pick up destroyers; they would serve only to attract torpedo fire. Starshell would be necessary. The system encountered difficulties even at 2,000 yards. In the 1911 battle practice, under ideal conditions, the guns averaged only 4.63 rounds and 2.89 hits per minute. Such weapons were unlikely to stop a determined division of 1,200-ton destroyers. An officer wrote that "the torpedo defense battery is a structure of cards. . . ."

By 1911, moreover, there were *10,000*-yard torpedoes in British service. Only very heavy high-velocity guns had flat enough trajectories at that range to have a fair chance of hitting a destroyer before it could launch. But now BuOrd reported that shrapnel, the ideal heavy-gun antidestroyer shell, could be fired only at low velocity, that is, only at short range.

By 1920, the clean lines of the *Nevada*s had become cluttered. The *Oklahoma* is shown at Guantanamo Bay, 1 January 1920, with flying-off platforms extended over both her superfiring turrets, her flying bridge transformed into an enclosed navigating bridge, and her torpedo-defense platforms enclosed in vee-front windscreens. Long-base armored range-finders surmount both navigating bridge and No. 3 turret. Note that three 5-inch guns are missing, one right forward and two aft, together with the single gun at the extreme stern. Unlike earlier battleships, these ships never had antiaircraft guns atop their derrick posts. One such weapon is visible abaft the 5in/51 gun on the 01 level. Other such weapons were added later. The two starboard 5-inch directors are visible, one just abaft her funnel and one abaft the break of her forecastle, abeam her mainmast. Note, too, the long-base range-finder installed atop No. 2 turret, at its rear.

Anchored in Panama Bay in the early 1920s, the *Nevada* shows four of her eight 3in/50 antiaircraft guns: two on the 01 level abeam her foremast and bridge, and two, less easily seen, on the deckhouse just inboard of her boat crane. She has an air catapult on her fantail, but no powder catapult on her superfiring turret aft, and she still has turret deflection markings. Note that octagonal tops were never fitted; this class retained essentially its 1920 appearance until it was rebuilt. The stubby cylinder of a Vickers-type 5-inch director is visible at the deck edge just forward of her large boat. Another was mounted aft, just forward of No. 3 barbette.

The newly completed battleship *Pennsylvania* is shown in Hampton Roads, 10 December 1916. Note that long-base range-finders have been built into all four turrets and that the two superfiring turrets carry unarmored range-finders. Note the canvas screens protecting the torpedo-defense stations on both masts.

Case shot was a point-blank antipersonnel weapon of no great utility and might well harm the gun firing it. That eliminated the heavy guns as an effective antidestroyer defense, leaving only the unsatisfactory 5in/51. It was, then, retained by default. This was a fortunate decision, as in later years destroyers adopted day attack tactics more amenable to such weapons, and director control markedly improved the accuracy of the secondary batteries. But in 1911–12 the retention of the 5-inch battery seemed a questionable decision at best.

On 9 June 1911, with the *Nevada* design nearly complete, the General Board issued 1913 characteristics: twelve 14 inchers, twenty-two 5 inchers, 21 knots, *Nevada* armor—essentially what it had wanted at first the previous year. The number of 5-inch guns was changed to eliminate the gun right aft, which was difficult to assign to a division for fire control purposes. In the new arrangement the six after guns formed two divisions, one for each quarter. Internal armor arrangement was to be determined by experiment. Special efforts were made to avoid the previous year's fiscal embarrassment; quite early the secretary of the navy was informed that the new characteristics would imply a C&M cost of about $7.5 million, a 25 percent increase that would buy about 10 percent more ship and 20 percent more main battery, as well as about twice as much underwater armor. Congress would prove reluctant to relax the earlier $6 million limit.

As usual, C&R tried to duplicate its latest design, objecting that it was the General Board's own policy to build in squadrons of four. Moreover, the state of battleship design was in such flux that it would pay to concentrate design efforts on yet more radical de-

partures for future construction. The General Board was unimpressed. The new ships would still be able to combine tactically with the *Nevada*s, even though they were 55-feet longer. There was no point in repeating inferior ships if better ones could be had.

C&R completed its first sketch design, Scheme A, on 19 January 1912. Draft was to be held to less than 30 feet and beam within 100 feet. In order to obtain sufficient waterplane area for the desired degree of stability (that is, for a large metacentric height), the preliminary design tried relatively long hulls, which in turn consumed considerable extra weight. Thus the 625-foot Scheme A (see Table 5-3) displaced 30,000 tons, yet the 2,500-ton growth was not sufficient to provide enough armor. The belt actually had to be *reduced* an inch, to 12.5 inches, tapering to 7 at the bottom.

This was unwelcome, and most of the evolution of the design was an attempt to achieve the desired characteristics on a hull of moderate size. Scheme B saved weight by eliminating the forecastle deck altogether, sloping the new flush weather deck down aft to save weight. Another possibility was to sacrifice metacentric height, reducing it from an estimated 6.5 to an estimated 4.5 feet. At this time calculations of damaged stability for the *Nevada* showed that a large metacentric height was not needed. The main effect of the choice of GM would be in the period of roll of the ship, significant for her gunnery performance. This was much the conclusion reached by British designers in the R-class battleships a few years later. The design book shows, however, that the preliminary design team remained skeptical, and the *Pennsylvania* was ultimately designed to have the usual great U.S. metacentric height.

Table 5-3. Origin of the Pennsylvania Class

Design	A	B	C	D
Date	19Jan12	22Jan12	26Jan12	29Jan12
Displacement	30,000	30,000	29,000	30,000 tons
Length	625	625	590	610 ft
Beam	94	94	95	95 ft
Draft	28.5	28.5	29.5	28.5 ft
Power	29,000	26,400	25,800	29,100* IHP
Speed	21	20.5	20.5	21 kts
14in Guns	12	12	12	12
Belt	12.5-7	13.5-8		in
Armor Deck	3	3		in
Splinter Deck	1.5/2	1.5/2		in
Weights:				
Hull&Fittings	13,490	14,220	12,995	13,430 tons
Underwater Pro.				tons
Armor	8200	8765	8340	8475 tons
Machinery	2230	2030	1900	2230 tons
RFW	193	176	165	194 tons
Battery	1550	1550	1550	1550 tons
Ammunition	1325	1325	1325	1325 tons
Equipment	1000	1000	980	1025 tons
Fuel Oil	1454	1454	1388	1435 tons

NOTE: Horsepower figures indicated by an asterisk are in SHP, for turbines; all the others are IHP, for reciprocating engines. Except as indicated, ships are armed with twenty-two 5-inch guns and with four torpedo tubes. In the lists of weights, equipment includes stores and outfit. Where an underwater protection weight is given, it is part of the hull weight and *not* a separate item. Weights *do not* include a margin (not listed) of about 300 to 400 tons, which is the difference between the total of items listed and the displacement given. In all cases, belt armor is 17 feet 4 5/8 inches wide, 8 feet 6 inches of it submerged at design draft, as in the *Nevada* class. BB 38 is the final preliminary design for the class, begun late in August 1912.

As for engines, the preliminary designers found themselves in the horsepower range in which turbines and reciprocating engines were competitive. They chose the former for most of the sketch designs on the ground that they were more compact and that turbine engine rooms would be 12-feet longer (at a cost of 140 tons). However, in February 1912 they shifted back, as turbines could indeed fit the 60-foot machinery spaces indicated. Moreover, by this time Fore River was promising better fuel economy for turbines: in a ship the size of the *Nevada*, 500 pounds per mile at 10 knots vs. 545 pounds was claimed by New York Shipbuilding for a reciprocating-engine ship.

All designs from C onwards had forecastles and full protection. The main sacrifice would be in speed or in metacentric height, as noted in Table 5-3. C&R argued that, since American ships usually made well above their designed speeds on trial, the paper loss of half a knot might be no real handicap. A new factor was added at the end of January, when the designers were ordered to provide another 600 tons of 3-inch external underwater hull protection against the Davis-torpedo. By way of contrast, the usual internal torpedo bulkhead weighed 200 tons. Tests later showed that external armor was counterproductive, as Naval Constructor Robinson, who headed the design team, suggested early in March.

By the end of February, skepticism over the reduced metacentric height had led to a new series of studies. Robinson tried for a 6.5-foot GM either by increasing beam and reducing length, which would cramp the ship internally, or by lengthening the wide-beam parallel midbody of the ship.

Four sketch designs, G, I, J, and K (Table 5-3), were presented to the General Board in March 1912. The first, G, satisfied the characteristics and was the largest at 31,300 tons. A reduction in speed by half a knot (K and I) could buy either a 500-ton reduction in displacement or a 15 inch - 9 inch belt and 14-inch barbettes; In the last alternative, J, the speed and protection of the *Nevada* were combined with the 1913 battery, to save 1,200 tons. In all four designs underwater protection was provided by a 3-inch belt extending from the bottom of the main belt to the turn of the bilge, a counter to the Davis-gun. However, many already suspected the splinter effect, and C&R reserved judgment on internal armor. In view of a BuEng statement that above 29,000SHP reciprocating engines showed no advantage, Scheme G (30,500SHP) was to have turbines.

The triple turret was as yet untested, and on 23 February BuOrd argued against arming two classes with an untried and therefore potentially faulty weapon. Should the turret fail, the only alternatives would be to fall back on the twin 14 inch or to go at

E	F	G	H	I	J
29Jan12	13Feb12	14Feb12	14Feb12	28Feb12	28Feb12
30,000	31,300	31,300	31,300	31,300	30,100 tons
605	650	630	620	610	595 ft
95	94.6	93	90.5	95.2	96 ft
29.5	28.5	28.5	28.5	29.5	29.5 ft
25,300		30,500*		27,100	26,000 IHP
20.5		21		20.5	20.5 kts
12		12		12	12
13.5-8		13.5-8		13.5-8	13.5-8 in
3.5		3		3	3 in
		1.5/2		1.5/2	1.5/2 in
13,510	14,765	14,490	14,395	14,224	13,867 tons
		630		660	660 tons
8700	8675	8575	8525	9094	8430 tons
1900	2120	2335	2550	2090	1990 tons
165	184	203	221	180	173 tons
1550	1550	1550	1550	1550	1550 tons
1335	1335	1335	1335	1335	1335 tons
1000	1025	1025	1025	1025	1025 tons
1435	1510	1463	1440	1445	1395 tons

once to the untried twin 16 inch. The bureau also wanted to eliminate the 5-inch battery in favor of additional underwater armor. The guns and their searchlights weighed 635 tons, and Battleship 1913 had only 400 tons of underwater armor. Alternatively, the 5-inch battery could be replaced by eight 6-inch guns in twin mounts, two at each end of the superstructure.

As for the triple mount, on 13 March 1912 Naval Constructor Robinson ordered his group to consider a ship with eight *15-inch* guns in twin mounts, and with 15-inch - 9-inch side armor. It became Scheme L. There is no indication in the record that this was the result of official fears of the failure of the 14-inch triple mount, and the U.S. Navy never had a modern 15-inch gun. It seems likely, however, that Robinson considered the 15 incher the natural alternative to the triple 14 incher. Neither Scheme L nor the slightly modified Scheme M was presented to the General Board, which chose Scheme G on 3 April 1912.

Even then the story was not quite over, as the tide began to shift toward greater metacentric height for survivability. The final version of the preliminary design appeared only in September 1912. A table compiled that December shows an initial objective of 5.5 feet (normal condition) but an estimated GM of 6.73 feet, because of the adoption of a longer parallel mid-body. By this time, too, the external anti-torpedo armor had been rejected, as a result of continuing experiments.

This work began in October 1911, using a caisson simulating a section of a battleship, with the usual inner and outer bottoms, a 0.75 inch STS bulkhead 6-feet 5-inches inboard of the former, and a second bulkhead 14-feet 6-inches inboard. In the first test an 8-inch Davis-shell penetrated the entire structure. The caisson was then raised and its outer bottom covered with 3-inch STS. In November, a Davis-shell did penetrate this armor, but it rebounded and exploded clear of the caisson. This success inspired the external armor of the new designs. In June 1912, however, the same caisson was attacked with a conventional torpedo. Armor, inner and outer bottoms were all blown through the STS bulkhead. This demonstrated that light external armor was worse than useless against ordinary torpedoes and that, for that matter, such weapons were more dangerous than the Davis-gun. As a result of these tests, the new *Pennsylvania* was built with a 3-inch STS torpedo bulkhead 9-feet 6-inches inboard of her outer bottom, the space between forming an explosion chamber; 30-inches farther inboard was a retaining bulkhead. Experiments in July and September 1914 showed that this sytem could withstand 300 pounds of TNT, considerably in advance of contemporary British and French protection practice and equivalent to later German systems incorporating coal.

The General Board asked for four ships in FY13, but Congress was extremely reluctant, given the rising cost. Senator Tillman of South Carolina went so far as to ask C&R where the inflation in battleship size and cost was likely to lead (see Chapter 6), on the theory that it was better to face the cost of building the ultimate battleship than to build a succession of ships each of which would soon become obsolescent. After all, it was only five years since a 20,000-

Table 5-3. Continued

Design	K	L	M	BB 38
Date	1Mar12	13Mar12	23Mar12	3Sep12
Displacement	30,800	31,000	30,500	31,000 tons
Length	620	605	610	600 ft
Beam	92.5	95.9	95.9	97.0 ft
Draft	28.5	28.5	28.5	28.5 ft
Power	27,400	28,300	30,500*	* IHP
Speed	20.5	20.5	21	21 kts
14in Guns	12	8 × 15in	8 × 15in	12
Belt	13.5-8	15-9	15-9	in
Armor Deck	3			in
Splinter Deck	1.5/2			in
Weights:				
Hull&Fittings	14,277	14,223	14,310	14,214 tons
Underwater Pro.	630			
Armor	8550	9100	8560	8534 tons
Machinery	2100	2167	2322	2595 tons
RFW	183	188	202	233 tons
Battery	1550	1280	1280	1550 tons
Ammunition	1335	1110	1110	1335 tons
Equipment	1025	1025	1025	1000 tons
Fuel Oil	1435	1442	1445	1425 tons

ton ship, the *Delaware*, had been the largest and most powerful battleship under construction anywhere in the world; now the standard was fully 50 percent larger. The House of Representatives actually refused to approve any new battleship; the Senate voted two, and the final compromise was for one, the limit on construction cost being relaxed. Battleship 38, USS *Pennsylvania*, was authorized on 22 August 1912 and ordered the following February for delivery in three years, equipped as a fleet flagship.

Now the General Board issued 1914 characteristics very similar to those for the 1913 ship, the chief differences being allowance for 6-inch secondaries (should that calibre prove superior to the 5 inch) and improved subdivision. The board was willing to forgo any immediate improvement because it had something more radical in mind for 1915. C&R as usual argued that even minor changes would require lengthy redesign, and on 8 February 1913 the board formally agreed. Battleship 1914 would duplicate Battleship 1913.

Congress once again refused to authorize more than one ship, although the secretary of the navy requested three, to maintain the average of two a year. It was possible, however, to speed up construction, so that the new ship, Battleship 39, USS *Arizona*, was authorized on 4 March 1913 but ordered from the New York Navy Yard before the end of FY13, on 24 June, for completion in September 1916. The use of the navy yard avoided any lengthy bidding process, and the new ship duplicated the *Pennsylvania* except for a smaller conning tower and flat armor over her uptakes, to simplify construction. She was

laid down less than five months after the *Pennsylvania*, and the gap in completions due to the low rate of authorization postponed to the next class, Battleship 1915.

European critics found the "all or nothing" scheme extremely bold, mainly because they had not followed the reasoning implicit in earlier designs. Thus *Jane's Fighting Ships* praised the *Nevada*s as opening "a new era in protection." There was also general admiration for the clean and rational design of these two classes, in which special efforts were made to reduce top hamper and the target it presented. *Jane's* considered the *Pennsylvania*s the most successful ships of their generation: simple and robust, roomy, well-ventilated, steady, excellent seaboats, and very economical steamers. Within the U.S. Navy, they were criticized only for their wet antitorpedo batteries. Alone of their generation the *Nevada*s and *Pennsylvania*s were optimized for long-range gunnery. The proof is that American battleships designed with the lessons of Jutland in mind had essentially the same deck armor. The splinter deck beneath the belt guaranteed that even shells passing through armor deck or belt would be unable to damage the vitals below it.

The subsequent designs, drawn up between 1913 and 1916, were dominated by the prospect of a new 16-inch gun, just as the prospect of the 14 inch had dominated the 1908–10 period (see Table 5-4). The increase of 2 inches in calibre promised nearly twice the muzzle energy in the 12-inch gun in service in 1913, and half as much again as the 14in/45, the largest gun then seriously in prospect. BuOrd first

Off New York City in December 1918, the *Arizona* displays 3-inch antiaircraft guns both atop No. 3 turret and just forward of the break of her forecastle. The only other major war modifications visible were vee-front screens for her mast platforms, and the removal of the eight wettest 5-inch guns, forward and aft.

By January 1920, the *Arizona* had been fitted with octagonal tops raised further up her masts, as shown in this photograph taken at the time at Guantanamo Bay. Note the flying-off platform atop No. 2 turret. A similar platform is barely visible atop No. 3.

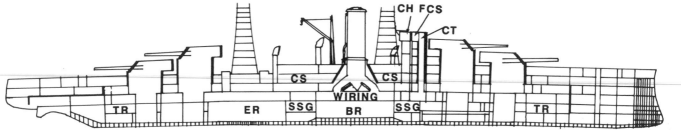

Pennsylvania inboard profile, from contract plans, 1913.

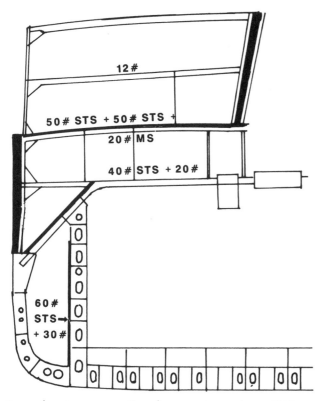

Pennsylvania cross section, from contract plans, 1913.

proposed the new weapon on 6 November 1911, the General Board approving it sixteen days later. The secretary of the navy, however, was leery of moving to a new calibre which might make expensive ships then only on the drawing board obsolete, so on 12 February he restricted BuOrd to blueprints only, as a hedge against foreign developments. Finally on 22 October 1912 he approved the construction of a prototype under conditions of extreme secrecy, using the cover designation "Type Gun, 45 calibres." Design work was completed in 1913, and the gun was very successfully fired in August 1914. At that time BuOrd considered the German 15in/45 (1,700-pound shell, 2,500ft/sec) its closest rival; the new gun (2,100-pound shell, 2,600ft/sec) "far exceeds it in power and energy per ton of gun. The Bureau believes our gun to be the most powerful in existence."

There were major foreign rivals. As early as 1 March 1911 the British *Naval and Military Record* reported a Royal Navy 15-inch gun, and on 14 April correctly reported its cover designation, "14 inch A." Two years later, in connection with consideration of new battleship designs, ONI compiled a list of unofficial naval publications referring to new heavy guns: at least Germany, Italy, and Japan were credited with 15-inch guns. Of these three, Japan actually chose its own 16-inch gun and placed the first such weapons in service, in 1920. It appeared that foreign navies were about to raise the standard of capital ship firepower. The board's foresight in advocating a new weapon seemed justified.

The board now proposed to abandon the *Pennsylvania* design for Battleship 1915 and to adopt the new main-calibre gun. At the same time it would introduce a new standard of armor protection, a new 6-inch antitorpedo gun, and the number of underwater torpedo tubes would be doubled to eight. The full menu of improvements would cost as much as 8,000 tons, twice the jump from *Nevada* to *Pennsylvania*. For the next three years, the issue was whether this new type of battleship would be adopted in place of a direct descendant of the existing standard battleship design exemplified by the *Pennsylvania*. Each time, President Wilson's secretary of the navy, Josephus Daniels, balked at the added cost, and each time overruled the General Board in favor of the existing type, albeit modified.

Thus he ordered that Battleship 1915 duplicate Battleship 1914. The General Board remained unconvinced, and for Battleship 1916 it submitted, early in 1914, the final 1915 characteristics the secretary had rejected the previous December. Daniels stood his ground, and for Battleship 1916 (*Tennessee* class) essentially duplicated Battleship 1915 (*New Mexico* class). At that time, July 1914, the 16-inch Mark I had not yet been test-fired. Once that had been done, the board revived its request for a very powerful ship with ten 16-inch guns. Daniels refused, but he did compromise, so that Battleship 1917 (*Maryland* Class) had eight 16-inchers in place of the earlier twelve 14 inchers. Finally, the cap on battleship size was lifted when six very large ships were approved as part of

The *Pennsylvania* steams through the Panama Canal about 1927. Note the catapult on her fantail. Catapults could not be mounted on turret tops until compressed air gave way to powder, as it was unacceptable to pierce turret armor for the necessary air lines. Note the paravane alongside the superstructure, just abaft No. 2 barbette, and the forward 5-inch director atop the flag bridge wing. The navigating bridge was one level higher than that in the *Arizona*, to clear the extra conning tower level.

Table 5-4. Comparative Penetrating Power of Guns

	6500	8000	10,000	12,000	14,000	16,000	20,000	22,000 yds
12in/50(2900)	18.7	17.3	15.6	14.1	12.8	11.7	10.0	9.5
14in (2600)	19.0	17.6	15.9	14.4	13.2	12.1	10.7	---
16in (2500)	---	---	19.6	18.2	---	15.9	---	13.8
16in (2400)	---	20.0	18.5	17.2	16.0	---	13.7	---

NOTE: This table was prepared by BuOrd in October 1913, to support its request for a new 16-inch gun. The figures in parentheses are muzzle velocities in ft/sec, and the numbers in the table are penetrations of Krupp Cemented armor in inches. The 13.5-inch belt of the standard U.S. battleship, for example, would be penetrated just beyond 14,000 yards by the high-velocity 14-inch gun, and beyond 20,000 yards by the 16-inch gun.

the 1916 naval program—the *South Dakota* class described in Chapter 7.

The General Board began work on Battleship 1915 in May 1913. In view of improvements in torpedo performance it decided to double the number of torpedo tubes to eight, and for the first time the board specified an antiaircraft battery, four 3-inch and four 37mm guns. To reduce wetness, only six of the twenty 6-inch antitorpedo guns would be in the forecastle, the remainder inboard on the upper superstructure. The belt amidships would be extended to the forward torpedo room and aft to the rudder post, the new sections to be carried to 2 feet above the waterline. The bulkheads joining these strips to the main belt would be inclined inwards, a concept probably derived from the "ironsides" project (see Chapter 6). The maximum thickness of the belt was to be increased by half an inch (to 14 inches) and the armor

Table 5-5. General Board Battleships, 10 October 1913

Design	1	2	3	4	5	6
Displacement	39,500	35,500	35,500	31,000	35,500	31,000 tons
Length	695	650	650	600	650	600 ft
Beam	98-6	95-6	95-6	94-0	95-6	94-0 ft
Draft	30-9	31-0	30-0	29-3	30-0	29-3 ft
Power	38,000	38,000	35,000	35,800	38,000	35,800 SHP
Speed	21	21	21	21	21	21 kts
16in Guns	10	10	8	8	6	6
Belt	16-10	13.5-8	16-8	13.5-8	19-11	17-10 in
Above Waterline		8-10.6				ft-in
Below Waterline		8-6				ft-in
Deck	3.5	3	3.5	3	4.25	3.75 in
Splinter Deck	1.5/2	1.5/2	1.5/2	1.5/2	1.5/2	1.5/2 in
Uptake	15	13	13	13	16	13 in
Barbettes	15,5.25	13,4.5	15,5.5	13,4.5	18,6.25	16,5.5 in
Turret Face	21	18	21	18	25	22.5 in
Turret Side/Rear	12/6	10/5	11.5/6	10/5	14/7	12.5/6 in
Conning Tower	16	16	19	16	19	17 in
Torp. Bhd.		3				in
Weights:						
Hull	18,664	17,134	17,117	17,757	17,322	14,990 tons
Protection	11,819	9660	10,178	8536	10,458	8831 tons
Machinery	2563	2550	2550	2400	2550	2400 tons
RFW	253	223	222	221	223	221 tons
Battery	1597	1597	1350	1350	1017	1110 tons
Ammunition	1530	1530	1277	1277	1024	989 tons
Equipment&Outfit	1275	1155	1155	1073	1155	1073 tons
Oil(2/3)	1799	1651	1651	1386	1651	1386 tons

NOTE: All had twenty-two-5in/51 and four torpedo tubes.

deck by 2 inches (to 5 inches). At this stage the main battery had not yet been set. It could be either eight 16-inch or twelve 14-inch guns.

C&R found this rather formidable specification impractical. The big underwater torpedo rooms would be difficult to fit in, and they would increase vulnerability to underwater damage. No more than ten 5 inchers could fit into the superstructure, if blast interference with the main battery were to be avoided. Worst of all, the new and much longer ship would have far too little armored freeboard. The high part of the belt now extended only between Nos. 3 and 4 turrets. As a result, "the *Pennsylvania* would be able to keep afloat after far greater punishment." The extra half inch of belt would buy very little, as the inner edge of the immune zone would be at 12,600 rather than 13,500 yards. The extra deck armor would be out of proportion to the belt.

Meanwhile, in view of mounting evidence of foreign advances, the board began to regard the 16-inch gun as the essential element of any new design. On 30 September 1913 it voted in favor of a change to ten 16-inch guns. At the same time, it investigated the new secondary gun. Some members wanted to shift to a new 3,000ft/sec 6in/50, but both BuOrd and C&R advised against. The new gun would not show much more chance per round of hitting (as it would not have a much larger danger zone), yet it would probably last only 300 rounds.

Chief Constructor Watts presented six sketch designs (Table 5-5) on 15 October. He preferred heavier armor to additional guns and wanted to exchange one turret for more armor. Similarly, he preferred twin to triple turrets, wishing to invest the weight of the third gun in armor. He showed various combinations of armor and armament on three alternative hulls: *Pennsylvania* (31,000 tons); 35,500 tons; and 39,500 tons. On the heaviest hull the board could have everything: ten 16-inch guns; 2.5 inches more belt armor (to 16 inches); 3 inches more on the turrets; 0.5 inches more on the main armored deck. On 35,500 tons it would have to choose between heavier armor (and eight 16-inchers) or *Pennsylvania* armor and ten 16 inchers. The sacrifice of another 16-inch turret would buy, on 35,500 tons, a 19-inch belt and a 4.25-in armor deck. Finally, the *Pennsylvania* hull could accommodate eight 16-inch guns with no improvement in protection. Ironically it was this last and, to the board, least satisfactory choice that became the final U.S. dreadnought actually completed, the *Maryland*, Battleship 1917.

In 1913 the 35,500-ton battleship with ten guns seemed the best compromise. Watts tried to sway the board to heavier armor, but even a 16-inch belt would extend immunity down only to 9,900 yards. In a battle with a *Pennsylvania*, such a ship would be immune between 13,500 and 9,900 yards while her opponent was not. It might take five minutes for the heavier ship to traverse those 3,600 yards. During that time each of her eight guns would be firing twice a minute; even 5 percent hits would ensure four *penetrating* hits. Of course, the ten-gun 39,500-ton ship would be better, but Watts estimated that she would cost $19 million, compared with $16.5 million for the eight-gun type and $12 million for a conventional type.

Rear Admiral Joseph Strauss of BuOrd discouraged reliance on the untried 16-inch gun. If in fact the effective battle range would be limited by visibility to about 12,000 yards, he saw little point in the larger gun. Below that range the 14-inch would penetrate as well, would have a greater danger space (hence a better chance of hitting), and on the same displacement half again as many could be mounted, which would again increase the number of hits. The board therefore gave up the 16-inch gun for the moment and sent Strauss and Watts back to propose a new and better-protected 14-inch gun ship. It would have to incorporate the triple turret, with its single slide. Critics charged that one hit could jam the slide and hence knock out all three guns in a turret. Hence Strauss suggested that new ships have their guns on separate gun recoil slides, cross-connected so that all three could still be controlled by a single pointer.

The bureau chiefs returned on 21 November with two proposals. The first was a slightly shortened 35,500 tonner with twenty 6 inchers. Watts shrank from so great an increase in size, which seemed to buy so little. He proposed a smaller version. By keeping to the former secondary battery of twenty-two 5 inchers and four torpedo tubes, and by shaving an inch from side and barbette armor and forgoing 2,000nm of steaming radius, he could cut his ship to 33,200 tons and save about a million dollars. Watts later defended his reduction in steaming radius on the ground that the requirement for 8,000nm had been predicated on war with Japan, which had become unlikely. However, so long a radius was still valuable. For example, it might enable a U.S. fleet to refuse action with another until the latter had exhausted much of its fuel. The thought that war with Japan was not so very unlikely over the next twenty or so years (the ship's lifetime) must also have colored the General Board's conclusions, since it had very recently advocated battle cruisers with just such a war in mind.

It was not surprising, then, that the board wrote its characteristics, issued on 10 December 1913, around the 35,500-ton design. The official view was that the 4,700 ton increase over the *Pennsylvania* was justified in view of the improvements it bought: (1) separate slides, which increased barbette diameter by 30 inches and cost extra armor weight; (2) 2.5 inches more belt and 0.5 inches more deck, to meet the new foreign 15-inch guns and to secure impenetrability throughout the expected battle zone of 10,000 to 14,000 yards; (3) an increase of 1 inch in the calibre of the antitorpedo guns, in view of the new long range torpedo "and the practicability of day torpedo attack, especially with the aid of smokescreens;" and (4) doubling of the torpedo battery itself, again in view of advances in torpedo performance.

As Watts and Strauss had suspected, the price was too high. On 3 January 1914, Daniels ordered that the next battleships, the *New Mexico*s (Battleship 1915), duplicate the *Pennsylvania*s except in that they might incorporate separate slides for their turret guns. Somewhat more was ultimately done, but first the General Board tried once more for a wholly new battleship design.

On 13 March 1914 the board reissued the characteristics it had drawn up the previous December, this time as Battleship 1916. Now Strauss admitted that the proposed 16 inch - 8 inch belt could not be manufactured, as it tapered too sharply. A 15 inch - 9 inch belt might barely work, but Strauss doubted that it would be worthwhile. From a manufacturing point of view, even the advance from 11 to 13.5 inches had been difficult. On the other hand, even 15-inch armor might be insufficient at battle ranges; BuOrd estimated that the British 15in/42 could penetrate 15.6 inches at 12,000 yards. The board chose the 15-inch - 9-inch belt, and a 3.5-inch deck.

The proposed secondary battery had by now been refined to sixteen 6 inchers in twin upper deck mounts, but there was neither a prototype 6-inch gun nor a prototype twin mount. Strauss could only report that twin 4-inch and 5-inch mounts were under design. He doubted the value of the 6-inch gun. Real improvement would require a much larger calibre, perhaps 7 inches, as in the last pre-dreadnoughts. Watts was developing a new, drier, secondary battery arrangement for the *New Mexico*s (Battleship 1915), in which eighteen guns would be mounted above the forecastle deck; it was incorporated in the new Battleship 1916 characteristics. There were to be at least eight antiaircraft guns, but the proposed torpedo battery was reduced to six to alleviate the squeeze on internal hull volume. Even to get these compartments, speed had to be reduced to 20.5 knots.

Daniels' axe fell on 30 July 1914. Battleship 1916, which became the *Tennessee*, would duplicate Bat-

Table 5-6. Battleship 1917 Alternatives (March, 1916)

Design	165	166	167	168	Tennessee
Turret Added	Amidships	Aft	Forward(Superfiring)	Amidships	---
Length	656	644	668	656	600 ft
Displacement	36,742	35,700	37,700	36,742	32,150 tons
Speed	20.4	20.5	20.25	20.4	21 kts
End Turrets Apart	390	378	384	390	334 ft
GM	5.1	5.6	3.8	5.1	4.8 ft
Trim	14S	37S	15S	13.5B	14S in
Weights:					
Hull	16,570	16,232	16,768	16,570	14,730 tons
Fittings	1467	1453	1480	1467	1399 tons
Protection	10,266	9571	10,391	10,266	8383 tons
Machinery(21kts)	2003	1964	2050	2003	1805 tons
RFW	193	190	200	193	173 tons
Battery	1881	1881	1881	1881	1887 tons
Ammunition	1536	1536	1536	1536	1423 tons
Equipment	536	520	550	536	466 tons
Outfit	670	660	685	670	607 tons
Fuel Oil	1720	1690	1750	1720	1267 tons

NOTE: The B or S in trim indicates a trim by the bow or stern, respectively. The distance between the end turrets is a measure of the hogging strain on the hull. In Design 165, the extra turret, four deck heights deep, was between the stacks amidships. In Design 166, that was reduced to two deck heights, and the mainmast moved forward to accommodate the extra turret just forward of the two after turrets. In Design 167, the extra turret, five deck heights deep, superfired *over* Nos. 1 and 2. Finally, in Design 168, the extra turret was mounted between the bridge and the funnels. Less space was available forward, so the cage mast had to be mounted atop the conning tower. When data were prepared for the General Board, two more designs were added: one with eight 16-inch guns (32,400 tons) and one with ten 16-inch guns in four turrets (33,200 tons). Designs 166 and 167 were such as to preclude the substitution of geared turbines for turboelectric drive, a contingency BuEng was then considering.

tleship 1915, except that its speed might be reduced to 20.5 knots to compensate for other improvements.

The next May the drama was repeated. This time the General Board could confidently request a 16-inch gun, and it could also somewhat relax armor requirements in view of the greater ranges actually being realized in battle in the North Sea. In any case the new 12,500-yard torpedoes would force battleships to fight at greater ranges. Now the ten-gun, 35,500 tonner of October 1913 made sense. On 28 September 1915 the General Board made it the basis of Battleship 1917.

C&R brought the 1913 ship up to date by incorporating developments in the five ships laid down after the *Arizona*: the new type of underwater protection; turboelectric propulsion (which made for more flexible internal arrangement); and the new secondary battery arrangement. The question of the value and arrangement of torpedo tubes remained unresolved, and there were still advocates of gunhouses for secondary guns. These were, however, minor issues. The major improvements over Battleship 1916, the *Tennessee*, (as designed and laid down) were to be ten 16-inch guns rather than twelve 14-inch and greater steaming radius, 10,000 rather than 8,000nm. As in ships designed since 1913, the armor deck was 3.5 rather than 3 inches. In Battleship 1916, for example, the extra half-inch cost 313 tons. This

increase explains the greater size of the 1915 ten-gun designs as compared with their predecessors (that is with 3-inch decks) of 1913.

As ususal, C&R wanted to avoid a new design. Its solution was to modify, to the least possible extent, the existing *Tennessee* (Battleship 1916) design: fortunately the twin 16in/45 approximated the existing triple 14in/50 in size and weight. Thus the characteristics might be met by inserting a fifth turret in the existing design. The extra turret might be inserted between the two funnels, forward of the two after turrets (as in the *New York*), between conning tower and forefunnel, or, most radically, between the conning tower and the two forward turrets as in the later HMS *Nelson*. Alternatively, triple 16-inch turrets might be placed in Nos. 1 and 4 positions.

Weight penalties varied according to the arrangement. Battleship 1916 was expected to displace about 32,200 tons, with an 8,000nm endurance. Another 25 percent of endurance would cost about 300 tons in fuel weight. However, substituting four twin 16in/45 for four triple 14in/50 would save about 200, including savings on reduced numbers of shells, 200 vs. 300 per turret. The existing hull could accept the greater barbette diameters of triple 16-inch turrets at the ends, as a displacement of 33,200 tons. Anything else would cost a great deal more, from 35,800 tons (and a length of 644 feet) for the extra turret

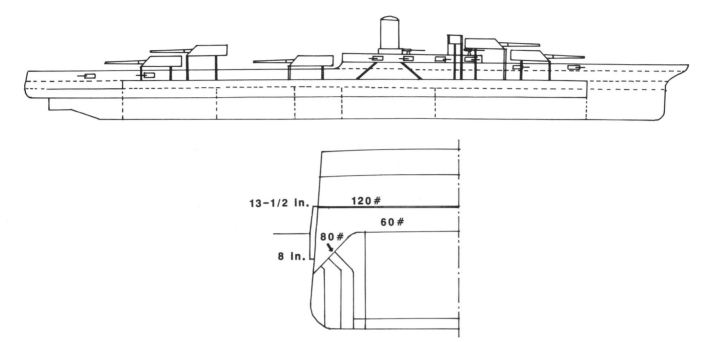

Battleship 1917, the General Board's big battleship as conceived by Preliminary Design in 1914. This version would have displaced 35,500 tons (650 feet wl × 100 feet × 30 feet) and would have been armed with ten 16-inch guns, four 21-inch submerged torpedo tubes, twenty-two 6-inch RF guns, and four 3-inch automatic antiaircraft guns. Armor would have matched that of the standard type, the cross section approximating that of the *Mississippi* actually built. This particular sketch was never completed. A pencilled note comments that it was "2 6in guns shy."

aft, to 37,500 tons (668 feet) for the *Nelson* arrangement.

On a subtler level, the new ship was to resolve the contradiction between the usual great U.S. metacentric height (GM, which made for a quick roll), associated with survivability, with the steadiness (that is, slow roll) associated with good gunnery. The proposed mechanism was artificial stabilization in the form of a 500-ton gyroscopic stabilizer, a large electrically run gyroscope deep in the ship. Previously "steadiness" had been equated with low GM, that is, with low resistance to capsizing after flooding damage. The U.S. Navy had resisted calls for steadier capital ships, in contrast to the Royal Navy, which deliberately built topweight into its *R* class. Several gyroscopes were tried about 1914–15, and in March 1916 one was ordered for the pre-dreadnought *Ohio*, to be fitted at the Philadelphia Navy Yard. At the same time stabilizers were specified for BB 43-48, the *Tennessee* and *Colorado* classes. The parts were not delivered on time, however, and installation was cancelled with the entry of the United States into the war in April 1917.

In 1915 C&R considered the gyro worth its weight (which might be cancelled out by reverting to the former standard cruising radius) "particularly where director fire is used," that is, particularly at very long range. Ironically, by the time the *Tennessee* (BB 43) was delivered, directors had improved to the point that roll damping was no longer necessary.

BuEng was unwilling to design completely new machinery, so it preferred the four-turret design. If five were required, it wanted to keep all of them outside the machinery spaces, concentrated either forward (as in the later British *Nelson*) or aft. Ironically, it was BuEng's achievement of turboelectric propulsion that had made exotic armament arrangements possible in the first place.

BuOrd appreciated the virtues of the four-turret design, but wanted to avoid designing twin and triple turrets simultaneously. It justified its preference for the five (twin) turret design by citing reports of fleet feeling against triple turrets—which had hardly been tested at sea. Moreover, by May 1916 the planned triple turrets were an entirely new multiple-slide type, so that even the accumulated sea experience was not quite relevant. The bureau announced that it was designing an even more powerful 16in/50 (2,800 ft/sec vs. 2,600 in the 16in/45). This may have been an attempt to get the General Board to retain the 14in/50 until the new weapon would be available. As for secondaries, a twin 4 inch would be ready for test about 1 October 1916. The single 5in/51 should be retained at least until then.

On 31 May the General Board chose the five-turret design, with three turrets aft. The board was reluctant to place three 16-inch guns in one turret. The other five-turret designs were rejected for excessive topweight, and eight 16 inchers did not seem a sufficient improvement over twelve 14in/50. On the other

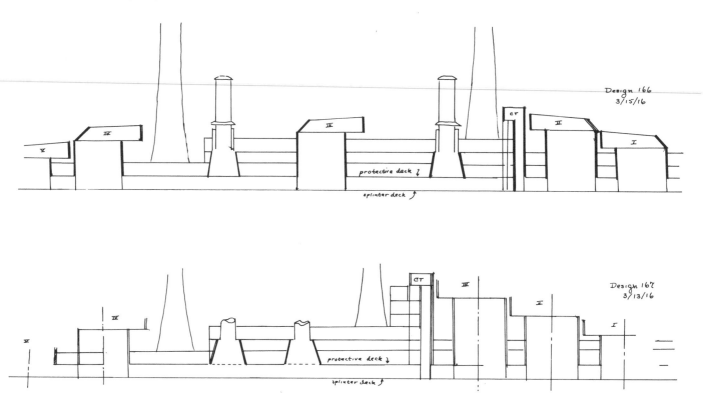

Alternative arrangements of ten 16-inch guns for the General Board (*above and facing*) March 1916. These designs were based on the *Tennessee*.

hand, the 16in/45 was a sufficient improvement that the board did not want to wait for the 16in/50. As part of its analysis, the board compared forty-gun fleets of eight- and ten-gun ships, the latter the five-turret type:

Guns/ship	Total tonnage(cost)	Personnel	Length of Torpedo Target
8	162,000	5,000	3,000 ft
10	143,000	4,300	2,560

The eight-gun ship required 8,100 tons/gun, but the larger unit could have two more for only 3,400 more tons, and the fifth turret would add only about seventy crewmen. The smaller fleet would also be easier to control and to maneuver and would be capable of more concentrated fire.

Daniels stood his ground again. On 28 June 1916 he ordered that Battleship 1917, the *Colorado*, duplicate Battleship 1916 except that the General Board might choose between 14 and 16-inch main batteries. It took the board only two days to choose the more powerful gun, as "guns of higher power than any now

afloat, including the 15 inch of several foreign nations, will soon be supplied to the ships of at least one nation." This may have been a reference to the British 18in/40. The board also used its reply to plead once more for its ten-gun ship, but Daniels would have none of that and on 22 August 1916 ordered again that the new ship duplicate Battleship 1916 except for main armament. A week later, as part of the enormous 1916 naval bill, Congress authorized four ships, BB 45–48, rather than the usual pair.

By this time the General Board already knew that Battleship 1918 (the *South Dakota* class, BB 49–54) would realize its desires; but the class was overtaken by the Washington Treaty. Thus the most advanced American battleships of the dreadnought era were the nine ships resulting from Daniels's consistent vetoes of General Board characteristics: BB 40–48, of which BB 47, the *Washington*, was also overtaken by the treaty.

Between January and June 1914, C&R revised the *Pennsylvania* design for construction as Battleship 1915. The basic change was in hull form, the ramlike plow bow being discarded in favor of a modest underwater bulb married to a graceful and very strongly

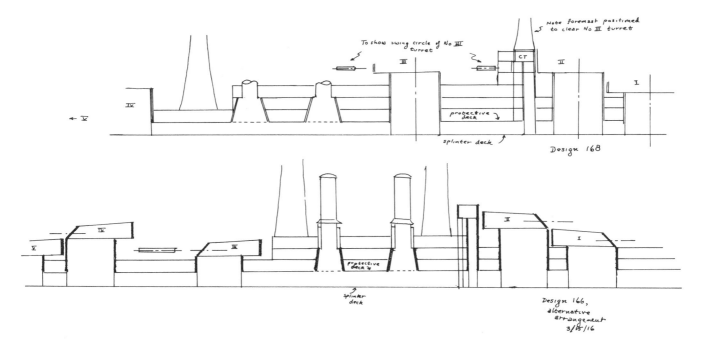

flared clipper form above. Officially this arrangement would "provide improved anchor-handling facilities," but in fact it probably answered charges of excessive wetness. At the same time most of the secondaries were moved into the superstructure away from seas breaking over the forecastle. Another new feature was four 3-inch AA guns. Detail weight economies permitted the designers to thicken the bulkheads enclosing the ends of the belt from 13 to 13.5 inches, and the deck from 3 to 3.5 inches. These figures became standard for subsequent designs. Secretary Daniels signed these plans on 2 July 1914, but the design process was far from over.

BuOrd had developed a new 14in/50 and suggested in August that it be incorporated in the new design. At a cost of 7.5 tons, much of it in stiffening to prevent the longer barrel from drooping, the new weapon achieved a muzzle velocity of 2,800 ft/sec, equivalent to 2 inches more penetration at 10,000 yards. Half of the improvement came directly from the greater length, half from an enlarged chamber that was useful only in a longer gun. Chief Constructor Watts approved the change in September, by which time it seemed that the design had to be frozen, for bids would be opened on 6 October 1914.

There remained, however, one further change, in some ways the most significant of all: turboelectric propulsion. Turbines are most efficient if they spin at high speed, but propellers are efficient only if they turn relatively slowly. Existing turbine ships were inefficient because propellers were directly con-

nected to the turbines, both turning at the same speed. Clearly some means of transferring power while reducing the rate of rotation was needed, and by 1914 a variety of systems had been proposed, including the reduction gearing which ultimately prevailed.

In the United States the General Electric Company advocated turboelectric drive, in which a turbine generated electricity that then ran a motor connected to a propeller. In theory this system had the enormous advantage that the turbine and motor could be remote from each other, the formerly located most efficiently both with respect to the boilers and with respect to subdivision. A collier, USS *Jupiter*, was built as a test bed, and her success induced BuEng and C&R to suggest on 17 October 1914 that one of the 1915 (*New Mexico*-class) battleships be turboelectric. GE had, in fact, already requested bidders' data and had submitted plans for an installation. It even turned out that the electric system cost $162,441 less than the less satisfactory direct drive.

BuEng claimed as major advantages that the turbines could be designed to run at very high (efficient) speed and that they would never run reversed, that is, they needed no astern stages. From a maneuvering point of view, it was important that full reverse power could be obtained instantly by reversing electrical polarity. The electric propulsion motors themselves could be designed to suit the most efficient propellers. Greater fuel economy at all speeds was expected. C&R expected weight savings in fuel, boilers, machinery, and feed water, as well as reductions in

The *Mississippi* is edged away from the dock at Newport News, 7 August 1917. She was the only one of her class ever to carry all twenty-two 5-inch guns called for by their design. Note, too, her extremely simple superstructure, typical of earlier U.S. battleships. Her long bridge wings are rigged, but no searchlight platforms have yet been fitted. Note the two open-mounted 5-inch guns on her 01 level, both pointing inboard at depressed angles. No 3-inch antiaircraft guns are in evidence. Since she has steam up, she is presumably headed for builder's trials. (E. P. Griffith)

boiler room floor area, allowing either a slight reduction in armored length or a slight reduction in the width of the boiler rooms. That would buy more underwater protection. Finally, the machinery spaces could be further subdivided, for better resistance to damage. These arguments convinced Secretary Daniels, who approved electric drive in one unit of the 1915 class, on 10 November 1914. USS *New Mexico* was quite successful, and all subsequent U.S. dreadnoughts, through BB 54, as well as the six abortive battle cruisers, had turboelectric drive. However, the *New Mexico* was not an experimental installation, in that by the time she had been completed in May 1918 plans for the later ships had for the most part been completed.

The *New Mexico* had two electric generators, which ran at 2,100 RPM at maximum power, generating 2 phase alternating current, at 4,242 volts, which drove a motor on each of the 4 shafts running at 173 RPM. By way of contrast, a typical direct-drive turbine installation, as in the *Arizona*, ran at 226 RPM. At 17 knots the ship consumed 187 tons of oil per day, compared with 226 tons for her sister ship *Mississippi* and 245 tons for her sister ship *Idaho* (these figures apply only to main engines). On trial, moreover, *Mississippi* was able to steam astern continuously for three hours, a performance well beyond the ability of any direct-connected turbine ship.

Steaming across the Atlantic to France in 1919 at a speed of about 15 knots, she required only one of her two generators, the other being kept ready at short notice. Her captain stated at the time that until his engine room crew was more fully trained, he would not take his ship to sea

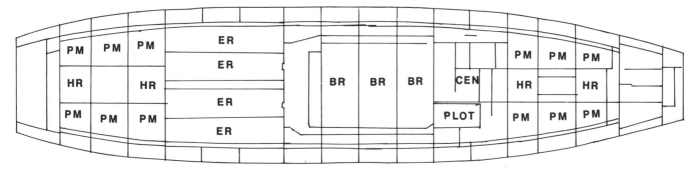

New Mexico machinery arrangement

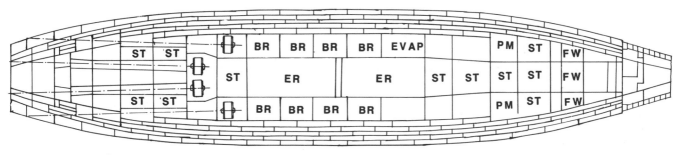

West Virginia machinery arrangement

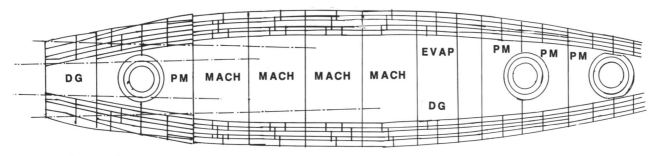

North Carolina machinery arrangement

Turboelectric power made it possible to subdivide machinery spaces very minutely, as illustrated by the *West Virginia*. Similar plans of the *New Mexico* (as completed) and of the *North Carolina* are provided for comparison. In theory, even a hit penetrating the *West Virginia*'s side protection would flood only a small fraction of her powerplant. The *North Carolina* and more modern U.S. warships are designed with a different philosophy. It is assumed that a penetrating torpedo will flood or damage either a fixed length (depending on the weapon) or a percentage of the total waterline length. Machinery spaces are, therefore, spread lengthwise so that one or two hits cannot immobilize the ship. Even such measures cannot protect against shock, which may affect an entire ship, or against the whipping effect of a large under-the-keel weapon. Such threats were virtually unknown during the First World War.

unless the generator not actually operating was ready for immediate use.

Although turboelectric drive was considered reliable, the next ship so propelled, the *Tennessee*, had one of her two main generators break down shortly after leaving New York Navy Yard in December 1920. It had to be removed for repairs in Pittsburgh, and Westinghouse, which had supplied it, complained that access was very difficult. The constructors had not cooperated with the electrical engineers in designing the ship. According to a British observer, "this had proved costly and in war might prove disastrous. The Navy Department has failed to order

hatchways of warships to be large enough to allow the removal and replacement of large machinery, without cutting away a large section of the ship. . .these defects were also in the battleship *New Mexico* and in the [turboelectrical] collier *Jupiter*."

A British constructor assigned to C&R during World War One, Stanley V. Goodall, who later became director of naval construction, later praised the turboelectric system for the better subdivision of machinery spaces which it permitted and for its flexibility. He commented, however, that turboelectric plants were much heavier than the geared turbines of British practice. The very powerful turbo-

The *New Mexico*, the prototype turboelectric battleship, is shown about 1920, after her flying-off platforms had been removed. The ships of this class could be distinguished by the size and shape of their enclosed navigating bridges. Note, too, the forward port 5-inch director on the 02 level forward and two of her four 3-inch antiaircraft guns, on the 01 level fore and aft of the after open-mounted 5in/51.

electric plant then planned for the U.S. battle cruisers (which became the *Lexington*-class aircraft carriers) *was* comparable in weight and volume to the geared turbine plant of the British *Hood*, but Goodall attributed that performance to the U.S. decision to use extremely large boilers, a decision he considered somewhat risky. He also feared that the turboelectric plants, so dependent on massive busbars to carry their high electrical currents, would be unusually vulnerable to the shock effects of battle damage and also to shorting-out through flooding. His comments were to some extent vindicated by the experience of the aircraft carrier *Saratoga*, laid down as a battle cruiser, which lost all power after a single torpedo hit in February 1942. In any event, the U.S. Navy was alone in building turboelectric battleships, al-

though several turboelectric merchant ships were built. The Japanese Navy considered adopting the system in 1919 and even ordered a turboelectric oiler, the *Kamoi*, in the United States, but the Washington Treaty intervened before she was delivered.

Congress wanted only two ships, but in 1914 the earlier pre-dreadnoughts *Mississippi* and *Idaho* were sold to Greece. The proceeds of their sale paid for a third unit, so that the original authorization of 30 June 1914 was supplemented a month later.

The *New Mexico*s were the most modern U.S. battleships in service during World War One, and as such they attracted great attention from British constructors, both those attached to C&R and those who had the opportunity to visit the *New Mexico* when she arrived in Brest in 1919. The new, very compact

The *Mississippi* is shown in the Hudson River off New York in 1919. Note how small her bridge is, compared with the *New Mexico*'s.

The *Idaho* is shown fitting out at the New York Shipbuilding Corporation, Camden, New Jersey, 23 June 1919. Note her small bridge, and the 5-inch director just abaft and below it. Her hull secondary gun ports have all been plated over, but before that was possible construction had proceeded far enough that they could not be faired into her hull. She has not yet been fitted with a range clock, but note the covering over the foundation for her pilot house roof range-finder.

Newly completed, the *Idaho* shows flying-off platforms atop her two superfiring turrets. Her antiaircraft battery appears to have been limited to a pair of 3-inch guns (abeam the derrick posts). The other six were later mounted on her 01 level, abaft the 5in/51 at its forward end.

turret design seemed particularly attractive to the Director of Naval Construction (DNC) department, the organization responsible for overall British warship design.

The main advantages of the U.S. turret were the elimination of shell rooms (with more than half the shells stowed point upwards inside the roller path support and ready-use shells in the turret and on the horizontal transverse platform at the rear of the guns); the elimination of hydraulic machinery; the elimination of walking pipes; simplification by using a fixed loading angle; and the elimination of a platform or supports behind the barbette armor. As a result, the internal diameter of barbette armor for three 14-inch or two 16-inch guns was 31 feet, little more than the 30 feet 6 inches required for only two British 15-inch guns. Moreover, American turrets were much lighter than the corresponding British types. The U.S. twin 16 inch had a revolving weight of 927 tons, compared with 884 tons for the British twin *15 inch*. Similarly, the U.S. 16-inch triple turret (which would appear in the *South Dakota*s) had a revolving weight of about 1,390 tons. The similar weight for a British-type triple 15-inch mounting would be about 1,175 tons. Of the difference of 215 tons, 84 tons was due to the difference in gun weights.

DNC argued that by making these turrets so compact and so light, C&R had gained major advantages; U.S. ships could mount a heavier battery on a fixed displacement. As a result, DNC argued, "British designs of Capital Ships must appear at a disadvantage as compared with those of the United States."

The British Director of Naval Ordnance (DNO) department, which was responsible for the British mountings, strongly disagreed:

The U.S. 16-inch turret designs which are taken for comparison as being the latest, cannot be equably compared to the British 15 inch, as in some respects, such as the gunhouse structure, they approximate more nearly to the *Dreadnought* designs [of 1905]. Omitting the weight of the armor, it would be interesting to know how the revolving weight of the 16-inch U.S. turret compared with the British 15 inch, as the large revolving shell room and the heavy longitudinal and transverse girders supporting the turret roof plates must add a good deal of weight.

Weight is however saved in that the Americans do not transport their projectiles *by power* to the extent carried out in British practice, relying more on [manual] parbuckling and rolling and sliding.

With heavy modern projectiles having long, flimsy ballistic caps, sliding and tilting methods are inadmissible. Power transport is considered an absolute necessity, if a rapid rate of fire is to be maintained, especially with motion on the ship. It is noted that both air power and electric power are used in the American turrets to some extent, including "run out" gear. Electric power has been ruled out as unsuitable for British turret machinery as a result of very exhaustive trials in [the battle cruiser] *Invincible*, and on the axiom that some sort of power is a necessity, hydraulic power has every advantage in reliability, simplicity, and ease of rapid repair, and quick detection of defects. . . .

As regards economy of weight by reducing the diameter of barbette armor, which means a reduction in diameter of roller path, [weight may be saved] at the expense of the efficiency of the turret as a fighting machine. . . . The roller path diameter of our 15-inch turrets is the same as that of 13.5 inch and this necessitated cutting away the structure supporting upper roller path to clear the loading arm of gunslide in 15-inch turret.

The length of projectile (which is tending to increase) and the Recoil Stresses which are taken on the Roller Flanges both tend to oppose any reduction in Roller path diameter. . . .

The American arrangement for transporting their projectiles from Shell Stowage to turret are inferior to our own.

It is understood that the American turret crews are far larger than our own, which would mean an increased allocation of weight for accommodation of the crew and the necessary stores.

It is also understood that since the American Fleet has been associated with the Grand Fleet their officers expressed preference for the British hydraulically worked turrets.

DNO did admit that fixed-angle loading might be worth adopting, DNC having observed that British ships usually loaded their guns at almost zero elevation, despite their arrangements for loading at greater angles. A fixed-angle turret would have a smaller barbette diameter and might be easier to make flashtight. On the other hand, a British visitor to the *New Mexico* at Brest found that although the U.S. powder hoists were provided with covers, "the arrangements for guarding against flash did not appear as complete as in British practice. The guns in the turntable are divided by vertical flashtight bulkheads with a flash door where the shell passes through at the rear."

Other British comments on the *Mississippi* design reflect (as in the case of the *New York* described in Chapter 4) the difference between U.S. and British practice. Most apply to the *New Mexico*, which Naval Constructor E. L. Attwood visited at Brest in March 1919.

Much greater use is made of electrical drives than in British ships, e.g. gun mountings, cable holders, steering gear and backing ovens are electrically worked either through hydraulic gear or direct.

The modern electro-hydraulic gear has many advantages for power purposes on board ship and it would appear desirable in any new design of vessel to investigate fully its possibilities before deciding to retain the proposed methods of operation.

The boiler rooms all get their air from a common downtake immediately before the foremast, but this is considered an undesirable arrangement, as if a shell burst in the downtake the fumes would affect the personnel in all the boiler rooms.

Gyroscopic Compasses are fitted in a number of places as is usual in the British service, with two Master compasses arranged in one compartment, and

the various officers spoke very highly of the reliability of the gyrocompass. There is one Standard Magnetic Compass fitted on a platform inside the cage mast, the platform and tubes in the vicinity being of brass, but it is thought that such a position for a standard compass would not be acceptable in the British Service, as the obstructions due to the tubes of the cage mast, superstructure forward and funnel aft would make it very difficult to take bearings. In our designs it is always a very difficult matter to find a satisfactory position for the standard compass owing to the requirements of the Compass Department in regard to the proximity of the mast and funnel and the heavy revolving masses of steel, and also the obtaining as nearly as possible of an all round view. These requirements in the U.S. service are evidently very much less exacting.

The Navigation Bridge is immediately behind the Conning Tower and has recently been closed in for protection against the weather; it is used purely for navigating. The steering pedestal is of the Tommy-handle type and although the officers express satisfaction with it, it is very doubtful whether it is definite enough in its operation. It is understood that considerable skill and experience is necessary to put the rudder exactly at any desired angle. The Admiral's Bridge is immediately above the main bridge with a small plotting room and a Radio Room.

A 12-foot rangefinder is fitted on the top of the Admiral's Bridge for the 5-inch control with a light tower attached, for protection. . . .

The mess decks had a very clear appearance between meals as the tables and stools are stowed out of the way between the beams; the tables and stools are very lightly constructed and when in position for use there are no arrangements for securing them. The CPO's mess is very well fitted with large tables and chairs, a steam coffee urn, hot closet, ice box and iced water, and CPOs sleeping compartments opens out of it with cots; each man is given a cupboard 6ft x 22in x 15in, the rear having slots for ventilation.

A spacious well fitted out reading and reception room for the crew is provided and was well filled with men reading and writing their letters at the time of the visit. . . .

Seamen's heads and washplaces are combined, the arrangements being distinctly inferior to those in the British service. . . .

The Officers' cabins were fairly large generally about 8ft wide and varying in length from 12ft to 18ft, in addition to the ordinary furniture, a settee is provided which can be used as a bed for additional officers drafted to the ship. The hand basin is provided with running water with a spring tap. . . . Inside the lock-up desk is a safe provided with a combination lock. . . .

The forward part [of the conning tower] is used wholly for navigation purposes and the slots provided are very few in number as compared with our practice and very narrow, and the opening is splayed inwards instead of outwards as with us; this not at all a desirable arrangement as it very much obstructs

The *New Mexico* is shown just before reconstruction, about 1930. She carries catapults on both her No. 3 turret and on the quarterdeck, and two 3-inch antiaircraft guns have replaced one of her two open-mounted 5-in/51 single-purpose guns. Her forward port side 5-inch director is partly obscured by the men on the 02 level, and her after director is visible just abeam her boat crane. The canvas-covered object abeam her foremast (and visible against her funnel) is an antiaircraft director, incorporating an altimeter. The *E* on her conning tower is presumably for gunnery.

the view. The after portion. . .is screened off with a 1.5in division plate for gun control with a number of periscopes sticking up through the top. . . .

The original secondary armament consisted of twenty-two-5in guns, four of these being on the Main Deck aft and four on the Upper Deck, forward. These eight guns have been removed, and the ports plated up. The remaining fourteen guns are not provided with shields. The ten guns on the Forecastle Deck are stepped back from the side. These guns are also bulkheaded round at the rear. The four guns on the Shelter Deck are in the open.

The openings for the guns on the Forecastle Deck are provided with port shutters, but these are stowed and only intended to be shipped in heavy weather. Canvas screens are provided for keeping out spray and rain.

Twenty-four rounds of shell per gun are arranged in racks. The shell, however, are not widely separated as is our recent practice.

Shell and ammunition are brought up by Dredger Hoists from below and on the Lower Deck there is a Travelling band for conveying ammunition from the magazine hatch to the hoists.

The gunnery officer is also the torpedo officer, and has control of the whole of the Ordnance. No range-finders are appropriated for the special use of the torpedo armament.

Four 5in directors in revolving hoods have been fitted precisely similar to our practice, the drawings having been supplied by us and the towers made in the United States.

The submerged torpedo room is forward, and is about 28ft long and the full width of the ship.

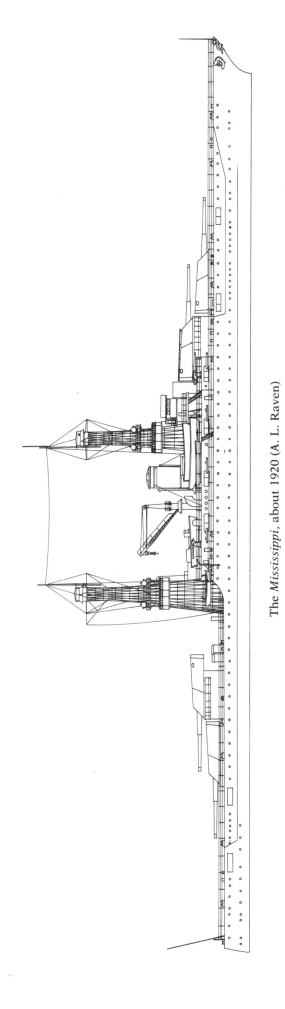

The *Mississippi*, about 1920 (A. L. Raven)

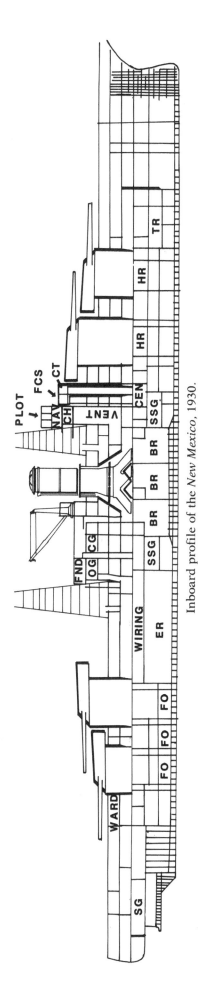

Inboard profile of the *New Mexico*, 1930.

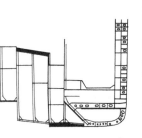

Cross section of the *New Mexico*.

Six torpedoes per tube are supplied, stowed in racks in two tiers 3 deep.

The tube is of the side-loading pattern. By a continuous action of handwheel, the side travels slightly to the rear to unlock and then turns the side of tube outward and then horizontal. The torpedo is then taken from the rack by a similar arrangement to the Vaughan's runway and placed in the side of tube and held there.

The side of the tube is then replaced by the turning of the wheel.

Inside the tube is a piston and shield which is run out with the torpedo in it, and on being run out the torpedo is released.

The sluice valve on ship's side is fitted vertically. An air compressor is fitted in the flat so that the room is self-contained. There are, however, two compressors amidships and one aft, and all are arranged to cut off when the desired pressure is obtained. A bulb angle is fitted around each tube for drainage purposes. It was stated they did not get any water on the deck and the hatch coamings on the flat were very low.

The voice-pipe installation appears very extensive and some of the leads are long, e.g., one from the fore bridge to the steering compartment.

The exchange board is fitted with 177 leads and 20 spares. There are a large number of "loud sounding" telephones with large bell mouths all over the ship, and a bugle call for instance from a central station can be heard immediately in all parts of the ship.

The armor bolt. . .is screwed into the back of the armor, a nut inside bearing on a steel washer with a grommet underneath. Generally speaking, the armor appeared to be very rough with indentations on the surface. Special care, however, is taken to avoid holes in the surface of the armor.

The framing behind armor is very light, being formed of 6in channel bars, but at the butts of the armor there was either a transverse bulkhead or a deep web frame. . . .

The watertightness of bulkheads and decks is not carried nearly so high up [in the ship] as in British practice.

The hatches generally are much larger than in British practice, and a number of them in the mess places are fitted with double ladders. The hatch covers in the thick decks are generally flush with the deck, and are provided with a spring below, powerful enough to lift the hatch. Armor gratings which have to be hinged for purposes of escape are similarly fitted. British practice has been to provide standing purchases for lifting heavy hatches, and for the purpose of escape a small manhole cover is provided fitted with spring hinges, and this has proved a satisfactory arrangement. The weak feature in the U.S. plan is that the edge of the hatch cover bears only on the under thickness of the deck and not on the full thickness of the deck, as with us. . . .

The structural work throughout the ship is of a very high class character and the fittings generally were elaborate and highly finished and compared with British practice must have been very costly. The ship generally gave one the impression that no expense had been spared to turn out a high class and well finished job.

The next step was Battleship 1916. Within C&R, as opposed to the General Board, it had been seen as an opportunity to build Taylor's "Ironsides" design (see Chapter 6), David Taylor having become chief constructor. On 14 January 1915, Preliminary Design was told to proceed instead on the basis of a modified Battleship 1916 design, the General Board's alternative characteristics having been rejected. As the design developed, it came to depend more and more on the outcome of experiments in underwater protection. Thus the plans for bidders were drawn to match Battleship 1916 protection while contracts were written "to permit a change within three months."

The new scheme was quite radical. It consisted of a sequence of thin vertical bulkheads forming four compartments roofed by the splinter deck, now flat rather than knuckled. A series of miniature experiments showed that the most effective arrangement was to fill the middle pair of spaces with fuel or water and leave the innermost and outermost void. A torpedo striking the side of the ship would produce a blast of gas and a shower of splinters; the former would expend its energy in deforming the liquid-filled compartments and the latter would be absorbed by the middle compartments. It was very important to the design that the walls of all these compartments as well as the side of the ship be as thin as possible so as to minimize splinters. The outer void was in part a shock absorber for the gas blast; the inner formed a flooding boundary before the liquid ("liquid loading") could flood the machinery spaces and magazines being protected. This system was adopted for all subsequent U.S. capital ships, and it was widely publicized after World War One. Many of the battleships of World War Two incorporated it in some form.

There were detail improvements as well. The main ventilation duct was moved from the second to the third deck to protect it from smoke and explosive gases. It was fed by a big air intake terminating under an enlarged pilot house and protected by 50-pound STS from the second deck to the superstructure deck. The forward torpedo room was moved forward to get it away from the magazines, "the torpedo room being a recognized weak place in the structure. . . ." It was protected above by a 5-inch deck at the first platform level, "and a cofferdam at the after end of the torpedo room affords some protection to the ship in case of explosions in the way of the torpedo room." Another protective measure was to hang the main belt armor outside the ship instead of on an armor

The *California* runs her trials in 1921: The 5-inch directors were incorporated into the large two-storey tops, served by small unarmored range-finders at the navigating bridge level. The main battery was served by a 20-foot range-finder atop the pilot house. Note also the squared-off shield on the forward open-mounted 5in/51 gun on her 01 level. Note that, unlike earlier U.S. battleships, she carried no searchlights at all on her foremast. The nearly identical *California* and *Maryland* classes were known collectively as the "Big Five."

shelf, so as to avoid a dangerous break in the continuity of the side structure. This did, however, break the smoothness of the ship's side, which a model basin test showed would cost about 400 EHP (about 800SHP) at the then-design speed of 20.5 knots.

A more substantial improvement was an increase in elevation of the main armament from 15 to 30 degrees. On 30 April 1915 Admiral Strauss (BuOrd) wrote that a slight change in turret design would buy 5 degrees more elevation, increasing gun range from 23,450 yards (21,140 in *Pennsylvania*) to about 28,325 at 20 degrees. He doubted that either figure would even be reached in action, but the extra elevation might compensate for the list of a damaged ship. C&R took the idea very seriously, and on 10 May suggested that 20 degrees be a *lower* limit. On 8 June it submitted sketches for turrets elevating to 20, 25, and 30 degrees (33,300 yards). Anything more would involve major structural changes, larger barbettes, and much more weight.

No. 4 turret presented special problems. At high angles of elevation, guns would recoil deeper in the ship. There was so little space under the turret that C&R proposed to limit it to 18 degrees elevation. For anything more, the barbette would have to be deeper (that is, would have to rise higher above deck). No. 3 turret would have to be raised to clear it. That in turn would require a disproportionate rise in total displacement for what was really a minor improvement.

The fleet thought otherwise. On 26 May the C-in-C noted that current reports from abroad indicated that German ships could elevate to 30 degrees (which was not true) and that engagements and bombardments had been carried out at extreme range (which was true). A newspaper clipping appeared to show elevations of about 30 degrees in the new British battleship *Queen Elizabeth*. Furthermore, in protracted engagements and under target practice conditions, where reduced charges would be used to conserve the guns, the ranges corresponding to great elevations would not be so very large. For example, at 2,100 ft/sec, the 12in/45 and 14in/45 would require 25 to 26 degrees to reach 20,000 yards; at the usual 15 they could reach only 10,000 or 12,000. Admiral Fletcher wanted a minimum of 38 to 45 degrees, but he got only 30. On 20 July Strauss asked C&R to rethink the problem of No. 4 turret, dropping its powder magazine and handling room within the ship. After a conference between C&R and BuOrd turret designers nine days later a design was worked out, which entailed a wider gun girder, hence a somewhat heavier turret, than on the *Mississippi* class.

Two ships, which became the *California* and *Tennessee*, were authorized on 3 March 1915. Bids were opened on 17 November, and both ships were assigned to navy yards. As a result, it was relatively easy to make postcontract changes. In particular, the turboelectric propulsion designed for Battleship 1917 was applied to Battleship 1916, formal redesign beginning on 13 December 1915. The new four-layer, torpedo-protection system was approved the following February, and the entire design was complete by March, but the ships were greatly delayed by the

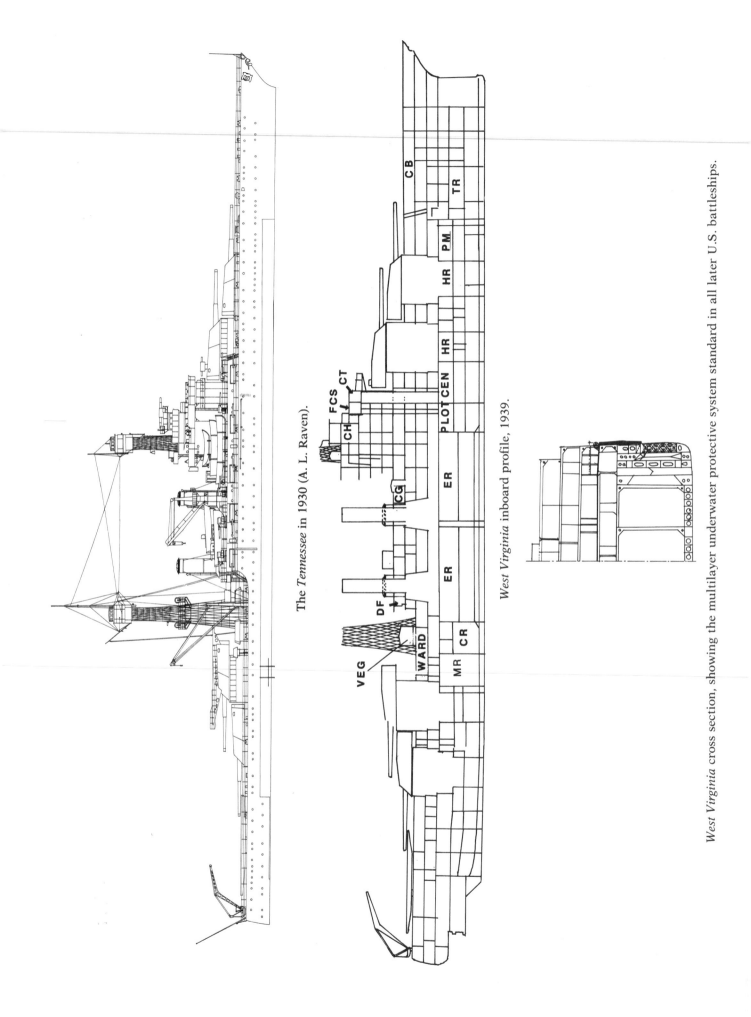

The *Tennessee* in 1930 (A. L. Raven).

West Virginia inboard profile, 1939.

West Virginia cross section, showing the multilayer underwater protective system standard in all later U.S. battleships.

About 1930, the *California* shows standard Vickers-type 5-inch directors occupying the navigating bridge level platform and also abeam her boat crane. Note also the shield on her forward open-mounted 5in/51 gun and the conning-tower roof range-finder for flag use, fitted at Puget Sound in October 1929. She retained the latter for many years. (Courtesy of H. F. Ailes)

war, emerging only in 1920–21 and then somewhat modified as explained in Chapter 8.

Turboelectric drive made for a very elegant form of underwater protection. No longer connected to the two propeller shafts, the turbines were mounted in tandem, surrounded by the eight boiler rooms in individual compartments. The latter were, in effect, the inner layer of the torpedo-protection system, since, even were the boilers on one side to be flooded, the turbines could continue to operate. The new boiler arrangement was reflected in a new uptake arrangement. In place of the single uptake of earlier ships there were two slender funnels, protected by truncated hexagonal pyramids of armor, the sides perpendicular to the centerline being thinner than the others (9 vs 13.5 inches). There were even weight savings, so that BuEng could achieve 21 knots despite the secretary's approval of a retreat to 20.5.

Battleship 1917, the *Colorado* class, was a straightforward development of the *Tennessee*, 16in/45 guns replacing the earlier 14in/50. Taylor approved the substitution on 17 August 1916, and the new plans (which were no more than redrawn *Tennessee* plans) were signed only five days later. Bids were opened on 18 October 1916.

This ended the development of the standard type of battleship which had begun with the *Nevada*s. The abortive *South Dakota*s of 1918 were an enlarged version, but they are treated separately in Chapter 7.

In February 1919, Preliminary Design (to which Goodall was still attached) assembled its ideas on the lessons of the recent war. They were, in effect, a critique of the standard type of battleship described in this chapter. The experience at Jutland, and the general advance in gunnery, convinced the U.S. analysts that battleships had to be armed with the heaviest guns, capable of firing at great angles of elevation. It followed that deck armor would be more and more important in the future. On the other hand, war experience was held to show that high speed was essential "for both strategic and tactical purposes, as well as for defense against torpedoes." These considerations together implied the demise of the standard slow U.S. battleship and its replacement by the sort of fast battleship proposed by David W. Taylor in 1918 (see Chapter 7 and also this author's companion volume on cruisers).

Efficient fire control would require at least four turrets, preferably grouped fore and aft, as in U.S. practice: "Out of twelve center turrets that have been in action, four have been hit and three put out of action, while out of thirty-six end turrets that have been in action, four have been hit and two put out of action." This was a small sample compared with

At Puget Sound on 5 April 1928, the *Colorado* displays her newly fitted 5in/25 antiaircraft battery and her Mark 19 directors, with their altimeters. She had also just been fitted with a protected flag battle station and with a powder catapult on her quarterdeck. Her bridge had been enlarged. During a previous refit she had been fitted with a 12-foot armored range-finder for flag use, on a platform just above the roof of No. 2 turret. At the same time, air coolers and purifiers had been installed for her plotting room, central station, internal communications room, and torpedo tracking room. All of the "Big Five" were similarly refitted at about this time.

the vast number of capital ships in the belligerent navies.

Secondary guns should be small enough to be handy and to be fired rapidly. They should be well placed to deal with torpedo craft; this is, high up and unprotected by heavy armor. "While this is prevailing British opinion and has resulted in the secondary armament of the latest ships [HMS *Hood*] consisting of 5.5-inch guns, there is a strong body of opinion that these guns are not sufficiently heavy [to deal with a modern light cruiser], and a 6-inch gun is advocated. . . ." For efficiency in fire control, the secondary weapons were best placed on either beam rather than on the centerline.

"Anti-aircraft armament need only be sufficient to keep enemy aeroplanes [*sic*] or airships high up. The best defense against aircraft is to possess superior air power." Every battleship should, therefore, carry two small aircraft.

C&R considered torpedoes aboard battleships increasingly important. One torpedo might well miss.

Battleships should be able to fire underwater salvoes, probably fired from above-water tubes, since the existing submerged type were heavy and bulky and reduced the effectiveness of torpedo protection.

As for protection, the key to the standard U.S. design, it now appeared that shells would (in future) fall so steeply that no reasonable weight of deck would stop them. Better to use a thin upper protective deck, which would set off their fuzes, and then a heavy main protective deck which would protect the vitals against the resulting splinters. Turrets clearly could not be protected this way. They would have to be provided with much heavier roofs, which would have to be free of sighting hoods.

On the other hand, since actions would generally be fought at very long ranges, side armor could be made thinner and lighter, its thickness fixed by what was now called a moderate range, 15,000 yards. Normal (perpendicular) impact would be nearly impossible, and further economies could be achieved by sloping the belt armor. Ideally, the belt would extend

Photographed on 23 August 1935, the *West Virginia* shows virtually her final prewar configuration, with a combination of 12-foot armored range-finder and Mark 19 director for secondary battery and antiaircraft control, an enclosed section of her signal bridge, and light antiaircraft guns in her tops and at the forward end of the signal bridge.

all the way up to the upper armor deck. That would be expensive in weight terms, however, and it might be well instead to use a secondary belt above the main belt and main armor deck. Like the secondary deck, the secondary belt would initiate fuze action. The main armor deck would stop the splinters. Without such an upper belt, the enemy might successfully use high explosive or gas shells. This amounted to a proposal to abandon "all or nothing" protection, although the logic of exploiting the fuzing of AP shells would still be the same.

Another bright spot was that heavy uptake protection might be unnecessary.

Gas shells were a new problem. In wartime, crews had been provided with gas masks, diaphragms had been fitted to block voice pipes, supply ventilators had been closed in action, and exhaust ventilation had been provided for the most important compartments. Over a decade later, members of the General

Board would admit that a gassed battleship would be impossible to decontaminate and would have to be scuttled.

As for steaming endurance, it was no surprise that the operations in the North Sea had not tested the 8,000nm endurance designed into U.S. ships. However, in view of "the demands for increased maximum speed involving. . .greatly increased power, and in consideration also of the probable increase in size of capital ships and of the present and prospective high speeds of submarines, it is believed that the present practice of specifying a radius at a cruising speed of 10 knots might well be changed to provide the same radius at a cruising speed of 15 knots or possibly more." For example, the losses (to submarine attack) among ships with speeds above 15 knots were negligible compared with the losses of ships with speeds as low as 10 knots. The increase in notional cruising speed was actually adopted when the

Unlike the *West Virginia*, the *California* was not fitted with a pair of 12-foot range-finders when light machine guns took over the previous flag range-finder position. Instead, it was moved to the roof of her conning tower. Note the removal of her searchlight-control platform. This photograph was probably taken during 1939. (Our Navy)

United States resumed battleship construction in the 1930s (see Chapter 12).

Preliminary Design naturally emphasized torpedo protection, but it appears that the U.S. Navy was quite satisfied with the multibulkhead system. Goodall described it as effective, but feared that in practice the fuel oil filling it would not be replaced by water as it was burned, greatly decreasing its value. Certainly the Royal Navy ultimately adopted a very similar system before World War Two. As evidence of its concern with underwater attack, Preliminary Design noted that, of 19,250 tons devoted to hull weight in the new *South Dakota* (BB 49), fully 3,380 tons were assigned to torpedo protection. Another large fraction of this total hull weight was assigned to deck armor, Preliminary Design's other great concern.

At this time (U.S.) Naval Constructor L. B. McBride was attached to the British DNC Department. He commented that,

In practically all classes of ships, you will find that their hull weights run considerably higher than ours. There are two main reasons. . . 1st—Their designers are in a far more subordinate position, especially as regards control by the Line, than are ours, with a consequence that when one of their vessels, under probably unusually severe conditions, shows a sign of local weakness, such as buckling of decks under heavy seas, or blasting of gunfire at extreme [angles of] train, or gun foundations appear a little too springy, they meet the resultant criticism by the addition of large quantities of weight without waiting to give thorough consideration as to just how probable the recurrence of the same conditions may be; 2nd—the fact that they pay considerably more attention to cheapness of construction than we do. In other words, although they acknowledge that a considerable number of tons can be saved, say in the hull of a destroyer, by the judicious use of lightening holes, they claim that it costs too much to do it. Although I think the above are the principal reasons for their heavy handed designs, their office organization is also, to a certain extent, responsible. Their draftsmen, as a whole, do not compare with ours, either in education or ability, with the result that practically all calculations, especially weight calculations, are made be Assistant Constructors, and as there are probably never more than two or three at the most available for such work on any one design, their calculations are nothing like so thorough as ours. Their final weight calculation for a design is just about comparable with the preliminary weight estimates which we make. . . . As a corollary, their weight records from the Building Yards are nothing like so complete, nor in such detail, as ours. . . . There is one thing which I have tried to get track of here and have not been able to do so, chiefly because data on the subject is non-existent: I am absolutely certain in my own opinion that nearly all British designs run way over weight. . . .

. . . the good side to offset the bad . . . is the undoubted fact that not only do they get out a design in far quicker time than we do, but their whole method is far more flexible and capable of meeting emergency conditions. . . . Shortly before I left the Bureau the last time, I had come to the conclusion that we were spending too much time on our designs in general, and particularly on the weight estimates. . . . The Bureau's record of the last ten years, during which there has not been a single design run overweight, is as good a demonstration as one could have to show that our methods of estimating are sound and are on the conservative side, with the result that I believe we have reached a stage where we could easily halve the amount of work and time put in. . . .

6

Alternatives to the Standard Type

The battleships laid down by the United States Navy between 1912 and 1920 show a remarkable uniformity of design. Indeed the progression is so logical as to appear to have allowed for almost no alternative concepts. Yet the Navy was very inventive, quite willing to try a variety of ideas. Two such were the "Torpedo Battleship" and "Ironsides." One might class the first as a radically different approach to the nature of the battle fleet itself. The latter was radical in its design, although not in basic concept. One other alternative deserves mention here—the "monster battleship" designed not for possible construction but as a test of the ultimate limit that rapidly growing U.S. battleships might reach.

A torpedo striking below the waterline would nearly always be deadlier than a shell striking above. This fact formed the basis of a series of proposals to substitute the former for the latter as the primary weapon of the capital ship.

Although battleships carried them as early as 1875, torpedoes were so feeble that they were not taken seriously until the 1890s. Later, torpedoes in above-water tubes presented a serious explosive risk, as demonstrated in the Spanish-American War. On the basis of that experience, the removal of capital ship torpedoes in the U.S. Navy was ordered. Later, when torpedoes had improved to a point where they could be considered a major offensive weapon of the capital ship, the General Board recommended that they be reinstated in battleships and large cruisers, observing (26 September 1903) that "the range, speed, and accuracy of torpedoes have so greatly increased within the last year or two . . . the torpedo may be considered a weapon of offense to be seriously reckoned with up to 3,000 yards, or even more. . . . Gun fire, in order to result in a decisive action, must be delivered at a range not greatly exceeding 3,000 yards. . . . Tactical war-games played at the Naval War College

between fleets with and fleets without torpedoes have been won by the former whenever the result of the game has been decisive. . . . The General Board recommends that every armored vessel of the Navy now building or being built be fitted with at least one submerged tube, and preferably two, on each side. . . ."

The next logical step was a capital ship armed primarily with torpedoes. W. L. Rodgers, later president of the Naval War College, proposed such a craft during the 1903 session of that institution. Although it was evaluated in some detail, Rodgers's proposal did not progress further, probably in part because of advances in gunnery that extended the likely battle range well beyond 3,000 yards.

The idea was revived three years later by Lieutenant Commander F. H. Schofield. On 3 January 1907, while serving in BuOrd, he proposed to the Navy Department a moderate-size, 23-knot ship, essentially unsinkable by shellfire. It would be armed with sixteen 21-inch submerged torpedo tubes, the largest guns being twelve 5in/50. The weight saved in armament would go into armor and engines. Schofield estimated a total ordnance allowance of only 700 tons, which might be compared with the 1,130 of the pre-dreadnought *Ohio*; this figure does not even suggest the saving due to the elimination of the barbette and turret armor. A displacement of about 14,000 tons was suggested on the basis of the big armored cruisers then being built. Such a hull could be armored so as to be impenetrable by shells outside of 6,000 yards.

Schofield reasoned that a torpedo hit would probably sink and would certainly cripple its target. Increased gun ranges made it unlikely that conventional battleships would be able to use their torpedoes, but conventional torpedo craft would find it difficult to attack "in the daylight conditions under which

The Panama Canal set an upper limit on U.S. battleship design. Here the reconstructed *Texas*, her beam set by the Canal, is towed through its Gatun Locks on 21 June 1937. She was then flagship of the Training Detachment of the U.S. Fleet. Note the standard 20-foot range-finder atop her bridge, and the "bird bath" for 0.50-calibre machine guns atop her fire controls.

decisive naval battles have been fought in the past." The new 3,500 yard, 26-knot torpedo could be fired into an 18-knot fleet with impunity by a ship steaming at 23 knots. She would be endangered only by shellfire. Tactical games showed that "a fleet accompanied by two such torpedo vessels, one at each end of the line, can attack with torpedoes with the vessel most advantageously placed, holding the other to reply to any attempt the opposing fleet may make to defeat the attack by change of direction."

So radical a suggestion was of great interest, not least as an "equalizer" to spring on numerically superior foreign fleets. The natural test was the well-developed gaming facility at the Naval War College. The main problem was how to interpret Schofield's assumptions concerning the vulnerability of his ship. Presumably it would have no advantage as far as underwater damage was concerned. In fact we can now see that even the assumption of parity would have been optimistic, as the spaces devoted to underwater tubes would have been weak points in any underwater protection system. Indeed, this was a major reason for the ultimate abandonment of submerged torpedo tubes. However, it was a point not sensed for some years.

As for shellfire, the Naval War College ultimately decided to allow the ship a life 50 percent greater than that of "a modern battleship of the usual type." Although she might not be sunk by shellfire, the ship would still be vulnerable to the destruction of such above-decks projections as conning tower and smoke pipes. In modern terms one might say that it would be impossible to kill her seaworthiness, but that the ship's mobility might be destroyed, which would be nearly as serious.

Games were played between a fleet of eight 18-knot battleships on one side and one of six battleships and two 23-knot "Schofields" on the other. A single Schofield could never secure a favorable position, but a fleet with two such ships nearly always won. The question was how nearly this conclusion might match with a reality that would cost the fleet two or three conventional battleships. After all, the Schofield was not the only unconventional capital ship being touted. There were also battle cruisers such as HMS *Invincible*, and a more heavily armored battle cruiser which had been devised at the Naval War College—General Board Summer Conference of 1904.

The Naval War College Committee observed in August that

the contemplated usefulness of a Schofield depends upon excess of speed, which must be considerable....The excess speed of a Schofield over the *Dreadnought* is only two knots.... The assumptions further included no vessel of the enemy capable of neutralizing the Schofields, which is not a safe as-

sumption.... The British *Invincible* type is actually two knots faster, has a battery superior to any battleship in commission excepting the *Dreadnought*, has a torpedo armament about half as great as the Schofield, but is not so heavily armored though still very well protected.... The *Invincible* would probably be as effective as the Schofield in a battleship fight, while of greater general usefulness.... The members of this committee believe that vessels of the type proposed by LCdr. Schofield would be powerful adjuncts tactically to a force of battleships; they also believe that vessels approximating to the *Invincible* type, but more heavily armored, such as were recommended by the Conference of 1904, would be still more useful. In either case, they should be provided in sufficient numbers so that both extremities of the enemy's formation can be threatened at the same time.

Schofield was not convinced. Surely on the same displacement a torpedo battleship would be faster than a well-armed fast battleship, simply because gun and turret weight could be exchanged for horsepower. Early in 1911 he resubmitted his idea with the backing of C&R, and once more a series of tactical games was played out. This time battle cruisers were included in the enemy fleet. It turned out that the greater gun ranges implied that the enemy fleet could always remain out of torpedo range until the torpedo battleship had been wiped out by shellfire. Any attempt by the torpedo battleship to close could be countered, and the attacker sunk by gunfire. Part of the reason was that although the torpedo could now be fired from 6,000 yards, the gun could hit at twice that range. In fact "any increased range of the torpedo up to and beyond gun range was a point more in favor of the destroyer type than of the torpedo battleship type.... To a large extent the limit of usefulness of the torpedo battleship lay in day attack; at night it was itself most vulnerable to attack from destroyers.... Money could be more advantageously expended on vessels of the approved battleship or destroyer type."

Schofield objected that the games had been rigged against his ship and the surprise offensive tactics she symbolized, but the torpedo battleship was not again taken up by the General Board.

Yet C&R continued to investigate the possible characteristics of a torpedo battleship during 1912. The work was carried out by R. H. Robinson, who headed the Design Branch, and the studies were intended for Schofield's use at Newport. They form an interesting contrast to Robinson's contemporary work on battle cruisers, which is described in the author's parallel volume on cruisers.

In both cases, high speed and heavy armor were demanded, and, in consequence, a very long hull had to be used. This in turn implied unusually great

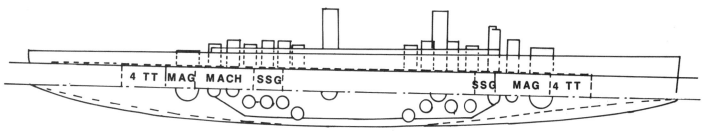

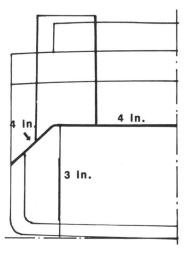

Sketch design for a torpedo battleship, 24 July 1912: 36,000 tons (890 feet wl × 90 feet × 28 feet 6 inches), capable of 31 knots on about 115,000SHP. Armament would have been two twin 14-inch turrets and forty 6-inch guns (locations for thirty-eight of which are shown), as well as eight underwater torpedo tubes, four in each of two torpedo rooms at the ends of the ship. The high-powered machinery would have required twenty-three boilers in eleven boiler rooms. Armor was limited to a 4-inch deck, 4-inch barbettes and turrets, and a 14-inch conning tower, with a 3-inch torpedo bulkhead. There was no conventional belt at all.

bending stresses, even (as here) in the absence of such concentrations of weight as gun mounts. To increase the effective depth of the ship girder, Robinson raised the protective deck (which acted as the strength deck) amidships, protecting it from broadside hits by raising the side armor as well.

By this time Schofield had accepted the necessity for some gun armament. One of his ideas was to use a single triple or even quadruple 14-inch turret forward. His ship would use her very considerable speed advantage to achieve a position from which she could rake a column of advancing ships. The target involved would be so large that the ship need not be a particularly steady gun platform to achieve hits. Hence a very large metacentric height, providing considerable security against underwater attack, would be acceptable.

Several of Robinson's studies are listed in Table 6-1. First he tried for high speed on a displacement limited to 30,000 tons. He could not, however, go much above 27 knots, and even then he had to eliminate the entire main battery in order to achieve a battleship scale of protection. At this time he was obtaining similar results in a study of more conventional battle cruisers.

In July and August he tried again, for 30 or 31 knots. There were to be four 14-inchers and as many as forty 6-inch guns, all protected by no more than splinter armor. Even at 36,000 tons it was difficult

to provide much side armor, and recourse had to be made to a protective deck. The result was a 31-knot protected cruiser. By mounting all four guns in a single thin turret and cutting a knot of speed, Robinson could get some belt armor, but clearly the torpedo battleship was not very practical.

The problem was the sheer weight of very high-powered machinery. The 31-knot ship required 115,000SHP, which would have required a machinery weight of 7,300 tons not counting reserve feed water. This plant was direct-connected to the propellers, and hence relatively inefficient. Only four years later the same weight of machinery would generate 180,000SHP in a battle cruiser.

Despite its rejection of the pure torpedo battleship, the General Board was much impressed with the potential of the torpedo aboard a capital ship. From the *New York* class on, a two-torpedo broadside was specified, first in the form of a twin tube in one room, and then, from the *Nevada* class onwards, two torpedo rooms, forward and aft of the main belt. These weapons were quite expensive both in terms of internal arrangement and in terms of underwater integrity, as C&R was quick to point out. Yet these sacrifices were made quite willingly.

In 1913, for example, in the tentative characteristics for Battleship 1915, the board specified a broadside of four torpedoes. The impetus was the development of a very-long-range (10,000-yard) tor-

Table 6-1. Torpedo Battleships, 1912

Date	15Aug12	24May12	31May12	31May12	23July12	24July12
Displacement	35,500	30,000	30,000	30,000	34,211	36,000 tons
Length	800	780	790	800		890 ft
Beam	91	87.7	85.7	83		90 ft
Draft	31	28.5	28.5	28.5		28.5 ft
Main Gun Battery	4 × 14	6 × 14	3 × 14	None	4 x 14	4 x 14 in
Secondary Battery	40 × 3	16 × 6	16 × 6	16 x 6	40 x 6	40 x 6 in
Torpedo Tubes	16(4 × 4)	8	12 21	18	8	8 21in
Belt	14-9	7.5-5.5	10	13-8	None	None
Width	18-6	25-5	25-5			
Armor Deck	3	3	3			4/4 in
Splinter Deck	1.5/2	1.5/2	1.5/2			
Turrets	18-10-5-9	18-10-5-9	18-10-5-9		4	4 in
Barbettes	13-4.5	13	13		4	4 in
Power	104,000	63,600	64,100	64,700	110,500	115,000 SHP
Boilers	31	21	21	21		33
Speed	30	27	27	27	31	31 kts
Weights:						
Hull	14,600	13,466	13,160	12,856	18,000	16,000 tons
Fittings	1770	1565	1572	1585		1880 tons
Protection	7144	6097	6854	7534	2035	4100 tons
Machinery	6600	3900	3930	3960	7300	7300 tons
RFW	693	424	428	432	767	765 tons
Battery	870	1032	790	578	1560	1567 tons
Ammunition	638	858	618	390	1224	1225 tons
Equipment	520	480	480	480	1300	520 tons
Outfit	735	596	598	600		775 tons
Fuel Oil	1740	1590	1605	1620	2025	1850 tons

NOTE: These designs were prepared to illustrate a lecture given by W. L. Rodgers at the Naval War College. The 24 May design had a belt extending from the usual 8 feet 6 inches below the waterline all the way to the 3-inch upper deck. At the level of the usual protective deck it had a 1.25-inch STS deck. All of these designs showed 3-inch (anti-Davis-torpedo) armor over their sides below their belt armor. Steaming radius in each case was set at 8,000nm at 10 knots. A C&R report on the May studies suggested that replacement of the after turret of the 27-knot ship by additional machinery would buy about 2 knots speed.

pedo, that is, of a weapon that could be used in co-ordination with the battleship gun, at gun range. C&R resisted because four tubes would entail four torpedo rooms. Surely two tubes each firing once every two minutes would suffice. Carried by a destroyer, the same weapon might be used from outside secondary-battery range, which is why the General Board badly wanted a 6-inch antidestroyer weapon.

Even though Secretary of the Navy Josephus Daniels rejected the General Board's concept, the board chose much the same characteristics, again with a very heavy torpedo battery, for Battleship 1916 (submitted May 1914). C&R argued that the extra torpedo rooms would reduce torpedo protection, since they would have to be cut through the torpedo bulkheads. Worse, structural bulkheads near No. 1 turret would have to be cut. Nor would it be possible to extend or enlarge the cramped after torpedo room—Preliminary Design argued for six rather than eight underwater tubes (for a broadside of three). Chief Constructor Watts finally suggested that lower-powered machinery be adopted, at the cost of half a knot.

It would be shorter, so the forward torpedo room might be lengthened. The General Board agreed, which shows how seriously it regarded the torpedo as a *battleship* weapon.

War experience soon suggested, however, that the underwater torpedo tube might not be so good an idea. In January 1916, BuOrd reported that torpedoes could not be fired at all at speeds much beyond 16 knots. Examples of underwater damage emphasized the weakness the after torpedo rooms represented, and in the end they were ordered omitted.

Policy changed again in 1921. From the *South Dakotas* (BB 49 class) on, ships would have only above-water tubes. Early plans for battleship reconstruction also included these weapons. Not until 1924 was the elimination of all capital ship torpedo tubes seriously advocated.

These developments roughly paralleled those in European navies. An element of considerable contrast was that, in its dreadnoughts, the U.S. Navy never had any great interest in bow and stern tubes. This may reflect concentration on broadside tactics.

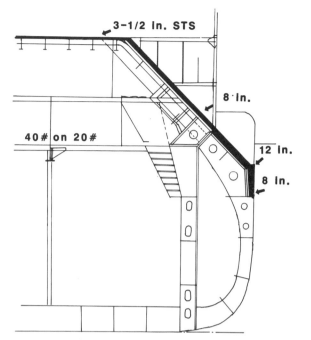

Cross section of the "Ironsides" battleship, showing its inclined belt, 1913.

"Ironsides," the other radical battleship design alternative, was an attempt to exploit the increased resistance encountered by a shell striking armor at an oblique angle. It is not merely that the shell must pass through a geometrically thicker piece of armor. The shell also has a tendency to skid over the surface of the plate. This accounts for the importance of sloped armor decks.

Early in 1913 David W. Taylor had the idea of using plates sloped at 45 degrees as the main side protection of a battleship. He hoped to save weight in two ways. First, he could use thinner belt armor. Second, he could reduce the area, hence the weight, of the flat armor deck covering the belt. The design history which has survived refers to a rough sketch in the workbook for a 25-knot battleship, all other references to which have disappeared. "Ironsides" differed from later attempts to use sloping armor in that the armor was inclined *inwards* as it rose out of the water, like an exaggerated protective deck. Battle ranges were as yet short enough that shells would still arrive on more or less horizontal trajectories. Later, as ranges opened and trajectories became steeper, the "Ironsides" idea would have been less attractive, since the inward slope *up* would only *decrease* the effective angle of impact. In later ships sloping armor was applied in the opposite way, at relatively shallow angles. From Taylor's point of view such an arrangement would have been self-defeating, since it would have required increased armor deck area, that is, increased weight.

Experiments at the Indian Head Naval Proving Ground at this time suggested that a 45-degree plate could stop projectiles with twice the velocity sufficient to penetrate a vertical plate of the same thickness. Since penetration is roughly proportional to the 1.4 power of velocity, five inches would do the work of 13.5. Taylor chose a more conservative figure in a cross section that shows 8 inches, with a conventional 3.5-inch flat deck on top. The lower edge of the sloped belt met a narrow vertical underwater belt tapering from 12 to 8 inches. The entire system was comparable in its depth to existing conventional ones, that is, about 8 feet 6 inches below and 9 feet above the waterline.

According to the design history, Chief Constructor Watts was much impressed and wanted the design kept as confidential as possible. Admiral Strauss of BuOrd "was also strong for this design, and several of the constructors examined [it] at various times."

By early 1914 Taylor was no longer thinking in terms of a fast battleship but rather of a ship in which the weight saved on side armor could be applied to improve secondary battery protection. Weight summaries dated 17 February 1914 show calculations for two- and three-gun six-inch secondary battery turrets with relatively thick armor: 9- and 10-inch face plates, 4- and 5-inch crowns, 13-inch barbettes. Typical batteries included eight secondary turrets, which might weigh as much as 1,600 tons, although initial design estimates had allowed for only 800.

A typical set of weights, dated 3 February 1914, showed twelve 14-inch, twenty 6-inch, and two underwater torpedo tubes on 32,000 tons, which with *Pennsylvania* machinery could be driven at about 20 knots. The weight devoted to protection, 9,149 tons, would approximate that of the *Pennsylvania* class (see Table 6-2).

With all parties so enthusiastic, Battleship 1915 (the *Tennessee* class) was initially to have been built to the "Ironsides" design. These plans were killed by stability calculations, however, which in this case were not begun until considerable design work had been carried out. They showed that, if the unarmored ends of the ship were riddled, water flooding into the triangular volume between the belt and the thin side of the ship would destroy so much stability that the ship would sink. In one such calculation, a ship which, intact, had a metacentric height of 4.51 feet would, riddled, displacing 32,230 tons rather than 32,000 tons, have a metacentric height of only 1.33 feet. Heeled over only 10 degrees, she would have a *negative* righting arm, that is, a tendency to keep listing until she turned turtle.

There was no real remedy. This kind of problem was endemic to all schemes incorporating internal armor. It was worst in a ship which actually lost waterplane area as she flooded. According to the design history, "the Chief Constructor [who was now Taylor] did not entirely give up the design, but appreciated the fact that to adopt sloping side armor

Table 6-2. "Ironsides"

Displacement	33,500 tons
Length	560 ft
Beam	105 ft
Draft	30.5 ft
Main Battery	12-14in/50 (4 × 3)
Secondary Battery	20 × 6in (4 × 3, 4 × 2)
Torpedo Tubes	2 (FWD)
Power	As *Pennsylvania*
Speed	20 kts
Armor Deck (Flat)	3.5in STS (2 layers)
Slope	8in
Splinter Deck	1.5in (2 layers)
Belt	12in - 8in
Main Turrets	18-10-5-9 in
Barbettes	15.5in
Secondary Turrets	9 - 9 - 4 - 7in (2-gun)
	9 - 9 - 5 - 9in (3-gun)
Weights:	
Hull	13,090 tons
Fittings	1266 tons
Protection	9149 tons
Machinery	2399 tons
RFW	209 tons
Battery	1632 tons
Ammunition	1484 tons
Equipment	450 tons
Outfit	582 tons
Fuel Oil	1548 tons

NOTE: These were preliminary data only. They are taken from calculations dated 3 February 1914 and November 1913. The 1914 calculation, which includes the weights, was based on a normal displacement of 32,000 tons, rather than on the 33,500 listed here. Powering calculations were based on the heavier displacement. Some of the 3-gun secondary turrets would have had 10-inch face and 5-inch roof armor; the conning tower would have matched that of the *Pennsylvania.*

we must retain the vertical armor up to the second deck. Any sloping armor above this would be effective, but would add considerable weight. He rather favored this arrangement, and the raising of the boilers ten or fifteen feet from the bottom of the vessel, if possible, getting the boilers above the level of the armored shelf."

Ironsides was officially abandoned (as a possible BB 43 design) on 14 January 1915.

The third departure from conventional design was a response to political pressure. Any observer of battleship development between 1905 and World War One would have been struck by the steady, apparently inexorable, increase in displacement, firepower, and, inevitably, cost. It was natural to ask whether there was any limit to the process. Both in 1912 and in 1916 C&R was made to examine the extent to which the Panama Canal limited the future U.S. battle fleet. Although the origins of the exercise were clearly political, the results are interesting as an upper bound on the technology of the time. The results of the 1916 study were published as a congressional document, and in 1934 the Japanese made a very similar study of U.S. battleship limits as a pre-

liminary to the *Yamato* design. They concluded that they could build a ship which would outclass anything the Canal-limited U.S. Navy could accomplish. Ironically, at about the same time U.S. designers were sketching a "maximum battleship" armed with 20-inch guns as a test of what the Japanese, who had announced that they were withdrawing from the treaty system, that is, from the limitation to 16-inch guns, could do. These 1934 sketches, which are described in Chapter 11, can be compared with the 1916 results to show the effects of improvements in battleship technology, particularly reductions in machinery weight per horsepower.

Both of the earlier studies were executed at the behest of Senator Benjamin R. Tillman of South Carolina of the Senate Naval Affairs Committee. The demand for the 1916 study was included in the language of the great 1916 Navy authorization bill which finally breached the size limit imposed by Secretary of the Navy Josephus Daniels.

Throughout this period, battleship tonnage growth often outstripped the language of the authorizing acts. For example, although the 1908 act called for construction of ships broadly comparable to the 20,000-ton *North Dakota*, the *Wyoming*s that were actually laid down displaced 26,000 tons, representing 30 percent growth in only one year. Senator Tillman objected to what he saw as a rather casual attitude toward Congress. If indeed the Navy needed much larger ships, then it should openly say as much.

In July 1912 he introduced a resolution asking the Navy "to investigate and report [on]. . . the maximum size of ship, whether battleship or cruiser; the maximum thickness of armor. . . the maximum size of gun. . . the maximum speed and the maximum desirable radius of action of such vessels that can safely be built as to navigate the ocean and enter the first class harbors of the world. . . and safely pass through the Panama Canal; the object to be. . . to make the very best battleship or cruiser that the world has ever seen or ever will see. . . . Let us find out just how far we can go. . . and go there at once. Let us leave some money in the Treasury for other more necessary and more useful expenditures."

Meanwhile the senator worried privately that the House Democrats would adopt too weak a ship for construction in Fiscal Year 1913: "it is very important, in my mind, to have one of the best battleships that we can build now, more so than to have two weaker vessels." His interest in the limit, then, was far from fanciful, a point he took pains to impress upon a resisting Navy Department. Ultimately C&R was ordered to make estimates, which show what the constructors of the time thought they could do, if they were freed from cost limitations.

The first estimate was an enlarged (twelve-gun) *Nevada*, with 17 inch-9 inch side armor, and a speed

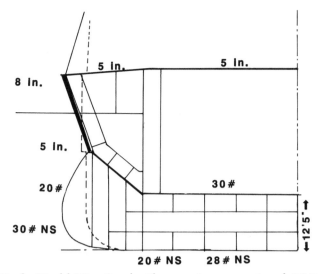

8 In.

5 In.

5 In.

5 In.

20#

30#

30# NS

20# NS   28# NS

↕ 12'5"

Early World War One battle experience convinced C&R that future naval battles would be fought at very long range, well beyond 10,000 yards. They therefore developed this inclined armor scheme, very much like later ones, in October 1915. It was rejected at the time as too speculative.

of 23 knots. It would displace about 38,000 tons, 6,500 more than what eventually became Battleship 1913 (*Pennsylvania*), with 3.5 inches more of side armor, and two knots more speed. Although she could easily pass through the canal, she could be drydocked only in two new West Coast facilities, and nowhere on the East Coast. Within two years, however, much larger ships would be routinely considered.

In 1912 C&R was appalled by the size and cost of such a ship, and it investigated the effect of cutting speed back to 20 knots. That would reduce displacement to 35,000 tons, and the shorter ship could dock at Norfolk and at New York. She would cost about $17 million, $1.5 million less than the first estimate, but $4 million more than the *Pennsylvania*. On the other hand, C&R had to admit that all of these ships were far below the ultimate limit on U.S. battleships, which was set by the locks of the Panama Canal: 1000 × 110 × 40 feet, which might admit a ship of 74,000 tons, costing as much as $34 million.

Tillman was unhappy with the low maximum speeds: "I hope the Department will not make any suggestion for less than 25 knots, and if we can get more, let us." C&R replied that even this small increment in speed would cost four 14-inch guns as well as substantial protection, on 38,000 tons. The result would be no more than a battle cruiser, which would stand little chance against a real battleship, for all its cost. Nevertheless, the Tillman resolution and its aftermath led to some study of the question of speed in the U.S. battle fleet.

Little came of either the resolution or the speed study. Congress voted funds for only one ship, which was a scaled-up *Nevada*. The impulse to growth was

checked by the decisions of the secretary of the navy, Josephus Daniels, to favor improvement of the "standard type" over the radical alternatives proposed by the General Board (see Chapter 5).

Senator Tillman remained powerful. In 1916, with massive construction once more in prospect, he was chairman of the Senate naval committee, and he revived his interest in the ultimate limits of battleship growth. This time an examination of harbor depths and dry dock dimensions showed that the Panama Canal was the main limit on length (975 feet) and beam (108 feet); harbor depths limited draft to 34 feet (about 32 feet 9 inches in normal condition). Preliminary Design considered three hulls: 70,000, 80,000, and 63,500 tons, the latter a finer hull for higher speed. In addition, C&R specified a normal cruising radius of 12,000nm.

Four separate studies stressed, in turn, armor, armament, speed, and a combination of heavy armor and armament. All had the type of turboelectric machinery just adopted for the 1916 battleships and battle cruisers, either the 180,000SHP battle cruiser plant or a 130,000SHP plant with eighteen rather than twenty-four boilers. The new battleship (which became the abortive *South Dakota*) was taken as a baseline. Minimum armament, then, was four triple 16in/50 turrets, minimum armor the standard combination of 13.5 inch-8 inch belt and double decks. BuOrd suggested that the most efficient way of increasing armament would be to adopt a *sextuple* 16-inch turret; sketches showed six guns semi-superposed, but no detailed drawings were ever made.

Two studies traded off armor and armament on 70,000 tons with a 130,000SHP (26.5 knot) powerplant. The belt and deck could be increased to 18 inch-9 inch and 5 inch-6.5 inch, or twelve more 16 inches could be added. Another study showed that merely increasing the speed of the projected *South Dakota* (BB 49) design would require growth to 63,500 tons, although other studies made in 1918 suggest that more could have been done on the displacement.

The fourth study combined heavy armor and armament on 80,000 tons (180,000SHP, 25.2 knots). Any of the four would have been extremely expensive, estimated prices ranging from a low of $24.8 million for the heavily armored type to a high of $27.7 million for the final project.

The usual resistance curves suggested that better performance could be achieved with deeper draft, but the Canal permitted drafts only up to 38 feet. The 80,000-ton hull could be made much finer at this increased draft, and it could achieve 28 knots on 180,000SHP. An increase to 90,000 tons could be tolerated before speed fell back to the 25.2 knots of the fourth study.

Meanwhile BuOrd suggested that an 18-inch gun be considered. As early as 22 June it had proposed a

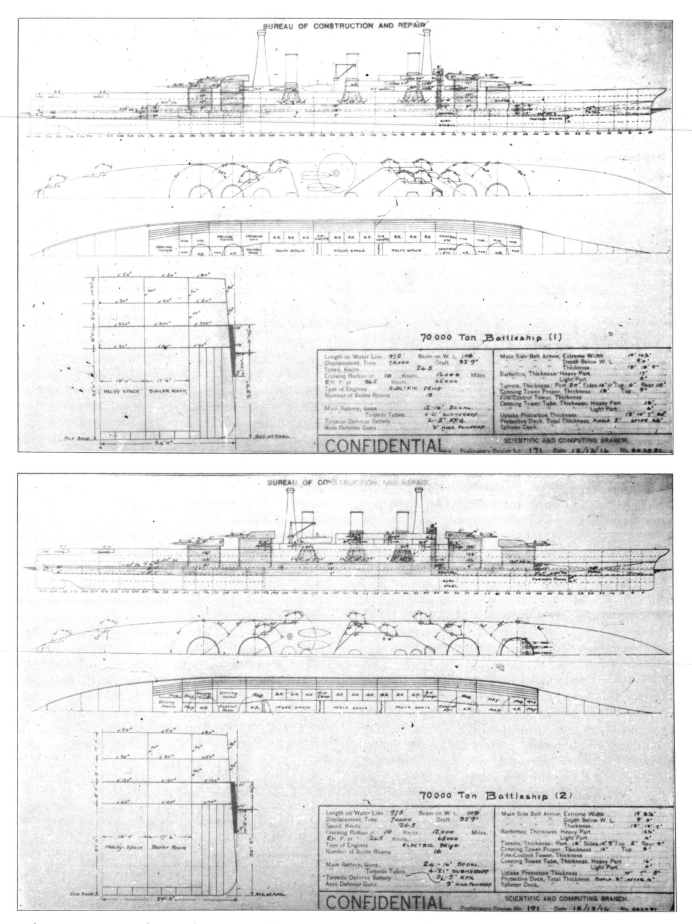

Preliminary Design made several attempts to determine the limit on U.S. battleship design, as set by the Panama Canal. These Spring Styles were drawn in December 1916 in response to Senator B. R. Tillman's demand for a concrete limit and represent alternative emphases. They were not conceived as approaches to practical designs. The figures for a

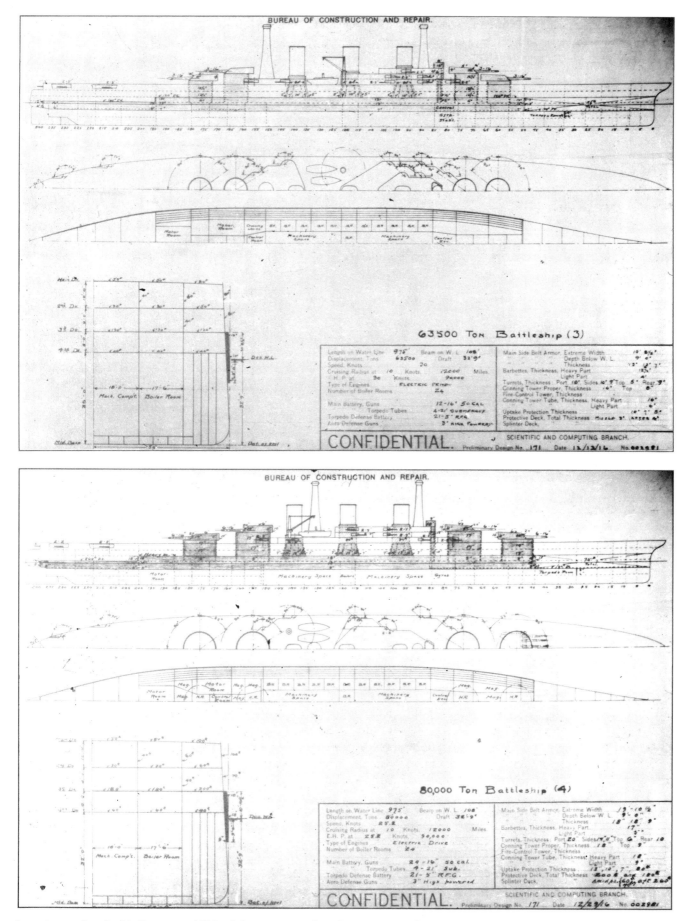

"maximum battleship" were published, however, and as late as 1940 the House Naval Affairs Committee complained that U.S. battleships were far from what they could be, that is, far from the Tillman ship.

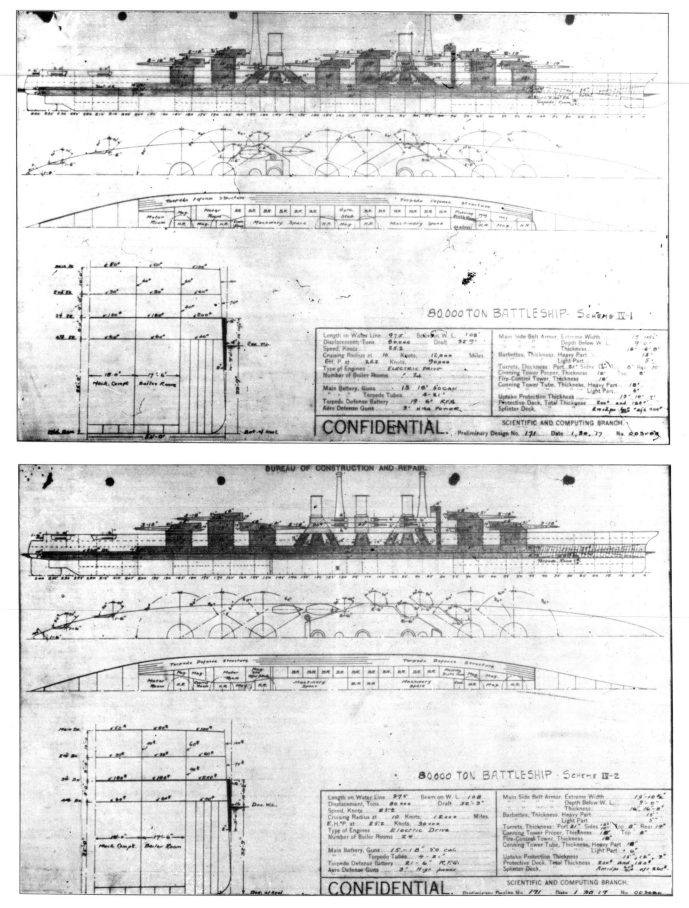

80,000 TON BATTLESHIP - SCHEME IV-1

CONFIDENTIAL   SCIENTIFIC AND COMPUTING BRANCH.

80,000 TON BATTLESHIP - SCHEME IV-2

BUREAU OF CONSTRUCTION AND REPAIR.

CONFIDENTIAL   SCIENTIFIC AND COMPUTING BRANCH.

Table 6-3. The Tillman Battleship (1916)

Design	1	2	3	4
Displacement	70,000	70,000	63,500	80,000 tons
Speed	26.5	26.5	30	25.2 kts
Power	65,000	65,000	90,000	90,000 SHP
Boilers	18	18	24	24
Main Battery	12	24	12	24 16in/50
Belt	18-9	13-7	13-7	18-9 in
Barbettes	17-5	12.5-4	12.5-4	17-5 in
Turrets	20-14-6-10	18-10-5-9	18-10-5-9	20-14-6-10 in
Conning Tower	18-9	16-8	16-8	18-6 in
Uptake	13	10	10	13 in
Armor Deck	5	3	3	5 in
Weights:				
Hull	33,613	31,813	30,150	35,000 tons
Fittings	3000	3000	3065	3300 tons
Protection	17,796	15,621	13,300	20,700
Machinery	5000	5000	6250	6250 tons
RFW	900	900	1200	1200 tons
Battery	2850	5197	2850	5197 tons
Ammunition	2000	3546	2000	3546 tons
Equipment	775	775	775	800 tons
Outfit	1050	1100	1050	1150 tons
Oil Fuel	3000	3000	2850	3200 tons
Cost:				
Hull	$17.1	17.2	15.5	18.1 million
Machinery	$ 7.7	7.7	9.6	9.6 million

NOTE: All four designs were provided with a secondary battery of twenty-one 5-inch guns, four 21-inch torpedo tubes, and antiaircraft guns. Hull dimensions were 975 × 108 × 32 feet 9 inches, and radius of action was set at 12,000nm at 10 knots.

60,000SHP, ten 18-inch design. In January 1917, the bureau claimed a substantial saving on the basis of one 18-inch for two 16-inch guns. If quadruple 18-inch turrets were practicable, the fourth design could mount four such turrets. BuOrd also doubted that 18-inch armor would be proportionately better than the usual 13.5-inch plating; the bureau had already argued that 13.5 inches was really the practical limit for armor production and that anything thicker would be inferior from a metallurgical point of view. BuEng argued that the allotted machinery spaces would not suffice for the big battle cruiser plant. The smaller 130,000SHP plant, good for 26.5 knots, they argued, would be much more practicable.

On 29 January 1917 Secretary Daniels directed C&R to develop the fourth study with 18-inch guns. The bureau compromised on side armor, reducing it to 16 inches. Three new studies were made, of which IV-2 was ultimately presented to Congress: fifteen 18-inch guns in five triple turrets, 80,000 tons, 180,000SHP for 25.2 knots—cost, $50 million.

Secretary Daniels reported that, for such ships to be worthwhile, they would have to be built in divisions of at least five (with an allowance of one ship under repair or in reserve), at an outlay of $250 million.

There had never been any prospect of actually building such a ship. The entire design effort was intended merely to explore the natural limits of U.S. battleship design. Yet it was important. For example, in 1921 the Navy could say that the 35,000 ton-limit set by the new treaty had nothing whatever to do with the Canal, that in fact "this limitation by the richest nation is deliberately giving away one of its points of advantage." The Navy actually did exceed the limit of the existing Canal locks in the *Montana* design which, although smaller than 80,000 tons, was too beamy to pass through them. However, that was not a fundamental change in U.S. policy. The *Montana* was planned in parallel with a new set of wider locks—which were not built because of the U.S. entry into World War Two.

The 80,000-ton Design 4 of December 1916 was developed further in January 1917 as Schemes IV-1 and IV-2, illustrated here by the usual Spring Styles. Note that the fanciful sextuple 16-inch mount of Design 4 has been replaced by a more practical triple 18-inch turret. At this time BuOrd had a design for an 18-inch gun, but it was nowhere near building one, and in fact the U.S. 18-inch prototype was cancelled in 1922 as a result of the Washington Treaty.

7

The Last Dreadnought:
The *South Dakota* Class

From 1905 onwards, Congress failed to maintain the steady tempo of two battleships per year which the General Board had proposed. Meanwhile, in the board's view, the U.S. fleet fell further and further behind requirements. Most of its ships were made obsolescent by the advent, first, of the *Dreadnought* and later by the super-dreadnoughts. In sheer numbers, it fell further and further behind the fleet of the most probable enemy, Germany, as the pace of German construction accelerated in its building race with Britain. German involvement in the Mexican revolution (1914) seemed to imply an attempt to seize a base in the New World, and there were also rumors of German interest in Haiti. Admiral Bradley Fiske of the General Board reported to Congress in 1914 that the planned German naval maneuvers that fall would include tactics far beyond the capabilities of the U.S. fleet.

For its part, Congress saw no point in vast naval expenditures, a sentiment mirrored in Secretary Daniels's rejection of the growth in individual battleship size (and cost) desired by the General Board. Nor did President Wilson favor increased defense spending. He concentrated mainly on domestic issues during his first fifteen months in office, apart from intervention, during 1914, in the Mexican revolution in the form of a naval occupation of Veracruz.

Once war broke out in August 1914, the issue of naval inferiority became more urgent. In its message to Congress early in 1915, the General Board renewed its call for forty-eight battleships by 1920 (see Chapter 1), claiming that this figure had been determined from "the known laws and prospective developments and aims of other countries." It therefore asked for four battleships (for FY16). The House Naval Com-

mittee refused, on the stated basis that not enough had as yet been learned from the war at sea to warrant major changes in the program. At this time the U.S. Navy had completed or had on order a total of fifteen dreadnoughts and super-dreadnoughts, excluding the slow *South Carolinas*.

Many within the Navy believed that, whatever President Wilson's desires for neutrality, the country would be forced into war. The U.S. Navy had long operated on the assumption that it would have no opportunity to move from a peace to a war footing. The whole theory of naval rearmament, from 1883 onwards, had been that a modern fighting navy could not be improvised. As the war in Europe continued, moreover, it became obvious that a citizen army could not successfully oppose a professional one. Late in 1914, a "preparedness" campaign began to promote the view that the United States might easily be invaded by a victorious Germany. A popular movie, for example, showed invaders (dressed as Germans) executing Civil War veterans as an example to the populace. The *Lusitania* sinking emphasized to many both the threat of Germany and the impotence of the United States.

For his part, President Wilson saw a powerful U.S. Navy as a lever he could use to bring the fighting powers to some equitable peace. German attempts to begin unrestricted submarine warfare helped convince the president that he needed a more powerful navy. In addition, the Japanese demands on China (the Twenty-One Demands), which amounted to excluding foreigners, were made public during the spring of 1915. By the fall of 1915, there were suggestions that Japan might well ultimately operate in alliance with the other probable enemy, Germany, abandon-

The *South Dakota*s were essentially enlarged versions of the earlier *Colorado* class, with triple rather than twin 16-inch turrets. Here, early in her career, *Maryland* approaches the New York Navy Yard. Her topmasts have been lowered to enable her to pass under the bridges. Note the unusual armored range-finder atop her No. 2 turret and the air intakes visible in the vent alongside of and beneath her bridge.

ing Britain. She might, for example, return to Germany the Pacific islands she had seized in 1914 in exchange for a free hand in the Dutch East Indies (Indonesia) and in French Indochina (Vietnam).

By the summer of 1915, the preparedness movement was strongly attacking the apparently poor state of the Navy, for which Secretary of the Navy Daniels was held personally responsible. The secretary vetoed a proposal by Admiral Fiske, a member of the General Board, that the 1915 naval maneuvers take the form of the defense of the United States against a German fleet and that the U.S. forces be overwhelmingly defeated to show the public just how much had to be done. Even so, Admiral F. J. Fletcher's official report of the maneuvers showed numerous deficiencies. The Office of Naval Intelligence reported that the United States stood fourth (after France) in tonnage.

With the sinking of the *Lusitania*, Secretary of State Robert Lansing, already strongly favoring the Allies, wrote a memorandum to President Wilson on policies to be followed in the event of war with Germany, including the purchase of the Danish Virgin Islands and the resolution of disagreements with Colombia to prevent the Germans from establishing a base there. Plans for the Atlantic Fleet to visit the Panama–Pacific Exposition in San Francisco were cancelled, the battle fleet remaining in the Atlantic. On 21 July 1915, ten days after receiving Lansing's memorandum, President Wilson ordered the secretaries of the Army and Navy to plan for mobilization.

The General Board's reaction was that the U.S. Navy must be equal, not to the navy of the most probable enemy, Germany, but rather to the most powerful navy in the world, the Royal Navy. The board justified this major change in policy on the ground that the next war would be fought for economic reasons and that whoever won the present conflict would have to fight the United States for the markets of the world. It suggested, for example, that the rivalry with Japan in the Far East was primarily due to a Japanese desire to eject the United States from the markets of Asia; the Philippines constituted a U.S. foothold in the economies of the area. As for the European powers, the General Board argued that, far from being exhausted by the world war, the winner would have a nearly unbeatable combination: millions of trained, battle-hardened veterans, and the war indemnity (paid by the losers) that would pay for the conquest of the United States. Nowhere was there any appreciation of the degree of exhaustion the European powers would experience.

On 7 October Secretary Daniels ordered the board to prepare a five-year program, to cost $100 million per year.

Given its standard figure of two battleships per year, the General Board called for a total of ten bat-

tleships within five years, together with battle cruisers and lesser craft. Wilson submitted this program to Congress in December. The small-navy forces seemed so strong, however, that for a time he was held to a one-year program of five battle cruisers, which apparently seemed (to the small-navy advocates) less expansionist than battle*ships*, although they were far costlier. By a remarkable coincidence, the battle of Jutland was fought while the House of Representatives was debating the bill, and many members saw in its outcome a justification for the battleship. The bill then expanded, to the point that the original plan passed, to be completed, not in five years but in three. Four ships were, therefore, authorized for fiscal year 1917, and three each in 1918 and 1919. Moreover, with public sentiment running strongly in favor of armaments, the six later ships, which became the *South Dakota* class (authorized on 19 August 1916), could be much more powerful than their predecessors.

This *South Dakota* class was the ultimate development of the series that had begun with the *Nevada*. Delayed by the First World War, the ships of the series were resumed as part of the postwar naval arms race with Japan and finally cancelled as part of the Washington Naval Arms Limitation Treaty. In the end, their main contribution to the U.S. fleet was in armor originally manufactured for them and then used in reconstructed capital ships. They indicate the direction in which U.S. design doctrine was running. Some of the alternatives proposed at the time by C&R show what the next stage would have been.

From the start the General Board wanted twelve 16-inch guns and higher speed, probably 23 knots. At hearings late in September 1916, representatives of the board told the bureau chiefs that the Royal Navy seemed to be going to 18- or 19-inch guns and that Japan seemed to be going toward fast battleships like the British *Queen Elizabeth*s. New ships were urgently needed, since Japan was becoming increasingly belligerent on the sensitive immigration issue. At this time it appeared that the new Japanese ships would mount ten 15-inch guns, but "we hear confidentially from England that they are building ships that will carry ten 18- or 19-inch guns; we want to get the largest ships possible. . . . Everybody is going up in speed [but] the Board does not believe in going for the present for more than two knots." In fact Japan was building her own equivalent of the *Queen Elizabeth*, the 26.5-knot *Nagato* mounting eight 16-inch guns (rather than the 15-inch of the British ship). U.S. intelligence was apparently unaware of such high speed for twenty more years.

A 700-foot ship could attain 23 knots and carry four triple turrets on about 40,000 tons. Alternatively, a longer and somewhat heavier ship could carry six twin turrets. Reducing speed by a knot would

An official waterline model shows how the *South Dakota* class would have appeared. Note the high elevation of the guns. The cage masts have been portrayed as solid. (National Archives)

save only about 1,000 tons, but eliminating two guns in the four-turret design would save about 3,000. More speed would be expensive. The board wanted to know how the British had attained 25 knots in their *Queen Elizabeth*s. Chief Constructor Taylor suspected that they had sacrificed armor, and believed, correctly, that some (in fact all) had failed to make 25 knots on trials. Moreover, the British carried far less fuel on trial: 900 or 1,000 tons vs. the U.S. figure of 2/3 of capacity, which might mean as much of a difference in speed as half a knot.

Preliminary Design therefore began work on the basis of twelve 16-inch guns and a speed of 23 knots but without any firm directives on armor or on secondary battery. Its six-turret sketch design was based on the Battleship 1917 study, but with three turrets superimposed forward. It had to be rejected, because it was expected to displace 46,000 tons. The more modest four-turret alternative was based on the *Maryland* design and was accepted by the General Board after successful salvo-firing trials by the new triple-turret battleship *Pennsylvania* (five hits out of twelve rounds fired at 19,500 yards). If guns were to be fired en masse, then, it was logical to mount them together.

Successful firing at ranges of 20,000 yards and beyond also clinched the argument for the largest guns. Admiral Strauss of BuOrd argued that his new 16in/50 gun could penetrate 13.5-inch belt armor (as in other U.S. battleships) at 20,000 yards, whereas the 14in/50 would penetrate it only out to 13,000. BuOrd claimed at this time that the 14in/50 was nearly as effective as the British 15-inch gun (which was expected to appear in new Japanese battleships), whereas the 16in/45 and the new 16in/50 were so clearly superior that they would place the new ship in a new category. As for the choice between the existing 16in/45 and the new gun, the weight differ-

ence per gun was only about 25 tons per gun, 300 tons per ship, or (in displacement) about 500 tons, a small price to pay for an enormous improvement in gun power. Strauss did not doubt that the new gun would succeed but asked that the formal characteristics of the ship be left open in the event of its failure, "I mean to say, there never has been a gun weighing 130 tons that we know of."

Given the existing standard of protection, the four-turret, 23-knot ship seemed to require a 660-foot hull and a 60,000SHP (twelve boiler) power plant, on a displacement of about 41,500 tons. Given the internal arrangement of the *Maryland* design, the boiler rooms were too widely dispersed for their uptakes to be trunked into two funnels. Quite early C&R had to accept that there would be four separate uptakes, two on each side of the ship. By early November 1916, it appeared certain that the General Board would choose the 50-calibre gun, and the designers reluctantly agreed to a displacement of 42,000 tons. They also sought steadiness, for good gunnery, by holding metacentric height to 5 feet. Hull scantlings (hence structural weight) would be cut by deepening the hull girder to reduce stresses.

BuOrd argued that so large a ship should be better protected than her predecessors, and Strauss convinced the board to call for half an inch more of both protective and splinter decks, and two inches more of belt armor. When the board realized how much the ship would grow as a consequence, it retreated to the original figures. C&R also sought better protection, by inclining the belt armor. It ordered tests of side armor inclined at 15, 20, and 22 degrees. In some sketches the belt above the splinter deck was inclined inboard (as in "Ironsides") to form a kind of turtle deck. But the chief constructor decided that existing data were too incomplete to justify so radical a step in so important a ship.

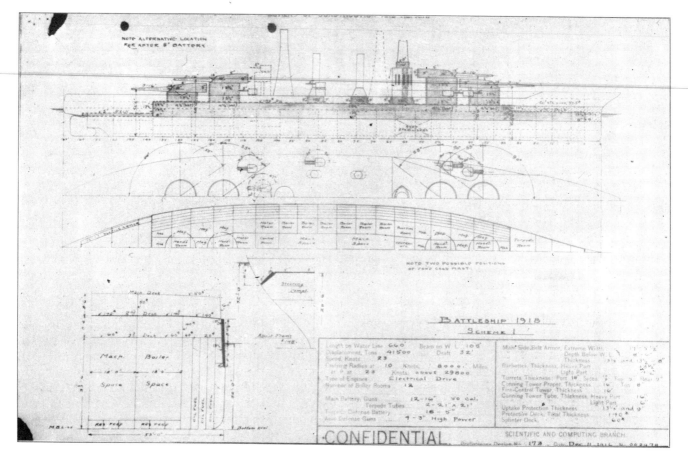

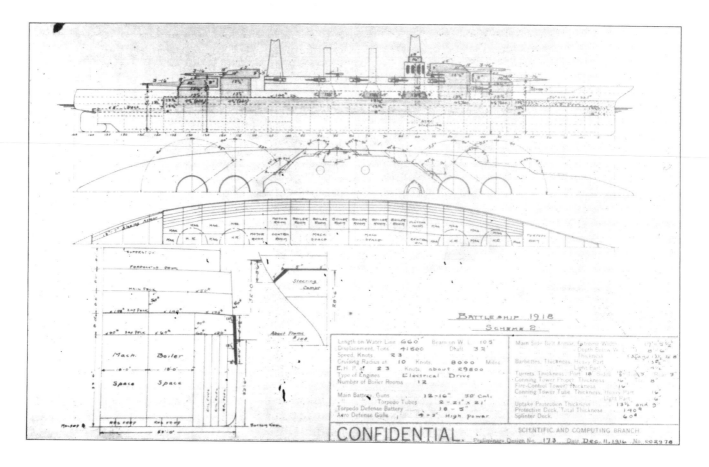

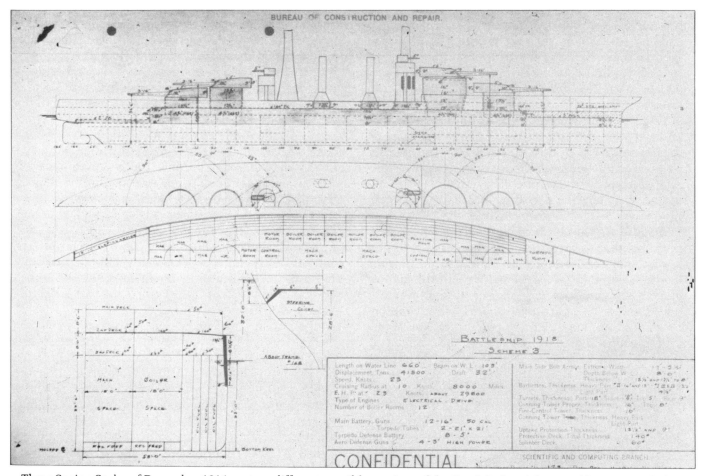

Three Spring Styles of December 1916 portray different possible versions of the *South Dakota* (*above and facing*), Battleship (Fiscal Year) 1918. Note the projected use of twin mounts for the secondary battery in Schemes 1 and 3. The latter was quite radical; the greatly enlarged No. 2 barbette would have doubled as a conning tower, with conning tower functions limited to an annulus around the barbette proper. The very limited secondary battery would have been raised on platforms. The other two schemes show the unsatisfactory location of the foremast directly on top of the conning tower, which it would have fouled had it been damaged in action. All of these designs show four separate smoke pipes.

Characteristics were approved by Secretary Daniels on 20 November 1916, and C&R now drew up a series of alternative sketch designs, or Spring Styles. They showed an improved armor scheme, in which a flat 5-inch deck (with 12 inch-7 inch slopes at its after end) ran aft over the steering gear. It replaced the lower (after) armored belt of previous designs. The weight saved was applied to a new lower belt forward, which was covered by a new forward 5-inch deck, in effect an extension of the splinter deck. In previous designs, a 5-inch deck on the first platform forward had covered the torpedo room. In these new designs, it was raised to third deck level and extended nearly to the bows. Above this deck the main belt extended as a 1 1/4 inch-STS layer, all the way to the bow, to reduce the effects of shell hits forward, which otherwise might force the ship to reduce speed. This change was based on reported European war experience.

As for the secondary battery, C&R argued that the four rather wet guns right aft might endanger the ship if their ports flooded in heavy weather. They were also too wet to be useful, and the bureau wanted them eliminated. The board approved, and decided that these four guns would also be removed from earlier ships under construction, BB40–48. The remaining guns were to be mounted as in the *New Mexico*s.

Topside arrangement was complicated by the great length of the machinery spaces. In particular, it appeared that there would be insufficient space between No. 2 barbette and the two forward smoke pipes to accommodate both the conning tower and the foremast. Unless the mast were well separated from the smoke pipes, its spotting position would suffer too much from smoke interference. The proposed solution was to combine conning tower and foremast. Yet C&R knew that the General Board had rejected earlier proposals to mount cage masts atop conning towers for fear that a falling mast would foul the main ship and fire control station.

C&R considered several unusual alternative secondary batteries. For some time BuOrd had been promising a blast-proof twin 5 inch mount. In Scheme 1, three of them were positioned on the main deck on each side, the two forward ones in a cut-out in the forecastle alongside Nos. 1 and 2 turrets. Another pair were atop pedestals alongside the two after turrets, to give them exceptional command. In an alternative sketch, the two after mounts were at conning tower level just abaft the mainmast.

Strauss argued that height and arc of fire, not the sheer number of guns, was essential, "In daylight a few can hold off an attack, at night not all the guns in the world can." In Scheme 3, then, the sixteen guns of Scheme 2 (the conventional design) were reduced to eight, in four twin mounts, all at conning-tower level or above near the two masts. Now, however, the conning tower itself would be blanked by the twin 5-inch mounts abeam it, and their blast might make it uninhabitable. C&R's imaginative solution was to use No. 2 *barbette* as a conning tower. Its diameter would be increased and an annulus around the barbette proper would form fire and ship control spaces. Admittedly there would be some interference because of the presence of the triple 16-inch turret right over the control positions, but the constructors thought that could be minimized by using periscopes held away from the guns.

The General Board and the Bureau of Navigation, responsible for the operating forces, were appalled. In action the triple turret would be far more than a minor irritation. It was hard enough to fight a ship using centralized instruments in a conning tower. How much worse with the instruments and personnel spread around a narrow gallery within a barbette? Even worse, for some time No. 2 turret had been used as a secondary fire control position. To use its barbette as the primary fire control would be to eliminate this reserve. Nor would it be popular to reduce the height of the main ship control position.

C&R retreated, discovering that it could solve its arrangement problem by trunking together the four uptakes into a single fat funnel. Now there would be space for a conventional foremast separate from the conning tower. This "quadruple funnel" was the major new feature of the design, the forerunner of numerous trunked uptakes in various navies during the interwar period. The trunking occurred entirely above decks and so did not affect the internal arrangement of the ship.

BuOrd was still dissatisfied with the secondary battery and with the proposed protection. It believed that, during a day action, the crews of open-mount guns would be disabled by the blast of the main battery. It also denied that the guns right aft would be too wet. It did, however, consider the usual pair of weapons right forward too wet. It suggested, too, that the usual quartet of guns atop the superstructure deck and the two in the superstructure abeam the after uptakes be eliminated. Two positions right aft could be restored, and the others replaced by twin mounts, for a total of twenty-four 5in/51. BuOrd also considered replacing the 5-inch altogether by a new 6in/53 but held back because the new weapon was not as handy and could not fire as rapidly. It was true that the 6-inch could hit at 12,000 yards, whereas the 5-inch would not hit beyond 8,000, but (reversing Strauss's view) the bureau argued that such weapons were primarily for short-range night work. In day actions destroyers would be dealt with by cruisers. The 6-inch shell was much more destructive, but the bureau noted that an 8-inch shell hit had failed to disable a British destroyer at Jutland.

The bureau also considered the 5-inch turret-top armor (compared to 8 inches for the conning tower roof) insufficient. It would be penetrated by 14-inch fire beyond 16,000 yards, and a single hit on a turret might destroy a quarter of the ship's firepower. During experimental firing against the former monitor *Puritan* (8 January 1917), 14in/45 shells at a simulated range of 16,500 yards just failed to penetrate 4-inch STS. Chief Constructor Taylor replied that any increase would be too costly in displacement, and the General Board and the secretary of the navy agreed.

The General Board effectively sealed the design on 24 January 1917. Twenty 5-inch guns were to be mounted in six twin and eight single mounts (with two twins atop the superstructure). By this time the General Board wanted to shift to 6-inch secondary weapons, and the chief constructor agreed that the fourteen 5-inch mounts of the 1918 ship could "without serious modification" become fourteen single 6in/53, with another two guns on the main deck. Located in the lower aft part of the superstructure, they would not suffer too badly from blast, although they might be wet. The board also wanted 4 inch rather than 3-inch antiaircraft guns.

The three ships of the 1918 program, BB49–51, should have been laid down in the fall of 1917 or early in 1918. World War One, however, intervened. Given the depredations of the U-boats, it was decided that all capital ship construction would be suspended in favor of destroyers, merchant ships, and ASW craft. The battleship designers were able to use their enforced idleness to refine their design. Early in 1917, it appeared that Battleship 1919 would be a modestly improved version of Battleship 1918. Given the suspension of new construction, however, both series would be built to a single improved design. Battleship 1918-19 became Battleship 1920-21.

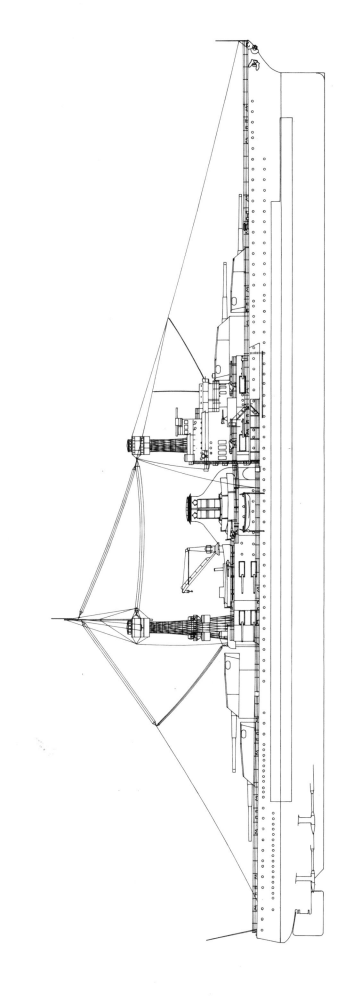

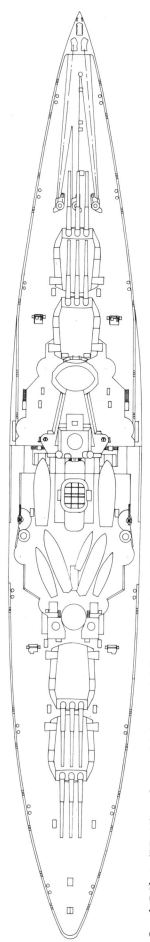

South Dakota (BB 49) as designed (above and following page), April 1919 (A. L. Raven)

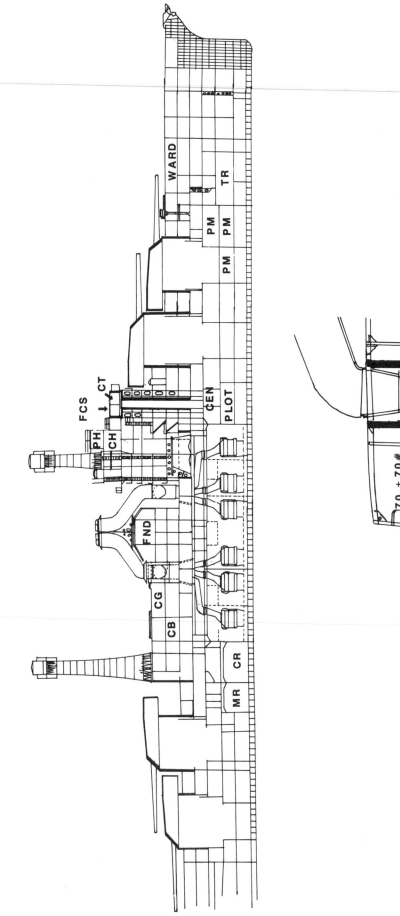

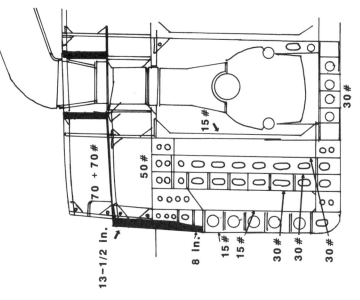

South Dakota (BB 49) (*above and preceding page*) as designed, April 1919 (A. L. Raven)

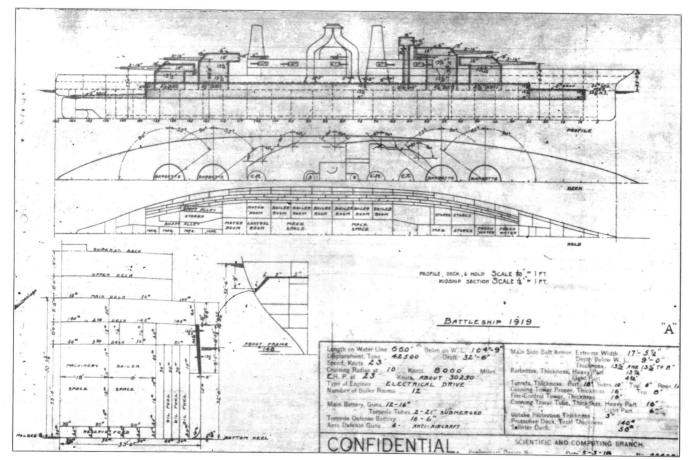

Battleship 1919, the *South Dakota* as designed, in a Spring Style dated 3 May 1918. The letter "A" indicates that this is Design A, to be compared with a range of fast capital ships described in this author's volume on cruisers. They were rejected by the General Board, which felt that a true fast battleship would be so revolutionary as to make all existing capital ships obsolete. This wartime design was substantially that chosen when the ships were actually laid down.

Influencing the revised design were very detailed accounts of British war experience, provided after the United States entered the war. In addition, the Royal Navy provided a young constructor, later the director of (British) naval construction, Stanley Goodall, who brought with him details of HMS *Hood*, with her inclined belt armor. A senior U.S. constructor, L. C. McBride, served on Admiral Sims's staff in London and thus became privy to much British experience.

The 1918 design was already quite tight. Its beam was limited to 106 feet by the Panama Canal, and draft was limited to a maximum of 32 feet 6 inches (fully loaded) for docking. The 1918 ship, however, was expected to draw 32 feet at *normal* displacement (41,500 tons), and draft would increase an inch for every 117 tons added. Even the usual allowance of 1/3 fuel oil between normal and full loads would bring the ship close to the limit. Thus, very small changes in the 1918 design would bring it outside the limits and would force a drastic redesign.

This point seems not to have been appreciated at the time. The delay caused by the war allowed BuOrd

once more to press for its favorite improvements. For example, in October 1917, its new chief, Admiral Ralph Earle, proposed again that the turret tops be 8 inches thick (and that they be flat, not sloped), to resist plunging fire. He also feared that, beyond 22,000 yards, the slope of the face of the turret would present a favorable angle to a plunging shell and argued that it should be as close as possible to the vertical, as in HMS *Hood*. The new threat of plunging fire made him suggest that the outer protective decks be 6 rather than 5 inches thick.

Earle also wanted greater elevation for the heavy guns, so that they could fire effectively at the greater ranges now apparently possible: 40 rather than 30 degrees. On the other hand, his bureau still objected to the 6-inch secondary gun, for its low rate of fire (with two bags of powder per shot) and its great flash (blinding effect). Surely the 5 inch would do. The British had just retreated from 6 inches to 5.5 inches in the *Hood* design. Earle speculated that they would have gone to 5 inches had a satisfactory weapon been available. He considered the 5in/51 perfectly satisfactory but wanted it in twin mounts because so few positions were available. Finally, Earle considered the 4-inch gun too large for efficient antiaircraft fire. Anything that could keep aircraft above a few hundred feet would make horizontal bombing ineffective. Nor was there any need for many such weapons—the British mounted only two in their battleships.

C&R was anxious to minimize changes from the 1918 design, in which so much effort had already been invested. Taylor wanted to keep the 5-inch secondaries but found that the 8-inch turret roofs would cost only 200 tons (including thicker turret backs, to balance the extra weight). He was also able to thicken the third deck aft (at a cost of 50 tons). He could not, however, provide vertical turret faces. In November 1917, Taylor estimated that Battleship 1918-19 would now displace 42,400 tons, and that it would draw 32 feet 5 inches, only an inch from the General Board's limit.

The other proposed changes would be more expensive: 120 tons for increased elevation (which would entail raising the turrets and dropping some of their machinery within the hull); 70 to provide 25-pound splinter protection between the secondary guns (a changed dictated by experience at Jutland); 120 tons for 6-inch guns; 6 tons to add more torpedoes (eight rather than six per tube); 99 tons for sturdier masts with splinter protection for spotters; 35 tons to thicken the third deck forward; 260 tons to increase deck height to allow for 6-inch guns. This total of 700 tons might almost be balanced if the 600-ton gyrostabilizer originally planned was abandoned. Even then, however, displacement would rise to 42,700 tons, and draft would increase to 32 feet 7 inches; the ship would have to be redesigned. Since he could alter neither the beam nor the draft, Taylor would have had to increase length to 675 or 680 feet, with attendant increases in armor weight. His assistants argued that, once such a redesign began, it would be wise to make generous allowances for improvements in torpedo defense, so that the ship might easily grow to 46,000 tons and a length of 725 feet.

The General Board could not accept so expensive a ship. It demanded that draft be held down but wanted the greater gun elevation, the thicker turret roof, and the thicker third deck. The secretary of the navy approved these changes on 29 January 1918. By now Taylor was very unhappy. His design kept growing in small ways, so that on 1 February he estimated a *normal* displacement of 42,000 tons (32 feet 3 inches) with a full load draft of 33 feet in prospect. The changes just approved would add another 800 to 1,000 tons. Perhaps the language of the board's characteristics could be changed so that the limitation would be on the *normal*, rather than the full load, draft. Meanwhile a redesign was in order.

Armor was a major weight, which could be reduced by sloping the side belt. Then thinner plating

would have the same ballistic effect as the 13.5 inches of the characteristics. In February, Goodall pointed out that at 20,000 yards, 12-inch plate would stop a 15-inch shell descending at an angle of 20 degrees. Perhaps, then, the constructors should try 12-inch plate inclined at 12 degrees. That would save 8.6 percent in weight. Angles of fall for 14-inch, 15-inch (British), and 16-inch shells at 16,000 and 20,000 yards were calculated, as it was assumed that battle range would be about 18,000. That gave an average angle of fall of shot of 16 degrees. In the end, the inclined armor was rejected for the battleship, but it was adopted for the contemporary battle cruiser design (described in the companion volume on cruisers).

Secretary Daniels was also unhappy. He had to order three battleships during fiscal 1919 and was therefore anxious for the General Board to make some definite choice. Taylor sought a fresh alternative, and on 9 April 1918 called a meeting of his designers, including Goodall, to work on a fast capital ship to replace both the battleship and the battle cruiser. This design, essentially a heavily protected battle cruiser, is described in the cruiser volume of this series. It was rejected by the General Board, which feared that the construction of a ship so obviously superior to all existing capital ships would touch off a building race.

That left some version of the 1918 battleship for the 1919 program. On 6 July the board accepted a normal draft of 33 feet and dropped the requirement for a gyrostabilizer, which in any case was suffering from very slow development. The final protection improvements amounted to the deck armor already noted, a 13.5-inch aft transverse bulkhead, and increases in air intake and uptake armor to 13.5 inch-9 inch. The latter amounted to a restoration to the original requirement after reduction to 3 inches to save weight.

Although a relieved Secretary Daniels signed the plans on 8 July 1918, construction could not begin until 1920–21. By that time the U.S. public was dissatisfied with the cost of naval construction, and pressure was building for suspension of battleship building. Compared with the other ships stopped by the Washington Conference, the *South Dakota*s would have been slower. They would also have been better protected than their Japanese rivals, particularly underwater.

In 1918, with the *South Dakota* design frozen, the battleship designers began afresh. They could expect to include multiple mounts for 6-inch guns, inclined armor, and possibly a new 18in/48 gun in any new design.

BuOrd considered casemate guns inefficient in their use of precious length, so that blast interference with the main battery was unavoidable. Toward the end of 1918 it began work on twin and triple 6in/53 mounts in gunhouses. A preliminary description of a triple mount was submitted to the chief of the bureau at the end of January 1919. All barrels were locked to a single slide, which could elevate to 75 degrees, the bureau already considering aircraft a major future threat. The guns had to be loaded at elevations of 20 degrees or less, and a powerful elevating motor would return them to the proper angle. Each gunhouse would stow 40 rounds per gun as ready service ammunition, with more in magazines.

One unlucky hit might now disable all three guns, but BuOrd expected future battles to be fought at such long ranges that hits would be few (only 8 percent at 20,000 yards) and randomly distributed. Then it might be argued that damage to the secondary battery would actually be reduced in that it would take up a smaller proportion of the deck area of the ship. As for fire control, each gunhouse would be equivalent to the group of individual casemate-mounted weapons formerly controlled together. Two triple turrets might be mounted on each beam. A fifth might replace the mainmast. In each case more gunhouses could have been worked into the available length, but BuOrd considered the arrangement chosen superior from the point of view of blast. It also calculated relative efficiencies. If a gun with a 360 degree command was rated at 100 percent, then the *South Dakota* battery could be rated at 36.87, the four gunhouses at 49.3, and the five at 54.44. The bureau also expected the five-gunhouse arrangement to save 165 tons compared with the less effective *South Dakota* battery. By the end of 1920, however, BuOrd was complaining that it had insufficient staff to complete the new gun-mount design in time for a proposed 1922 program.

Armor was another sore point. The new 16in/50 was so powerful that BuOrd and C&R agreed that much heavier protection was needed if a new ship was to be restored to the old standard of being protected against her own guns. The earliest idea was to increase the armor deck to 5 inches and the vertical side thickness to 16 inches. The thick part of the barbettes would have to be increased to 16 inches as well. Some weight could be saved by reducing the splinter deck from 1.25 to 0.75 inches in view of the increase in armor deck thickness. If these changes were applied to the existing *South Dakota* design, however, they would amount to a direct addition of 2,113 tons. The final change in displacement would be far greater. The *South Dakota* was already very tight, and its stability was not great. Although a metacentric height of not less than 5 feet had been specified, by the end of 1920 estimates were down to 3.45 feet. Since the curve of metacenters was still falling at the draft attained, additional weights, *even were they low in the ship*, would further reduce stability.

Any major weight addition would have to be bal-

anced. One candidate for weight reduction was the prized turboelectric power plant. The adoption of geared turbines would save 450 tons directly, and BuEng thought that two uptakes would then suffice, for a further saving of 180 tons. The light parts of the barbettes, shielded by a heavier armor deck, could be reduced from 4.5 to 2 inches (153 tons). The flat parts of the third deck could be reduced an inch (86 tons). The thin part of the conning tower could be reduced from 6 to 3 inches (8 tons). Perhaps, then, 969 tons could be saved but that still left 1,144 in direct weight. The deck and side armor of the new design would weigh 10,211 tons, compared with 8,631 for the original one.

The next possibility was inclined armor. C&R tried seven distinct schemes, developing three in some detail. In the simplest, Scheme 2, the 16inch - 10inch belt was inclined at 23.5 degrees. It would be impenetrable by the 16in/50 gun beyond 13,750 yards. The 5-inch deck would be proof inside 22,350 yards, although the 16in/45, falling more steeply, would penetrate at 21,000. By way of contrast, the *South Dakota* would have been penetrable at all ranges. However, Scheme 2 would have been expensive, total side and deck armor amounting to 10,770 tons.

Scheme 5 was an alternative. The designers reverted to the old "Ironsides" concept, in which some armor was inclined upwards, like the slopes of a protective deck. It would be most effective at short range, where shells would have flat trajectories. At long ranges they would strike at favorable angles. For example, a 10-inch plate inclined at 30 degrees to the horizontal would be immune between 15,000 and 21,000 yards, beyond which the ship would suffer in any case because of penetration of her deck armor. Total armor weight could be reduced to 9,570 tons.

The final step (Scheme 7) was to combine the two, to get the most out of the lower belt armor, in a "sawtooth" arrangement effective between 13,750 and 21,000 yards, at a cost of 9,685 tons. Another 430 tons would buy another half inch on deck and slope. Sloping the upper belt at 20 rather than 30 degrees would make this scheme more effective (8.5 inches at 20 degrees would match 10 inches at 30). However, C&R considered that this scheme was far too complex and preferred Scheme 2, which was only about 3 percent heavier.

The bombing tests of 1920 impressed BuOrd with the need to protect against this new weapon. Aircraft at 4,000 feet were able to make eleven hits on a ship dead in the water. Dropped from that altitude, a 16-inch shell would fall at 500 ft/sec and would penetrate 3.76 inches of armor. *If* a bomber could hit from 10,000 feet, the same weapon could penetrate 7 inches of armor. High explosive bombs could stop a ship by destroying her uptakes. BuOrd wanted an inch of armor to protect them.

The General Board met in November 1920 and then in January 1921 to draw up characteristics for a proposed Battleship 1922. The constructors abandoned any attempt to adapt the existing *South Dakota* design, and instead concentrated on much larger ships, of 45,000 or 50,000 tons, 695-feet or 710-feet long, capable of 23 knots. Beam was limited by the Canal to 106 feet. To gain sufficient internal volume within this limitation, both hulls were filled out to maximum beam over 20 percent of their waterline lengths, in contrast to previous U.S. designs which had had very limited parallel (full-beam) mid-bodies. Estimated metacentric heights were, respectively, 7.2 and 8.5 feet, with drafts of 31 and 31.5 feet. Speed would have matched that of the *South Dakota*, 23 knots. The program ended before detailed designs could be developed, but these figures suggest the trend.

The General Board appears to have had the existing 16in/50 battery in mind, even though BuOrd was well advanced with a new 18in/48. Work had begun in 1916, and in 1920 the bureau estimated the effect of mounting eight or twelve such weapons on a *South Dakota* hull (with armor unchanged except for turrets and barbettes). The resulting displacements were 44,500 and 50,000 tons. However, the gun was still incomplete, work stopping in 1922 when the Washington Treaty banned anything beyond 16 inches. It was completed as a 16in/56. Presumably the General Board preferred not to recommend it until it had been proof-fired. Very little correspondence concerning it has survived. Some estimates of the force it would exert when fired were used to suggest that it could not have been mounted in triple turrets.

Battleship 1922 never materialized. Several programs were proposed to follow the 1916 program, but none received popular support, and U.S. dreadnought battleship construction ended with the Washington Treaty. In the fall of 1924, however, Preliminary Design estimated weights and costs of a U.S. "treaty" battleship (that is, one limited to 35,000 tons). Presumably they were only for long-range planning purposes, since the treaty banned any new construction before 1931.

In its final version, the *South Dakota* was expected to displace 43,200 tons, which equated to a standard displacement of 41,400. Hence the 1924 study had to eliminate another 6,400 tons. Alternatives tried were a reduction to eight or ten 16in/50, and a reduction in speed to 21 knots (40,000 rather than 60,000SHP). In both cases the secondary battery would have been sixteen 6in/53 in single casemates and two above-water torpedo tubes. Machinery weight would have been saved by substituting geared turbines for the earlier turbogenerators, and protection would have matched that of the *South Dakota*, except that turret tops would be only 6.5 inches thick. June 1919 tests

had shown that this would suffice out to 25,000 yards. It was also assumed that underwater protection could be simplified, to save another 600 tons. Even so, not much was left for the belt, which could be no thicker than 11inch-6.5inch.

These estimates were revived in 1925 for the 1926 program estimates, and they probably formed part of the basis for the more extensive calculations begun in 1927.

The battleship design group also investigated some radical alternatives. Two series of studies deserve mention: an attempt to resolve the stability problems of the *South Dakota*; and a series of small-battleship studies.

The first series, dated June 1921, was prompted by the failure of the attempt to increase protection. C&R proposed that, when about to enter action, the ship take on considerable quantities of water in deep bottom tanks. It was inspired by design work on a large submarine, which showed that a low center of gravity (that is, a low metacentric height) could be coupled with a very large range of stability, even though it would also be coupled with limited reserve buoyancy. The latter would be acceptable if the ship were provided with such effective torpedo protection as to be virtually immune from flooding. So much

Table 7-1. Battleship Proposals for FY25 and FY26

Design	FY25	FY26
Length	640	625 ft
Beam	106	106 ft
Draft	31	31 ft
Main Battery	8	10 16in/50
Secondary Battery	16	16 6in/53
Torpedo Tubes	2	2 above water
Hull Weight	20,070	20,580 tons
Protection	6960	7180 tons
Machinery	2300	2800 tons
Power	40,000	60,000 SHP
Speed	21	23 kts
Cost		
Ord	$12.9	$13.7 million
Machinery		$4.8 million
C&R		$14.1 million
Equipment		$0.8 million
Ammunition		$4.5 million

NOTE: Side belt armor was to have been 11 inches thick, 16 feet 6 inches wide, tapering to 6.5 inches over the lower 6 feet 6 inches. Turrets: 16-inch face, 8-inch side, 6.5-inch crown, 9-inch rear; 11-inch barbettes with 2-inch bottom section. The ten-gun design differed from the eight-gun type in having triple turrets in Nos. 1 and 4 positions (barbette diameter 35 rather than 32 feet). Note the absence of antiaircraft weapons in the armament lists. Compared with the *South Dakota*s, these ships dispensed with torpedo bulkhead No. 3, saving about 600 tons. Machinery would have been geared turbine rather than turboelectric. These estimates were dated October 1924.

Table 7-2. Small Battleship Designs (1919)

Design	G1	H1	A7	B5	C5	D11	E3	F3	Louisiana
Speed	20	29	20	23	26	29	20	18	18 kts
Belt	13.5	13.5	12	12	12	12	12	12	11 in
LWL	520	710	520	570	650	710	530	500	ft
LOA	---	---	522	582	666	724	542	512	ft
BWL	93	98	92.5	94	95	96.8	94.5	87.3	ft
Bext	---	---	100.5	101.3	102	103	103	---	ft
Draft	26.5	31	26.5	28.6	30.1	30.4	27	26	ft
Displacement	25,000	37,750	24,000	28,500	33,400	37,000	26,250	21,500	16,000 tons
Power	14,800	62,000	14,200	28,400	43,200	62,000	15,200	8400	EHP
Weights:									
Hull	12,000	18,900	11,700	14,000	16,650	18,850	12,700	10,450	6352 tons
Fittings	1100	1750	1085	1300	1550	1750	1180	970	755 tons
Torpedo Protection	375	550	360	435	500	550	410	320	tons
Side Armor	5600	6900	4950	5500	5900	6140	5220	4800	3992 tons
Machinery	1420	3950	1350	2370	3250	3950	1400	800	1500 tons
RFW	185	500	175	350	500	500	190	105	50 tons
Armament	1000	1000	1000	1000	1000	1000	1350	1000	945 tons
Ammunition	790	790	790	790	790	790	1040	790	394 tons
Equipment	400	630	390	470	560	630	425	350	351 tons
Outfit	300	465	290	345	415	465	310	260	219 tons
Stores	340	530	330	390	470	530	355	295	228 tons
Fuel Oil	1440	1830	1375	1500	1665	1830	1500	1170	900 tons

NOTE: All of the sketch designs except E (six guns in two turrets) showed four (2 × 2) 16in/50 guns. The planned secondary battery was twelve 6in/53 in four triple blast-proof gunhouses. All were designed for a cruising radius of 8,000nm at 10 knots, compared with about 5,000 for the pre-dreadnought *Louisiana*, which is listed for comparison. Note that power is expressed in *EHP*, not in SHP. Depending upon propulsive efficiency, SHP would be about twice EHP. Note that, although she had much the same total weight of battery, she carried far less ammunition. The vast differences in hull weight can be attributed to the heavy deck protection of the 1919 designs.

of the hull would be below the waterline that a very narrow belt would suffice. Proposed protection consisted of a flat 5-inch deck with 10inch-4inch slopes, as in Scheme 5 (less the side belt). The propellers and rudders were also to have been protected. Sketches show auxiliary rudders and very widely separated propellers, and some form of tunnel stern may have been contemplated.

There would have been a number of problems. Internal space would have been severely limited by the very deep bottom tanks, and in action freeboard would have been small. It also seems not to have been appreciated that even the elaborate side protective systems of U.S. battleships of this period would probably have failed to protect against bottom explosions (in which all of the force of the explosion vents straight up). Much of the effect of a torpedo exploding against the side of a ship is dissipated as gas vents into the air. There might also have been structural problems. The proposed ship would have displaced 43,500 tons in normal condition and 56,000 when fully ballasted, with metacentric height reduced from 8.5 to 3.9 feet.

The other major alternative design was a small capital ship, an internal C&R study ordered personally by the Chief Constructor, Rear Admiral David W. Taylor. A man of independent thought, Taylor

may well have felt that ships were already much too large, and that important features were being sacrificed in futile attempts to prune back growth. As early as 1919 he must have seen that a properly redesigned *South Dakota* would displace 50,000 tons or more, far beyond what the General Board would accept.

That March, he asked Preliminary Design to prepare a series of designs with two twin 16-inch guns, 12-inch armor, the usual underwater protection, and speeds of 20, 23, 26, and 29 knots, one object being to show the effect of speed on displacement. This seems to have been the first U.S. attempt to design a small capital ship since the *Mississippi* of 1903. Taylor was very hopeful, he expected a ship about the same displacement as the pre-dreadnought *Maine* (13,000 tons) but longer, for higher speed. The last U.S. pre-dreadnought, the 16,000-ton, 18-knot *Louisiana*, was used as a point of departure.

Taylor's hopes were misplaced. The smallest of the new sketches, Design A (20 knots) came to 21,000 tons, heavier than the early dreadnought *Delaware*. The two twin 16 inchers equated to two triple 14 inchers, which shows the effects of deck and side protection: in 1908 designers had been able, on slightly greater displacement, to provide eight 14in/45 in twin mounts.

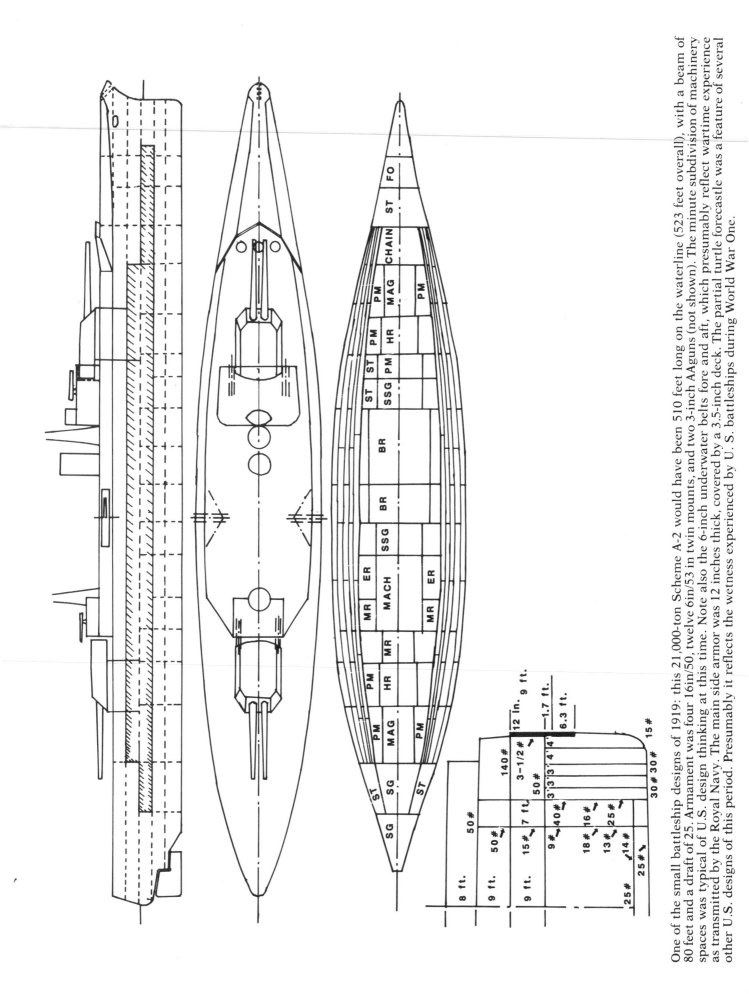

One of the small battleship designs of 1919: this 21,000-ton Scheme A-2 would have been 510 feet long on the waterline (523 feet overall), with a beam of 80 feet and a draft of 25. Armament was four 16in/50, twelve 6in/53 in twin mounts, and two 3-inch AAguns (not shown). The minute subdivision of machinery spaces was typical of U.S. design thinking at this time. Note also the 6-inch underwater belts fore and aft, which presumably reflect wartime experience as transmitted by the Royal Navy. The main side armor was 12 inches thick, covered by a 3.5-inch deck. The partial turtle forecastle was a feature of several other U.S. designs of this period. Presumably it reflects the wetness experienced by U. S. battleships during World War One.

Worse was to come. With secondaries in triple turrets and *South Dakota*-style protection, Design A would displace 24,000 tons. The 29-knot ship, Design D, was far worse—38,000 tons. Even the 23-knot ship would be about as large as the new battleship *Maryland*. It appeared that two knots equalled two 16-inch turrets. This calculation was complicated by the use of a larger 16-inch gun, and by the use of 6-inch guns in gunhouses, but even so the results of the study were sobering. In each case the estimated displacements could be pared somewhat by making more careful calculations, but they were still badly disappointing.

In April a new cycle began, Design A being modified with triple 16in/50 turrets as Design E, with a lower speed (18 knots) as Design F, and with a thicker (13.5-inch) belt as Design G. Design H was the fast ship, D, with the thicker belt. The results were uniformly unpleasant. Merely to modernize the old *Louisiana* while redistributing her battery in fewer turrets would add 5,500 tons (Design F). Design E, with half the battery of the *South Dakota* and with far less speed and armor, would require about 63 percent of her displacement, 27,250 tons. The fast ship with standard armor came to 37,750 tons, or 88 percent of the *South Dakota*.

Small battleships did not pay. Taylor's next answer to the inadequacies of Battleship 1919 was to add another 1,500 or 6,500 tons on the theory that growth just could not be checked. Later the U.S. position at disarmament conferences would be that adequate ships could not be built on very low displacements. This was largely because of the need to devote considerable hull volumes to underwater protection, just the factor that had driven up the displacement of the 1919 designs.

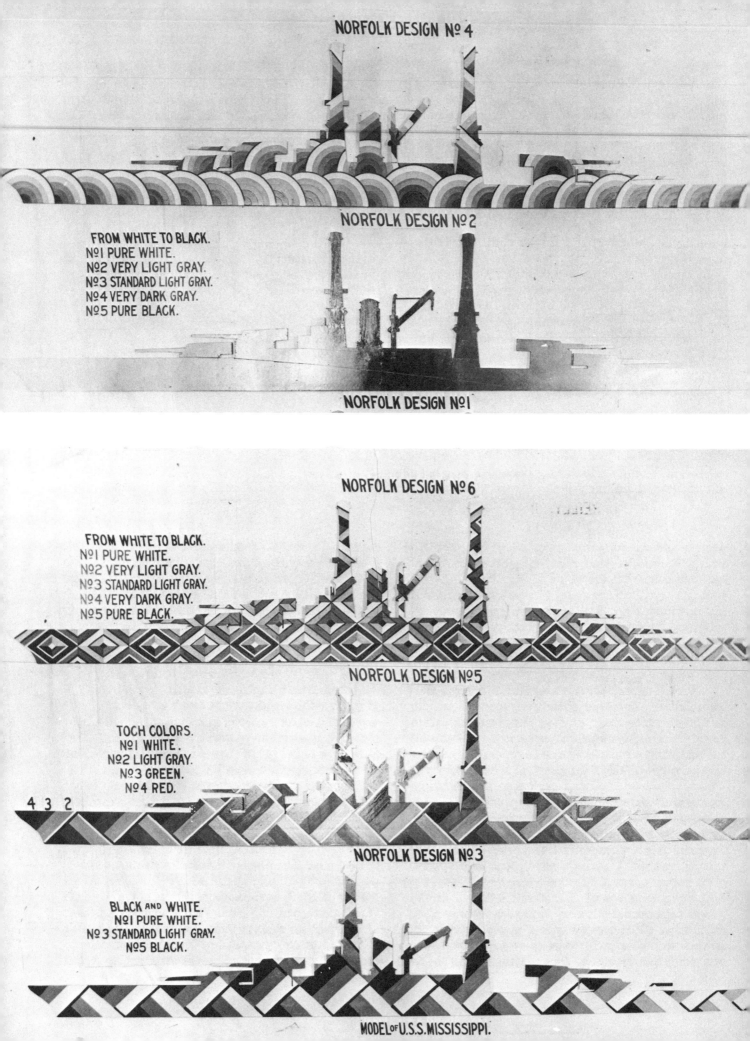

NORFOLK DESIGN № 4

NORFOLK DESIGN № 2

FROM WHITE TO BLACK.
№1 PURE WHITE.
№2 VERY LIGHT GRAY.
№3 STANDARD LIGHT GRAY.
№4 VERY DARK GRAY.
№5 PURE BLACK.

NORFOLK DESIGN № 1

NORFOLK DESIGN № 6

FROM WHITE TO BLACK.
№1 PURE WHITE.
№2 VERY LIGHT GRAY.
№3 STANDARD LIGHT GRAY.
№4 VERY DARK GRAY.
№5 PURE BLACK.

NORFOLK DESIGN № 5

TOCH COLORS.
№1 WHITE.
№2 LIGHT GRAY.
№3 GREEN.
№4 RED.

4 3 2

NORFOLK DESIGN № 3

BLACK AND WHITE.
№1 PURE WHITE.
№3 STANDARD LIGHT GRAY.
№5 BLACK.

MODEL OF U.S.S. MISSISSIPPI.

8

World War One

The U.S. battle fleet had only a very limited role in World War One, but, even so, wartime experience had enormous postwar influence. To a large extent that was because the war brought the fleet into contact with the most experienced battle fleet in the world, the British Grand Fleet. U.S. and British officers exchanged information very freely, and the Americans in many cases revised their practices on the basis of British experience. Moreover, operations with the Grand Fleet constituted the *only* American wartime operational experience between the Spanish-American War and 1941—and the only wartime operational experience with large modern battle fleets. The attitudes and practices adopted were, therefore, important in shaping the fleet of the interwar period.

There were two major themes. First, the ships had to operate in much worse weather than had been experienced in home waters. Problems of wetness, important enough prewar, were much magnified, and the physical appearance of the ships changed materially as a result. Second, although the prewar U.S. Navy had prided itself on its gunnery, it proved far inferior to the British in this respect, and U.S. fire control systems had to be revised. The improvement in U.S. gunnery continued in the postwar era, and it accounts for some of the important attitudes adopted during the 1930s, for example with regard to the value of surface ship torpedoes.

By far the most important U.S. contribution to the Allied naval war effort was in ASW, in the form of destroyers and subchasers. The pre-dreadnought battleships and armored cruisers were employed in training and in ocean convoy-escort roles. On the outbreak of war, only a few of the *Virginia*s and *Connecticut*s remained in active service, but all of the other pre-dreadnoughts were soon reactivated. The elderly *Oregon* became flagship of the Pacific Fleet. She escorted U.S. troops to Siberia in 1918–19.

Cruiser escort of convoys, particularly troop convoys, began as early as mid-1917. The armored cruiser *San Diego* (ex-*California*) was torpedoed on this service on 19 July 1918, sinking in twenty-eight minutes, the only major U.S. wartime naval casualty. Battleships were assigned as convoy escorts from September 1918. The *Georgia, Nebraska, Rhode Island, Virginia, Louisiana, New Hampshire*, and *South Carolina* served in this role. *Louisiana* escorted only a single convoy to Halifax; the others operated across the Atlantic, turning over their charges to local ASW escort forces in the eastern Atlantic. A typical fast convoy run might last a week, and most of the battleships covered one or two convoys. For example, on 17 September 1918 the *Nebraska* departed New York as principal escort of an eighteen-ship fast convoy, returning to Hampton Roads on 3 October. On the 13th she sortied with the large armored cruisers USS *Montana* and HMS *Edinburgh*, covering a twelve-ship convoy. She sortied with her last convoy on 13 November, in company with the armed merchant cruiser HMS *Teutonic* and the destroyer HMS *Talbot*. The pre-dreadnoughts helped carry troops home from France after the Armistice, much as their successors would in 1945–46.

More importantly for the future, six modern U.S. battleships were assigned to the Grand Fleet, as the Sixth Battle Squadron. Even though the Royal Navy already enjoyed a substantial numerical superiority, there was always a fear that the Germans would choose their time so as to take advantage of the need to refit British ships. Intelligence concerning the German capital ship program was, moreover, extremely poor. Through 1917 and 1918 the British believed that new German battle cruiser construction had already given them a substantial edge. Admiral Sir David Beatty went so far as to convince the War Cabinet to try to purchase some or all of the Japanese

Visually, the most striking World War One change to warships was dazzle camouflage, designed both to confuse submarine commanders and to frustrate enemy range-finders, the latter by breaking up the vertical lines used by coincidence devices. In practice, U.S. destroyers were camouflaged, but, except for some bow and stern painting, battleships were not. (Office of Naval History)

The *Florida* is shown in experimental antirange-finder camouflage at Norfolk, 23 November 1917. Note the triangles (baffles) on her foremast, and the broken shapes painted on her funnels and on her turrets. The stripes at the bow would confuse a submarine commander attempting to estimate her inclination, that is, her course. Note that she has already been fitted with permanent windscreens for her navigating bridge and torpedo-defense platforms, as well as an enclosed pilot house and 3-inch antiaircraft guns.

Kongo-class battle cruisers. On the other hand, it does not appear that the British encouraged the U.S. Navy to push completion of the six battle cruisers of the 1916 program, perhaps because they could not be ready in time.

By 1917, U-boat attacks on British trade had been so successful that oil stocks in the United Kingdom were quite low; the U.S. ships based at Scapa were all coal burners, using fuel readily available in Britain. On 25 November 1917 the *Delaware*, *Florida*, *Arkansas*, and *New York* departed Lynnhaven Roads for Scapa Flow, joining the Grand Fleet on 17 December as the Sixth Battle Squadron, part of the "fast wing" of the fleet—which says something for the speed capabilities of these U.S. ships, nominally no faster than their British counterparts. The *Texas* joined in February 1918, and late in July the *Arkansas* relieved *Delaware*. At least twice these U.S. ships accompanied the Grand Fleet on sorties.

During 1918 the British began to fear that the Germans would send one or more of their battle cruisers out into the Atlantic to attack a convoy, perhaps sinking troopships. Although the battle cruiser might ultimately be lost, such an attack would greatly improve German morale. Moreover, most of the Grand Fleet had to be available to meet the threat of the main German fleet. To some extent, these fears may have been fed by the German attack, early in 1918, on a convoy to Norway and by the failed High Seas Fleet sortie of April 1918. To counter this threat, the *Nevada* and *Oklahoma* were based at Bantry Bay, Ireland, from 23 August 1918. The *Utah* joined them on 10 September.

Of the remaining dreadnoughts, the *North Dakota* remained in American waters throughout the war, as did the *Pennsylvania*, the flagship of the Atlantic Fleet. She escorted President Wilson to and from France in 1918–19. Her sister, *Arizona*, arrived at Scapa Flow only on 30 November 1918, at which time resumption of hostilities still seemed possible. Neither the *New Mexico* nor *Mississippi* left U.S. waters for the duration.

Perhaps the greatest shock of contact with the Grand Fleet was the realization that U.S. naval gunnery was deficient. For example, a 1917 British divisional practice selected at random showed two minutes of trial salvoes, then four five-gun salvoes on target in 50 seconds. By way of contrast, a recent U.S. battle division practice (in which the salvoes were full broadsides, averaging ten shells) showed nineteen hits on a target at 20,000 yards in two minutes. American ships seemed to show excessive dispersion of fire, particularly at long range. Patterns as large as 800 yards were reported, although by June 1918 the *New York* was down to 400. BuOrd suspected that the secret was reduced muzzle velocity. However, the U.S. Navy was again plagued by excessive dispersion during the 1920s.

Unlike the Royal Navy, the U.S. Navy fired full (rather than half) salvoes, one officer suggesting that they made for much better spotting and hence for quicker hitting; another officer claimed that the second salvo would generally straddle the target.

American observers were impressed by British attention to massed fire. At Jutland they had found that, although four or even eight ships sometimes could see only one or two targets, they could not concentrate their fire effectively. By 1917, British officers claimed that the massed fire of one or two battle divisions could break up an enemy line, as Nelson had done. Without massed fire, they would be condemned to the indecision of Jutland. Thus the fleet fired by divisions, the flag or second ship acting as the master. Data were transmitted via a net of plotting room radios. Each ship determined an average range using her several range-finders, then radioed to the other ships in line. Firing was in successive time blocks. The master fired her salvo, at which time the others started their stop watches, which were marked in sectors. The master ship fired at one range, the next ship up 400 yard, and so on. All spotters in the division would observe the fall of shells. The allotted time per division, fourteen or fifteen seconds, was determined by the period of roll of the ships. The external indications of these concepts were the range clock, a visual indicator of the range at which a ship was firing, and the bearing marking painted on the side of the turrets.

Several U.S. observers concluded that, although the American fire control system was fundamentally superior, it was not nearly as well developed. In each case, the central problem was to determine the future range and relative bearing of the target ship. At long range, a shell took an appreciable time to reach its target. The guns also had to be fired at the appropriate point in a ship's roll. Both navies employed a form of centralized control (director firing), but they differed in the extent of centralization and in the means used to estimate future target position.

Position estimation was partly a matter of mechanical computation and partly a matter of the overall structure of the fire control/gunnery system. Target position had to be estimated on the basis of a series of range and bearing observations. Dr. Jon Sumida has pointed out that accurate projection required the solution, in effect, of a differential equation. The Royal Navy adopted the Dreyer Table, which employed a geometric (straight-line) approximation, mathematically deficient. The U.S. Navy ordered its

first Ford Rangekeeper in 1916, receiving it a year later. It was an analog computer that could actually solve the differential equation. Dr. Sumida has suggested that the rangekeeper was developed from, or at least closely related to, the Pollen "clock," a British instrument which was used in limited numbers during the war and which later evolved into the Admiralty Fire Control Table of the *Nelson*s and later British battleships. Ford computers were the basis of the very rapid postwar development of U.S. naval gunnery, and Navy confidence in such equipment also led to the development of such diverse mechanisms as the Norden bomb sight and the successful dual-purpose directors of the 1930s and 1940s.

The secrets of such computers were very closely guarded, but their characteristics determined battle line tactics through World War Two. In particular, successful gunnery required relatively slow maneuvering, to permit the computer to settle down to a solution. U.S. ordnance experts were, therefore, surprised by the radical maneuvers which the Japanese Navy adopted in connection with torpedo (fire and forget) attacks. The success of the Ford Rangekeeper and its successors also convinced the U.S. Navy that it was possible to hit consistently at very long ranges, so that aerial spotting was well worthwhile.

In U.S. ships, data were fed into a plotting room deep in the ship, where gunnery officers used their instruments to estimate appropriate ranges and bearings. More important, they plotted the trend of the data, and thus could (at least in theory) spot errors. Although the spotters and range-finders aloft were individually vulnerable, the plotting room was well protected, so that in theory the system as a whole could survive considerable battle damage. In U.S. practice, too, the role of the "directorscope" aloft was merely to sense the roll of the ship so that guns could be laid and fired properly. The British system was dominated by the director tower aloft. The compartment below decks was designated a "transmitting station." It housed the analog predictor (the fire control "table") which automatically processed data. U.S. gunnery officers claimed at the time that their system placed greater demands on the skill and intelligence of the gunnery team and consequently paid greater dividends.

The other major issue was the extent to which positive commands were fed to the guns. In 1917 the U.S. Navy transmitted only gun elevation. In a confused action, then, individual turrets might be firing at different targets at different ranges. The standard system, devised by the British, was "follow the pointer," in which a master indicator drove indicators at the guns. The gun crews in turn matched their own dials to those of the transmitters. A follow-the-pointer elevation system was introduced in 1918. The British transmitted bearing as well, so that the captain could designate a target, using a special pelorus in the conning tower. By late 1917, BuOrd was fitting spotting glasses with a bearing repeater which could match this feature. New fire control systems were fitted to the dreadnoughts *South Carolina, Michigan, North Dakota, Florida, Utah, Wyoming,* and *New York* during their yard periods, and to the others by a travelling team of BuOrd technicians, working aboard ship. The later pre-dreadnoughts were fitted with a simpler director system, since it was impossible to find sufficient space for plotting rooms. Ironically, the British had no repeaters to transmit turret bearing back into the plotting room, whereas U.S. ships had been so fitted even before 1917. As a result, British ships tended to show greater deflection (bearing) errors, although they found the range rapidly enough.

The most important elements of the new main battery systems were internal, but at this time ships also sprouted numbers of new long-base range-finders. Even before 1917, some dreadnoughts had had long-base turret-top instruments, free to rotate independently of the turrets, but only in wartime were large navigational range-finders atop their bridges. In addition, the pre-dreadnoughts were fitted with range-finders atop their turrets and forebridges.

U.S. observers were also impressed with the British practice of director control for the secondary battery, to the point that the U.S. Navy actually built duplicates of the British Vickers system. In 1917, U.S. secondary guns were individually sighted, with group control (and searchlight control) exercised by a fire control party in a "torpedo defense station" on each cage mast. The Vickers system automated this control by connecting "follow the pointer" indicators at the guns to a computer in the director. The main virtue of the director system was that it moved the sights well above the smoke and spray, for much better visibility and clarity. In October 1917 BuOrd planned to install two directors on each beam of the dreadnoughts, which were actually fitted postwar. Generally one was mounted on each side abeam the bridge on the 01 or 02 level, with another farther aft on the weather deck directly above the bulk of the secondary battery. In the flush-deck coal burners the after director was bracketed to the after end of the deckhouse amidships. It would later be claimed that such low positions were too wet to be useful.

The other aspect of war experience was the need to plate in bridgework and fire control tops in the face of North Sea weather. Prewar doctrine had been for ships to be controlled entirely from within the conning tower, to the point that the General Board tried to make open bridges so uncomfortable that captains would command from inside even in peacetime. U.S. officers in the Grand Fleet discovered that the Royal Navy considered its conning towers virtually useless, partly because good visibility was so

important in fleet steaming. Meanwhile, the captain of the fleet flagship *Pennsylvania* asked for greater space for a flag plot. The British had found that a fleet commander needed such a facility if he was to envisage his own and the enemy's formations.

Since plotting data automatically went to the central fire control station, it was natural to construct a rudimentary flag plot adjacent, on the fourth deck, directly beneath the conning tower. However, fleet commanders tended to stand on the bridge or in the conning tower, overseeing the fleet by eye as well as by plot. That was, at the least, a necessary corrective to possible plotting errors.

Moreover, the conning tower, even one so spacious as that fitted in the *Pennsylvania*, was relatively crowded, leaving space neither for the fleet commander nor for his own staff. He would, therefore, have to stand on the open bridge, and his staff on the signal bridge would block the view of the torpedo-defense party nearby. Enlarging and enclosing the bridge was the only solution.

Contemporary British practice varied: Admiral Beatty preferred the open bridge, whereas his predecessor as commander of the Grand Fleet, Admiral Sir John Jellicoe retired into the conning tower when the fight became general, that is, when he could no longer either see or really control his fleet. It followed that both captain and admiral needed the best possible vantage, at least up until the moment when smoke obscured the view of the nearby fleet. For example, in the new *Hood* the navigating platform had been adapted as a captain's position, and a separate bridge fitted for the admiral. The conning tower, however, was also enlarged, special captain's and admiral's positions being provided. The need for submarine lookouts high in a ship was yet another consideration.

The other side of the coin was fear that shells hitting the conning tower would burst and kill everyone on the unarmored bridges.

The General Board acted in March 1918. It distinguished ship control before an action (that is, from a navigating bridge) from control *during* action (from the conning tower). In the past, it had demanded that the open bridge actually be removable, to limit its obstruction to the view from the conning tower. Now it relaxed that requirement to allow for weather cover and splinter mattresses. It also demanded separate bridges for the admiral (signal bridge) and the captain (navigating bridge), so that the two would not interfere with each other. During the approach and during the action proper, the admiral might well wish to remain on his open bridge while the captain fought his ship from inside the conning tower. The admiral would, therefore, be provided with a narrow gallery around the conning tower; he could speak to the captain through the vision slits. The enclosed chart house atop the signal bridge would be divided into charts and navigational facilities for the captain and a flag section including a flag plot, bridge radio, telautograph,* and communication deck.

A flag range-finder atop the navigating bridge would provide data to flag plot.

C&R had, then, to modify existing bridges while designing a future standard type. The latter, developed by April 1919, consisted of a large chart house built on the after end of the platform surrounding the conning tower. Except for the first of the class, the *New Mexico*s were not yet in service. They were fitted with a rudimentary bridge structure rising from their 01 level, surmounted by an enclosed navigating bridge. The entire structure was dominated visually by a large octagonal torpedo-defense station.

Ships already in service went through two sets of alterations: emergency war modifications and then 1919–20 refits. In the former, bridges were enclosed and raised 8 feet to clear conning towers. Flag plot was located in the mast at the new bridge level. In the second series, from the *Florida*s on, an enclosed navigating bridge was built well above conning tower level, in many cases supported entirely by stanchions and by the foremast. This new structure was retained even when the coal-burning battleships were rebuilt later in the 1920s.

Distinctive angled baffles were fitted around torpedo-defense platforms and fire control tops, the latter being roofed and glassed-in. Postwar, the modern battleships were fitted instead with large octagonal (flat-sided) torpedo-defense platforms, which were covered over and glassed-in. The first to receive them was probably the *Mississippi*, which had them in the positions formerly occupied by the baffled platforms, that is, low on her masts, at funnel top level on the foremast, but considerably lower on the mainmast. Platforms above both carried four searchlights each. Her two sisters had their octagonal platforms considerably higher, about halfway up the masts, and so can be distinguished in contemporary photographs. *Pennsylvania* and *Arizona* were similarly refitted in 1919–20, but for some reason *Nevada* was not. The coal-burning *Arkansas* and *New York* classes were similarly refitted, the after top below funnel-top level to avoid smoke interference. The earlier classes were not modified; for example, *Utah* had no octagonal torpedo-defense platform until her reconstruction in the 1920s.

The mast head was clearly the best position of all for secondary fire control, but the cage masts fitted to existing ships (that is, through the *New Mexico* class) could not take much weight very high up. However, the *Tennessee*s introduced a new and much stronger cage mast. Their secondary battery controls were located in the lower of two enclosed mast-top levels. The upper level housed a main battery director. This arrangement was advantageous because it placed the main battery control on the centerline but allowed for division of secondary control between port and starboard batteries. The 5-inch directors proper were located in the bridgework and on the weather deck near the boat cranes, as in the *Idaho*s.

The next and final step was to move the 5-inch directors into the now much-enlarged control stations. In the "Big Five" (BB 43–48) this was done either soon after completion or even while the ships were under construction (in the case of the *Maryland* class). The instruments, after all, accounted for little of the weight of the enclosed director towers. In March 1925, the captain of the *Arizona* suggested that directors in his ship be relocated to the existing secondary control platforms up the masts. Although BuOrd strongly supported him, the work was not carried out, probably because the bureaus considered a move only half way up the mast an insufficient improvement. However, to provide heavier masts in all of the dreadnoughts would have been too expensive, in a time of fiscal stringency. The change was effected only when ships were rebuilt with strong tripod masts.

The secondary batteries themselves were rearranged. They had been considered wet even before the war, but only after the war was any action taken. In 1917–18, moreover, there was an urgent need for weapons to arm merchant ships. Thus on 26 April 1917, soon after the U.S. declaration of war, BuOrd was authorized to remove twelve 5in/50 and thirty-six 6in/50 from battleships and cruisers, together with one-hundred-twenty-four 3in/50 and twelve 4in/50. Two days later another one-hundred-eighty 3in/50 were earmarked, but by 1 October most of this supply had been exhausted, and a new wave of removals (twenty-eight 3inch, two 4inch, and twenty-six 5in/51) was approved. On 7 December twenty 5in/51, twenty 6in/50, four 5in/50, and twenty-six 3in/50 were ordered removed. Deliveries of new weapons from war production did not begin until the following April.

Many of these weapons came from the pre-dreadnoughts, because of the wetness of their secondary batteries. However, even guns high in some ships were removed. For example, by 1918 the *Indiana*s were down from twelve to four 3-inch, and *Iowa* had only four 4 inch left. The *Kentucky*s were cut to eight 5 inch (end guns only) and the *Alabama*s and *Maine*s to eight 6 inch (retaining all forecastle guns, but only four on the main deck). These ships were employed in home waters and were unlikely to see combat.

The much larger *Virginia*s and *Connecticut*s were employed as ocean convoy escorts. Guns were initially removed on an ad hoc basis. By January 1918,

---

* A device for automatically transmitting a handwritten message as it was written.

for example, the *Virginia* had removed two amidships 6-inch guns on each side, leaving four. The captain of the *Minnesota* wanted to retain the two forward groups of broadside guns. He considered these 7-inch guns useful only for torpedo defense and was willing to exchange them for upper-deck 6 inchers. Late in January, however, Secretary Daniels vetoed any further removals and ordered a study of the practicality of installing upper-deck 6-inch guns in the *Maine*, *Virginia*, and *Connecticut* classes. In fact many guns were removed, but the ports were not sealed, at least through late 1918.

The dreadnoughts were liberally stripped, because they were least likely to see combat. Some commanders argued, too, that hull ports right aft represented a positive danger to the ships. According to the captain of the *Pennsylvania*, the British battleship *Audacious* would not have been lost had she not flooded through her after gun ports. In general the foremost and aftermost weapons were removed. Ships with forecastles had all the after guns landed (for a total of eight weapons in the *Pennsylvania*s and later ships, and nine in the *Nevada*s, which had three guns on each side aft and a seventh on the centerline right aft). The flush-deck *New York* and *Arkansas* classes lost five each including, respectively, the second gun on each side forward and the 01 level open-mount (which was exposed to the blast of No. 2 turret). The guns were removed in stages. For example, by July 1918, *Arizona* had removed six 5 inchers (two out of four forward), among the oil-burners only *Oklahoma* retained her centerline gun right aft.

Ships serving with the Grand Fleet were spared until the end of the war. As for new construction, on 4 February 1918 the Navy Department officially authorized the deletion of all hull secondaries (four forward, four aft) in the *Tennessee*s, and on 7 February followed suit for the *New Mexico*s (although the first of the class was completed with all twenty-two guns). As the latter were well advanced, the eight casemates involved were plated over, but not faired in. The *Tennessee*s were completed without any evidence of the missing weapons.

War service in the Grand Fleet prompted many commanders to suggest that all main deck guns be landed, even if they could not be replaced. For example, the captain of the *Texas* wrote in May 1919 that during his entire wartime service, only four guns, the two open 5 inch and the two 3-inch AA guns atop the boat cranes, were ever manned at sea. They were also the only weapons he manned when at Battle Condition Three postwar. He found it quite rare to be able to use the lower-deck guns. Moreover, the sheer number of men required to man the lower-deck guns crowded his ship. Multiple mounts would be a better alternative. BuOrd considered a twin best, having rejected a triple as impractical. A special board,

formed in June, seconded this proposal. Only the aftermost two or four gun deck weapons would be retained. In the *New York*s, for example, there would also be four enclosed multiple mounts: on the centerline; abaft No. 5 turret and between Nos. 3 and 4; and on each side in place of the existing exposed single mount on the 01 level. The 5-inch battery would, then, be reduced to twelve guns (sixteen if BuOrd could be convinced to use a triple mount), but the broadside would be ten (thirteen with triples), comparable with that provided by the original twenty-one guns.

The arrangement in the two *Arkansas*-class ships would be similar, except that there would be only one centerline mount (No. 6 turret was so far aft that there was no space abaft it); the *Utah* and *North Dakota* classes would have two mounts on the 01 level and two on the main deck near No. 3 (superfiring) turret. BuOrd complained that in all of these schemes main deck guns would be subject to blast interference, and C&R believed that the centerline mounts would fall victim to splinters created when shells hit nearby turrets and barbettes. Admiral Rodman, who had commanded the U.S. battleships in European waters, particularly objected to guns mounted between turrets aft. He did want an improved secondary battery arrangement but preferred to retain the existing weapons until a satisfactory twin mount became available, because he considered it essential that some torpedo defense guns be available for drill.

Secretary Daniels steamed to Honolulu aboard the *New York* in August and was much impressed by the wetness of the lower-deck weapons. Given the need to lay up ships and reduce crews, he suggested that the time was ripe to decide definitely the torpedo-defense batteries of the dreadnoughts. If all the work were done promptly along standardized lines, the ships would be ready for the new crews, the men being recruited to replace the wartime Navy. Alterations would be kept to a minimum to save money, "and with due regard to the age of the ship."

The *New York* and *Texas* had already had additional guns removed, respectively, the remaining two and four foremost guns, leaving totals of fourteen and twelve 5in/51. C-in-CPac authorized these changes on 9 and 12 July 1919. On 23 September, however, the department ordered all but the four aftermost gun deck guns (two after most in the *North Dakota*s) removed from the coal-burners. As of 19 November, only the *Texas* retained her gun deck weapons.

The General Board concluded that the proposed alterations substituted blast for weather interference. On 13 November it suggested what it considered the best of several bad alternatives. The earlier dreadnoughts would retain single 5-inch guns as both interim and ultimate batteries, since they had only limited operational life remaining to them. The *New York* and *Arkansas* classes would be refitted with single 5-inch guns in new positions as space reservation for the planned ultimate twin-gun batteries. For a time they would, therefore, have to operate with half-batteries of eight guns each. They would have two positions on each side right aft on the gun deck, one on the main deck and one on the 01 level right above.

Quite soon, however, BuOrd had to admit that its twin 5-inch mount was nowhere near completion. On 22 November the program was abandoned, and by December the yards were reinstalling guns in their original positions. The *North Dakota*s and *Florida*s were returned to their former state. In the *Arkansas* and *New York* classes, the only weapons eliminated were the five originally ordered landed. In theory, the foremost guns were eliminated to improve watertightness, and the centerline gun right aft could not fit properly into the new quadrant broadside fire control system.

The entire story is worth telling because it suggests the extent of dissatisfaction with the original designs. This view would reemerge within a few years as the battleships surviving the Washington Treaty axe were rebuilt.

At this time, too, the U.S. Navy began to employ antiaircraft guns. The first were 3-inch guns atop the turrets of the *Texas* in 1916. In wartime, the standard battery in the coal-burning dreadnoughts was a 3-inch gun atop each of the two derrick posts. The oil-burners incorporated antiaircraft weapons into their original designs.

At the end of the war, the standard battery was doubled to four 3in/50, and extra guns were installed during the big postwar refits. At this time turret-top weapons reappeared in the *New York*s, pairs surmounting Nos. 3 and 4 turrets. In the *Pennsylvania*s two guns were mounted atop No. 3 turret, with two more on forecastle platforms just forward of the secondary directors.

In 1921 the standard was again doubled, to eight 3in/50, two guns on each side replacing one of two open 01-level 5in/51 antidestroyer guns. The standard battery, then, was twelve 5in/51 and eight 3in/50; the *Colorado*s were completed in this form.

The value of the unique American cage mast came into question at this time, for two reasons: *Michigan*'s mast collapsed dramatically in a gale; and officers serving with the Grand Fleet had their first opportunity to compare their own masts with the heavier British tripods.

One night in January 1918, the *Michigan* was rolling heavily in a gale so severe that four ships of Battle Squadron Two had already lost their topmasts. She rolled heavily to port, then almost immediately lurched back to starboard, whipping the top violently to port. The mast failed at its narrowest point,

the heavy fire control top falling to port, and the mast snapping at about the level of the torpedo-defense station. The collapse was not particularly violent, and both men in the top at the time survived. However, any such failure had to bring the structural integrity of the entire mast into question.

The *Michigan* was to some extent a special case. Her mast had originally been mounted atop her chart house, and when that was removed, it was bodily lowered to the deck, elements being added to the upper end to obtain the necessary height. Diameter at the base was therefore increased from 9 feet 6 inches to 14 feet, concentrating stresses at the weakest point in the mast. No stress calculation was, however, done by the yard. Moreover, when the mast buckled, stresses were not taken up by other structural members, as they should have been. Some time before, one of the ship's 12-inch guns had exploded, fragments being driven through the mast just about where it later failed. Repairs had not included the reconstruction of the mast as a whole.

An emergency inspection of existing masts showed some buckling in the *Connecticut*. C&R concluded that, as a corrective, new masts should have a greater diameter at the top, and that all elements should be continuous from bottom to top. One problem appears to have been the sheer difficulty of inspecting cage masts or, for that matter, of replacing defective elements. During the 1920s and 1930s there were periodic scares. Every so often wholesale inspection would show large numbers of corroded elements, particularly in mainmasts exposed to funnel gases.

Many serving officers charged that C&R defended the cage mast more out of conservatism than logic. Those with the Grand Fleet were particularly impressed by the British tripod, which they had never seen at firsthand. The constructors argued that first impressions could be misleading. For example, although only the tripod was stable enough to carry a range-finder at its head, funnel smoke from other ships often made that instrument unusable. Although the tripods did not vibrate at speed, an American gunnery officer, Lieutenant Commander W. R. Furlong (later chief of BuOrd), considered motion upon firing a salvo fully as violent as that atop a cage. Officers of both navies believed that the cages were taller than the tripods, and hence more visible at a distance, but in fact both were about the same height. Finally, the tripod with its large fire control top weighed about three times as much as a cage mast.

Any decision to abandon the cage mast would have been costly. Twelve battleships (BB 43–54) and six battle cruisers were either on order or under construction. All would have the heavier cage mast and the more massive fire control top. Even so, the extra weight of tripods would probably have precluded installation of a second fire control top aft. Moreover, the cage mast still seemed to offer greater survivability under fire. The C-in-C Atlantic Fleet noted, too, that abandonment of the mainmast would greatly reduce radio range, which he considered very important: "It does not follow that because British ships in the North Sea are using radio only for short range work, American vessels will never have long range work to do. The opposite conclusion is more reasonable."

In June 1918, C&R asked Stanley Goodall, who represented the British constructors in Washington, to have the British DNC department make its own analysis of tripod vs. cage masts. The British view was that American practice would necessarily follow the British, with more and more fire control structures high in the mast. The new battle cruiser *Hood*, for example, had a 15-inch control tower, two 5.5-inch directors, a 15-inch director with a 15-foot range-finder, and two 9-foot range-finders for her 5.5-inch guns, all atop the mast, plus a torpedo lookout, and a searchlight platform. Goodall himself had made a point of being in the tops of the *Courageous*, *Glorious*, and *Furious*, in the latter when the heavy gun was fired, and was much impressed with the rigidity of the top. However, (U.S.) Naval Constructor W. G. DuBose (later chief of C&R), found the top of one of the *Royal Sovereign* class inferior to the tops of cage masts. "I cannot combat this statement, as the only time I have been in the top of an American ship at sea was in the *Mississippi*, when the speed was only 12 knots and the sea was quite calm." However, "only this week [July 1918] an American officer told me that he was in the top of the *Mississippi* when a broadside was fired, and he was thrown down as a result. I have never heard of any similar experience in the top of British ships." Goodall quoted DuBose as stating that the vibration in the top of the ship of the *Royal Sovereign* class at about 20 knots was very severe whenever the helm was used.

The Royal Navy also reacted to its exposure to American standards. A postwar summary of remarks by British constructors claims that in sanitation, living conditions, and ventilation

the latest British ships are far ahead of . . . U.S. battleships. . . . In the installation of what are conceived to be luxuries for the men there is no doubt that the American ships are ahead of ours. Whether this is a desirable position or not is an open question. It must be remembered that American Blue jackets are not seamen by birth and tradition, and, moreover, in many respects they are drawn from a class which is more used to luxuries than that from which British seamen are recruited. Hence it is essential that provision should be made in American ships for what are regarded as luxuries in the British service. The reports make it very clear that the provision of such luxuries in a fighting ship is difficult, and has been made at the expense of what is really more essential, namely, good sleeping accommodation. In the *Mississippi* and *New Mexico*, men were sleeping in conditions which could be regarded as untenable according to latest British standards. As these reports, however, rightly state, it is probable that American Blue jackets would prefer to have these luxuries at the expense of better sleeping accommodation, although the wisdom of such a preference is doubtful. . . .

In view of the difficulties which, as these reports indicate, arise from the provision of such luxuries, it is evident that it would be undesirable to force them into British ships ahead of their time.

With regard to office accommodation, to organization, and equipment of American offices ashore are more elaborate than is the custom in Great Britain, and it is natural that a similar comparison would hold between office organization and equipment in British and American ships. Several American officers have given their opinion to me that the clerical work in American ships is much overdone, and that specialist officers as a result spend too much time in keeping their papers in order, and too little time in developing the efficiency of their departments. In this particular it seems advisable to take American experience in the light of a warning, and attempt to slow down the pace at which increased numbers of offices and increased clerical work have been introduced into the British Navy. . . .

While at the Bureau of Construction and Repair, Admiral Rodman's report was considered by Naval Constructors in conjunction with me, and it was generally conceded that the demands of the Navy for offices could only be met at the expense of accommodation.

The remarks on the greater extent of space given to workshops and the larger extent of repairs carried out in American ships is of interest, but again the conditions in the American service differ from those in the British. The voyage of the American fleet around the world during President Roosevelt's administration led to the adoption of the present policy. The British Navy is in general more fortunate on account of the number of bases from which ships can work and again it would seem desirable to profit from American experience and if possible reduce the amount of space given to workshops.

The conning tower slots in British ships were much favored by American officers, but the U.S. Naval Constructors pointed out that the small slots in American conning towers were introduced as the result of experience in the Russo-Japanese War, they rather doubted the wisdom of discarding this experience merely because it had not been repeated during the recent actions.

The consumption of fresh water in American ships is notoriously great. Again, this is partly due to living conditions in the United States. Americans drink immense quantities of water and use shower baths freely. These, coupled with a more elaborate system of steam heating necessary as the American cannot live in

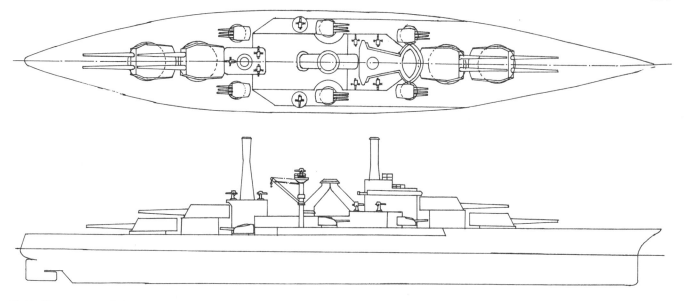

BuOrd's concept of the battleship of the future, a sketch dated 14 August 1919, drawn to accompany a proposal for triple 6in/53 secondary mounts. The main battery is eight 18in/48, a gun then under development, and the nine anti-aircraft guns were probably 5in/25's. No dimensions were given; this sketch was intended only to show the advantages (in terms of arrangement) of the triple 6in turret, six of which are shown. Each gun would have elevated to 75 degrees.

temperatures to which Englishmen are accustomed, and the fitting of a laundery, result in a larger consumption of fresh water.

However, the final DNC report, prepared in March 1919, attributed much of the congestion of U.S. ships to additional complement due to war alterations and cautioned that the Royal Navy, too, had had its share of excess office requirements. In some ways, too, the U.S. Navy had advantages in the sophistication of its equipment. For example, it was able to operate ships from the conning tower partly because it could rely on the gyrocompasses much more than on the magnetic compasses, in distinct contrast to the Royal Navy.

Finally, during World War One the U.S. Navy encountered a Grand Fleet liberally supplied with ship-launched fighters. Prewar U.S. interest in shipborne aircraft had been concentrated on catapult-launched reconnaissance seaplanes. In the Grand Fleet, however, the aircraft were fighters, intended to deny the air to German reconnaissance zeppelins and seaplanes. They were launched from short runways built over the gun barrels of superfiring turrets.

The *Texas* was fitted with such ramps on her Nos. 2 and 4 turrets, possibly as early as March 1918. She flew off an airplane while anchored at Guantanamo Bay, 9 March 1919. On 2 July similar installations were authorized for all of the existing oil-burners, and all were completed by September 1920. Each had four turrets, with two superfiring.

Experience was not entirely satisfactory. In November 1919, for example, the captain of the *Pennsylvania* complained that, when an airplane was on the forward flying-off platform, it masked the view from the navigating bridge for 25 degrees to each side, so that the ship could not be conned. In the *Nevada*, the guns could be elevated only to 5 degrees, and that very slowly. When the guns were depressed, they vibrated badly; it was impossible to fire the superfiring guns. C&R recognized the problem and unsuccessfully sought alternative locations. By September 1920, it was hoping instead to fit turntable catapults (then already under development) on the weather deck fore or aft. In October, the General Board formally rejected flying-off platforms for the *South Dakota* class, preferring catapults.

The construction of a prototype catapult at the Philadelphia Navy Yard was authorized in January 1921. That April, BuAer suggested that the *Colorado*s be fitted with two catapults each, one forward and one aft. The OpNav Plans Division wanted one catapult for every battleship, battle cruiser, and light cruiser. By June, the department was asking for bids for installations in the *Nevada* and *Oklahoma* ($21,823 for the catapult and $3,574 for installation). The prototype was installed aboard the *Maryland*, and five more ships (*Idaho, Mississippi, New Mexico, Tennessee*, and *California*) were to be fitted with a more powerful Mark II (6,000 rather than 3,000 pounds capacity). The *Arizona* and *Pennsylvania* had to wait for later installations.

9

The Washington Treaty

Every battleship built in the world after 1918 was greatly affected by the Washington Naval Arms Limitation Treaty of 1922, both directly, by limitations built into the treaty, and indirectly, by what other nations—potential opponents—had been able to modify from existing hulls or build afresh. Another important factor was the sharp contraction of the world's arms industries because of the slowdown of major naval construction immediately after the conclusion of the treaty. This chapter is concerned not so much with the origins of the treaty but, rather, with its consequences.

Throughout the interwar naval treaty negotiations, the massive industrial strength of the United States was a key factor. It was most evident during and after World War One but remained important even during the Great Depression. The major rival powers, Britain and Japan, were both far weaker. Although Britain led the world in naval construction before 1914, the strains of war were severe, and companies such as Vickers never really recovered from it. Japan severely strained her own economy while trying to match U.S. naval strength during and just after the war. Of the other major powers, France was essentially bankrupt and Germany, the theoretical prewar adversary, disarmed.

At the end of World War One, only one capital ship of the 1916 program, the battleship *Maryland*, had been laid down, and enormous sums remained to be spent. Britain had four fast capital ships under construction, but the Admiralty had already decided to complete only one of them, HMS *Hood*. In American eyes, well trained by exchange naval constructors such as Stanley Goodall, the *Hood* was extremely impressive, clearly the prototype of future

fast battleships. Americans were also aware of the extensive modifications carried out in the Grand Fleet after Jutland, for example, reinforcement of deck armor and improvements in fire controls and in torpedo protection. "Bulges" or "blisters" were added—streamlined cofferdam structures built outside the original hull—to keep torpedo explosions away from the vitals of the ship. The makeshift character of these improvements and the superiority of the American oil-burning battleships of the *Nevada* and later classes seem to have made little impression on the U.S. Navy. A dispassionate analysis of British finances and commitments in 1918–19 would have shown very little capacity for an extended program of new construction.

Japan, on the other hand, was unbloodied. In 1915 her government obtained statutory authority for an "8–4" fleet, consisting of eight battleships and four battle cruisers, all under age. This was increased to 8–6 in 1918–19 and to 8–8 in 1920, when it was planned to lay down two capital ships per year for the next eight years. It could be assumed that the Japanese were well aware of British war experience, and Japanese secrecy made it difficult for the United States to obtain details of the new ships.

Perhaps the greatest factor of all was the very general feeling that World War One had been fought to end wars for some considerable time. It was impossible to reconcile this view with any major program of new naval expenditure. Moreover, many believed that the pre-1914 Anglo-German naval arms race had contributed to the outbreak of World War One. The U.S. Congress was, therefore, reluctant to appropriate sufficient funds to complete the 1916 program. However, it was clear that only the United States

The Washington Treaty provided both for discarding large numbers of ships and for reconstructing the survivors. The first U.S. all-big-gun ship, *South Carolina*, was used to test the torpedo-protection blisters planned for reconstruction of the existing battleships. She is shown at the Philadelphia Navy Yard, 26 May 1924, before and during the first explosion. The blister is the dark area amidships. Another experimental blister was built on her other side. Note the removal of her turrets and her fire control tops, as a measure of demilitarization in compliance with the new treaty.

had the industrial strength to win a naval arms race, and it was this last perception that ultimately brought Britain and Japan to the negotiations.

The U.S. government was well aware of the leverage it held. In December 1918 the Wilson Administration presented a new three-year program including ten more battleships and six more battle cruisers. The threat that it would be implemented was used to force Britain to support the League of Nations and to adopt a clause in the League Covenant supporting the Monroe Doctrine. The British knew that Congress was reluctant to support the new program, but they could not afford to chance its adoption.

Through 1919 and 1920 the General Board continued to consider new construction programs, albeit considerably smaller ones: two battleships and one battle cruiser for FY21 (December 1919); then a three-year (FY22–24) program (July 1920) including three battleships, one battle cruiser, four aircraft carriers, and thirty cruisers. Meanwhile the 1916 program ground ahead.

The Admiralty, with a pre-Jutland fleet subject to decidedly post-Jutland conditions, sought eight new ships: four battle cruisers to be laid down in 1921; and four battleships in 1922. The Japanese 8–8 program would have built up a fleet of twenty-seven capital ships by 1927.

This was a naval race no one really wanted. As early as October 1920, the influential Senator William E. Borah called for a disarmament conference. Congress showed a marked reluctance to fund the completion of the 1916 ships. On 8 July 1921 the U.S. secretary of state, Charles Evans Hughes, invited Britain, Japan, France, and Italy to meet in Washington. He opened the conference on 12 November with a striking proposal. He suggested that all ongoing programs should cease and that there should be a ten-year holiday in naval construction, at least in capital ships; that further reductions should be made through a program of scrappings; that the general balance of naval power (measured through total capital ship tonnage) should be maintained. The main exception to the tonnage ratio was an attempt to limit the number of modern (that is, post-Jutland) battleships. No effort was made to distinguish between the U.S. and Japanese ships, and there is no evidence that the U.S. Navy had any evidence of the details of the Japanese ships. The simplistic tonnage measurement was characteristic of the naval arms limitation treaties, and ultimately it was subject to a remarkable range of sophistry and outright cheating. Even so, it exercised great influence on the design process.

As for the overall ratios, the main effect was to legitimize the U.S. demand for parity with Great Britain, in the famous 5:5:3 ratio (the low end for

Japan). Hughes offered to scrap fifteen of the sixteen 1916 ships, as well as fifteen older U.S. battleships (up through the *South Carolina*s). By this time the first twelve U.S. battleships (pre-dreadnoughts) had already been stricken, and the oldest units on the effective list, the *Virginia*s, were already scheduled for scrapping. As for the Royal Navy, Hughes wanted the four 1921 ships stopped and nineteen older ones, all dreadnoughts, scrapped—all of the 12-inch gun ships, the battle cruisers of the *Lion* and earlier classes, and the *Orion* class 13.5-inch "super-dreadnoughts." Japan would cancel eight ships and scrap seventeen more, leaving her with one 16-inch ship, four 14-inch battleships, four 14-inch battle cruisers, and one surviving 12-inch dreadnought, *Settsu*.

Although these proposals were greeted with horror, in fact they merely called for the elimination of many older ships which would in any case soon be relegated to minor roles. It is, however, striking that Britain alone would have to scrap dreadnoughts, some of them newer than ships the other parties would be retaining. On the other hand, the British ships had seen hard war service and many were already, in 1921, on the sale list. For example, in November 1921 an Admiralty report listed the two remaining semi-dreadnoughts, *Commonwealth* and *Agamemnon*, in subsidiary roles (paid off and fleet target service, respectively). HMS *Dreadnought* had already been stricken. Of the next nine ships, *Bellerophon* had already been sold, and *Vanguard* blown up in 1917. *Superb* was in commission for experimental work, which in her case meant shell attack. *Colossus* served as a cadet training ship, about to be replaced by the super-dreadnought *Orion*. A few battle cruisers and the early super-dreadnoughts were already in reserve. Unless some new war were to come very soon, none of these ships could realistically be considered a national resource.

The Hughes proposals formed the basis of the treaty, although there was considerable negotiation. For example, the Japanese attempted to raise their ratio from 60 to 70 percent, dropping their demand only when the United States agreed not to fortify Pacific islands. The Japanese also claimed that one of the ships listed as under construction, the *Mutsu*, was complete and thus should not be scrapped. She was exchanged for the *Settsu*. Japan now had two post-Jutland ships armed with the new 16-inch gun, which had to be balanced by new U.S. and British ships: two more *Maryland*s and two new British ships, which became the *Nelson*s. As compensation, the United States agreed to scrap two more dreadnoughts, the *North Dakota*s, and Britain the three *King George V* class super-dreadnoughts and HMS *Erin*, all armed with 13.5-inch guns roughly comparable to the U.S. 14 inch. The United States would then have eighteen and Britain twenty capital ships.

The *Nelson*s would be the first capital ships built under the treaty, which had to provide qualitative limits to be imposed on any future ships: the 16-inch gun and a *standard* displacement of 35,000 tons. Standard condition was defined as ready for sea, but without fuel and reserve feed water. This definition was intended to reduce the disparity between long- and short-range battleships, for example, between British and Italian practice. An American attempt to exclude stores as well was, however, defeated. The 35,000-ton limit has been attributed to the British, the DNC having estimated what he needed to accommodate the necessary post-Jutland features.

At the same time future *total* fleet size (tonnage) was fixed. The treaty also limited modernization of existing battleships, which, nevertheless, was the major capital ship design activity of the next decade, as described in the next chapter.

The total size of cruiser fleets was unregulated. It was, then, important to maintain a gap between cruisers and capital ships, as otherwise ships nominally built as cruisers might fill capital ship roles. Hence the significance of the 10,000-ton limit on cruiser tonnage and of the 8-inch limit on cruiser gun calibre. Ironically, the Germans, who had never been invited to sign the Washington Treaty, were limited by the Versailles Treaty to *battleships* of 10,000 tons mounting 11-inch guns. They chose instead to build what amounted to super-heavy cruisers, which fell exactly between the cruiser and battleship classes: the "pocket battleships." Since the treaty had spared few battle cruisers, the new German ships inspired the construction, where possible, of a new generation of very fast battleships, which in turn destroyed the neat distinctions set up in 1921.

As for Pacific tensions, the United States gained abrogation of the Anglo–Japanese Alliance in favor of a more general Pacific security system. On the other hand, Japan gained a U.S. pledge not to fortify Pacific bases, which materially simplified the Japanese advance twenty years later.

Probably the main effect of the treaty was the abrogation of traditional battleship functions. That is, afterwards there were so few battleships left in any navy that they were automatically considered too valuable to risk for most purposes. The best illustration is probably Japanese naval operations in 1941. She had twelve battleships, including the four rebuilt *Kongo*-class battle cruisers. Her strategy was predicated on a climactic engagement in home waters with the U.S. fleet; the battleships were saved against that eventuality. Only the less valuable *Kongo*s and the cruiser-destroyer forces could be spared to escort the Japanese carrier task force to Hawaii and the Indian Ocean.

Through early 1942 the United States similarly husbanded what was left of its battle line. However,

even before the war U.S. strategists had taken a more positive view of the value of the aircraft carrier and hence were more willing to risk the new battleships. As a result, American (but not Japanese) battleships saw considerable action, though generally in a subsidiary role.

Note, too, that by the outbreak of World War Two there was no reserve of obsolete battleships available for risky enterprises, as there had been in 1914. There was no equivalent of the pre-dreadnought fleet sacrificed at Gallipoli. Only the United States built enough new battleships before and during World War Two (ten in all) to make her older ones truly second-line. In Britain, for example, even Winston Churchill was unable to convince the Admiralty to rebuild the least effective of his ships, the "R" class, for coastal warfare. In a broader sense, in the absence of powerful battle fleets, large cruisers became more and more important; in wartime they sometimes functioned almost as junior battleships. Their proliferation in turn inspired the construction of fast battleships such as the *Iowa*s.

For the United States, the most important effect of the treaty regime was an imbalance between the U.S. and Japanese navies. It is interesting as an *indirect* effect of the treaty and as a parallel to similar effects under SALT. That is, in 1922 the treaty left the United States in a commanding position, with the only truly modern 16-inch battleships in the world, with arguably the only deck armor truly effective against long-range fire. All that the United States had to do was to build up its carrier and cruiser forces to match. What happened was that the public and Congress saw the treaty *itself* as proof that the underlying tensions in the Pacific had been eliminated, and naval construction was severely restricted. The symptom was mistaken for the disease. Japan, with a much more autocratic political system, embarked on an intense building program, the consequences of which were obvious in 1941.

On the other hand, it seems specious for Americans to regret the loss of the 1916 ships as a sacrifice unequalled by other navies. For example, some of the Japanese ships were at least as advanced, and their relatively high speed might have made them superior in combat. A great part of any judgment as to the winner of the Pacific naval race would have to rest on exactly *when* the race terminated. Congress might, for example, have been most reluctant to approve totally new types of U.S. capital ships, which might have made the 1916 ships obsolete.

What was perhaps most remarkable was that U.S. intelligence was poor enough that this point may have been missed altogether. The U.S. Navy simply did not know the characteristics of the new Japanese ships, nor, it seems, did it sufficiently understand the advantages of its own.

Shown at Puget Sound in September 1934, the *Nevada* (*above and facing*) was typical of the battleships rebuilt under the Washington Treaty. Note the antiaircraft range-finders on the foremast platform above her bridge. The director proper was located one level down, at the rear end of the range-finder platform. Its front end carried the 20-foot armored range-finder (for the secondary battery) atop her pilot house. As in the "Big Five," the three-level masthead tops carried, from top to bottom, a main battery director (Mark 20), a platform for main battery control and spotting, and a platform for two secondary battery directors. The lower mainmast platform carried the 12-foot range-finder for the secondary battery. Just visible under the foremast itself is the diamond-shaped loop of the radio direction-finder. The large oval openings just below the flag rack, which were characteristic of this class, were air intakes leading into ducts installed as part of the modernization. The port duct is visible as a square structure just below the signal searchlight forward of the flag rack. In the view looking forward, note the searchlight platforms on the funnel, which were characteristic of many of the rebuilt battleships, with their controls below them. (U.S. Navy via Don Montgomery)

For example, the claimed speed of the two Japanese *Nagato*s, the latest ships actually completed, was 23.5 knots. They were actually designed for 26.5, but the Office of Naval Intelligence does not appear to have understood that. The significance of the 3-knot difference is that, with such ships, the Japanese might have been able to "cross the T" of the slower U.S. fleet, much as the British hoped to be able to do with their own fast *Queen Elizabeth*s. The two *Kaga*s (one of which became a carrier, the other being sunk in tests) were designed to mount ten 16-inch guns and to make 26.5 knots. However, in October 1920 a U.S. agent reported that they were designed for 25 knots, and the next February a British source reported that their extra displacement was due to armor and fuel, not guns. As late as November 1921 an account of the launching of the *Kaga* gave the correct armament (from press accounts!) but a speed of only 23 knots.

Nor was there reliable information on British plans. For example, in 1920 Preliminary Design was ordered to work out sketch plans for a *Hood* modified to carry 20-inch guns, on the basis of a report in the Chicago *Tribune*.

Even so, the lesson remains that it matters very much *where* in the action-reaction spiral of an arms race a halt is called. In particular, in the case of capital ships not much could be done to change a design once construction had begun, so that in principle all of the major powers should have been willing to spend a great deal on intelligence. That this was manifestly not the case, at least for the United States as late as 1941, is remarkable.

For all three major treaty signatories, a major consequence of the agreement was that modern capital ships became available for weapon tests. The *Maryland*-class battleship *Washington*, the old *South Carolina*, and the *North Dakota* were all used.

The *South Carolina* was used to test features planned for the reconstruction of the existing ships. By August 1923 plans had been drawn for blisters to simulate those of a coal-burner on her starboard side and a rebuilt oil-burner on her port side. She had been laid up at Philadelphia since December 1921 and was demilitarized, her turrets removed. About 98 tons of blister and 100 tons of new internal bulkheads were built into her, and she was ballasted to a draft of 28 feet 1 inch, similar to that expected for the modernized ships. Work was completed about the end of April 1924, and she was tested with 400 pound TNT charges at a depth of 15 feet. These were proof shots rather than pure experiments.

North Dakota was converted into a radio-controlled target, her guns removed and many of her spaces plated over. Her geared turbines, installed in 1917, were removed for later use. It appears that

some of the earliest firings against this ship provided important data on the shock effect of hits on turrets.

The new *Washington* had been completed up to the boilering stage, that is, she had her full armor and underwater protection. She was chosen for tests of underwater explosions at various stand-offs, such as would be experienced with mines or near-miss bombs. Then there were contact explosions by the standard U.S. charge of 400 pounds of TNT, and finally she was sunk by bombing and gunfire. In contrast to the better-known Army tests of 1921, the Navy was able to control conditions and record data after each explosion. The tests were run in deep water so that stand-offs as great as 100 feet could be tried.

One account of the test series indicates that it began with two 400-pound torpedo hits and three 2,000-pound near misses. The ship then withstood three days of heavy seas without repairs, listing only three degrees. She remained afloat another two days, and was finally sunk by fourteen 14-inch shells fired by the *Texas*. In another test, fourteen 14-inch shells were dropped on her from 4,000 feet, but only one penetrated. It was offically estimated on the basis of these tests that a modern ship of this type could withstand eight torpedo hits, if they were well distributed, and that shellfire would be far more destructive than either torpedo attack or bombing. One consequence of the tests was a better understanding of the effect of near misses, including depth charges exploding near submarines. A major lesson was that future battleships should have triple bottoms; another was that existing deck armor was inadequate. Both were applied to the plans for battleship reconstructions.

The Washington Treaty inspired further attempts at limitation, culminating in a second treaty signed at London in 1930. This time cruiser and even destroyer construction was limited, and battle fleets further reduced. The United States had to give up the two *Utah*s and the *Wyoming*, the British the *Iron Duke*s and the battle cruiser *Tiger*, and Japan the battle cruiser *Hiei*. The ratio in *numbers* of capital ships was thus reduced to 15:15:9. In this case a ship could be demilitarized rather than scrapped, if the process was complete enough to preclude restoration to combatant status. Thus the *Utah* became a radio-controlled target ship, and the *Wyoming* a training ship. Neither ever saw combat service, although the remilitarization of the latter ship was seriously considered in 1940–41. Japan was unique in rearming her *Hiei* after withdrawing from the treaty structure.*

* The British retained the *Iron Duke* as a training ship and the older *Centurion* as a radio-controlled target, in analogy to the U.S. *Wyoming* and *Utah*; the analogous Japanese ships were the *Hiei* and the *Settsu*.

The 1930 treaty also extended the building "holiday" for another five years, to the end of 1936. Probably the world economic depression was the greatest factor in its success, since none of the major navies could afford new capital ships during this period. However, by 1936 a new naval race had begun. Even under the original Washington Treaty, both France and Italy had each been permitted to lay down 35,000 tons of new capital ships before 1931. Replying to the German "pocket battleships," France had laid down the first modern fast battleship, the *Dunkerque*. She in turn elicited an Italian reply, a full-size battleship, which in turn called for French replies. The U.S. Navy was not directly involved, but it was certainly affected by the appearance of new ships radically different from the standard types it had developed.

Japan, no longer willing to accept treaty-mandated inferiority, announced in 1934 that she would withdraw from the treaty system. A conference at London in 1935 was unable to resolve the problem, and in the end the system of ratios was abandoned altogether, although limits on battleship size and firepower were retained. However, an "escalator" clause permitted the signatories to revise these limits if Japan were unwilling to abide by them, as was indeed the case. For the United States, this escalation led to the design of the *Iowa*s.

10

Reconstruction

In the aftermath of the Washington Conference, the U.S. Navy was left with three groups of battleships: the old coal-burners, deficient in deck, side, and underwater protection and whose only deck armor consisted of a thin waterline deck; the *Nevada*, *Pennsylvania*, and *New Mexico* classes, deficient in underwater protection; and the satisfactory turboelectric battleships of the *Tennessee* and *Colorado* classes. The question, then, was to what extent the first two groups could be brought up to the standard of the third.

The treaty-mandated cancellations of seven battleships and four battle cruisers left a mass of material that might be used in reconstructions of existing ships: boilers for at least five battleships and three battle cruisers; turboelectric machinery for a battleship; 80 percent completed sets for five more and 60 percent completed sets for two more, some of which were destined for *Colorado*-class ships yet to be completed. As for the battle cruiser power plants, four were 70 percent complete, two 30 percent complete. C&R considered turboelectric drive the key to effective underwater protection. This mass of nearly complete machinery therefore represented an opportunity to bring the entire battle fleet up to the standard of the *Tennessee* class. Much of the armor planned for the cancelled ships had also been manufactured and was therefore available for any reconstruction program.

The treaty banned reconstruction "except for the purpose of providing means of defense against air and submarine attack," at the cost of an increase in displacement of up to 3,000 tons. Blisters and increased deck armor were specifically permitted. Apparently at the request of the British, however, alterations in side armor or in the "calibre, number, or general type of mounting of main armament" were forbidden. The Royal Navy had already modernized its battleships with increased gun elevation (for greater range) as a result of the experience at Jutland, and the clause prevented its rivals from following suit. On the other hand, the modernization clause did tend to maintain the ratio of battleship strength against other battleships (side armor and guns) while permitting defense against threats not regulated by treaty, that is, air and submarine attack. However, it left major loopholes.

Reconstruction could include improvement to fire control, which might make fire at much longer ranges possible. It was by no means clear, moreover, whether increased gun elevation (to take advantage of new fire controls) would fall under the restrictive clause. Deck armor, moreover, would be the *primary* means of protection at very long ranges. In April 1922, the General Board ruled that the word "blister" had been used to limit changes *outside* the hull, that is, that the treaty framers had explicitly restricted armor and main battery because those elements could easily be altered if a ship were blistered. Hence there would be no restriction on internal changes if they were intended to counter air or underwater attack. Almost any internal modification could be justified in this manner. Modifications to the secondary battery were entirely outside the treaty structure.

C&R and Steam Engineering began joint studies of reconstructions as early as March 1922, using the *New York* class as a basis. Eight *South Dakota*-class boilers would replace the former fourteen coal-burning units, and the machinery would be arranged as in the *Tennessee*s, the turbogenerators on the centerline. Rated power would increase from the original 27,000 to 60,000SHP, although the ship would normally operate at two-thirds power, 40,000SHP. Such a ship could make 21 knots using only three boilers. She might be considered overpowered, but the bureaus were loath to rely on only a single turbogenerator (a 30,000SHP plant). Conversion could,

The *Oklahoma* was one of thirteen U.S. battleships modernized under the Washington Treaty. She is shown newly completed at Philadelphia, 19 August 1929.

moreover, be justified on the basis of fuel economy. Cruising radius would increase by about 50 percent because of an improvement of 25 to 40 percent in fuel economy.

The new power plant would also be considerably more compact, leaving space between it and the side of the ship for increased underwater protection. Two new torpedo bulkheads would be added on each side, outboard of the turbogenerators and outboard of the boilers. The former centerline machinery space bulkhead would be eliminated. Electric motors would occupy the former engine room. In addition, the former longitudinal bunker bulkheads would be reinforced and made watertight. The resulting multiple-bulkhead system would be similar to that of the *Tennessee* and later designs.

It was not clear whether sufficient deck protection could be provided. For example, the new 8-inch cruiser gun could penetrate the existing 9-inch upper belt at 7,100 yards, and a 2-inch deck (the heaviest which could be provided) at just under 19,000. To cover the entire weather (upper) deck with 70-pound (1.75-inch) STS would cost 909 tons, which was considered excessive. That could be reduced to 764 tons by restricting the 70-pound STS to areas covering the boiler and engine rooms. Elsewhere the thickness was reduced to 1 inch (40 pounds). In this scheme the original diagonal armor bulkheads were replaced by 40-pound splinter armor, and 3-inch armor added to the lower barbettes of Nos. 2 and 3 turrets, which had been covered by that diagonal plating. The inner bottom would be thickened, either by replacement by half-inch plating or by doubling with $\frac{3}{8}$ inch. The turret tops would be reinforced by 40-pound STS. They had already been doubled to 4 inches. Such reconstruction would cost $5 to $10 million, over one to two years.

As an alternative to this radical surgery, the bureaus suggested merely blistering (bulging) without replacement of the machinery. This would provide sufficient volume for improved underwater protection by adding spaces outside the hull. Internal changes would be limited to replacement of the boilers and conversion to oil burning. Deck armor would be improved as in the more complex scheme. In each case new fire controls on heavier (*Tennessee*-type) cage masts would be installed, and the former underwater torpedo tubes replaced by a pair of above-water tubes abeam the after two barbettes.

The General Board preferred the simpler of the two alternatives. It could not recommend immediate modernization in view of the anti-naval atmosphere reflected by the treaty itself. However, other navies would surely modernize their own ships, and the United States must be able to follow suit. It should, therefore, retain enough boilers from the scrapped ships to reboiler the six coal-burners; retain the tur-

boelectric machinery for future use (although it was not to be used for the present); and prepare plans and estimates. Plans for the *Nevada*, the oldest ship satisfactorily protected against shellfire, would have the highest priority.

The *Nevada*s would be bulged to a beam of 105.2 feet. At a displacement of 28,500 tons they would require about 1 percent more power at full speed, 18,125 rather than 17,874EHP. In one scheme, 2 inches of deck armor (at a total cost of 1,300 tons) would have been added. The *Pensylvania*s would have been fitted with six battle cruiser boilers, allowing space for two more torpedo bulkheads. Six twin 6-inch mounts and eight 5in/25 AA guns would replace the former 5-inch and 3-inch secondary battery. On the other hand, reconstruction of the *New Mexico*s would be limited to improvements in underwater protection—a new 15 pound inner bottom and a new 30-pound STS torpedo bulkhead inserted between the former inner boiler room bulkhead and the old light bulkhead which had formed the outer wall of the boiler room escape passage.

By December 1922, the General Board was far less willing to forgo reconstruction. In its view, the core of the Washington Treaty had been equality with Britain, yet the Royal Navy still had a much superior battle line. For example, the U.S. 12-inch gun would not penetrate British belt armor beyond 15,000 yards, where the British 13.5-inch gun would still be effective against U.S. armor. Moreover, the British ships had all been modernized, with blisters, added deck armor, and increased gun elevation. At a recent battle practice, the British fleet had opened fire at 30,000 yards, whereas most U.S. ships could not fire beyond about 21,000. Worst of all, only Britain was permitted by treaty to build two new battleships. It appears that the General Board was unaware of the considerable superiority of recent American battleships, with their "all or nothing" protection, heavy deck armor, and advanced torpedo protection.

The U.S. battle line could gain a range advantage through a combination of better ballistics (new shells) and gun elevation. The choice in ballistics lay between higher velocity (that is, shorter gun life) and a heavier shell. For example, the 1,400-pound shell fired by the 14in/45 could penetrate 15.4 inches of side armor at 15,000 yards. A 100 ft/sec increase in velocity would add 1.2 inches of penetration. Alternatively, a lower-velocity 1,570-pound shell could penetrate 16 inches. As for gun elevation, at 30 degrees the 14in/50 could reach 33,500 yards, the 12in/45, 32,000. Contracts for the first two ships, the *Florida* and the *Utah*, were signed in December 1922. It was estimated then that the work would take about three months and cost $465,000 per ship. BuOrd claimed that such changes were permissable under the treaty.

On this basis, in January 1923 Congress authorized $6.5 million for increased elevation for BB 30–42. On 26 February, however, the First Lord of the Admiralty denied that Britain was increasing the elevation of her battleship guns and charged that any U.S. action would violate the reconstruction clause of the treaty. Although U.S. legal opinion differed from his, the U.S. government denied any desire to begin a new naval arms race. Work was suspended pending congressional reconsideration, and authority was rescinded in the FY25 naval bill.

By this time BuOrd expected to increase deck armor in the coal-burners to 2 inches on each of the weather and main protective decks, plus another inch in a splinter deck. In weight terms, that was 5 inches, but, because it was divided into three thicknesses, it was ballistically equivalent to only 3.15 inches. C&R wanted to eliminate both the gun deck secondary 5-inch guns and their relatively thin side armor. That would expose the 5/16inch (12 pound) deck atop the main side armor, which C&R wanted to thicken to two layers of 70-pound (3.5inch total) STS. In a ship like the *Florida*, that would add 800 or 900 tons of armor. Blistering would provide both the additional stability and the additional buoyancy (about 1,500 tons) to compensate. Additions to deck armor would be the most complex and difficult aspect of modernization.

The value of increased gun range depended upon improvements in fire control. BuOrd claimed that beyond 20,000 yards spotting, which was necessary for effective fire, would have to be by aircraft. Catapults and aircraft thus became so important that considerable sacrifices were made to accommodate them. BuAer went so far in March 1922 as to promote increased gun elevation on the basis of the improvements in air spotting it had already achieved. The bureau wanted to operate a mix of aircraft from each capital ship: two fighters, one spotter, and one torpedo bomber. The latter would be used in a one-time strike before the fleet closed to gun range. The fighters would help assure U.S. gunnery superiority by denying the air over the battle to enemy spotters, while protecting friendly ones. By November, with true aircraft carriers clearly about to be built, the General Board dropped the torpedo bomber in favor of a second spotter.

Catapults could be located either on the quarterdeck or atop the turret closest to the superstructure. Only the oil-burners had enough quarterdeck space for the former. In the coal-burners, it appeared that No. 3 turret was so close to the mainmast that no catapult could be mounted unless the mast were removed.

The first compressed-air Mark I catapult was fired aboard the *Maryland* on 22 May 1922, and installations aboard the *Nevada* and *Oklahoma* soon followed

during overhauls at Norfolk and Puget Sound Navy Yards. Catapults were installed aboard the *Mississippi*, *Idaho*, *California*, and *Tennessee* during fiscal year 1924. By early 1926 all of the oil-burners had been fitted.

BuAer feared that aircraft stowed on these quarterdeck catapults would be swept away by a seaway. It wanted covered aircraft stowage on the superstructure, perhaps serving a superstructure-deck catapult. The Royal Navy actually adopted this configuration in the form of a fixed cross-deck catapult, but senior U.S. seagoing officers commanding the battle force and the U.S. Fleet rejected it. The best alternative was a powder-driven turret-top catapult. Compressed air could not be used because no air line could be run up to the turret top. The prototype was tested aboard the *Mississippi* on 14 December 1924, and from then on standard policy was to provide both turret-top and quarterdeck catapults to each four-turret battleship. Only the *Mississippi*, *California*, and *Colorado* classes were so fitted before reconstruction.

Reconstruction of the six coal-burners had the highest priority, because they were least able to survive under modern conditions. Congress was reluctant to spend this money, but serious deficiencies became obvious during the 1924 winter maneuvers. The *Utah* and *Arkansas* classes had to be restricted to 14 knots. Temporary repairs were soon made, but the *Florida* had to be laid up in June 1924. Congress may also have been affected by the new race among foreign navies to build the large cruisers permitted under the treaty. Clearly, naval competition was continuing. On 18 December it authorized the reconstruction of all six coal-burners within the treaty limits, which (as then understood) meant without increases in gun elevation. New fire control systems were authorized for the *New York* and *Texas*.

C&R's basic concept followed its 1922 ideas, with two 70-pound STS layers over the length of the second deck between the end barbettes. This deck already had 12-pound plating under the secondary battery amidships. The original waterline armor deck served as a splinter deck beneath it. In addition, 70-pound STS was added to the third deck fore and aft of the main belt, in areas where there was already considerable protection (for example, 1.5 inch forward in the *Florida*s). The turret and conning tower roofs, already "doubled" during or just after World War One, were given additional layers of 70-pound STS.

In the *Florida*, the 70-pound STS plate was laid atop a layer of 70-pound nickel steel. Over the boilers, inboard of the 12-pound plating, there was a third layer (50-pound STS), for a total of 4.75 inches. Fore and aft of the casemate bulkheads the original second deck had consisted of two layers of 20-pound

The two *Florida*s were the oldest battleships retained under the treaty. The *Florida* is shown at Hampton Roads, 25 October 1929. Note the 20-foot range-finders atop Nos. 2, 4, and 5 turrets. They were necessary because long-base range-finders were not built into the turrets. All but No. 1 turret also had 1pdr sub-calibre guns for training. There was also a 12-foot range-finder atop the pilot house, offset to starboard so as to provide space for a large radio direction-finder loop antenna. The detail view shows *Utah*, which differed in details, such as the shape of the sponson carrying her 5-inch guns. Note the Vickers-type 5-inch director just inboard of the 5in/51 gun on her 01 level. A chart house, which is barely visible, occupied the base of the cage foremast. The navigating bridge above carried a 3-inch range-finder/altimeter at its after end; it had not yet been mounted at this time. The level above carried 3-inch fire controls and lookouts. The empty sponson was reserved for a main battery director(scope), with spotters in the masthead. Note the pair of 3-pounder saluting guns at the forward end of the 01 level and the range clocks on both masts.

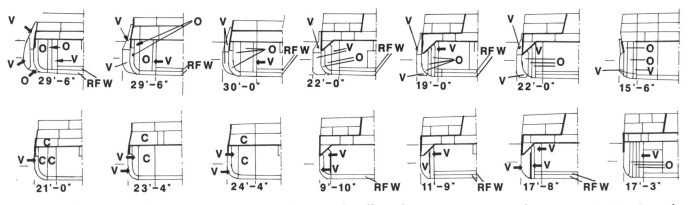

Comparative cross sections (at the boiler room) illustrate the effect of reconstruction on underwater protection. In each case the dimension given is the total depth of protection, from the outside of the ship to the inner torpedo bulkhead. The upper row of cross sections illustrates ships as reconstructed, except for the rightmost case, the carrier *Lexington*, which was built with what was considered adequate protection. The lower row illustrates ships as completed, with the *Tennessee*, the first adequately protected class, on the right. From left to right, the others are *Florida, Wyoming, New York, Nevada, Pennsylvania*, and *New Mexico*. Loadings have been indicated as follows: V for void, C for coal, O for oil, and RFW for reserve feed water. This chart was prepared about 1924.

mild steel, so that the new total was 4.5 inches. *Utah* differed in that both layers were STS, the upper layer being reduced to 50 pounds, so that her total was 4.25 inches. She had 30-pound reinforcement over her original battery deck plating, for a total there of 4.05 inches.

In the other four ships the protective deck forward of the casemate was the half deck, protected for the length between end bulkheads by two 70-pound layers (the lower one nickel steel in the *New York*s). Local stiffening was 50-pound STS over the boiler rooms (total 4.75 inches) and 30-pound STS over the engine rooms (in the *Arkansas* class only). In all four ships, areas of deck near magazines were already protected by 40-pound plating, so that total thicknesses were about 4.5 inches. On the third deck aft, 70-pound STS was provided to protect the steering gear.

All six were fitted with oil-fired boilers taken from scrapped capital ships, and uptakes were altered for a single funnel. In each case, oil-firing in itself increased endurance, and the big blisters also greatly increased fuel capacity. For example, at 10 knots the coal-burning *Arkansas* was rated at a 6,700nm radius of action. She had been designed for 8,000. In 1925 it was expected that as rebuilt she could make 11,000. The *Florida*, with a coal-burning radius of 7,200nm, was expected to make 16,500.

The old engines were not replaced, but the ships lost little or no speed. The changed midsection coefficient (and hence changed prismatic coefficient) due to bulging actually *reduced* resistance at constant displacement, so that the added weight of blister and armor increased resistance less than might otherwise be expected. For example, on trial at 24,700 tons *Florida* made 22.25 knots at 43,610SHP. On her orig-

inal trials, she made 22.09 knots at 40,511SHP at 21,240 tons. The bulges did increase resistance at cruising speeds, in a region of the resistance curve dominated by wetted surface area rather than by wave making.

The blister itself was first tested on the discarded battleship *South Carolina*. It was a single-skin structure, kept empty to dissipate the energy of a torpedo exploding against it. In the *Florida*s a new bulkhead was inserted between the former bulkhead dividing the coal bunkers longitudinally and the boiler room bulkhead. Outboard of it were two oil tanks comprising the former outboard bunker and half of the former inboard bunker. The former void inner bottom extending around the bilge was kept empty, and a new void consisted of the space between the new torpedo bulkhead and the boiler room. The four later ships had wider bunker spaces, so that the new bulkhead could be installed about three-quarters of the way inboard in what had been a single large bunker. Outboard of this had been a void and then the void of the inner bottom. Now the inner void was filled with oil, since an additional void, the blister, had been added outboard. The new bulkhead in way of the boiler rooms was built of 30-pound STS. Existing boiler room bulkheads were doubled to 15 to 20 pounds, and an additional double bottom was added under the boiler rooms, to resist the effects of near-miss bombs.

As aircraft were now considered an essential element of fire control, it was necessary to trade off aloft fire control stations (that is, masts) against catapults on turret tops. The ideal solution was to eliminate the mainmast altogether, but that could be done only if, in normal operation, the foremast sufficed. C&R proposed a lower after control station. Searchlights,

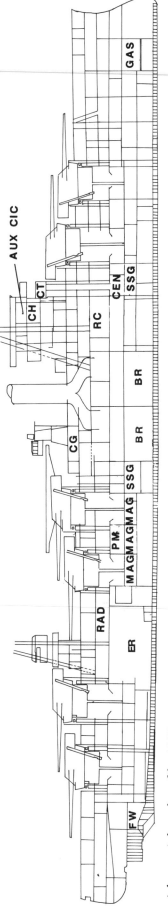

Arkansas inboard profile, 1945.

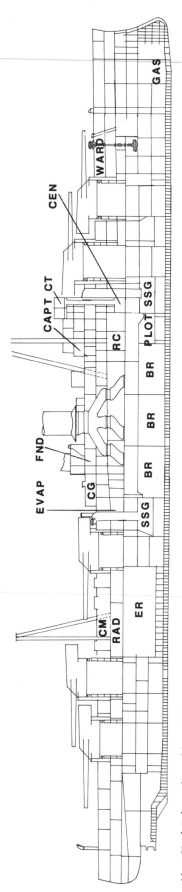

New York inboard profile, 1945.

The rebuilt *Arkansas* is shown in October 1931. Note her three turret-top range-finders, two of which survived to the end of her career. Her one cage mast carried a main battery fire control station at its head, with an antiaircraft control station inside the mast atop the torpedo-defense station (5-inch fire control). A flag plotting room occupied the base of the cage mast. The structure abaft the funnel was the after control station, with a range-finder atop it, the structure on the mainmast carrying controls for the searchlights above it. The *Arkansas* was the last reconstructed battleship to retain her cage mast, and by 1941 replacement by a tripod (for a configuration similar to that of the *New York*) was planned.

normally on the mainmast, would be mounted instead on the funnel. Reconstruction was also an opportunity to replace the existing cage masts with tripods.

The General Board canvassed battleship commanders. At this time the five active coal-burners formed the scouting force, and the twelve oil-burners constituted the battle force. With shorter-range guns, the scouting force commanders were much more willing to give up mainmasts. The captain of the *Texas* even argued that it was too easy to estimate the course of any ship with two tall masts. He also wanted the shape of the superstructure simplified to make chemical decontamination easier; gas shells were a major perceived threat of the interwar period. Much the same consideration would be raised in connection with nuclear fallout twenty years later.

The commander of the scouting force argued, too, that the foretop was obscured by funnel gas and smoke no more than 10 to 15 percent of the time. However, the main top was usually untenable, either because of smoke or hot gases which disrupted optical instruments. Modernization with oil burning was unlikely to eliminate such gases.

The battle force, more concerned with long-range fire, was unwilling to forgo a second elevated fire control position. The foremast might well be put out of action by enemy fire early in an action, but without such a position fire control would be ineffective beyond 17,000 yards. C&R's proposed lower station would probably be effective only out to 15,000 yards,

and would suffer blast from No. 3 turret. In theory, airplanes carried on board might replace such positions, but success required a combination of air superiority, reliable radio communication, and sufficient airplane performance. In any case, the four-turret ships of the battle force could have both catapults and two masts. For them the argument was academic.

The cage mast argument recalled the 1918–19 controversy. Postwar experience showed that, although the masts whipped as the guns fired, that did not make fire control impossible. Spotters reported, for example, that whipping (which made instruments unusable) lasted for only five to ten seconds, which was far less than the interval between salvoes. The captain of the *Tennessee* went so far as to argue that his spotters would probably outlast his turret personnel in a long action.

The net result was that, in the *Utah*s, a pole mainmast was fitted to carry radio antennas. There was no space for a secondary fire control position. In the longer *Arkansas* and *New York* classes the second main battery position was just abaft the single funnel, forward of No. 3 turret. A dwarf tripod aft supported radio antennas and searchlights. Only in the newest units, the *New York*s, were the main battery fire controls replaced. The new weight required a new mast. C&R chose a tripod, which it considered steadier than the cage. Its STS legs protected wiring leads. Similar masts were considered for the other ships, but they were rejected as being disallowed by the restrictive language of the authorizing act.

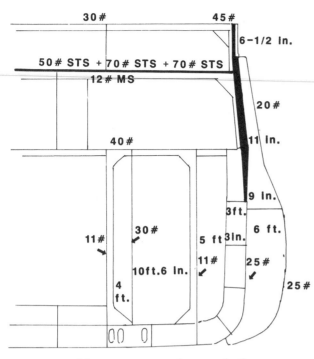

Arkansas cross section as rebuilt.

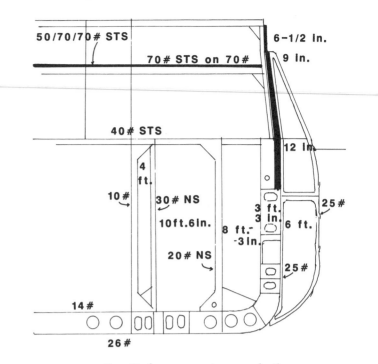

New York cross section as rebuilt.

C&R took this opportunity to relocate secondary batteries. In the *Florida*s, a sponson was built out at main deck level just abaft the pair of guns already mounted there (that is, *in* the forecastle). Another 5in/51 was sited on the 01 level on each side in the bridgework. Only the four hull guns right aft were retained. As first completed, *Florida* retained another four hull guns, but they were soon removed. The eight 3in/50 AA guns were resited atop the sponson.

The analogous modification in the flush-deck *Arkansas* and *New York* classes was a sponson on the main deck abeam the bridgework, mounting six guns, with two more in the open atop it on the 01 level. Eight more guns remained in the hull, four just abaft the sponson and four right aft as in the *Florida*s. The eight 3in/50 were mounted atop the sponson. This neat arrangement was to be followed in later reconstructions.

Although the 5in/25 was now the standard battleship AA gun, the coal-burners were not fitted with it in view of their age and the shortage of funds. The *New York*s, however, were fitted with hoists large enough to take 5-inch shells.

The original reconstruction plans called for installation of above-water torpedo tubes, but in the end the ships carried no tubes at all.

Blistering did not improve the seagoing behavior of these ships. In 1928 the captain of the *Texas* reported that his ship was slow to start to turn, but unusually quick once she had started to swing. She "rolls excessively when anchored in an open roadstead, as shown at Corinto, Nicaragua, and it would be impossible to fuel from a tanker alongside under these conditions. This in an overseas campaign would be a grave handicap." She was very stiff and did not roll in a rough or choppy sea, but rolled excessively in a swell from abaft the beam.

The roll was, moreover, irregular and unpredictable. Even the new General Electric fire control gear had lags built into it that could reduce accuracy considerably if the roll were not uniform. Moreover, it often seemed that the blistered ships rolled far more heavily than did other ships of similar tonnage. The captain of the *Texas* complained that at times his ship wallowed so badly that it was unsafe to serve the guns, whereas ships like the *California* did not even realize she was in trouble. C&R blamed such behavior on very great metacentric height. The crews would surely be grateful if their ships were damaged, for their steadiness as weapon platforms would actually improve.

The blisters had been made from extremely thin plating to reduce splintering in the face of underwater explosions, but that made it vulnerable to collision damage. For example, the captain of the *New York* claimed that he could not fuel from a tanker in anything but a very well protected anchorage. At Honolulu, for example, he could not take a tanker alongside without risking leaks, and he wondered what would happen in an overseas campaign. In all six ships, practice torpedoes dished in the thin blisters, and C&R had to strengthen them.

During this period, too, the reciprocating engines of the *New York* and *Texas* caused considerable trouble. It is not clear whether this was a new problem, but it appears to have come to the attention of C-in-

The reconstructed *New York* was broadly similar to the *Arkansas*, except that totally new fire controls, like those of the "Big Five," were fitted. The structure abaft the funnel had to be very low to avoid smoke interference. Note the eight 0.50-calibre machine gun tubs on her two masts, and the armored range-finder on No. 3 turret. Her 3-inch range-finders (altimeters) occupy the small platforms at the after end of her range-finder platform, above her bridge.

C U.S. Fleet (CINCUS) only after the rebuilt *Texas* became his flagship. At least as early as his FY28 report, CINCUS stated that *Texas* had a critical speed at which torsional vibration was particularly bad: 12.5 to 14.5 knots (12.4 to 14.3 for *New York*, 11.0 to 12.6 for *Oklahoma*). It was feared that propeller shafts might crack at such speeds which were, unfortunately, within the range of standard fleet cruising speeds. The problem was so severe that CINCUS asked that the engines be replaced by turbines in his FY34 report. This engine trouble continued through the 1930s. In 1936 CINCUS complained that the reciprocating-engine ships "are not able to take and maintain their place in the battle line over long periods. Either they should be re-engined . . . or they should be replaced. The latter is considered the more economical and desirable alternative." By 1939 only *Oklahoma* remained in the first line, and she continued to give trouble: "If it is planned to keep [her] in commission for several years to come, her reciprocating engines should be replaced by turbines." That was never done, however.

The four earliest oil-burners, BB 36-39, form very nearly a homogeneous group. As of January 1925, the modernization of the seven remaining substandard battleships (BB 36-42) was third in priority on the Navy's list, after the modernization of the coal-burners and the completion of the two new carriers, *Lexington* and *Saratoga*. However, in March 1926,

with the coal-burning conversions well under way, the General Board suggested that all seven be done under the FY28 program. The work was actually stretched out over several years: *Nevada* and *Oklahoma* under FY28, *Pennsylvania* and *Arizona* under FY30, and the *New Mexicos* beginning with FY31.

Congress was now willing to allow higher gun elevation. In all seven oil burners, elevation was doubled to 30 degrees. New fire control systems were fitted, atop tripods in the *Nevada* and *Pennsylvania* classes. At the same time turret catapults were added, and the quarterdeck units were replaced by powder-fired catapults. All hull secondaries were removed, ten being remounted in a much enlarged deckhouse. Two 5in/51 were mounted in the open atop it, together with eight 5in/25 AA guns. The secondary battery directors, which had been at weather deck level, were raised to the tops, fire controls externally similar to those of the "Big Five" being mounted at masthead level. *Pennsylvania*, the designated fleet flagship, was fitted with a greatly enlarged conning tower, and all four ships had their bridges much extended, with provision for antiaircraft controls at an upper level.

Added protection was much simpler than in the coal-burners: a 70-pound (80-pound in the *Nevada*s) layer was added to the 3-inch second deck, for a total of 4.75 or 5 inches. These total thicknesses were not, however, equivalent to a single plate. In the *Nevada*s

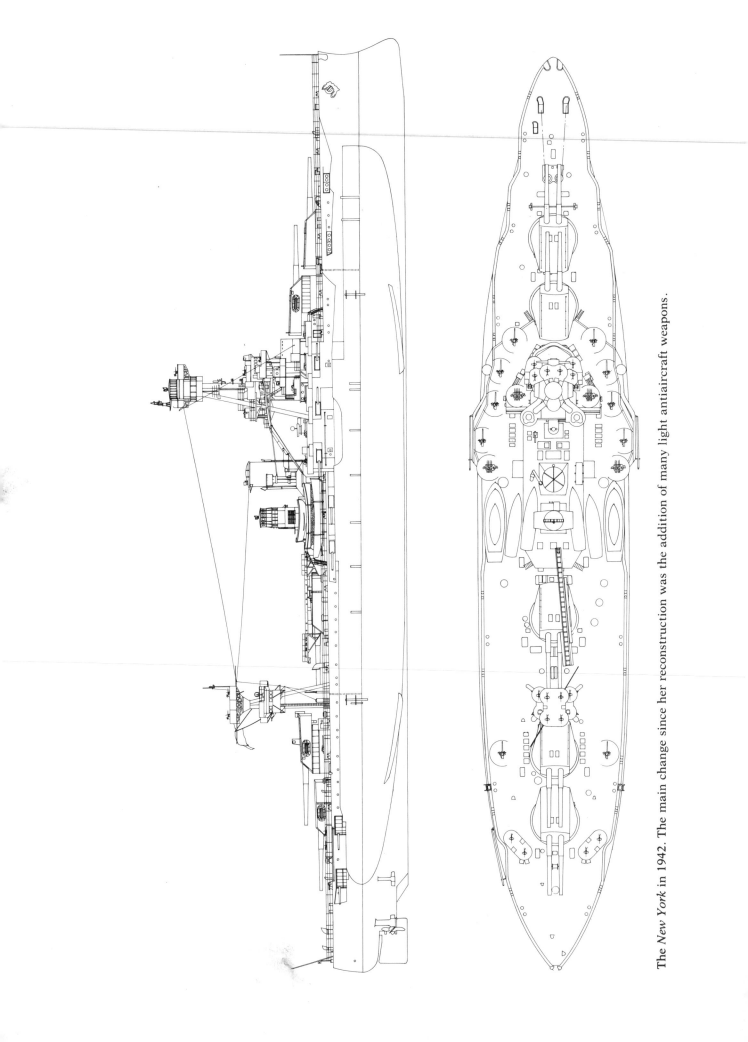

The *New York* in 1942. The main change since her reconstruction was the addition of many light antiaircraft weapons.

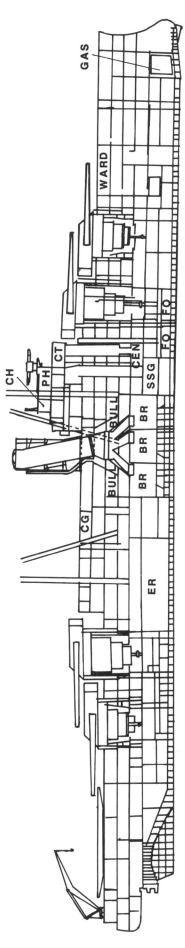

Oklahoma inboard profile, 1941. Note the skeg added aft in a 1936 Puget Sound refit. The vertical tube abaft No. 2 barbette was a 3-inch ammunition hoist, for the antiaircraft weapons added as an emergency measure. Note also the big protected air duct installed during modernization, similar to that in the later U.S. dreadnoughts.

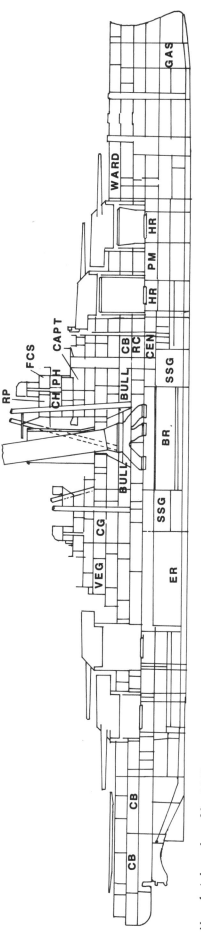

Nevada inboard profile, 1945.

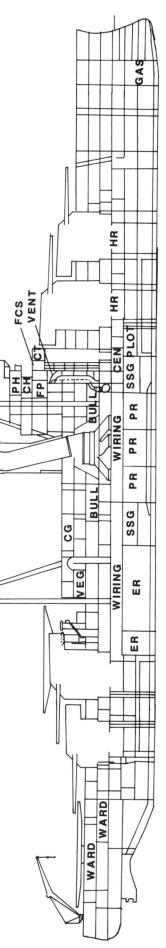

Arizona inboard profile, 1941.

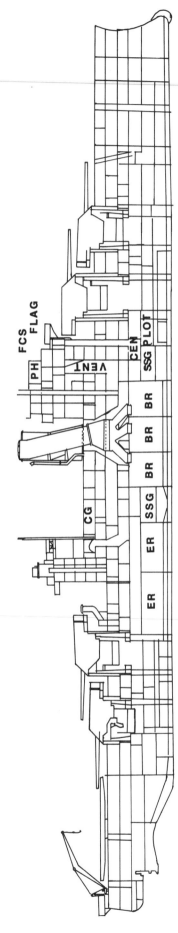

FCS
FLAG
PH
VENT
CEN
SSG PLOT
BR
BR
BR
CG
ER SSG
ER ER
ER

Pennsylvania inboard profile, 1945. Note that her conning tower has been removed.

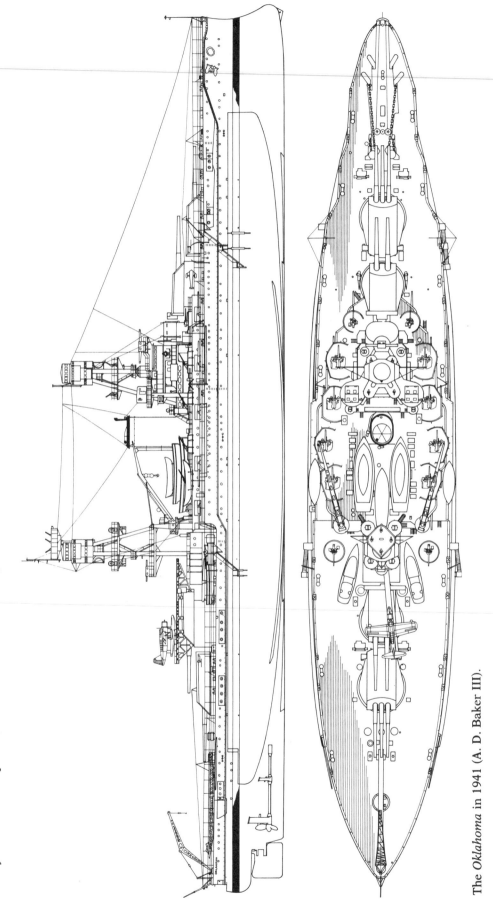

The *Oklahoma* in 1941 (A. D. Baker III).

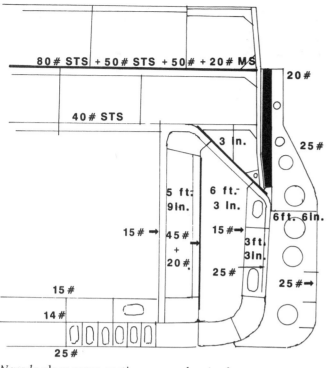

Nevada-class cross section, as modernized.

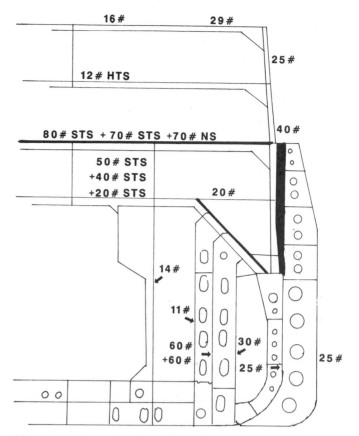

Mississippi-class cross section as modernized.

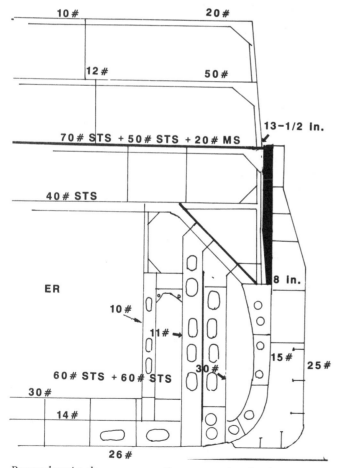

Pennsylvania-class cross section, as modernized.

an additional 15-pound torpedo bulkhead was worked in through the boiler rooms. The extra bulkhead in the Pennsylvanias was 30 pounds, outboard of the former torpedo bulkhead. All four were fitted with an additional inner bottom under the boiler rooms, and all were blistered.

Internally, six small-tube boilers replaced the former twelve, and the turbine ships were reengined. In each case the single funnel was moved slightly aft to clear the forward superstructure. Nevada received the geared turbines originally fitted to the North Dakota in 1917. Machinery ordered for the Colorado-class battleship Washington was used for both the Pennsylvania and Arizona. In the latter, the high-pressure (but not the low-pressure) turbines were replaced by high-pressure geared units from the cancelled ship. Power increased sufficiently to balance off the resistance of the new blister. Nevada made 31,759SHP (20.28 knots) at 31,961 tons; Pennsylvania, 34,001SHP (20.89 knots) at 37,132 tons; Arizona, 35,081SHP (20.70 knots) at 37,654 tons. By way of contrast, without additional power, Oklahoma was reduced to 19.68 knots at 32,338 tons (23,599IHP, as standardized).

The most complete reconstruction was reserved for the last three ships, the New Mexicos. Two-inch (80-pound) STS was added to their 3.5 inch armor decks, for a total thickness of 5.5 inches, and the

The *Nevada* is shown at sea, 6 April 1937. By this time four 0.50-calibre machine guns had been mounted in a "bird bath" on her mainmast. Additional guns were mounted on the two mast platforms. The two vertical 5-inch antiaircraft range-finders are just visible on the foremast platform.

Very few photographs of the battleships taken between 1939 and 1941 have survived. This is the *Oklahoma* during her last Puget Sound refit, February 1941. Her antiaircraft directors and range-finders had been consolidated into the large armored box visible at the rear end of her range-finder platform. The structure at the base of her foremast leg was a new air defense control station. Four locally controlled 3in/50 guns were also added. One is visible, in its tub, alongside the conning tower. They were to have been replaced by quadruple 1.1-inch machine cannon. The existing 5in/25 battery was provided with splinter protection. At this time, too, the four-36 inch searchlights were relocated from the funnel to the mainmast, and the 0.50-calibre machine guns formerly mounted on what became the searchlight platform were moved up into a "bird bath" at the masthead. Similar guns are visible on the foremast platform. The 24-inch searchlights on the signal bridge had to be relocated to clear the new 5-inch (Mark 19) director support. (Gerald Forman, *Oklahoma* Association)

splinter deck over the machinery was reinforced (50 pounds added to the existing 60, for a total of 2.75 inches). An additional 30-pound torpedo bulkhead was built outboard of the previous one, and the ships were all blistered.

Although the *New Mexico* was already fitted with turboelectric drive, she, like her two sisters, received new propelling machinery. Reportedly the decision to buy identical machinery for all three ships saved $300,000. As in previous refits, the increased power was needed, not to increase but merely to maintain speed as displacement increased. Also as in earlier ships, the original nine boilers were replaced by six new small-tube ones. The new 40,000SHP plants were expected to drive these ships at 21.3 knots at 37,000 tons. In fact *Mississippi* made 21.68 knots on trial

(power and displacement unreported), and *New Mexico*, 21.8. In 1945 the official register *Ships Data* reported *Mississippi* good for 21.7 knots at 36,977 tons, and *New Mexico* for 21.8 at 36,985. These data probably reflect postmodernization trials.

The major new feature of these modernizations was a new tower bridge, inspired by that of the British *Nelson*. BuOrd proposed it in September 1930, arguing along the same lines which, we now know, had justified the British design—increased resistance to shellfire and blast. Although some in the fleet were unwilling to accept materially lower fire controls, the secretary approved the plans the following April. The tower carried a 5-inch director superimposed above a main battery director on its centerline. To avoid smoke interference, the after controls were

The *Pennsylvania*, the fleet flagship, is shown on 31 May 1934. At this time she carried machine guns on both masts, and she could be distinguished from the *Arizona* by her higher conning tower. Note the ventilation trunking on her turrets. Below her pilot house is the emergency cabin platform, with the chart house and the admiral's and chief of staff's emergency cabins. Below that is the flag bridge, with the flag plotting room and the 12-inch and 24-inch signal searchlights.

below the funnel cap. Searchlights were grouped around the funnel. The mainmast, for signal hoists, was stepped from the after tower. The entire arrangement was remarkable in that the fleet accepted a relatively low position for fire controls, only about 90 feet above water. This acceptance may have represented increased faith in air spotting.

That left the "Big Five," the best protected of the U.S. dreadnoughts. The bureaus began to make estimates in October 1931, based on experience with the *New Mexico*s. Improvements would have included gas protection, a thicker protective deck (80-pound STS added, at a cost of 1,319 tons), thicker turret tops, improved ammunition hoists, modernized fire controls, and new main battery projectiles. They would have been fitted with two quadruple 1.1-inch machine cannon, and their machinery would have been replaced to maintain speed. Blisters would have provided added buoyancy to compensate for the added weights, as well as for weights already added during their service careers. Details are lacking, but a January 1932 order to the David Taylor Model Basin requested power figures for a blister increasing beam to not more than 106 feet and displacement to not over 35,600 tons at a draft of 30 feet 9 inches. The latter was important because it determined the extent to which the side armor would be submerged.

This modernization would cost about $11 million per ship, exclusive of ordnance ($4 million). Money was scarce, however, and the CNO proposed to save $3 million per ship by reconditioning the main machinery rather than replacing it. The president of the Naval War College agreed that a loss of up to 1 knot could be accepted. Other savings could be realized by eliminating gas protection and the new shell, so that the bill for five ships would fall from $71,723,000 to $45,098,000. By October 1932, however, the bureaus had returned to their original proposal, now modified to include four quadruple 1.1-inch guns.

The cost would now be $15 million per ship, and the bureaus asked the secretary of the navy to request funds for FY33. Ships would be withdrawn one by one for modernization, beginning with the *Tennessee*. Their rationale was that new battleship construction was unlikely; the United States must make the most of her existing ships. In fact, the Great Depression deepened, and no ships at all were requested for FY33. Modernization planning, however, continued.

Within a few years there was a new factor. All five ships were grossly overweight, their armored freeboard insufficient. This was partly a consequence of the standard practice of going to sea with emergency oil aboard, for increased range. Thus in June 1935, *Tennessee* reported an operating displacement of

The *Arizona* in the mid-1930s (the aerial photograph was taken in September 1936). Note the walkway around her pilot house, which distinguished her from the *Pennsylvania*. Antiaircraft range-finders are visible on her range-finder platform, with 5-inch directors at the emergency cabin level (that is, the level below the navigating bridge), one of them visible against the after leg of the tripod foremast. In a Puget Sound refit completed in March 1939, the funnel searchlights were relocated to the mainmast machine gun platform, their own platform being taken over by a pair of 0.50-calibre machine guns. Like *Oklahoma*, she was modified extensively just prior to World War Two, completing a Puget Sound refit in June. Her antiaircraft directors and range-finders were consolidated and enclosed. Foundations for 1.1-inch guns were installed (although not the guns themselves). The directors would have been installed on the emergency cabin level (below the signal bridge), about where the 5-inch directors are shown in this photograph. Fixed splinter shields were installed, and the flag bridge was extended. Machine gun platforms were installed on the maintop (four guns) and on the foremast (two guns), for a total of eight 0.50-calibre machine guns.

The three *New Mexico*s were the last to be rebuilt. They could be distinguished by their searchlight platforms. The *Mississippi* and *Idaho* had theirs far above their controls, with long struts, but the *New Mexico* had her control cabins directly under the lights. Quite unlike their predecessors, they had tower masts supporting Mark 28 5-inch directors, the first to combine range-finder and calculator in a single unit. The small cylinders were Mark 31 directors, with an armored range-finder at the forward end of the bridge structure. Below it were secondary battery controls and battle lookout stations (note the eye slits), with the navigating bridge below that, then the chart house platform, the radio direction-finder platform, and the conning tower platform. Note the four 0.50-calibre machine guns visible on the latter. The radio direction-finder itself was housed between the funnel and the bridge structure. The *Idaho*, fitted as a flagship, had a flag bridge below her navigating bridge. Her chart house was on the radio direction-finder platform. The *New Mexico* (aerial view) and *Mississippi* are shown.

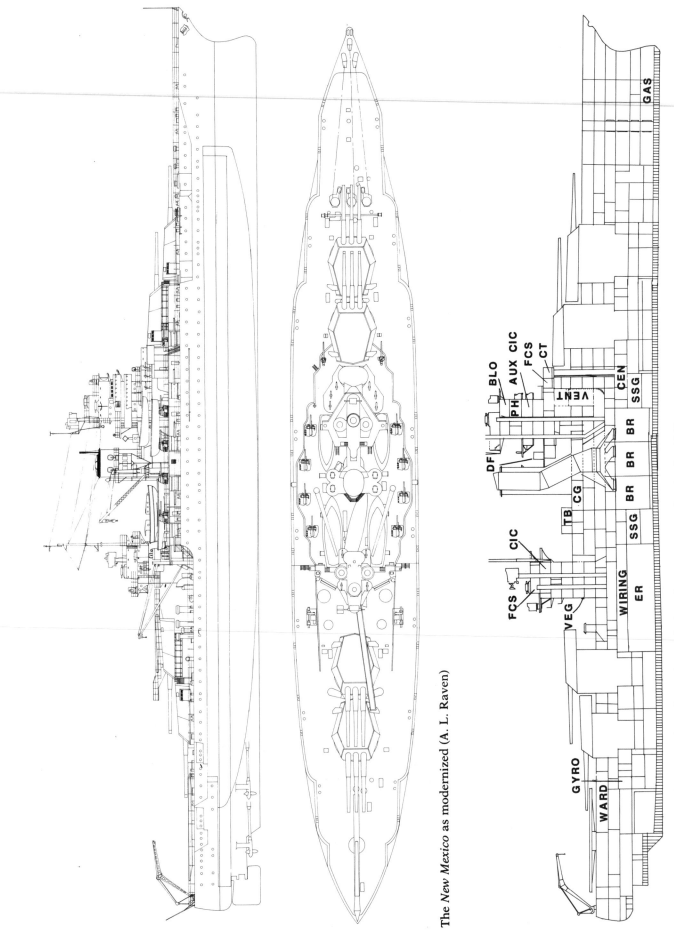

The *New Mexico* as modernized (A. L. Raven)

Mississippi inboard profile, 1944, largely unchanged since her reconstruction in the 1930s.

GAS

BLO
DF
PH
AUX CIC
FCS
CT
VENT
CEN
SSG

CIC
TB
CG
BR BR BR
FCS
SSG
WIRING
VEG
ER

GYRO
WARD

38,200 tons, 2,050 tons above her designed *emergency* load, or 5 feet 4 inches deeper draft than that originally contemplated. Her belt was only 2 feet 5 inches out of water.

Early the next year there was some interest in modernizing fire controls in the *Tennessee*s, with tower structures to replace the original cage masts. However, C&R considered the proposed increase in weight, 258 tons, unacceptable. The bureau wanted the ships blistered to restore buoyancy: a blister displacing 2,884 tons (and weighing 1,142) could bring the ships 17 inches out of the water at a cost of $438,000. C&R wanted the *Maryland*s blistered as well (20 inch rise, 2,000 tons). In each case, work would take about a year: one month's docking so that templates of the detailed hull shape could be made; six months to fabricate the blister while the ship operated; and five months for installation.

Early in 1937 the bureaus held a conference on a partial modernization for the "Big Five." No deck armor would be added, but they would be reboilered, to gain internal space for new fire control instruments. New 5-inch AA controls would be fitted, as well as new main and secondary fire controls atop the cage masts. There would also be new turret rangefinders and new main battery plotting room instruments (stable vertical and range-keepers). The new antiaircraft directors, presumably Mark 33s, were needed to keep up with increasing aircraft speeds. To carry them, the bridge would have to be strengthened, adding about 20 tons. New masthead fire controls would be too heavy for the existing cage masts. The 0/.50-calibre machine guns might be removed, and the mainmast cut down. New blister studies, for a beam of 108 feet and a displacement of 39,600 tons, were ordered. The increase in beam was justified on the basis of handling experience with earlier blistered ships.

By October 1938 the bureaus had developed a range of plans costing (per ship) from $8,094,000 to $38,369,000. None would be a complete reconstruction, but any such expenditure would have to come out of funds available for new battleships. That was unacceptable, and in November the secretary of the navy formally rejected reconstruction, since even then the ships would be inferior to new ones. In 1939, however, Congress was persuaded to appropriate $6.6 million for large refits, including the blistering C&R believed essential.

With the war came the King Board on antiaircraft improvement. British experience in Norwegian waters made it painfully clear that much had to be done. King Board improvements in turn made blistering essential, not to improve underwater protection, but to preserve armored freeboard. In September 1940 the new Bureau of Ships reported that, given their existing overloads, a single torpedo hit would prob-

ably cause the ships to list so badly that the top of the side belt and probably the second deck would be submerged, even though the torpedo protection was rated at 400 pounds of TNT. It might be objected that a foot of freeboard could be recovered by leaving one layer of torpedo protection compartments empty. However, that would considerably reduce the value of the system as a whole. A single torpedo or heavy bomb would bring the main deck edge under water, the ship listing about 12 degrees. BuShips sought to solve this problem by blistering, at an estimated cost of $750,000 per ship and three to four months in dock.

The King Board proposed that armor decks be strengthened and that twin 5in/38 dual-purpose secondaries be fitted. However, the CNO wanted such major alterations delayed, given a precarious world situation. The secretary of the navy approved the limited blistering program on 4 October 1940. All work was to be done at Puget Sound, three months per ship. The planned schedule as of 7 October 1940 was:

	Planned Refit	*Actual Refit*
Maryland	17 Feb 41-20 May 41	Completed 1 Aug 41
W.Virginia	10 May 41-8 Aug 41	Not Carried Out
Colorado	28 Jul 41-28 Oct 41	Completed 26 Feb 42
Tennessee	19 Jan 42-21 Apr 41	Not Carried Out
California	16 Mar 42-16 Jun 42	Not Carried Out

The *Colorado* was actually under refit at the time of Pearl Harbor. The *West Virginia* and *Colorado* refits were interchanged in December 1940, which explains why the *West Virginia* was not refitted. The work took far longer than estimated; at that time Puget Sound offered to complete *Maryland* in 123 calendar days (four months) working shifts, six days per week, based on priority equal to that of a refit of the carrier *Saratoga* and ahead of new construction.

The blister differed from earlier ones in having a flat top, sloped outward just enough to provide drainage. It met the side of the ship just above the belt and in some photographs may be mistaken for belt armor. Although beam was increased to 108 feet, it was never considered adequate. Thus as early as 17 December 1940 commander, battleships, battle force complained that armored freeboard would be increased only to a point 2 1/2 to 3 feet *below* the 8 feet considered optimum for gun engagements. Matters could only become worse if other essential improvements were made.

The major wartime refits showed just how much would have been required. They will be described in detail below, but it may be noted here that they included the addition of 1,400 tons of deck armor and a 114 foot blister. The cost was far beyond anything imaginable before the war.

11

Design Studies, 1928–34

The Washington Treaty transformed the world of the U.S. battleship designers. A combination of World War One and the treaty-enforced, battleship-building "holiday" froze much of capital ship technology in most foreign navies at 1914 levels. In particular, the wide proliferation of such extremely powerful weapons as the 16in/50 and the 18 incher, which had inspired the armor studies of Battleship 1922 (see Chapter 7), was no longer to be feared as a likely feature of the near future. On the other hand, the treaty had not constrained the development of fire control for very long ranges (generally via spotter aircraft) or that of aerial and underwater weapons. Future designs would have to emphasize horizontal and underwater protection, the former against plunging shells as much as against bombs, and far more effort would have to go into antiaircraft batteries. Both protective features were potentially large consumers of weight, a quantity in short supply in view of the treaty limit of 35,000 tons. Considerable effort, therefore, went into various expedients for weight saving.

The Royal Navy was the great exception to the technology freeze. It was permitted by treaty to build two battleships, the *Nelson* and the *Rodney*. In the U.S. Navy these two units of unusual design were taken as a probable standard against which to measure U.S. design. This standard included what was considered an unusually high speed, 23 knots. It seems remarkable in retrospect that U.S. naval intelligence had little success in penetrating their mysteries—or, for that matter, that details of their designs became so freely available after their completion in 1927. For example, the first scanty outline details, including the unusual battery arrangement, became available in the fall of 1924. Preliminary Design was asked to work out a series of sketch designs by means of which the possible details of the British ship might be explored. The American constructors were puzzled by

the unusually great length of the ship, where "good design practice based on the most economical weight for hull, machinery, and protection would require length of only 625 feet with about 53,000SHP on a trial displacement of 36,500 tons. The reported HP of these vessels is, however, only 40,000 and this is very closely the power required to drive a 700-foot ship of 36,500 tons displacement at 23 knots." C&R also knew that all nine 16-inch guns would be concentrated forward, and indeed that the British "super *Hood*s planned in 1921 would have had all of their guns forward. Preliminary Design concluded, incorrectly, that this unusual arrangement had been adopted to provide a flight deck abaft the funnel. It assumed that the hull had been made unusually long in order to provide sufficient space for flight operations.

Nor did the American designers understand the British concept of protection, despite the recent close collaboration between C&R and the British DNC department during World War One. U.S. practice was to armor a fixed percentage of the waterline length to protect buoyancy and stability. Long hulls were therefore heavy hulls, since the longer the hull, the greater the investment in side armor. *If* the very long *Nelson* were armored on U.S. lines, then she could not have very thick side armor. Preliminary Design reported that

a large amount of 7-inch armor plate was under manufacture in Great Britain at a time prior to its requirement for the construction of their present light cruisers. . . . Armor of this thickness if inclined at an angle of 30 degrees to the vertical would have resistive quality equal to that of a 12-inch vertical plate at ranges greater than 16,000 yards. . . . Certain reports indicate, however, that the side belt armor plates are about 13 or 14 inches in thickness. Further reports on the pre-Treaty British battleships of 48,000

U.S. battleship designs of 1928–34 show the same features that were applied to battleship modernization. The *New Mexico*, shown here, might have been typical.

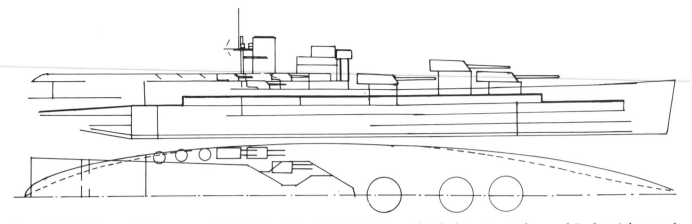

After the Washington Conference, only Britain had the right to build new battleships. Her *Nelson* and *Rodney* (*above and facing*) therefore excited enormous interest—and enormous curiosity. In October 1924 Preliminary Design tried to deduce their characteristics from the scanty information available, with the two results shown: These flight-deck battleships were probably heavily influenced by an article in the 1923 *Brassey's Naval Annual*, by a senior British naval architect, George Thurston. Most striking is that, even though U.S. constructors had been intimately exposed to British thinking during World War One, they were unable to project reliably British ideas after the war. For example, they had no idea that the British had changed their criterion for waterline protection, and therefore that the concentration of machinery and magazines was seen as a weight saver. To U.S. constructors determined to armor a fixed fraction of the waterline, it had to be a means to leave space for some other function—probably aircraft-related. This was not simple mirror-imaging, in that U.S. interest in hybrid warships was still several years away. For example, the ships were relatively long for their speed of 23 knots. To the British, that saved machinery weight (at 700 feet they would need only 40,000SHP, compared to 53,000 for Preliminary Design's optimum length of 625 feet). The U.S. designers also recalled that the 48,000-ton British battle cruisers cancelled as a result of the Washington Conference had a clear deck aft—which was interpreted as a flight deck. Similarly, Preliminary Design concluded from relatively sparse information that the British had decided not merely to slope their belt very steeply but to use only 7-inch armor. The arrow in one of the plans indicates the extent of 7-inch plating, the rest of the belt being even thinner, 5 inches. Inclined at 30 degrees to the vertical, a 7-inch plate would be equivalent to a 12-inch plate, given the steep angle of fall of shells at ranges beyond 16,000 yards. It was believed that the inclined internal side belt would help to vent the gases produced by underwater explosions. Some of the conclusions were valid, but most were not—reverse naval architecture is difficult at best. No records of attempts to estimate Japanese designs have been found, but throughout the treaty period Preliminary Design was asked to develop in design form the consequences of various treaty proposals. Some of them are illustrated in this chapter.

tons indicated that the side protection extended only in way of magazines and conning tower. Thirteen-inch or 14-inch side belt protection could be carried on the weights if its length were limited to the extent specified.

All of this showed that battleships conforming to the Washington Treaty could not be designed like pre-treaty capital ships. The British had simply given up the American requirement for waterline protection. Then length could be chosen to minimize power (hence, machinery weight) to achieve a given design speed. Battery arrangement was dictated by a desire to concentrate the vitals and hence to reduce armor weights. The American designers refused to recognize the new conditions and tried hard to design treaty battleships to pre-1921 standards, only to be forced in the end to expedients they did not particularly like, such as inclined armor and geared turbines. Their studies convinced them that 35,000 tons was at best a bare minimum for a satisfactory battleship—a conclusion of great consequence in subsequent treaty negotiations.

Politically, the Washington Treaty failed to defuse U.S.–Japanese tensions in the Pacific. The Navy continued throughout the interwar period to regard Japan as by far the most likely future adversary. The

U.S. Fleet was concentrated in the Pacific, and new warship designs were generally evaluated in terms of their performance in a Pacific war (see Chapters 12 and 14, in particular).

In the treaty-making process, however, the British were the most immediate adversary. Throughout the interwar period, they sought to reduce the cost of sea power through agreements to reduce the maximum size of all warship classes, including battleships and aircraft carriers.* The U.S. perception was that, having clearly lost economic and industrial superiority, Britain was trying to preserve her naval supremacy by disarming the United States at the conference table. The British were accused of exploiting assymmetries between their position and that of the United States by demanding symmetrical arms reduction. The chief assymmetry was in bases. The Royal Navy could expect to fight hundreds of miles from its major bases in the event of the Pacific war that both it and the United States feared. American ships, on the other hand, would have to cross much

---

* In 1929 the United States compromised with Britain by accepting 6 inches as the future cruiser gun calibre. In 1935, however, the United States refused to reduce battleship size below 35,000 tons, although it did accept a 23,000-ton limit on aircraft carriers and an 8,000-ton limit on new cruisers.

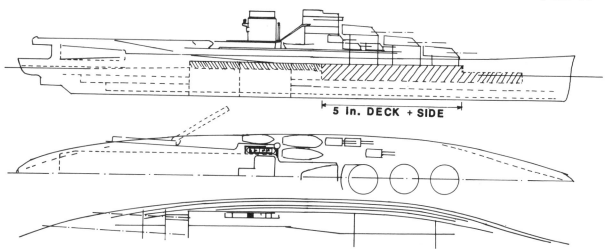

5 In. DECK + SIDE

greater distances—and would have to recross them if they were to return after suffering battle damage. A member of the General Board observed that "in effect, bases equal more ships."

The British had clearly benefited from the common upper limit achieved at Washington. Moreover, they had benefited from the U.S.–Japanese agreement to forgo island fortifications, since many of their own bases were already both well established and well protected. It appeared to the U.S. Navy that the British were determined to press matters further by achieving reductions in the capabilities allowed each capital ship—a change from which they would benefit, since the less effective U.S. ships would find it harder to cross the wider oceans before them.

At Geneva in 1927 the British proposed that future battleships be limited to 13.5-inch guns and 28,500 tons. To Americans this meant a fleet limited to the obsolescent dreadnoughts built before 1912 and in future to 12-inch gun ships, as the United States would be unlikely to invest in a wholly new gun design. But the British would have 13.5-inch weapons comparable ballistically to the American 14 inch. Moreover, they would have the last of the 16-inch ships, since the lives of the *Nelson*s would necessarily expire long after those of the newest U.S. *Colorado*s. A twenty-five-year age limit was generally accepted, which would mean British superiority in 1948–52. Finally, sheer size would favor the British. Their smaller ships would be viable in the face of aerial and underwater attack because, even heavily damaged, they could limp home to nearby bases, whereas comparable American ships would probably founder en route home.

For their part, the British saw their proposals as a means of maintaining a worthwhile fleet in the face of a deepening financial crisis. Britain had never really emerged from the post–World War One financial trauma, and many of the British government's efforts were directed toward maintaining a very expensive Empire on less and less secure assets. Successive British treaty proposals for small battleships demanded U.S. replies, and Preliminary Design had to

evaluate the possibilities inherent in reduced size ships. These studies, many of which are listed in this chapter, were not so much design sketches for prospective construction as technical support for treaty negotiation. The "defensive series" of designs developed in parallel with the earliest *North Carolina* designs fit into this category (see Chapter 12). At the other end of the scale, when Japan announced her prospective withdrawal from the treaty structure in March 1934, Preliminary Design had to estimate the possible technological consequences.

Although the battleship-building holiday did suspend preliminary design work on battleships, there was never any serious expectation that such construction would not one day resume. Thus, the bureaus were always interested in developments which would be applicable to future battleships, and in particular BuOrd retained considerable interest in new main battery guns. Its most interesting study, in December 1926, was inspired by the construction of a very long (56-calibre) 16-inch gun.

This weapon had originally been ordered as a prototype 18in/48, but as such a calibre was prohibited by the Washington Treaty, the incomplete gun was lined down to 16-inch calibre and completed as such in 1925. The results of extensive test firing were compared with the performance of existing 16-inch guns. They are of interest here because both the 16in/56 and the 18in/48 were later considered as alternatives to more conventional weapons. The results of the 1926 evaluation carried over to later ones. The longer barrel brought higher muzzle velocity, 3,000 ft/sec as against 2,800 for the 16in/50 and 2,600 for the 16in/45, at the cost of much-reduced barrel life, 125 vs. 180(16in/50) rounds. Since standard policy was to reline whenever *remaining* barrel life was equal to the ammunition allowance, 100 rounds, the 16in/56 would have to be relined every 25 rounds. On the other hand, if it were fired at a reduced charge to give it the muzzle velocity of the 16in/50, the 16in/56 would last 225 rounds.

The three guns were evaluated against a hypothetical ship with 13-inch side armor and a 3.5-inch

Table 11-1. Hitting Probabilities: Percentage of Hits at Various Ranges, on Side and Deck Armor. The Percentage of Hits That Would *Not* Penetrate Is Given in Parentheses for Each Range and Each Gun.

Gun MV Range	16in/56 3000			16in/50 2800			16in/45 2600ft/sec		
	Side	Deck	Total	Side	Deck	Total	Side	Deck	Total
15,000 yds	50	(50)	50	50	(50)	50	50	(50)	50
20,000	40	(60)	40	40	(60)	40	40	(60)	40
21,000	38	(62)	38	38	(62)	38	38	(62)	38
22,000	36	(64)	36	36	(64)	36	36	(64)	36
25,000	30	(70)	30	30	(70)	30	(30)	(70)	---
28,000	24	(76)	24	(24)	76	76	(24)	76	76
30,000	(20)	80	80	(20)	80	80	(20)	80	80

NOTE: These data were assembled for the Special Ordnance Board in 1926. They refer to a 13-inch belt and 3.5-inch deck, immune against the 16in/56 between 23,800 and 28,000 yards; against the 16in/50 between 25,200 and 26,300 yards; and against the 16in/45 between 22,000 and 24,800 yards. Note that the *lower velocity* guns are actually more effective, because so many of the shells strike the deck and because, the slower the shell, the more steeply it plunges.

deck. Hits were expected to be equally distributed between side and deck at 15,000 yards, beyond which deck hits would increase until they accounted for 80 percent at 30,000 yards. The test ship would have no immunity at all against the 16in/56 (side penetration out to 28,800 yards, deck penetration beyond 28,000 yards). Below 28,000 yards, however, most hits would be on the deck armor (74 percent at 27,000 yards), and they would fail to penetrate, because of the relatively flat trajectory of the long gun. The 50-calibre gun would penetrate side armor out to 25,200 yards, and deck armor inside 26,300, at which range about 72 percent of hits would be deck hits. With its steeper trajectory, the 16in/45 would begin to penetrate deck armor at 24,800 yards but would not penetrate side armor beyond 22,000.

These figures must be evaluated in light of the very small number of hits to be expected in battle. World War One experience was commonly held to show that 5 percent would be a great deal. At 26,000 yards (28 percent hits on side armor) that would mean, overall, 1.4 percent of shells fired hitting side armor, and 3.6 percent decks. At Jutland, the British fired 4,598 heavy shells for 100 hits (2.17 percent); the Germans, 3,597 heavy shells, for 120 hits (3.33 percent). However, 37 of the German hits were by shells fired at short range at the three British armored cruisers *Black Prince*, *Defence*, and *Warrior*. At long range, then, every hit would have to count heavily. Steeply plunging shells hitting deck armor were potentially the most important, since they might well damage machinery or destroy magazines. Hence it could be argued that a gun optimized toward penetrating side protection would be of little value in the naval battle of the future.

There was also the impact of the new gun on the ship as a whole. It weighed 168 tons and cost $353,000, compared with 128 tons and $286,000 for the 16in/50, and with 105 tons and $235,000 for the 16in/45.

Relining would cost $46,000 (compared with $38,000 and $30,000, respectively). A twin mount would weigh 1,190 tons per gun, a triple 974; by way of comparison, the 16in/50 cost 1,030 or 843 tons. On the ordnance weights of the *Maryland*, 7,560 tons, nine 16in/50 could be accommodated in three triples, but only six or seven 16in/56 (two triples for as little as 5,844 tons, three twins for 7,140, or two triples and one twin on 7,682 tons).

In effect, 200 ft/sec added 3,500 yards in maximum range of side penetration, but cost 2,000 yards in deck penetration. The likely percentages of hits on side and deck were such that these changes in immune zone were nearly equivalent. There was little to choose from, and BuOrd concluded that a battery of nine 16in/50 was by far the best investment, particularly since the 50-calibre guns had already been built for the cancelled capital ships of the 1916 program. Moreover, they would fire more shells and so achieve more hits, per unit time, than would the less numerous battery of 16in/56.

One conclusion was important for future development: the Special Board on Ordnance, which conducted the study, noted that "studies made over a period of about ten years seem to indicate a considerable advantage to having whatever gun we finally adopt fire a projectile somewhat heavier than present projectiles of our Navy, but using a muzzle velocity somewhat less. . . . The erosion would be the same; accuracy might possibly be increased, and penetration, particularly of decks, would certainly be improved. . . . A 16in/50 gun looks like the gun to use. . . . The indicated line of improvement is thought to lie not so much with the gun itself as with the projectile. The development of a heavier projectile for the 16in/50 (using some of the money saved by not having to build new guns) has much to recommend it. . . . All of the foregoing is presumed on adhering to the present 16-inch limitation. . . otherwise

Table 11-2. 16in/50 Armor Penetration

Target Angle Range	Deck	90 degree Belt	60 degree Belt
18,000 yds	2.65	17.5	inches
22,000	2.8	15.0	14.0
24,000	3.2	14.0	13.1
26,000	3.6	12.9	12.4
28,000	4.0	12.1	11.5
30,000	4.5	11.0	10.6

NOTE: These data were prepared by BuOrd in 1926. They refer to a gun firing a 2,100-pound shell at a muzzle velocity of 2,800 ft/sec. The bureau considered 30,000 yards the ideal fighting range. By way of comparison, at 28,000 yards a 16in/45 could penetrate 5.6 inches of deck armor or 9.5 inches of side armor, compared with 2.65 and 16.7 inches at 18,000 yards.

one would probably increase the calibre and decrease length." That is exactly what happened. By 1929 BuOrd was working on a 2,400-pound, 16-inch shell to replace the existing 2,100-pound type, and later a 2,240-pound shell would enter service. In 1939, moreover, BuOrd formally proposed a new super-heavy 2,700-pound shell. The bureau considered a 16in/50 firing its new shell superior to the 18in/48 firing a more conventional shell.

The other major relevant technical development of the 1920s was the relatively light and reliable geared steam turbine. Numerous treaty battleship design studies foundered on the weight of the turboelectric plant, which C&R espoused for its suitability to minute compartmentation. Treaty cruiser construction required the development of relatively light, high-powered plants. For example, the *Salt Lake City,* the first U.S. treaty cruiser, developed 107,000SHP on 2,176 tons of machinery at the same time that Steam Engineering estimated 2,560 tons for a 40,000SHP turboelectric plant.

Another machinery system was often considered but never adopted. Diesel power allowed for very low fuel consumption and very long endurance, the latter a feature dear to U.S. strategists. Diesels were rejected on grounds of unreliability—it would be too bad were a battleship to have to have her armored decks ripped out to get at a faulty cylinder. The Japanese were to make a similar decision a decade later on their *Yamato.* But the Germans decided in favor of the diesel for their commerce-raiding "pocket battleships," which were designed at just this time.

As originally envisaged, the battleship-building "holiday" was to have terminated on 31 December 1931, that is, during FY32, the budget for which would have to be passed in the spring of 1931. Budget figures would have had to be submitted no later than

the fall of 1930, based on concrete designs. C&R and the General Board both recognized that a treaty design would be different enough from previous practice to require an early start, so they began work in 1928. There was as yet no hint of the depression to come, and congressional support of the ambitious cruiser program promised similar support for new capital ships, especially in view of the two Britain had just completed. A further hopeful sign was congressional support for the extensive (and expensive) battleship reconstruction program already under way.

Considerable material remained from the cancelled *South Dakota* class, including triple 16in/50 turrets and what amounted to a pair of complete sets of armor. The cancellation of the 1916 ships had wiped out much of the domestic heavy armor plate industry, which made use of the existing armor attractive, although it might be argued that purchases of fresh armor would be necessary to preserve a vital industrial asset.

About mid-July, 1928 the secretary of the navy asked for characteristics for the next class of battleships. On 19 July Chief Constructor J. D. Beuret asked the General Board for some parameters:

—Should we consider only 35,000-ton types, or smaller ones as well?

—Should we accept maximum beam and draft of 106 and 33 feet? Although the *West Virginia* drew only 31 feet 6 inches maximum, the *South Dakota* required 33 feet.

—We assume a minimum speed of 21 knots and a maximum of 23. Are speeds beyond 23 knots to be considered?

—Should the previous endurance requirement of 10,000nm at 10 knots be retained?

—Is turboelectric drive so valuable that geared turbines and diesels are not to be considered? The General Board rejected both alternatives, and ordered turboelectric drive retained.

—Should only 16-inch guns be considered? Beuret suggested eight to twelve gun studies. He wanted to know how important a symmetrical arrangement was—nine guns in triples weighed roughly as much as eight in twins if armor, protection, barbettes, and ammunition were included.

—Secondary battery: should gunhouses be used? If the AA guns were to be 5 inch or larger, it seemed wise to consider a dual-purpose battery. At this time BuOrd was already working on what would become the 5in/38, the success of which appeared to hinge on that of an aluminum cartridge case. There was also the question of torpedo tubes. The General Board called for a conventional secondary battery of twelve 5in/51 single-purpose guns and eight 5in/25 AA, with four 0.50-calibre machine guns in each mast top

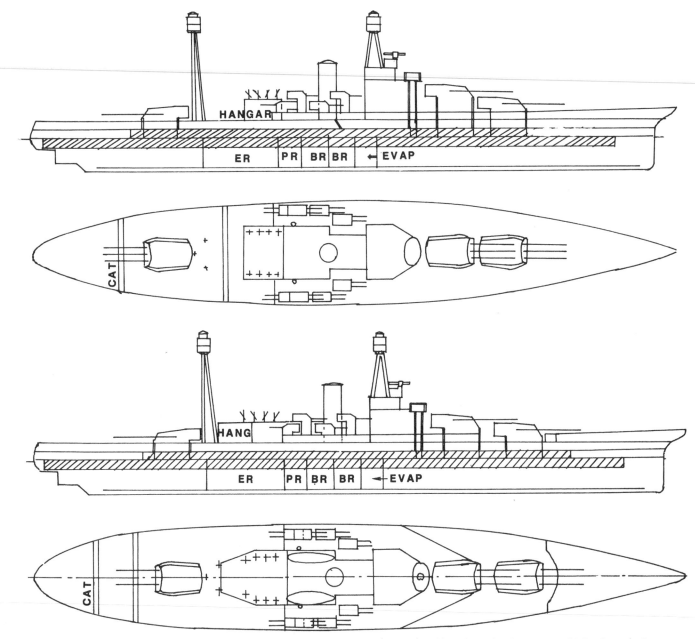

Sketch designs for battleships prepared in 1928 for the General Board show how barbettes could be lowered to save weight. Each ship is armed with nine 16in/50 and with sixteen 6in/53; note the fixed cross-deck catapults. The first design is entirely conventional, with a 16 feet 6 inch-wide belt and two protective decks. All the turrets are substantially lowered in the second design, through the use of a broken forecastle forward of No. 1 turret.

to defend against strafers. Alternative designs with and without above-water torpedo tubes were to be worked out.

—How important was it to provide two elevated main battery fire control positions?

—Beuret wanted to assume the classical protection parameters of 16-inch shellfire, 400-pound TNT (underwater), heavy case bombs equivalent in charge to 16-inch shells, and light case bombs with charges up to 1,000 pounds.

Beuret ordered two preliminary design studies, one with ten 16in/50 and a speed of 21 knots, the other with eight guns and a speed of 23 knots. He demanded immunity between 18,000 and 28,000 yards, at which ranges penetration was estimated at:

	16in/ 50:18,000	28,000	16in/ 45:18,000	28,000 yds
Deck	2.65	5.3	2.65	5.6 in
Side	17.5	11.6	16.7	9.5 in

The thickest available side armor was 13.5 inches, so that the inner edge of the zone would have to be well beyond the desired 18,000 yards. This plate would defeat the 16in/45 of the *Nelson* beyond 20,000 yards. All of these figures were predicated on a target angle of 90 degrees, that is, with the shell striking at right angles to the belt armor. A more realistic figure like 60 degrees would allow considerable relaxation of requirements. For example, at that angle, 14 inches would stop a 16in/50 shell at 22,000 yards, compared with 15 inches at 90 degrees. The idea of relaxing requirements for side armor was particularly attractive if one assumed that there would be few hits on the side at very long ranges.

These considerations became even more interesting if the low-velocity American 16in/45 were taken as the standard of protection. It could penetrate 16 inches at 20,000 yards *at a 90 degree target angle*, but only about 11.25 at 60 degrees. Even more could be achieved by the use of internal (inclined) armor, as in HMS *Nelson*.

Preliminary Design now proceeded to trade off speed, firepower, and protection. Its sketch design would have resembled the reconstructed *Nevada* and *Pennsylvania* classes, with a single prominent funnel and two tall tripods surmounted by fire control. In the following table, an asterisk on the side armor indicates internal armor; 10-45 means ten 16in/45. All ships displace 35,000 tons (standard), and all have 1.5-inch splinter decks. An asterisk in the speed column indicates geared turbine, rather than turbo-electric propulsion.

Speed	Guns	Deck	Side Armor
23	10-45	3	12.5
23	9-45	3.25	13.5
23	8-50	2.625	13.5
23*	9-50	4.0	13.5
23*	9-50	4.75	15.0 over magazines
		2.75	11.0 over machinery
23*	9-50	5.25	13.5*
21	10-50	1.875	12.5
21	10-45	3.5	12.5
21	9-50	3.75	13.5
21	8-50	3.125	13.5
21*	10-50	2.375	12.5
21*	10-50	3.375	12.5*
21*	9-50	4.5	13.5
21*	8-50	3.625	13.5
24	9-45	3.75	13.5

These represented the alternatives available to the treaty battleship designer. He had to give up the protective effect of turboelectric power to save weight. He could not really afford the symmetry of twin turrets fore and aft, either. If, further, he wanted to achieve really effective deck protection he had to adopt inclined armor or else vary the thickness according to the importance of what was being protected. All of these approaches can be seen in ships built later under treaty restrictions.

By September, the chief constructor had sketches in hand. He reported to the General Board that on 35,000 tons the choice of 23 rather than 21 knots would cost 12 feet more length, 1.5 less beam, and about 275 tons in engineering weight, equivalent to about half an inch of deck armor. A switch to geared turbines might buy back the half inch. These conclusions were nearly constant in all of the existing studies. Three triple turrets would weigh materially less than four twins, and about 1,500 or 1,600 tons less than ten guns in two twin and two triple mounts. The chief constructor found little saving in a *Nelson*-like arrangement, although that may well be because he was unwilling to give up the long waterline belt of standard U.S. practice. On the other hand, he could save a great deal by substituting 45- for 50-calibre guns: about 850 tons on nine guns, 1,000 on ten, so that ten 16in/45 might just be squeezed into 35,000 tons, while ten 16in/50 would be too heavy.

BuOrd much preferred the 16in/50, whose greater range would take full advantage of new developments in fire control, such as air spotting. As for secondary weapons, the bureau greatly preferred dual-purpose guns, which would require fewer separate fire control positions. Were that not acceptable, the bureau proposed the 6in/53 as an alternative to the existing 5in/51. It weighed about twice as much, but would be far more effective against the new 10,000-ton cruisers (albeit about as effective against the chief surface threat, the destroyer, except possibly in a mass attack on the bow at long range). The 1926-27 gunnery exercises showed that the 6in/53 achieved 35 percent more hits per gun per minute than the 5 inch firing at full charge, although at reduced charge the 5 inch did 30 percent better.

The best single-purpose antiaircraft gun was clearly the 5in/25 then mounted in the *Colorado*s and the *Tennessee*s. Were a single secondary weapon to be adopted, its calibre would be limited by the requirement to load at high angles. The heaviest dual-purpose gun would probably be a 5.3-inch weapon firing a 75 pound shell. BuOrd envisaged a dual-purpose battery of sixteen weapons in twin gunhouses or else the maximum single-purpose battery plus eight AA guns. In the latter case it would be best to mount the guns in twin gunhouses with maximum elevation, three or four on each beam, the inner mounts firing over the outer ones. The key question was whether aircraft or destroyers constituted the primary threat. Twin mounts had been scorned in the past as much less effective than singles, but BuOrd

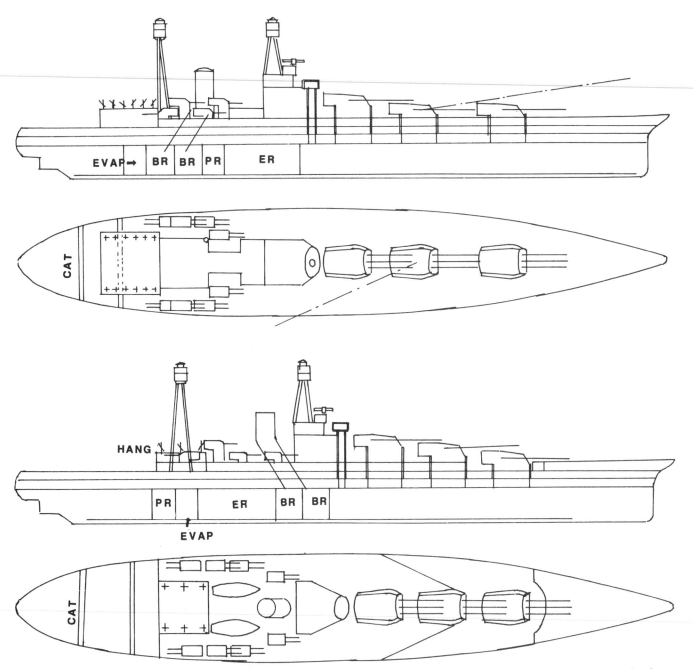

Arrangements (*above and facing*) with all turrets forward were also extremely difficult. The most conventional scheme had a 48 degree dead zone aft. Lowering the guns saved weight, and as the turrets spread out the dead zone aft was reduced to 16 degrees. However, No. 2 turret could not fire dead ahead at less than 9 degrees (17,400 yards). This ship had a narrow (12-foot) belt, and one rather than two protective decks. The exotic alternative was an asymmetrical turret arrangement, as shown, which reduced the dead zone aft to 6 degrees. All of these Schemes showed a length of 640 feet.

felt that they were quite as effective as long as power could be supplied to them.

A light AA battery of ten machine guns was suggested, mounted on masts and superstructures, as in the reconstructed battleships. In future this might be supplemented by machine cannon; BuOrd then had a 37mm weapon under development. Finally, the bureau rejected torpedo tubes as hazardous, because of the danger of flooding underwater tubes or of explosions in above-water warhead stowage.

Steam Engineering found arguments on both sides of the turboelectric/geared turbine issue. The former was more reliable and more economical, partly because in a geared turbine installation all auxiliaries had to be kept on line continuously. Now, however, fuel weight no longer figured in standard displacement. Therefore it might be argued that bare machinery weight and volume alone should determine the choice of engine, and in that case the geared turbine was more attactive because of its compact-

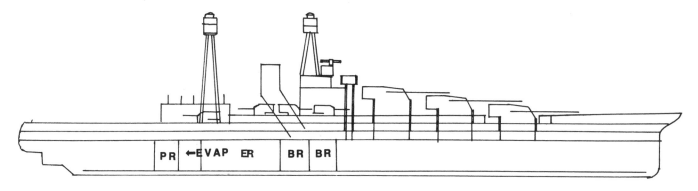

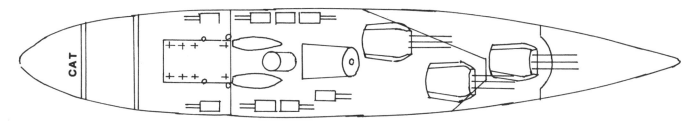

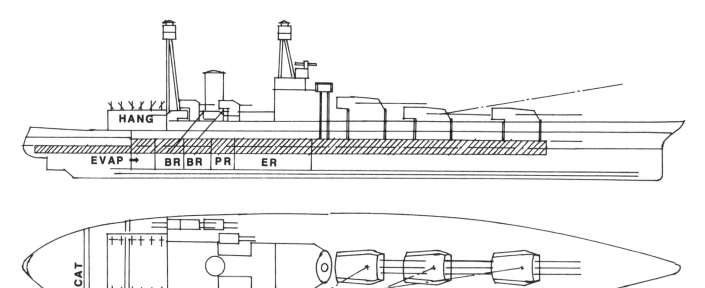

ness. It would save about 20 feet in length as well as some beam. Moreover, the dead weight of fuel storage tanks would count for little, as these tanks would in any case have to be provided as part of the torpedo-defense system.

The War Plans Division of OpNav noted that these ships would not be completed until 1934 and that they would probably serve through 1959. They would, therefore, be the nucleus of a new battle fleet. War Plans wanted a maximum ship, partly in view of Pacific requirements. It favored high speed (by which it meant 23 knots), arguing that at higher power weight per horsepower would fall off, "The tendency of design is toward increased speed. . . .We are justified

in making some sacrifice in other qualities in order to increase the speed of future battleships, thereby providing for a future fleet whose speed as a whole will compare favorably with the speed of foreign fleets." Unconstrained by technical problems, War Plans pushed for at least ten 16-inch guns. It opposed the *Nelson* arrangement in view of the danger of lucky hits. As for secondary weapons, it seemed to War Plans that torpedo development would lead to longer ranges and hence to the need for heavier rather than lighter torpedo-defense guns. There should be at least sixteen 6 inchers.

War Plans was impressed with the longer gunnery ranges now possible. At such ranges most shells would

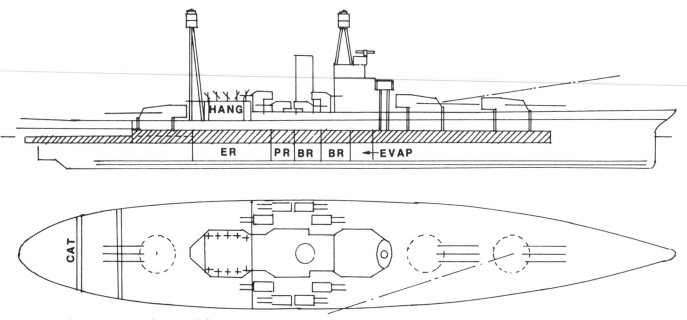

The 660-foot Scheme (*above and facing*) was prepared to show the sacrifices entailed in mounting ten 16-inch guns (45 rather than 50 calibre) on 35,000 tons. No. 2 turret cannot fire dead ahead at elevations of less than 8 degrees (that is, to less than 16,000 yards), and the belt is just 12-feet high, with only a single protective deck. Alternatively, nine 16in/50 could be carried on a 640-foot hull, again with the severe range limitation.

plunge steeply into the deck of a battleship. The division proposed that armor be devised to burst such shells before they struck the main protective deck. This idea and a similar one about bombs led eventually to a characteristic feature of American battleship protection, the "bomb deck." This was splinter armor spread over the main or weather deck and intended to detonate bombs before they struck the main protective deck, so that their bursts would not damage the upper part of the hull.

The director of war plans concluded by asking for a greater steaming radius, at least 12,000nm at 10 knots, and four aircraft on two catapults. He wanted to retain the well-tested turboelectric propulsion of previous classes. Battleships were not to be considered experiments. The War Plans staff went further, citing studies of Pacific warfare to show a need for a radius of 16,000nm at 10 knots, as well as resistance to at least six underwater hits. As for deck protection, priority should be given first to magazines, second to machinery, third main armament, and fourth to ship control.

Fleet Training questioned the reliability of the triple turrets, particularly the sleeve type introduced in the *New Mexico*s. It did, however, favor the dual-purpose secondary gun. Such a compromise weapon would necessarily have a limited range, since to attain a high rate of fire (for antiaircraft employment) it would have to use a shell and cartridge case of limited weight. The division argued that this was no great sacrifice. Few hits on surface craft would be made at extreme ranges, since spotting of the splashes

from such small weapons was considered impossible beyond about 12,000 yards. The fleet wanted a multiple AA machine gun, preferably eight mounts per ship. Gas attack was a new issue, "Experiments [show] no certain means of removing mustard gas from battleships. It might even be necessary to sink a ship that has been thoroughly gassed."

Fleet Training also advocated, apparently for the first time, a tower-mast of the *Nelson* type, which it considered far superior to the existing separate conning tower, bridge, and mast. Finally, it pressed for multiple catapults in view of the long firing interval between launches and the possibility of casualties—current types could fire every five minutes, a new one every two. Catapults were essential to the view of very long-range battle which was expressed elsewhere in high gun elevations and in heavier deck armor. Without aircraft to spot, ranges would be limited, and hits mostly on side armor the thickness of which would have been reduced precisely to allow for the heavier decks required to protect at longer ranges. Ships designed for battle beyond 20,000 yards would be penetrated again and again. It was, therefore, worthwhile to make considerable sacrifices to ensure air spotting.

The General Board reconvened about three weeks later, on 16 October. It favored a nine-gun, 23-knot ship with a 4.7-inch deck that would guarantee immunity against the 16in/50 out to 30,000 yards. The C&R studies appeared to show that the guns would be limited to 45 calibres, and Admiral William Leahy, the chief of BuOrd, remarked that two knots (that is,

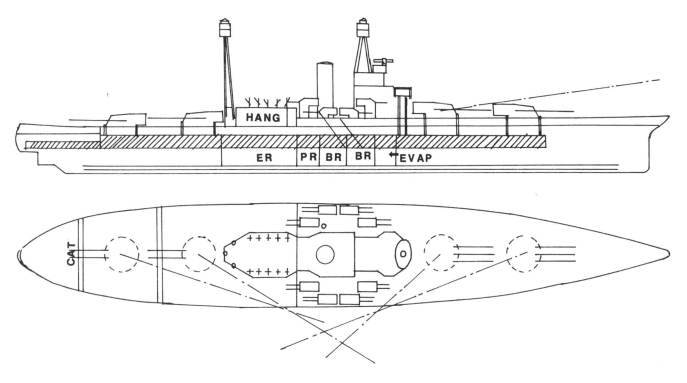

HANG

ER | PR | BR | BR | EVAP

CAT

23 to match the British and perhaps the Japanese) were valuable enough to warrant a careful study of the two alternative guns. The armor immediately available from the cancelled ships would provide immunity against 16in/50 fire between 23,000 and 26,000 yards (between 17,000 and 26,000 at a 60-degree target angle). Alternatively, it was possible to choose a single battle range and use that to determine both side *and* deck armor. For example, at 30,000 yards one might choose 11-inch side and 4.5-inch deck, at 22,000, 14 and 3.1 inches. Leahy reviewed these figures for the distribution of hits between side and deck at long range and noted further that he expected on average 0.64 hits per gun per minute at 14,000 yards and only 0.18 at 24,500. He concluded by observing that the 16in/50 had the great advantages of current availability, a flatter trajectory (for greater accuracy), and about 4,500 yards greater maximum range. The 16in/45 would penetrate deck armor better at range and would weigh less—which would be reflected in higher speed.

Our studies show that for the general average of present battle ranges and at all target angles their effectiveness is not very different.

If ranges should by the assistance of aerial observation and further development of indirect fire reach out beyond the present maximum battle range, the 16in/50 would have a marked advantage. If in battle the range should close to where there is no danger of deck penetration, their flatter trajectory and their advantage in a narrow zone where the 45-calibre gun lacks penetration recommend the 16in/50. . . . It is my present opinion that a decisive battle is not likely to be won at long range. . . . That commander who forces fighting to close range should, other things being equal, win the battle. For this speed is essential, and those guns that are more effective at close range are to be preferred.

This added up to nine 16in/50, 23 knots, a 13.5-inch side, and perhaps sacrifices in deck armor. But Leahy would, in the end, sacrifice guns for speed, "The speed of late foreign battleships, the advantage in battle of choice of range and choice of favorable target angle, and the ability to accept or decline action, that are given by superior speed, all point to the necessity of accepting the small disadvantage of the 45-calibre gun in order to obtain the advantage of 2 or 3 knots additional speed."

Characteristics issued on 27 February 1929 called for nine 16 inch in triple mounts, eighteen 5.3-inch DP guns,* and a speed of 22 knots. Protection would match that of the *South Dakota* (BB 49), except for a thicker deck (4.5 vs. 3.5 inches), which would be costly in terms of weight. Steaming radius would be the classical 10,000nm at 10 knots, twice that with emergency fuel load. Preliminary Design had already found even these modest requirements impossible to meet, as they would cost about 37,000 tons. It had continued battleship work until late October 1928, at which time the limited number of designers were

---

* This weapon was never built. It was superseded by the famous 5in/38, just as a later conceptual 5.4-inch dual-purpose gun became the 5in/54 (see Chapter 15).

Table 11-3. Sketch Designs of October 1928

Design	A	B	B1	C	D
Dimensions			640 × 100.6 × 32		
Gun	16in/50	16in/45	16in/45	16in/50	16in/45
IZ VS	16in/45	16in/50	16in/50	16in/45	16in/50
IZ	28-30	27.5-30	28-30	26-28	26-28
(60′ T.A.)	22-30	21.4-30	22-30	20-28	20-28
Deck (in)	4.85	4.75	4.75	4.25	4.15
Belt (in)	10	12.4	12.2	11.2	13.3
SHP	60,000	48,000	53,000	48,000	48,000
Speed(kts)	23.5	23	23.2	23	23
Hull					
Fittings					
Protection					
Machinery					
Battery					
Ammunition					
Eq't &Out.					
Stores					
Aero					
Displacement					

NOTE: Apart from Scheme 7, all had nine 16-inch guns of varying lengths, as indicated.

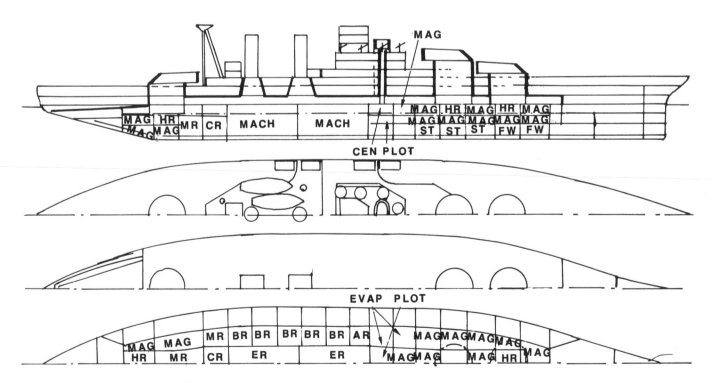

Scheme D for a conventional battleship, dated April 1929: 35,000 tons (standard) (612 × 104.5 × 32 feet), with a steaming endurance of 20,000nm at 10 knots. She would have been powered by turboelectric machinery (41,000SHP = 22 knots). Note the wing locations of her ten boiler rooms (as in earlier battleships). Armament would have been eight 16in/50 and sixteen 5.3-inch DP guns in twin mounts, plus eight 37mm antiaircraft guns. The 13.5-inch belt would have been 16 feet 6 inches wide, covered by a 3.75-inch deck (1.5-inch splinter deck). Although not indicated in detail, there were conventional torpedo bulkheads, as in Schemes F and G.

F	G	G1	7
			660 × 100.3 × 32
16in/45	16in/50	16in/45	10 - 16in/45
	20 - 28		
4.3	3.9	3.9	
11.2	12.6	12.6	
48,000	60,000	66,000	46,300
21.1	22.9	23.85	23
17,786	17,325	17,325	18,267
1715	1715	1715	1720
7716	8179	8179	7052
2360	2750	3150	2575
2180	1905	1905	2048
1794	1686	1905	1793
620	620	620	620
400	400	400	400
35	35	35	35
34,606	34,615	34,015	34,510

switched to more urgent work on submarines and destroyer leaders. By that time a variety of sketch designs showing more or less desperate attempts at weight saving had been worked out.

For example, in the last of the outline designs the splinter deck had been reduced to a structural deck. The weight of STS otherwise worked into it went instead into a thicker main protective deck (5.75 inches). The belt was made narrower, the turret roofs thinner (6.5 rather than 8 inches). No. 2 turret was even lowered to only 2 feet higher than No. 1 to save barbette height and therefore weight. The second turret had to be moved far enough aft to clear the first. Such a ship could manage nine 16in/50 and South Dakota protection on 35,000 tons, or alternatively ten 16in/45 and turboelectric machinery for 23 knots.

These types did not quite meet General Board requirements. When Preliminary Design returned to battleship work in April 1929, it felt forced to consider still more radical ideas. There was already a 1928 study of savings that might have been made in the Maryland by various means, including using lighter scantlings, aluminum superstructure, welding, and thinner teak decking. The structural changes saved 830 tons. Using them, a ship with a displacement of 31,500 tons could have one of the following sets:

—eight 16in/45 in three turrets, 3.75- and 2.25-inch decks, a 17-foot wide, 14.5in-9in belt, and 7-inch (rather than 5-inch) turret crowns

—nine 16in/45 and 21 knots with 15-inch barbettes, 20-inch face plates, and 4.5-inch plus 2.25-inch decks

These structural measures engendered more radical ones. Deck and side armor were the two greatest weights in these ships. Any reduction in armored length would, therefore, greatly reduce displacement or else would free weight for thicker armor. The British had realized as much in the Nelson, but Preliminary Design was unwilling to abandon its requirement that a fixed fraction of the total waterline length be protected. Modern battleships had limited freeboard, that is, a small range of stability. "Therefore it appears obvious that the maintenance of the waterline intact throughout the half or 5/8 length amidships is essential. Further, the grave difficulties resulting from the loss of considerable amounts of buoyancy forward [where the Nelson is unarmored] were repeatedly emphasized during the great war." Then it seemed that the best way to cut armor weights was to cut the length of the ship and compensate for the increased wave-making resistance by using higher-powered but lighter-weight machinery, as in the new cruisers.

As in the 1928 study, the other available weight savers were reductions in fittings and in the hull scantlings (that is, in the weight of the hull structure itself) and extensive use of welding and of aluminum structure, as in the new cruisers.

A series of these short battleship studies was done, including one only 530 feet long (Scheme G); it turned out that on 576 feet (Nelson was 700) 23 knots could be attained and the belt made a foot wider than on the South Dakota while at the same time the deck protection increased to 4.25 inches. The only real difficulty was in deck arrangement. For example, to get in the secondaries in their gunhouses the stacks had to be pushed aft; even then only four gunhouses could be accommodated. As in the Nelson, engine rooms had to be forward of the boilers.

By the summer of 1929, it was by no means clear that any battleships would be laid down in FY32. Britain and the United States were loath to spend money on such expensive ships, both hoping to use the forthcoming London Naval Conference to put off such expenditures. In preconference conversations the British once more proposed to reduce battleship tonnage and gun calibre, but President Herbert Hoover and Secretary of State Henry Stimson preferred to delay any new battleship construction for five more years without prejudicing this issue. In particular, presumably on the basis of (no longer surviving) C&R studies of smaller battleships, they told the British that the United States could not consider using 12- or 14-inch guns in future battleships because the 16-inch gun gave the U.S. fleet a slight advantage over the Japanese.

The conference opened formally on 21 January 1930, with the world economy already sliding toward

Table 11-4. Short Battleship Designs, April 1929

Design	D	E	F	G
LWL	612	576	554	530 ft
Beam	104.5	106	106	104 ft
Depth	49	49	49	47 ft
SHP	46,000	81,000	71,000	53,500
Speed	22	23	22	20.5
Machinery	TE		CL GT TYPE	
Protected Length	73	72.1	71.5	77.5 %
Deck	3.75	4.25	5	5.25
Belt Width	---	+ 1	+ 1	− 1 ft
Hull	17,885	17,472	17,196	16,646 tons
Hull Fittings	1700	1685	1670	1655 tons
Protection	7345	8325	8768	9654 tons
Machinery	2870	2265	2067	1723 tons
Battery		2085 tons		
Ammunition		1630 tons		
Eq't&Out.		620 tons		
Stores		400 tons		
Aero		35 tons		
Margin	430	483	529	552 tons
Displacement		35,000 tons		

NOTE: Note the dramatic savings on machinery weight when cruiser geared turbines (CL GT) were adopted. They required half the volume per unit power of battleship turboelectric engines. Belt width is relative to the *South Dakota* (17 feet 5 inches wide).

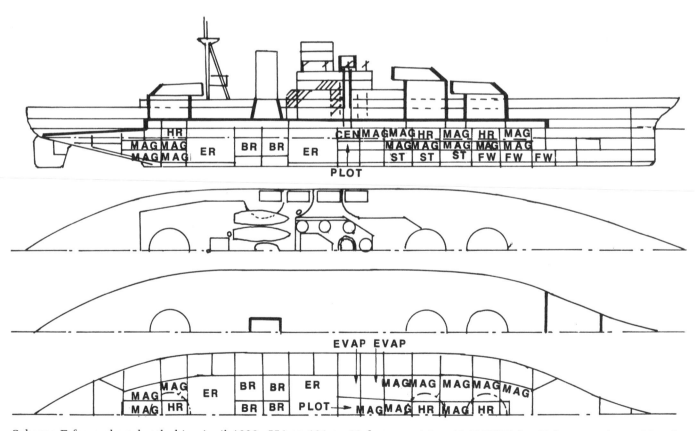

Scheme F for a short battleship, April 1929: 554 × 106 × 32 feet, requiring 65,000SHP for 22 knots and capable of steaming 17,500nm at 10 knots. She would have been powered by geared turbines, with six boilers, each in its own room. The belt would have been 17 feet 6 inches wide, as in earlier U.S. battleships. The protective deck would have been 5.25 inches thick, with a 1.5-inch splinter deck below it. Armament would have matched that of Scheme D.

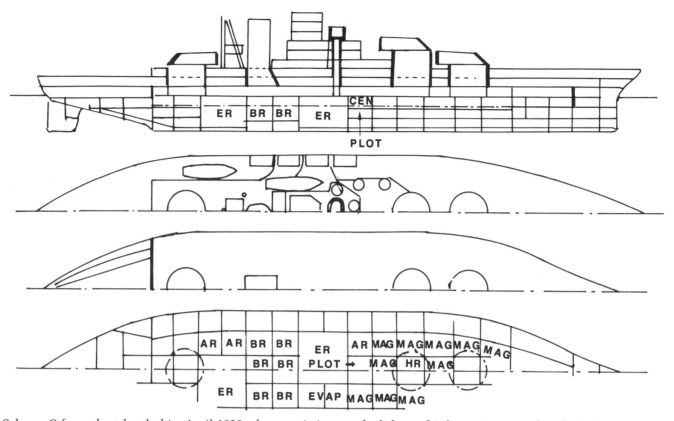

Scheme G for a short battleship, April 1929: characteristics matched those of Scheme F, except that the belt armor was only 15 feet 6 inches wide, 15 inches-9 inches thick. In the short designs, the turrets had 18-inch faces, 10-inch sides, 8-inch crowns, and 10-inch rears; conning towers were 18-inches thick. These figures compared to 13-inches port, 7-inches side and rear, and 6.5-inches crown in Scheme D, which had a 13-inch conning tower.

depression. Japan agreed to the extension of the building holiday to 31 December 1936 (with a new conference scheduled for 1935 to discuss further limits), partly because she could not then afford new capital ships. The situation was not quite as it had been in 1921, however. Both France and Italy had been permitted by the Washington Treaty to lay down new ships. Each might have laid one keel in 1927 and another in 1929. Neither had done so, because, even before the onset of the Great Depression, neither could really afford to.* In 1929, however, Germany laid down the first of her "pocket battleships," a type of ultra-heavy cruiser which the Washington Treaty had specifically sought to outlaw.

Such a unit could be hunted down and destroyed with certainty only by fast capital ships, that is, only by a new type of battleship. Otherwise it would be an extremely efficient commerce raider, as the cruise of the *Graf Spee* showed in 1939. Unfortunately any specialized killer of pocket battleships would *also* be an extremely efficient commerce raider, requiring as a counter a still more powerful, specialized, very fast battleship or battle cruiser. Such a spiral of construction would soon break through the 35,000-ton limit. In addition, the construction of fast and well-protected battleships would very quickly make the world's battle lines obsolescent, so that strong pressures for rearmament would be generated by an increase in world tensions.

At least that was the way matters appeared to stand in 1930. The pocket battleship would prove vulnerable to cruiser fire and certainly to air attack, but in 1930 no one could know how effective carriers would be a decade hence. Certainly, the French could not. In 1932 they laid down a fast battleship, *Dunkerque*, of 26,500 tons with 13-inch guns. She was still within treaty limits, but that was mainly because the French wanted to build a number of *Dunkerque*s with which to track down pocket battleships, and they had to work within a *total* tonnage limit as well as within a limit on individual ships. Even so, their adoption of the 13-inch gun in itself countered

* Both France and Italy considered new capital ship construction at this time. Each would have built fast, lightly protected units comparable in concept to the "pocket battleships," but much larger and somewhat faster. The prospective French "cruiser-killer" received considerable publicity during the mid-1920s. It was credited with eight 12in/55 guns in two quadruple turrets on a displacement of 17,500 tons. There is no indication of whether these data were correct.

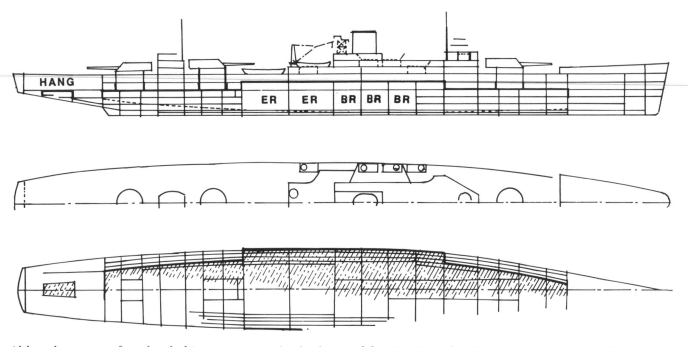

Although not part of any battleship spectrum study, the design of this 30,000-ton battle cruiser contributed to Preliminary Design's understanding of the problems of high-speed capital ships. Displacing 33,500 tons (30,000 standard), it was designed for 31.5 knots (130,000SHP geared turbines, six to nine boilers), and carried nine 14in/50 and sixteen 5-inch dual-purpose guns in twin mounts. Dimensions were 760 feet (wl) × 92 feet × 32 feet. Armor comprised a 12-foot wide, 12-inch belt and a 5-inch (6-inch over magazines) deck; the shaded portions of the drawing indicate the extent of the deck armor. Turrets had 14-inch faces, 8-inch sides and rears, and 6-inch tops. This sketch was dated June 1933. The genesis of this design is described in the author's companion volume on cruisers.

the British campaign to reduce the standard battleship gun to 12 inches. And the mere existence of the French project allowed the Italians to counter it by laying down the first of the series of full-size treaty battleships, the *Vittorio Veneto* (1934). These ships established a new standard of speed, about 30 knots, which had been made possible by engineering developments originally tested in the treaty cruisers of the 1920s.

From the fall of 1929 through 1932 Preliminary Design developed a large number of sketch studies of battleships as a basis for U.S. evaluation of British proposals for smaller battleships. The first series, completed by early 1930, covered displacements between 25,000 and 35,000 tons, with 12-, 14-, and 16-inch guns and geared turbines for 21 to 23 knots. It was concluded that the United States needed ships of maximum displacement for maximum protection and firepower but that high speed would be undesirable. Too little remains of these studies to show how these conclusions were reached, but clearly 23 knots was no longer being described as high speed. However, characteristics developed for the 1930 studies proved useful when the General Board reopened the question of battleship size in 1931.

On 31 March of that year the board convened to discuss "Reductions in the Displacement and Armament of Capital Ships," that is, the U.S. reply to the next British assault on 35,000 tons/16-inch guns. Admiral G. C. Day of the board opened by remarking that the next conference would surely have before it a displacement below 35,000 tons and a reduction to 12-inch guns. Rear Admiral G. H. Rock of C&R demonstrated the possibilities inherent in various displacements:

35,000 tons	9 16in/50	12 5.3in DP	23 knots 6.25 + 0 in deck*
30,000 tons	12 12in/45	16 5.3in DP	22 knots 3.75 + 1.5
25,000 tons	8 12in/45	12 5.3in DP	21 knots 4.0 + 1.5

*No splinter deck in this case

These were optimum designs: a 30,000-ton ship could mount ten 14in/45 or six 16in/50; 25,000 tons sufficed for six 14in/50 or four 16in/45. Similarly, the 35,000 ton ship could be made to carry fifteen 12in/50 or twelve 14in/50. As in the last of the 1929 studies, all of these ships would be driven by geared turbines, and all would have complete underwater protection (no treaty would limit torpedoes or mines). A treaty would probably limit gun calibre and thus might reduce the required weight of armor.

Rock analyzed the possibilities available on the 25,000-ton displacement favored by the British as a new treaty limit. Such a ship could have a 12-inch belt and a 4-inch deck, for immunity against 12in/50 fire between 16,700 and 30,800 yards (or 21,000 to 30,300 vs. the 14in/50). It would be quite vulnerable to the 16in/45, as shells would be able to penetrate the side out to 23,700 yards and the deck from 23,200 out. At a 60- rather than a 90-degree target angle, however, the belt would be proof beyond 16,000 yards. A 35,000 tonner would have a 14-inch belt, and it would cost marginally less per ton, $1,150 vs. $1,200. In effect 5,000 tons might be equated to $5.5 million or four 12-inch guns, four DP guns, and one knot of speed.

Admiral Leahy of BuOrd saw no advantage for the United States in adopting a 25,000-ton/12-inch limit. The economic superiority of the United States would be cancelled out, since the British would be able to build up to the uniform limit in numbers of ships at a reduced cost. Nor could the United States hope to equal either the firepower of the *Nelson*s or the protected high speed of the *Hood*. Worst of all, Leahy argued, the battle line was the only possible substitute for fortified bases in an overseas campaign—such as the primary U.S. scenario, the fleet projection against Japan (ORANGE).

By this time the United States had been committed to achieving naval parity with Britain for about fifteen years. Acceptance of the 12-inch gun limit would preclude parity until after the demise of the *Nelson*s (1951, if the proposed twenty-six-year lifetime were accepted). Leahy's proposed alternative was not merely to limit new construction but also to require that existing guns be replaced by 12-inch weapons on a one-for-one basis—which would overwhelm the British, as their eight-gun ships would face U.S. units armed with twelve guns (originally 14 inch vs. British 15 inch).* Studies already showed that the alternative, for 12-inch ships to face the 16-inch *Nelson*s, would be as ruinous as the situation of the wooden ships at Hampton Roads exposed to the *Merrimack* before the appearance of the *Monitor*. At 20,000 yards, a 12-inch shell would penetrate only 9.6 inches of belt and 2.4 of deck, compared with 15 and 3.4 for the 16in/45. Leahy clearly considered the regunning proposal a bargaining tactic to be used at the coming London Conference, "It would be very pleasing to me if the U.S. could get an advantage at one of these conferences." He found it particularly unfortunate that the public could not understand that the British system of overseas bases unbalanced any *apparent* equivalence between the two navies achieved by treaty.

Alternatively, the United States might offer to scrap her two latest battleships in return for the two *Nelson*s. Admiral William V. Pratt, the CNO, rejected this idea. It was all very well to use the rivalry with Britain for domestic political gain, but Japan was the real potential enemy. Sacrificing the two best U.S. battleships would be far worse than accepting British superiority. Worse, Congress, intent on saving money, might use willingness to scrap the newest battleships as an excuse to wipe out the expensive battle line altogether. Perhaps most important, Pratt was not so very sure that the *Nelson*s would be superior to the modernized *Colorado*s. Pratt did consider the U.S. battle fleet inferior in speed, and, what was worse, he could not hope for any relief. The plans to modernize the *Tennessee* and *Colorado* classes called for improved protection rather than higher speed.

Partly as a result of these discussions the chief constructor began a new series of studies of the relation between battleship size and effectiveness. "It is a form of naval suicide to force individual ships to fight more powerfully armed enemies, and this statement holds in spite of the fact that we ourselves have and will have for a certain indefinite period of time, more powerful ships than some of the old and all of the new ones our rivals will build under an agreement limiting gun calibres to 12 inches on replacement ships." He tabulated the displacements needed to protect ships against the more powerful guns they might have to face. For example, a ship with nine 12in/45 protected against 12-inch guns could be built on 25,000 tons. To protect the same ship against the 16 inch, however, she would have to grow to 31,000 tons, at about twice the cost, $32.2 vs. $16.75 million. As a rule of thumb, at 30,000 tons, 3 inches of side armor would cost 845 tons in direct weight but 1,440 tons in total displacement. It would be worth, at about 20,000 yards, protection against 2 more inches of enemy gun calibre. An inch of deck armor would cost 650/1,140 tons and would extend the outside edge of the immune zone about 3,000 yards at 30,000.

Torpedo protection would also drive up the size of the ship, as on 25,000 tons it would be barely possible to get in the conventional five-skin system. It would be entirely impossible if the speed of the ship were to drive up machinery weight and volume. Even antiaircraft armament would be limited by total ship size, as deck space and available topweight would be limited. It might be necessary even to reduce speed below the older 21-knot standard, and at the least lightweight machinery would have to be adopted. For example, although turboelectric plants were commonly rated at 12.5 to 16 SHP/ton, and battleship geared turbines at 14.5 to 18, figures such as 53.5 were common in cruisers.

---

* It was argued that 16-inch guns could be replaced by larger numbers of 12-inch guns: three for every two U.S. 16-inch. Quadruple turrets were considered impractical, so there was the delicious possibility of *Nelson*s armed with nine 12-inch facing *Colorado*s armed with twelve such guns.

Table 11-5. Battleship Studies, 1931

Design	1	2	3	4	GB-1	GB-2
Date			31 March 1931		9 April 1931	
Displacement(std)	35,000	30,000	25,000	25,000	34,000	30,000
LWL × Beam (ft)	600 × 106	590 × 98	562 × 93.5	616 × 104	616 × 104	594 × 100
Speed(kts)	23	22	21	21	23	23
SHP	62,000	42,000	27,000	52,000	52,000	49,000
Main Battery	9 -16/50	12-12/45	8-14/45	8-12/45	12-12/50	9-12/50
Mountings	3 × 3(fwd)	4 × 3	2 × 3, 1 × 2	2 × 3, 1 × 2	4 × 3	3 × 3
Secondary Battery	12 - 5.3	16-5.3	12-5.3	12-5.3	16-5	12-5.3
Mountings	6 × 2 DP	8 × 2 DP	6 × 2 DP	6 × 2 DP	8 × 2	6 × 2DP
Belt (in)	12 - 8	12 - 7.5	11.5-7.75	12 - 8	13.5-8	13.5-8
Turret(in)	18-10-8	14-8-5	16-8-6	14-7-5	18-9-5	18-9-5
Barbette(in)	15-3.5	12.5-3.5	12.5-3.5	12-3.5	13-3.5	13-3.5
Conning Tower(in)	16	16	16	16	16	16
Conning Tower Roof(in)	8	6	6	6	8	8
Uptake Protection(in)	3	3.5	3	4.5	9	9
Torpedo Bulkheads(no.)	5	5	5	5	5	5
Splinter Deck (in)	---	1.5	1.5	1.5	1.5	1.5
Armor Deck (in)	6.25	3.75	3	4	5.5	5.5
Machinery	GT	GT	GT	GT	TE	TE
Deck (12in)						
Belt(16in/50)						

NOTE: Belt penetration is computed for a 60-degree target angle.

Table 11-6. Battleship Studies for Capt. Greenslade, 26 December 1931

Design	1	2	3	4
Displacement(std)	27,500	29,000	32,450	36,500
LWL × Beam (ft)	580 × 95.5	592 × 97.5	633 × 100.2	685 × 102.6
Speed(kts)	21	22.5	25	27.5
SHP	33,000	45,500	77,000	101,000
Main Battery		9 - 12/50		
Mountings		3 × 3 (2 - A - 1)		
Secondary Battery			12 - 5/40	
Mountings			6 × 2	
Belt (in)		9 - 8		
Turret(in)		14 - 8 - 5.5		
Barbette(in)		11		
Conning Tower(in)			16	
Conning Tower Roof(in)			8	
Uptake Protection(in)			4.5	
Torpedo Bulkheads(no.)			5	
Splinter Deck (in)			1.5	
Armor Deck (in)		4.125		
Machinery			TE	
IZ (own guns)		16,000 - 28,000 yds		

Further studies were now carried out, both the three listed above and three more presented to the General Board on 9 April 1931:

GB-I   34,000 tons   12 12in/50   8 × 2 5inch   23 knts
GB-II 30,000 tons   9 12in/50   6 × 2 5inch   23 knts
       27,500 tons   9 12in/50   8 × 2 5inch

The two GB studies answered a board request for ships with 12-inch guns and with deck protection superior to that of the *South Dakota* (if one deck, that was to be 5 inches thick), a speed of 23 knots, and an endurance of 10,000nm at 12 knots. Both a 5.5-inch deck and a 1.5-inch splinter deck could be provided, as well as turboelectric drive and 13.5-8inch

a	b	c	GB-X1	GB-X2	a	b
	20 Apr 1931		2 December 1931		14 December 1931	
25,000	27,500	27,500	32,250	35,250	28,350	29,300
562 × 93.5	577 × 95.5	577 × 95.5	620 × 101	650 × 106	580	585
21	21	21	25	27.5	22.5	25
27,000	27,500	27,500	87,000	132,000	46,000	80,000
9-12/45	9-12/45	10-12/45	9-12/50	9-12/50	9-12/50	9-12/50
3 × 3	3 × 3	2 × 3, 2 × 2	3 × 3	3 × 3	3 × 3	3 × 3
16-5.3	12-5.3	12-5	12-5	12 -5	12-5.3	12-5.3
8 × 2DP	6 × 2DP	6 × 2	6 × 2	6 × 2	6 × 2DP	6 × 2 DP
11.5-7.75	12-7.5	12-7.5	12-8	12-8	9-8	9-8
14-8-5	14-8-5	14-8-5	18-9-5	18-9-5	14-8-5.5	14-8-5.5
12.5-3.5	12.5-3	12-3	13-3.5	13-3.5	11-3	11-3
16	16	16	16	16	16	16
6	6	6	8	8	8	8
3	4	3	9	9	3	3
5	5	5	5	5	5	5
1.5	1.5	1.5	1.5	1.5	1.5	1.5
3.25	4.75	3.875	4.625	4.625	4.125	4.125
GT	GT	GT	TE	TE	GT	GT
			30,000	30,000	28,000	28,000 yds
			18,000	18,000	14,700	14,700 yds

5	6	7	8	9
31,400	33,250	38,250	36,250	37,000
596 × 100.5	615 × 102.2	680 × 104	600 × 106	608 × 106.5
21	22.5	25	20	21
34,000	46,000	76,000	32,500	38,000
	9 -14/50			9 - 16/50
	11.5 - 8			13.5- 8
	16 - 9 - 6			18 - 10 - 7
	13			15
	4.625			5.5
	16,000 - 28,000			16,000 - 28,000

belt armor. This success suggested that something useful might be done even on the British 25,000-ton limit. On 18 April Pratt asked for nine 12 inchers on 25,000 tons, 21 knots and nine or ten 12 inchers on 27,500 tons with the same speed. On 27,500 Preliminary Design tried two 16in/45 or 16in/50 triple turrets (one forward and one aft), both of which weighed less than ten 12in/45 in two triple and two twin mounts. Alternatively, there could be eight 14in/45 in two triple mounts and one twin. A 25,000-ton ship could carry five 16 inchers (one twin, one triple). Both hulls could carry only limited protection, however.

There was also interest in higher speeds. For example, in September estimates were made for the

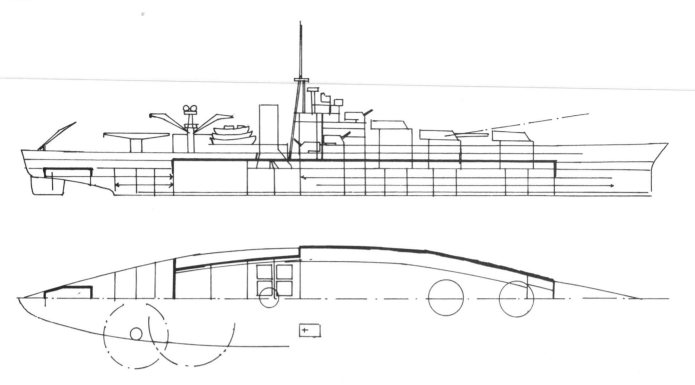

Scheme A of 30 August 1933: 675 feet long on the waterline, with all turrets forward and with a protected hangar for at least five aircraft. Freeboard was 29 feet forward and 18 feet aft, and the triple turrets left a blind arc of 42 degrees around right aft. Note that Turret 2 was limited in its minimum elevation, as in the 1928 sketches. This is not the Scheme A of the September 1933 comparative tables.

34,000 type with its speed increased to 25 and 27.5 knots. At a length of 700 feet, GB-I/27.5 knots would require 103,000SHP, at a *direct* cost of 1,850 tons. Actual growth would be several times greater, as allowance had to be made for the longer hull and the greater weight of protection: the design would grow beyond the 35,000-ton treaty limit. Even to increase speed from 23 to 25 knots would be impractical. For example, if length were increased from 616 to 650 feet, power would have to be increased from 52,000SHP to 68,000SHP. Machinery weight alone would grow by 600 tons.

There had to be some alternative. Further study of the nine-gun type showed that sufficient weight could be saved on armor. A 2 December 1931 calculation showed that, if belt armor was reduced to 12in-8in and the main protective deck to 4.625 inches, 32,250 tons would suffice for turboelectric machinery of 87,000SHP which would drive a 620-foot ship at 25 knots. On 35,250 tons, barely over the limit, a 650-foot, nine-gun ship could be driven at 27.5 knots. The belt would still resist 16in/50 shells fired at a 60-degree target angle at 18,000 yards.

These estimates showed that any future fast battleship design would have to involve painful choices, as will be even more obvious from the painful development of the *North Carolina* design described in

Chapter 12. A series of studies culminated in nine-gun (12, 14, or 16in/50) ships of various speeds. A 30-knot turboelectric battleship armed only with nine 12in/50 guns and protected only by an extremely thin belt (9in-8in) far exceeded the treaty limit, with a standard displacement of 41,700 tons, a figure which is difficult to reconcile with the very similar tonnage of the earlier British *Hood*, which was faster and better armed. Part of the difference was the much greater heavily armored area of standard U.S. designs. For ships armed with 14-inch guns, the treaty limited speed to 25 knots (37,500 tons), and, for a 16-inch battery, at 22 knots (38,000 tons).

High speed, therefore, required C&R to abandon its favorite turboelectric machinery in favor of the new lightweight geared turbines. Other design economies would probably also be required, but no records of geared-turbine studies made in 1931 have survived. Nor did work continue into 1932. In the Great Depression there was no great interest in resuming capital ship construction, and indeed no new naval construction at all was voted that year.

By 1933, however, it must have been obvious that capital ship building would soon resume in some form. With the *Dunkerque* under construction, it seems remarkable that the British were still pressing for a new, very low, treaty limit. C&R began two new se-

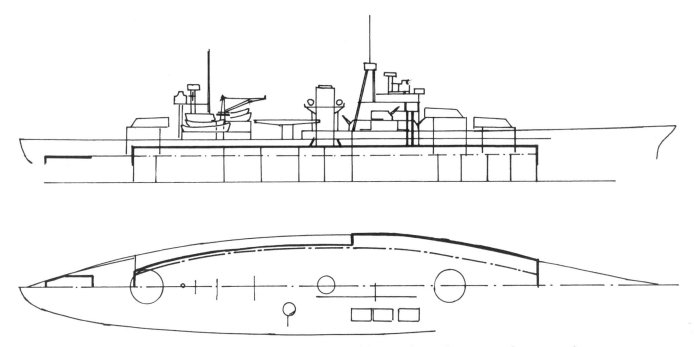

Scheme B of 21 August 1933: 675 feet long, with the protected hangar limited to two or three aircraft.

ries of sketch designs: a series of battle cruisers specifically requested by Admiral Pratt (and described in the companion volume on cruisers); and a long series of battleship sketches intended once more for guidance at the next naval conference. Work began in August, as "it is understood clearly that the Department must be prepared to take a position relative to capital ship size and type, if not in the immediate future, at least in time for the general naval conference anticipated in 1935-6."

Basic requirements were: *Armor:* immunity against 14-inch guns between 18,500 and 31,000 yards; or against 16 inch between 21,500 and 28,000 (in both cases requiring a 14inch-8inch belt and 5.75-inch deck); later immunity against the 12in/50 between 17,000 and 29,000 yards (11.5inch-6.5inch belt and 4.5-inch deck) was also considered. Full underwater protection was to be provided.

Battery: Only 12- and 14-inch guns were considered, as previous studies had shown that the 16in/50 could not be accommodated within the treaty limits. There were to be twelve guns in triple turrets, except that equality of firepower to the eight or nine 16 inchers of the British and Japanese fleets demanded twenty 12 inchers, which would have to be mounted in quadruple turrets—and whose weight would of necessity limit armor and arcs of fire. An important consideration was the effective limit of spotting, which BuOrd set at 25,000 to 28,000 yards. Air spotting would help, but to what extent was not yet clear, "It cannot be *relied* on absolutely to utilize the range advantage of the heaviest guns."

Machinery: Geared turbines, but *not* the lightweight type, would be adopted. In this wholly C&R study the speed was set at 22 knots on the basis of the 1929 General Board characteristics.

These were unambitious requirements for their date. Four sketch designs were prepared: A, 35,000 tons and twenty 12in/50; B, 34,000 tons and twelve 12 inch; B', 30,000 tons, protection at 12-inch level; and C, 35,500 tons, twelve 14in/50. The latter could probably be kept within the treaty limits by more careful design, but there was no hope of raising A above 12-inch protection, which amounted to only 23,000 to 26,500 yards of immunity against 16-inch fire. All four types were to have twelve 5-inch DP guns in twin mounts. Very roughly, the addition of 15,000SHP (600 tons) would add a knot. A reduction of 10,000 (400 tons) would reduce speed by about as much.

These pedestrian designs were valuable mainly for educating Preliminary Design in details of battleship protection and arrangement. By October enough had been learned to warrant a special series of designs, of 25,000 to 35,000 tons, 21 or 22 knots, and 12- , 14- , or 16-inch guns. The displacement limits were set by U.S. preference for retaining the upper end of the scale, and British insistence on the lower. In view of the existence of the *Dunkerque*, however, it seemed unlikely that anything below 26,500 tons would be accepted. Moreover, there was a case for a very high speed battleship, which C&R argued should further incline the United States against a reduced battleship tonnage limit.

Table 11-7. Battleship Studies, September 1933

Design	A	B	B'	C
Displacement	35,000	34,000	30,000	35,500 tons
Length	630	600	590	600 ft
Beam	104	104	100	106 ft
Power	43,500	46,500	40,500	46,500SHP
Speed	22	22	22	22 kts
Main Battery	20 × 12	12 × 12	12 × 12	12 × 14 in
Secondary Battery	12 × 5	12 × 5	12 × 5	12 × 5 in
Belt	11.5-6.5	14-8	11.5-6.5	14-8 in
Barbettes	12, 3	15,4	12,3	15, 4 in
Armor Deck	4.5	5.75	4.25	5.75 in
Splinter Deck	1.5	1.5	1.5	1.5 in
Ct	13	16	13	16 in
Immune Zones(thousands of yards)				
vs. 12in/50	17-29	13-33	17-29	13-33
vs. 14in/50	22-26.5	18.5-31	22-26.5	18.5-31
vs. 16in/45	26.5-23	21.5-28	26.5-23	21.5-28
Weights(tons):				
Hull	16,690	16,803	14,809	17,349
Fittings	1700	1635	1480	1670
Protection	8100	8400	6875	8600
Machinery	2560	2630	2390	2630
Battery	2377	1473	1473	1896
Ammunition	1743	1229	1229	1625
Equip&Outfit	500	491	450	491
Stores&FW	713	647	608	647
Aero	35	35	35	35
Margin	582	514	465	524
Std Disp't	35,000	33,857	29,814	35,467
RFW	300	310	290	310
Fuel Oil	2000	2000	2000	2000
Design Disp't	37,300	36,167	32,104	37,777
Deck Armor	3702	5005	3651	5111
Torp.Bhds	2500	2330	2190	2370

NOTE: In the list of Immune Zones, the first figure refers to range *beyond* which belt *cannot* be penetrated, the second to range *within* which the deck *cannot* be penetrated. Thus when the first figure is larger, the ship has a *negative* zone, that is, it is not immune at any range. All of these ships were powered by geared turbines.

Table 11-8. Battleship Studies Program, October 1933

Design	1	2	3	4	5	6
Speed	22	21	30	30	32.5	32.5 kts
Endurance(15kts)	13,500	10,700	12,000	9750	12,000	9750 nm
Endurance(10kts)	20,000	16,000	18,000	14,500	18,000	14,500 nm
T Bhds.	5	4	5	4	5	4
Immune Zone (thousands of yards):						
vs.16in/45	21.5-28	---	---	---	---	---
vs.14in/50	18.5-31	21.5-28.5	28.5-21.5	23-28	23-28	---
vs.12in/50	13-32.5	16-30.5	16-30.5	18-30	18-30	24-26

NOTE: Endurance figures are with emergency fuel.

That is, in a war with Britain, France, or Japan (all of whom possessed high speed capital ships), U.S. cruisers would be unable to operate freely, yet the 21-knot U.S. battle line would itself be severely restricted. Against Germany or Italy, which had no modern battle lines, "what useful service would be assigned to our own powerful but excessively slow battleships? Apparently the active operations of such a war would fall almost entirely upon cruisers, carriers, and destroyers. . . . The forgoing is not intended to throw doubt upon the value of a strong battleship fleet. The possession of such fleets by both Great

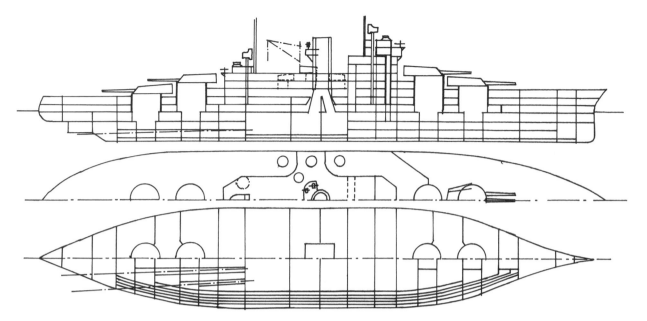

A 32,000-ton slow battleship design of September 1934, typical of a series that included ships with eight or nine 16-inch guns: This one had twelve 14in/50 plus twelve 5in/38 in twin mounts and four quadruple 1.1-inch machine cannon. Normal displacement would have been 35,000 tons (586 feet wl × 104 feet × 31 feet) and she would have made 21 knots. In effect, she was an updated *Tennessee*. The 13-inch belt would have been relatively narrow, 6 feet 11⅜ inches above and 8 feet below the waterline, covered by a 5-inch deck with a 1-inch splinter deck below it. Note the tradeoff of side armor for thicker deck armor, to fight at longer ranges. Turrets: 14-inch faces, 10-inch sides, 5-inch roofs, 9-inch rears.

Britain and Japan is sufficient to necessitate our maintaining in an efficient condition an adequate number of such ships. However, it is intended to bring attention to what seems a real lack in the make-up of our fleet. It appears that this lack might be met by two or three fast vessels as heavily armed and protected as practicable within the limits placed upon displacement. Such ships should be capable first of at least 29 knots under service conditions and second of accepting action with the *Repulse, Renown, Dunkerque, Kongo*, etc. upon even terms."

C&R also proposed a combination fast battleship-carrier, to overcome recent fears of the effect of surprise air attack on carriers. "As the airplane carrier is inherently at a disadvantage in self-defense, there appear to be only two general means to help her, that is, by putting more planes in the air and keeping them there, and by greatly increasing the number of AA guns on the vessels assigned to operate with or escort the airplane carrier.... It appears desirable to design a vessel having a trial speed of 32.5 knots or more; carrying an unusually large number of 5-inch and 1.1 inch AA guns; having stowage below decks for at least eight fighting or scouting planes; with facilities for taking planes aboard as in the proposed 10,000-ton, 6-inch cruisers and having two or possibly four catapults. Such a vessel might carry either two triple 14in/50 or two triple 12in/50 turrets."

A detailed program of studies was laid out on 20 December 1933:

Scheme	Disp't	Speed	Main Battery	Radius at 10kts
1	35,000	22	9 16in/50	17,000
2	35,000	22	12 14in/50	17,000
3	35,000	30	8 16in/45 or 9 14in/50	15,000
4	31,000	21	9 14in/50	15,000
5	31,000	21	12 14in/45	14,000
6	31,000	25	9 14in/50	13,250
7	31,000	30	8 14in/50	13,250
8	31,000	30	12 12in/50	13,250
9	26,500	21	8 14in/45	13,000
10	26,500	30	9 12in/50	11,400
11	28,500	32.5	6 14in/50	
12	24,000	32.5	9 12in/50	
13	19,500	32.5	6 12in/50	

The last three were to have been carrier escorts, and were not assigned any particular desirable radius. They would have steamed at higher speeds consistent with carrier operations.

BuOrd envisaged as a secondary battery six twin 5in/38, one each on the centerline fore and aft, and two on each beam. In addition the new battleship would have four quadruple 1.1-inch machine cannon, and eight or ten single 0.50-calibre machine guns.

All of these Schemes were to have geared turbines. The required endurances are impressive reminders of the Pacific bias in American thinking, even when it is thinking connected to a memorandum which

Table 11-9. Typical Battleship Characteristics, September 1933

Std Disp't	LWL	Max Speed	Machinery	%Torp.Pro.(1)	Main Battery
35,000(2)	600	23	GT	100	9-16/50
35,000	600	22	GT	100	9-16/50
35,000	600	22	GT	100	12-14/50
35,000	630	22	GT	100	20-12/50
34,000	616	23	TE	100	12-12/50
34,000	600	22	GT	100	12-12/50
33,250	615	22.5	TE	100	9-14/50
33,500(4)	600	21.5	GT	100	12-14/50
31,400	596	21	TE	100	9-14/50
31,500(BB 45)	600	21	TE	100	8-16/45
30,000	590	22	GT	100	10-14/45
30,000	590	22	GT	100	9-14/45
30,000	590	22	GT	100	8-14/45
30,000	590	22	GT	100	12-12/45
30,000	590	22	GT	100	12-12/50
29,000	592	22.5	TE	100	9-12/50
28,350	580	22.5	GT	100	9-12/50
28,500	583	22	GT	100	10-12/45
27,500	577	22	TE	90	8-14/45
27,500	577	22	GT	100	8-14/45
27,500	577	22	TE	90	10-12/45
27,500	577	22	GT	100	9-12/45
26,500	571	22	GT	100	9-12/45
25,000	562	22	TE	80	8-12/45
25,000	562	22	GT	80	8-12/45
25,000	562	21	GT	100	8-14/45

NOTE: These figures summarize many C&R studies made at various times and were not meant for direct comparison. (1) Torpedo-protection figures are based on the *West Virginia*. (2) This ship has only a single protective deck and a side belt only 14-feet wide, as in the British *Nelson*. (3) Belt thicknesses are maximums; all belts are tapered. (4) Figures for *New Mexico* as modernized. (5) Where deck armor is applied in layers, the ranges given are for "equivalent" single thicknesses of armor. This table was dated 20 September 1933.

almost avoids mention of the Japanese fleet. The low speeds in most of the Schemes are also noteworthy. A fourteenth ship, perhaps the battleship-carrier, was later added, but its details do not appear to have been worked out in any detail. Scheme 2 was essentially C of the earlier series.

This ambitious program was never completely carried out. Work began in January 1934 on Schemes 4 and 5, on the theory that the slow 35,000 tonner had already been dealt with. As in 1929, weight-saving studies turned toward shorter and shorter hulls. Thus Scheme 4 came out to 560 feet, rather than the 580 originally envisaged.

By late March Captain A. H. Van Keuren, heading Preliminary Design, had decided to explore fast battleship design with Scheme 7. Once more length was a major question, since shorter length meant thicker armor on a given displacement, as long as the additional power required to overcome increased wave-making resistance did not cost too much in weight. The predilection for protection shows in Van Keuren's remark that this was "not to be an old type battle cruiser. It is more properly described by the term fast battleship. It is intended to be capable of withstanding heavy blows. To this end protection against the 14-inch gun over a reasonable range is essential. If this proves impossible the type is worthless."

The design which emerged presents very considerable contrasts to the pessimistic attempts at fast battleship design of only a few years before. In particular the designers began by adopting the compact machinery of the new carrier *Yorktown* (CV-5), which at 2,600 tons (including a large electrical plant of 474 tons) was rated at 120,000SHP, 46SHP/ton. By way of contrast, 2,150 tons had been allowed for the 38,000SHP of the 21-knot, 31,000-ton type.

It was surprisingly easy to produce a well-rounded fast battleship, but some of the problems encountered are interesting as indications of those in the later, fast battleship designs. Internal hull volume for torpedo protection was particularly difficult to find. Preliminary Design began with the hull form of the successful *Lexington*-class carriers (ex battle cruisers), which had a very low prismatic coefficient,

Turret Arrangement	Pro. Dk	Spl. Dk.	Belt(3)	IZ(12in/50)	IZ (14in/50)	IZ (16in/45)
3 × 3 (all fwd)	6.25	---	14/12	13 - 32.5	18.5 - 31	21.5 - 27.5
3 × 3 (2-A-1)	5.75	1.5	14	13 - 32.5	18.5 - 31	21.5 - 28
4 × 3	5.75	1.5	14	13 - 32.5	18.5 - 31	21.5 - 28
5 × 4	4.25	1.5	11.5	17 - 29		
4 × 3	5.5	1.5	13.5	14 - 32	19.5 - 30.5	22 - 27
4 × 3	5.75	1.5	14	13 - 32.5	18.5 - 31.5	21.5 - 28
3 × 3	4.625	1.5	11.5	17 - 30	22 - 28	Vulnerable
4 × 3	5.5	1.0	13.5	14 - 31.5	19.5 - 30	22 - 26.5
3 × 3	4.625	1.5	11.5	17 - 30	22 - 28	Vulnerable
4 × 2	3.5	1.0	13.5	14 - 26	19.5 - 23.5	Vulnerable
2 × 3, 2 × 2	4.25	1.5	12	16 - 29	21.5 - 26.5	Vulnerable
3 × 3	4.75	1.5	13	14.5 - 30.5	20 - 28.5	23 - 24.5
2 × 3, 1 × 2	4.875	1.5	13	14.5 - 31	20 - 29	23 - 25
4 × 3	3.75	1.5	12	16 - 27	21.5 - 24.5	Vulnerable
4 × 3	4.25	1.5	11.5	17 - 29	22 - 26.5	Vulnerable
3 × 3	4.125	1.5	9	22 - 28.5	Vulnerable	Vulnerable
3 × 3	4.125	1.5	9	22 - 28.5	Vulnerable	Vulnerable
2 × 3, 2 × 2	3.75	1.5	12	16 - 27	21.5 - 24.5	Vulnerable
2 × 3, 1 × 2	4.5	1.5	12.5	15.5 - 29.5	20.5 - 27.5	Vulnerable
2 × 3, 1 × 2	4.625	1.5	12.5	15.5 - 30	20.5 - 28	Vulnerable
2 × 3, 2 × 2	3.875	1.5	12	16 - 27.5	21.5 - 25	Vulnerable
3 × 3	4.5	1.5	12	16 - 29.5	21.5 - 27.5	Vulnerable
3 × 3	3.75	1.5	12	16 - 27	21.5 - 24.5	Vulnerable
2 × 3, 1 × 2	3.875	1.5	11	18 - 27.5	23 - 25	Vulnerable
2 × 3, 1 × 2	4.0	1.5	12	16 - 28	21.5 - 25.5	Vulnerable
2 × 3, 1 × 2	3.0	1.5	11.5	17 - 23.5	Vulnerable	Vulnerable

Note the absence of studies of fast battleships, even though C&R had recently completed a series of battle cruiser sketch designs for Admiral Pratt. Immune zone (IZ) ranges are in *thousands of yards*, for protection against the guns listed in parentheses. In the machinery column, GT is geared turbine; TE is turboelectric.

that is, the hull did not fill out at the curve of the bilge. Volume was particularly scarce at the quarters, which in a battleship would be abeam the fore and after turrets—and their magazines.

Another problem was great hull length. The longer the hull, the heavier, which would mean less weight available for protection. A shorter hull might also have meant a fuller hull form, with more internal volume per unit length. However, any reduction in length would increase wave-making resistance and hence power required. However, power was now relatively inexpensive in weight terms, a point first made in the abortive 1929 designs. Thus "from a compartment length standpoint we might get down to 652 feet but would have to increase the machinery plant to say 155,000SHP and would need say 30 feet more machinery spaces. This would bring us up to 682 feet and we could reduce power plant [in view of reduced wave-making resistance]. Perhaps 675 feet is the shortest length." It turned out that 670 was optimum, requiring 140,000SHP, although 147,000 was allowed.

Protection was a 13in-6in belt, and a 5-inch deck (4.5 inches over machinery). The only splinter deck, however, was 1 inch over the torpedo bulkheads. This scale of armor would protect against 14in/50 fire between 20,000 and 27,000 (25,000 for machinery) yards; the barbettes would be proof beyond 18,700. The 16in/50, however, would penetrate the belt at 24,000 yards, and the deck over machinery at 22,700 (magazines at 24,500). However, the scale of protection was still impressive in comparison to more conventional battle cruisers. Perhaps the United States *could* answer HMS *Hood* within the treaty limit.

A peculiarity of the design was the stowage of six aircraft below decks aft, with two catapults. The other, slower, designs of the series had only half this air complement and only one catapult. Moreover, they stowed their aircraft in the open, where they would be vulnerable to gunfire, as in the reconstructed battleships. It may be that the designers envisaged the fast battleship as an independent unit, which would have to furnish its own air group, whereas the battleships of the fleet could use each other's aircraft,

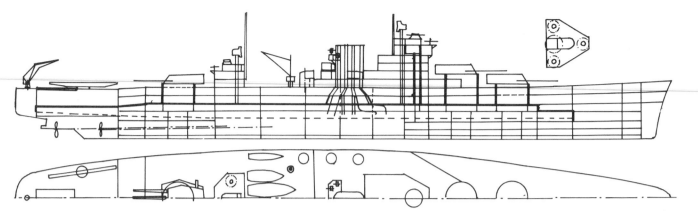

A 31,000-ton fast battleship (33,900 tons normal displacement) dated July 1934: 670 × 101.5 × 29.4 feet, 147,000SHP for 30 knots, with an endurance of 15,000nm at 15 knots. Armament was nine 14in/50, twelve 5in/38 (in twin mounts), and four quadruple 1.1-inch. The 13-inch side belt extended 8 feet below the waterline and was covered by a 4.5-inch deck (5-inches over magazines), with a 1-inch splinter deck (over the torpedo bulkheads), ¾-inch inboard. Turrets: 16-inch face, 9-inch side, 7-inch top, 8-inch rear.

Table 11-10. Battleship Studies, July 1934

Design	1	2	3	4
Displacement	32,500	31,000	35,000	35,000
Normal Displacement	35,550	33,900	38,250	38,250
Length	586	670	600	710
Beam	102	99.5	104	101.6
Draft	31.4	29.4	32.4	30.6
14in/50	12	9	12	12(?)
Power	38,800	147,000	40,000	182,000
Speed	21	30	21	31.5
Cruising Speed	10	15	10	15
Radius	20,000	15,000	20,000	15,000
Aircraft	3	6	3	
Stowage	On Deck	Below Dk	On Deck	
Catapults	1	2	1	
Deck Over Magazines	5	5	5.75	
Deck Over Machinery	5	4.5	5.75	
Splinter Deck	1	1(T Bhds)	1.5	
Torpedo Bhds-Heavy	3	2	3	
Torpedo Bhds-Light	2	2	2	
Belt	13	13	14.5	
Barbettes	14	14	15.5	
Turret Faces	18	18	18	
Immune Zone				
vs. 14in/50	20-28.5	20-27(Mag)	18.2-31.7	
vs. 16in/50	24-25.6	24-24.5	21.3-29.3	
Weights:				
Hull	14,852	14,559	16,510	
Fittings	1670	1700	1685	
Protection	7925	7600	8646	
Machinery	2150	3300	2200	
Battery	2000	1560	2000	
Ammunition	1500	1200	1500	
Equ't & Outfit	478	510	508	
Stores, Etc.	454	520	481	
Aero	30	51	30	
Deck Protection	4284	3205	5257	

NOTE: All are armed with twelve 5in/38 in twin mounts and sixteen 1.1-inch machine cannon in four quadruple mounts. Study No. 4 was not carried out in detail; see the series for September 1934.

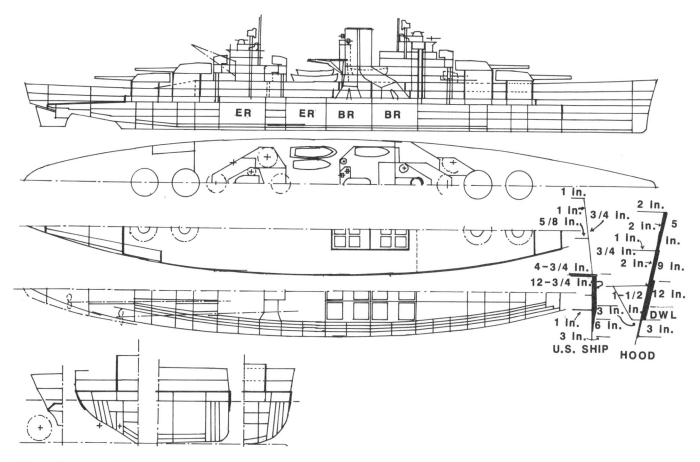

A large fast capital ship of 22 September 1934, described in its Spring Style as a "*Hood* type": 35,000 tons (standard; 38,250 normal), 710 × 101.5 × 30.76 feet, 160,000SHP = 30.5 knots, endurance 15,000nm at 15 knots. She carried eight 16in/45, fourteen 5in/38 in twin mounts, and the usual four quadruple 1.1-inch guns. Main belt was only 12.75-inches thick, tapering to 6 and then to 3 inches below the waterline, as shown in the large armor sections. Turrets: 15-inch face, 9-inch side, 6-inch top, 4-inch rear. The smaller cross sections show her torpedo protection. The sloping cross section shows the protection of HMS *Hood*, for comparison.

and so could consider their spotters less vulnerable through redundancy.

In any case the success of the fast ship encouraged the designers to try to get more out of the slower types. In particular they could not but expect to trade off some of the speed of the 30-knot ship for a fourth triple 14-inch turret. This turned out to be practicable on a length increased to 580 feet, but the armor weight was not quite sufficient. A satisfactory ship could be had on 32,500 tons and 586 feet, that is, a new *California* on roughly the same tonnage as the earlier ship. In this design the belt armor was increased to the 13.5 inches of earlier American battleships. The designers commented that the after turrets were still somewhat cramped and that a truly satisfactory four-turret ship would require about 35,000 tons.

These characteristics were embodied in a 28 May 1934 General Board request for an estimate of the standard displacement of a 21.5-knot, twelve 14in/

50 battleship to be protected against 14in/50 fire between 20,000 and 30,000 yards. It is not clear whether the board was seeking data for treaty negotiation or for new construction. Preliminary Design quoted 32,000 tons, on the basis of its 586 foot study, which "represents a saving of from 2,000 to 2,500 tons over what would have been required to produce a *California*, at her time, to the above general characteristics. This saving represents modern refinements in design, involving extensive welding, the use of light-weight high strength materials whenever possible, and latest practices in the general system of construction employed."

By early July there had been added to the two 31,000-ton studies a pair of 35,000-ton ships, each with twelve 14in/50 and with speeds of 21 and 31.5 knots. At the lower speed, the addition of 2,500 tons would buy 14.5 inches of belt armor and 5.75 of deck, with the splinter deck increased from 1 to 1.5 inches. Against 14in/50 fire, the immune zone would be in-

Table 11-11. Battleship Studies, September 1934

Design	2	3	4	5	6	7
Displacement	35,000	31,000	35,000	35,000	35,000	32,000 tons
Normal Displacement	38,500	33,900	38,250	38,250		35,000 tons
Length	710	670	600	600	616	586 ft
Beam	101.6	101.6	106.3	106.3	106.3	104 ft
Draft	30.76	29.4	32.42	32.42	31.6	31 ft
Main Battery	8-16in/45	9-14in/50	8-16in/50	9-16in/50		12-14in/50
Secondary	14-5in/38	12-5in/38	12-5in/38	12-5in/38	16-5in/38	12-5in/38
AA Battery	4Quad 1.1	4Quad 1.1	4Quad 1.1	4Quad 1.1		4Quad 1.1
Power	160,000	147,000	40,000	40,000		SHP
Speed	30.5	30	21	21		21 kts
Cruising Speed	15	15	10	10		10 kts
Radius	15,000	15,000	20,000	20,000		20,000 nm
Deck Over Magazines	4.75	5	5.75	6	5.5	5 in
Deck Over Machinery	4.75	4.5	5.75	6	5.5	5 in
Splinter Deck	1	1(0.75inbd)	1.5	1.5	1	1 in
Belt	12.75	13	13.5	13.5	13.5	13 in
Barbettes	13	14	13.5	13.5	13.5	13 in
Turret Faces	15	16	18	18	16	14 in
Torpedo Bhds--Heavy	2	2	3	3	3	3
Torpedo Bhds--Light	2	2	2	2	2	2
Immune Zone (thousands of yards) vs. 14in/50					19.3-31.4	20-30
Weights(tons):						
Hull	17,644	14,559	17,682	17,840	17,703	15,857
Fittings	1750	1700	1685	1685	1700	1670
Protection	7758	7600	8593	7893	8355	7970
Machinery	3600	3300	2200	2200	2200	2150
Battery	1740	1560	1993	2171	2050	2000
Ammunition	1129	1200	1485	1627	1573	1500
Equ't & Outfit	540	510	508	508	1019	478
Stores, Etc.	481	460	481	481		455
Aero	55	51	30	30		30
Margin	303	300	346	505	400	390
Fuel Oil	2750	2600	3000	3000		2770
Deck Protection					5095	4271

creased from 18,200 to 31,700 tons, and even against the 16in/50 the ship would be immune between 21,300 and 29,300 yards.

Work on the fast type, in effect a counter to the *Hood*, began early in September. The July estimates had been no more than powering studies which showed that a 710 foot hull of reasonable form could be driven at 31.5 knots on 173,000SHP (182,000 with margins). In fact it appeared that 31 knots would suffice against the *Hood*. That would have to be achieved on a design displacement of about 38,250 tons, that is, 35,000 plus 500 tons of reserve feed water and 2,750 of fuel.

BuEng had just completed the design of an 80,000SHP twin-screw plant for the carrier *Wasp* and expected to be able to achieve 160,000SHP on about 3,800 tons, about 42SHP/ton, which was actually pessimistic considering its achievement in the *Yorktown*. A radius of action of 15,000nm at 15 knots was

envisaged, but finally it had to be admitted that maximum speed at design displacement would be no more than 30.5 knots.

A battery of four twin 16in/45 was assumed, and in the end there were seven twin 5in/38, an extra mount being required because there was no space on the centerline for one between No. 2 turret and the conning tower. Weight was available for four torpedo bulkheads, a 4.75-inch deck, a 1-inch splinter deck, and a 12.75-inch belt. Some unusual sacrifices had to be made in reducing armor thickness below the waterline, but on the whole this was a well-protected ship.

The ship had a forecastle with a ramp leading down to the fantail, presumably to permit the movement of embarked aircraft. The provision of catapults is not clear from the sketch produced.

This was a remarkable achievement, and it finally shows what could be done with the new technology

Table 11-12. Battleship Designs, September 1934

Design	No. 7	No. 6	Weights No. 7	No. 6	Ranges for Penetration by 14in/50 Gun No. 7	No. 6
Displacement	32,000	35,000	32,000	35,000		
Length	586	616				
Beam	104	106.3				
Draft	31	31.6				
Hull (incl spl deck)			9764	10,600		
Main Armor Deck	5in	5.5in	3473	4215	30,000	31,400
Torpedo Bulkheads	1in	1in	1822	2000		
Hull Fittings			1670	1700		
Machinery			2150	2200		
Battery			2000	2050		
Ammunition			1500	1573		
Equ't & Outfit			963	1019		
Margin			390	400		
Main Belt	13in	13.5in	2722	3230	20,000	19,300
Bulkheads	13in	13.5in	324	344	20,000	19,300
Turrets	14-10-5in	16-10-6in	1100	1168	5000 20,000	1000 19,300
Barbettes	13-3in	13.5-3in	2210	2290	20,000	16,500
Conning Tower	13-5in	16-6in	384	471	Splinter Protection Only	
Air Induction	2.5in	2.5in	150	165	Splinter Protection Only	
Uptake	2.5in	2.5in	128	145	Splinter Protection Only	
Secondary Battery Pro.	2in	2in	324	407		
Armor Backing			96	100		
Armor Bolts			32	35		
Secondary Battery	12-5in	16-5in				

NOTE: All weights are in tons; penetration ranges are in yards.

of the 1920s and early 1930s. Full waterline protection was provided, certainly against 14-inch shells. In fact the protection was equal to or better than that provided HMS *Hood*, on a far smaller displacement. In particular, the main part of the belt was wider, 7.17 feet above the waterline as compared with 5.5 in the British ship. The total width of the British main belt was greater—the 12-inch portion extended 3 feet below the waterline—but it can be argued that the sloping belt was *effectively* far narrower as far as plunging shells were concerned. Nor was there any comparison in deck armor, a deficiency often credited with the loss of the *Hood*.

In September, Preliminary Design prepared a set of comparative sketch plans for seven Schemes: two versions of the *Hood*-like fast capital ship, the 31,000-ton fast battleship, slow 35,000-ton ships with eight or nine 16in/50 or twelve 14in/50; and (Scheme 7) a 32,000-ton slow battleship with twelve 14in/50. That low speed was still considered the convention for American battleships shows in the proportion of fast to slow types worked out in detail. Undoubtedly Preliminary Design expected that some version of the 35,000-ton, 16-inch type would be built.

By this time preliminary discussions for the pre-treaty conference of 1935 were already taking place

between the British and the Americans, and the British were still trying to reduce the upper limit on battleship size, despite the new French and Italian projects. Moreover, in March 1934 the Japanese had announced their intention of leaving the treaty system, so that they would be entirely unconstrained in any new construction they might undertake after March 1937. Even so, during June and July 1934 the British showed American negotiators plans for a new 25,000-ton battleship they hoped to build should their proposals be accepted.

Preliminary Design regarded 32,000 tons as a possible compromise, which made Scheme 7 the most important of its sketch designs. "Superficially this is an attractive scheme. Actually it shows in many places the results of skimping. Note [for example] side belt 15 feet wide as compared with old standards of about 17 feet; reduced thickness of turret port and top plates of conning tower and communication tube. . . . The serious nature of sacrifices in protection thickness are emphasized by our possible inability to produce heavy armor of great thickness today. Horizontal protection is emphasized in all schemes, when compared with wartime standards. However, in Scheme Seven we have nothing to spare even in this respect. . . . We probably have an im-

Table 11-13. Proposed 25,000-Ton Battleships, 1934

	Scheme 2	Scheme 5	British Proposal
LWL(Ft)	557	610	610
Beam,Mld(Ft)	99.2	100	100
Draft(Ft)	29.17	27.9	26(?)
Displacement(Tons)	27,300	27,140	
Period of Roll(Sec)	17 1/4	17 1/4	
SHP, 23 Kts	48,000	37,500	45,000
Cruising Radius, 10kts(NM)	15,000	15,000	10,000(Speed?)
12inGuns(Twin)	8	8	8
Secondary Guns(Twin 5in/38)	12	12	
AA Guns(Quadruple 1.1in)	4	4	
Deck Armor	3.75	3.5	
Splinter Deck	1	1	
Side Belt	12	11	
Barbette	12	11	
Conning Tower	12	12	
IZ VS 12in/50(Yds)	11,300	8100	
Weights(Tons):			
Bare Hull & Margin	6845	7114	
Hull Fittings	1090	1170	
Battery Foundations	433	433	
Armor Supports	170	170	
Machinery Fndns	270	250	
Torpedo Bhds(Mild Steel)	627	657	
Hull, Total	9435	9794	10,400
Armament & Ammunition	1975	1975	
Main Turret Pro.	737	730	
Protection for Other Guns	243	243	
Turret Framing, Machinery	417	417	
Aeronautics, Misc.	130	130	
Armament, Total	3502	3495	4190
Main Machinery	1750	1600	
Boats, Hoists, Airplane Gear	100	100	
Steering Gear	90	100	
Warping&Towing Gear, Lube Oil	70	65	
Machinery, Total	2010	1865	2050
Side Armor	2358	2402	
Transverse Armor	355	272	
Armor Backing & Bolts	105	105	
Barbette Armor	1857	1715	
Conning Tower & Tube	350	350	
Uptakes, Air Intake Protection	273	344	
Splinter Pro. for Bridges	200	200	
Torpedo Bhds(STS)	627	656	
Decks(Protective & Splinter)	3000	2947	
Misc. Splinter Pro.	130	130	
Protection, Total	9255	9021	7400
Equipment and Outfit	408	430	
Stores & Fresh Water	240	245	
Complement	150	150	
Standard Displacement	25,000	25,000	25,000

NOTE: This table illustrates a U.S. attempt to compare U.S. with British design practice. Schemes 2 and 5 were U.S. approaches to a small battleship under a proposed 25,000-ton treaty limit. The British figures were given to the United States in July 1934. The only other details were that it was intended to resist 12-inch shell fire, a 750-pound torpedo warhead, and a 1,000-pound bomb. The detailed breakdown of weights in the U.S. columns illustrates standard British practice. The British provided only the outline information given, including the speed of 23 knots. The U.S. 12-inch gun would have been a 12in/50. The displacement given is the designer's figure, the figure on which the design is predicated. It includes fuel oil and reserve feed water. In a memorandum submitting these data to the General Board (27 October 1934), the chiefs of BuEng and C&R observed that "a detailed knowledge of these data would define for a competing power the design attitude of the United States. An example of this is already at hand in the interest shown by the British in the relatively small allowance for hull weight presented to them for discussion."

Table 11-14. Maximum Battleship Studies, November 1934

			Montana	*Yamato*			
Displacement	66,000	72,500	60,500		50,000	50,000	63,000 tons
Length	975	975	890	840	740	740	900 ft
Beam	107	107	120.7	127	108	108	108 ft
Draft	33.5	37	36	35.5	34	34	34 ft
Power	88,300	220,000	172,000	150,000	70,000	70,000	85,000SHP
Speed	25.3	30	28	27	23	23	23 kts
Main Battery	8-20	8-20in	12 - 16in/50	9 - 18.1in/45	9-18in/45	12-16in/50	10-18in/45
Secondary Battery	20-5	20-5in	20 - 5in/54	12 - 6.1in/55			
AA Battery	16-1.1	16-1.1in		12 - 5in/40			
			40 - 40	60 - 25mm	14.5	14.5	17 in
Belt	16	16	16.1	16.1			
Barbettes	16	16	21.3	21.7	6.5	6	8.8 in
Armor Deck	6.5	6.5	6.2	7.9			
Splinter Deck	1.5	1.5	0.6	0.4			
Weights (Tons):							
Hull	32,682	33,700	29,781	20,327			
Fittings	2610	2670	2152	1930			
Protection	13,447	14,563	15,538	21,727			
Machinery (Wet)	3930	7350	4738	5043			
Battery	3456	3456	4018	11,914			
Ammunition	2984	2984	2700	---			
Equ't&Outfit	614	650	991	440			
Stores, Etc.	720	872	418	600			
Aero	55	55	54	109			

NOTE: These figures are approximate. Weights are provided for comparison with studies for the *Montana* class (see Chapter 15). *Yamato* data are from Japanese sources; note that the distribution of weights did not follow U.S. practice, so that precise comparison is difficult. The Japanese figures for battery include ammunition as well as turret armor. The last three columns are Japanese estimates of the largest ships the U.S. Navy could build, prepared in 1934 at the time the *Yamato* was designed. There was also a 53,000-ton, 33-knot ship (190,000SHP), armed with nine 16in/50, and protected by 9-inch side and 4-inch deck armor. All of these displacement figures are "normal" tonnages including two-thirds loads of fuel and reserve feed water, following Japanese practice.

mune zone against 14-inch shells of 9,000 yards (20,000 to 29,000 yards). This is reasonable rather than generous and there are only 2,000 yards against the 16-inch guns (23,000 to 25,000). . . ."

It was necessary, however, to answer the British proposal. On 19 October the chairman of the General Board asked C&R to work out sketches for ships similar to the British design but incorporating U.S. practice. In an effort to answer U.S. charges that smaller capital ships would not be able to survive full-size bombs and torpedoes, the British had claimed for their ship resistance to a 750-pound underwater explosion and to a 1,000-pound bomb, the former in excess of U.S. standards. They claimed further a speed of 23 knots, an endurance of 10,000nm, and protection against 12-inch fire—which would make sense were the 12-inch gun to be the future standard.

C&R suspected that the British design worked mainly because it avoided American standards of hull protection, in which case its relatively long hull (610 feet) would save on machinery weight. A 25,000-ton, 535-foot, 21-knot, eight 12-inch type had already been designed (sketch design 11 October). C&R reported a pair of studies to the board, 557 and 610 feet long, protected from 12-inch fire over immune

zones 11,300 and 8,100 yards wide. The design was, therefore, practicable, if only barely so, and only were the limit to 12-inch guns to be accepted, which in the past the General Board had never agreed to. The board had asked further whether higher speed could not be obtained on 610 feet. In fact this would be possible without an excessive powerplant, but only at the sacrifice of already-scarce armament or protection. Probably 27,000 tons would be more realistic for a battle cruiser with eight 12in/50.

There was one other interesting result of this study. The original British proposal had been made in the course of an exchange of technical data in July 1934. In describing their responses to the General Board inquiry, the bureaus argued that any detailed U.S. counterproposal would reveal "the design attitude of the United States. An example of this is already at hand in the interest shown by the British in the relatively small allowance for hull weight presented to them for discussion. . . . Such information should be retained by the United States solely for its own use. Accordingly, it is urged that no measures be sanctioned which might lead to further detailed exchanges of information or discussions of our design material with representatives of competing powers."

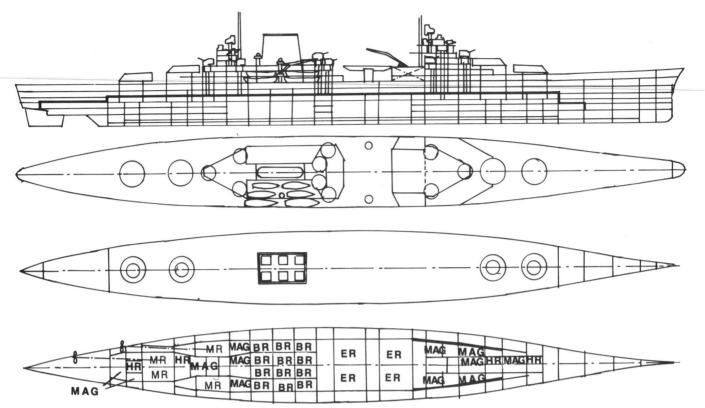

Maximum battleship, dated November 1934: 66,000 tons (975 feet wl × 107 feet × 33.5 feet), capable of 25.3 knots (88,300SHP) with turboelectric machinery. The main battery was eight 20-inch guns, with twenty 5-inch DP in twin mounts, and four quadruple 1.1-inch machine cannon. The side belt would have been 16-inches thick, with a 6.5-inch armor deck, and a 1.5-inch splinter deck. Turrets would have had 18-inch faces, 11-inch sides, 7-inch tops, and 9-inch rears. Note that U.S. designers no longer used heavy uptake protection; even in this large a ship it was limited to 3-inch to 2-inch plating.

Meanwhile the General Board began to think more and more seriously about actually building battleships. On 16 October one of its staff officers telephoned C&R to ask for cost estimates for a variety of ships, including 23-knot battleships of 32,000 and 35,000 tons. Then the board asked for yet another pair of studies, this time of two ships each with nine 14in/50, of 23 and 30 knots. The new feature was an unusually great spacing between the guns in each turret, in an attempt to overcome problems then being experienced with the triple 14in/50 turrets. In passing from the original 5 feet 11 inches between guns to 10 feet 6 inches the constructors had to increase barbette diameter from 31 to 38 feet, with a great weight increase. Even an intermediate expansion to 8 feet 2 inches (35-feet diameter) was expected to cost 605 tons in total armament weight, including barbette armor.

Both of the new studies showed 13-inch belt and 5-inch deck armor, which would protect against 14-inch fire. Both could be built within the treaty limit, at 31,000 and 34,500 tons, respectively, but neither would be a very great bargain for the weight of armament to be carried. As a test of the effect of bore

spacing, Preliminary Design also calculated details of a ship with eight 14-inch guns in four twin turrets, each with a 31-foot barbette, that is, each equivalent in size to the 14in/50 *triple* then in service. The direct cost was 500 tons, but this would increase the displacement of the 30-knot ship by a thousand tons, that is, would push it over the treaty limit.

There was one other series of design studies, to examine the upper limits of battleship design, apparently in view of Japanese abandonment of the treaty regime. On 19 August 1934 Preliminary Design was asked to prepare a study of the largest possible battleship, to mount 24-inch guns. Later the calibre was reduced to 20 inches. As in the case of the 1916 ships, the primary limit was the dimensions of the Panama Canal locks. However, Preliminary Design eschewed really large ships on the theory that speeds of at least 25 knots were desirable. Characteristics of the 20-inch gun were obtained by extrapolation, and armor was far from exotic: a 16-inch belt and 6.5-inch deck (1.5-inch splinter deck) would be in line with such powerful ordnance.

The attitude toward speed is interesting. In the letter of submission of the studies (14 November 1934) the designer notes that "this vessel is capable of 25 knots [which] might be considered satisfactory in the same sense that 21 knots for our present capital ship has been accepted. However, if it is accepted that among the duties of a vessel of this type will be the running down and destroying of other fast capital ships such as the *Hood*, a minimum speed of 30 knots is essential. . . . It will be necessary either to reduce the offensive power or, while holding the offensive power as originally assumed, to force up the speed by increasing the power of the machinery plant, while at the same time accepting fuller coefficients of underbody in order to increase displacement [so as to accommodate the extra machinery on fixed dimensions]. . . . The second alternative has been adopted, with the results that upon the dimensions originally selected a displacement of 72,500 tons [compared with 66,000] has been obtained." It turned out that 220,000SHP would drive the larger ship at 30 knots. The smaller type would require only 88,300. Both had eight 20-inch and twenty 5-inch in the usual twin mounts. A sketch of the 25-knot type shows a conventional flush-decker with catapults amidships, as in current cruiser practice, and a single fat funnel just abaft them.

Copies of this design appear in the classified correspondence of the secretary of the navy, but it is not clear whether the study had any great effect on U.S. estimates of unconstrained ships Japan might build.

1934 ended, then, with a variety of design studies but without any clear General Board policy—except that the slow ships far outnumbered the fast ones, and the fast ones look very much like special-purpose designs.

As late as May 1935 some effort was being expended on lightweight battle cruisers. A sketch design for a 23,500- to 24,000-ton type with six 14in/50 and sixteen 5in/38 is dated 3 May 1935. She would have required 120,000SHP for a speed of 30 knots on a waterline length of 650 feet. The design was developed from the 31,000-ton fast battleship and may have been the end result of General Board inquiries as to the practicality of 25,000-ton battle cruisers. Still later (2 July) Captain Van Keuren directed Preliminary Design to prepare fast and slow 25,000-ton types protected against 12-inch fire and with dimensions of 610 × 100 × 26 feet. They would be armed with eight 12in/50. They were essentially the studies of the previous October, and it is difficult to see why new ones were needed. They are described specifically as "a basis for reply to the probable British insistence on reduced displacements." The characteristics were those claimed by the British the previous year. As for speeds, it was hoped to achieve 23 (as in R.N. designs) and 30 (as in *Dunkerque*) knots. They would later be developed into a series of "defensive studies" for the General Board's consideration (see Chapter 12).

12

The *North Carolina* Class

Through 1934 and early 1935 Preliminary Design proceeded on the premise that, when the United States resumed capital ship construction, the ships would be what it called "conventional," that is, heavily armored with a speed of about 23 knots. Perhaps a few would be fast battleships intended as replies to specific foreign types. Instead, the United States built *only* what could be described as fast battleships, although in fact by the late 1930s the standard of speed in other navies had so advanced that some of the new American ships were considered slow. What happened was a combination of the tactical and strategic requirements for a few very fast ships with the sudden discovery that the most likely enemy, Japan, already posessed a substantially faster battle line. Thus the two *North Carolina*s were envisaged almost from the first as specialized fast battleships, but the *South Dakota*s which followed them might well have been substantially slower but for intelligence received late in 1936. Both classes, moreover, were much affected by the details of the London Naval Treaty of 1936, which replaced the Washington Treaty of a decade and a half earlier.

Japan announced in March 1934 that she intended to abandon the treaty regime. The remaining signatories (Britain, France, and the United States) wanted to continue the treaty process but needed some means of convincing Japan to limit herself. Otherwise she would (as she did) build super-battleships capable of overwhelming the treaty ships. Their device was the "escalator clause"—the treaty limits could be relaxed if a nonsignatory failed to agree to them or if one of the signatories felt that its national security was threatened. In the case of the *North Carolina*s, the key clause limited gun calibre to 14 inches. Japan refused to agree, and the limit was increased to 16 inches, too late to affect the protection of these

ships, but early enough to change their weapons. About a year later the tonnage escalator clause was invoked, resulting in the design of the *Iowa* class.

Compared with previous U.S. battleships, the new generation had to contend with two new threats: bombing and underwater shell hits, the latter in view of increasing battle ranges. At the same time they had to survive against larger underwater explosions, and they had to be much faster. The C&R solution was a combination of innovations, including a new form of deck armor, inclined side armor, and high-temperature, high-pressure machinery.

It appears that the U.S. Navy first recognized underwater shell hits as a threat about 1935, although the Japanese had noted (and exploited) their potential after tests on the cancelled battleship *Tosa* as early as 1924. At very long ranges, shells would strike the water steeply enough to retain considerable velocity for short distances; at shorter ranges they would richochet. Caisson experiments appeared to show that such hits would produce severe damage, even if they failed to penetrate. C&R reported that "plates [frequently] were set back so that the backing and the hull plating below the bottom edge of the belt opened up." The problem was appreciated only after the new design series began, and the designers could only provide an auxiliary thin STS belt below the main one. They recommended a tapered belt, 7-feet wide, with an average thickness of 3.5 inches, which would cost 420 tons. Even this was impossible in the series of 35,000-ton designs, which were extremely tight. Ultimately the *North Carolina*s could be provided only with patches of internal armor over their magazines. Such patches presented further problems, in that they had to interfere with the elastic deformation of the usual multibulkhead torpedo-protection systems. At its worst, such construction, in the next

At the end of the war, the *North Carolina* (*facing*) could be distinguished from her sister ship by the platform built around her secondary conning level, halfway up her forward fire control tower. This postwar photograph shows a drastic reduction in light antiaircraft weapons, such as the wet main deck 40mm and 20mm mounts. On the other hand, she had been fitted with modern radars, including an upward-looking SCR-720, in the dark radome on her forefunnel, and a tilting SR air-search set on her mainmast. Her siren is visible on the port side of her fire control tower. Her whistle was on the other side. She is shown on 3 June 1946.

(*South Dakota*) class, could nearly negate the value of the entire system.

All U.S. battleships of the treaty period were designed to resist a 700-pound charge of TNT, this number having emerged from a 1935 intelligence study of major foreign torpedoes and mines. The U.S. Navy remained blissfully unaware of the Japanese heavy torpedo until well into World War Two. To achieve this protection the designers generally provided a sandwich of void and filled compartments: a void outboard against the shell, then a liquid layer to absorb the shock of explosion and to catch fragments of the hull, and then a void to back up the liquid layer, as in the "Big Five" and later ships. In the designs of the late 1930s, the splinter deck formed the upper boundary of the entire system, holding it together under the impact of underwater explosions. The splinter deck had to be kept watertight, as it was generally below the waterline, and had damage-control passageways running along its sides. Caisson experiments in 1934 showed that even 60 pounds (1.5 inches) was not too heavy a plating for the splinter deck, and the 50 pounds of the early U.S. treaty designs was considered a bare minimum.

The building holiday decreed at London in 1930 was scheduled to end on 31 December 1936, midway through the FY37 program. Lead times were such that the General Board formally asked for design studies in May 1935. This was already quite late. In theory, a preliminary design should have been ready by 1 December. Given the economic strains of the Great Depression, however, the board could not have hoped for any earlier start.

The design of the last generation of U.S. battleships began, then, with the board's 11 July call for three alternative sketch designs for fast division flagship battleships (A, B, and C) armed with the secondary battery of the 1934 studies, twelve 5in/38 in single or twin mounts. All three were to have "complete" torpedo protection, the best possible protection against gas, and the very long endurance of 15,000nm at 15 knots. Propulsion was not fixed. Preliminary Design could choose between turboelectric and single- and double-reduction geared turbine powerplants. It was soon obvious that only geared turbines would be light enough to power such fast ships.

Unlike previous designs, intended to make their speed at a fixed fraction of *endurance* fuel, they would have to make their speed carrying half of the *maximum* fuel oil. Existing ships often incorporated considerable emergency tankage beyond that required to meet their designed radius of action. These extra tanks were usually filled in service, often adding so much draft that belts were nearly submerged (see Chapter 16). Scheme A was a conservative alternative, a 30-knot ship armed with nine 14-inch guns,

all mounted forward and protected against 14in/50 shellfire between 22,000 and 27,000 yards. That equated to an 11.5-inch side and a 4.5-inch deck. Protection at similar ranges against the U.S. 16in/45 would require 15-inch side and 5.2-inch deck armor.

Schemes B and C would be 30.5-knot ships protected against 14in/50 shellfire between 19,000 and 30,000 yards and armed, respectively, with twelve 14-inch triple turrets and with eight 16in/45 in twin turrets. This standard of protection equated to 13.25-inch belt and 5.25-inch deck armor. Protection at similar ranges against the U.S. 16in/45 would require 16.6-inch side and 6.2-inch deck armor.

U.S., rather than foreign, guns were always used as the standard for penetration. For example, at this time the Japanese 16in/45 was credited with a 2,205-pound shell and a muzzle velocity of 2,592 ft/sec,* compared with 2,250 pound, 2,500 ft/sec for the U.S. 16in/45. For the design A immune zone, then, protection against it would require 13.6-inch side armor and 5.4-inch deck armor. By way of comparison, to resist a new U.S. super-heavy (1,500-pound) 14-inch shell, Scheme A would require 13.3-inches side and 4.4-inches deck armor, not so very far off.

All three sketch designs showed alternating engine and boiler rooms as insurance against being immobilized by lucky underwater hits, as well as the big tubular fire control tower characteristic of the American capital ships built a few years later. They also saved weight on torpedo protection, eliminating one of the usual five bulkheads on the theory that a fast ship would have a better chance of evading torpedoes.

At 32,150 tons, Scheme A was well within the treaty limit. Schemes B and C showed just how tight that limit was. Their additional armor thickness translated to 4,286 (vs. 3,683) tons of deck and 4,095 (vs. 3,478) tons of belt armor, an increase of 1,220 tons. Merely to use four rather than three barbettes cost 375 tons (plus 260 on the turrets). That pushed them beyond the limit, at 36,800 and 36,500 tons. A new BuOrd super-heavy (1,500-pound vs. 1,400-pound) shell made matters worse, since it became the standard for protection. Now A needed 13.5 inches of belt armor, and B and C, 15 inches. Schemes A1, B1, and C1 were all attempts to modify the initial Schemes to resist the new shells at the original ranges. A1 remained barely within the treaty limit at 34,500 tons, but B1 and C1 were altogether impossible at 39,550 and 39,500 tons. There was, then, no hope—without unconventional practices—of combining earlier standards of armament and protection with high speed.

---

* This intelligence data was substantially confirmed postwar. The Japanese gun initially fired a 2,205-pound shell; later it fired a 2,260-pound shell at 2,560 ft/sec, according to the *U.S. Naval Mission to Japan.*

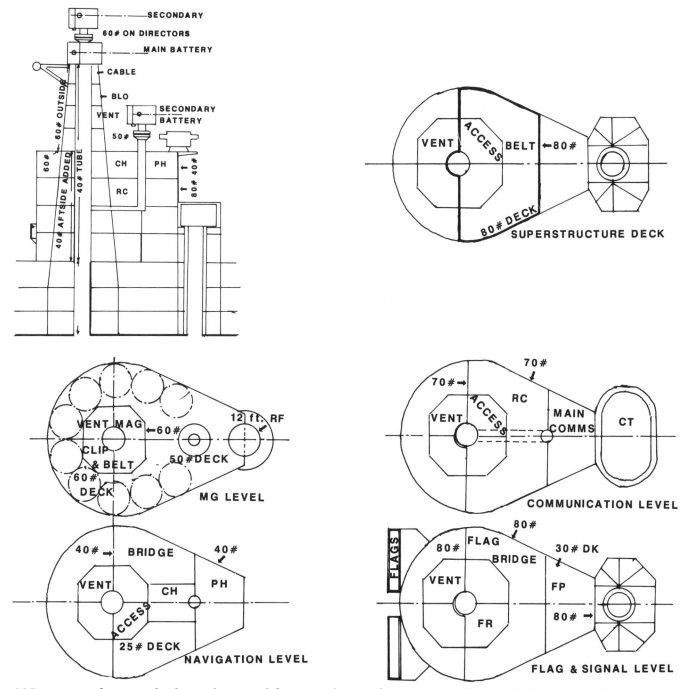

C&R concept of a tower bridge and armored fire control mast, for Schemes I through IV, December 1935. Note the extensive areas of splinter protection. Although the United States ultimately abandoned the concept of placing secondary and main battery directors one atop the other on a common shaft, both France and Italy incorporated such arrangements in the battleships they designed in the 1930s. The broken circles on the upper superstructure levels are the working circles of ten 0.50-calibre machine guns.

Scheme A mounted her No. 3 turret above the other two, so that all nine guns could fire ahead at roughly 4.5 degrees elevation, at a range of about 10,000 yards. Like that of the French battleship *Dunkerque*, this was ideal for a fast ship designed for pursuit. It also protected aircraft, vital for scouting (by a solitary fast capital ship) or for fire control (for

the battle line) from the blast of the heavy guns. However, from a weight point of view it was more expensive than a more conventional arrangement. That was not realized for several months.

These tentative studies were by no means a directive for the next class of U.S. capital ships. Rather, the General Board seems to have seen them as a

Table 12-1. Battleship Designs, 1935

Design	A	A1	B	B1	C	C1	D
Length	710	710	710	710	710 ft	710	750
Beam	102	102	105	105	106 ft	106	106
Draft	28.5	29.725	30.65	32.63	30.43 ft	32.63	32.00
Battery	9 X 14	9 X 14	12 X 14	12 X 14	8 X 16 in	8 X 16	9 X 16
Belt	11.5	13.5	13.25	15	13.25 in	15	17
Deck	4.5	4.5	5.25	5.25	5.25 in	5.25	6.25
Weights(Tons):							
Hull(Bare)	8054	8262	8654	8993	8614	8993	9314
Fittings	1760	1760	1760	1800	1760	1800	1890
Belt	3478	4095	4095	4843	4095	4868	5110
Controls(STS)	494	820	494	825	494	820	820
CT	283	328	340	378	340	378	487
Uptakes	366	366	416	366	410	410	412
Deck Protection	4406	4403	5205	5205	5205	5198	5449
Torpedo Protection	2042	2042	2196	2320	2196	2320	2451
Turrets	700	747	960	1058	1057	1168	1183
Barbettes	1864	2174	2239	2535	2230	2514	2643
Secondary Armor	122	289	122	289	122	289	289
Equip&Outfit	450	450	450	460	450	460	510
Battery	2757	2757	3559	3559	3174	3174	3232
Ammunition	1430	1430	1722	1722	1630	1630	1813
Machinery	3350	3500	3600	3950	3600	3950	3700
Stores	550	550	575	550	575	575	625
Aero	52	52	48	48	48	48	52
Margin	392	475	440	510	560	398	580
Std. Dispt.	32,450	34,500	36,800	39,550	36,500	39,500	40,500
RFW	315	315	330	330	330	330	350
Fuel Oil	2550	2550	2600	2650	2600	2650	2880
Design Dispt.	35,615	37,365	39,730	41,930	39,430	41,980	43,730
Speed	30	30	30.5	30.5	30.5	30.5	30.5
Power	160,000	166,500	180,000	200,000	180,000	200,000	185,000
Immune Zone	22-27	22-27*	19-30	19-30*	19-30	19-30*	19-30†

NOTE: Weight data for designs J through L are arranged differently from data for earlier designs and so are not directly comparable. Thus the entry for belt armor includes the armor and splinter decks; turrets include not only armor but also weapons and ammunition as well as the weight of the conning tower; secondary armor includes not only protection for the secondary guns but also the guns and their ammunition; fittings have been lumped with equipment and outfit; the entry for conning tower is actually miscellaneous splinter protection; the entry for the battery is limited to miscellaneous ordnance weights. Immune zones are calculated against old-type 14-

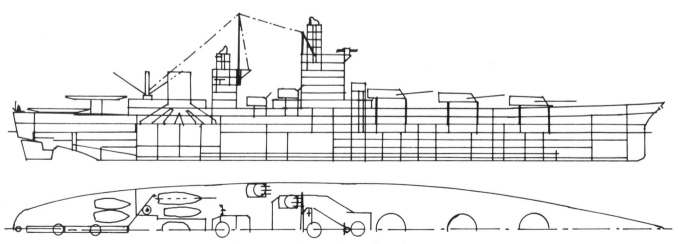

Scheme A, the 32,500-ton fast battleship that began the *North Carolina* design series.

E	F	G	H	J	J1	K	L
750	680	590	598	710	710	710	710
106	101	105	106.5	105	105	102	102
32.00	28.82	30.60	30.64	32	30	30	30
8 X 16	8 X 14	9 X 14	9 X 14	12 X 14	12 X 14	9 X 14	12 X 14
17	13.5	13.5	15	12.5	8	15	12.5
6.25	4.5	4.5	5.25	5.25	5.25	5.25	4.5
9353	8022	7145	7414	8770	8770		8641
1890	1760	1780	1764	2260	2260		2210
5110	3534	3720	4134	8570	7317		7574
820	634	634	634	820	532		541
427	328	328	378	190	100		100
440	366	286	286	220	220		176
5306	4409	4206	4607				
2489	2051	2150	2180	2260	2260		2260
1371	678	793	793	8550	7924		7980
2824	1014	2400	2400				
289	289	289	289	970	893		893
510	450	450	450				
3174	2353	2757	2757	150	150		150
1630	1334	1430	1430				
3700	3450	2010	2010	3550	3550		3550
625	550	550	550	570	570		570
48	95	32	32				
494	433	567	406	500	454		400
40,500	31,750	31,500	32,500	37,383	35,000	35,000	35,045
350	315	300	300				
2880	2450	2150	2150				
43,730	34,082	33,950	34,750				
30.5	30	23	30	30	30	30.5	30
185,000	160,000		65,100	190,000	170,000	170,000	170,000SHP
19-30†	22-27*	22-27*	19-30*	22-30*	-30*	19-30*	22-27* Kyds

inch guns, except where indicated: one asterisk (*) indicates the new-type 14-inch gun; a dagger (†) indicates the new-type 16-inch gun; a double dagger (‡) indicates the existing 12-inch gun. Scheme *M* was Scheme *L* with one of the quadruple turrets moved aft, the weight saved (200 tons) going into increased deck armor (4.75 inches rather than 4.5 inches, for an immune zone extending from 22,000 to 27,700 yards). It is not described in this table. Note that the belt of *J1* is penetrable at all ranges: she has no immune zone at all. Immune zones for *J*, *L*, and *M* are all calculated for *75 degree* rather than 90 degree target angles.

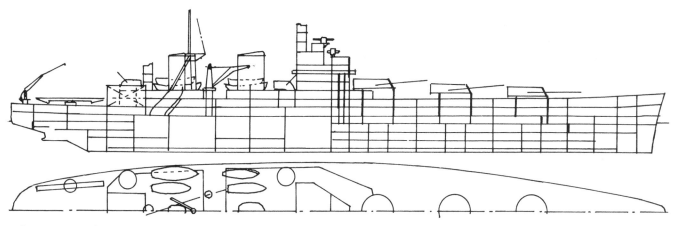

Scheme A1, with alternating engine and boiler rooms.

Table 12-1. Continued

Design	1	3	4	5
Length	542	562	660	660
Beam	99	103	103	103
Draft	26.5	30.5	29.90	29.90
Battery	8 X 12	8 X 12	8 X 12	6 X 14
Belt	10.5	14	14	14
Deck	3.25	5.25	5.25	5.25
Weights:				
Hull (Bare)	6034	6850	7733	7733
Fittings	1250	1370	1630	1630
Belt	2534	3658	4218	4218
Controls	494	450	450	450
CT	264	416	416	416
Uptakes	155	255	366	366
Deck Protection	2355	4341	4936	4936
Torpedo Protection	1310	2360	2150	2150
Turrets	652	920	920	767
Barbettes	1621	2180	2180	1567
Secondary A	122	122	122	122
Equip&Outfit	350	390	410	410
Battery	2048	2048	2048	2110
Ammunition	1041	1041	1041	1114
Machinery	1570	1850	3600	3600
Stores	450	500	550	550
Aero	48	48	48	48
Margin	1202	330	629	452
Std. Dispt.	23,500	29,000	32,500	32,500
RFW	160	210	300	300
Fuel Oil	1575	2100	2185	2185
Design Disp.	24,033	31,300	34,985	34,985
Speed	23	23	30	30
Power	57,500	67,500	180,000	180,000
Immune Zone	19-24.7‡	20-30*	20-30*	20-30*

means of filling out its menu of alternatives. It went so far as to ask the Naval War College whether the next battleship should be a conventional 23-knot type with eight or nine 16-inch guns and 15- or 16-inch armor, or a fast type such as A, B, or C. On 23 August C-in-C U.S. Fleet argued for a conventional slow battleship with a very great endurance, 18,000nm at 15 knots. It also had to keep in mind the possibility that the next London Treaty (which would be signed in 1936) would add new restrictions.

In 1934, the British had proposed a further reduction to 25,000 tons and 12-inch guns. The United States refused any reduction in net tonnage, arguing that tonnage bought both range and resistance to damage—and that bombs and torpedoes would not be correspondingly limited. The British therefore proposed a gun limit of 14 inches, possibly because their own studies suggested that a balanced 16-inch gun battleship could not be built on less than 40,000 tons. The United States ultimately agreed to the 14-inch limit only if the other powers agreed to do so. Hence the escalator clause in the treaty ultimately

adopted. It was important, from a U.S. point of view, to demonstrate the futility of British proposals for smaller battleships; on 21 August the CNO asked for a series of designs emphasizing defensive features on *minimum* displacement. None was particularly attractive. In fact, Preliminary Design characterized the worst (eight 12-inch guns, 25,000 tons, 23 knots, protected against 12-inch fire) as a deathtrap.

C&R returned to its 35,000 tonners. Given the failure of B and C, it tried five alternatives late in September: D, E, F, G, and H. The latter two were traditional slow (23-knot) designs armed with nine 14-inch guns and protected against the new 14-inch shell between either 22,000 and 27,000 (G) or 19,000 and 30,000 (H) yards. They were direct descendants of the 1933-34 designs, well within the treaty limits, and with five rather than four torpedo bulkheads (a slow ship would be easier to hit with torpedoes). Compared with A and A1, they were a hundred feet shorter, with one fewer catapult and one fewer control position. Preliminary Design considered H particularly well balanced. But because they did not

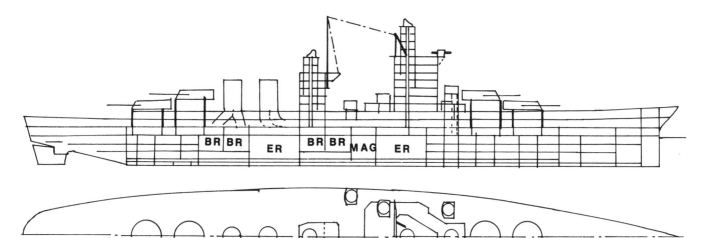

Scheme C.

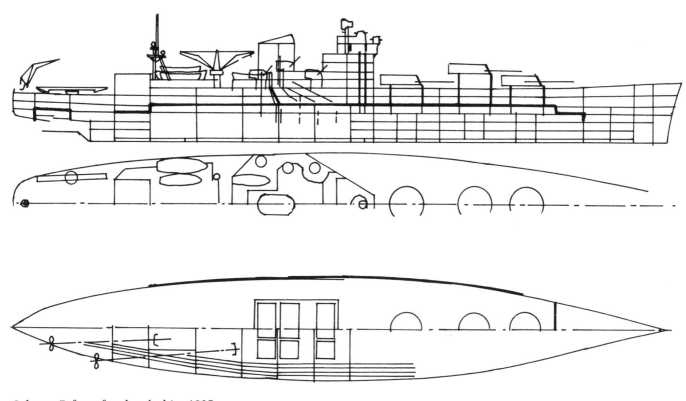

Scheme D for a fast battleship, 1935.

correspond to the General Board's interest in fast, multipurpose ships, they went no further.

C&R's first major weight reduction was a narrowing of the belt from 17.5 to 15.5 feet. It was justified by the assumption that ships would generally enter battle at almost a fixed draft. Torpedo protection depended so critically on the extent to which layers of side (fuel) tanks were filled that captains could be expected to fill those tanks with seawater as fuel oil was burned. The width of the belt should not have to take into account the range of possible variation

of displacement, for example, between design and emergency conditions.

On the other hand, there was a good possibility that the new standard battleship gun would be the 16 inch. Designs D and E were, therefore, armed with and protected against a new 2,250 pound 16in/45 shell, analogous to the new 14 inch, between 19,000 (17-inch belt) and 30,000 (6.25-inch deck) yards. The ships had to be lengthened to 750 feet to take the larger weapons. That, in turn, somewhat reduced required power. Even so, they were altogether im-

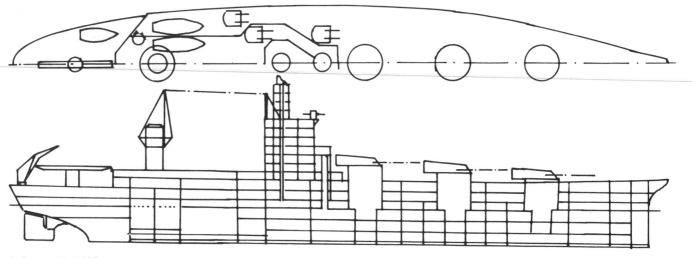

Scheme H, 1935.

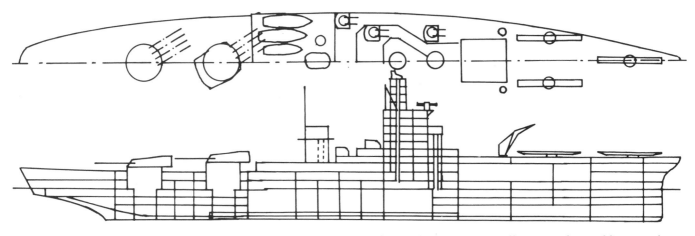

Scheme F, the hybrid battleship-carrier with three large catapults forward, 1935. Reportedly, it was favored by President Roosevelt.

practical, as they would displace 40,000 tons (standard).

Study F was a radical alternative, descended from the carrier escorts of 1933: a battleship emphasizing aviation features but retaining a strong battery. She would have two catapults forward, the hangar below them holding ten bombers with their wings folded. Two quadruple 14-inch turrets were mounted aft, neither superfiring, to save weight on barbette height. Preliminary Design considered the bombers compensation for the loss of the forward main battery turrets. Although it was unconventional, it had "merits warranting further investigation." Displacement was well within the limit, at 31,750 tons. It was by no means considered impossibly eccentric. Several navies were interested in hybrid ships, and the U.S. Navy had just come quite close to ordering a "flight deck cruiser," with her main battery forward and a full flight deck aft, and Sweden actually built a somewhat similar ship, the cruiser *Gotland*. At about the same time, however, interest in catapult-launched combat aircraft began to wane because of the performance penalties they had to pay for having floats allowing them to alight on the sea for recovery after flight.

These studies define the problem. The United States could choose either a relatively lightly armed (and armored), 30-knot ship (Design A) or a slower but better armed ship (which became the *North Carolina*). Heroic measures would be required if the ship were to be protected against 16-inch fire (as in the case of the *South Dakota* described in the next chapter). For the present, only A was really viable, albeit too lightly armed and protected.

Now Preliminary Design could add armor to A or scale B down. It submitted five more studies on 8 October: J, J1, K, L, and M. J and J1 were the last gasp of the four-turret designs, gaining weight at the expense of armor. J1 showed that the belt had to be cut to 8 inches (and even then at a width of only 13.3 feet) if it were to remain within the treaty limit. That left the field to the three-turret designs. It did not prohibit a twelve-gun ship, since BuOrd could develop a quadruple 14-inch turret, as in the contemporary French *Dunkerque*.

Design K was armored up from A1. To gain weight for additional armor, the belt was narrowed to 14 feet and the after control tower and second inner bottom eliminated. The 1,450 tons saved equated to a 15-inch belt and 5.25-inch deck, corresponding to the immune zone of design B1, 19,000 to 30,000 yards (against the super-heavy 14-inch shell). Preliminary Design considered K attractive, but feared that it was so tight that any further development would bring it over the treaty limit.

L was the twelve-gun alternative, employing quadruple turrets. As in J, the belt was cut to a thickness of 12.5 inches and a width of 13.3 feet. The armor deck was cut to 4.5 inches (27,000 yards), the splinter deck to 1 inch, and the barbette, conning tower, and tube to 12.5 inches, which corresponded to a smaller immune zone than did the belt, since these circular structures never presented other than a 90 degree target angle. As in Designs A and K, L had all three turrets forward. Another 200 tons (125 tons in barbette armor, 75 tons in armored length) could be saved by moving one turret aft (Design M); it bought a quarter inch of protective deck, or 700 yards of immune zone. Both L and M were so close to the treaty limit that Preliminary Design feared they could not be developed into detailed designs without exceeding it. That left design K as the best compromise.

The General Board decided in October to proceed with it rather than with a more conventional design, largely on the basis of its expectations of a Pacific campaign. Admiral William H. Standley, the CNO, argued for four fast battleships, to form two task forces with the two heavy carriers *Lexington* and *Saratoga*. He did not want carrier speed, 33 knots, for the new battleships, but rather enough to overtake and engage the fastest capital ships in the Pacific, the 26-knot *Kongo*s, that is, he wanted a minimum of 27 knots.* Yet Standley also expressed concern with Japanese heavy cruiser and carrier forces, which the slow U.S. battle line could not bring to action and which could certainly outrun any 27-knot battleship as well.

---

* The U.S. Navy was unaware of a major reconstruction of these ships, which increased their speed to 30.5 knots. Nor did it know that Japan planned to remilitarize the fourth ship of the class, *Hiei*. The available records do not always explicitly indicate what intelligence material was available. The case of the *Mutsu* (see Chapter 13) is an important example. One might, for example, conclude that the insistence on high speed in the *Iowa*s was linked to the revelation of the higher speed of the *Kongo*s, about 1938.

Admiral William S. Pye, then president of the Naval War College, emphasized the threat of the *Kongo*s. He doubted that the Japanese would risk their main fleet unless they could wear down the U.S. battle line first. That was, in fact, their policy in 1941. War College exercises consistently showed that the three fast Japanese capital ships, which the United States could oppose only by air and by torpedo-carrying craft (submarines, cruisers, and destroyers), could exercise enormous influence during the early stages of a Pacific war. They were "a thorn in the side of the U.S. Fleet." He therefore favored a speed of at least 28 knots, so as to have an edge of 2 knots or more. As for the tightness of the fast battleship designs, Pye suggested that the margin built into battleship designs might be abandoned, "We must not lose ten percent in margin. We should be willing to accept ten per cent *over* in the first ship of a class."

The senior officers afloat favored the "battle cruiser" by a 9 to 7 margin. The strategists were even more enthusiastic. Thus, of the six line officers immediately concerned with strategic planning within the War Plans Division, five, including the director, favored fast units. However, no officer wanted to make the fast capital ship the standard for all future U.S. construction. The majority wanted only three; one wanted four; another, as many as in any other navy. The most radical choice was two for every Japanese one. However, one officer argued that the Japanese capital ships could be taken care of more simply by air attack alone.

As might be expected, BuOrd much favored the 16-inch gun and would accept design A only if it were forced to do so by the treaty. For example, U.S. guns firing the new 2,250-pound shell could deny the Japanese *Nagato* (13-inch side, 4-inch deck) any immune zone. The new 14-inch gun, however, would not penetrate the side of the ship beyond 22,600 yards nor the deck inside 25,200. The British *Nelson* (14-inch side, 6.25-inch deck) would be immune to both guns. Her immune zone against the 14 inch, however, would be 13,000 yards wide, whereas it would be limited to 6,600 yards against the 16in/45.

BuOrd also wanted to space guns more widely in each turret, to reduce interference (but also to simplify shell handling). It was then trying to solve interference patterns in the new heavy cruisers, whose weapons were relatively closely spaced. From C&R's point of view, however, any increase in spacing would cost barbette diameter and gun-mount weight. For example, in the *Tennessee* the spacing was 71 inches, gun diameter to gun diameter, corresponding to a total armor weight for barbettes alone of about 400 tons. However, spacings of 10 or 11 feet, as in some of the 1934 studies, would increase the weight per barbette to 500, and the weight of rotating turret armor would rise as well. It appeared that 85 to 95

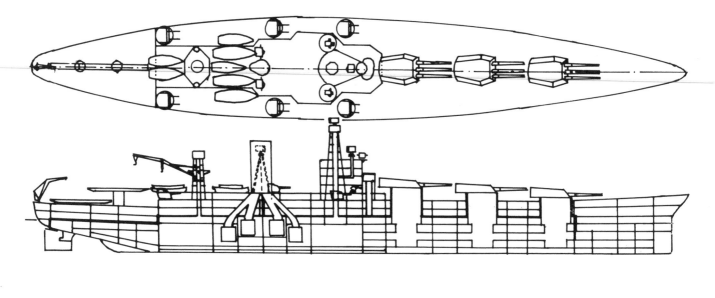

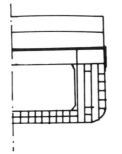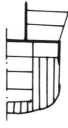

Scheme I, the beginning of the final preliminary design series, 1936.

inches would be a good compromise, for an average of 900 tons per turret in fixed and rotating armor. Finally, the bureau called for a heavier secondary battery: twelve dual-purpose guns seemed a poor substitute for the combination of twelve single-purpose and eight antiaircraft guns mounted by existing battleships.

Design K was really the only practicable alternative. The General Board sought immunity between 20,700 yards (14-inch belt) and 30,000 yards (5.25-inch deck) against the 14in/50 gun. Corresponding zones against 16in/45 and 16in/50 guns would be 23,900 to 26,100 and 26,300 to 26,900 yards. Either a conventional configuration or the all-forward arrangement of 14-inch guns could be tried.

Ultimately, a developed version of Design K was actually selected for construction, then rejected at the last moment in favor of a slower but more heavily armed ship. The twists and turns of the design give some idea of the problems that both designers and policy makers encountered. Sketch designs evolved in the next stage were denoted by Roman numerals;

a total of thirty-five have been identified in the surviving documents.

The first series, I through V, were submitted to the General Board as early as 15 November. Weight was clearly critical, and they incorporated a characteristic feature of later U.S. calculations, the "paper" weight reduction. In their case, the fraction of ammunition stowage to be counted within the standard displacement was reduced. It had been customary to allow for 100 rounds per gun plus 100 more for the ship. Now the latter was eliminated. This was a purely paper saving, since the ship was designed to accommodate the larger allowance. It was the forebear of much larger paper weight reductions, all well worthwhile in ships so close to the treaty limit.

Schemes I and II were the two alternative versions of K requested by the Board, II having one of the low turrets moved aft. Scheme I showed that K had been overoptimistic. Side armor had to be reduced from 15 to 12.25 inches, moving the inner edge of the immune zone from 19,000 out to 22,600 yards. It was also difficult to fit large machinery spaces (for

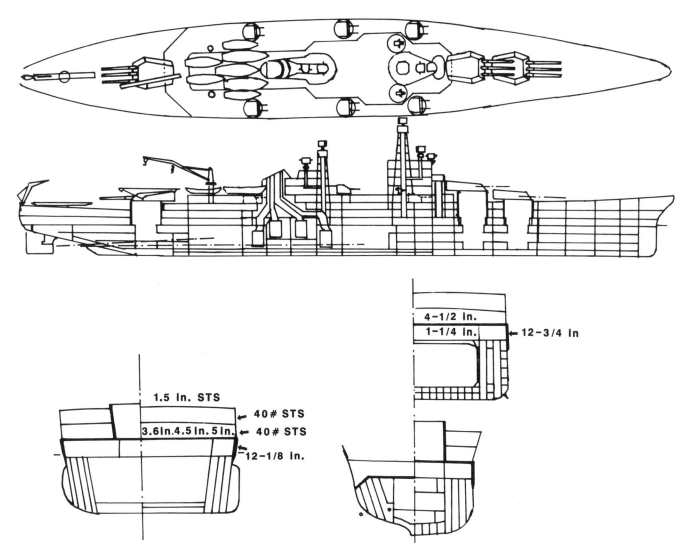

Scheme II, 1936, the first with guns aft. Scheme III differed only in that it had sloping armor, as in the cross section at left. Even the barbettes were sloped (coned).

165,000SHP for 30 knots) within the torpedo-protection aft.

Nor could much be saved by moving one turret aft. Scheme II would probably displace 35,745 tons, even if the margin were kept unrealistically small. Therefore armor was further reduced, in Scheme II-A, to 12.75 inches. The new turret was difficult to locate aft, due to its greater depth and diameter. Depth precluded lowering it, whatever weight saving might be entailed. Diameter was a problem in that both magazine and torpedo protection had to be worked in at a point where the hull had to narrow for a good flow to the propellers. On the other hand, since BuOrd demanded two fire control towers at least 75 feet apart, Preliminary Design could not realize what might have been a major saving in a design with all turrets forward, the elimination of the after director.

Another issue was how much of the waterline to armor. As it went to longer hulls, C&R had to abandon the traditional policy of fixing the armored length by buoyancy and stability criteria. For example, Scheme II was armored over only 63.6 percent of its length, compared to 68.6 for the earlier *West Virginia* (but only 58.4 for the British *Nelson*, which reflected a different design philosophy). It might be argued that the hull lines necessary for high speed would place far more of the buoyancy of the hull in that central 64 percent than would be the case in a slower ship. Even so, C&R felt compelled to justify these figures by their application to a fast capital ship, that is, to a specialized type that presumably would not have to stand the continuous pounding expected for the battle line. The subtle switch away from a fixed fraction of waterline length made long hulls (as in the *Iowa*s) practical.

Table 12-2. Designs for the *North Carolina*, 1935–36

Design	I	II	II-A	III	IV	IV-A	IV-B
Date	15Nov35	15Nov35	15Nov35	15Nov35	15Nov35	10Apr36	10Apr36
Length	710	710	710	710	725	725	725
Beam	106-6	106-6	106-6	107-6	107-6	107-9	107-9
Draft	32	32	32	31-8	31-7	31-9	31-1
Battery	9 X 14	9 X 14	9 X 14	9 X 14	9 X 14	9 X 14	9 X 14
Belt	12.25	14	12.75	12.125*	12.125*	12.125*	12.125*
Deck	5.25	5.25	5	3.6-5	3.6-5	4.1-5.5	4.1-5.5
Weights:							
Hull	17,390	17,640	17,450	18,000	18,086	18,079	18,617
Fittings	1730	1730	1730	1730	1760	1587	1587
Protection	7578	8050	7508	7001	6971	7010	7121
Equip&Outfit	520	520	520	520	520	538	538
Battery	1696	1696	1696	1696	1696	1716	1798
Ammunition	1300	1300	1300	1300	1300	1276	1345
Machinery	3560	3560	3560	3560	3419	3588	3588
Stores	669	669	669	669	689	633	633
Aero	75	75	75	75	75	54	54
Margin	482	503	492	449	566	668	257
Std. Dispt.	35,000	35,743	35,000	35,000	35,000	35,000	35,000
RFW							400
Fuel Oil							6644
Design Dispt.	42,050	42,050	42,050	42,050	42,050	42,050	42,044
Deck Protection	4796	5155		5600	5601	6127	6127
Torpedo Protection	2400	2310		2605	2605	2490	2490
Speed	30	30	30	30	30	30	30
Power	165,000	165,000	165,000	165,000	165,000	165,000	155,000
Immune Zone	24.1-27.4	20.7-30	23.1-29.3	21.4-30	21.4-30	21.4-30	21.4-30

Design	IX-C	IX-D	IX-E	X-A	X-B	XI-A	XI-B
Date	6May36		19May36	29May36			
Length	725	725	725	690	690	706	706
Beam	107-9	107-9		107-9	107-9	107-9	107-9
Draft	31-9	31-9		32-7	32-7	31-9	31-9
Battery	8 X 14(Q)	8 X 14(Q)	8 X 14(Q)	10 X 14	9 X 14	10 X 14	9 X 14
Belt	13.375*	13.125	13.125*	13.125*	13.325*	12.625*	12.625*
Deck	4.1-5.5	5-5.5	5-5.5	5.75	5.75	5.75	5.75
Weights:							
Hull	18,283	18,283		17,797	17,841	17,971	18,138
Fittings	1668	1668		1585	1585	1589	1589
Protection	7111	6869		7562	7516	7439	7335
Equip&Outfit	538	538		536	536	538	538
Battery	1692	1702		2030	1902	2030	1902
Ammunition	1315	1161		1351	1262	1351	1256
Machinery	3588	3588		3100	3150	3100	3250
Stores	633	633		633	633	633	633
Aero	54	54		54	54	54	54
Margin	118	500		352	527	295	325
Std. Dispt.	35,000	35,000		35,000	35,000	35,000	35,000
RFW							
Fuel Oil							
Design Dispt.							
Deck Protection	6463	6463		5442	5534	5517	5679
Torpedo Protection	2460	2460		2440	2440	2410	2430
Speed	30	30	30	26.8	27	27	27.5
Power	155,000	155,000		112,500	116,000	112,500	122,000
Immune Zone	19-30	19-30.4	19-30.4	19-30	19.5-30	20.3-30	20.3-30

*Belt sloped at 10 degrees.

IV-C	V	VI-A	VI-B	VII	VIII	IX-A	IX-B
10Apr36	15Nov35	10Apr36	10Apr36	10Apr36		6May36	6May36
725	660	725	690	640	690	725	725
107-0	107-6	107-9	107-9	107-9	107-9	107-9	107-9
31-9	33.7	31-9	32-6	33-4	32-6	31-9	31-9
9 X 14	8 X 16(Q)	8 X 14	8 X 14	12 X 14	10 X 14	8 X 14(Q)	8 X 14(Q)
12.125*	15.5	9.875*	13.375*	12.125*	12.125*	12.125*	13.375*
4.1-5.5	6.3	4.1-5.5	4.1-5.5	4.1-5.5	4.1-5.5	4.1-5.5	4.1-5.5
18,095		18,296	17,718	17,680	17,849	17,881	18,283
1634		1608	1600	1587	1600	1587	1668
7010		7039	8246	7908	7762	6253	6898
538		538	533	524	533	538	538
1902		1688	1688	2343	1971	1598	1708
1416		1287	1287	1719	1440	1250	1315
3588		3588	3000	2340	3000	3588	3588
633		633	633	633	633	633	633
54		54	54	54	54	54	54
130		271	241	212	158	1718	315
35,000	35,000	35,000	35,000	35,000	35,000	35,000	35,000
42,500	41,922						
6127		6127	5890	5868	5890	6113	6463
2490		2590	2490	2460	2490	2460	2460
30	27	30	26.5	22	26.5	30	30
155,000	130,000	155,000	116,000	50,000	116,000	155,000	155,000
21.4-30	20-30†	25.8-30	19-30	21.4-30	21.4-30	21.4-30	19-30

XII	XIII	XIII-A	XIII-B	XIV	XV	XV-A	XV-B	XV-C
	29May36			29May36	2Jun36			
674	725	725	725	725	725	725	725	725
107-9	107-9			107-9				
33-2	31-9			31-9				
9 X 14	9 X 14	9 X 14	9 X 14	10 X 14	11 X 14	9 X 14	10 X 14	10 X 14
14.75*	13*	13*	13*					
4.9-5.5	4.9-5.5	4.9-5.5	4.9-5.5					
17,884	18,206			17,913	18,005	17,400	17,293	17,535
1583	1610			1610	1610	1610	1610	1610
7571	7320			6183	7648	7259	7366	7469
534	538			538	538	538	538	538
1902	1806			1928	2056	1800	1928	1928
1256	1256			1256	1256	1256	1256	1256
3100	3250			3250	3250	3500	3200	3500
633	633			633	633	633	633	633
54	54			54	54	54	54	54
483	328			453		950	1122	477
35,000	35,000			35,000	35,000	35,000	35,000	35,000
					400			
					6644			
					42,044			
5688	6240			6183	6752	6309	6195	6343
2420	2510			2510	2430	2490	2430	2510
26.6	28.5	30	28.5	28.5	28.45	30.05	28.45	30.05
112,500	123,000			123,000				
17.9-31.8		19.8-30	19.8-30	30-30				

†Immune against 16- rather than 14-inch shellfire.

Table 12-2. Continued

Design	XV-D	XV-E	XVI	XVI-A	XVI-B	XVI-C	XVI-D
Date		19Jun36	20Aug36				
Length	725	725	714		725	725	725
Beam							
Draft							
Battery	10 X 14	12 X 14	12 X 14		10 X 14	9 X 14	
Belt			11.2*		13.5	13.6	12.8
Deck			5.1-5.6				
Weights:							
Hull	17,420	17,447					
Fittings	1610	1610					
Protection	7417	7764					
Equip&Outfit	538	538					
Battery	1928	2184					
Ammunition	1256	1256					
Machinery	3400	3200					
Stores	633	633					
Aero	54	54					
Margin	744	314					
Std. Dispt.	35,000	35,000					
RFW							
Fuel Oil							
Design Dispt.							
Deck Protection	6273	6195					
Torpedo Protection	2470	2430					
Speed	29.2	28.45	27	30	30	30	30
Power							
Immune Zone							

Despite its interest in underwater protection, C&R was now willing to concentrate the boilers in four adjoining boiler rooms between the engine rooms, so as to minimize the length of steam lines. The end rooms each contained two boilers abreast, the central ones three. The latter had to be raised to clear propeller shafts from the forward engine room. They could not be covered by the splinter deck.

Schemes I and II showed that armor was the main bar to successful treaty battleship design. At about 20,000 yards, 100 tons of vertical armor would buy 500 yards more of immune zone. At about 30,000, the same weight invested in deck armor would buy only 300 yards, since any given thickness of deck armor had to cover a vastly greater area than an equivalent thickness of side armor.

Scheme III was an attempt to overcome such limits by using more sophisticated forms of protection, inclined side armor and a bomb deck. Deck heights were also reduced by 3 inches to cut hull weight by 66 tons. Of the two expedients, inclined side armor was well known and had been used in the 1919 battle cruisers, which became the carriers *Lexington* and *Saratoga*. A 10 degree slope would save 1 3/8 inches on the thickness required at 19,000 yards. Even though the plates would have to be slightly wider, that would save 260 tons. That was still too little, and the de-

signers had to settle for 12 1/8 rather than 13 5/8 inches, that is, an inner edge at 21,400 yards. A related measure was to slope the barbette outward, as in the heavy cruiser *Wichita*. A 5 degree cone saved 3/4 inch, or a total of 240 tons for the ship.

The inclined belt presented some problems of its own. Maximum beam above the waterline was set by the Panama Canal, and the inclined beam sloped inwards from it. In consequence, beam (hence waterplane, for stability) at the waterline was somewhat reduced. Moreover, were the slope to continue below the waterline, there would be insufficient volume for torpedo defense—as the British had found with HMS *Hood*, and as, for that matter, the Americans found in their 1919 battle cruiser design. The solution in all three cases was the same: a blister to restore underwater beam. In Scheme III the blister actually increased the depth of underwater protection as compared with Schemes I and II. It proved possible to insert an additional (fifth) bulkhead abeam the magazines fore and aft. This 200 tons was released by other weight-saving measures (see below). The designers remarked that had it been put into armor the immune zone could have been expanded by another 1,000 yards at its inner edge.

The bomb deck was a much more radical idea. It was intended to answer the threat of large, light-cased, high-explosive bombs, which could be stopped by 1.5 or 2 inches of STS. C&R feared that, unless such a deck was provided, bombs might tear up the structural decks and topside plating above the main armor deck, causing large craters. Armor piercing bombs would penetrate easily enough, but the bomb deck would initiate their fuze action, and they would burst harmlessly against the main armor deck. In addition, shells passing through the bomb deck would find it more difficult to penetrate the armor deck below it. Only shells striking the armor deck through the unarmored side of the ship would be unaffected. They in turn would strike the outer edge of the armor deck. The inner portion, which would be shadowed by the bomb deck, could be thinned.

In Scheme III only the maximum armor deck thickness of 5 inches was maintained over only the outer 13.5 feet. For 11 feet inboard of this on either beam the thickness was reduced to 4.5 inches, and over the next 6.5 feet it tapered to the 3.6 inches of the central part. These reductions held the *net* increase due to the provision of a bomb deck to only 35 tons out of a total deck armor weight (excluding splinter deck) of about 5,550 tons. It was expected that another quarter inch (150 tons) could be skimmed from the splinter deck in view of the protection added. Later on, much more would be cut. On the other hand, it was necessary to cover the space between the two armor decks with 1-inch splinter armor.

Both inclined belt and bomb deck characterized all later U.S. battleship designs.

The turrets were lowered closer to the deck on their barbettes. This was possible because the earlier requirement for clearance *below* the rear end of the turret (for a trapdoor) was abandoned, a door being cut in the rear plate of the turret (and the consequent weakness being accepted). That in turn lowered the conning tower, whose height was fixed by the requirement to see over No. 2 turret. Such savings could add up to 150 tons. The height of the turret itself was reduced by lowering its rear end, its height fixed by the height of the turret officer's booth. The booth itself was lowered into a deepened turret overhang. There was no longer any need for clearance below the overhang of the turret (for the trapdoor). Now the turret could have a flat roof, superior ballistically to a sloped roof, hence thinner. Hundreds of tons could be saved on the thinner roofs, lower barbettes, and lower conning tower.

In Scheme IV the hull was lengthened from the previously standard 710 feet to 725 feet, which actually *saved* weight by reducing the required power. A longer hull could be driven more easily, particularly in bad weather, and it would also make for better habitability. The hull itself, however, would have to be heavier, it would be less maneuverable, and it would be more difficult to provide sufficient

underwater protection within its finer lines. For all of these reasons, the American designers argued that "the shortest ship capable of making the required speed and accommodating the vitals has the least displacement." Preliminary studies seemed to show that 710 feet would be adequate.

All of this was predicated on similarly proportioned armor suits. However, armor weight could actually be reduced by lengthening the hull. That is, when hull length grew to 725 feet in Schemes IV and V, power was reduced 10,000SHP, and the machinery space (hence the armored length) shortened by 8 feet. On the other hand, some side armor had to be provided to link the main belt with the steering gear. That reduced the net saving to 47 tons. That is, the bare hull had to be increased from 7,630 to 7,782 tons, and hence hull fittings from 1,730 to 1,760. But 76 tons were saved on protection (12,601 reduced to 12,525), 143 on machinery (to 3,417), and 20 more on hull features related to machinery, such as foundations. In addition one of the three boilers in each of the two amidships boiler rooms could be eliminated. The remaining two could clear the wing shafts, and the splinter deck could be restored. In the lengthened Scheme IV the margin of Scheme III could be restored to a realistic figure.

BuOrd would still have preferred a 16-inch ship, and Scheme V was armed with eight 16in/45 (which weighed roughly as much as nine 14in/50) but protected only against 14-inch fire. Preliminary Design chose to trade off speed for armor, reducing the 710-foot hull by one boiler room length, to 660 feet (130,000SHP, 27 knots). In December 1935 it produced a design with two triple turrets forward and one twin turret aft, immune between 19,000 and 30,000 yards. Later two quadruple turrets would be proposed instead. In outline, these results are close to what later became the *South Dakota*, although it is clear from surviving documents that there was no connection between the two designs. Scheme V was cramped, and it had the shortest armored length, 61 percent (vs. 61.2 in Scheme IV, the next worst). Moreover, its 14-inch protection could not be satisfactory as long as foreign navies could build 16-inch battleships.

Scheme IV was clearly the best of the lot, and on 3 January 1936 the General Board selected it as the basis for further development. Even though it was clearly extremely tight, the board asked for major improvements. It wanted sixteen 5-inch guns, as the twelve previously accepted seemed far too few in view of the size of the battery already mounted on earlier battleships. By March, tentative characteristics called for twenty 5-inch guns, a combination of single mounts and either four, six, or eight twin mounts. They would be supplemented by two quadruple 1.1-inch machine cannon and at least eight

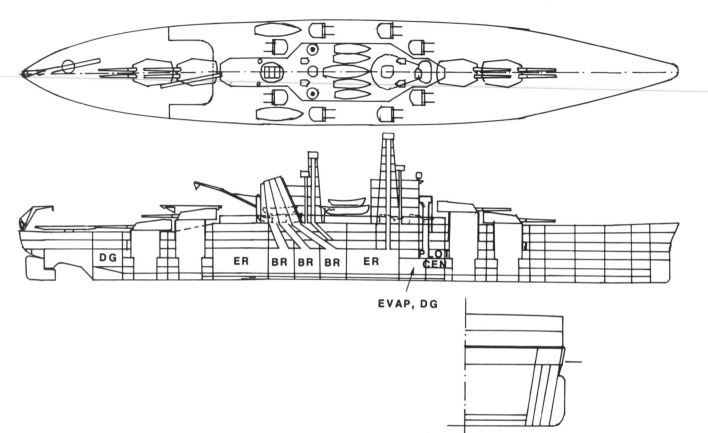

Scheme VIB: 690-feet long, 26.5 knots, eight 14in/50 guns, protected against 14-inch fire between 19,000 and 30,000 yards. Note the ramps connecting the forecastle with the quarterdeck. They carried stresses over, to avoid weakness in the hull. Weight was saved by the reduction in hull structure aft. These ramps were common to many of the *North Carolina* preliminary designs, but the ship actually built was flush-decked.

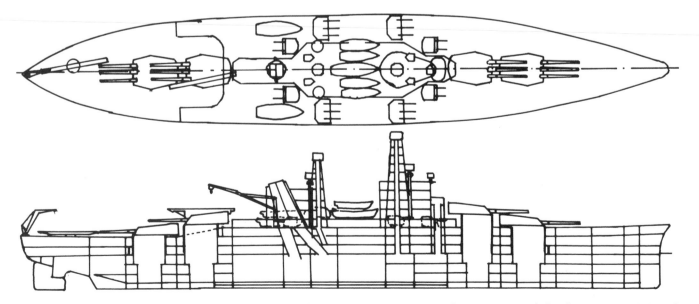

Scheme VII, a slow battleship: 640 feet, 22 knots, twelve 14in/50 guns, protected against 14-inch fire between 21,400 and 30,000 yards.

0.50-calibre machine guns. The immune zone was to be 19,000 to 30,000 yards against the new 14-inch gun, the speed 30 knots, and the endurance 15,000nm at 15 knots.

Nor did the board fully accept the lessons of earlier designs. It asked informally for a new series of four-turret sketch designs, which became Schemes VIA and VIB. Preliminary Design also developed Scheme VII, a return to the old twelve-gun, low-speed (22-knot) studies, and VIII, an intermediate ten-gun type. Both VII and VIII were three-turret designs. Thus, VII makes an interesting comparison with the twelve-gun ship actually built. However, the main line of development continued in three sketch designs submitted in April, Schemes IVA through IVC.

As might be expected, these designs were extremely tight. For example, to get extra 5-inch mounts in Scheme IV, Preliminary Design had had to dispense with the 1.1-inch mounts, despite the board's desire for both. Worse, it had been discovered that a lower-velocity, 14-inch gun would actually penetrate deck armor more effectively than the high-velocity 14in/50, because its shell would fall more steeply, hence striking the deck at an angle closer to the vertical. It now became the standard for the outer edge of the immune zone, and IVA was re-rated at 21,400 to 27,000 yards, despite an increase in deck armor to 2.6 to 4 inches laid atop 1.5-inch plating. Scheme IVB had eight twin 5in/38, and Scheme IVC six twins and eight single mounts. For the 5-inch guns alone, that meant a total of 805 tons in IVB and 861 in IVC, compared with 597 in IV or IVA, not including ammunition: 500 rounds per gun in IV (304 tons), but 450 in IVC (438 tons). In each case the allowance included a total of 800 illuminating rounds for the ship.

C&R complained that on 35,000 tons it was being asked to equal the British *Hood*, balancing the 5,000- to 6,000-ton advantage of the earlier ship by improvements in machinery design and by using triple rather than twin turrets. Moreover, safety margins had to be abandoned. For example, "the torpedo bulkheading is intended to just defeat one torpedo at a given point. The side belt has just sufficient freeboard to keep the heavy protective deck out of the water after one torpedo hit." Power sufficed to meet the required speed only in smooth water with a clean bottom.

Even then the General Board requirements could not be met. For example, to thicken the belt (to 13 3/8 inches) to meet the 19,000-yard standard would cost 270 tons; half an inch more deck, another 400; the increase in 5 inch guns, 398; the increased hull depth to take account of ambiguities in the definitions of trial and battle displacements, another 360; BuOrd's desire for 6-inch rather than 3-inch armor over the light part of barbettes, another 140. These

and other *direct* increases would amount to 2,075 tons, and the actual increase in displacement would be far greater.

C&R needed a way out. One possibility was to reduce the number of barbettes and turrets by using two quadruples in place of the earlier three triplets (IXA, B, and C). There was enough weight to provide full belt protection (IXB) and even twenty 5-inch guns (IXC), albeit, in the latter case, at the price of nearly the entire margin. In IXD deck armor was increased at the cost of some splinter deck armor and some secondary ammunition, and in IXE both quadruple turrets were mounted forward. Now No. 2 barbette had to be raised, at a cost in armor weight. The margin, which had reached a low of 145 tons in IXC, fell from the 456 tons of IXD to 395 tons. These were all 30-knot, 725-foot designs. None appears to have been satisfactory.

The board now began to waver in its affection for very high speeds. On 15 May it asked for a nine-gun ship which would trade off speed (27 knots) for armor. Variations on this theme were to be the addition of a tenth gun, and a loss or gain of half a knot. In Scheme XA, the tenth gun was added by replacing one forward triple with a quadruple turret. Length and power could be reduced (690 feet, 112,500SHP for 26.8 kts). Armor roughly met the board's standards. The General Board hoped to save more weight by eliminating the bomb deck, but the constructors argued that nearly as much plating was needed merely for structural strength. Speed still seemed slow, and in Scheme XIA the ship was lengthened to 706 feet (XIA) at a cost in belt armor (13 1/8inches reduced to 12 5/8inches, for immunity at 20,300 rather than 19,500 yards). XB and XIB were nine-gun equivalents, with somewhat more power and, in XB, a quarter inch more belt armor. Scheme XII tested the possibility that a small further cut in speed (to 26.6 knots) would add armor.

The constructors felt that XII sacrificed too much to protection and that there might be some way of increasing speed at a minimum price. That meant going back up to 725 feet for Schemes XIII (nine guns) and XIV (ten). Now 123,000SHP, much as in XIA, would drive a ship at 28.5 knots. Weight savings included the elimination of four single 5in/38. In addition, the requirement that No. 1 turret be able to fire dead ahead at zero elevation was abandoned. This turret could now be dropped as much as 8 or 9 feet, for substantial savings in barbette and conning tower armor. The extra gun in XIV was bought by eliminating the after control tower, which had contributed so much to the failure of the original Scheme I. Alternatively, in XIIIA, the extra control tower was traded for more power, so that the ship could make 30 knots on 150,000SHP. XIIIB was equivalent to XIII except that a half inch of bomb deck was added.

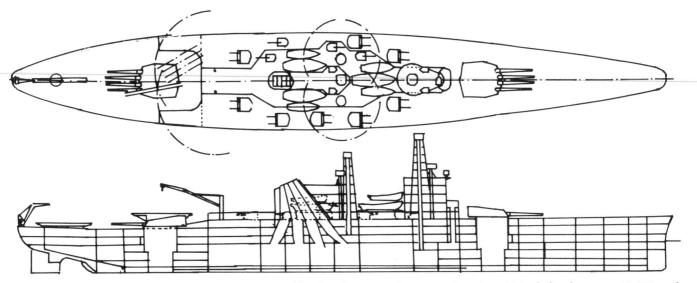

Scheme IX: 725-feet long, eight 14in/50 guns, capable of 30 knots, and protected against 14-inch fire between 19,000 and 30,000 yards. Two alternative secondary battery arrangements are shown.

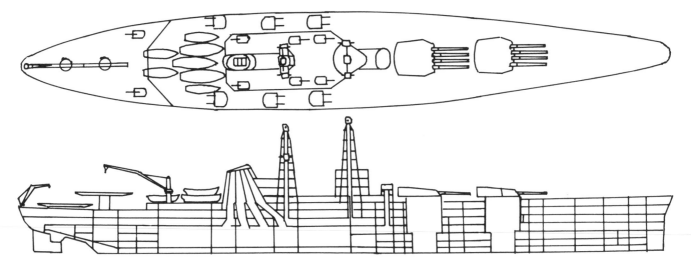

Scheme IXE: 725-feet long, eight 14in/50 guns, with speed reduced to 28.5 knots, protected against the new 14-inch shell (1,500 pounds) between 19,000 and 30,400 yards.

The constructors also sketched a longer (740-foot) hull that could achieve 29 knots on the original 123,000SHP, with eleven guns (two quadruple turrets, fore and aft), but it was impractical. Its eleven-gun battery was attractive, however, and it appeared in the next serious sketch design, XV, of early June 1936. At that time alternatives with nine, ten, and twelve (XVE) guns were also considered.

Preliminary Design described IXD and IXE as emphasizing speed and protection at the expense of firepower; XIII and its derivatives as more or less balanced compromises; and XIV as emphasizing firepower at the expense of speed. By this time the General Board was leaning toward the relatively slow eleven- and twelve-gun designs. Impatient with arguments concerning design margin, the board ordered C&R to redesign XV and XVE, distributing their 450 tons of margin among protective features. The existence of these schemes encouraged the board to issue new tentative characteristics on 25 June.

They called for a 28.5-knot ship with eleven 14-inch guns and sixteen 5in/38 (twelve in twin mounts), weight being saved by restricting ammunition (in standard condition) to 900 14-inch and 6,800 5-inch,

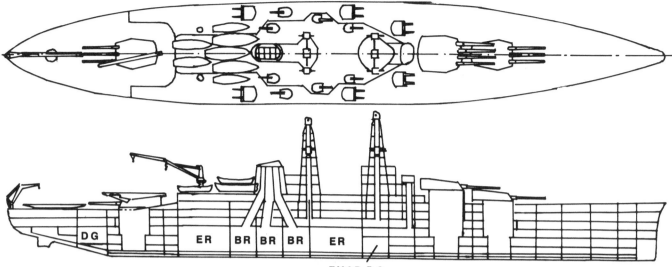

Scheme XA: 690-feet long, 26.8 knots, ten 14in/50 guns (note the quadruple mount in No. 2 position), protected against the new 14-inch shell between 19,500 and 30,000 yards.

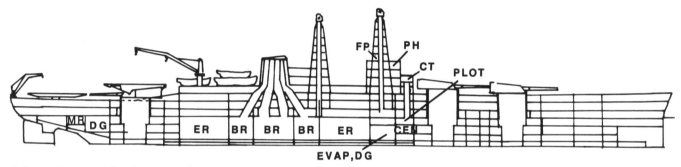

Scheme XIII: 725-feet long, 28.5 knots, nine 14in/50 (three triple mounts), protected against the new 14-inch shell between 19,800 and 30,000 yards.

although capacity would be much greater. In accordance with C&R experience, the quadruple 1.1-inch machine cannon would be omitted, the only light AA battery being eight 0.50-calibre machine guns. The immune zone would extend between 19,000 and 30,000 (33,000 over magazines) yards. With a bomb deck, that would require a 5.6 inch-6.25 inch main armor deck and a 1.25inch-0.75inch splinter deck. In a major triumph for C&R, trial speed was to be calculated with full loads of oil, stores, and ammunition.

In his covering letter to the secretary of the navy, the chairman of the General Board commented that the usual weight margin had been forgone, so that it might be necessary, in the course of the design, to reduce some of the characteristics so as to remain within the treaty limit. In that case, the board proposed to cut the number of 14-inch guns from 11 to 10 rather than to reduce protection. On the other hand, it might be possible, by refining the design, to increase the battery to twelve guns. The CNO added

informally that he would be glad to see an extra gun at the expense of speed. However, at least on the surface, the characteristics seemed to be a victory for the constructors' view that a battleship design could be balanced between effective protection, moderately high speed, and battery. The dominance of the 14-inch gun in these studies was due to London Treaty negotiations rather than to any technical decision. BuOrd still favored the 16-inch gun.

Preliminary Design responded by shaving XVE down to 714 feet and 27 knots (as Scheme XVI, 20 August 1936). No reduction in protection was contemplated, partly because two new threats had just been discovered. Model tests showed that at high speed, 20 to 27 knots, the system of waves generated by the ship would uncover parts of the lower edge of the belt forward and aft, unfortunately, just over the magazines. At the same time, BuOrd discovered that underwater shell hits were a major menace in the 20,000- to 30,000-yard range band. The most logical counter would be internal patches of armor over

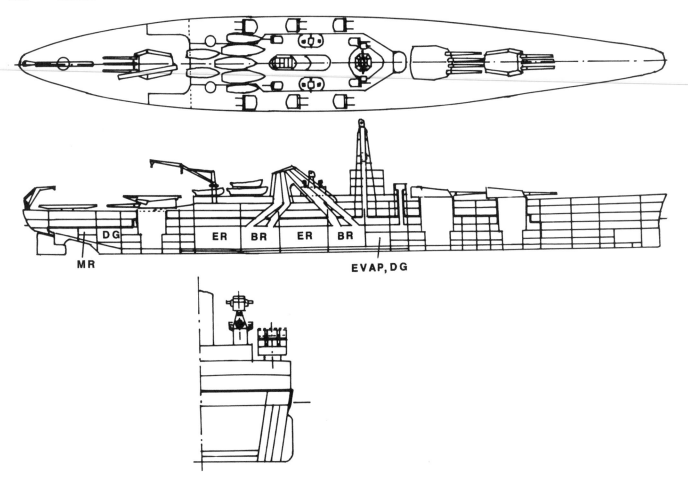

Scheme XIV: 725-feet long, 28.5 knots, ten 14in/50, protected against the new 14-inch shell between 20,000 and 30,000 yards.

the magazines, but the constructors feared that such hard patches would render the torpedo-protection system ineffective. BuOrd also feared that the divided-armor formula used to compute the benefits of the bomb deck was overoptimistic. Finally, the bureau suggested that it was wrong to taper the lower edge of the forward transverse bulkhead below the waterline to match the tapering belt armor. Clearly shells travelling through the water to strike the belt would lose power but that could not be said of projectiles plunging through the soft bow of the ship.

The design was already tight, and each suggestion threatened to make it altogether impractical. For example, a deeper belt forward and aft (4.4 and 3.7 feet, respectively) would cost 490 tons. The internal patches, about 3 inches thick, would cost another 787 tons, and about 340 would have to be added to the main armor deck. Against this, on 7 August BuOrd agreed to reduce the splinter deck to a half inch, compared with 1.25 inches over magazines and 0.75 inches elsewhere in Scheme XVI. However, structural strength demanded a minimum of 5/8in every-

where and stiffening over the torpedo bulkheads by another eighth of an inch, so that only 118 tons were saved. At the same time, BuOrd's insistence on an after director limited savings due to the elimination of its tower to only 50 tons. BuOrd began to demand a second plotting room, despite the volume problem that would entail. BuEng was willing to substitute six boilers for the former eight, saving 6 feet of machinery-room space (on 184 feet) and perhaps 100 tons, but there were good operational reasons to favor eight boilers.

The point of this rather lengthy and erratic design history is that, although one might see the *North Carolina*s in several of these designs, that was not in fact so. The General Board was never entirely sure of what it was willing to give up to achieve some kind of ship within the treaty-limited displacement. As its membership changed, moreover, so did its ideas. The fast capital ship with nine guns and a speed of 30 knots, yet having good protection, was ultimately rejected in favor of a ship that sacrificed both speed

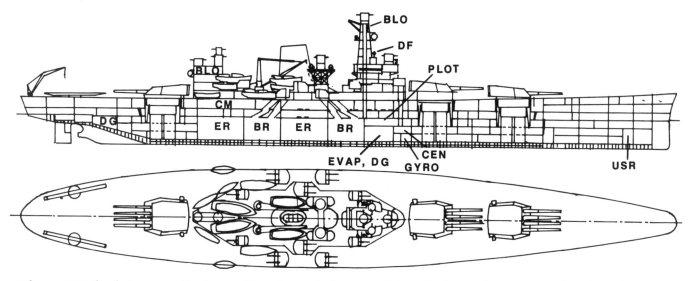

Scheme XVI, the design actually chosen. Note the single funnel and the mixed secondary battery of single and twin 5in/38 mounts.

and protection for firepower, a combination unprecedented in American capital ship development.

In October Preliminary Design could propose three alternatives. First, it could restore speed to some extent by increasing length back to 725 feet. On that basis, eleven 14-inch guns could be mounted, but then the belt would be only 10.1 inches thick (equivalent to a range of 25,000 yards), and there would be no extra underwater protection. The eleventh gun could be traded for another 3.4 inches of belt armor (18,700 yards). The tenth gun could be traded for increased speed (30 knots) and another tenth of an inch of belt armor (18,500 yards). It was designated Scheme XVIC. All three alternatives incorporated the usual deck armor, rated at 30,000 yards except over magazines, where it was thickened to be impenetrable out to 33,000.

On 5 November the General Board once more reversed itself and came out strongly for Scheme XVIC, the same kind of fast, well-protected, but relatively lightly armed type it had earlier rejected when setting characteristics. Once again, as in 1935, the new ship was perceived as a specialized carrier escort. She would be well enough protected to fight in the battle line, yet fast enough to be part of a detached wing. She could also support light forces and cruiser-carrier raiding groups. Again, as in 1935, such a ship was essential to U.S. operations in the long period of commerce warfare that was expected to precede the decisive battle line engagement. The board clearly saw this as a specialized design, not more than three of which should be built. Even so, it could not be sure that future ships would retreat to the low speed of the existing U.S. battle line. The new French and Italian ships were very fast (at about 30 knots), and

no one knew what the British or the Japanese planned.

Scheme XVI was rejected as "not being a true battleship," too slow and deficient in armor; the board preferred the much faster XVIC, hoping that some armor could be traded for a better secondary battery. A BuOrd suggestion that provision be made to substitute 16-inch for 14-inch guns was rejected.

However, Admiral J. M. Reeves of the General Board (who had been responsible for much of the development of U.S. carrier tactics) argued that XVIC was neither fast enough to work with the carriers, nor powerful enough to justify its high cost. He wanted instead to modify XVI to provide the added underwater protection which the BuOrd tests showed was needed, by abandoning uniform protection. The belt, which covered both machinery and magazines, was sharply reduced (to 11.2 inches, effective beyond 23,000 yards), and the protection of the magazines increased with local patches of internal armor (so that they were immune beyond 19,000 yards to both above-water and underwater hits). At the same time, the outer edge of the immune zone was moved outward from 28,200 to 30,000 yards (33,000 over machinery). That is, the characteristics were not quite attainable on the limited displacement. In October the General Board had to go through yet another round of revisions.

Reeves convinced the CNO, Admiral W. H. Standley (who was acting secretary of the navy). Although the General Board held out for XVIC, the secretary signed the revised characteristics, with the added proviso that it be possible to substitute triple 16-inch turrets for the planned quadruple 14 inch, "should that be found desirable." That really meant, should

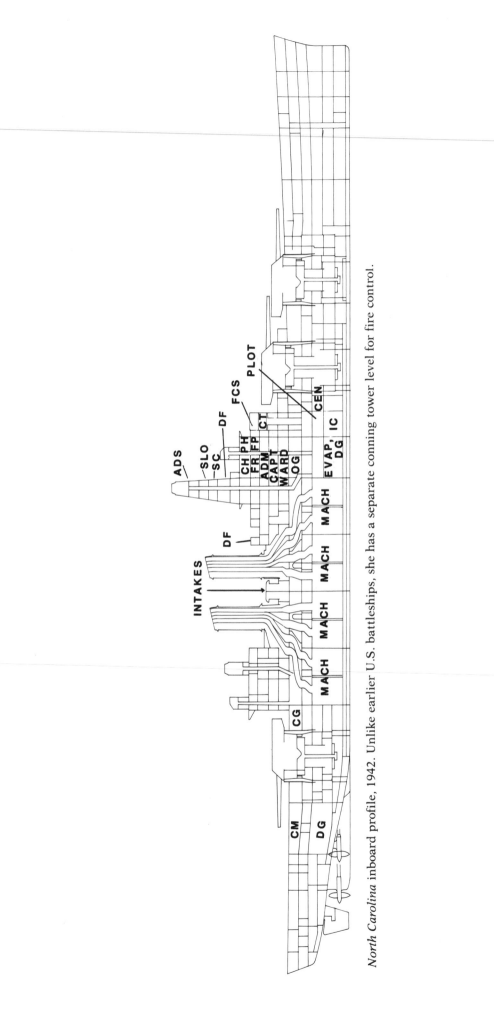

North Carolina inboard profile, 1942. Unlike earlier U.S. battleships, she has a separate conning tower level for fire control.

The *Washington* (with a British battleship in the background) and *North Carolina* illustrate the design for this class, which included a 12-foot range-finder atop No. 3 turret. Neither had yet been fitted with main battery directors or with 1.1-inch machine guns. Note the 1.1-inch director platform above the after starboard machine gun tub in the *North Carolina* photograph. Note, too, that the after main director tower has not yet been braced against vibration.

the release clause in the 1936 treaty be invoked. This was not done until March 1937.

The design for what became the *North Carolina* class was now largely fixed. At a conference in the office of the CNO on 18 November, C&R was asked to add a few final touches: four more secondary guns; a thicker belt to make the inner edge of the immune zone uniform at 20,000 yards; a higher barbette for No. 2 turret so that it could fire over No. 1 (and, incidentally, so that it could be moved closer to No. 1, leaving more room for machinery between No. 2 and No. 3). Surely these small improvements could be attained by a minor cut in power and hence in speed.

That was not the case. Scheme XVI was extremely tight. On the 714-foot hull then planned, the im-

provements would cost a total of 782 tons, which equated to a reduction (in the rather light-weight power plant) to 65,000SHP (24 knots). Even then too much metacentric height would be lost. Alternatively, the hull could be shortened to 702 feet, which would involve considerable cramping in an already crowded design. On the weights then available, the ship might perhaps develop 87,000SHP (25.25 knots), but it was by no means certain that there would be sufficient internal volume for such a plant.

C&R therefore proposed to minimize changes. The belt might be thickened at a cost of 379 tons. To replace the four single 5-inch mounts with four unprotected twins would cost another 88. The design was already fairly tight, but it seemed wise to let it proceed through the final design stage and then trim it by skimming off some of the armor weight. C&R very much wanted to avoid raising No. 2 turret, as that would simultaneously add considerable weight and subtract metacentric heights.

The bureau now submitted a detailed design both to the General Board and to the other technical bureaus. This was essentially the design adopted, so it is worth describing in some detail. As compared with the late versions of Scheme XVI, it (and its successors) incorporated a more deeply sloped (13 rather than 10 degrees) belt. This increase (which was changed to 15 degrees in the fall of 1937) was intended to move the inner edge of the immune zone back to a range of 20,000 yards at a minimum cost in weight. The patches of armor over the magazines were 3.75-inch plate thinning to 2 inches, and they were roughly parallel in slope to the belt, albeit lower and inboard.

The belt was designed to protrude 6 feet 6 inches above the *maximum* draft (32 feet 4 inches) in battle condition, and a similar depth below the *minimum* draft at the end of a long engagement (31 feet 1 inch). A depth of 14.25 feet would, therefore, suffice. The 6.5-foot figure was chosen so that the belt at neither end would be entirely submerged or exposed by the effect of a single torpedo hit before counterflooding. The lower edge of the belt was shaped to cover hollows in the wave profile at speeds of up to 27 knots. The design papers show no concern with increased displacement due to additions in service, although it was already becoming clear that they were a major problem in the older battleships. As for variations in displacement, the designers claimed that they had only to take account of the 15-inch difference in draft between a ship entering battle and one which had fired off the bulk of her ammunition.

The torpedo-protection bulkheads were inclined parallel to the belt armor to increase the depth of the system toward the turn of the bilge. As in the earlier design studies, there were four bulkheads, the liquid now being in two rather than three layers. Proof tests appeared to show that the systems would perform as designed. The ship was expected to be able to withstand three hits on one side before becoming unstable or losing enough buoyancy to sink. Special attention was paid to counterflooding. It was expected that the list due to flooding from a torpedo hit could be eliminated in less than five minutes. The third deck was the damage-control deck, that is, the watertight deck that was expected not to flood in the event of underwater damage. All bulkheads below it were unpierced, so that it was the lowest deck along which men could pass fore and aft.

The splinter deck over the magazines was thickened from the specified 1.1 to 2 inches; the other thicknesses remained at 0.75 inches over the torpedo bulkheads, and 0.625 over the machinery.

In the original design, six of the secondary gun mounts were protected with 2.5-inch STS, but the other four, one deck above, were given only blast and weather cover. Later all were made uniform (2-inch STS), at a cost of 117 tons. This was justified, it appears, largely to simplify manufacturing. The light AA battery was set at eighteen 0.50-calibre machine guns, fourteen of them on portable hand trucks, with four quadruple 1.1-inch machine cannon in the superstructure. The machine cannon were more than antiaircraft guns. They were also intended to counter motor torpedo boats, which in 1937 were considered a major threat to capital ships in confined waters. Two were therefore arranged so that they could fire across the bows even at zero elevation.

All major calibre ammunition was stowed on the first and second platforms, well below the waterline, for protection from shellfire. Although the ammunition capacity was generous (1,400 14 inch plus 25 to 30 rounds per gun of target ammunition, plus 8,800 rounds of 5 inch, or 440 per gun), much of it was not counted in the standard displacement.

The main battery was to be served by three directors: one on the upper level of the conning tower; one in a fire control tower forward; and one atop a built-up structure aft. The four secondary directors were widely separated so that no more than one would probably be destroyed by a lucky hit. In addition, two had to be available on any bearing, so that the ship could simultaneously engage surface and air targets, that is, so that the dual-purpose performance of the secondary battery could be fully exploited in the event an enemy could coordinate air and surface attacks.

Through most of the design period, it was assumed that the machinery would be divided into separate engine and boiler rooms. In August 1936, for example, an arrangement of alternating engine and boiler rooms was compared with a lighter arrangement in which two boiler rooms (each with four boilers) were set between two engine rooms. However, by January

The *North Carolina (facing page)* is shown on 11 December 1941 (side view) and on 17 April 1942 (aerial view), essentially as completed. The most visible changes are added 20mm cannon on the main deck and 01 level forward and replacement of the 12-foot range-finder forward with a fifth quadruple 1.1-inch cannon. The ship retained her 0.50-calibre machine guns at this time. The short cylinder abaft her forward 5-inch director is a 1.1-inch director atop a 20mm clipping room. The objects projecting from her fire control tower are, top to bottom, a masthead light, the ship's bell, and a strut carrying a towing light on top and a radio direction-finding loop below. Internally, this level was a secondary conning station (Battle-2). The ship's bell hung from a battle lookout station, at the after end of which was a 24-inch searchlight. The

platform atop the tower was for secondary battery control; it carried six target designators and the sky lookouts. At this time the ship carried no radar on her after Mark 37 (5-inch) director, but both main battery units were equipped with Mark 3 fire control sets. The big air search set was a CXAM-1, and there was no surface search set.

The *North Carolina*, 3 June 1942.

1937 the design called for a unit arrangement, each of four units containing high and low pressure turbines driving a propeller shaft through double-helical double-reduction gears, a steam turbogenerator, other auxiliaries, and two air-encased boilers fed by four turbine-driven blowers. An 8,000SHP astern turbine was incorporated in the low-pressure casing, and a cruising element in the high-pressure casing. Since each unit was self-contained, the effect of a single torpedo hit was minimized. This divided plant required two uptakes, and it was impossible to provide the kind of uptake protection formerly standard in U.S. battleships. There were four turbogenerators and three diesel generators, one of the latter aft. In the course of design development a fourth diesel generator would be provided aft. A measure of the congestion of the hull was that the after diesel room was *abaft* the after turret.*

The design initially called for 115,000SHP, for 27 knots, using conventional medium-temperature, medium-pressure boilers. However, the design of these ships coincided with the adoption of high-pressure, high-temperature steam plants in U.S. destroyers. The entire subject was highly controversial. Rear Admiral H. G. Bowen, who as chief of the Bureau of Engineering was responsible for the change, had suggested that some of the shipbuilders, who manufactured the conventional turbines in their ships, were unwilling to abandon this business. The higher-pressure turbines were all manufactured by Westinghouse and General Electric. Nor, in 1937, had sufficient experience with the new destroyers of the *Mahan* and later classes been accumulated. Experience with power stations on land showed that efficiency would improve, and the new high-speed machinery would be much lighter, but there was a strong feeling that battleships were far too important to be the subject of experiments. Ultimately BuEng triumphed, although by no means without a fight. Steam conditions were to be 565 pounds per square inch and 850 degrees F, in contrast to 300 psi/572

degrees in recently completed heavy cruisers and 400/648 in recent aircraft carriers of the *Enterprise* (CV 6) class. However, because the improved steam conditions were approved only very late in the design period, the turbines had to be designed for lower pressure and temperature, and some of the gain to be expected was lost.

As early as November 1936, BuEng had claimed that adoption of a radical 1,200 psi/950 degree F plant would save about 8 percent (250 tons) compared with the then-planned 600 psi/700 degree F plant. Oil consumption would be reduced by about 10 percent. At this time it appeared that a 120,000SHP plant might be substituted for the planned 115,000SHP one. A little over a year later, however, the bureau was far more optimistic. It believed that power could be boosted to 130,000SHP at no cost in space or weight, by going to 850 degree steam. Early the following year the machinery specifications were changed to reflect the increased temperature, but contract power was raised only to 121,000SHP, and propeller speed from 192 to 199 RPM.

Unlike earlier U.S. battleships, these ships were longitudinally rather than transversely framed. That in turn required deep transverse frames, so that the deck heights had to be unusually great, 8 feet 3 inches on the centerline and 7 feet 9 inches at the side. Great deck height was also used to obtain the requisite freeboard and girder strength. It in turn led to the adoption of four-high berthing amidships. Forward, where the deck height would have increased even more because of the sheer at the bow, the officers were housed on a half-deck. Even so, space was so scarce that some of the crew had to be accommodated forward of the forward transverse armored bulkhead, with a passageway on the second deck so as to avoid breaking through it. Crewmen also had to be accommodated on the third deck, in artificially lighted and ventilated quarters. In the end all scuttles had to be omitted, as they would break the 1-inch splinter armor on the upper side of the ship.

The new ships also had an unusual hull form, their two inboard shafts emerging from the hull in deep skegs, or keels. The hull design series begun in 1934

---

*These were *main* generators; there were also two 200 kW diesel emergency generators.

Model basin models of the *North Carolina* hull show the unusual twin-skeg configuration adopted for this class.

was based on the old battle cruisers (later carriers) of the *Lexington* type, shortened and with the quarters filled out. Speed characteristics were deliberately sacrificed to provide sufficient volume for torpedo protection. A model basin memo of October 1935 noted that the form "is not expected to be a record breaker." In November 1937, Admiral DuBose, chief of C&R, explained the twin skegs as a means of providing sufficient protection around the after magazines while reducing the cross sectional area of the hull aft to reduce resistance in a relatively fast ship. With area removed by means of the tunnel formed by the skegs under the hull, the ship could be beamier aft. The *North Carolina* was the first application of this technique, and the subsequent *South Dakota* was a more extreme form. For example, at the 26-foot draft waterline, a ship with a twin-skeg hull form might have her No. 3 magazine as much as 15 feet from the outside of the ship, versus 11 in a more conventional hull. DuBose also argued that the twin keels would help protect off-side propellers and shafts from stern hits, since no hit would be likely to stop more than two of the four shafts.

It was also claimed that the new form improved propulsive efficiency by making for a cleaner flow aft. DuBose in fact claimed a propulsive coefficient of 0.602, compared with 0.595 for a conventional hull form. In the final design, however, the claimed coefficient was only 0.590, which was no gain at all. All of these designs showed improvement over earlier high-speed hull forms, such as that of the carrier *Lexington* (0.565). DuBose commented only that he had not done as well as expected in this direction, which is another way of saying that the new hull

form had been chosen primarily for protection. Protective depth was needed that far aft only because the treaty had forced the designers to accept a very cramped design.

From about 1937 onwards, however, C&R and BuShips accounts of the design came to suggest that the skegs had been adopted specifically for higher propulsive efficiency. It was believed that the inboard propellers, on their deep skegs, would behave like single propellers. A 1945 model basin report admitted that, "although the early model tests indicated that this would not be achieved, the deep skegs were nevertheless retained to serve as docking keels, . . . to add to the longitudinal stiffness of the ship girder, . . . and to act as torpedo protection for the propellers on the unengaged side."

There was some fear of transverse vibration associated with the unusual hull form. In 1937 constructors testifying before the General Board went to some length to show that unusual vibration would not occur. In fact it did not. However, both ships were plagued with *longitudinal* vibration and for some time were under speed restrictions.

Twin rudders made for excellent manueverability. When the *Washington* operated with the British Home Fleet in 1942, she could easily turn inside British carriers and battleships, and the British naval constructors were severely criticized on this point. Their defense (see below) was that the price of quick turning was lower maximum speed; they also referred their critics to the performance of British ships of First World War vintage, which had twin rudders and which had comparable turning circles at comparable speeds.

Newly fitted with 40mm guns, the *North Carolina* is shown on 15 November 1942. Note that her forward and after main battery fire controls have different Mark 3 antennas and that a Mark 4 radar has finally been fitted to her after 5-inch director. The heavy bracing of her after main battery director is also visible.

As the first battleships to be built by the United States since 1921, the two *North Carolina*s were controversial. Because he did not want to upset pacifist sentiment in the United States during the 1936 election, President Roosevelt delayed the two new battleships, Numbers 55 and 56, from the projected FY37 program to the FY38 program. The act of 3 June 1936 stated specifically that "the commencement is authorized of . . . not more than two capital ships, to be undertaken only in the event that the President determines . . . that capital-ship replacement construction is undertaken by any of the other signatory powers to the Treaty . . . signed at London."

President Roosevelt waited until after the 1936 elections to so certify. Once they had been ordered, however, work began very rapidly. The *North Carolina* was laid down at the New York Navy Yard in October 1937, for completion in September 1941. She was actually completed much earlier but could not enter service for some months because of vibration problems.

The decision in favor of the 16-inch gun (the invocation of the escalator clause) was, if anything, even more delicate. France, Britain, and the United States signed the new London Treaty, incorporating the escalator clause, on 25 March 1936. Although Japan refused to guarantee that she would honor the treaty limits, President Roosevelt was loath to invoke the escape clause in an election year. He remained reluctant even after the election. The United States could not lightly abandon efforts at arms control. In the absence of very clear evidence of Japanese intentions and actions, evidence extremely difficult to obtain in the face of Japanese secretivenss, Congress would be unlikely to allow invocation of either the gun calibre or the tonnage escalation clause. Moreover, popular sentiment in the United States was running strongly against any expenditure on arms, let alone on battleships, and particularly on any battleships beyond the treaty limits.

Although the General Board pressed for the 16-inch gun on 29 March 1937, the secretary of the navy did not approve this recommendation until 15 July, and orders were not actually given to the yards until after the keel of the first ship, the *North Carolina*, had been laid. Similarly, studies of a follow-on class, which became the *South Dakota*, showed 14-inch guns as late as July 1937.

Studies by BuOrd and the Naval War College, as well as proving ground experiments, all showed that nine 16-inch guns would provide far more offensive power than twelve 14 inch. Rate of fire would suffer little if at all, and Fleet Training argued that fire would actually be more accurate because it would be easier to spot splashes from a smaller number of guns. Moreover, a quadruple turret would be a far greater experiment than a triple. The United States had already built triple battleship and cruiser turrets.

With the adoption of the 16-inch gun, the *North Carolina* design took on much its final form. It had been well enough balanced on the basis of 14-inch shellfire, but that was no longer the case. Exactly how much worse is hard to say, since the armor thicknesses varied back and forth during 1937. As of November, protection against the existing 16-inch gun firing a 2,250-pound shell was estimated, in terms of immune zone, as 21,000 to 27,700 yards over magazines, versus 23,200 to 26,000 yards over machinery. This was disappointing at best, but the design was too far along (and far too tight) for much to be done about it. Only in the next (*South Dakota*) class could a balance against 16-inch shellfire be attained.

Even that protection was insufficient against the guns these ships actually carried, which fired, not the 2,250-pound shell, but a new super-heavy, 2,700-pound type BuOrd proposed in 1937. Although the new shell was not tested until 1939, the 1936-37 designs had sufficient deck height in their magazines and shell hoists to accommodate it. The bureau claimed that its new shell made a 16-inch gun equivalent to the 18-inch weapon which had been proposed on and off since 1916. Range would be sacrificed, but there were already rumors (which were correct) that Japan had decided to adopt the 18-inch weapon. Compared with a conventional shell, the super-heavy one fell more steeply, penetrating decks more effectively at maximum range. That would be particularly valuable if, as many believed, most combat would occur there and most long-range hits would be on deck rather than on side armor.

Another measure of the power of the 2,700-pound shell was that not until the huge *Montana* was a U.S. battleship designed to be fully protected against it.

Despite General Board suggestions that the United States should be willing to accept a 10 percent overweight in its new battleships, the administration wanted badly to remain clearly within the treaty limits. By 26 April 1937 detailed weight estimates showed the design 435 tons, over 1 percent, over-

weight. This did not yet include the proposed protection for all of the 5-inch mounts, or the thickening of the thin parts of the barbettes from 2 to 3 inches, or the carrying of the full barbette thickness around the forward sides, to improve the immune zone against fire from 60 degrees off the centerline. These improvements would add another 193 tons, for a total of 628.

The bureaus suggested a number of minor weight reductions: all 5-inch mounts would be protected by 2-inch rather than 2.5-inch STS (46 tons); splinter protection for their handling rooms (as well as flag plot, radio and signal shelters) was all reduced similarly (161 tons); the belt taper started at a draft of 31feet1inch rather than 36 inches further down (110 tons); and that six of the 0.50-calibre machine guns be deleted (13 tons). That left 298 tons to cut, and it seemed that this weight could come only from the main armor. The bureaus proposed a uniform 2 percent cut of all but splinter armor and material contributing directly to the structural integrity of the ship. This course was justified on the ground that, since the overall design was well balanced, the cut would automatically preserve its balance. The immune zone (at this time still calculated in terms of the 14-inch gun) would be reduced by about 500 yards at its inner and 300 at its outer edges. Alternatively, the cut could be limited to heavy forged armor (belt, turrets, upper barbettes, bulkheads). That would mean 4 percent in weight, 900 yards in immune zone. A similar cut in decks and splinter armor would cost 650 yards at the outer edge of the immune zone.

The CNO and the secretary of the navy approved the overall 2 percent cut on 1 May 1937. That was not, however, quite the end of the story. There appears to have been grumbling within the service concerning the unusually high speed of the new ships, and also their inadequate protection against 16-inch fire. The assistant secretary of the navy therefore convened a special Battleship Design Advisory Board on 8 October 1937, to consist of William F. Gibbs, the well-known naval architect, William Hovgaard, the dean of American naval architects, John F. Metten, president of the New York Shipbuilding Corporation, Joseph W. Powell (chairman), and retired Admiral Joseph Strauss, a former BuOrd chief.

The board considered protection nearly adequate, but suggested that an inch be moved from deck to side so as to move in the inner edge of the immune zone. It seemed, too, that there was still some fat that could be taken out of the ship by a more careful calculation of standard displacement. The board estimated that about 360 tons could be transformed into a higher speed, 29.4 knots. This would come from reductions in habitability features; in stores normally carried (62 tons if a uniform standard of two months' stores were enforced); in potable water (100 tons out of 136 in view of the capacity of the

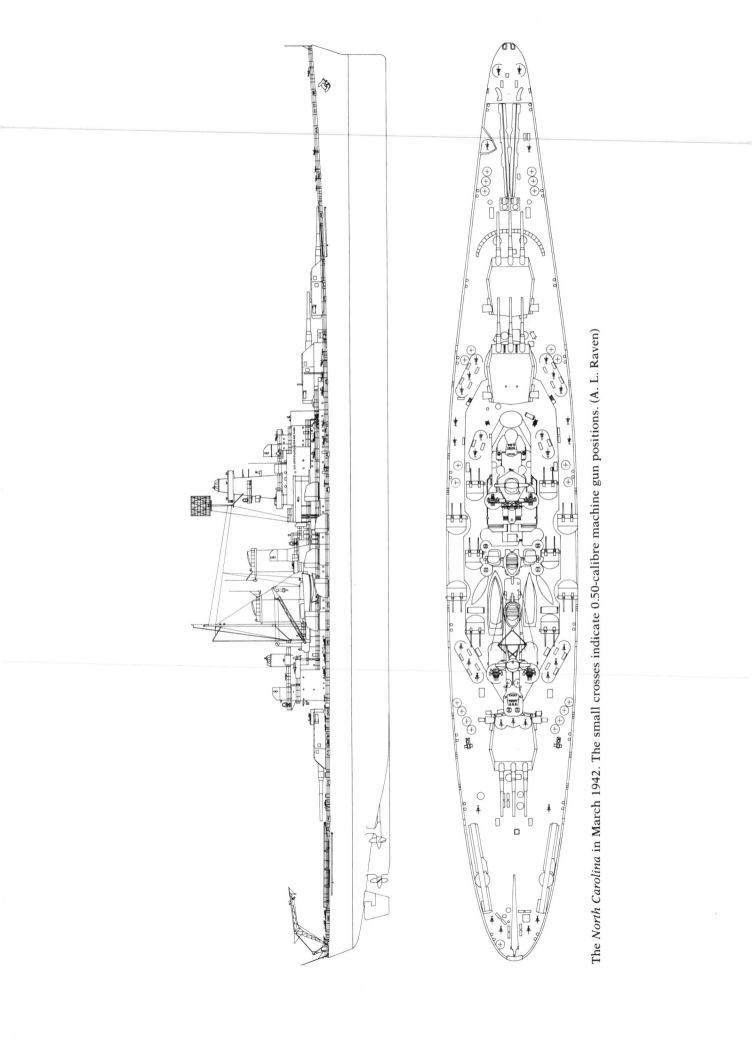

The *North Carolina* in March 1942. The small crosses indicate 0.50-calibre machine gun positions. (A. L. Raven)

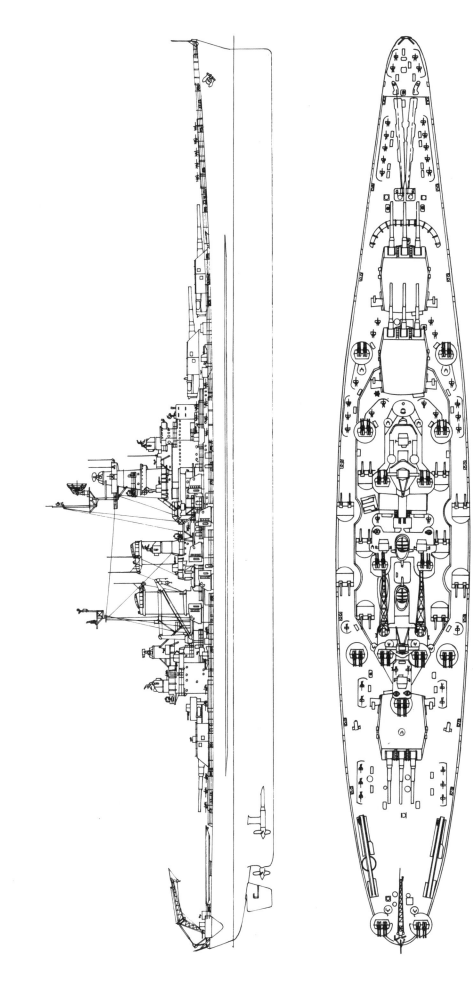

The *North Carolina* in 1945 (A. L. Raven)

Washington shows much her final configuration in this 29 April 1944 photograph: fifteen quadruple 40mm guns and fifty-six 20mm guns. An open bridge, valued for air defense, has replaced the 1.1-inch mount atop her pilot house. Note, too, the brace connecting her after main director and her after 5-inch director.

distilling plant); in boats which in wartime would not be carried and therefore did not have to be counted against the total standard tonnage (25 tons, a purely paper saving); even in stores normally carried for sale aboard ship (10 tons out of 30). The important point in each case was that standard displacement was defined as the displacement of a ship ready for battle but without fuel oil or reserve feed water, *not* as her displacement in peacetime rig excluding those liquids. Hence her displacement should be calculated on the basis of a stripped-down condition. A considerable paper weight saving had already been made by the restriction of the *theoretical* standard ammunition supply to 75 rounds per gun.

The General Board saw these 360 tons as an opportunity to recoup the losses of protection sustained earlier. It was reluctant to increase the speed of the new battleships. Earlier in the year it had asked several prominent officers whether the new ships should become the speed standard for any new battleship or whether they should constitute a fast wing. The general conclusion was that 27 knots was a useful battle line speed and that nothing slower should be accepted. However, there was no sentiment favoring any reduction in protection. Hence the board preferred to add armor: it was able to restore the cuts on side and deck, and the belt was actually thickened, from 11.2 to 12.2 inches. As in the case of the belt, the same thicknesses of deck covered both machinery and magazines: 5 inches inboard (3.6 inches on a layer of 1.4-inch plate) and 5.5 inches outboard (4.1-inch upper layer).

Such arguments over very small weights were typical of the treaty period. The irony is that ships so very rarely were completed at their designed tonnage. Even before weights had been added in wartime, the *North Carolina*s displaced about 36,600 tons in standard condition, according to BuShips figures of December 1941. As the discussion above demonstrates, the very definition of standard displacement was sufficiently ambiguous to allow for thousands of tons of movement up or down.

Preliminary builder's trials of both ships revealed severe longitudinal vibration. As of June 1941, although both had been commissioned, neither had been run up to full power. On her first sea trial *North Carolina* was run up to 70,000SHP (about 25 knots) at which point "unexpected longitudinal vibration developed which made continued operation at higher speed appear inadvisable." The vibrations ran along the propeller shafts themselves, up to the shaft braces, the gearing, even the turbines themselves. Special instruments were installed, and she was run up at 90,000SHP (over twenty-six knots) in hope of discovering its cause. A variety of experts on hand felt that although the ship could make her full speed in an emergency, "danger of injury to the machinery does exist, and . . . continuous operation should until corrective measures are effected be limited to not over 23 knots." The *Washington* encountered similar problems in her first trials at 100,000SHP and about 27 knots. At this time 28 knots were expected at a maximum power of 120,000SHP.

The problem must have been terrifying. Unless it was solved, the two most modern U.S. battleships would be unable to operate with fast carriers. The design practices that had led to the new hull form and to the new generation of lightweight machinery extended to large numbers of other ships, including three more battleship classes. It was, therefore, conceivable that the *entire* modern U.S. battle line would prove a failure. In a 24 June 1941 letter to Senator David I. Walsh, Secretary of the Navy Frank Knox described the vibration as "of a type which was en-

The *North Carolina* as refitted at Puget Sound, 24 September 1944. Note the extra fire control mast platform, which distinguished her.

tirely unexpected and which has not been experienced heretofore in such degree as to attract or require attention. The cause is not easy to isolate, being the result of resonance in the very complex mass-elastic system of propellers, shafting, machinery, and hull, with vibratory impulses which are always present in some degree with a propeller which necessarily has a small number of blades in order to obtain acceptable efficiency." The propeller shafts themselves were vibrating. Secretary Knox described three cures: new propellers; stiffer machinery foundations; and restraining blocks for the shafts, the last of which was considered (at the time) the most promising. Later the same year the light cruiser *Atlanta* would also require extended modification to cure a severe vibration problem. Her hull form was quite different, but her hull *structure* was similar in concept, and she used the same sort of new-generation machinery.

A BuShips, Taylor Model Basin, and Philadelphia Navy Yard conference called in July 1941 concluded that vibration felt in the engines and in the fire control systems could be laid to alternating thrust by the propellers; increasing the number of blades on the inboard shafts to five would, it was hoped, improve conditions there as much as the increase to four had helped on the outboard shafts. More drastic steps, such as installing restraining blocks on the shafts, could be put off. Changing the propellers would, in theory, move the frequency produced by their blade motion away from some resonance in the ship structure. The ships were completed with three-blade propellers on the outboard shafts, and four-bladed propellers inboard. In June 1941 trials were run with three-bladed propellers cut down from 17feet 3inches to 16feet 4inches 5/8in diameter, and interchanged with the four-bladed ones. Most of this work was carried out aboard the *North Carolina*, which made so many day trips out of New York harbor that she was nicknamed "The Showboat."

On 1 August 1941 the secretary of the navy was able to report to Congressman Carl Vinson of the House Naval Affairs Committee that *Washington* had "operated at sea again at full power with very great improvement. . .still further improvement is expected." On 3 August it was possible to run builder's trials at 123, 850SHP at 44,400 tons. In December, *Washington* was running with four-bladed propellers outboard and five-bladed propellers inboard. On 19 February 1942 she ran full-power trials with spacers between her reduction gearing and her turbines, achieving 127,100SHP at 44,000 tons. The following day, with spacers (restraining blocks) removed from all but No. 4 shaft, she ran at full power, 121,000SHP (191.4 RPM). Speeds could not be measured accurately, but on 2 December *Washington* made 121,100SHP (196.5 RPM) at 42,000 tons, and her pitometer log showed 25.9 knots.

Even so, the after range-finder still vibrated excessively. Ultimately the turbine and gear casings had to be braced. The after fire control tower required external braces, which are quite visible in photographs of the ships. As late as 1943 the propellers were still being changed. In September 1943, the ships had reduced-diameter three-bladed propellers inboard and four-bladed propellers outboard and were scheduled to receive five-bladed propellers inboard. When she served with the British Home Fleet in 1942, *Washington* was still having problems. The British director of naval construction (DNC) remarked the following year that "it is understood that conditions are still not very good at full speed."

When the *North Carolina* ran standardization trials at Guantanamo on 30 September 1941, on her shakedown cruise, she made 26.15 knots at 43,166 tons at 199.1 RPM (SHP not recorded). The *Washington* departed Philadelphia on 1 December not as yet standardized, but accompanying destroyers reported her speed as 28 to 28.2 knots at 42,100 tons. A full power trial, on 27 December 1941, showed less vibration than formerly and generally no vibration below 24 knots. She made about 27.1 knots at 45,000 tons at full power.

Vibration was never completely cured. The *Washington* ran special vibration trials in Puget Sound as late as April 1944, with four-bladed propellers outboard and five-bladed inboard. A David Taylor Model Basin report suggested that the problem had been partly solved, but that vibration at 17 to 20 knots was still unacceptable.

In common with other classes of U.S. warships, these battleships grew considerably in weight during the war. By 1945, they displaced about 46,800 tons fully loaded, a growth of about 960 tons since September 1941. Both were considered good for 26.4 knots at full power and full load at this time, which corresponds roughly to 27.3 knots at the designed trial figure of 42,100 tons. A similar figure was obtained from model basin tests: *Ships Data* 1945 shows 27.6 knots at 42,000 tons. At that time, with all U.S. warships rapidly gaining weight, BuShips assigned a limiting (that is, maximum desirable) displacement of 48,000 tons (draft 35 feet 4 inches, armored freeboard 5 feet 7 inches).

Perhaps the two most striking wartime changes were the adoption of radar on a very large scale and the great increase in light antiaircraft weapons. The modern U.S. battleships were all designed before the advent of radar and therefore were liberally supplied with optical range-finders, both for fire control and for navigation. Both ships were completed with 12 feet navigational range-finders atop No. 3 turret and the pilot house roof, with a 15-foot spotting glass/range-finder atop the conning tower (for the fire control station in its upper level). Longer base stereo instruments were housed in the turrets, and in Mark 38 directors aloft fore and aft. Both navigational range-finders were replaced by 20mm guns between the end of 1941 and about mid-1942. The spotting glass or auxiliary main battery range-finder remained until 1944, when it was replaced by a Mark 27 microwave radar. It was supplemented during 1942 by a third Mark 3 fire control radar.

Both ships were originally scheduled to receive a CXAM air search radar on the foremast, plus two Mark 3 main battery fire control radars and three (not four, because of potential interference between the after directors) Mark 4 secondary battery sets. By November 1942, however, the *North Carolina* carried a fourth Mark 4 aft, raised above the line of sight of the nearby main battery director on a tall support. By this time she also had an SG surface search set on a foremast bracket *below* her main air search antenna. By April 1944, the *North Carolina* had assumed the standard battleship configuration, with air and surface search antennas (SK and SG) on her foremast, an auxiliary SG surface search set on her mainmast, and Mark 8 radars for her main battery. One of her Mark 3s had been retained, presumably as an auxiliary main battery fire control set. Its antenna was mounted on the forward side of her fire control tower. In a September 1944 refit her mattress-type SK air search antenna was replaced by the big dish of SK-2, and her Mark 4s replaced by the standard combination of Mark 12 and Mark 22. This latter had a much heavier antenna, and the antenna of the after director had to be relocated directly atop the director roof. The *Washington* was similarly refitted but never received SK-2. At the end of the war, the *North Carolina* was again refitted, with a secondary air search set (SR) on her mainmast and an SCR-720 zenith search radar in a radome on her forward funnel. The *Washington* was refitted just after the war. In March, 1946 she had SK forward and SR aft, with SG fore and aft, and a TDY jammer on her forward fire control tower.

Another visible change was the elimination of the large prewar complement of ships' boats: two 40-foot motor boats, one 35-foot motor boat gig, three 50-foot motor launches, two 40-foot motor launchers, two 26 foot motor whale boats, and one 40-foot barge, plus pulling boats. However, both retained their two massive boat cranes through the war, despite plans to remove one.

The ships were designed to mount four quadruple 1.1-inch machine cannon in suitably elevated and protected gun tubs in their superstructures. As of the summer of 1941, these weapons were scheduled for replacement by the much heavier quadruple 40mm Bofors gun on a one-for-one basis. As in the cases of the other modern battleships, additional positions, progressively more and more subject to blast and weather, and less and less convenient to ammunition supply, were added as the war progressed. The *North Carolina* may have had a quadruple 1.1-inch machine cannon atop her pilot house, replacing her 12-foot range-finder; it did not last long in any case. Both were fitted with a pair of quadruple machine cannon which replaced two of the searchlights around the barbettes of each of the two beam Mark 37 directors abreast 1 funnel. Only the *Washington* had 1.1-inch guns in this position (fitted in the fall of 1942); both ultimately received 40mm mounts there. However, as refitted following torpedo damage in November 1942, the *North Carolina* had two quadruple Bofors mounts abaft her catapults but none around the Mark 37 barbettes. At this time she also had two quadruple mounts on each side, on the main (weather) deck fore and aft of her 40mm battery, for a total of ten mounts.

Through most of 1942 both ships were scheduled for a total of six quadruple 40mm guns, a figure raised to ten in November. As noted, the *North Carolina* was refitted to this standard late in 1942. By March 1943, however, the "ultimate" 40mm battery had been increased yet again, to fourteen quadruple mounts, and the *North Carolina* had attained this figure by June 1943. A fifteenth mount (atop No.3 turret) was added to the "ultimate" battery in June and installed aboard the *North Carolina* in November 1943. Unlike many other modern U.S. battleships, these two never had 40mm guns atop their superfiring forward turrets. Any such mount would have blocked the sight lines of the lower (ship control) conning tower level.

The *Washington* did not have her six quadruple 1.1-inch machine cannon replaced by ten quadruple 40mm guns until the summer of 1943. By August, she had all fifteen mounts.

Beyond the first six mounts, the remaining eight were located as follows: two on the main (weather) deck just abeam No. 2 barbette; two on the 01 level superfiring over them; two on the weather deck abeam the after fire controls; and two on the fantail, abaft the two catapults.

The planned free-swinging antiaircraft armament was twelve 0.50-calibre machine guns, all but two of them on portable hand trucks: two on each side abeam No. 2 barbette, four on each side on the 01 level abeam conning tower and bridge, and four on each side abeam No. 3 turret. The permanent positions were on each side on the 02 level above the second 5-inch mount on each side (just forward of the waist Mark 37 directors). All were scheduled for replacement (on a one-for-one basis) by 20mm cannon. However, in April 1942 the *North Carolina* had forty 20mm guns *and* twelve 0.50-calibre machine guns aboard, and the *Washington* had twenty 20mm and twelve 0.50-calibre. By June, the number of 0.50s had increased to twenty-eight in each ship, with the number of 20mm guns constant. The heavier *North Carolina* battery was the approved standard, attained in her sister ship by September. Both ships briefly carried all forty 20mm, but the *Washington* had five removed late in 1942 (together with her remaining 0.50s) when two more 1.1-inch mounts were added amidships. The *North Carolina* had her 0.50-calibre machine guns removed and six 20mm guns added (for a total of forty-six) during her major refit after torpedoing, late in 1942.

By April 1943 the *Washington* had twenty-nine 20mms guns added, for a total of sixty-four. The *North Carolina* had seven 20mm (for a total of fifty-three) added in March 1944, but at the end of April *Washington* had one single 20mm removed and a quadruple 20mm cannon installed. By November 1944, each ship had been assigned a total of forty-eight 20mm guns. However, during 1945 eight single 20mm were ordered replaced by twin mounts, and that April the *North Carolina* was assigned a battery of fifty-six 20mm guns, and the *Washington*, seventy-five. As of August 1945, each had aboard eight twin 20mm; the

North Carolina also had twenty single mounts, and *Washington* had sixty-three single mounts and one quadruple 20mm. Each ship also ended the war with fifteen quadruple 40mm guns.

Oerlikons could be easily fitted at facilities in forward operating areas, but the heavy quadruple Bofors were added only during major refits. Thus changes in the heavy antiaircraft battery corresponded to a few large refits for each ship. For the *North Carolina*, the first major refit was due to battle-damage repairs after torpedoing by the Japanese submarine *I-15* on 15 September 1942. The ship was repaired at Pearl Harbor between 30 September and 17 November. She again refitted at Pearl Harbor during March, April, and May 1943, when new fire controls and new radar were added. She had a major refit, with major alterations, at Puget Sound between 23 July and 1 October 1944 and later was refitted for peacetime service at New York Navy Yard. Corresponding major refits for the *Washington* were carried out at New York Navy Yard (23 July–23 August 1942); Pearl Harbor (28 May–27 July 1943); Puget Sound (March and April 1944, after her collision with the *Indiana*); and Puget Sound (23 June–mid-September 1945).

It is difficult to evaluate any warship design, particularly one incorporating so many novel features. Clearly the *North Carolina*s performed quite adequately in wartime. Clearly, too, they were successful enough for the *North Carolina* herself to be retained briefly postwar as an active Naval Academy training ship. Another evaluation of the design was provided in 1943 by the British DNC (ship construction) department (see Table 12-3). By this time many British officers believed that the U.S. Navy had somehow managed consistently to achieve higher speeds, better protection, and bettery armament than had British designers, and DNC compared U.S. to British practice in battleships (*North Carolina* vs. *King George V*), cruisers (*Belfast* vs. *Cleveland*) and destroyers ("Battle" vs. *Fletcher* and *Sumner*). The exercise is reminiscent of more recent comparisons between U.S. and Soviet practice, the answer always being, of course, that the foreign design represents an alternative series of trade-offs on the same displacement. It must, of course, be understood that there was an element of self-defense in the DNC remarks which will be quoted below. Even so, such comparisons are useful, given the extent of the information exchanged between the U.S. and British navies in wartime. They are, therefore, quite different from comparisons between U.S. and Soviet design practice, in which the estimate of modern Soviet practice is itself subject to considerable uncertainty.

As to armament, the U.S. turrets were clearly more heavily protected, "but arrangements for handling shell are simplified to a degree which would not be

Table 12-3. Comparison, *North Carolina* vs. *King George V*

	King George V	*North Carolina*
Length (WL)	740	714 ft
Beam (Ext)	103-0	108-3 ft-in
Draft(Deep)	32-9	33-4 ft-in
Displacement(Std)	36,730	36,600 tons
Displacement(Full Load)	42,080	44,800 tons
Weights(Tons):		
Equipment	1150	1200
Machinery	2770	2900
Armament	6570	7000
Protection	12,460	11,300
Hull	13,780	14,200
Oil	3770	5500
Power	110,000	121,000
Speed(Deep)	28.25	26.5
Main Battery	10-14in	9-16in
Belt	15in(magazines)	12in(sloped)
	14in(machinery)	
Barbettes	13in	16in
Conning Tower	4in	16in
Turret Face/Rear	13in/6in	16in/7in
Deck	6in(magazines)	3.6&4.1 on
	5in(machinery)	1.375in
	5in-2.5in(fwd)	None Fwd
	4.5in(aft)	6in(Steer Gear)
Freeboard(Deep)	18-0	16-0 ft-in
Armored Freeboard(Deep)	9-9	5-0 ft-in
GM(Deep)	8.0	8.5 ft
Tactical Diameter(14.5kts)	930	575 yds

accepted in H.M. service. The 5-inch turrets. . .are very close together [which is objectionable] on the score of possible damage."

Compared with the British battleship, the U.S. design showed much less armored freeboard and an inferior armored deck (in that the British deck was applied in a single layer, which was more effective than two layers adding up to the same total thickness). Although the British conning tower was much thinner, the total protected volume of the British ship was much greater and the armor thicker. Although DNC did not cite immunity zones, the British had designed their magazine armor for immunity against 15-inch shells between 13,500 and 33,500 yards, and their machinery spaces for 15,600 to 29,500 yards. They also claimed that their 14-inch side armor would withstand the British 2,375-pound 16in/45 shell at 20,000 yards, and their 6-inch deck at 31,000 yards. In this sense the *King George V* design demonstrated that, given British technology, it was possible to protect a modern battleship *against* 16-inch fire but not to arm her with such heavy guns. Note that in December 1941, in connection with a

study of the German *Bismarck*, BuShips estimated that the magazines of the British ship would be immune to attack by the U.S. 16in/45 gun firing a 2,240-pound shell between 23,000 and 31,000 yards and that her machinery would be immune only between 25,000 and 28,000 yards. Her barbettes, however, would be penetrated at 27,500 yards.

As for underwater protection, DNC considered *North Carolina* inferior in that the chance of flooding the third deck was much greater, due in part to the smaller armored freeboard of the U.S. ship. He cited the recent torpedoing of the *North Carolina* as evidence. Although the U.S. ship had a triple bottom, war experience had shown that it gave no appreciable advantage over a double bottom of similar weight and depth, and indeed later U.S. ships had reverted to the simpler double bottom. DNC noted, too, that the U.S. designers had had to accept very large compartments in their machinery spaces when they combined engine and boiler rooms. BuShips remarked that the British design standard for underwater protection was a 1,000-pound charge, whereas the U.S. Navy designed for a 700 pound charge. However, amidships the British system was only 13-feet deep, whereas the U.S. system, installed in a beamier ship, was 18.5-feet deep.

The U.S. ship gained only slightly in metacentric height compared with British ships, despite her greater beam. DNC attributed this to additional top-weight in the U.S. ship, principally the massive superstructure and heavy conning tower. He argued that in the "riddled" condition the ship might suffer in comparison with *King George V* because of her soft ends.

Endurance and turning performance were particular sore points with British officers who had worked with the *Washington* in the Home Fleet during 1942. DNC pointed out that endurance was difficult to compare, but that the U.S. ship did have a 50 percent greater fuel capacity as designed. He also noted that the U.S. ship could stow another 500 tons forward, but normally did not, to reduce draft there (that is, to increase freeboard forward, for dryness). He suspected that the U.S. ship had been designed for most economical operation at 18 to 25 knots, the British ship at full power. Here U.S. practice reflected the need to steam great distances in the Pacific, and the relatively poor steaming economy of British battleships would be very noticeable during the Okinawa campaign.

As for turning performance, there could be no question of the inferiority of the British ship. DNC claimed that the price of maneuverability in the U.S. ship had been greater underwater resistance, so that the U.S. ship required more power to make a lesser speed at a given displacement.

In theory, battle is the ultimate test of any warship design, yet the accidents of different circumstances make it an ambiguous test at best. Certainly the *Washington* was fortunate in the night battle of Guadalcanal, when she sank the Japanese battle cruiser *Kirishima* with radar-directed 16-inch fire: she suffered no counterbattery fire. Her unlucky companion, the *South Dakota*, achieved little except to demonstrate that even modern battleships could be severely damaged at short range by cruiser and destroyer fire, since such ships could not be heavily armored in their superstructures. On this basis, the success at Guadalcanal would seem to be more a success of fire control (and of turret operation) than of the design as a whole.

The other major wartime test came when the *North Carolina* was torpedoed on 15 September 1942. The torpedo, with a 660-pound warhead (that is, somewhat smaller than the charge for which the protective system had been designed) struck on the port side just abaft No. 1 turret, blowing a 32 × 18 foot hole in the side of the ship and admitting about 970 tons of water. Armor above the hole cracked, and the second and third decks buckled. Although the ship was able to accelerate to 24 knots within a few minutes, she later had to slow to 18 to avoid strain on shoring around the large hole. Moreover, structural damage below No. 1 turret put it effectively out of action, and shock disabled the main search radar.

This incident excited very considerable interest, since it was the first case of torpedo damage to a modern U.S. capital ship during World War Two. Many officers felt that it showed that too much had been sacrificed in battleship design, since the torpedo-protection system had come close to failure in a crucial area, abeam magazine spaces. The General Board, for example, wanted the last two *Iowas*, *Kentucky* and *Illinois*, redesigned, blistered abeam their magazines. BuShips argued that its system had performed much as designed, and no major changes were actually made.

13

The *South Dakota* Class

The two *North Carolina*s were to have been authorized as part of the FY37 program, and the General Board met in July 1936 to discuss the FY38 program. It wanted two more identical battleships, but the CNO, Admiral Standley, disagreed. He wanted a fresh design. Thus the next U.S. battleship class, which became the *South Dakota*, was scheduled for FY39, the fiscal year beginning 1 July 1938, even before the *North Carolina*s had been delayed to FY38. Design work for this "Battleship 1939" began in March 1937, and on 23 June the secretary of the navy formally approved the drafting of characteristics for two battleships for the FY39 program. Characteristics were approved on 4 January 1938, and the two ships were appropriated as part of the act of 4 April 1938. In fact, as the international situation deteriorated, Congress added another two, under a Deficiency Authorization of 25 June 1938. By that time the United States had already invoked the tonnage "escalator clause" of the London Treaty and was already developing the *Iowa* design. However, Congress offered two *35,000-ton* battleships, and President Roosevelt was glad to accept what he could. Thus the total of four *South Dakota*s.

Probably none of the participants in the design and characteristics-making process had been completely happy with the *North Carolina* design. To the strategists of the General Board, she was far too slow, particularly for carrier escort. To Admiral J. M. Reeves, who had forced upon the board the 27-knot twelve-gun type, she was too weakly protected against 16-inch fire. By early 1937 it must have seemed clear that in future the 16-inch gun would be the world standard. To the technical bureaus, the design was a patchwork of old and new technology. The very important new threat of underwater-trajectory hits had been appreciated only very late in the design process, by which time matters had gone so far that only the magazines could be protected at all. It was

not at all clear whether the deck protection could perform as advertised, according to the "divided-deck formula." Even the turbines were only a compromise between the new high-temperature, high-pressure technology and the older technology represented by recent cruisers and carriers.

Surely the next class of battleships could be better. By taking a series of radical steps Preliminary Design achieved, in the *South Dakota*, a treaty battleship armed with and protected against the 16-inch gun and yet capable of the same 27 knots as her predecessor. On the debit side, the new ship was extremely cramped, and the new system of protection against both underwater-trajectory shellfire and 16-inch shells precluded effective protection against torpedoes. This last sacrifice was largely unexpected and was discovered too late in the design process for full correction to be possible. Even so, the *South Dakota* was a remarkable achievement within very constricting treaty limits. Most of this was due to a series of innovations suggested by Captain A. J. Chantry, who headed Preliminary Design at this time.

It was a measure of Chantry's triumph that the new design, despite its tightness, could accommodate fleet (force) flagship facilities, whereas the ostensibly roomier *North Carolina* could not. Yet by mid-1939 it was essential that a fast battleship be so adapted, given the expectation that the U.S. Navy would operate battleship-carrier task forces. The *North Carolina*s were limited to division flagship accommodations and facilities. The new design was developed as a force flagship, and a division flagship variant (which became BB 58-60) developed from it.

The problem was weight, an expected direct increase of 145 tons, including 117 tons merely to enlarge the upper level of the conning tower to accommodate personnel and their equipment. The treaty ships, however, were designed right up to the treaty limit, essentially without weight margins. Over-

The *Alabama* is inclined during a Puget Sound refit, 25 February 1945. The walkway in front of her conning tower had just been enclosed. The antenna mounted above her secondary conn has not been identified, but it was probably a jammer. Note the manholes atop her exposed outer tankage.

weight equated directly to loss of military capability. Thus in April 1937, it was necessary to shave 298 tons of protection from the *North Carolina*, equivalent to a reduction in the immune zone of 800 yards; another 145 tons would equate to about 400 yards more. It was not that the *South Dakota* was in any sense a looser design, it was merely more adaptable. In the end the trade-off was two twin 5-inch mounts for an extra conning tower level in the *South Dakota* herself.

The preliminary designers cannot have been very sure, in March and April of 1937, of exactly what the General Board would want in the next battleship. Their fast battleship design, Scheme XVIC, had come very close to satisfying the board the previous November. On the other hand, since that time the extremely destructive 16-inch gun had become the standard. Nor was it at all clear whether future U.S. battleships would have to be much faster than the existing ones. The *North Carolina*s could be seen as a special type. Thus the designers turned to a type emphasizing protection and the 16-inch gun at the expense of speed. Scheme XVIC had typified the alternative of high speed at the expense of firepower. Preliminary Design's guess is illustrated by the first entry in the *South Dakota* design notebook, dated 30 March 1937, a pencilled requirement for nine 16-inch guns, at least 23 knots, and an immune zone with its outer edge set at 30,000 yards. That in turn implied at least 5.9 inches of deck armor, representing a weight relatively easily accommodated within treaty limits.

Side armor was much more of a problem. Even at 25,000 yards a 16in/45 could penetrate 13.5 inches, the thickness of existing U.S. armor belts. To move the inner edge inward to 21,000 yards would require 15.5 inches, which was well beyond the weights such a ship could carry. It was inevitable, then, that some form of inclined armor would be used. It could not be much thicker than that employed in the *North Carolina*, given the weight constraints of the treaties. It would, therefore, have to derive its increased protective power by being more steeply inclined. That in turn implied that it would have to be internal, inside the outer shell of the ship, a step already taken by the French in their *Dunkerque* class. The step to internal armor was not taken lightly, because it implied problems even in ship construction and, moreover, in repair after battle damage—the external side plating would have to be removed in order to get at it. However, this design expedient appeared to be inescapable.

Sloping the outside of the hull would have had two effects: it would have drawn in the waterline; and it would have enlarged the decks above water, compared with a ship that had a conventional, nearly vertical, side. The first reduced stability because it reduced waterplane area. The second worsened the problem, since it increased the area, hence the weight,

of the thick armor deck covering the belt. The steeper the angle of slope, the worse the problem. By moving the belt inside the hull, the designers could maintain waterplane area and avoid excessive armor deck area, so that normal standards of stability could be met—as long as the unarmored waterline *outside* the belt remained more or less intact. Were the waterline shattered, however, it would be as though the ship had a steeply sloped external belt. To limit the consequences of such damage, Preliminary Design had to endow its ship with a great metacentric height, and also to limit the space between the unarmored outer hull and the belt.

Its proposed solution was ingenious. The inwardly sloping belt was not continued all the way up to the armored deck. Instead, it met an upper belt that sloped back toward the deck, so that the upper portion of the armored citadel was reminiscent of the old flat/sloped protective decks. This had several effects. First, it minimized the space between belt and outer hull. Second, it reduced the area, hence the weight, of the flat armored deck. At long range, the upper belt was at a considerable disadvantage, since its slope made shells strike nearer the perpendicular, that is with greater effect. On the other hand, at relatively short range, most shells, following nearly flat trajectories, would strike the upper portion of the belt armor, since they would not be plunging toward the lower belt. Its slope would be effective. The split between upper and lower belts allowed provision of a thicker upper belt, effectively moving the inner edge of the immune zone inwards. The added thickness might make up for the loss of effective sloping at long range.

The unusual double-angled belt appeared in the earliest cross section in the design book (2 April), when the immune zone was only to have been 5,000 yards wide, and it survived through most of the preliminary design stage. In its ultimate form, it consisted of an upper belt (11.5 to 13 inches) sloping at 44 degrees, and the lower (12.4 to 2 inches) at 15. The main armored deck would be 5.1 inches on 30 pound backing, covered by a 1.5-inch bomb deck. Because it was entirely inboard of the main torpedo bulkheads, and therefore no longer a vital stiffener of the torpedo-protection system, the splinter deck could be made a uniform 25-pounds (5/8-inches) thick.

This combination was expected to satisfy the design requirement (at that time 20,000 to 30,000 yards) against 16-inch fire and would provide immunity against 14-inch fire between 17,200 and 33,500 yards. In a departure from earlier practice, the thickness of the bulkheads enclosing the ends of the belt was calculated on the basis of a 60 degree target angle, as a weight saver. Up to 30 degrees off the beam, these 12.8-inch bulkheads would be equivalent to 16 inches or better. However, if the ship were pursuing her adversary (target angle between 0 and 30 degrees off the centerline), they would be effectively thinner, and the ship would not be immune to 16-inch fire inside 22,700 yards.

An internal belt had another advantage: it could be continued down to the inner bottom (tapered, of course, to save weight) and so could protect against the newly understood menace of underwater-trajectory hits. It was hoped, then, the entire vital area of the ship, not merely the magazines, could be so protected. The downward extension of the belt armor would also form part of the torpedo protection, as a torpedo bulkhead.

In the end, the complicated double-sloped belt was abandoned when it was discovered that reversion to a simpler tapered single-sloped belt saved several hundred tons of badly needed weight (see below). The greater complexity of the knuckled armor appears not to have figured in this decision. Indeed, Captain Chantry of Preliminary Design, who had originated it, considered it easier to build. He did admit that the new single slope simplified the arrangement of the oil tanks. The belt was initially to have been 11.3 inches thick at its upper edge, but it was thickened to 12.2 inches when the inner edge of the immune zone was set at 18,000 rather than 20,000 yards (by a directive issued 14 April 1938).* At the same time its backing was reduced from 35- to 30-pound STS. The belt tapered to 10.7 (later 11.25) inches, and then to 5.9 inches, 25.6 feet above base (that is, 7 feet below the designed waterline, at 33.6 feet) and finally to 1.75 inches at the inner bottom, and sloped at 19 degrees. At first, it appeared that this steeply sloped belt would save about 0.4 tons per foot of armored length, beside a saving of about a ton per foot due to a narrowing of the armor deck.

However, the nature of the design required additional armor, which effectively cancelled out the weight advantage due to internal protection. First there was external belt armor to protect the waterline (60 pounds or 1.5 inches, equivalent to 10.4 tons per foot). It also served as a rubbing strake. Then there was additional framing to support the lower portion of the belt against underwater explosions. Then, since it was now expected that shells might actually strike the lower portion of the belt, splinter protection had to be provided inboard of it. In practice that meant that the holding bulkhead of the torpedo-protection system had to be increased from 17.5-pound mild steel (MS) to 25-pound STS.

The preliminary *South Dakota* design also incorporated water-excluding material, reminiscent of that used early in the century, between the second and third decks to help deal with the threat of flooding outboard of the belt. In theory it would swell to fill about half the volume involved if the side of the ship were shattered. In practice, however, no suitable material was found, and this vulnerability remained.

The outer-hull armor, which initially was to have been 2 inches thick, was arranged to follow the wave contour, 4 feet above and 2 below the waterline. In addition the main belt armor was knuckled to follow the wave contour at the point of 10.7-inch thickness. It was covered by a main armor deck graded to take advantage of the 1.5-inch bomb deck, varying from 5.3(outboard) to 5.1(inboard) inches on 30-pound STS backing, with a 25-pound splinter deck below it. Protection was uniform over machinery and magazines. However, the boilers (see below) penetrated the third (splinter) deck and had to be covered by a secondary splinter deck only 30 inches below the main armor deck, an unusual arrangement tested at Dahlgren Proving Ground in 1939. In addition, initially the outer parts of the second deck (below the bomb deck) were to have been 2.25-inch STS, partly to protect the oil tanks below them and outboard of the belt. However, the ships were actually built with only 0.5-inch STS on the outer part of the second (armor) deck, and with an additional layer of 5/8-inch STS sloping above that.

When BuOrd introduced a new 2,700-pound 16-inch shell in 1939, the zone of immunity was recalculated. Belt and deck retained some of their effectiveness (20,500 to 26,400 yards), but the turrets, with their 17-inch faces sloped inwards, could be penetrated out to the maximum range of the gun, 41,700 yards. Turret face armor was, therefore, increased to 18 inches. As weight compensation the turret sides were reduced from 10 to 9.5 inches, on 30-pound MS backing.

The designers hoped that, by contributing strength to the torpedo-protection system, the lower part of the belt could increase its effectiveness and thus substitute for weight and volume, both in very short supply in a treaty-limited ship. They observed that, in caisson tests, belt armor tended to limit the vertical extent of torpedo damage without itself being deformed. It seemed to follow that the sheer mass and strength of the internal belt would tend to stabilize the holding (inner) bulkhead. The torpedo-defense system was cut from five to four bulkheads, and its depth (measured by the distance from shell plating to holding bulkhead halfway between waterline and bottom) from 18 feet 7 inches to 17 feet 11 inches. There was also the hope that, given the slope of the inner belt, an underwater explosion would tend to vent upward, thus reducing the force on the interior bulkhead.

Perhaps it was not clear at the time that this added up to a radical change in approach. Earlier torpedo-protection systems had been based on the deformation of relatively thin, elastic bulkheads. This one incorporated a very rigid layer of ballistic armor,

---

* As weight compensation, the conning tower and turret tops were reduced by three quarters of an inch. An inner limit of 17,500 yards had also been proposed. It would have required a 12.6-inch belt tapering to 11.4 rather than 11.25 inches.

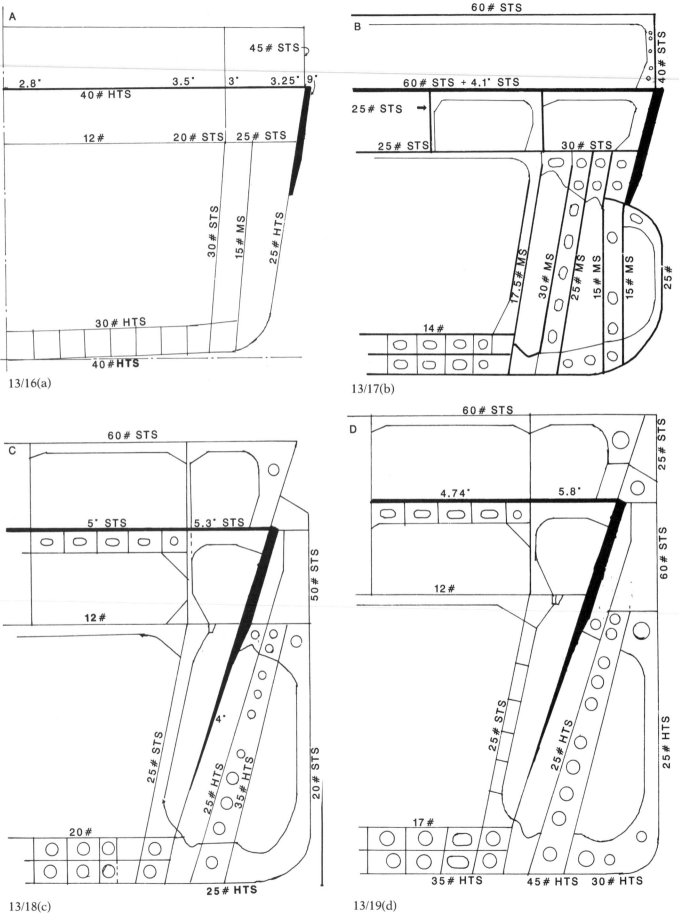

A

45# STS

2.8"   3.5"   3"   3.25" 9"
40# HTS

12#   20# STS   25# STS

30# STS
15# MS
25# HTS

30# HTS

40# HTS

13/16(a)

B

60# STS

40# STS

60# STS + 4.1" STS

40# STS

25# STS →

25# STS   30# STS

17.5# MS
30# MS
25# MS
15# MS
15# MS
25#

14#

13/17(b)

C

60# STS

5" STS   5.3" STS

50# STS

12#

4"

25# STS
25# HTS
35# HTS

20# STS

20#

25# HTS

13/18(c)

D

60# STS

25# STS

4.74"   5.8"

25# STS

60# STS

12#

25# STS
25# HTS

25# HTS

17#

35# HTS   45# HTS   30# HTS

13/19(d)

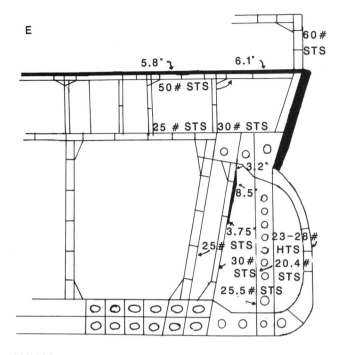

E

13/20(e)

Comparative cross sections show the development of U.S. battleship armor schemes, from the *North Carolina* on. The *Alaska*, a large cruiser often classed with capital ships, is shown for comparison. All but the *Montana* (engine room) are shown at the boiler room. Key: (a) *Alaska*, (b) *North Carolina*, (c) *South Dakota*, (d) *Iowa*, (e) *Montana*.

necessarily rigid given its role in stopping armor-piercing shells. In any case, it appears that the construction of the new battleships was too urgent to allow for caisson tests until all four were well under construction. Then, in 1939, C&R discovered that its new system was considerably *less* effective than earlier ones. The best it could do was to fill the outboard spaces, which in earlier systems had been left empty, on the theory that what really counted in underwater protection was an inboard void and the deepest possible liquid layer. Note that these developments occurred not only after four ships were under construction but also after the next design, the *Iowa*, was substantially complete. Hence the *Iowa* protective system substantially reproduced that of the *South Dakota*. This point would come up again after the torpedoeing of the *North Carolina*, when the General Board made a critical reexamination of the protection of all the new American battleships.

In sum, then, Preliminary Design was able to provide not merely excellent protection against conventional 16-inch fire, but also protection, over both machinery and magazines, against the new threat of shells striking underwater. It paid two prices, only one of which was obvious at the beginning: a cramped, short, ship; and a loss of underwater protection. The

former had to be accepted because, no matter how much weight could be saved on a tons-per-foot basis, 35,000 tons allowed for only so much total armor weight, which translated into only so many protected feet of length. U.S. design practice further complicated matters in that it sought to protect a fixed percentage of overall ship length, whatever the actual length of the vitals requiring protection. That is, waterline protection was considered protection of the buoyancy and stability of the ship, as well as protection of magazines and machinery. On the other hand, any attempt to shorten the ship, that is, to constrict her vitals, would run up against the need to provide sufficient secondary weapons far enough from the 16-inch turrets to avoid their blast.

More generally, ship length had to be balanced against speed. For a given power plant, the shorter the ship, the slower. Alternatively, for a given speed, the shorter the ship, the more power would be required. Without some innovation, more power would require more power-plant length. The *South Dakota*s were appreciably shorter than the *North Carolina*s, and it was a considerable achievement for Preliminary Design to make them just as fast, by drastically shrinking their machinery spaces. At the outset of the design process, however, it appeared that the heavier protection could be purchased only by cutting speed.

Thus the earliest Preliminary Design sketches called for speeds of 23 or 24.7 knots. A rough sketch dated 2 April shows a three-turret, 606-foot ship for which $61,700EHP$ sufficed to achieve 24.7 knots at 42,300 tons. That level of *effective* power is roughly equivalent to the $115,000SHP$ of the *North Carolina*—which (in that ship) required too much length. These were guesses, as the General Board had (as yet) made no determination. An undated handwritten memorandum in the design notebook argues that the two key figures would be the speed of opposing battleships (estimated at 22 knots fully loaded) and the need to escape surfaced submarines (by a speed margin of 20 to 25 percent over their average sea speed of 18 knots). That implied a speed of at least 22.5 knots.

It now appears, however, that late in 1936 U.S. cryptanalysts learned that the reconstructed Japanese battleship *Nagato* had exceeded 26 knots on trials. The Japanese battle fleet, previously credited with a maximum speed of 22 knots, was clearly much faster. This information appears nowhere in the surviving General Board files, but it is striking that the board consistently demanded higher speeds. Thus a Preliminary Design computation sheet of 8 April shows speed studies for ships 640-, 650-, and 660-feet long, for speeds of between 19 and 27 knots. Something between 25.8 and 26.2 knots could be obtained *if* the *North Carolina* plant could be shrunk to fit a short hull.

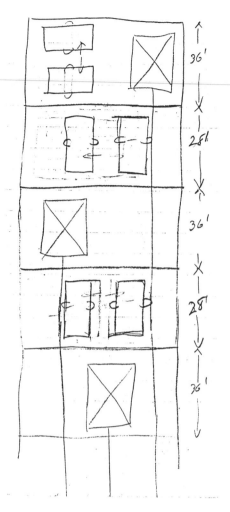

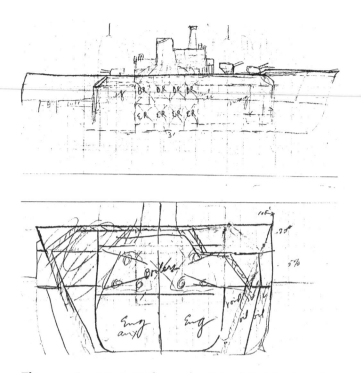

These are Captain A. J. Chantry's original sketches for what became the *South Dakota*. Although extremely crude, they clearly show his radical concept of mounting boilers *above* the engines, to shorten the machinery spaces. Note also the unusual double-sloped armor, with two liquid layers outboard. The plan view shows the engineering spaces with an inscription by Rear Admiral Edward L. Cochrane, a chief of the Bureau of Ships. The crossed-out signs at the top are Chantry's estimates of the total length of the machinery spaces, which he sought to minimize.

Once more Preliminary Design had to seek a novel solution, in which the boilers would sit directly *above* the turbines. This was reminiscent of the first designs for the 1916 battle cruisers, but here there could be no boilers in the open above the armor deck. Rather, that deck would jog up over the machinery spaces. The 2 April cross section shows the double deck: a flat layer amidships, then a short 14.8-inch thick vertical strake, then another flat deck outboard, and finally the belt. Captain A. J. Chantry, who as head of Preliminary Design was responsible for these concepts, hoped to save 64 feet (out of 176), although by early May that estimate had been halved, to allow some staggering between machinery spaces that otherwise would have been abreast. Even so, the saving was expected to make a 650-foot, 25-knot design practical.

Ultimately the staggering went so far as to move the boilers alongside the turbines. They no longer extended above the flat armor deck, although they had to protrude through the splinter deck to clear propeller shafts running beneath them. Each pair of high- and low-pressure turbines formed a unit with two boilers and one or two turbogenerators. As a result, electrical generating capacity was so widely dispersed that there was no longer a need for a separate forward diesel generator room, as in the *North Carolina*. The length of the machinery spaces was further cut by installing all evaporators and distilling equipment in the main machinery spaces. These savings in turn left enough protected space that, although it was much shorter, the new ship could be provided with two (rather than one, as before) separate plotting rooms.

The new design reverted to all-steam electric generators, with seven 1,000 kW units distributed within the unit machinery spaces. There were no separate main diesel generators. However, as in contemporary U.S. warships of other classes, two 200 kW emergency diesel generators were fitted, forward and aft.

In the end, 135,000SHP was installed on a shorter length than the 115,000 required in the earlier ships. That in turn made it possible to achieve 27 knots, the speed the General Board ultimately demanded, in a ship short enough to be protected against 16-inch fire. The one problem of length that could never really be solved was limited superstructure length.

Given the expected saving in machinery length (and 8 feet more shaved from the magazines), it appeared that the 714-foot *North Carolina* could be reduced to 638 feet. Captain Chantry proposed a 650-foot, 25-knot ship on this basis on 12 April. For its part, the General Board was as yet by no means sure of what it wanted. At a session held at this time, the Preliminary Design notetaker suggested that "we might get across a two quad 14-inch turret high speed design." Presented with claims of the benefits of internal armor in a new design, members of the General Board wanted to know whether the *North Carolina* could not be improved by using it. Chantry replied that if they wanted the 27 knots of the earlier ship, it would be better to develop a new design than to attempt to adapt the existing one. As a result, Preliminary Design developed the 666- and 682-foot designs that led directly to the *South Dakota*. By 13 May, calculations showed that, *if* citadel length could be held to that used in the 650-foot design, a 666-foot hull could be driven at 28 knots by 135,000SHP. This design already incorporated external splinter armor.

Serious problems remained: the length of the soft hull forward approached, if it did not exceed, what C&R considered acceptable. Too, the hull had to be quite narrow at the quarter-points fore and aft. Turrets could be placed only where there was sufficient beam to provide torpedo protection outboard of their magazines. The end turrets, then, would have to be brought well inside the quarter-points, and that would cramp the superstructure.

The necessary narrowing (actually a reduction in cross-sectional areas) fore and aft made for further complications. In more conventional designs, the forepart of the ship was nearly vertical, for minimum underwater resistance. However, stability (the large metacentric height required to make up for the possibility that the side plating would be penetrated and the space between it and the belt flooded) demanded maximum waterplane area, that is, as much beam as possible as far fore and aft as possible. The hull had, therefore, to slope upward and outward, which increased resistance and required more power. The first weight estimate showed about 300 tons too much, and worse was in store: 130 tons for 16 feet more of hull; 250 for 20,000 more SHP. The total was about 400 more tons compared with the 650-footer.

Problems were even greater aft, where the hull had to narrow just about where the magazines of No. 3 turret would be located. Here the solution was ingenious. The magazines required beam, so that there would be enough torpedo protection outboard of them. Hydrodynamics required, not so much that the hull narrow, as that its cross-sectional *area* decrease smoothly. The designers therefore cut the necessary area out of the bottom of the hull, forming a tunnel. Its outer limits were defined by the massive skegs carrying the two outboard shafts; the two inner shafts projected through it. The twin-skeg stern had the

incidental virtue of protecting the inner shafts against torpedo hits, but General Board testimony makes it clear that it was adopted entirely for hydrodynamic reasons. Like the internal armor and the two-story machinery, it was a radical step. In its case, the chief risk was vibration due to interaction between the propellers and the skegs. Special model tests were run, and the then-chief constructor, Admiral DuBose, assured the General Board that there would be no difficulties, and it appears that in service these ships suffered much less than did the *North Carolina*s.

Finally, any reduction in length (compared with the *North Carolina*) had to be compensated for by increased draft, since displacement (and, therefore, underwater volume) did not change, and since both ships had the maximum beam permissable to pass through the Panama Canal. Thus the new design showed the unusually deep draft of 35 feet. Critical depths (drydock sills) at major bases at this time were:

Pacific:	Hunters Point	37ft7in
	Panama	41ft6in
	Pearl Harbor	32ft6in
	Puget Sound	35ft0in
Atlantic:	Boston	42ft3.5in*
	Philadelphia	39ft11.5in†
	New York	32ft11.5in

*Channel only 36ft.
†Channel only 34ft6in.

Although Chief Constructor DuBose was confident that he could control weights, the General Board correctly suspected that the new ship would far exceed her planned draft in service. The *Massachusetts* passed through the Panama Canal in February 1943 drawing 37.4 feet, the record for any ship transiting the locks up to that time.

Although the 666-foot ship was the principal C&R design, alternative studies had to be prepared against the possibility that the General Board would once again turn to a faster ship, or perhaps abhor the radical internal armor. During May 1937, the General Board held an informal hearing and asked for a heavily protected fast battleship with nine 14-inch guns or with two quadruple 14-inch turrets. Preliminary Design prepared a series of alternatives:

—Design A was the *North Carolina*, still armed at this point with 14-inch guns.
—B was a 30.5-knot, 765-feet ship with nine 14-inchers and a 12-inch belt.
—C, D, E, F were 680-foot, 24-knot types emphasizing either protection or firepower. Thus C had the three quadruple turrets of the *North Carolina* but a 15.5-inch belt. D had the more popular quartet of triple turrets but had to sacrifice belt

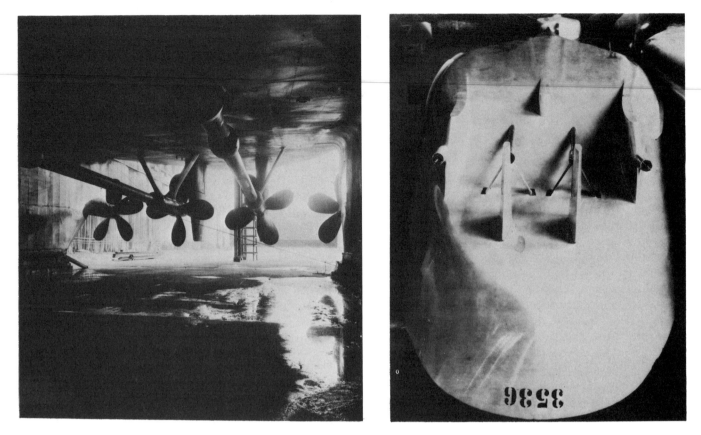

A tank test model and the *Indiana* illustrate the tunnel stern characteristics of the *South Dakota* class, with skegs on the outer, rather than the inner, shafts. The *Indiana* photograph looks aft, out of the tunnel. It was taken on 13 March 1942. Note that the outer propellers are five-bladed, the inner ones, four-bladed.

Table 13-1. BB 57 Studies, 1937

Design	A	B	C	D
Length (ft)	714	680	680	680
Beam (ft)	108	108	108	108
Draft (ft)	31.5	31.5	31.5	31.5
Displacement (tons)				
Speed (kts)			24	
Power (SHP)			75,000	
14in Guns	12		3 × 4	4 × 3
5in Guns				
Barbettes (in)	14.7	15.5	19	16.45
Belt (in)	11.2	12.0	15.5	12.75
Weights (tons):				
Hull	17,744	18,042	17,132	17,398
Fittings	1547	1590	1516	1516
Protection	7911	7683	9453	8982
Machinery (wet)	3098	3550	2390	2390
Armament	2596	2294	2470	2643
Ammunition	1290	1077	1290	1432
Equipment	531	531	531	531
Complement	190	190	190	190
Stores	470	470	432	451
Aeronautical	54	54	54	54
Std. Displacement	35,431	35,481	35,443	35,438

NOTE: G1 is dated 22 May 1937; *A* was the *North Carolina* design *as then agreed*. The increase in belt armor between *A* and *G2* moved the inner edge of the immune zone inwards from 20,400 to 19,200 yards.

armor (12.75 inches). E demonstrated that two of the triples could be traded for quadruple turrets at the cost of 2.5-inches of belt. In F, 1.25 inches of belt was restored at the cost of one gun(three rather than two triple turrets). None was pursued in great detail. Early in June, however, the General Board circulated three of them to the C-in-C U.S. Fleet, to commander battle force, to commander battleships of battle force, and to the president of the Naval War College:

—*North Carolina*, immune, against the *14-inch* gun, between 19,500 and 30,500 yards (magazines).

—Design C which, given its limited amidships length, could accommodate only sixteen 5-inch guns. It was also difficult to find room for control stations and boats, and living spaces would be cramped. The inner edge of the immune zone moved to 12,500 to 13,300 yards. If some of the weight of protection were used instead to shift to triple turrets, the inner edge would move out to 16,500 to 17,500 yards. However, to replace *triple* 14 in turrets with 16-inch would be "less simple" than in the case of quadruple 14-inch mounts.

—Design G, with deck protection as in the *North Carolina* but side armor increased to give inner limits of 18,200 and 19,300 yards, respectively. This nine-gun ship would be difficult to adapt to the 16-inch gun.

The board mentioned that an alternative armor scheme, which would confer substantial immunity to 16-inch fire on a ship otherwise similar to the *North Carolina*, was "under study." It would yield the best returns in a 27-knot ship, next best in a 30-knot design, and would make the least difference in the slow, heavily protected ship.

The board's memorandum gives no direct hint of the new information on Japanese developments, although it did observe that (from the sketch information in hand) all the new European battleships would be quite fast. Given recent improvements in machinery design, it might no longer be necessary to sacrifice speed. "The General Board has for some time been of the opinion that some of the improvement should go into speed—battle line speed, 'fast wing' speed, or both. . . ."

All three officers argued for a combination of better protection (that is, a shorter minimum battle range, represented by a reduced inner edge immune range) and continuation of the 27-knot policy represented by the *North Carolina*s. They believed that battles would be won at relatively short ranges, that long *gun* range was useful mainly because it would permit very early hits to register. The thicker the belt armor (that is, the shorter the minimum safe battle range), the more effective the gunnery. Protection would be more valuable than *nominal* firepower, because it would increase the effectiveness of the guns by decreasing the range at which they would have to fire. Ironically, the development of radar fire control in World War Two would permit decisive engagement at long ranges, but such a possibility was not envis-

E	F	G	G1	G2
680	680	725		725
108	108	108		108
31.5	31.5	31.5		31.5
				42,000
		30		30
				157,000
2 × 4, 2 × 3	1 × 4, 3 × 3	9		9
				20
13.8	15	14.2		15.4
10.25	11.5	10.7		11.8
17,742	17,579	17,881	17,683	
1516	1516	1556	1556	
8275	8641	7281	7725	
2390	2390	4150	3650	
2858	2752	2294	2294	
1432	1361	1077	1290	
531	531	531	531	
190	187	190	190	
470	460	470	470	
54	54	54	54	
35,454	35,471	35,484	35,443	

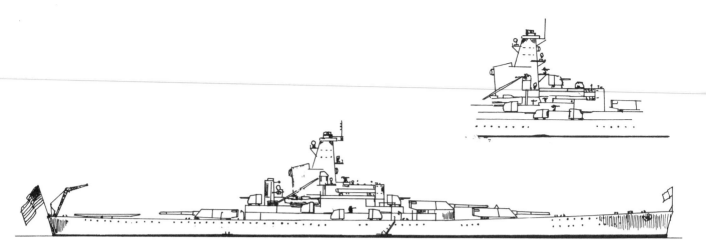

Sketch design for the *South Dakota*, as presented to the General Board in August 1937. The inset shows the division, as opposed to fleet, flagship version. At this stage the fleet flagship had a two-level conning tower, flag facilities being accommodated in the after half of the navigational level. Note the centerline 5-inch guns.

aged in 1937. The concept of radar does not appear even in the highly classified papers of the General Board of that time.

None of the officers the board consulted had any concept of what short-range protection would entail. For example, CINCUS imagined it would be easy to bring the immune zone up to 12,000 yards to 30,000 yards against the *16-inch gun*. He was willing, however, to accept an inner edge set at 15,000 yards. Calculation showed that to achieve his minimum zone on 666 feet would require a reduction in speed to 21 knots. On 666 feet and 27 knots, there would be an overweight of 2,750 tons. A comparable 714-foot, 27-knot ship would displace about 40,000 tons standard, which might as well have been learned from some of the 1935 studies. Yet CINCUS was unwilling to reduce speed below 25 knots.

The battle force argued for 27 knots for tactical homogeneity. The president of the War College also wanted high speed, although he recognized that the U.S. Navy would continue to operate 21-knot ships until the "Big Five" were due for replacement in the 1950s. He argued that, from what amounted to an isolationist point of view, the U.S. Navy would have to defend very distant sea frontiers in mid-Atlantic and mid-Pacific and that only fast ships could respond in time to distant threats. It seems remarkable in retrospect that he considered an aggressive campaign against Japan (that is, Plan Orange, the main U.S. Pacific war plan) an unlikely contingency. Speed would be clearly valuable in that case.

Only the radical C&R proposal could satisfy the demand for speed, protection, and the 16-inch gun. Work proceeded rapidly enough for C&R to circulate its design under a date of 6 August 1937.

Two interrelated themes characterized the detailed development that followed: weight saving, to keep the ship within the 35,000-ton limit without wasting any of the available weight; and the problem of accommodating necessary features within a very cramped midships section. The hull was so filled with machinery and magazines that officers would have to be housed above the main deck. Space was made in this deckhouse by moving the 5-inch magazines down into the boiler room wings below the main armor deck.

Perhaps the control arrangements were the clearest indication of just how cramped the new ship would be. Conning tower, pilot house, flag plot, and navigating bridge were all placed on the same superstructure level, and some of the usual superstructure was eliminated on the basis of using the conning tower for ship control in both peace and war. This idea, which had been standard in the U.S. fleet before World War One, had the virtue of forcing upon personnel during peacetime the procedures that would be best in battle. As in World War One, however, it greatly limited visibility for maneuvering. Thus, the only navigating bridge would be *abaft* the conning tower, so that the captain or OOD would be able to see forward only through the conning tower ports. Otherwise he would have only the bridge wings, and both vantage points would be unsuitable in fog or in confined waters. There would be, moreover, no astern view whatever. Surely this was a lot to give up in a battleship worth $55 or $60 million. At an 8 September General Board hearing, Captain R. C. McFall of Fleet Training asked for a real navigating bridge, not merely a catwalk around the front of the conning tower, "where the Captain has to run around and shout orders in through peep holes in the conning tower."

As for secondary guns, it appeared that the space between Nos. 2 and 3 turrets could not accommodate

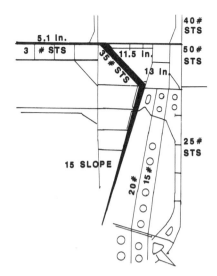

The complex belt arrangement originally planned for the *South Dakota*. Note that the outboard torpedo-protection space was to have been filled with oil, as was ultimately the case.

ten twin gunhouses (as in the *North Carolina*) without risking blast damage. Instead, Preliminary Design proposed to fit four on each beam, with one more on the centerline aft, to give a total of ten guns on each broadside. Later this was cut to three on each side, with another gunhouse on the centerline forward, although Admiral Furlong (BuOrd) held out for a total of twenty 5-inch guns.

Even the centerline positions were unattractive, since they would be vulnerable to blast. Admiral W. H. Allen of the General Board went so far as to ask in September whether these four guns might not be placed in old-style between-decks (casemate) mountings. Captain McFall of Fleet Training doubted their value, particularly in a fast battleship. The freeboard of the new design matched that of the *California*, whose forward casemates had to be closed up to keep solid water out in a moderate sea at 15 knots.

Chantry returned on 13 September with a series of alternatives designed to unclutter the superstructure amidships. Scheme 1 was the original 666-foot ship, already 558 tons overweight, with Nos. 2 and 3 turrets able to fire, respectively, 60 degrees abaft and before the beam, that is, with total arcs of 300 degrees each. The alternatives could be graded on turret separation and on allowed arcs beyond dead abeam. The more restricted the arcs, the more blast-free space could be provided for secondary guns between the turrets. They were not entirely comparable to Scheme 1, however, because Preliminary Design had taken this opportunity to add a fourth dual-purpose director aft and to eliminate blast interference already present, so that Chantry could claim that the result was little worse than that presented by the *North Carolina*.

As the table below shows, for example, Chantry could choose either to add 16 feet amidships between the two turrets, as in Scheme 2, or else to restrict their arcs by 5 degrees each. The extra 16 feet of hull cost 750 tons. Were the 750 tons of added overweight to be eliminated by cutting an equivalent weight of side armor, the ship would lose 3,500 to 4,500 yards of immune zone. Scheme 2 also introduced a pair of single open-mounted 5-inch guns, which would be useful for star shell or for quick and easy maneuvering in a night destroyer attack.

The other Schemes were attempts to cut the overweight of Scheme 2 (which was otherwise quite attractive) at minimum real cost, initially by keeping the turrets spread 16 feet farther apart but otherwise holding to the original 666-foot hull. In Scheme 3, 435 tons of overweight (compared with Scheme 1) equated to a narrowing of the immune zone by 2,000 yards. That was the limit which could be achieved by restrictions on the turrets; the ship could be made no shorter. Any other improvement would have to be more fundamental. In Scheme 4, Chantry abandoned his complex belt armor and was somewhat surprised that he could actually save weight in the process. Scheme 5 reintroduced the uniform secondary battery of twin mounts, and overweight, compared with Scheme 1, increased from 249 to 361 tons.

The only alternative left, Scheme 6, was to accept the original turret spacing and, therefore, reduced arcs of fire. Overweight now fell to 191 tons, a weight of armor equivalent to about 1,000 yards of immune zone. Chantry considered it the best compromise, given the demand for a 10,000-yard-wide immune zone.

By now Battleship 1939 had very nearly reached its final form. Some minor improvements remained. In November, in response to General Board suggestions, C&R enlarged the deckhouse sufficiently to mount the 5-inch guns on top of it, that is, on the 01 and 02 levels, where they would be acceptably dry. That and the abandonment of the inward-sloping portion of the belt armor in turn added badly needed internal space. The navigating bridge was enlarged, and it proved possible once more to separate Nos. 2 and 3 turrets by 16 more feet and so to increase their arcs to 57.5 degrees beyond the beam. This increased separation in turn made it possible to mount four twin 5-inch on each beam plus a 1.1-inch quadruple AA machine cannon. It was also now possible to provide, as requested, a secondary battery director at the after end of the superstructure. Preliminary Design observed that its clear sight arcs extended to 40 degrees before the beam. A third 1.1-inch quadruple cannon would be mounted aft, between the secondary and main battery directors. Thus the sacrifice of one mount as compared with the *North Carolina* would not reduce the 1.1-inch broadside, although, as no

Newly completed, the *South Dakota* (*above and facing*) is shown in the summer of 1942. At this time she had only seven quadruple 1.1-inch machine cannon (note the two on the stern) and many 20mm and even 0.50-calibre machine guns.

Battleship Alternatives, September 1937

Scheme	2	3	4	5	6
Length	682	666	666	666	666ft
Training Arc	60	55	55	55	55 degrees
5-inch Twin Mts	18	18	18	20	20
5-inch Single Mts	2	2	2	--	--
Overweight	1,308	993	827	919	749 tons

NOTE: In this table, "Training Arc" is the angle No. 2 or No. 3 turret could reach, respectively, abaft or before the beam.

one pointed out, it would certainly reduce effectiveness in the event of attacks from both beams. Finally, as for habitability, with the superstructure considerably lengthened and widened, many of the crew could be berthed at its after end, near their stations in the 5-inch battery.

All of this cost some weight, but model tests appeared to show that the ship could make her speed on somewhat less power than initially expected, and the projected weight saving on machinery would more than make up for the extra structural weight.

In the division flagship version of the design, a fifth twin 5in/38 would be mounted in the space used for a quadruple 1.1-inch gun on the fleet flagship, for the desired total of twenty guns. The 1.1s were placed higher up in the bridge structure. The large conning

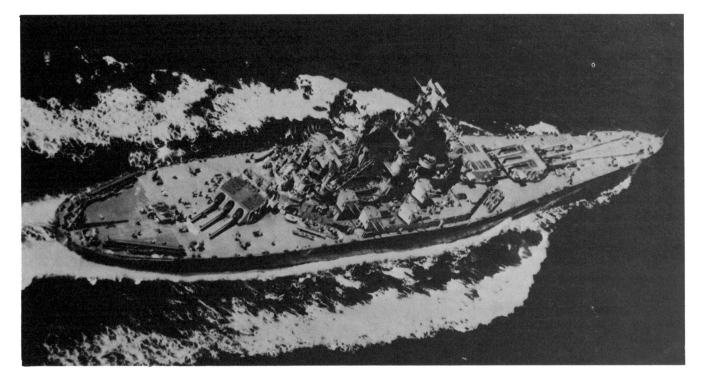

tower of the force flagship was reduced in size and the bridge rearranged. The addition of two twin 5 inchers more than made up for the weight saved, particularly since more men were actually required for the extra guns. Preliminary Design estimated that the division flagship would displace 140 tons more than the force flagship, arguing that this difference should be accepted rather than cut the protection or armament of the division flagship.

The effect of adding the large deckhouses on the main deck amidships was to fill most of the deck area, so that fueling ports could not be placed on deck. This may also have been a consequence of the use of an internal belt. The solution, an external catwalk set into the side of the ship below the weather deck, became a prominent visual feature of the *South Dakota* class; it covered the fueling ports.

Reductions in machinery weight helped make these improvements possible. Thus, as completed *South Dakota* machinery came to about 3,306 tons (dry), which is only 9 percent more than the 3,020 of the *North Carolina*, despite a 17 percent increase in power. Moreover, many "luxury" features were eliminated to save weight. For example, there would be no airports, so the interior of the ship would have to be artificially ventilated. Nor could the crew enjoy large separate berthing and messing spaces. Ensigns would have to share bunkrooms, lieutenants j.g. and warrant officers would be housed in double staterooms, and the single staterooms would be far smaller than in previous ships. Even captain's and admiral's spaces would be reduced. Detail changes might save weight—

wood weather decks were to be eliminated, as well as many of the ship's boats.

Even so, there was overweight trouble. A weight sheet of 22 December 1937 shows an expected displacement of 35,412 tons for the force flagship version. Rather than shave protection, the CNO, Admiral Leahy, turned to a more careful definition of standard displacement itself. First, standard displacement was defined in terms of the condition of the ship "ready for sea" in wartime. It was therefore possible to deduct equipment and stores, particularly boats, which were carried only in peacetime. For example, four 50-foot launches, two 40-foot launches, and two 35-foot motor boats would interfere with No. 3 turret. Two racing cutters would not be carried in wartime, and two whalers would interfere with the 5-inch battery. These boats totaled 71.46 tons. It might be possible not to count water in the machinery (94.7 tons), as well as part of the 16.5 tons of lubricating oil. Drill ammunition amounted to 39.77 tons. The nominal "standard" supply of ammunition could be reduced by 49 tons by reducing the theoretical supply of 5 inch to 4,800 rounds plus 800 of starshell. The designers had already imposed a theoretical supply of 675 rounds for the main battery—although space was provided for a "mobilization supply" of 495 more, a total of 1,170 rounds, 130 (rather than the paper 75) per gun. Similarly, 101 tons could be saved by setting the nominal potable water allowance at only 5 gallons per man, which could be justified in view of the power of the distilling plant on board. Finally 45 tons might be saved on stores. By such expedients the *designed* standard displacement was shaved to an acceptable 35,024 tons, all without any *physical* change in the ship. As with the *North Carolina* design effort, the lesson to be learned here is that standard displacement was a far less well-defined term than anyone had realized at Washington in 1921–22.

Of the four ships authorized, BB 57-60, the first was built as the fleet flagship *South Dakota*. The others were fitted as division flagships. New York Shipbuilding Corp. served as lead yard for BB 57 and 59, and Newport News for the other pair. All four were rushed through after Pearl Harbor, dock trials and inspections being accepted in place of the normal sea trials. Informal sea trials were combined with their brief shakedown cruises. Fortunately, they did not suffer nearly so badly from vibration as did the *North Carolina*s.

All ships but *Indiana* were completed with four-bladed propellers on each shaft. Extensive model tests showed that five-bladed propellers on the skegs and four-bladed propellers inboard would be superior, and *Indiana* was completed in this form. Vibration trials (*Indiana*) in September 1942 showed this arrangement superior to the 4 blade outboard/3 blade inboard combination then being installed aboard the *South Dakota*, and the 5/4 combination was installed aboard the *Massachusetts* (1944) and *Alabama* (1943). The *South Dakota* reverted to all four-bladed propellers in 1944, however, and the *Indiana* was fitted with three- (instead of four-) bladed inboard propellers in the summer of 1945, as a result of the 1945 vibration survey of *Alabama*.

On trial, 1 June 1942, the USS *Indiana* was run up to 27.8 knots (27.5 on her pitometer scale) at 41,700 tons, in a vibration test. Presumably this approximated full power behavior. Her captain reported that handling was very easy. Model tests predicted a speed of 27.77 knots on 130,000SHP at 42,900 tons, somewhat lighter than actual full load. Similarly, the BuShips figures prepared for the General Board in November 1944 show 27.4 knots at 44,700 tons, or 25.8 knots if a 25 percent effective power reduction were credited to fouling or bad weather. As in the case of contemporary U.S. carriers and cruisers, none of the ships was run back and forth over the measured mile upon completion, for fear of U-boat attack. *Alabama* was standardized off San Clemente in March 1945, achieving 27.08 knots at 42,740 tons on 133,070SHP at 180.54 RPM. At 44,840 tons, she made 26.70 knots on 135,420SHP.

This last trial did show severe fore-and-aft vibration at full power, due to the inboard propellers, and less severe athwartship vibration due primarily to the outboard propellers on the skegs. The test report recommended a change of propellers, to four blades inboard and three blades outboard.

The design was very tight, and even before completion it appeared to be overweight. Thus in July 1938 Final Design calculated the standard displacement of the *South Dakota* as 35,447 tons, and of the others as 35,678 tons. In December 1941, BuShips estimated that they would displace about 35,900 tons in standard condition. On trial, the ships were expected to displace 42,888 tons, about 900 more than the *North Carolina*s. Wartime changes, particularly additions to the light antiaircraft battery, added considerable weight. As completed, it was estimated that the ships would be as much as 1,500 tons overweight. Moreover, in seeking a shorter hull form the designers had accepted relatively deep draft in the first place. Any further increase in draft would reduce armored freeboard and might also reduce very considerably the value of the torpedo protection, which was most effective at designed draft.

For example, in July 1943 the "optimum battle" displacement of the *Massachusetts* was calculated at 43,884 tons, for a draft of 34feet 7.5inches. On average in service she actually displaced 46,041 tons (draft 36feet 1inch). The situation was aggravated by the need to carry additional light antiaircraft ammunition, extra fuel oil (to fuel escorts), and additional stores and fresh water (for long-range Pacific operations). Thus she typically carried 6,400 tons of fuel rather than the optimum figure of 5,089; 2,600 tons of ammunition (vs. 2,339); 245 tons of stores (vs. 107); 500 tons of provisions (vs. 213); and 625 tons of fresh water (vs. 558). The situation was so serious that a reduction to 85 rounds per 16-inch gun had recently been authorized. In 1945, BuShips established a limiting displacement of 47,000 tons for the entire class, for a draft of 36feet 9inches and an armored freeboard of 5 feet.

The principal wartime alterations were the addition of radar (and a consequent reduction in the number of range finders); alterations to the bridge in which the walkway around the front of the conning tower was enlarged and then enclosed; and a massive increase in light antiaircraft weapons. The only major weight compensation available was removal of ship's boats and of the two cranes serving them. The *South Dakota* and *Alabama* were to have none, the other two only one each. In fact, however, only the *Alabama* was completed without either boat crane. The *South Dakota* was completed with both boat cranes but had both of them replaced by 20mm guns during her big refit early in 1943. The others were completed with both boat cranes, but the *Massachusetts* and *Indiana* had their portside cranes removed during 1944 and 1945 refits and replaced by a gallery of 20mm guns.

As designed before the radar era, these ships were to have had, beside the usual complement of turret and main battery director range-finders, three 12feet

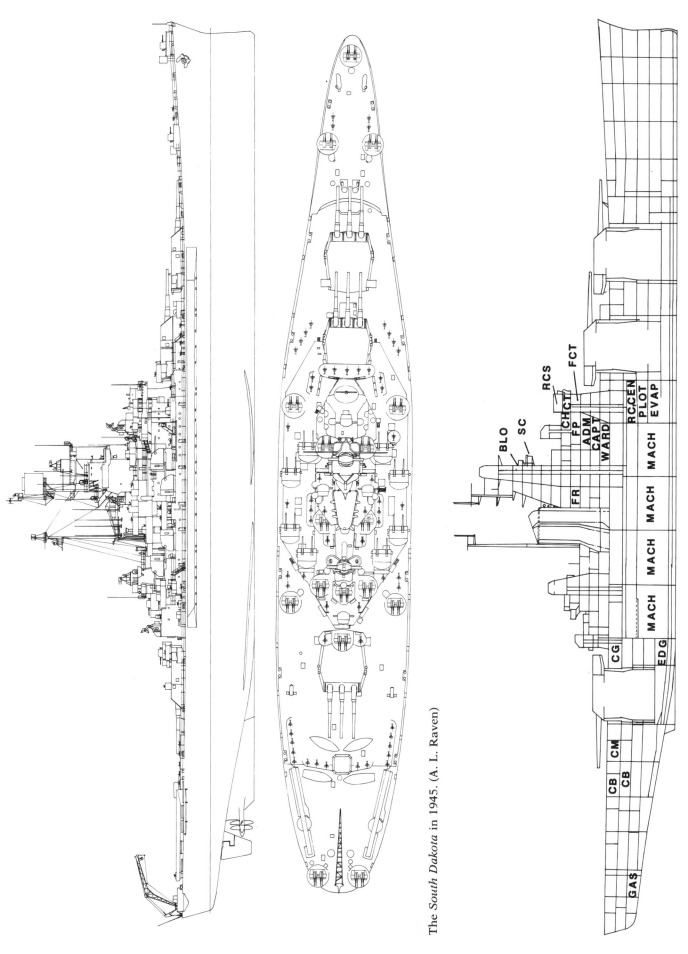

The *South Dakota* in 1945. (A. L. Raven)

The *Alabama* inboard profile, 1945.

BLO

SC

RCS

FCT

CHCT

FP

ADM/CAPT

WARD

RC.CEN

PLOT

EVAP

FR

MACH

MACH

MACH

MACH

CG

MACH

EDG

CB

CM

CB

GAS

The *Indiana* is shown in Hampton Roads, 20 May 1942. Note her rudimentary bridge, with an enclosed gallery below it. The object atop her conning tower is a spotting glass; it was ultimately replaced by a Mark 27 radar. Slits in the fire control tower were for battle lookouts.

navigational range-finders (two on either side of the forward superstructure, just abaft the forward secondary director and one atop No. 3 turret) and a 15-foot spotting glass/auxiliary main battery range-finder atop the upper level of the conning tower, which served as a fire control tower. The navigational instruments were never fitted, but all four ships had the spotting glass through 1944–45, when it was replaced by the new Mark 27 microwave radar. From 1943 onwards, all but the *Massachusetts* had Mark 3 main battery fire control radars atop their conning

towers in order to supplement the optical range-finder.

Searchlights were also a major fixture of the pre-radar era. The *South Dakota*s were designed to carry six 36-inch lights, two on their boat crane kingposts and four on the main fire control tower. Only the *South Dakota* herself was delivered with all six, the two on the crane posts being removed when she was fitted with 40mm guns and directors. The *Indiana* and *Alabama* each had two on the forward side of the main battery tower at the secondary conning level and two on its after side at the fifth level. The

Massachusetts had one on the centerline, atop her superstructure just forward of the barbette of her secondary director, two on the after side of the main battery tower at the fifth level, and one on the after side of her after (stub) main battery director tower. By way of contrast, by February 1942 the planned complement of the *Iowa*s and *Montana*s had already been cut to four 36-inch searchlights, in a lozenge pattern to be determined in detail during construction. The *North Carolina*s, completed with six search-lights, were having two (amidships) replaced by 20mm guns, and the two after lights were to have been moved when 40mm mounts were fitted.

Radar was first specified in the summer of 1941, as a CXAM air-search set on the foremast. They were actually fitted with SC, and later with SK or the dish-shaped SK-2. In addition, they had the SG surface-search radar, initially atop a platform just forward of the forward main battery director. Later, after waveguide problems had been solved, it was moved to a topmast. A second SG was fitted (on the main-mast) as a result of experience at Guadalcanal (see below). By 1944 battleships were ordered fitted with auxiliary air-search radars on their mainmasts. That required a much heavier (and taller) mainmast, first installed in the *Massachusetts*, during her major refit in June-July 1944. In 1945, then, all but the *Indiana* (which had an SP height-finder) had an SR (two-dimensional air search) radar antenna on their main-

Having completed a Norfolk refit in August 1943, the *Alabama* (*left and below*) displays the full antiaircraft battery of ten quadruple 40mm guns. Note that the flag bridge level has been plated in. Circles indicate the very minor changes during this particular refit: an enlarged radar platform for the small SC air search set forward, soon to be replaced by SK; and a pair of light antiaircraft directors amidships.

As inclined in February 1945, the *Alabama* (*above and facing*) shows a pair of Mark 577 antiaircraft directors abaft her after main battery fire control tower, as well as the vent trunking, range-finder and sights of her No. 3 turret. Note also the large vent just below the 40mm mount. The forward main-battery fire control tower carries another of the unidentified flat antennas, just below the searchlights. The photo of her rig, dated 13 March, shows the small radome of an SU, which replaced her forward SG surface-search set. Below it is the fat radome of a TDY-1A jammer, sharing a platform with an SK-2 air-search antenna. The mainmast air-search antenna is an SC-2. The spike just visible on the forward edge of the fire control tower was presumably associated with the flat-faced antenna there.

masts, with SG bracketed beneath it. All but the *Indiana* ended the war with the SK-2 dish air-search antenna forward, and the *Alabama* had the small enclosed SU surface-search radar in place of the usual SG. All four had the standard TDY jammer on a bracket on the forward side of the fire control tower, with two searchlights below it.

By February 1942, each ship was to have been fitted with a pair of Mark 8 main battery radars and four Mark 4 for her Mark 37 secondary directors. The *South Dakota* herself was too far advanced to wait for the Mark 8, so she was fitted with a pair of Mark 3 instead. The *Indiana* was the first ship fitted with Mark 8 (August 1942), and at first it was on her for-

ward main battery director only. As in other battleships, all were fitted at first with Mark 4 and later with Mark 12/22 for secondary fire control.

The designed light antiaircraft battery was initially three quadruple 1.1-inch machine cannon and twelve 0.50-calibre machine guns, the after 1.1-inch mount being on the centerline forward of and above the after secondary battery director. The flagship *South Dakota* had five 1.1-inch mounts, two of them abaft and below the after centerline mount. She alone was completed with 1.1-inch guns. Her three half-sisters were completed with the quadruple 40mm guns scheduled (by mid-1941) to replace the 1.1 on a one-for-one basis. In place of the single after mount,

they had two quadruple 40mm, for a total of four mounts in the superstructure. Before any of the class had been completed, another pair of heavy machine cannon mounts was added right aft, abaft the catapults, and all four ships were completed with six (seven in the *South Dakota*) mounts. By that time the 1.1-inch gun had been ordered replaced by the much more effective (but much heavier) quadruple 40mm Bofors on a one-for-one basis in battleships. The *South Dakota* was completed with thirty-four 20mm (increased to thirty-five very shortly) and eight 0.50s; the other three were completed with thirty-five 20mm Oerlikon machine cannon (including three atop each of Nos. 2 and 3 turrets) but without any 0.50s. The new weapons were in relatively short supply, and in September 1942 *South Dakota* was actually fitted with eight more 0.50s, for a total of sixteen. The machine guns were soon replaced by Oerlikons, so that by November 1942 *South Dakota* had a total of fifty-seven 20mm guns.

By that time, too, she had a mixed battery of 1.1-inch and 40mm guns. During repairs at Pearl Harbor after she grounded at Tongatabu, two of her 1.1s were replaced, and two more quadruple 40s added, for a total of four quadruple 40mm and five quadruple 1.1-inch. Her 1.1-inch guns were not removed until February 1943, when thirteen quadruple 40mm guns were added, for a total of seventeen mounts:

the ten of the other ships (see below), plus the one superfiring, plus three forward, plus two alongside her funnel (replacing her boat cranes), plus one atop No.3 turret. She never carried a 40mm gun atop her No. 2 turret, probably because it would have blocked the sight lines of the slits in her extra lower (flag) conning tower level. *Iowa* had the same problem. In both ships only 20mm guns could be carried atop No. 2 turret. This battery had been approved in December 1942, together with eighty 20mm. The unique mount virtually over her forefoot was installed at the personal suggestion of her gunnery officer. Since the ship pitched deeply in service, particularly in some ground swells, it often flooded and had to be evacuated to save the crew from drowning. It was never removed, however, and was a distinguishing feature of the ship between 1943 and 1945.

The three force flagships were all completed with six quadruple 40mm guns, and by November 1942 the planned "ultimate" battery was ten such mounts. The extra four mounts (two mounts on the 01 level just abaft the conning tower, and two mounts on the main (weather) deck just forward of No. 3 turret) were added to the *Indiana* and *Massachusetts* late in the year. Meanwhile the planned battery increased to twelve mounts in December, with the addition of guns atop Nos. 2 and 3 main battery turrets (installed in the *Indiana* and *Massachusetts* in February 1943).

After her 1942–43 postbattle-damage refit in New York, the *South Dakota* (*above and facing*) carried a total of seventeen quadruple 40mm mounts, including the wet one in her bow. Note how the platform of her secondary conn dips down at its forward end, unlike those of other ships of this class. She is shown after a second 1943 refit, at Norfolk, in which a large SK antenna replaced the small SC-2 on her foremast. Note the small SG surface-search antenna on the secondary battery control platform under her forward main battery director. (Detail photographs courtesy of R. F. Sumrall).

At this time the approved ultimate 20mm battery was fifty-two guns, which was reached in stages. For example, in December 1942 the *Massachusetts* added thirteen (total forty-eight), with two more a short time later. In January 1943, the *Indiana* added eighteen (total fifty-three). In February 1943, the *Massachusetts* added eleven 20mm, for a total of sixty-one barrels. The *Alabama* added eight barrels only in May 1943. She never operated with the ten-mount 40mm battery, adding six mounts to reach the new standard of twelve only in November 1943.

The Oerlikon continued to be extremely popular through 1943, the *Indiana* adding nine (total sixty) as late as December 1943. By early 1944, however, there were suspicions that the 40mm Bofors was the minimum really effective antiaircraft weapon, and in June 1944 the ultimate (planned) battery of the force flagships was increased to eighteen quadruple 40mm: two mounts on the weather deck just forward of the catapults; two on the weather deck just abeam No. 2 turret; and two forward of the main battery turrets. The latter two were accepted even though limitations due to blast cut 15 degrees of effective train from the arc of No. 1 turret, and even though the turret could no longer be fired at elevations of less than 2 degrees.

The 20mm battery was to be reduced to thirty-three barrels, which in the *Massachusetts* would ultimately include the two existing experimental weapons of this calibre: one quadruple and one twin mount. She actually had forty-three Oerlikons on board in September. The new battery was actually installed in October 1944, but with thirty-two rather than thirty-three 20 mm guns. By July, the *Indiana* was down from sixty-three to fifty-five 20mm, and *South Dakota*'s ultimate 20mm battery had been reduced from eighty to seventy-six barrels. The *Alabama* and *Indiana* never received the final six 40mm

The *Massachusetts* (*above and facing*) was refitted just after the war at Puget Sound. She is shown on 22 January 1946, her 40mm battery sharply reduced to save weight and manpower. Note that the quadruple mount atop No. 2 turret has been replaced by 20mm guns and that the very wet forward 40mm mounts, which obstructed the line of sight of No. 1 turret, have been removed, leaving a total of fifteen (rather than eighteen) quadruple 40mm.

mounts. As of 1945, their approved "ultimate" batteries included fourteen quadruple 40mm guns. The two extra ones would have been forecastle mounts, as in the *Massachusetts*. At the end of the war, the *South Dakota* had seventy-two 20mm guns aboard, all single mounts. The *Indiana* had fifty-two singles. The *Massachusetts* had thirty-two singles (plus one twin and one quadruple mount). And the *Alabama* had fifty-six singles. Approved ultimate batteries at this time were, respectively, eighty-four (8 twin), forty (8 twin), forty-three (1 quadruple, 8 twin), and forty (8 twin) 20mm guns.

With their low freeboards reduced further by overloading, all of these ships were quite wet, their forward quadruple 40mm guns virtually useless in most weather. In August 1945, then, the new Ship Characteristics Board agreed with the *Massachusetts*'s captain that her two forecastle mounts should be removed as they were only of limited value. Both were removed during her postwar refit. At the same time the 40mm mount atop No. 2 turret was landed. That presumably reduced any tendency to trim by the bow, and so reduced wetness. Before she was laid up, the *South Dakota* suffered similar reductions. Her

bow 40mm mount and its gun tub were removed, although the stub projecting above the bow remained. The two forecastle mounts were also removed, although their gun tubs, gun foundations, and wiring were retained. These changes are evident in photographs taken when she was towed to the breakers in 1962.

All of this light antiaircraft battery required extra manpower. As designed, the force flagships had a total complement of 1,849, increased by 99 in February 1942, because of war conditions. The *Alabama* had 2,300 men on board by that December, and by the end of the war these ships typically accommodated about 2,350 officers and men.

Perhaps the best verdict on the class as a whole is that it showed, first, that a ship armed with and protected against the 16-inch gun *could* be built on 35,000 tons, and, second, that such a design would entail major sacrifices in seakeeping ability (particularly dryness forward) and in habitability. The *South Dakota*s were badly cramped internally.

As for the test of battle, the only battleship-on-battleship engagement one of them experienced was the night battle of Guadalcanal, 14–15 November

1942, in which the *South Dakota* herself engaged the Japanese battle cruiser *Kirishima* as well as lesser craft, in company with the USS *Washington*. At this time she had only a single SG surface-search radar. The ship sustained at least twenty-six hits, including one 14 inch, eighteen 8 inch, six 6 inch, and one 5-inch. Although her main armor was never pierced, she was badly damaged topside, particularly in her fire control tower structure. Her air-search radar antenna was torn away. More significantly, damage to cabling in the superstructure put most of her internal communications and fire control circuits out of action. All radars except the Mark 3 atop her after main battery director were knocked out. Short-circuits resulting from this damage temporarily overloaded her interior communication (IC) switchboard, and interior communication circuits throughout the ship were disrupted for about three minutes.

BuShips concluded that structural damage to the ship was limited because she was hit by armor piercing rather than high-explosive shells, that is, because her thin superstructure plating did not detonate them. That had, after all, been the logic of U.S. "all or nothing" protection for about thirty years. The effect of the thin plating was accentuated by a peculiarity of Japanese shells. They had been designed to penetrate a ship's armor after striking the water short and traveling underwater. Therefore they had relatively long fuze delays: 0.08 seconds for 6 inch, 0.4 seconds for 8 inch, and above, compared with 0.02 to 0.035 seconds for U.S. shells. They also had special caps designed to break off upon striking the water, leaving a shape better suited to an underwater trajectory. Many of the clean entry holes found in the ship were accompanied by small fragment holes clearly due to these shields. Thus, even when fuze action was initiated, the Japanese shells often passed through the ship before exploding. The problem of underwater hits by just such shells had been a major factor in the *South Dakota* design. It is ironic that such shells, if they hit *above* water, were substantially less effective than conventional ones.

The *Alabama* after her refit, 22 March 1945. Note how wet she was.

Quite aside from damage done by the Japanese, the shock of No. 3 turret firing astern caused some electrical problems. Later, during the battle, the blast of the same turret set catapult aircraft afire. The next salvo knocked them overboard, and put out most of the small fires.

Operationally, perhaps the greatest shock of the battle was the effect of losing the sole surface-search radar. Even though radar was relatively new, there was a terrible feeling of blindness associated with its loss. Even the temporary loss of the radar picture, when the sole SG was out of action for a few minutes, caused severe tactical confusion. In its report, BuShips emphasized that the ship was never in any real danger, that her hull and her main battery were never really affected. However, as a fighting unit, *South Dakota* succumbed almost completely to what would now be called a "soft kill," some of it self-inflicted.

Her captain considered the battle clear evidence of the value of the heavy conning tower. Had the ship control party been in the open, losses would surely have been severe. As it was, many of the antiaircraft gun crews took cover in the unarmored fire control tower, and suffered as it was repeatedly hit. Others agreed, and efforts to eliminate the heavy conning towers of the modern battleships were abandoned.

14

The *Iowa* Class

The four *Iowa*s were the only U.S. battleships to remain in active service after World War Two, and, as this is written, they are all returning to active service once more, probably for the rest of this century. They are certainly the best known of U.S. World War Two battleships. Were they also the most successful, *as battleships*? Apart from abortive engagements at Leyte Gulf, none was tested in battle because each entered service too late. Perhaps their main virtue, and the one which kept them in service for a decade after the war, was their high speed, which made them ideal companions for the fast carriers. Later, when they were the sole battleships remaining in Navy hands, the Marines prized them for their heavy gun batteries—which were common to all battleships and to the much cheaper monitors as well.

If these four were among the most elegant capital ships of the Second World War, they were also among the most puzzling. For half a century prior to laying them down, the U.S. Navy had consistently advocated armor and firepower at the expense of speed. Even in adopting fast battleships with the *North Carolina* class, it had preferred the slower of two alternative designs. Great and expensive improvements in machinery design had been used to minimize the increased power on the designs rather than to make extraordinarily powerful machinery (hence much higher speed) practical. Yet the four largest battleships the U.S. Navy produced were not much more than 33-knot versions of the 27-knot, 35,000 tonners that had preceded them. The *Iowa*s showed no advance at all in protection over the *South Dakota*s. The principal armament improvement was a more powerful 16-inch gun, 5 calibres longer. Ten thousand tons was a very great deal to pay for 6 knots.

The General Board was willing to pay that price because it wanted fast capital ships to fight its version of a future Pacific war. The U.S. ORANGE war plan envisaged a fleet advance through the Central Pacific, at the end of a long line of communication

that would attract Japanese cruiser-carrier attacks. For its part, the U.S. 21-knot battle force would be unable to bring these Japanese task forces to battle. Detached carriers might have a chance, but their cruiser escorts would be unable to defeat the three Japanese *Kongo*-class battle cruisers, which might well be detached from the Japanese battle force as cover for the lighter units. This actually happened in 1941. By 1939 it was also argued that fast-striking groups might be needed merely to bring the Japanese fleet to battle.*

As the story of the *North Carolina*s shows, these were not new ideas. The C&R design files show a June 1936 study of a 33-knot, 35,000-ton battleship based on Scheme XVA. It appeared that 191,000SHP would be needed at a waterline length of 788 feet. One triple 14-inch turret would have to be sacrificed, and the immune zone (against 14-inch fire) would shrink in total width from 11,000 to about 9,500 yards. Another 10,000 tons, and more sophisticated engines, bought a great deal: the *Iowa* carried nine much heavier guns and was much better protected than the *North Carolina*s.

The new factor in 1938 was the tonnage escalator clause of the London Treaty. The gun-calibre escalator had already transformed the *North Carolina*s. Rumors of Japanese super-battleships first began to circulate in November 1937. They specified three ships of 46,000 tons armed with 16-inch guns, and there were vaguer rumors of even larger ships with 18-inch guns, which were proven correct only at the end

---

* In 1939–40 the U.S. Navy appears not yet to have been aware that the fourth *Kongo*, *Hiei*, had been resurrected from the training to the operational capital-ship category. This information would have become available (probably through traffic analysis) only well after the ship had reentered service in January 1940. Nor does it appear that the last reconstruction of the *Kongo*s, which increased their speed from 26 to 30 knots, was known. Thus ONI 222, a list of Japanese warships published in December 1942, showed the speed of the four *Kongo*s as 26 knots.

The *Missouri* lies at anchor, probably at Ulithi, in 1945.

Table 14-1. Slow Battleships of 1938

Date	Jan. 1938	April 1938 (I)	28 Jun 38	28 Jun 38
Length(Wl)(Ft)	770	800	785	800
Beam(Ext)(Ft)	108-3	108-3	108-3	108-3
Draft(Max)(Ft)	35-0	35.96	35.96	35.96
Dispt(Max)(Tons)	54,200	56,595	55,397	55,338
Draft(Battle)(Ft)	33-9	34.71	35.24	35.19
Dispt(Battle)(Tons)	51,500	54,495	54,077	53,984
Dispt(Std)(Tons)	45,000	45,495	45,292	45,099
Speed(Kts)	27	27.5	27	27
SHP	170,000	130,000	130,000	130,000
Radius(15 Kts)	15,000	15,000	15,000	15,000
Main Battery	12-16in/45	9-18in/48	12-16in/50	12-16in/50
Secondary(Twins)	16-5in/38	20-5in/38	20-5in/38	20-5in/38
Quad 1.1in	3	3	3	3
0.50 cal MG	12	12	12	12
Protection:				
IZ VS 16in/45	20-30	12.15-30	18-30	18-30
IZ VS 18in/48		20-29		
IZ VS 16in/50		16.5-32.3	21.8-32.1	21.8-32.1
Belt(19 Deg on 30#)	11.3	14.75	12.2	12.2
Heavy Deck	5.1	5.1	5.1	5.1
Bomb Deck	60#	60#	60#	60#
Splinter Deck		25#	25#	25#
Barbettes, CT	16	21	17.3	17.3
Turret Face	18	20	18	18
Turret, CT Roof	8	10	7.25	7.25
Transverse Bhds.	10.4	16.75	11.3	11.3
Splinter Pro.	100#	100#	80#	80#
Weights(Tons)				
Hull	22,405	2115		
Hull Fittings	1580	1697		
Protection	10,845	13,037		
Engineering(Wet)	4200	3500		
Armament	3218	3464		
Ammunition	1576	1638		
Equip&Outfit	540	476		
Complement	227	192		
Stores & Fresh Water	518	322		
Aeronautics	54	54		
Margin	300	--		
Reserve Feed Water	747	650		
Fuel Oil	6860	8000		
1/3 Stores & F.W.	259	350		
Designed Full Load	53,329	54,495		
Belt	4880	6226		
Heavy Deck	4130	4010		
Bomb Deck	2260	1344		
Splinter Deck	507	454		
Torpedo Bulkheads	3310	3310		

of World War Two.* There was not enough concrete evidence to permit any of the treaty signatories to invoke the escalator clause, but at the same time intelligence evidence was growing.

If the U.S. Navy invoked the escalator clause without sufficient evidence, that would only invite the wrath of a still-isolationist and pacifist Congress. Too, there was a feeling that any major leap forward in battleship characteristics would make the new 35,000-ton ships obsolete, before any of them had been com-

* U.S. intelligence was certainly aware of the *Yamato* and *Musashi* (by name) by late 1942. ONI 222 of December 1942 listed them with approximately the correct length but with far too little beam (only 110 rather than the correct 127 feet) and as displacing 40,000 to 57,000 tons (rather than the correct figure of 64,000). Armament was given officially as nine 16-inch guns as late as July 1945 (ONI 222-J).

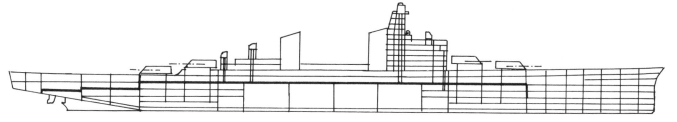

The C&R fast battleship design, 1938, to mount four triple 16-inch turrets.

pleted. It was clear from the beginning, however, that a well-designed 45,000-ton battleship would be much superior to the existing, very tight, 35,000 tonners.

It was not until 31 March 1938 that the three treaty powers, the United States, Britain, and France, exchanged notes invoking the clause. In June they signed a protocol to the London Treaty raising the maximum capital ship displacement to 45,000 tons, but retaining the 16-inch limit on gun calibre.

At this point the U.S. designers could continue their combination of heavy weapons and heavy protection; the 18-inch gun was the natural weapon. Alternatively, 10,000 more tons could buy a very fast cruiser-killer, a type first suggested by Admiral A. J. Hepburn, C-in-C U.S. Fleet, late in 1937. C&R developed both in parallel, but ultimately a variant of the second became the *Iowa* class. Early in 1938 Preliminary Design began work on the first at the request of Admiral Thomas C. Hart, chairman of the General Board.

The first approach was to add another triple 16in/45 on a lengthened *South Dakota* hull, the extra tonnage being absorbed in extra hull structure, in extending the armored box, and in adding power (to maintain 27 knots). Alternatively, nine 18-inch guns could be accommodated (the United States did not accept the 16-inch limit in the new "escalated" treaty until after these schemes had been worked out).

There was also the cruiser-killer. On 17 January 1938 Captain A. J. Chantry, head of the Design Division, asked his group to study a ship unlimited in displacement, although able to pass through the Panama Canal. She would be armed with twelve 16-inch guns, as well as the usual secondary battery of twenty 5-inch guns, and to be capable of 35 knots, with an endurance of 20,000 (rather than the previous 15,000)nm at 15 knots. Unlike full battleships, she was to be protected against 8-inch shellfire between 10,000 and 30,000 yards. The inner edge of the immune zone (and, for that matter, of the cruiser-killer *Alaska*-class cruiser designed two years later) corresponded to the sort of range at which a solitary ship might have to fight in, for example, poor visibility. A battleship could be designed to fight at a much greater range, since she would have a screen of lighter ships that could be expected to encounter

an approaching enemy even in the worst weather.

This was primarily a killer of raiding Japanese cruisers, although she would also be an ideal weapon to use against the Japanese lines of communication stretching among the Mandated Islands. The first sketches showed a standard displacement of over 50,000 tons. Chantry sought something more flexible if no less expensive. At the end of January he called for three more studies, all protected against 16-inch shellfire: one with nine rather than twelve 16-inch guns, the others (with nine or twelve guns) having speed reduced to 32.5 knots (with nine or twelve guns). The fast ship would have to be justified as a combination cruiser-killer and true battleship.

These were still very large ships. For example, the new Scheme B, nine 16-inch and 32.5 knots, would displace nearly 53,000 tons. She had been scaled down from the twelve-gun ship, and it seemed that some weight could be saved by shortening still further. Studies made at the end of February, however, showed that the best that could be done was 50,714 tons on a length of 850 feet, far above what it seemed that Congress and the General Board would buy.

But the fast battleship idea was far from dead. On 8 February 1938 the Battleship Design Advisory Board (see Chapter 12) submitted its report. About a month later the designers were asked what would be required to increase the speed of the 35,000-ton battleships to 30 knots, with particular emphasis on the features of the newest class, the *South Dakotas*. A preliminary estimate showed that the higher speed could be achieved on a standard displacement of only 37,600 tons, which encouraged the constructors to try for 33 knots. A rough calculation showed that an 800-foot ship based on the *South Dakota* and displacing only 39,930 tons could make 33 knots on 220,000SHP. This result was far lower than estimates based on scaled-down versions of the earlier fast battleship. It may be that in scaling down the constructors had kept too much of the heavier structure associated with the larger ship.

The General Board discussed the Advisory Board report on 10 March 1938 and a week later called for a new battleship design, a 33-knot *South Dakota* which it was hoped would displace about 40,000 tons. This became the *Iowa* design. It appears that the designers used their fast battleship studies as a basis. Scheme

Table 14-2. Fast Battleships, 1938

Scheme	8in	A	B	C
Length	980	960	920	960ft
Beam	108	108.25	108.25	108.25ft
Draft(Max)	35	37.5	37	37.5ft
Dispt(Std)	50,950	59,060	52,707	55,771 tons
Dispt(Max)	62,700	70,750	63,500	67,280 tons
Speed(Kts)	35	32.5	32.5	35
SHP	285,000	277,000	225,000	300,000
Radius(15 Kts)	20,000	20,000	20,000	20,000
16in Guns(Triple)	12	12	9	9
Secondary (Twins)	20-5in	12-6in	12-6in	12-6in
IZ	10-30	20-30	20-30	20-30 Kyds
VS	8in	16in	16in	16in
Belt (On 30#)	8.1	12.6	12.6	12.6in
Heavy Deck(On 30#)	2.3	5.0	5.0	5.0in
Vertical	10.5	16	16	16in
Turrets	9-6-5	18-10-8	18-10-8	18-10-8in
Splinter	70#	100#	100#	100#
Length of Belt	584	556	496	512ft
Weights(Tons)				
Hull	26,450	29,505	27,450	28,011
Hull Fittings	2002	1966	1885	1967
Protection	10,019	15,139	12,889	13,137
Machinery(Wet)	6000	5700	4750	5910
Armament	3249	3377	2742	2742
Ammunition	1657	1781	1479	1479
Equip&Outfit	665	685	656	669
Complement	252	252	236	236
Stores & Fresh Water	575	575	540	540
Aeronautics	80	80	80	80
Reserve Feed Water	1024	1000	820	1090
Fuel Oil	9439	9400	8700	9150
1/3 Stores & F.W.	288	288	270	270
Full Load	61,700	69,748	62,497	66,281
Max Displacement	62,700	70,748	63,497	67,281
Torpedo Bulkheads	4155	4020	3590	3700
Bomb Deck	2120	2020	1805	1860
Heavy Deck	2830	5100	4536	4670
3rd Deck Aft	369	677	782	819
Splinter Deck	687	661	590	610
Belt	5000	7802	7111	7305
Turrets	1092	1728	1296	1296
Barbettes(Heavy)	2399	3650	2625	2625
Conning Tower	324	496	496	496

B had, after all, incorporated protection identical to that of the *South Dakota*s. The effect of the 40,000-ton estimate had been to convince the General Board that the 33-knot battleship was a practical proposition under the new "escalated" treaty limits.

More detailed work began late in March. It seemed to the designers that a fast ship would require more freeboard—both unarmored freeboard forward and another foot of armored freeboard amidships. Perhaps the main armored deck could be sloped up forward as well. This might add about 1,375 tons in direct weight. But when such a weight was added, other weights in the ship had to increase proportionately—structure weight, for example, and horsepower (hence machinery weight)—so that a net increase of about 2,400 tons was expected. The 33-knot ship would reach 43,000 tons or even to the new limit of 45,000 tons. What had seemed a comfortable cushion of 5,000 tons between the initial design and treaty limit was beginning to shrink.

It had not disappeared entirely, however. To the General Board it seemed that there must be some way to gain more than 6 knots on an investment of 10,000 tons. Many 16in/50 guns, manufactured for the battleships and battle cruisers cancelled in 1922, remained in storage. Although they were heavier, for their size, than the more modern 16in/45 adopted for the 35,000-ton battleships, they were considered ballistically superior even to a proposed 18-inch gun. Surely their increased weight would matter very little on so great a displacement as 45,000 tons. On 14 April 1938 the General Board directed that the 33-knot study incorporate the more powerful weapon.

In March 1938 the hull designers began with dimensions of 880 × 108 × 33 feet, the great waterline length having been chosen to minimize wave-making resistance. On the basis of an estimated standard displacement of 43,000 to 45,000 tons, the full-load figure was set at 53,600. On this basis the ship would need about 230,000SHP, which could be supplied by eight boilers. By this time unit machinery arrangement was standard, and high power implied a great unit (turbine/boiler) compartment length of 64 feet. One torpedo hit could flood a space 128 feet long.

When the General Board decided to switch to the 16in/50 gun, it also relaxed its previous restriction on draft. Deeper draft made the hull easier to drive, the beam-to-draft ratio being second only to the length of hull in determining wave-making resistance. Now the power requirement could be cut, perhaps even to 200,000SHP. Shortening the hull would save weight. More weight was saved by concentrating the hull volume (and buoyancy) amidships where the heavy weights were. This accounts for the very unusual forward hull form which, because of its lack of buoyancy, made the ships wet. Finally, given deeper draft, it would be easier to position the the very large propellers required to transmit very high power into the water. The new hull also showed a pronounced bulbous bow and a twin-skeg stern generally similar to that adopted in the *North Carolina* class. It was justified partly on the ground of providing a clean flow of water to the propellers without entailing the weakness aft which might have been associated with a more conventional form sharply cut away. Outboard skegs (as in the *South Dakotas*) were rejected because they could not be aligned with the propeller shafts.

The twelve-gun, 27-knot, 45,000-ton study proceeded in parallel. It appears that the General Board wanted it to become the standard battleship type, the 33-knot ships being for special duties. Ultimately the slower ship evolved into the *Montana* class.

The development of the faster ship showed how little 10,000 tons actually were. On 16 April 1938 the designers presented their studies to the board. The 16in/50 turret weighed about 400 tons more than that already in use. There was an additional penalty due to its greater barbette diameter, 39feet4inches rather than the 37feet3inches of the 16in/45. The total was 1,600 tons, including barbette armor, and net impact on the ship was estimated at nearly 2,000 tons. Estimates showed 44,682 tons for the 16in/45 version of the 33-knot ship, compared with 46,551 for the 16in/50. Careful detail design might cut the latter figure but not by enough. The treaty had been stretched by 10,000 tons, but it was not to be broken.

The General Board's only hope was a lighter turret installation. BuOrd appeared to promise just that: a table of alternative turrets showed one carrying the old 16in/50 in a new slide on a barbette diameter of 37feet3inches; and a rotating weight per turret of 1,663 tons, a net saving, on three turrets and three barbettes, of 825 tons. The constructors estimated a net saving of 785 tons by adopting the new turrets and hoped for another 435 by minor reductions, such as a thinning of the underwater belt, half an inch cut from splinter protection, and a relaxation of the standard of protection to be given by the transverse armored bulkheads. Just as added direct weight produced far more added displacement, this reduction of 1,220 tons saved about 2,000 in final displacement, so that on 25 May the designers could claim that a 16in/50 ship could be built on 44,559 tons. They described the additional protection equivalent to the remaining 440 tons, but in fact everyone realized that the ship as built would grow by detail changes and that 440 tons was little enough margin.

This triumph was presented to the General Board on 2 June 1938, just as the three treaty powers agreed to the new 45,000-ton limit.

While C&R pressed ahead with contract plans, so that bids could be advertised for and contracts signed, BuOrd, entirely independent, proceeded with its turret design—the wrong turret design. Instead of the lightweight design it had listed, BuOrd developed a 39-foot barbette diameter type, a scaled-up version of the turrets of the *North Carolina* and *South Dakota* classes. The lighter weight alternative had been no more than a paper study, in which weight and volume were saved by excluding most of the advances incorporated in the new 16in/45 turrets.

For some reason neither bureau realized that ship and turret could not go together. That became obvious only when plans for both were virtually complete, in November. The General Board was incredulous. Detail work had eaten up the 440-ton margin, so that estimated displacement was already 45,155 tons. Clearly any gross redesign to accommodate the larger turret would breach the treaty limit. Chantry and his staff testified that their ship could not accept even a two-foot increase in barbette diameter. Since they represented larger holes in the upper (strength) deck, the forward barbettes would have to be farther apart if the length of solid deck between them (that is, deck strength) was to be maintained at its former value. No. 1 turret would therefore have to be farther forward, where the sheer rose rapidly (to keep the ship dry at 33 knots). It would therefore have to be

Table 14-3. Evolution of the *Iowa* Design, 1938

Scheme	I	IV	V	BB 61
Main Battery	9-16in/50	9-16in/45	9-16in	9-16in/50
Secondary Battery	20-5in/38	20-5in/38	20-5in	20-5in/38
Length(Wl)(Ft)	860	832	860	860
Beam(Ext)(Ft)	108-3	108-3	108-3	107-3
Std Dispt	46,585	44,540	44,560	45,155
Draft(Max Load)	35.96	35.96	35.96	35.65
Displacement(Max Load)	57,935	55,620	55,710	56,088
Draft(Battle)	34.71	34.71	34.71	34.55
Displacement(Battle)	55,685	53,440	53,460	53,959
SHP	230,000	230,000	200,000	200,000
Speed(Kts)	33	33	33	33
IZ(16in/45)	18-30	18-30	18-30	20.5-26.5*
IZ (16in/50)	21.8-32.1	21.8-32.1	21.8-3	24.5-28.5*
Radius (15Kts)	15,000	15,000	15,000	15,000
Belt(19 Deg on 30#)	12.2	12.2	12.2	12.1
Heavy Deck(On 30#)	5.1	5.1	5.1	5.1
Bomb Deck	60#	60#	60#	60#
Splinter Deck	25#	25#	25#	25#
Barbettes, CT	17.3	17.3	17.3	17.3
Turret Face	18	18	18	18
Turret, CT Roof	7.25	7.25	7.25	7.25
Transverse Bulkheads	13.5	13.5	11.3	11.3
Splinter Pro.	100#	100#	80#	
Armored Length	480	480	464ft	464
Weights(Tons):				
Hull	22,964	22,240	22,127	22,852
Hull Fittings	1756	1726	1756	1788
Protection	11,298	10,524	10,433	10,252
Machinery(Wet)	5000	5000	4700	4660
Armament	3187	3160	3160	3188
Ammunition	1310	1310	1310	1314
Equip&Outfit	505	498	505	471
Complement	192	192	192	232
Stores & Fresh Water	322	322	322	345
Aeronautics	54	54	54	54
Reserve Feed Water	500	500	500	760
Fuel Oil	8000	7850	7800	7621
Designed Displacement	55,088	53,376	52,859	53,959
Belt	5913	5730	5655	5322
Main Armored Deck	4440	4440	4300	4300
Bomb Deck	1892	1892	1830	1830
Splinter Deck	655	655	615	615
Transverse Bulkheads	734	626	626	569
Barbettes (Heavy)	1760	1590	1590	1584
Torpedo Bulkheads	3442	3442	3330	3488

NOTE: Scheme I is dated 20 April 1938, Schemes IV and V dated May 1938. Transverse bulkheads were generally designed for a 60 degree target angle, except for Scheme V, at 50 degrees. Compared with Scheme I, Schemes IV and V show weight savings due to a new type of 16in/50 turret with a barbette diameter of 37 feet 3 inches (BuOrd Scheme C), a thinner underwater belt, thinner splinter protection, and thinner transverse bulkheads. Barbette thicknesses on the centerline could also be reduced. Scheme IV had the same power as Scheme I but was shorter, for a saving of 1,700 tons. In Scheme V, length matched that of Scheme I but power was reduced. This saved not only direct weight but also weight due to the length of the armored box. The next step, the initial *Iowa* design, is dated November 1938, although studies designated "BB 61" had been made as early as June 1938. Asterisks indicate immune zones calculated on the basis of the 2,700-pound shell rather than the earlier 2,240-pound shell.

higher above the waterline. Now No. 2 turret would have to be made higher to clear it, and the conning tower would have to be raised as well, to keep sight lines clear. A member of the board asked the chief of BuOrd whether it did not occur to him, "as a matter of common sense," that C&R was vitally interested in which turret he was developing.

On the other hand, to go back to the 45-calibre gun would mean that 45,000 tons would have bought nothing more than six knots. Very fortunately BuOrd

The *Iowa*-class preliminary design model shows the kinship between this class and the *South Dakota*s. Note the hull slot, which was faired over when the ships were built. The model also shows the usual prewar complement of 12-foot navigational range-finders (including one atop No.3 turret) and range clocks (the forward one is just visible under the platform atop the forward fire control tower). Note, too, the usual pair of boat cranes. They were never fitted, and the planned boat stowage was replaced by three quadruple 40mm mounts on each side, on high platforms. When the *New Jersey* was being refitted in 1982, workmen found the original boat skids *under* these platforms. The object atop the conning towers is a spotting glass, which actually was installed aboard the *South Dakota*s but not aboard these ships.

was able to save the day by developing a new light-weight 50-calibre gun, whose smaller outside diameter permitted installation in a turret of the required dimensions. Remarkably, there were no reprisals. A somewhat analogous scandal of destroyer overweight, ascribed at this time to conflicts between C&R and BuEng, led in 1940 to the amalgamation of the two bureaus as BuShips and to the virtual demise of the BuEng hierarchy.

The design was essentially complete by the end of 1938. Detail design was assigned to the lead yard, the New York Naval Shipyard. Its main contribution was to devise a new machinery arrangement, more effectively subdivided, in November 1939. Caisson tests had shown that the planned system of underwater protection would break down over the unsupported length planned, about 64 feet. Additional

transverse bulkheads were needed. The yard's design staff broke up the "unit" spaces, the boilers paired side by side in separate compartments. Three new transverse bulkheads were added, and boiler rooms and engine rooms alternated. The engine rooms contained the main condensers and paired 1250 kW turbogenerators, and other auxiliaries were placed below the boilers. The prospective effect of flooding was roughly halved and the number of uptakes and hence of openings in the third deck greatly reduced. This was certainly worth the extra weight. Since the ships were being built in navy yards, no cost was associated with revising contract plans after contracts had been let. The increased subdivision added weight, which was acceptable because Britain and France had suspended the 1936 London treaty limits at the outbreak of war. Added draft was not acceptable; the yard added a foot of beam to provide the necessary underwater volume, for a total of 108 feet.

The *Iowa*s all shared the relatively unsatisfactory torpedo-protection system devised for the *South Dakota*s. Detail improvements in the last two ships, the *Illinois* and *Kentucky*, were proposed on the basis of new caisson tests made in 1943, in connection with the design of the *Midway*-class aircraft carriers. These changes were expected to improve protection by about 20 percent and would also reduce flooding in the event the system were penetrated. However, neither ship was ever completed, and the improvement could not be applied to the first four units of the class.

As a further complication, the fine (high-speed) hull form was very narrow near the end turrets and therefore near their magazines. For example, early in detail design it became necessary to correct a trim: the center of gravity was too far aft relative to the center of buoyancy of the hull. The simplest solution would have been to move the center of gravity of the ship forward by shifting the internal weights of the ship within the hull. However, No. 1 turret already had too little hull volume (for torpedo protection) abeam it. To move it forward would have made matters even worse. The designers therefore had to move the center of buoyancy (that is, some of the underwater hull volume) aft. They actually gained some protection (volume) around No. 3 turret.

The protection of No. 1 turret was discussed again in connection with the torpedoing of the *North Carolina* and the proposed improvements to the last two ships. After all, the only torpedo damage suffered by any of the new U.S. battleships had been in the same area on the *North Carolina*. The minor changes under consideration might have saved her from extensive flooding, but to provide No. 1 turret with protection similar to that of the rest of the ship would have required a blister and a consequent loss of 1.5 knots at full power. The General Board rejected it. Ten thousand tons had been spent to buy six knots; the General Board was not going to surrender a quarter of that gain.

Protection against shellfire duplicated that of the *South Dakota*, with an immune zone of 18,000 to 30,000 yards against the 16in/45 gun firing a 2,240-pound shell. It corresponded to 21,700 to 32,100 yards against the higher-velocity and hence flatter-trajectory 16in/50 firing the same shell. However, the armored box of the new ships was 464-feet long, compared with 360-feet for the *South Dakota*s, with a proportionate increase in weight. Just as the *Iowa*s were being designed, BuOrd adopted a new 2,700-pound, 16-inch shell, a magnificently destructive projectile, which shrank the immune zone (against the 16in/45) to only 5,300 yards (20,200 to 25,500

yards). A similar shell fired by the *Iowa* 50-calibre gun would penetrate anywhere except in the band between 23,600 and 27,400 yards. There could be no hope of providing protection against such attack and yet retain high speed on a reasonable displacement.

For example, the 12.2-inch sloped belt was equivalent to a vertical thickness of 13.5 inches, as in earlier U.S. battleships. It would have to be thickened to be equivalent to 16.4 inches, and the armor deck increased from 6.2 to 6.75 inches. The net increase in armor weight, including deck armor, would be about 2,300 tons. A July 1940 sketch design of a ship equivalent to the *Iowa* but protected against the heavy shell (and carrying the new 5in/54 secondary gun) showed a displacement of 51,500 tons. Even to hold it to this figure, the hull had to be filled out to such an extent that the 212,000SHP of the *Iowa* would suffice only for a little beyond 28 knots.

The side belt was closed fore and aft by 11.3-inch transverse bulkheads, which were expected to protect against shells striking at angles of 50 degrees or less, that is, from ships more than 50 degrees from dead ahead, at battle ranges. This had been relaxed from a 40 degree requirement to save 110 tons. However, a fast ship might well expect to come upon enemy units from very nearly dead astern, and in August 1940 it was proposed that the forward transverse bulkhead be increased to 14.5 inches, corresponding to an angle of 25 degrees from dead ahead (2,240-pound shell, 18,000 yards). At 25,000 yards such a bulkhead would protect at all angles. For the 2,700-pound shell fired by the 50-calibre gun, protection would be effective at all ranges for angles beyond 45 degrees, and beyond 23,000 yards at 30 degrees. Similar improvements were suggested in the other vertical armor, the conning tower, and the barbettes. BuShips estimated that the bulkhead would cost only 90 tons, the barbettes another 42. At so low a price there was no question of approval. On 27 August 1940 the secretary of the navy signed his endorsement for the change on BB 63-66. Armor had already been purchased for the first two ships, and their completion was considered too urgent to be worth delaying, even for considerably improved protection.

The main belt was continued aft by a narrow strake 13.5 inches thick, also sloped at 19 degrees, to protect steering leads and propeller shafts. In this area there was no STS in the outer hull, as flooding would be of relatively little consequence. The aft belt terminated as protection for the steering gear, which was covered by a 6.2 inch deck.

There was one effort to counter the new shell, in the turret face, whose area was so limited that improvement in it would cost very little. The original 18-inch face was replaced by a 17-inch plate backed

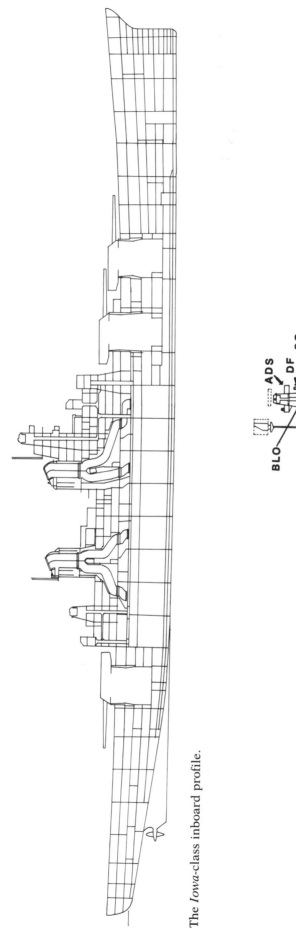

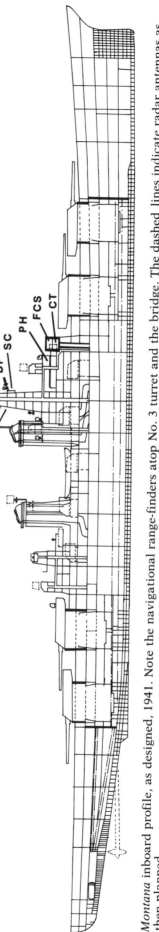

The *Iowa*-class inboard profile.

ADS

BLO

DF

SC

PH

FCS

CT

Montana inboard profile, as designed, 1941. Note the navigational range-finders atop No. 3 turret and the bridge. The dashed lines indicate radar antennas as then planned.

Newly completed, the *Iowa* (*above and facing*) is inclined at the New York Navy Yard, 28 March 1943. Her three conning tower levels, the lowest for the fleet commander, are visible. As in other U.S. battleships of this period, the upper level was a fire control station, with periscopes and radars protruding from it. The large platform above was the primary conn. By this time it was clear that the constricted walkway around the conning tower could not suffice. Moreover, an open bridge was useful (even essential) in air action. The mast structure accommodated a small chart room, which supplemented the chart house at the navigating bridge level further down. Surface lookouts occupied the next level, with its slits. The uppermost platform was the forward air defense station, with a 24-inch searchlight at its after side. It carried two sky lookout positions and two target designators.

by 2.5 inches of STS to give the equivalent of a single plate 18.75 inches thick. This added 17.5 tons to the turret weight. To compensate, the turret side plating was altered from 10 inches on 3/4 inches of mild steel backing to 9.5 inches of armor on 3/4 inches of STS (splinter armor) backing. The result could resist the heavy shell (fired by the 16in/45) at 20,000 yards. Even the improved turret face, however, could always be penetrated by the more powerful 16in/50—which suggests why the U.S. Navy considered that gun perfectly sufficient.

When the *Iowa* was laid down her design displacement was up to 45,873 tons, less than 2 percent over the treaty requirement. She was completed at a far greater displacement, but that was due in large part to the mass of light antiaircraft guns added during her construction.

Contracts for the first two ships, the *Iowa* (BB 61) and *New Jersey* (BB62), were signed on 1 July 1939 as part of the FY39 program. Both were built in navy yards because the three experienced private builders, Bethlehem Quincy, New York Shipbuilding, and Newport News, were all fully occupied with the previous *South Dakota* class.

No battleships were authorized under FY40, but in FY41 the Navy wanted to order two more, BB 63 and BB 64. The General Board originally planned to buy only three *Iowa*s but held a hearing on the new building program in June 1939. Admiral Robert L. Ghormley, the director of War Plans, argued that although three 45,000-ton battleships might match three Japanese *Kongo*s, the new Japanese battleships might well also have to be matched. Further, "in the strategic studies . . . the value is apparent of a strong

really threatening striking force of fast battleships accompanied by carriers and destroyers. . . . With four fast battleships, we would always be able to assemble such a striking group with at least three of them present."

The board concluded that both FY41 ships should be 33-knot types: the *Missouri* (BB 63) and *Wisconsin* (BB 64) were ordered on 12 June 1940. Subsequent battleships, however, would be of the heavier, slower type. Four fast battleships would be quite enough. Studies of the slower type were resumed under the tentative designation BB 65.

They in turn fell afoul the need for industrial mobilization. Numbers of ships, in capital classes as in destroyers and cruisers, could be attained only by means of a design freeze. On 19 July 1940 Congress authorized a large emergency program, partly to make up for the new threat created by the fall of France. The secretary of the navy ordered that most new ships duplicate the latest classes already on order. Despite General Board objections, two more *Iowa*s were ordered on 9 September: the *Illinois* (BB 65) and *Kentucky* (BB 66). Neither would be completed.

The first four ships were very nearly identical, except that USS *Iowa* was fitted as a force flagship and

so had an enlarged conning tower, as in the *South Dakota*. As a consequence, unlike her sister ships, the *Iowa* was never fitted with a quadruple Bofors gun atop No. 2 turret. Unlike the earlier ship, the *Iowa* did not sacrifice 5in/38.

The *New Jersey* ran her standardization trials in shallow water in October 1943. At 55,500 tons she required 162,277SHP to make 29.30 knots. She did not run such trials at higher speeds because results in shallow water were considered unrepresentative. In December, she attained 31.9 knots at 56,928 tons on about 221,000SHP. On the basis of model tests these results were equated to a trial speed of 32.5 knots at design power (212,000SHP) at a designed trial displacement of 53,900 tons. Later self-propelled model tests (January 1945) showed a speed of about 34 knots at 225,000SHP at the relatively light displacement of 51,209 tons. All of these data taken together suggest an operating speed of about 31 knots, bottom fouling and sea state having been taken into account. In the Pacific Fleet the *Iowa*s were considered good for 30.7 knots under average conditions. It appears that none of the ships ever ran full-power trials over a measured mile in deep water. By the time the *New Jersey* had been recommissioned in 1968,

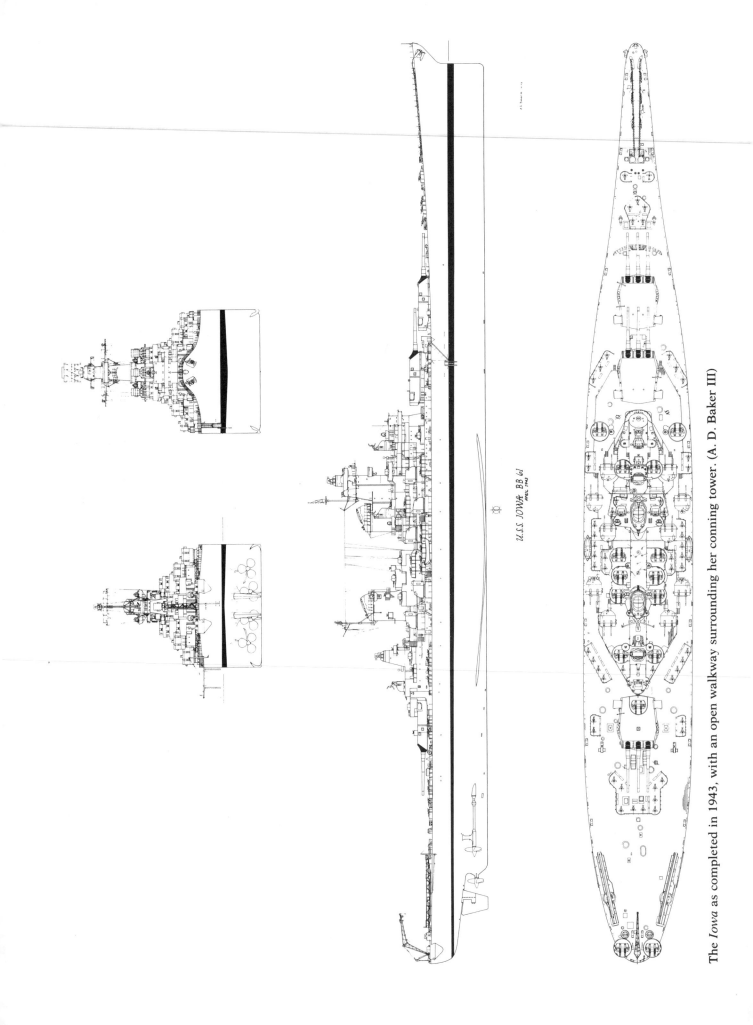

U.S.S. IOWA BB 61
APRIL 1943

The *Iowa* as completed in 1943, with an open walkway surrounding her conning tower. (A. D. Baker III)

The *Iowa*'s bridge structure is shown a few months after completion, with baffles installed to protect her primary conn and the open platform (which could serve as an open bridge) surrounding her forward 5-inch director. A Mark 51 director (for 40mm fire control) occupies the small tub just outboard of this open platform. The roof of the conning tower shows four periscopes and a Mark 3 fire control radar, an electronic analog to the optical spotting glass installed aboard the earlier modern battleships. Note also the radio direction-finding loop abaft the forward 5-inch director.

standard practice was to run machinery up to full power but not to run formal measured-mile trials.

The power plant was designed for up to 20 percent overload, that is, up to 254,000SHP, which might have allowed a fully loaded *Iowa* to reach about 33.5 knots or a lightly loaded ship to touch 35.4 (51,000 tons). Certainly the latter speed would be an unusual performance. In October 1948 BuShips estimated that, at full load, adding or subtracting 1,000 tons was equivalent to a quarter-knot, which suggests that 35 knots could be attained without grossly overloading the boilers only at a very light displacement indeed.

The endurance requirement was met and exceeded. In part this was a consequence of the enormous tankage. The USS *Iowa*, for example, could carry up to 9,520 tons of oil, of which she required only 7,892 to achieve her radius of action, fully 7,019 tons of which were necessary to fill her underwater protective system. On trials, USS *New Jersey* showed fuel consumption equivalent to a cruising radius of 20,150 miles at 15 knots, 4,830 at full power.

As built, all four ships differed in their bridgework and in their light AA batteries. The *New Jersey* and *Iowa* were completed without the Oerlikons right forward which later distinguished the entire class. *Iowa* never carried a quadruple Bofors on her No. 2 turret, since they would have blocked sight lines to the lower level of her enlarged conning tower. She

The *Iowa* is shown at sea in 1944, little changed since her commissioning. Note the 20mm guns atop No. 2 turret. *Iowa* was unique in never carrying a bulky 40mm mount there. It would have blocked the view from the lower row of conning tower slits, for flag use. The *South Dakota* had much the same limitation. The *Iowa* was not refitted with an enclosed bridge until late in the war.

did, however, carry gun tubs with Oerlikons in that position.

It was originally intended that all four ships be fitted with a narrow walkway around the conning tower, an arrangement similar to that in the *South Dakota*s. Experience during *Iowa*'s shakedown cruise showed that it was unsatisfactory. The *New Jersey* had the platform above her pilot house extended and the space between this level and the navigating bridge enclosed, the result being a prominent bridge with a curved front. The *Missouri* and *Wisconsin* were completed with similar but more spacious square-fronted bridges, a modification extended to the *New Jersey* during her 1945 refit. *Iowa* was fitted with the standard squared-off bridge at this time. Up to that point she could be distinguished by her open walkway and exposed conning tower.

Like the other modern battleships, the *Iowa*s were equipped with three main battery directors: two Mk 38 atop control towers, and a Mk 40 in the conning tower. There were also the usual quartet of Mk 37s for 5-inch control. Radar was not an element of the

original design, but by February 1942 plans called for one SK air-search radar, one SG surface-search set, and Mk 4 and Mk 8 radars for their Mk 37 and Mk 38 directors. In view of the requirement to keep waveguides short, Radar Plot was sited close to the main air-search antenna, halfway up the forward fire control tower in the *Iowa* and *New Jersey*. At the same level a big open bridge was built, so that the captain could be near Radar Plot during an air action. Before the ships could be completed, the *South Dakota* action had shown the urgent need for a second surface-search set. As they were fitted out, the first pair of ships had SGs fitted on a prominent platform above Radar Plot on the foremast and on the pole mainmast. In addition, on postshakedown refit both ships were fitted with a big Mark 3 ranging radar directly atop the conning tower, the analog of the rotating radar mounted on the conning towers of earlier U.S. battleships. It was later replaced by the much smaller Mark 27.

By 1944 the waveguide problem had been solved. The *Missouri* and *Wisconsin* did not have SG mounted

The *New Jersey* was completed with a *South Dakota*-type bridge, but it was soon enclosed, and she spent most of the war with the curved structure shown. Note the SG surface-search radar mounted on the face of her forward fire control tower. Such microwave radars originally had to be mounted close to their transmitters and receivers, to avoid major losses in waveguides. Once the problem had been solved, they could be moved to topmasts above the big air-search radars. The position thus vacated was then occupied by radar jammers.

before the fire control tower but rather on a fore topmast, which provided a 360 degree vantage. In addition, the *Missouri* had the new SK-2 parabolic dish in place of the previous SK. Both had the new Mk 27 ranging radar atop their conning towers, and Mk 12/22 on their 5-inch directors. Both earlier ships were refitted in 1945. *Iowa* received a new foremast with SK-2 and an SU surface-search radar in a radome on her topmast. Her after SG was relocated to a topmast, and a big SC-2 secondary air-search set fitted. As refitted in 1945, the *New Jersey* received SK-2 but not SU. She was fitted with a new lattice mainmast designed to accommodate flag hoists, as she was fleet flagship. It could, more importantly, support an SP height-finding radar. The new mast stood away from the second funnel, which supported it. The surface-search (SG) radar previously atop this mast was mounted on a bracket on its after leg. Both ships had their Mark 3 radars replaced by the new Mk 27 and their Mk 4s replaced by the newer Mk 12/22. Postwar the combination of Mk 12 and Mk 22

was replaced by the single dish of Mk 25, which appeared in these ships from 1952 onwards. For a time in 1953 the *New Jersey* had the new set only on her end directors.

In 1945 it was intended that all four ships receive the SP height-finder aft, but the *Wisconsin* refitted in 1945–46 with the SR "mattress" on her pole mainmast, and she went into reserve before anything else could be fitted. The *Iowa* and *Missouri* were fitted with SP and with a *New Jersey*-type lattice mainmast. Both of the active ships, the *Missouri* and *New Jersey*, were fitted with the new SR-3 air-search radar in 1948, the former ship retaining it, with a variety of later antennas and other modifications, through the Korean War. The other three were fitted with the related but more effective SPS-6 when they returned to service for Korea. The *Wisconsin* alone was later fitted with SPS-12. The *Missouri* was fitted with the SG-6 surface- and zenith-search radar in 1948, the others following suit when they were reactivated for Korea. The *Wisconsin*, which had never been fitted

The *Missouri* and *Wisconsin* were completed with enclosed square-faced bridges like this one. There were no baffles, but glass windshields could be raised to protect both primary and secondary conning positions. Note the siren bracketed to the side of the forward fire control tower, and the small Mark 27 radar that replaced the Mark 3 of earlier battleships atop the conning tower. Abaft it is a 36-inch searchlight. The newly completed *Missouri* is shown at the New York Navy Yard on 23 July 1944.

with the small SP dish, was refitted instead in 1953 with the new SPS-8 height-finder, which required a massive new mainmast. Her sisters were similarly refitted, and in the case of the *Iowa* the new mast was combined with kingposts for at-sea refueling in a 1955 refit. This system was later extended to the *Wisconsin*. All ships were laid up soon afterwards, the *Missouri* alone retaining the lattice mainmast fitted after World War Two.

Finally there was ECM equipment, most prominently the TDY jammer fitted in 1945–46, which in

the *Iowa* and *New Jersey* replaced the SG formerly mounted on the forward fire control tower. In the *Wisconsin* it occupied a platform projecting aft atop her fire control tower.

There was also the usual vast increase in antiaircraft weapons. The original design called for four quadruple 1.1-inch machine cannon (one each side above the bridge wings, one each side abeam the after control tower), and twelve water-cooled 0.50-calibre machine guns. In April 1941, they were ordered replaced by, respectively, quadruple 40mm and

The *Missouri* lies in Tokyo Bay, 27 August 1945. Additions include Mark 57 radar directors on the after fire control tower and just abaft the forward 5-inch director. She also has a TDY radar jammer just beneath her air defense station.

20mm guns. BuShips complained that this would add 100 tons and wanted any further 40mm compensated for by the removal of twin 5in/38s. The General Board refused. Surely a battleship had enough reserve weight to accept such additions. By 1945 the antiaircraft battery included twenty quadruple 40mm weighing (not including directors or splinter shields or even ammunition) 222 tons, which compares with 545 tons for the ten twin 5in/38.

Blast interference with either the main or the secondary battery governed the initial choice of 1.1-inch sites, but, as in other classes, it was ignored as the demand for light antiaircraft weapons grew. The *Iowas* benefited, compared with their 35,000-ton predecessors, from their great length, which allowed for a much better arranged antiaircraft battery. By October 1942, the assigned AA battery was six quadruple Bofors and forty Oerlikons, and BuShips had been ordered to increase this to ten quadruple Bofors and fifty-five Oerlikons. The *Iowa* was completed in February 1943, with *fifteen* Bofors and no fewer than sixty Oerlikons. Two additional 40mm guns were placed right aft abaft the catapults: three on each side abeam the after funnel on a special built-up structure (which replaced the boat stowage initially planned); one on each side on the 01 level abeam the

conning tower; and one on No. 3 turret. Oerlikons were added atop No. 2 turret and in other locations after her shakedown cruise in the summer of 1943. The *New Jersey* was completed with a quadruple Bofors atop No. 2 turret, for a total of sixteen. On postshakedown refits both ships were fitted with two mounts on the main deck just forward of No. 3 turret and with two forward of No. 2 turret, for a total of nineteen and twenty such mounts, respectively, including four main deck ones particularly subject to gun blast. The *Missouri* and *Wisconsin* were completed with all twenty quadruple 40mm.

On their postshakedown refits, the *Iowa* and *New Jersey* were fitted with an unusual position for two 20mm right in the bows, a feature that became characteristic of the entire class.

All of this extra armament cost weight, as BuShips had foreseen. By May 1945 full-load displacement was about 3,000 tons above the original design figure of 56,270 tons. The extra weapons and the radars also added men. The *Iowa* was designed for 91 officers and 1,760 enlisted men but ended World War Two with accommodations for 151 officers and 2,637 men, figures exceeded by the other ships in the class.

On the whole the *Iowas* seem to have been the only satisfactory American battleships of the Second

World War. The *North Carolina*s were deficient in ballistic protection. The *South Dakota*s were regarded as cramped even before they were laid down. The *Iowa*s were long enough to mount extensive light AA batteries and radar suits without very much interference. Almost above any other qualities, they were fast enough to keep up with the fast carriers. That alone dictated their retention in service to the exclusion of earlier classes.

In 1944, as new cruisers were being designed, a commander in BuShips, P. W. Snyder, reviewed the basic characteristics of the *Iowa*s. He felt that they incorporated a variety of errors, all of which could be corrected if speed were allowed to fall to about 30 knots. Snyder argued that the *Iowa*s were about 40 feet too long but that they needed about 6 feet more beam to achieve better torpedo protection and the more highly subdivided machinery arrangement of the new *Midway*-class carriers. A fuller hull form would also better protect No. 1 turret. Armor protection might then be increased to provide full immunity against the 2,700-pound shell. If the boilers could be lowered under the third deck, there would be no need for a splinter deck just under the second deck. Armored wiring tubes (as in the *Montana* design) could be used abaft the after armor bulkhead, and the extension of the armor deck aft to the steering gear eliminated. Finally, the machinery itself could be redesigned to save weight and space, and more emergency diesel generators could be provided. The ships had only two 250 kW units.

A more detailed analysis was made by a committee appointed by the commander-in-chief Pacific Fleet to make recommendations on the characteristics of ships and aircraft types based on war experience. The committee's 13 December 1945 report was based on extensive interviews with senior personnel who had had battle experience, and it is probably the best source for any evaluation of the *Iowa*s in action.

The report envisaged a postwar need for heavy support ships. The *Iowa*s were the ideal prototype.

> Any later postwar ship must have a speed at least equal to that of the postwar carriers. The *North Carolina*s and *South Dakota*s do not have such a speed. The *Iowa*s do. This quality, plus the lack of any major inherent deficiency or weakness, makes the *Iowa* class the logical prototype for future development. . . in all, the *Iowa*s must be considered better ships than any American or foreign predecessor or comtemporary. . . .
>
> In open sea and off soundings these ships are highly maneuverable, are not unwieldy or unhandy, and easily keep pace with carriers and smaller ships. The only time they seem uncomfortably large is when they are being handled in certain restricted harbors and inland waterways. . . . [Their] seaworthiness is excellent. They are steady gun platforms and have good stability in all conditions of loading and weather.

They have a good freeboard but are wetter, from Turret Two aft, than seems proper for ships of their size. This wetness seems due to the sudden and extreme widening of the hull lines just forward of Turret One. . . . The wetness of the present ships has been of no concern in the normally smooth South and Central Pacific but would be a decidedly undesirable feature if they were to be employed in other waters such as the North Atlantic. . . .

The report considered the loaded speed of about 31 knots inadequate for task force operations. This note was common in U.S. naval writing of the time and resulted in a demand for increased operating speed in such new ships as the *Mitscher*-class large destroyers. In addition, "destroyers report that the *Iowa* class are difficult to refuel from because of the bow wave peculiar to the class. Consideration should be given to relocating the fueling station to a better

The *New Jersey* (*above, facing, and following page*) was refitted in 1945, with the now-standard square-faced bridge. She is shown being inclined at Puget Sound on 24 June 1945, and on post-refit trials, 30 June 1945, at 18 knots. Her conning tower carries one large periscope (for her captain) and two smaller ones, with a Mark 27 radar abaft them. She has also been fitted with Mark 57 radar directors for her 40mm guns. Note the floater nets on No. 3 turret, and the folded-down splinter shield for the Mark 51 director controlling the 40mm guns atop it. The rails carried inclining weights. By measuring the changing list of the ship as the weights were moved, naval architects could calculate the ship's precise displacement and stability. The bow view emphasizes the unusual hull form of this class, with a long, narrow entry and then a sudden widening to a parallel midbody. It was not altogether successful, and it has been argued that a more conventional form might not have required as much power. However, the combination of displacement *and the Panama Canal limit* made the long parallel (constant-beam) section inevitable, and the unusual hull form was the result.

The *Wisconsin* at sea off Japan, 22 August 1945. Note that her mainmast carried, not the usual surface-search radar, but a second air-search set, an SC-2.

position.''* Berthing was cramped, a design complement of about 2,000 having grown to over 2,500, while at the same time masses of electronic equipment (with accompanying spare parts) had invaded the interior of the ship.

The bridge structure came in for special criticism. The board wanted to eliminate conning towers altogether. Many previous such proposals had been defeated entirely on the basis of the experience of the *South Dakota* during the night battle of Guadalcanal, which was surely not representative. Yet another defect was the arrangement of light antiaircraft guns. Surely the light weapons could be moved futher aloft to give them better sky arcs. And surely

* The fueling-at-sea station was moved further aft when the ships were modified with kingposts, or when they were reconstructed in the 1980s.

there was a better way of arranging the 5in/38s than to place them in two parallel lines on either side of the ship, where they had inadequate end fire.

But for all this, the *Iowa*s were the only American capital ships suited to postwar carrier task force operations, and in that capacity they often served as fleet flagships in the postwar period—and sometimes bore out the board's dismal view of their suitability for the North Atlantic. Their long endurance and high sea speed inspired their use in a number of projects—missile ships, fast transport/fire support, underway replenishment—to use them even after the battleship as a type had been declared obsolete. (Indeed, turbines intended for the unfinished BB 65 and 66 ended up in four underway replenishment ships.) Finally, their endurance and speed (and firepower) have led to the current program of modernization and reactivation (see Chapter 17).

15

The *Montana* Class

If there is a moral to the story of these, the last U.S. battleships, it is that even when designers are nearly unconstrained in displacement, they find it very difficult to meet a wide range of conflicting requirements. The *Montana*s were the culmination of the American tradition of emphasizing firepower and protection at the expense of speed. They began as an elaboration of the slow battleship studies of 1938, that is, of the more traditional alternative to the fast *Iowa*.

The most important factor in the new design was the new 2,700 pound 16-inch shell, which greatly increased the penetrating power of existing guns. There was also interest in a heavier secondary weapon, to deal with large Japanese destroyers. For a time BuOrd hoped that its new 6in/47 dual-purpose gun, which was also planned for the new 8,000-ton light cruiser, would be adopted. In fact this weapon was not ready until after World War Two, but the *Montana* design included a new 5in/54.

In mid-1939, with the FY41 program under consideration, two fast battleships (BB 61 and 62) were included in the FY40 program. These were clearly a special type. The only question was when the navy should revert to a slower and more conventional battleship. Several witnesses at a General Board hearing that June strongly advocated two repeat *Iowa*s for FY41, and slow ships from FY42 onwards. On this basis it could be assumed that BB 65 would be the prototype slow battleship.

The General Board now asked C&R to sketch 45,000-ton, twelve-gun battleships protected against the new shell, and capable of 27 knots or more. C&R referred back to its 1938 studies, showing that 785 to 800 feet was the optimum length for a four-turret battleship capable of 27 knots using the *South Dakota* power plant. Any shorter hull would require greater engine power, and the extra weight would offset any saving

in hull weight. Moreover, the armored box could not have been shortened because the distance between Nos. 2 and 3 turrets was already at a minimum.

On these weights, the best C&R could do was protect against the 2,250-pound shell, and even then the design was very tight. Scheme BB 65A, with twenty 5in/38, essentially a *South Dakota* with an additional turret and 50-calibre 16-inch guns, would displace 45,435 tons (standard). C&R estimated that the same ship, protected against the 16in/45 firing the heavier shell, would displace about 47,800 tons. In BB 65B, with twelve 6in/47, displacement rose to 45,658 tons. The addition of four more 6in/47 would cost 492 tons directly, plus more for the longer armored box. In BB 65C, adoption of quadruple turrets saved 800 tons on the turrets and another 800 on the armored box. Because this ship came to only 43,800 tons, it was suggested that perhaps protection against the 2,700-pound shell could be provided. Finally, BB 65D was 65C with twelve 6in/47 and came in at 44,021 tons.

Given the obvious potential of the quadruple-turret designs, C&R tried to protect them against the heavy shell at ranges between 18,000 and 26,000 yards. Thus, the BB 65E (revision of 65C) would displace 44,684 tons. Deck armor would match that of the *Iowa*, the increased smashing power of the shell being reflected in a reduced immune range. Most of the additional weight would go into the belt. To achieve an *Iowa*-class immune zone (18,000 to 30,000 yards) would take a 16.4-inch belt and a 6.75-inch deck, with 21.1-inch (rather than 17.3-inch) barbettes. Captain Chantry, chief of Preliminary Design, suspected that the ship should displace 50,000 or even 55,000 tons.

Moreover, it was by no means clear that the proposed design was feasible. The quadruple turrets would be extremely heavy, with a weight on rollers of 2,064 tons, compared with 1,622 for the triple 16in/

This model, prepared by the New York Navy Yard in November 1941 shows almost the final version of the design, with 40mm guns aboard; four quadruple mounts are visible; and the ship carries radars and directors typical of the first year of the war.

Table 15-1. Design Studies of July 1939

	Iowa	*BB65A*	*BB65B*	*BB65C*	*BB65C-1*	*BB65C-2*
Main Battery	9-16in/50	12-16in/50	12-16in/50	12-16in/50(4)	11-16in/50(3)	12-16in/50(4)
Secondary Batt.	20-5in/38	20-5in/38	12-6in/47		20-5in/38	20-5in/38
Displacement	45,075	45,435	45,658	43,800	43,580	46,168
Max. Load	55,710					
Length	860	800	800	800	800	800
Beam	107-3	108	108	108	108	108
Draft	35.96	36	36	36		
Power				130,000		
Speed				27.5		
Belt	12.1	Protected				
Deck	4.75	As				
IZ Vs.	16in/45	*Iowa*				(1)
IZ	18-30					
Power	200,000	130,000	130,000	130,000		
Speed	33	27	27	27		
Weights(Tons):						
Hull	23,807	22,554	23,134		22,077	22,592
Fittings	1757	1570	1506		1616	1616
Protection	10,163	11,016	11,444		10,037	11,674
Engineering(Wet)	4389	3300	3452		3852	3952
Battery	3092	3954	3214		3371	3591
Ammunition	1422	1646	1749		1645	1761
Equip&Outfit	502	455	439		439	439
Stores	489	546	489		489	489
Aero	54	54	54		54	54

Table 15-1. Continued

	BB65F	*BB65G*	*BB65H*	*BB65I*	*BB65J*
Main Battery	9-16in/50	9-16in/50	9-16in/50	9-16in/50	12-14in/50
Secondary Batt.	20-5in/38	20-5in/38	20-5in/38	20-5in/38	20-5in/38
Displacement	41,627	44,654	43,466	44,432	44,380
Max. Load					
Length	800	800	800	800	800
Beam	108	108	108	108	108
Draft					36
Power					
Speed					
Belt	Protected	15.4	15.4	15.4	14.3
Deck	As	6.2		5.5	5.5
IZ Vs.	*Iowa*	16in/50(Heavy)	16in/45(Heavy)	16in/50(Heavy)	16in/50(Heavy)
IZ		18-30	18-30	18-30	20-30
Weights(Tons):					
Hull	21,426	22,598	22,598	22,239	22,407
Fittings	1616	1616	1616	1616	1616
Protection	9487	11,342	10,154	11,279	11,081
Engineering(Wet)	3652	3652	3652	3652	3752
Battery	3042	3042	3042	3042	2817
Ammunition	1422	1422	1422	1422	1225
Equip&Outfit	439	439	439	439	439
Stores	489	489	489	489	489
Aero	54	54	54	54	54

NOTE: Except as noted, immune zones (in thousands of yards) are against 16in/45 guns firing light (2,240-pound) projectiles. The 18,000 to 30,000 yard zone corresponds to 20,500 to 26,500 yards against a heavy (2,700-pound) projectile, and to 24,600 to 27,700 yards against a 16in/50 firing the heavy projectile. Note that data for *Iowa* refer to the design as ordered in 1939, *not* to the modified design actually built. Main battery arrangements: (1) is triple-triple-quadruple; (2) is quadruple-twin-quadruple; (3) is quadruple-triple-quadruple; (4) is three quadruple mounts. Protection: (1) belt vs. 16in/56 at 21,000 yards, deck vs. 16in/45 at 27,000 yards; (2) belt vs. 16in/56 at 22,000 yards, deck vs. 16in/45 at 26,000 yards.

BB65C-3	BB65C-4	BB65C-5	BB65C-6	BB65D	BB65E
11-16in/50(3)	11-16in/50(3)	10-16in/50(2)	10-16in/50(1)	12-16in/50(4)	As C But
20-5in/38	20-5in/38	20-5in/38	20-5in/38	12-6in/47	New Main Protection
45,191	45,272	44,793	44,840	44,021	44,793
800	800	800	800	800	800
108	108	108	108	108	108
				36	36
	14.9	14.3	14.3	12.1	13.2
	4.8	5.5	5.5	4.75	4.75
(1)	16in/50(Heavy)(2)	16in/50(Heavy)	16in/50(Heavy)	16in/45	16in/45(Heavy)
	19-27.8	20-30	20-30		18-26.5
22,373	22,102	22,413	22,394		
1616	1616	1616	1616		
11,352	11,104	10,704	10,795		
3852	3852	3752	3752		
3371	3371	3288	3263		
1645	1645	1538	1538		
439	439	439	439		
489	489	489	489		
54	54	54	54		

50 of the *Iowa*s. That in turn would require increased electrical power, probably 10,000 kW rather than the 7,000 kW of the *South Dakota*s. BuEng estimated that this would increase the length of the power plant (that is, of the armored box) by 16 feet, adding 400 tons. C&R had allowed for only 205 tons of growth.

At the subsequent General Board hearing the issue of the 18-inch gun was raised, but Admiral Furlong of BuOrd argued that a 16in/56 (a conceptual gun) would be even better, with a greater range. That option was later rejected because it had a gun tube life of only 120 rounds. Finally, the War Plans Division clearly favored firepower (four three-gun turrets) over protection.

Preliminary Design now sacrificed one triple turret for protection, leaving three. This series began with BB 65F, essentially a 16in/50 version of the *South Dakota* with *Iowa* splinter and secondary protection, at 41,627 tons. The next step was vertical protection against the 16in/50 (18,000 yards), and horizontal against the 16in/45 (30,000 yards), both with the heavy shell, at 44,654 tons (BB 65G). BB 65H and BB 65I were slightly modified versions, with protection adjusted against, respectively, the 16in/45- and /50-calibre guns.

Chantry knew that none of these alternatives would particularly excite advocates of increased firepower. However, that all were feasible suggested that ten or even eleven guns might be mounted on a 45,000-ton hull. For example, a 4-3-4 gun arrangement and *Iowa* protection displaced 43,580 tons. Belt protection against the 16in/56, the best penetrator (21,000 yards), and deck protection against the 16in/45 (27,000 yards) increased this to 45,191 tons, just over the limit. A slight relaxation of the immune zone (to 22,000-26,000 yards) and a 4-4-3 arrangement could be had on 44,672 tons, which must have been very encouraging. A ten-gun ship (4-2-4) protected against the 16in/50 between 20,000 and 30,000 yards (14.3-inch belt on 351-pound STS backing and 5.5-inch deck on 1.25-inch backing) would displace only 44,793 tons.

Finally, BB 65J sacrificed gun *calibre* for protection. Four triple 14-inchers and full protection against the 16in/50 between 20,000 and 30,000 yards would cost 44,380 tons. Chantry suspected that one of the turrets could be replaced by a quadruple mount on about 45,000 tons.

On the other hand, the properly protected four triple 16in/50 ship would displace 46,668 tons. If it were shaved to 45,000 tons, it would actually have a *negative* immune zone against the 16in/50, its belt penetrable at a range 700 yards less than the range of deck penetration. Chantry was also able to rule out the 18-inch ship. On 45,000 tons he could provide only six guns. He favored a 3-3-4 arrangement, which

The New York Navy Yard model seen from astern. Note the radar mast bracketed to the after funnel. Presumably, had the ship been built, 40mm guns would have been mounted on the two superfiring turrets and abaft the catapults. Others would have replaced the boats and the boat cranes.

would place the heavy quadruple turret aft, where there would be plenty of buoyancy to support it. During the summer and fall of 1939, this version was developed with sixteen, eighteen, or twenty of the new 5.4-inch guns.* The General Board met on 15 September to develop final characteristics, but clearly

---

* The 5.4-inch gun was never built. By 1941 it had been superseded by a 5in/54, which was produced and which became the secondary battery planned for the *Montana*s. It was never actually mounted in twin form, but in single form it armed the *Midway* class.

no one was very happy with the quadruple turret. Even the escalated treaty limit of 45,000 tons was proving too tight.

With the outbreak of war, however, the London Treaty of 1936 was clearly abrogated, a situation that also saved the contemporary *Cleveland*-class cruiser design. On 24 October 1939, Admiral John W. Greenslade of the General Board asked for two twelve-gun battleship studies, each protected against the 16in/50 with heavy shells, at ranges between 18,000 and 30,000 yards, one design for 27.5 and one for 32.5 knots. Each would have a secondary battery of about twenty 5in/38. Rough estimates based on the earlier four-turret studies suggested that the first ship would displace about 50,000 tons. The second estimate was based on the *Iowa*, with an extra turret, increased armor, and increased length to maintain speed: 55,000 tons. At this time beam was still limited by the dimensions of the Panama Canal locks.

Both estimates turned out to be wildly optimistic. As the design grew, Preliminary Design was periodically asked to develop an *Iowa*-like ship with improved protection as a more economical alternative. At the same time, there was a prospect that the fundamental Panama Canal limit itself might be relaxed. As early as March 1938, C&R, mindful of the advantages of increased beam, had agitated for new wider locks and also for wider graving docks at the naval shipyards (132 feet at Puget Sound and Pearl Harbor). On 12 February 1940 the secretary of the navy asked the secretary of war to make the new (third) set of locks 140-feet wide. He therefore removed the old limit on battleship beam. Money was appropriated in the FY40 budget, for completion about 1945-46. The new wide locks would be armored against air attack, and they would normally be reserved for U.S. warships. Merchant ships and foreign warships would be able to use them only when another set of locks was being overhauled or when the remaining set could not handle the load. Even that would not be permitted in any crisis. The new lock project was suspended in wartime, but it was briefly revived postwar, and the estimated new lock dimensions set the beam of the first postwar carrier design.

In mid-January 1940, Preliminary Design reported that the 27.5-knot ship, powered by a *South Dakota* plant and immune between 20,000 and 30,000 yards, could be built on 51,500 tons (840 x 114 x 36 feet). If the new 5in/54 (which had replaced the 5.4in) replaced the 5in/38, displacement would rise to 53,500 tons. The fast battleship, 1,000 x 115 feet, would be much larger. A speed of 33 knots would require 318,000SHP (63,500 tons standard, 76,200 tons fully loaded). The existing *Iowa* power plant could drive a 58,000-ton hull at 31.75 knots. Alternatively, the larger power plant could drive a slightly smaller hull (61,500 tons) at just over 34 knots.

Table 15-2. Sketch Designs of August–September 1939

	BB65-A	BB65-B	BB65-C	BB65-D	BB65-E
Main Battery	12-16in	12-16in	12-16in(3 × 4)	12-16in/50(4)	12-16in/50(4)
Secondary Batt.	20-5in	12-6in/47	20-5in	12-6in	20-5in/38
Secondary Pro.	2.5	2.5	2.5		
Displacement Max. Load	46,668	46,896	45,000	45,308	44,793
Length	800	800	800	800	800
Beam	108	108	108	108	108
Draft	36	36	36	35	
Power	130,000	130,000	130,000		
Speed	27.5	27.5	27.5		
Belt				Protected as *Iowa*	
Deck					
IZ Vs.	Protected as *Iowa* Class				16in/45(heavy)
IZ					18-
Weights(Tons):					
Hull	23,219	23,643	22,535	22,959	22,535
Fittings	1616	1506	1616	1506	1616
Protection	11,413	11,684	10,454	10,825	10,847
Engineering(Wet)	3952	3959	3952	3952	3972
Battery	3725	3380	3700	3355	3700
Ammunition	1761	1749	1761	1749	1761
Equip&Outfit	439	439	439	439	439
Stores	489	489	489	489	489
Aero	54	54	54	54	54

In each case, protection followed that of the *South Dakota* and *Iowa* classes, with an internal sloped belt 14.2-inches thick (on 35-pound STS backing) and a 5.5-inch armor deck (50-pound STS backing). To bring the inner edge of the immune zone in 2,000 yards, to 18,000, would require that the belt be thickened to 15.3 inches. Similarly, to extend the outer edge by 2,000 yards, to 32,000, would require an increase in deck armor to 6.2 inches. Any internal belt would be combined with 60-pound (1.5-inch) STS plating spread over the outside of the hull at the waterline. Equivalent external belts would be 14.6- and 15.75-inches thick, without any outer layer, but it would be difficult to work a 19 degree slope into the ouside of the hull.

On 16 February the General Board asked for new studies, all with draft limited to 36 feet:

—A modified *Iowa* (BB 65-1) trading slightly reduced speed (31 knots) for extra protection (18,000 to 30,000 yards) and an enlarged *Iowa* (BB 65-2) with heavy protection and 33-knot speed. The latter, 980-feet long, would displace 53,500 tons.

—A twelve-gun type (BB 65-5) immune to 32,000 yards, with a speed of 28 knots: 57,500 tons, 930 feet, 150,000SHP.

—A twelve-gun, 31-knot ship (BB 65-6), 1050 x 118 feet, 64,500 tons with an *Iowa* power plant, 212,000SHP.

—A 33-knot, twelve-gun ship (BB 65-7), protected to 30,000 yards: 65,000 tons, requiring 320,000SHP.

—A corresponding ship (BB 65-8) protected between 18,000 and 32,000 yards, on the same hull, which would displace 67,000 tons, with 366,000SHP.

BB 65-3 and -4 were more developed versions of the earlier 28-knot, twelve-gun designs, with an immune zone extending from 20,000 yards and displacing 52,500 and 54,500 tons, respectively, with 5in/38 or 5in/54 secondaries. They had excessive draft because they had been developed before the decision had been made to limit draft to 36 feet.

In each case except for the very large BB 65-7 and -8, machinery plants would be based on existing ones: the 130,000SHP of the *South Dakota*, the 150,000SHP of two *Atlanta*-class light cruisers, or the 212,000SHP of an *Iowa*. Anything larger would require turbo-lectric drive, which in turn would increase weight and volume out of proportion. For example, 320,000SHP would fill 308 feet of a 590 foot armored

Table 15-3. Designs of January–February 1940

	BB65-1	BB65-2	BB65-3	BB65-4	BB65-5A	BB65-6
Main Battery	12-16in/50	12-16in/50	12-16in/50	12-16in/50	12-16in/50	12-16in/50
Secondary Batt.	20-5in/38	20-5in/54	20-5in/38	20-5in/54	20-5in/54	20-5in/54
Displacement	51,388	53,312	51,500	53,500	56,600	62,000
Trial Disp't		53,500	61,700	64,000	67,800	74,400
Length	840	860	840	870	900	1000
Beam	113	113	114	114	114	115
Draft	36	34.5	36	36	35	36
Power	130,000	130,000				
Speed	27.5	27.5				31
Belt	15.3	15.3	14.2	14.2	15.3	15.3
Deck	5.5	5.5	5.5	5.5	6.2	6.2
IZ Vs.	16in/50(Heavy)	16in/50(Heavy)	16in/50(Heavy)	16in/50(Heavy)	16in/50(Heavy)	16in/50(Heavy)
IZ	18-30	18-30	20-30	20-30	18-32	18-32
Weights(Tons):						
Hull	25,268	26,151	25,402	26,549	28,197	31,925
Fittings	2140	2200	1837	1884	1900	1950
Protection	12,468	12,764	12,823	13,176	14,273	15,530
Engineering(Wet)	3952	3952	3952	3952	3952	3952
Battery	3730	1/2 5990	3730	4046	4046	4046
Ammunition	1773	1/2	1773	1903	1903	1903
Equip&Outfit	500	520	500	500	500	575
Stores	553	675	552	562	565	565
Aero	54	54	54	54	54	54

box. By way of contrast, the 130,000SHP *South Dakota* plant, which was relatively compact, was only 176 feet long.

The other major design issue was internal vs. external armor. By now, with treaty restrictions gone, it was no longer clear that the weight saving inherent in internal armor was worthwhile. External armor would be less expensive to install and would be much easier to repair in the event of battle damage. Finally, waterline hits would flood portions of any internally protected ship.

Initial studies showed that internal armor saved about 2 tons per foot of waterline armor in the 57,500-ton, twelve-gun design and that it would be difficult to protect an externally armored ship against underwater-trajectory shells. Even so, by mid-March, external armor had been chosen. The main problem was that the slope of the armor left too little waterline beam for stability after battle damage. The designers could either thicken the belt (and reduce its slope) or move the belt bodily outboard, increasing beam and retaining the full 19 degree slope. They tried a series of alternatives, beginning with internal armor on a 114 foot waterline beam. If beam at the protective deck (that is, armor deck weight) and immersed section area were held constant (the latter by blistering underwater), waterline beam shrank to 108 feet, and stability was inadequate. If the belt

were sloped much less steeply, to maintain waterline beam, it had to be made much thicker. Ultimately, therefore, both waterline beam and beam at the protective deck had to be increased. The design finally submitted to the General Board, about 21 March, showed a waterline beam of 116 feet and an underwater beam of 118. The cost was 707 tons: 504 tons for 504 feet of armored box and 203 for additional deck armor (0.4 tons per foot).

At this stage the designers had not yet provided special protection against underwater hits. The protection inherent in the earlier internal-armor designs had been lost.

Two more schemes, BB 65-9 and -10, were developed late in June. BB 65-9 was BB 65-3 with the inner edge of the immune zone moved inwards to 18,000 yards (it matched BB 65-5 except that the outer edge was moved inwards from 32,000 to 30,000 yards). It lay between the two, 880 feet long, 53,500 tons, 130,000SHP for 28 knots. BB 65-10 was a similar ship with nine guns, 48,000 tons. The range from BB 65-1 through -10 covered the entire spectrum of possibilities: fast ships, slow but well-protected ships, and intermediates.

The General Board met again on 9 July 1940. With the fall of France, Congress was about to pass a massive new authorization program (for the "two-ocean Navy") and there was intense pressure to build up

BB-Y1	BB-Y2	BB-Y3	BB65-7	BB65-8B	BB65-8C
12-16in	12-16in	12-16in	12-16in/50	12-16in/50	12-16in/50
20-5in/54	20-5in/54	20-5in/54		20-5in/54	
63,500	58,000	61,500	63,000	66,000	66,700
76,200	69,500	73,700	75,500	79,000	80,000
1000	1000	1000	1000	1050	1100
115	115	115	118	116	116
36	35	36	35	35	35
318,000	212,000	318,000		320,000	
33	31.75	34 +		33	
14.2	14.2	14.2	14.2	15.3	15.3
5.5	5.5	5.5	5.5	6.2	6.2
16in/50(Heavy)	16in/50(Heavy)	16in/50(Heavy)	16in/50(Heavy)	16in/50(Heavy)	16in/50(Heavy)
20-30	20-30	20-30	20-30	18-32	18-32
32,026			31,880	33,648	34,358
2610			1950	1984	1984
14,544			15,037	16,000	16,000
		5700	5700	5700	5700
5990			4046	4046	4046
			1903	1903	1903
620			575	600	600
750			565	565	565
60			54	54	54

sufficient numbers of ships to fight both Germany and Japan. Many feared, for example, that Britain, too, would fall, and that the United States would have to deal with the bulk of the Royal Navy, in German hands. Under these circumstances, the decision was made to freeze designs for speed of production. That is why, for example, the interim *Cleveland*-class light cruiser was built despite the existence of sketch designs for a much more satisfactory, albeit larger, ship. The General Board argued against this policy, fearing that it would result in large numbers of inferior ships. In each warship category, it tried to gain an agreement that the design freeze would extend only so far and that a superior design would be adopted within a short time. In the case of the battleship, it sought a design change beyond BB 66.

That would leave the United States with six very fast battleships and six slow ones. The new battleship, then, might well be considered the prototype of the *next* six. The very large fast ships were clearly too expensive. Captain R. S. Crenshaw of War Plans favored an intermediate speed, 30 or 31 knots, on the ground that Japan had already gone to 30 (which we now know was untrue). A slow battle line might be unable to force an inferior enemy to battle. Admiral Greenslade of the General Board favored BB 65-5 as the ultimate in sturdiness, but Crenshaw objected that 8,000 tons and 3 knots bought only a triple turret

and 0.7 inches in deck armor. Was an extra turret worth 10 or 11 percent more displacement (as in BB 65-9 vs. BB 65-10)? Any very large ship would be limited in her ability to use existing harbors and drydocks.

Captain Griffin of Fleet Training considered very high battleship speed excessive, given limitations on supporting ships. Cruisers could not reach 35 knots, so it seemed unwise to demand 33 in battleships. Admiral Leigh Noyes of the Communications Division agreed. He preferred BB 65-5.

Admiral Van Keuren, chief of BuShips, testified that he could no longer design a satisfactory battleship on 45,000 tons. Displacement might go as high as 100,000 but in that case the draft might be excessive. He preferred BB 65-6, a 31-knot, twelve-gun ship protected between 18,000 and 32,000 yards.

BuOrd favored the twelve-gun designs. Armor would be the major bottleneck. Existing output was 40,800 tons per year, which was scheduled to rise to 52,000 tons per year within six months. After that a new plant (25,000 tons per year) would be required. Plant construction would take about another year. Even then a new ship would be delayed six to seven months, because of armor production limitations. As the new plant would cost $36 million, the bureau was anxious to know whether it would be needed. The first small increase in armor production would

Table 15-4. Sketch Designs, March–July 1940

	BB65-1	BB65-2	BB65-3	BB65-4	BB65-5	BB65-6
Main Battery(16in/50)	9	9	12	12	12	12
Secondary Batt.	20-5in/38	20-5in/38	20-5in/38	20-5in/54	20-5in/54	20-5in/54
Displacement	50,500	53,500	52,500	54,500	57,500	64,500
Trial Disp't	60,000	63,000	62,500	64,500	68,000	76,000
Length	900	980	860	870	930	1050
Beam(Wl)	110	111	114	114	116	118
Beam Below Wl	112	113	116	116	118	121
Draft	34.5	34.5	36	36	35	35
Depth of Hull	54.5	56	54.5	54.5	54.5	56
Est. GM	8.76	9.95	8.77	7.77	8.80	8.72
Power	212,000	212,000	130,000	150,000	150,000	212,000
Speed	31	33	28	28	28	31
Belt	15.75	15.75	14.6	14.6	15.75	15.75
Deck	5.5	5.5	5.5	5.5	6.2	6.2
IZ	18-30	18-30	18-30	20-30	18-32	18-32
Weights(Tons):						
Hull	25,647	27,733	26,106	27,324	29,239	33,600
Fittings	1806	2022	1837	1884	1900	1950
Protection	12,111	12,610	12,873	13,176	14,273	15,694
Engineering(Wet)	4390	4390	3952	3952	3952	4689
Battery	3042	3042	3730	4046	4046	4046
Ammunition	1422	1422	1422	1903	1903	1903
Equip&Outfit	460	483	500	500	500	575
Stores	524	524	555	562	562	565
Aero	54	54	54	54	54	54

NOTE: All immune zones are computed for the 16in/50 gun firing heavy projectiles. They are expressed in *thousands* of yards.

be felt in about eight months, the second in six more, and full production would be available eighteen months from go-ahead. That was quite apart from problems in producing very thick armor, due to limitations in the capabilities of the armor presses themselves. For example, in the *Iowa*s it had been necessary to use a 17-inch turret face plate on 2.5-inch backing rather than a single 18-inch thickness.

Preliminary Design now conducted a fresh series of studies at the request of members of the General Board:

—BB 65-5A, in which power (212,000SHP) was traded for length.

—A pair of studies, not completed, for ten-gun (3-2-2-3) ships, one limited to the old Panama Canal dimensions (975 x 108 feet) and one unlimited. The former lacked stability, and the latter was dropped in favor of twelve-gun ships.

—Nine-gun studies derived from BB 65-1 and -2: BB 65-11 and -12. In BB 65-11A, 212,000SHP drove an 820-foot, 52,000-ton hull, protected between 18,000 and 32,000 yards, at 28 knots. BB 65-12 was a 54,000-ton, 32-knot ship with an *Iowa* power plant and 5in/54 secondaries.

—BB 65-13 was similar to the *Iowa* except for full protection, 5in/54 secondaries, and trial draft increased from 34.5 to 35 feet. Speed fell to 28 knots. The object was to develop a fully pro-

tected battleship capable of transiting the Panama Canal (that is, with a 108-foot beam), with minimum length, and with her underwater body filled out to match the required displacement. This proved difficult. On 51,500 tons the ship could barely make 28 knots, and any increase in topweight would be disastrous. The underwater hull would have to be filled out to add stabiliy, and speed would be lost. Moreover, this design had to be internally armored.

The General Board had already decided in favor of BB 65-5A, the twelve-gun ship with the *Iowa* power plant, protected against heavy shells beween 18,000 and 32,000 yards. By this time the formal characteristics included references to a lower armor belt that would protect against underwater shell hits. This was an internal sloped belt, similar in principle to the magazine protection of the *North Carolina*, but made continuous to cover the machinery spaces as well.

Hoping that a new battleship design would be approved for BB 67 and beyond, the General Board submitted new characteristics, which Secretary of the Navy Frank Knox approved on 19 August 1940. This approval did not *in itself* imply approval of construction. Characteristics for improved light cruisers, which were never scheduled for production, were also approved at about this time. Given the new bat-

BB65-7	BB65-8	BB65-9	BB65-10	BB65-11	BB65-11A	BB65-12	BB65-13
12	12	9	9	9	9	9	9
20-5in/54	20-5in/54	20-5in/38	20-5in/38	20-5in/54	20-5in/54	20-5in/54	20-5in/54
65,000	67,000	53,500	48,000	52,000	52,000	54,000	51,500
77,000	82,000	63,700	57,500	61,500	61,500	63,500	62,500
1000	1050	880	830	860	820	950	860
118	120	114	110	112	112	112	108
121	125	116	112				
35	35	36	36	35	35	35	35
56	58	54.5	54.5				
8.72	8.93						
320,000	320,000	130,000	130,000	150,000	212,000	212,000	212,000
33	33	28	28	28 +	28 +	32	28 +
14.6	15.75	16.2	16.2				15.2
5.5	6.2	5.5	5.5				
20-30	18-32	18-30	18-30	18-32	18-32	18-30	18-32
33,880	37,448	26,423	24,073				25,887
1950	1984	1880	1720				1800
15,037	16,200	13,484	11,584				12,418
5700	5700	3952	3952				4389
4046	4046	3730	3042				3375
1903	1903	1773	1422				1576
575	606	510	500				501
565	565	552	524				522
54	54	54	54				54

tleship characteristics, BuShips began fresh studies.

The first, BB 67-1, was limited by the characteristics to 890 feet (compared with the 880 of BB 65-5A and the 930 of BB 65-5). The origin of this length limitation is unclear. It may have been no more than an attempt to restrain growth beyond BB 65-5A. Certainly it was later associated with the size of the new building docks then being constructed at Norfolk and Philadelphia Navy Yards. Displacement grew from 58,500 tons to 61,200.

Meanwhile, BuOrd continued to improve the 16in/50, whose muzzle velocity had increased from 2,470 to 2,500 feet per second. That in turn increased the armor thickness necessary to maintain the required immune zone. The belt, 15.75 inches on 35-pound STS, would have instead to be 16.1 inches thick. Deck armor, however, could be thinner (5.8 rather than 6.2 inches on 50-pound STS), because the shell would have a flatter trajectory.* The corresponding BB 67-2 study displaced 200 tons more than BB 67-1. As in

previous types, the main protective deck was tapered to take account of the effect of the bomb deck, which in this class consisted of 60-and 30-pound layers of STS, a total of 2.25-inches. The outer part of the main protective deck was thickened to 6.1 inches and the side above the belt covered with 60-pound STS to provide a ballistic equivalent to the bomb deck.

As a weight saver, the after belt connecting the main armored box to the box protecting the steering gear was eliminated in favor of armored tubes carrying the wiring leads to the steering gear. The designers argued that, as the top of the former belt was at the waterline, it did not contribute to the watertight integrity of the ship and merely wasted weight. This change, which could hold displacement to 59,700 tons, was important enough to require General Board approval (January 1941).

BuShips also added protection against underwater shell hits. It consisted of armor added to No. 3 torpedo bulkhead (30-pounds STS), which was sloped at 15 degrees. The thickness of this secondary belt was set by the ratio of *Iowa* to BB 67-1 main belt thicknesses applied to the thickness of the *Iowa* armor below 8 feet below the waterline, that is, where it protected primarily against underwater shell hits. In addition, a 35-pound doubler was applied to the 35-pound torpedo bulkhead, so that maximum ballistic thickness would be 7.74 inches. Armor weights

* It was customary to develop required zones of immunity in terms of U.S. guns, for which complete data existed. U.S. intelligence of foreign developments, such as the Japanese 18.1-inch gun, was sketchy at best. It was simpler to require that a ship be capable of surviving the fire of her own guns. Note, too, that BuOrd believed that its super-heavy shells made the 16in/50 the most powerful naval gun in the world, superior to any 18-inch weapon firing a shell of manageable size.

The *Montana* design was very considerably modified during 1940-41. The all-white preliminary design model shows typical prewar features, such as 12-foot range-finders forward (on a pedestal) and aft (atop No. 3 turret). The second model is dated November 1941. Note that the secondary guns in both cases are long-barrelled 5in/54s, rather than the 5in/38s of earlier U.S. battleships.

were later redistributed, so that in the end the inner (lower) belt was thicker over the magazines (8.5 inches tapering to 1.5 inches) than over the machinery (7.1 inches to 1 inch). In each case these thicknesses were added to the original 30-pounds STS of the torpedo bulkhead.

Even so large a design was very tight. For example, the new battleship was initially designed to carry six quadruple 1.1-inch machine cannon. In January 1941 BuOrd decided to substitute first twin and then quadruple 40mm cannon on a mount-for-mount basis. BuShips objected to the extra weight, which was no more than about 100 tons on 60,000. In March, two more quadruple mounts were added, and drastic measures for weight compensation, such as removing half an inch of armor from the turret tops, were proposed. In the last version of the design, completed in June 1942, yet another pair of quadruple Bofors was added, in a commanding position at the extreme stern, for a total of ten quadruple 40mm. There were as yet none on the turret tops,* and certainly many

more would have been mounted had the ships actually been built.

Even so, 40mm arrangement was difficult. In November 1941, after inspecting the detailed model shown in this chapter, the Interior Control Board recommended two major modifications. Two of four forward 36-inch searchlights fitted for high-angle search would be eliminated and the other two relocated higher up; two more further aft would be retained. In addition, the 12-foot navigational range-finders atop the pilot house roof and No. 3 turret would be eliminated. Their function could be assumed by 40mm and 5-inch director range-finders, and they interfered with gunnery lines of sight. Sim-

---

*In November 1941, BuOrd rejected a June 1941 BuShips proposal that 40mm guns be mounted atop the superfiring turrets. Each mount, exclusive of director, would add 22,500 pounds plus 2,875 for ammunition; the director would add another 7,500 pounds.

The director would not be far enough from the mount to avoid smoke and blast interference. The mount itself would probably block the periscopes in the turret officer's booth, and the mount on No. 2 turret would block sight lines from the ship and flag level of the conning tower. Ammunition supply would be difficult, and the 40mm mounts would suffer from 16-inch blast. Finally, guns atop the 16-inch turrets would be unable to train fast enough to remain on target while the 16-inch turrets trained. The battle force proposed in September the two stern positions or, alternatively, sponsons on either side of the after smoke pipe. It considered the position atop No. 2 turret particularly important "as experience in this war indicates the great importance of adequate anti-aircraft gunfire on this bearing."

Table 15-5. BB67 Design Studies of November 1940–January 1941

	BB67-1	BB67-2	BB67-3	BB67-4
Main Battery	12	12	12	12-16in/50
Secondary Batt.		20	20	20-5in/54
Displacement	61,000	61,333	59,700	60,500
Trial Disp't	73,000	72,300	70,600	70,500
Length	890	890	890	890
Beam(Wl)	115	115	115	
Beam Below Wl	118	118	118	118
Draft	36	35.9	36	36
Power	212,000	212,000	172,000	172,000
Speed	28	28 +	28	28
Belt	15.75	16.1	16.1	
Deck	6.2	5.8	5.8	
IZ	18.6-33.1	18-32	18-32	18-32
Weights(Tons):				
Hull	31,091	30,454	29,688	29,907
Fittings	2368	2138	2138	2238
Protection	14,473	15,493	15,128	15,211
Engineering(Wet)	4690	5145	4770	4550
Battery	4062	3940	3961	3972
Ammunition	1903	1826	2769	2663
Equip&Outfit	515	515	515	495
Stores	616	568	568	568
Aero	54	54	54	54

NOTE: Differences in armament and ammunition weight are due partly to radical increases in light AA battery in the course of these design studies. BB67-1 and -2 each had six quadruple 1.1-inch machine cannon, whereas BB67-3 and -4 had six quadruple 40mm guns. BB67-1 standard displacement included 75 rounds per 16-inch gun, with a "mobilization supply" of another 495 rounds (allowing for a total *capacity* of 96 rounds per gun). This low figure followed U.S. practice in calculating standard displacements under the arms limitation treaties. In BB 67-2, which followed the new General Board characteristics, the standard figure was increased to 100 rounds of 16in per gun (plus 360 as a "mobilization supply"). Similarly, the standard for 5-inch guns was 340 rounds (with a mobilization supply of 2,800) in BB 67-1. The mobilization supply was increased to 4,000 rounds in BB 67-2. BB 67-3 and -4 were designed to carry 500 rounds per 5-inch gun plus 600 illuminating rounds for the ship, a total of 10,600 rather than 9,600 rounds. Of the full load ammunition supply in BB 67-4, 3226 tons, 1,880 tons was 16-inch shells, and 544 tons was 16-inch powder. The 5-inch battery contributed another 526 tons, and the 40mm battery another 240 tons (2,400 rounds per gun). The difference in ammunition weights between BB67-3 and BB67-4 was entirely due to a difference in light antiaircraft ammunition, 342 tons of it in BB 67-3.

ilar modifications were made on the other modern battleships at this time.

Although the January 1941 hearing had been called to discuss the proposed wiring tubes, it allowed considerable criticism of the design as a whole. The General Board now relaxed both length and displacement limits, the former to 910 feet. The extra 20 feet was not needed, however, and the final versions of the design were all 890-feet long. The outer limit of the immune zone was brought in to 31,000 yards, so that deck armor thicknesses could be reduced slightly. BuShips now began work on what it called BB 67-3, in which 1,800 tons were shaved from BB 67-2: 1,200 forward, 600 aft, to keep the center of buoyancy aft, so that balancing the ship did not unduly constrict No. 1 turret and magazine. It appeared that the new hull would need less power to make the required speed.

BB 67-3 was based partly on the discovery that BB 67-2 was overpowered. On 212,000SHP the 890-foot ship would make 29 knots. The last knot was

very expensive; 170,000SHP would suffice for 28. Finally a new 172,000SHP plant was chosen. Machinery redesign was an opportunity to improve compartmentation. BuShips revived the arrangement used in the old *Lexington*-class battle cruiser/aircraft carriers, in which a central turbine compartment was flanked by boiler rooms. Because the turbines no longer drove electric generators, the wing-shaft turbines had to be placed outboard, at the after end of the machinery spaces. To avoid the vibration problems then being experienced in the *North Carolina*, the designers separated the main thrust bearings from the reduction gear casings. This arrangement saved space, so that the length between Nos. 2 and 3 turrets was now determined by deck space requirements rather than by the sheer size of the machinery spaces. This was a net weight saver: 250 tons because of a reduction of 12 feet in armored length, and 600 because of a reduction in power. The only direct cost was 200 tons in extra bulkheads. However, BuShips also extended the bomb deck aft, at a cost of 230

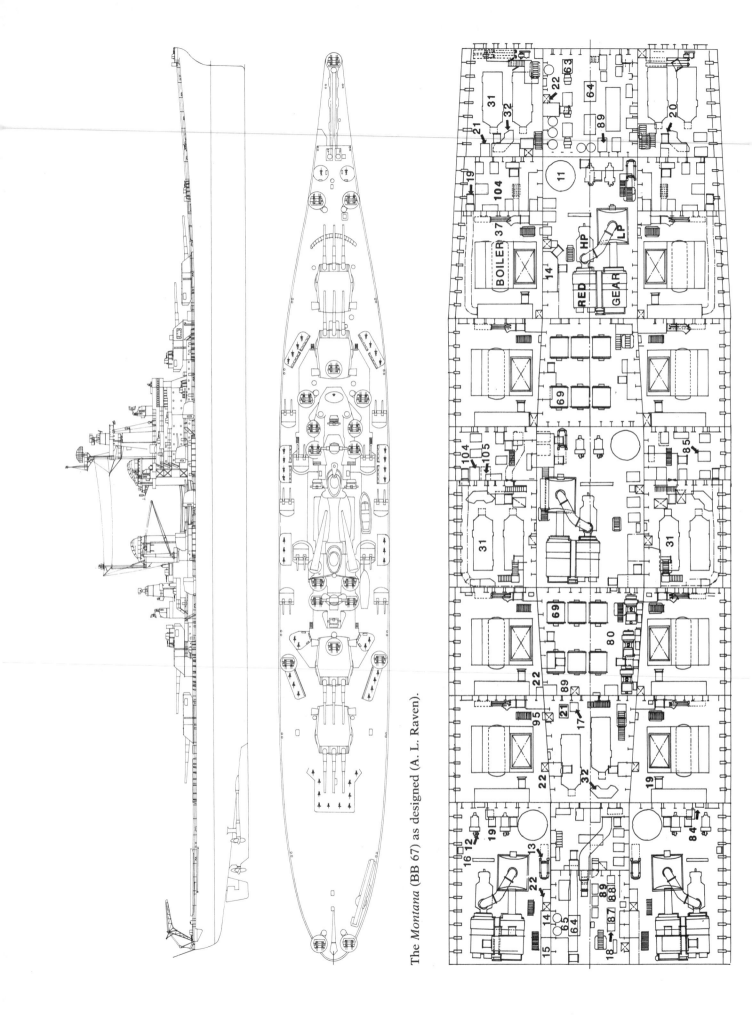

The *Montana* (BB 67) as designed (A. L. Raven).

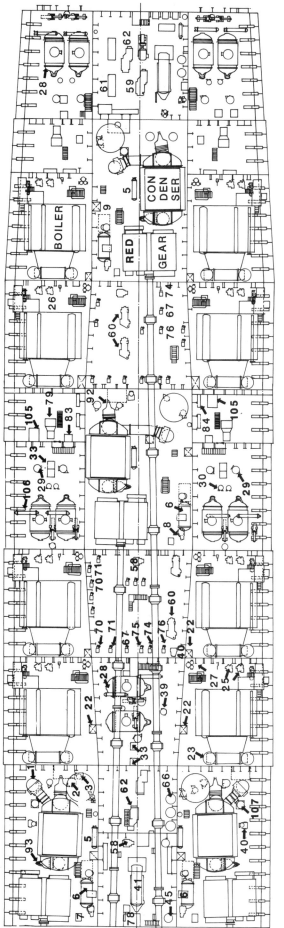

The complex machinery arrangement planned for the *Montana* class is shown in these two drawings, adapted from plans developed by the New York Naval Shipyard in 1941. Shapes have been simplified slightly for clarity. The key to auxiliaries has been taken directly from the original drawing; omitted numbers were omitted in the original. It indicates the range of equipment to be found in all modern U.S. battleship (and other warship) engine rooms, as of the beginning of World War Two. Note the special degaussing motor-generators to combat the new threat of the magnetic mine. (a) is the upper level, (b) the lower. *Key*: B, boiler; BR, boiler room; CON, condenser; DGR, diesel generator (and air compressor) room; ER, engine room; EVR, evaporator and degaussing room; HPT, high pressure turbine; LPT, low pressure turbine; RG, reduction gearing; SWR, switchboard room; TGR, turbogenerator room. Auxiliaries (not all shown in each case): 1, main condenser circulating pump; 2, main condenser condensate pump; 3, main feed booster pump; 4, auxiliary machinery cooling water service pump; 5, main engine gland steam condenser; 6, main engine lube oil cooler; 7, main engine lube oil purifier; 8, main engine lube oil pump (turbine); 9, main engine lube oil pump (motor); 10, main engine lube oil strainer; 11, deaerating feed tank and heater; 12, main feed pump; 13, main condenser air ejector; 14, main lube oil storage tank; 15, main lube oil settling tank; 16, main gage board; 17, telephone booth; 18, log desk; 19, ventilation exhaust fan; 20, ventilation supply fan; 21, circuit breaker (turbogenerator); 22, escape trunk; 23, forced draft blower; 24, fuel oil service pump—port and cruising; 25, main fuel oil service pump (turbine); 26, main fuel oil hand pump; 27, emergency feed pump; 28, dynamo condenser; 29, dynamo condenser circulating pump; 30, dynamo condenser condensate pump; 31, turbogenerator; 32, turbogenerator control board; 33, generator field rheostat; 34, freon compressor; 35, freon condenser; 36, dynamo condenser air ejector; 37, fuel oil heater; 38, fuel oil strainer; 39, dynamo condenser—gland steam condenser; 40, bilge pump; 41, diesel generator; 42, diesel generator switchboard; 43, diesel oil purifier; 44, diesel oil service pump; 45, diesel oil filter; 46, drinking fountain; 47, diesel lube oil purifier; 48, diesel lube oil filter; 49, diesel lube oil standby pump; 50, lube oil hand service tank; 51, diesel gage board; 52, diesel air starting bottle; 53, diesel generator lighting transformer; 54, diesel oil service and day tank; 55, diesel lube oil tank; 56, diesel lube oil settling tank; 57, combined diesel lube oil and jacket water cooler; 58, fuel oil booster and transfer pump (turbine drive); 59, fuel oil booster and transfer pump (electric drive); 60, fire and flushing pump (turbine drive); 61, fire and flushing pump (electric drive); 62, HP air compressor; 63, MP air compressor; 64, LP air compressor; 65, LP air accumulating tank; 66, MP air accumulating tank; 67, evaporator feed pump; 69, LP distilling plant; 70, 1st effect tube nest drain pump; 71, fresh water distillate pump; 72, fresh water pump; 73, link box; 74, distillate condensate pump; 75, circulating water pump; 76, brind overboard discharge pump; 77, fresh water test tank; 78, steam heating drain collecting tank; 79, motor generator set (for searchlights); 80, degaussing motor generator set; 81, degaussing motor generator set control panel; 82, AC distribution panel; 83, DC distribution panel; 84, load center switchboard; 85, main distribution panel; 86, 117 volt distribution panel; 87, controller and generator circuit breaker; 88, bus transfer panel; 89, breaker (bus tie circuit breaker); 90, work bench; 91, 5-pound tank for pneumatic tube system; 92, main injection gate valve; 93, main overboard discharge gate valve; 94, main circulator suction gate valve; 95, power panel; 97, cleaning gear cabinet; 98, burner rack; 99, main injection check valve; 101, fuel oil inspection tank; 102, main condenser circulating pump check valve; 103, controller for degaussing motor generator set panel; 104, turret breaker; 105, shore line breaker; 106, turbogenerator oil cooler; 107, bilge injection.

tons. Changes in the light gun battery cost 20 tons in guns and 248 tons in ammunition.

The final version, BB 67-4 of March 1941, was 60,500 tons, 890-feet long, with minor changes, primarily an increase in armored freeboard from 8 to 9 feet.

This design was circulated among senior commanders afloat, who were surprised that so little could be obtained on so much displacement. Commander battleships of battle force, for example, was disappointed that there was no increase in the number of secondary guns compared with the *Iowa*. He could not understand how, on a reported displacement of 45,000 tons, the designers of the German *Bismarck* had crowded in a total of twenty-four secondary guns (twelve 5.9 inch and twelve—there were actually sixteen—4.1 inch). He also considered the locations of the 40mm guns defective, particularly since dive and torpedo bombers would probably attack simultaneously, on as many different bearings as possible. Admiral E. J. King, the Atlantic Fleet commander (who would soon be CNO), had been responsible for the last attempt to prune back the size of these ships, BB 65-13. He objected that the ships were too large and that dimensions should be limited to those of the *Iowa*s.

Although the General Board thought in terms of four ships, five were included in what became the *Montana* class: BB 67–71. They were authorized as part of the "Two-Ocean Navy" Act of 19 July 1940, which included 385,000 tons of battleships: BB 65 and 66 plus five more of about 59,000-tons each. All were to have been built at Navy Yards: three at Philadelphia, one each at New York and Norfolk. However, none was ever laid down. Industrial bottlenecks precluded laying down any of these ships as planned in 1941.

With the outbreak of war, fresh industrial problems arose, and President Roosevelt ordered all five suspended in April 1942 in view of a shortage of steel. The same steel shortage caused cancellation of the new Panama Canal locks. The issue was priorities. The president strongly favored aircraft carriers over battleships.* The General Board later claimed that the apparent shortage had been due more to improper distribution and improper assignment of priorities than to limitations in U.S. industrial capacity and complained that such assumed limitations had been used as a pretext to end battleship construction with inferior *Iowa*-class ships. Only a *Montana* could stand up to the new 16in/50 gun with the super-heavy shell. The board therefore called for the construction of the *Montana*s, perhaps in place of the last two *Iowa*s. However, all five were formally

cancelled on 21 July 1943, the last U.S. battleships to be designed.

Since their designs were still active projects in the spring of 1942, they were subject to suggested changes that reflect early war experience, most notably the effects of air attack. Deck armor seemed more and more important. For example, it was argued that with the outbreak of war new foreign battleship construction would cease, so that the gun threat to future battleships might well cease to improve. However, bombers and their weapons would continue to develop. Thus it might be reasonable to reduce the side armor to *Iowa* thickness, using that weight to thicken the decks. A BuShips memo of 14 May suggested that the bomb and protective decks could be thickened to a total of 10.4 (rather than 9.24) inches, ballistically equivalent to 8.3 (rather than 7.3) inches, which could stop a U.S. 14-inch armor-piercing bomb dropped from 19,000 feet. Alternatively, a 14-inch belt could be combined with the ballistic equivalent of an 8-inch deck, effective against the bomb dropped from 17,500 feet. This armor would be immune against the old 2,250-pound, 16-inch shell between 16,500 and 34,500 yards. A 3-inch bomb deck would defeat 500-pound heavy-case bombs dropped from 14,000 feet. No one yet realized that it was almost impossible to hit moving ships from such altitudes.†

The General Board never acted on these proposed changes.

BuShips did develop one more set of sketch designs. On 31 January 1942 the chairman of the General Board asked for three Spring Styles for ships protected as the *Montana*s, but with speed reduced to 27 knots and lengthened amidships so that all secondary and antiaircraft guns might be mounted on no more than two deck levels. Particular attention was to be paid to clear antiaircraft arcs:

—Twelve 16in/50, and alternative secondary batteries: (a) sixteen 5in/54, eight twin Bofors, twenty-four 20mm; (b) twelve 5in/54, eight twin Bofors, twenty-four 20mm; (c) no 5in/54, sixteen twin Bofors, twenty-four or more 20mm.
—Nine 16in/50, secondaries as above.
—Nine 16in/50, and somewhat higher speed.

No sketch designs appear to have survived, although the fact that BuShips was still actively investigating the *Montana* design as late as May and June 1942 suggests that some work was done. The

---

* His efforts on behalf of escort and light carrier construction illustrate his air-mindedness. See this author's *U.S. Aircraft Carriers: An Illustrated Design History* (U.S. Naval Institute, 1983).

† The vital caveat was that, once radio controlled bombs had been perfected, high-level bombers *could* hit maneuvering ships. This occurred for the first time when the Germans sank the Italian battleship *Roma* at sea, 9 September 1943. Several Allied warships, including the British battleship *Warspite* and the U.S. cruiser *Savannah*, were hit soon afterwards, at Salerno. This new weapon, rather than the Kamikaze, was the inspiration for U.S. antiaircraft guided missiles, which would be able to engage the bomber before it could reach an attack point.

all-machine gun secondary battery is noteworthy and suggests fleet frustrations with heavy antiaircraft fire control very early in the war.

Interest in new battleship designs persisted for some time. As late as 1944, an officer in Preliminary Design, P. W. Snyder, was drafting modified *Iowa*-class characteristics, clearly based on discussions of the faults of that class within BuShips. Even at the end of the war, a special Pacific Fleet board on warship and aircraft characteristics reaffirmed the value of the battleship as a support type and suggested improvements for future designs. The two last *Iowa*s, the *Illinois* and *Kentucky*, were still being built at the end of World War Two, the latter having been laid down as late as 6 December 1944 and the *Illinois* on 15 January 1945. However, there is no evidence of anything concrete in the way of a fresh design.

The U.S. Navy was by no means alone in retaining interest in battleship design after 1942. In 1945 the British Admiralty still intended to build two new battleships, the *Lion* and *Temeraire*, which had been suspended since 1939. The British were fully aware of the details of both the *Iowa* and *Montana* designs, and their plans contrast with those of the U.S. ships. As of 1945, Design B for the *Lion* was expected to displace 59,100 tons (standard) and 69,140 tons fully loaded. It would, then, have been quite comparable with the *Montana*. Yet its main battery would have been only nine 16-inch guns, and armor would have been limited to a 14-inch belt and a 4 inch-6 inch deck. The great displacement would have bought a very powerful secondary battery, twenty-four 4.5-inch guns in twin dual-purpose mounts and sixty-eight 40mm. More impor-

tant, the armored box would have been expanded to enclose much of the internal space, and freeboard would have been increased. The British also planned to use a very large 16-inch turret. One contribution to the growth of the design was the need to defeat a new weapon, the "Uncle Tom" rocket, which was designed to strike the side of a ship underwater. The British had not shown great interest in underwater shell hits, and "Uncle Tom" must have presented them with much the same problems which the United States designers faced after 1936 onwards.

The dimensions of the 1945 battleship would have greatly exceeded those of the *Montana*: 960(wl) x 120 x 35 feet.* The only problem was the British drydocks and other facilities effectively limited a new capital ship to about 44,000 tons (standard; about 850 x 115 x 34 feet). In 1945–46, then, the British tried to develop a modern battleship of what they thought of as restricted dimensions, very much as BuShips had tried to do in 1942. No final design was developed, but it appears that the main battery would have been limited to two turrets (six 16-inch guns)—a remarkable decline from the nine 16-inch guns of the 40,000-ton *Lion* designed in 1938. The United States was not alone in discovering that, even at the end of a long period of battleship evolution, there were intense pressures for growth.

---

* The ship would have carried 7,870 tons of oil fuel, for an endurance of 8,000nm at 20 knots. By way of comparison, the British credited the *Iowa* with 11,800nm at 20 knots on 8,050 tons of oil. They expected to achieve 29 knots fully loaded with a clean bottom compared with 30.65 knots for an *Iowa* in comparable condition.

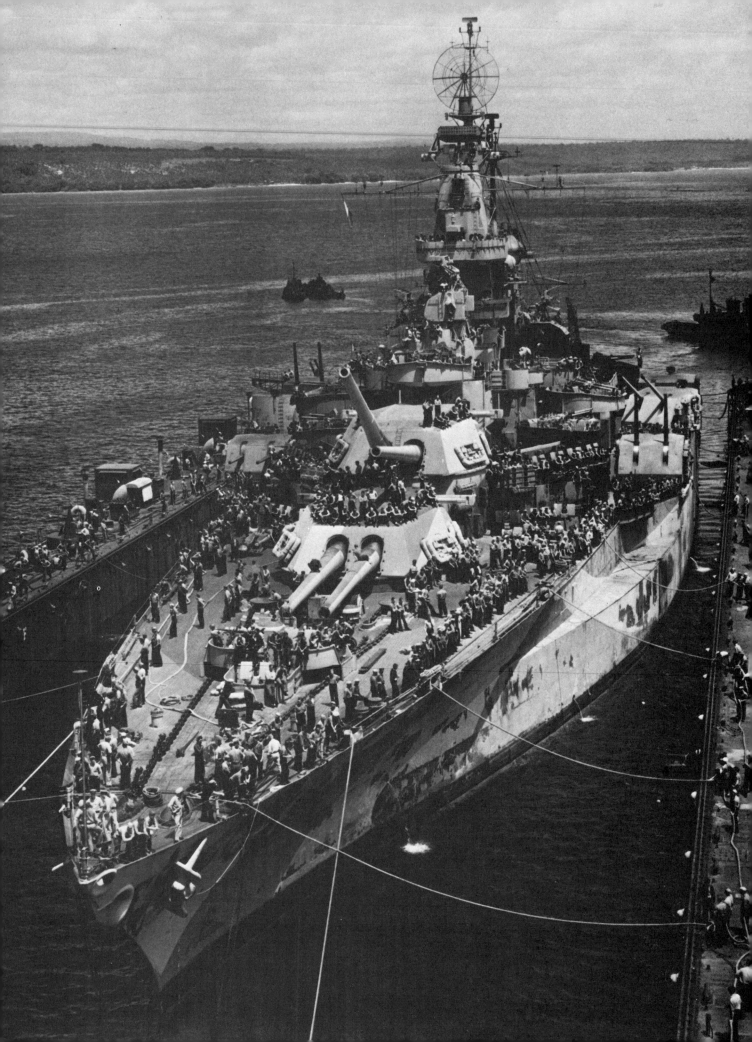

Battleships at War 1941–45

By 1941 there were, in effect, two battle fleets: the much-modernized ships that had been designed and built before, during, and just after World War One; and the new fast capital ships, designed at least partly to operate with fast carriers. Although all of these ships bore the same type designation, the two groups fought markedly different wars.

The old battle fleet was tested at Pearl Harbor, where two of its ships, the *Arizona* and the *Oklahoma*, were permanently out of action. So was the old target/training ship *Utah*. Of the remaining ships, the *Nevada*, *California*, and *West Virginia* all required large refits, which in the latter two cases became total reconstructions. Only the *Pennsylvania*, *Tennessee*, *Maryland*, and *Colorado* (which had been under refit at Bremerton at the time of Pearl Harbor) could be brought into action in a short time. They were soon reinforced by the three *New Mexicos*, which had been transferred to the Atlantic the previous summer. This fleet of seven battleships operated during 1942 as a fleet-in-being, a reserve against any Japanese attempt to penetrate to the West Coast. Only in October was the situation sufficiently stable to permit the *Pennsylvania* and *Idaho* to be taken out of service for major refits (in the former case, for removal of single-purpose secondary guns). During late 1942 and early 1943 several ships escorted South Pacific convoys.

The old ships in the Pacific, however, did not begin to see real action until May 1943, when U.S. forces invaded Attu in the Aleutians. The northern covering force consisted of the *Pennsylvania*, *Nevada*, and *Idaho*, covered by the escort-carrier *Nassau* and eight destroyers. Other fire support units in this operation consisted of cruisers. In July, the *Mississippi*, *New*

Mexico, *Idaho*, and the rebuilt *Tennessee* and *Pennsylvania* supported the occupation of Kiska. From November 1943 on, the old battleships formed a mobile fire support force for landings in the Central Pacific: Tarawa/Makin, the Gilberts, Saipan, Leyte, Lingayen Gulf, Iwo Jima, Okinawa. In these operations the fast carrier task force struck at the Japanese defenses and provided distant cover, while the slow battleships remained on station to provide softening-up fire and then call fire. Only once, at Surigao Strait, did the old battleships see classical battleship employment: for the last time in U.S. naval history, the *Pennsylvania*, *Mississippi*, *Tennessee*, *California*, *Maryland*, and *West Virginia* formed battle line and helped sink a Japanese battleship.

For much of the war the three ex-coal burners remained in the Atlantic. All three covered some of the high-value Atlantic convoys. The *New York* and *Texas* helped cover the North African landings. The former actually engaged the half-finished French battleship *Jean Bart*, while the latter served as flagship of the northern attack group. The *New York* operated as a gunnery training ship in 1943–44. The *Nevada* joined the old Atlantic battleships after Attu, and all four (now including the *Arkansas*) supported the Normandy and southern France landings. Then they shifted to the Pacific for Iwo Jima and Okinawa.

The fast battleships fought a very different war. In 1941–42 the main reason for operating battleships in the Atlantic was the German *Tirpitz*, which clearly required one or more modern capital ships to match her. In addition the Germans had the two battle cruisers *Scharnhorst* and *Gniesenau*, which could operate out of Norwegian ports to threaten convoys to Russia. Thus a major consideration in U.S. fleet em-

The *West Virginia* was perhaps the most dramatic example of U.S. battleship rehabilitation. Torpedoed and sunk at Pearl Harbor, she was raised and completely rebuilt, with a broad blister and an entirely new superstructure. Although she superficially resembled the more modern battleships, she was rather differently arranged, with her conning station on the level just under her forward main battery director, and the forward surface lookouts on the flag bridge below. This conning position was chosen at the same time as those in the *Iowa*, *Alaska*, *Oregon City*, and *Fargo*, for its clear overhead view. She is shown in floating drydock ABSD-1, 9 November 1944.

The *New York* (*above and facing*) is shown off Hampton Roads, 14 November 1944. She had just been fitted with Mark 50 directors to control her 3-inch anticraft battery, one atop her bridge, one atop her stub tripod mainmast.

ployment through 1943 was reinforcement of the British Home Fleet. Several new battleships saw their first service there: the *Washington* (March through July 1942), the *Alabama* (May through August 1943), and the *Iowa* (August through October 1943).

The Pacific was, however, paramount. The *North Carolina*, *South Dakota*, and *Indiana* were sent there upon completion of shakedown. The *Massachusetts* was an exception, beginning service with the North African assault force, in which she covered the central attack group. She duelled with the *Jean Bart*. Once in the Pacific, most of the fast battleships covered fast carriers. Their most valuable feature was their powerful antiaircraft batteries. Only rarely did they find employment for their heavy guns.

One of those occasions was the battle for Guadalcanal. On the night of 14–15 November 1942 the *Washington* and *South Dakota* engaged a Japanese force led by the *Kongo*-class battle cruiser *Kirishima*. A series of accidents aboard the *South Dakota* confused her radar plot and made her vulnerable to Japanese fire, which wrecked her superstructure. The *Washington*, however, sank the Japanese ship with at least nine 16-inch hits. The lessons of this engagement, particularly the need for auxiliary radars and the perceived need for a conning tower, were important in subsequent war refits of American capital ships.

There were no other classical engagements for the fast battleships to fight. They very nearly had their

opportunity in the battle for Leyte Gulf, when a fast battle force was detached to run north and attack what turned out to be the Japanese decoy group. The Japanese attack on the U.S. escort carriers off Samar, however, forced the recall of the fast battleships shortly before they would have come into gun range.

The fast battleships did engage in some shore bombardment, and at the end of the war they were shelling Japanese industrial targets in the Home Islands.

Both groups of battleships faced enemy attack by shore batteries, aircraft, and submarines. For the newer battleships, the two most significant cases of battle damage were the torpedoing of the *North Carolina* by a Japanese submarine on 15 September 1942 and the gunfire damage to the *South Dakota* the following November. There was also some relatively minor kamikaze damage.

The older ships suffered more heavily, partly because they were tied to invasion beaches accessible to Japanese air attack. Thus the *Nevada* was hit by a kamikaze (26 March 1945); the *Pennsylvania* was torpedoed and nearly sunk (12 August 1945); the *New Mexico* was hit on her bridge by a kamikaze (6 January 1945) and by another amidships (12 May 1945); the *Mississippi* by kamikazes (9 January and 5 June 1945); the *California* by a kamikaze (6 January 1945);

the *Colorado* by a kamikaze (27 November 1944); the *Maryland* was both torpedoed (22 June 1944) and hit by kamikazes (29 November 1944 and 7 April 1945); and the *West Virginia* was hit by a kamikaze (1 April 1945). This list does not include gunfire damage, nor does it include minor kamikaze hits, in which the attacking airplane bounced off its target into the sea.

Finally, there was the danger of collision at sea. Battleships were relatively unwieldy and often had to operate at close quarters, in darkness. On the night of 1 February 1944 *Washington* rammed *Indiana* as the latter turned out of line to fuel destroyers before dawn. Some 200 feet of plating were sheared off, and *Washington*'s forecastle crumpled. Subsequently the *Indiana* was refitted at Puget Sound. As might be expected from their extreme beams, the rebuilt "Big Five" were particularly unwieldy, and on 24 August 1944 the *California* collided with her sister ship *Tennessee*, but the damage was repaired locally. As late as 1956 *Wisconsin* would ram the destroyer *Eaton* in heavy fog. This problem was not, of course, unique to the battleships.

With the end of hostilities, the bulk of the battle fleet was hastily refitted for troop-carrying service. Operation Magic Carpet was the transport home of troops by combatant ships, from cruisers up. The older battleships and then the treaty ships were soon

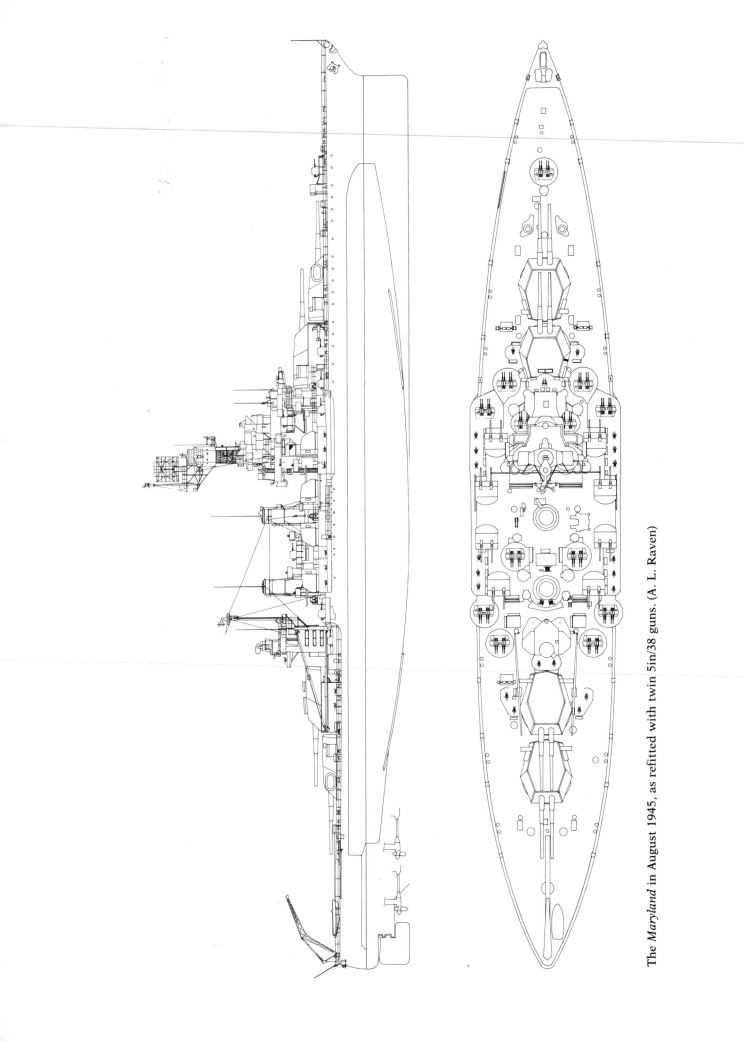

The *Maryland* in August 1945, as refitted with twin 5in/38 guns. (A. L. Raven)

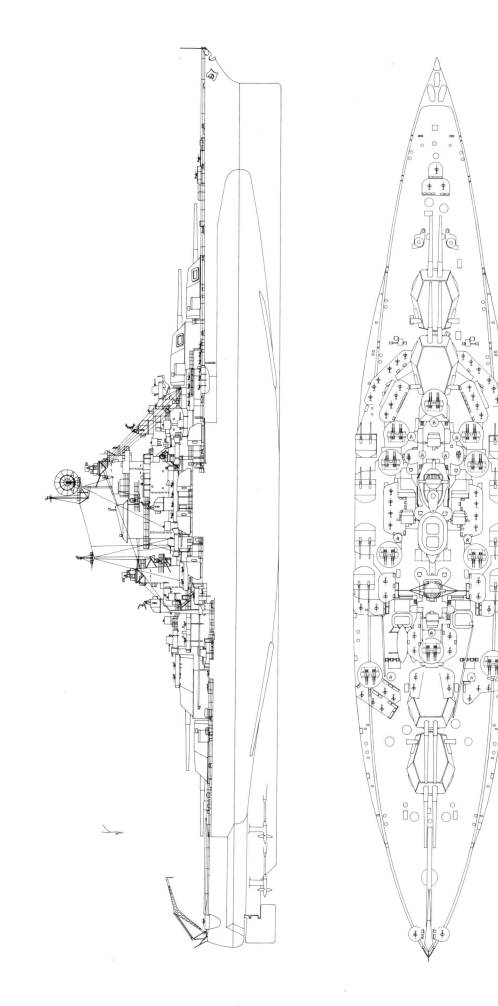

The *West Virginia* in late 1945. (A. L. Raven)

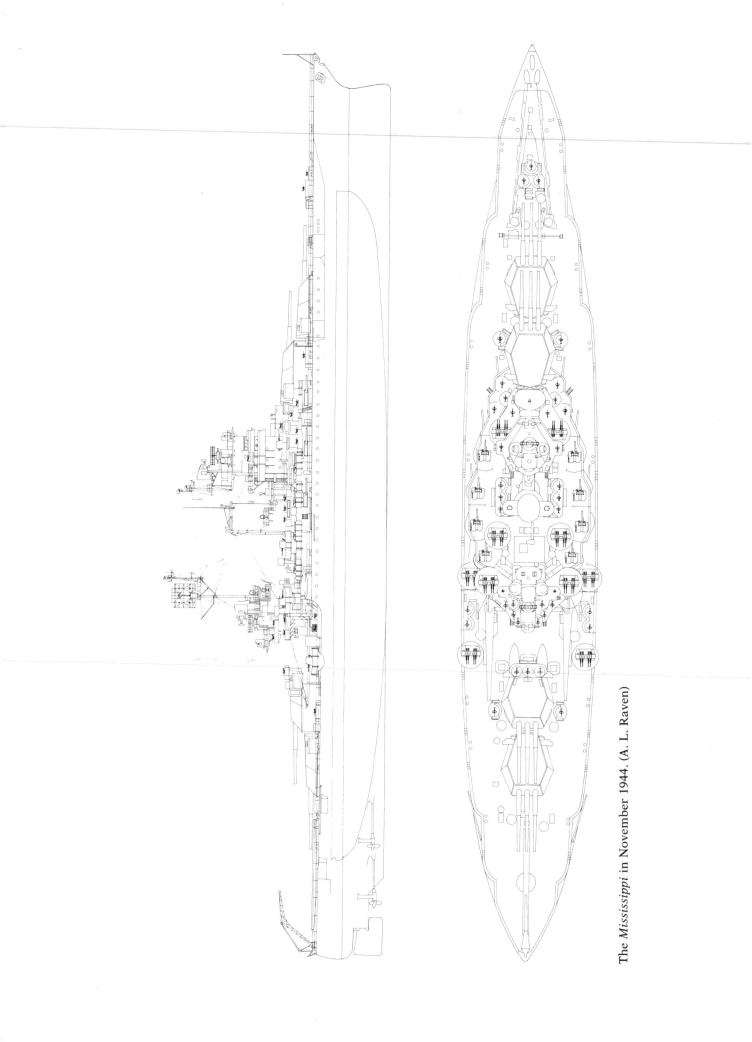

The *Mississippi* in November 1944. (A. L. Raven)

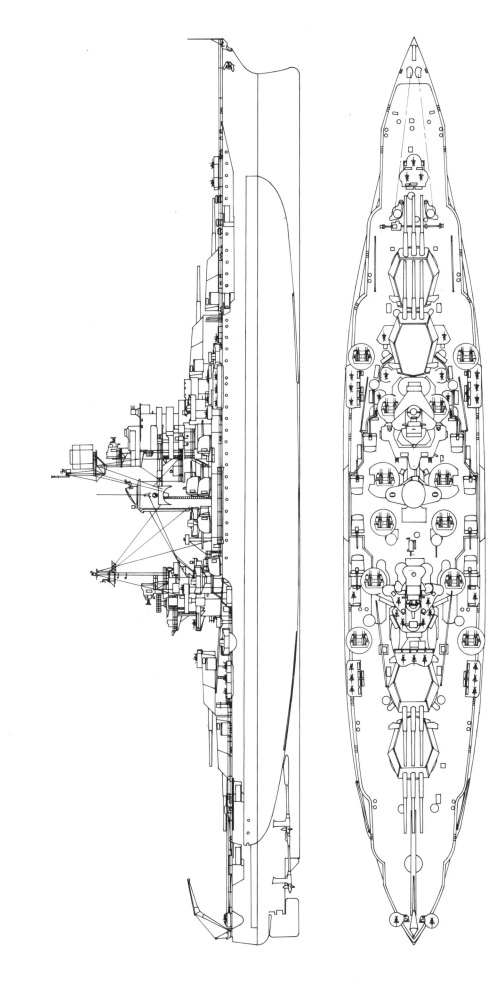

The *Idaho* as refitted, with single 5in/38 guns. (A. L. Raven)

laid up in mothballs, and by 1947 only the "Big Five" and the later ships remained in existence as battleships. The *Mississippi* had been converted into a gunnery experimental ship (which will be described in a later chapter) and the *Pennsylvania, Nevada,* and *New York* remained afloat as hulks after the nuclear tests at Bikini. The *Texas* was given to her name-state as a memorial. She is the last survivor of the dreadnought era.

At the beginning of the war the three *New Mexico*s were clearly the most modern of the older U.S. battleships. As such, one of them, the *Idaho,* was the subject of an unusual experiment. Admiral King, the CNO and C-in-C U.S. Fleet, ordered her to fire her entire complement of main battery ammunition (to "fire to exhaustion") as a test of the ability of battleships to maintain their rate of fire during a protracted engagement—or a protracted shore bombardment, as actually occurred during the war. The ship actually fired off 100 rounds per gun of her two forward turrets on the morning of 10 October 1942. Witnesses included eight BuShips and four BuOrd observers, the CinCPAC gunnery officer, thirty-five Pacific Fleet battleship officers (for spotting training), and eight Army officers from the Western Defense Command. Most of the 156 salvoes were fired at 21,000 yards, but range varied from 19,000 to 28,000 yards; some of the salvoes were air spotted. The sea was calm, the ship moving at about 15 knots.

Each turret had a crew of ninety-eight men, and of the 300 shells per turret, 67 were on the turntable, 185 on the fixed structure of the shell deck, 30 in the lower handling room, and 18 in the lower shell circle in the fixed stool structure immediately below the turret shell deck. Modifications since the original design of the ship made it somewhat more difficult to handle the shells in the lower shell circle. Instead of being hoisted directly, they had to be lowered into the lower handling room before being hoisted. Each powder charge consisted of four 110-pound bags, taken initially from the wing magazines on either side of each handling room. Later it had to be taken from the powder magazines between the two turrets, the starboard magazine supplying No. 1 turret.

The BuShips report commented that complications in powder supply had been accepted as inevitable when the turrets were modernized and elevation increased from 15 to 30 degrees. That is, bags passed by hand into the lower handling rooms were carried into separate upper handling rooms where they were transferred into upper hoists discharging into transfer rooms at the loading level, where four bags were sent from each of two hoists to its wing guns, and two bags from each hoist to the center gun.

This complex system, depending largely on muscle power, worked quite well. Only five times before the 148th salvo did any gun fail to fire because it lacked powder, and only once because a shell was not available. BuShips commented that "for a good portion of the time, shell and powder handling lines were crossing each other in the lower powder handling room without causing any confusion. In fact, the flexibility of the powder handling system was most impressive, especially with the relatively green crew manning these stations. . . . 2400 bags of powder were handled without any breakage. Considerable strength and dexterity were exhibited by the shell handlers as they 'walked' the projectiles to any desired location by rocking and turning the shells so their points moved in a horizontal circle of about 6 inch diameter. This indicates the importance of acquired skills in any ammunition handling problem."

Only in twenty cases did all six guns fire. More often (forty-seven times) five of the six could fire together. There were twenty-two 4-gun salvoes, thirty-one 3-gun, twenty-five 2-gun, and eleven 1-gun. On average the interval between salvoes was 1 minute 24 seconds. However, a 5-gun salvo was fired only forty-nine seconds after the previous salvo, and salvoes sixty to eighty, mostly 5-gun salvoes, were fired at an average interval of sixty-seven seconds. By the end of the exercise, all firing was delayed by slow arrival of shell and powder, and salvoes 148 to 156 were all (except for one 2-gun salvo) 1-gun salvoes with an average interval of two minutes. Guns generally failed to fire for minor reasons: the need to adjust or replace a gas check pad (seventy-eight times); the need to adjust a rammer (seventy-five times); or a misfire (thirteen times).

BuShips concluded that the magazine arrangements of the old battleships should be satisfactory, although it had reservations about the performance of the system in heavy weather. Certainly there was no need to install mechanical powder handlers within the lower handling rooms, as in the newer ships. It did endorse the practice of cooling the lower handling rooms of turrets, which had been begun on the basis of simulated protracted firing in tropical waters by the *North Carolina.* It also suggested that, although it was possible to manhandle the 14-inch shells of the *Idaho,* BuOrd had been wise to insist on mechanical handling of the much heavier 16-inch shells of the new battleships.

The major wartime main battery modification to the older ships was remote power control of the guns, linked to Mark 34 directors. The combination of such control, backed by an effective spotting radar (the Mark 8), was demonstrated at Surigao Strait in 1944, when ships so fitted performed extremely well, whereas the *Pennsylvania,* with her earlier fire control system, could not locate the target at all. The *Mississippi,* with the best of the prewar systems (but with Mark 3 radar), fired only a single salvo, the last in the battle. The *Maryland* fired only six (by ranging

The *Tennessee* and the *West Virginia* underwent the most radical of the World War Two reconstructions. The *Tennessee* is shown on postmodernization trials in Puget Sound, making 20 knots on 12 May 1943. Except for improved electronics, she was not again altered in wartime.

on *West Virginia*'s splashes). The other ships fired ten salvoes or more, and all had firing solutions long before the enemy had come within range.

Other wartime modifications to existing battleships were carried out on two levels. First, there was the attempt to strengthen antiaircraft batteries at a minimum cost in structural change. Second, many ships underwent less radical reconstruction.

The program of antiaircraft improvements to the existing old battleships can be traced back to the King Board of 1940–41. In March 1940 the board proposed that ultimately the 01 level be cleared of existing weapons and the deck over the broadside

guns cut away to provide sky arcs. The existing 5in/51 single-purpose guns would be replaced with dual-purpose weapons on a one-for-one basis. Four more dual-purpose guns could be mounted on what was left of the 01 level, inboard of the previous locations of 5in/25 guns 3, 4, 5, and 6. Six quadruple 1.1-inch machine cannon could be located inboard of guns 1, 2, 7, and 8, that is, at the fore and after ends of the 01 level. There would, then, be a total of fourteen 5in/38 and six quadruple 1.1 inch. The board suggested further that splinter protection be added over bridge and antiaircraft positions and that upperworks be cut back as necessary to clear sky arcs.

Photographed at Norfolk on 31 December 1941, the *New Mexico* (*above and facing*) illustrates King Board improvements: splinter protection and quadruple 1.1-inch machine cannon. She had just been fitted with 20mm guns and still retained her 0.50-calibre machine guns, two of which are visible on the direction-finder level below her navigating bridge. Her range clocks have been removed. Two radars have been fitted—a Mark 3 atop her forward main-battery director and an SC air-search set on her mainmast.

By 1941 the board was calling for far more ambitious modifications. Each ship would ultimately be armed with eight of the new twin 5in/38 gun mounts, with four quadruple 40mm Bofors guns (in place of the inadequate 1.1 inch), and eight 20mm Oerlikons. There was some question as to whether the older ships could accommodate this much topweight, but that issue was deferred.

Such modifications would require considerable yard time, and the situation in the Pacific prohibited lengthy refits. Thus the board sought an interim policy: adding four quadruple 1.1-inch machine cannon. Two would replace the 5in/51s mounted on each side of the forward end of the 01 level. Two more would be mounted abaft the break of the forecastle. They were on the upper deck in surviving flush-deck ships. But the rate of 1.1-inch production was slow, and the board approved the locally controlled 3in/50 as an interim measure. Splinter shields would be built around the new gun positions as well as around the exposed 01-level 5in/25 guns. In the *New Mexicos* and the "Big Five" the forward gun tub was raised to about the 02 level, and in the former class the after gun tubs were also raised.

A 10 June 1941 status sheet shows 3-inch guns in all the battleships, except for *Arizona* and *Nevada*, which had only empty gun tubs. By 1 November, 1.1-inch guns had already been installed in the three

elderly Atlantic battleships, which were both deficient in heavier antiaircraft fire (having 3-inch rather than 5-inch guns) and closer to being in a war zone. Of the battle force, only the *Maryland* had the new weapons. The *Colorado*, refitting on the West Coast, would soon have them, but further installations would have to wait for the new year: the *West Virginia* in February, the *Tennessee* and *Idaho* in March, the *Mississippi* in July. In each case two power- and two hand-operated quadruple 1.1-inch mounts would be provided.

Thus the ships at Pearl Harbor were largely bereft of modern light antiaircraft weapons, each ship having the mixed 3- and 5-inch battery, plus eight (nine in *Pennsylvania*, eleven in *West Virginia*) 0.50-calibre machine guns. Only the *Maryland* had the 1.1s.

The other major pre-Pearl Harbor modification program was the installation of splinter protection, particularly at the antiaircraft guns. The commander of the battleships was particularly concerned to protect the 5in/25 gun crews because they could not seek cover during an air attack. On the other hand, the pedestal mount might become too heavy and, worse, unbalanced, so that protection would cost some fraction of the handiness which made the 5in/25 an effective antiaircraft weapon. A prototype quarter-inch shield, which weighed 1,600 pounds, was developed aboard the *West Virginia* in June and more were fabricated at Pearl Harbor. The *West Virginia* had at least one at the time of the attack; the status of the other ships is less clear. Soon after the attack, however, the *Pennsylvania*, *Tennessee*, *Colorado*, and *Maryland* all carried them. The last two ships still had them as late as 1945. The *New Mexico*s were never fitted with these shields, even after they had come to the Pacific after Pearl Harbor.

By September 1941, the battle force commander was pressing for splinter protection for light antiaircraft weapons as well as bridges and fire controls. Reports of naval combat in Europe had convinced him that, without shields, gun crews would be unable to remain at their weapons during intense air attacks. "There should be no near [by] position more attractive from a protection standpoint than their stations firing the guns." Similarly, he feared the effects of strafing directed against bridges and fire controls. Such attacks had been a staple of U.S. and foreign naval air tactics for many years, and it is interesting that splinter protection against them was not seriously advocated before World War Two.

In November, however, BuOrd cited new intelligence reports describing a series of severe air attacks by groups of fifty aircraft at fifteen minute intervals, over a period of six hours, on the British cruisers *Dido* and *Orion* and three destroyers near Crete. In this case "pompom [AA] crews in particular stuck to their posts without flinching. In large part the performance...is attributed to the fact that the gun captains on the pompoms were especially capable and experienced men." The CNO therefore disapproved a proposed shield for the new twin Bofors (40mm) gun, although he approved one for the quadruple mount. No shield was to be added to the existing 1.1-inch machine cannon because it would reduce the field of vision of the pointer and trainer and would make training difficult if power failed. The King Board had already pressed for gun tubs as a much better alternative. Nor were shields to be added to 0.50-calibre machine guns.

At this time a distinction was made between "real" protection against bomb-case fragments and splinters and "morale" protection against low-flying aircraft. The former had to extend all around a position. Bombs would generally burst below topside stations, so that armor would have to consist of low bulwarks and reinforced deck. "Morale" protection would consist of a shield rotating with the guns.

Ten-to-twenty-pound STS bulwarks and partial overhead protection were to be applied to the pilot house, flag bridge, and signal bridge. Aloft controls were a more difficult problem, since the cage masts of the "Big Five" could not take any additional weight. Machine guns were already being moved from them to decks and kingposts, and radar installations were a serious weight problem.

Initial war modifications continued the prewar weight-saving ideas and the King Board antiaircraft recommendations, but major refits were no longer possible. For a time, all the West Coast ships were held at forty-eight hours' steaming notice. On the other hand, the ships severely damaged at Pearl Harbor became available for reconstruction, as long as graving docks could be spared. At the time of the attack, the *Colorado* was refitting at Puget Sound and the three *New Mexico*s were in the Atlantic on convoy duty, as were the two *New York*s. The *Arkansas* was laid up. At once the *New Mexico*s were refitted with radar and with 1.1-inch rather than 3-inch guns and dispatched to the Pacific.

Of the ships already there, the *Pennsylvania* was hardly damaged, and both the *Tennessee* and *Maryland* would return to active duty before the end of 1941. The *California* and *West Virginia*, on the other hand, clearly required major reconstruction. In fact they would not rejoin the active fleet before 1943–44. The *Nevada*, which was burned out, required a large refit but clearly not such a radical one as the other two. Of the two remaining ships, the *Arizona*

had been so completely destroyed that she could not be resurrected. The *Oklahoma*, capsized, could be salvaged, but was never restored to service because she was only of marginal value by the time she had been salvaged in 1944. She sank while under tow to the West Coast.

On 17 December 1941 commander, battle force, renewed his suggestion that cage mainmasts be removed from the "Big Five" as an unjustified weight and an obstruction to antiaircraft fire. He also wanted boat cranes removed. The *Colorado* was under refit, but she was so urgently wanted that nothing could be done beyond the addition of radars (one SC, two FC), splinter protection, and light antiaircraft weapons (four quadruple 1.1-inch, fourteen 20mm). Meanwhile, the *Maryland* and *Tennessee* were rushed through Puget Sound Navy Yard. The former received sixteen Oerlikons, splinter protection for bridge and pilot house, and radar. The latter had to be regunned, which left time for more elaborate modifications. Her mainmast was replaced by a stump tower, the top of which carried her after fire controls. She received her four quadruple 1.1-inch mounts and sixteen Oerlikons. She was fitted with SC and FC radars forward, but nothing aft, and no FD radars for her pair of Mark 33 directors. Although moderate blistering, as in the *Colorado*, had been planned, there was not enough time for it. All three ships retained turret catapults and boat cranes at this time, although both features would soon go.

Anything more elaborate would require extensive yard work. In January 1942, the CNO ordered the fabrication of tower mainmasts for the *Colorado* and *Maryland*. On the basis of the experience with the *Tennessee*, commander, battleships, thought that replacement might require about three weeks per ship. However, the ships were still being docked on the basis of *forty-eight hour* readiness. The *Colorado* still had the stump of her cage mainmast as late as November 1943. This represented a considerable sacrifice in her combat capabilities, in that she had been reduced to the single main battery director in her foretop.

Meanwhile, the *Pennsylvania*, the only other undamaged battleship, continued to operate in essentially her pre-Pearl Harbor configuration, except that now all of her 5in/25 guns were shielded and she had considerable additional light AA weapons: the now-standard four quadruple 1.1 inch and sixteen 20mm Oerlikons.

The VCNO announced a battleship modernization policy on 25 May 1942. The primary possible alterations were improvements to armor (particularly deck armor), the installation of modern dual-purpose secondary batteries, and blistering, which would restore some or all of the buoyancy lost by the other changes. It had already been decided that the severely damaged *West Virginia* and *California* would

The *Pennsylvania* survived Pearl Harbor virtually without damage. She therefore preserved some of the features installed on the Pacific Fleet battleships before their destruction, as shown in this 2 March 1942 Mare Island photograph. They included the installation of enclosed Mark 19 directors (on the range-finder level), the King Board's quadruple 1.1-inch guns (abeam No. 2 turret here), and extensive splinter protection. The shields for the 5in/25 guns were a Pacific Fleet initiative and survived through the war aboard the *Colorado*. Note, too, the air defense position at the base of the foremast and the radar, which was scheduled for installation aboard all of the battleships. The 20mm guns were a postattack addition.

Again refitted, the *Tennessee* steams through Puget Sound in January 1945. Note the SP height-finder on her mainmast and the small Mark 27 radar on a platform above her navigating bridge.

be blistered to a beam of 113 or 114 feet to balance off the addition of about 1,400 tons of deck armor. The *Tennessee*, too, would be rebuilt, but the VCNO was unwilling to remove her from service for a sufficient period just then. The blistering program itself was limited because there were only four large-enough drydocks on the West Coast—three at Puget Sound and one at Hunters Point. One at Puget and the one at Hunters Point had to be reserved for emergencies as well as minor and routine docking. Because the installation of "ultimate" dual-purpose batteries (twin 5in/38) would take six to seven months, it was deferred.

The *Pennsylvania* would have her mainmast replaced by a stump tower to open sky arcs. Conning towers would be removed to save weight. For example, in the *New Mexico*s the tower proper weighed about 175 tons, its tube another 225. Since the latter could not be removed during an eight-week overhaul, removal of the former would not be worthwhile. However, the two-level flagship conning tower of the *Pennsylvania* weighed about 400 tons, its tube another 250. Hence substantial weight could be saved if both levels were removed and the upper one replaced by 50-pound STS around the steering gear and fire control instruments formerly located in the upper conning tower level. A way around this problem of rearrangement was to replace existing conning towers with structures of similar shape built of 50-pound splinter armor. Such substitutions were authorized on 10 November for the *New Mexico*s, but it appears they were not carried out.

C-in-CPac argued that the dual-purpose secondaries would be extremely valuable. He suspected that the time to install them had been overestimated. As for conning towers, all of the older battleships trimmed by the head when loaded, so that the removal of these structures might well be more beneficial than a weight analysis alone might show. Armored freeboard continued to be a major problem. Unless some major alteration were made, it would only be possible to gain 6 inches.

Partially stripped, the *West Virginia* was inclined as she was "mothballed." She is shown at Puget Sound, 12 April 1946. Note the two small radars (Mark 27s) on either side of her No. 3 turret, replacing the optical range-finder it normally carried. She and her sisters survived in reserve until 1959.

The *Tennessee* (*above and facing*) had her mainmast replaced by a short prefabricated tower. The detail views were taken at Puget Sound on 19 February 1942. The overall aerial view, showing another pair of quadruple 1.1-inch guns, dates from June. The two mounts shown in the detail views were initially installed as a King Board measure.

A month later the VCNO suggested an interim modification, in which two 5in/51 would be replaced by two 5in/25 aboard the *Tennessee*. At the same time two twin 40mm and perhaps two 20mm would be added. As for the other ships, the upper conning tower of the *Pennsylvania* might be removed, but in the others removal would require rewiring, which would double refit time. He suggested that blisters be enlarged and that ultimately both conning towers and boat cranes be removed.

Very little was acutally done. In September, the *Tennessee* reported to Puget Sound for reconstruction. On 21 October the VCNO authorized removal of all 5in/51 as well as turret catapults from the *Idaho* and *Pennsylvania*. Light antiaircraft batteries would be increased to forty to forty-five Oerlikons and, respectively, ten and six quadruple 40mm guns. This order led to the reconstruction of the *Pennsylvania*

to parallel that of the *Nevada*. The *Idaho* was not reconstructed, nor were her two sisters, nor the *Colorado* and *Maryland*.

The *New Mexico*s were too urgently needed in the war zone for much to be done to them. The *Idaho* was refitted at Puget Sound between 14 October and 28 December 1942, but her two sisters remained near Hawaii. On 15 October commander, service forces, Pacific, suggested that it was so urgent to remove dangerous top hamper above their antiaircraft batteries that they should be refitted at Pearl Harbor without waiting for either the plans of the *Idaho* refit or some of the material which might later be needed. Their yard period was extended through 29 November, and 5in/51 guns Nos. 7, 8, 9, and 10 and the after secondary directors were removed, two quadruple Bofors with their directors being installed on the upper deck at Frame 89, port and starboard. Two

Little changed by the war, the *Mississippi* is shown at San Pedro in June 1942. Her elaborate searchlight controls have been removed, and a few 20mm guns supplement her four quadruple 1.1-inch mounts. Note the tall periscopes emerging from the roofs of her two superfiring turrets. Her two open-mounted 5in/51s had already been removed as part of the King Board antiaircraft improvement.

Oerlikons replaced the after secondary directors, and four more appeared on an extended signal bridge level. The four existing quadruple 1.1-inch gun tubs were modified for later installation of quadruple 40mm, for an ultimate total of six. The large searchlight platform on the stack was replaced by a much smaller one, with only two lights. In fact the four 1.1s were not landed until October 1943, at which time they had four quadruple and two twin 40mm. Oerlikon batteries increased to twenty-four (*New Mexico*) and twenty-nine (*Mississippi*). By January 1943, they had increased sharply to, respectively, forty-three (then forty-six) and fifty.

By way of contrast, as early as November 1942, their "temporary approved" battery was no 5in/51 at all, eight 5in/25, ten quadruple 40mm, and forty to forty-five Oerlikons. The *Idaho* was so modified during her big 1942 refit, except that as late as December she had only sixteen Oerlikons. There were twenty-two and then twenty-seven the next January, and by February she had a total of forty-three. The others did not reach ten quadruple 40mm until late in 1944.

The *Idaho* alone was extensively refitted at Puget Sound, between 22 October 1944 and 1 January 1945. Ten single enclosed 5in/38 replaced her open 5in/25s. She retained her ten 40mm mounts and her forty-

three Oerlikons. At this time her two sisters had total batteries of six 5in/51, eight 5in/25, ten quadruple 40mm, and, respectively, forty-six and forty Oerlikons. The *Mississippi* was rearmed at her captain's request at Pearl Harbor during kamikaze damage repairs, 3 March through 18 April 1945. All the remaining 5in/51 were removed, and she emerged with sixteen 5in/25, twelve quadruple Bofors (a thirteenth being added later in 1945), and forty Oerlikons. Much of this battery was controlled by individual Mk 51 directors. Her conning tower was finally removed as weight compensation, replaced by a 60-pound STS structure. BuOrd was concerned at this time that the eliminaton of the 8-inch conning tower roof would leave a dangerous gap in her horizontal protection and wanted to fill in the deck armor below the conning tower. That was never done.

Fire controls in the *New Mexico*s were also modernized, Mark 33 dual-purpose directors replacing the earlier and less capable Mark 28. The latter, unlike their counterparts in many other ships, were fitted only with the Mark 28 radar. As for the main battery directors, in 1944 the two Mark 3 radars originally provided began to be replaced in 1944 by Mark 28 (Mark 8 in the more extensively rebuilt *Idaho*). Toward the end of 1944 Mark 27 standby fire control radars began to be installed.

The *Mississippi* (*above and following page*) was refitted at Pearl Harbor in the spring of 1945, many antiaircraft weapons being added on her captain's initiative. Her remaining 5in/51s were removed, and their casemates plated up. Eight 5in/25 were added, doubling the battery in that calibre. Two were mounted on the 01 level aft and four on the main deck, two in new splinter shields, and two displacing quadruple 40mm guns. She now mounted twelve quadruple 40mm guns: two new ones on the centreline; six raised above the 01 level; and four abaft the break of the forecastle.

Like the *New Mexico*s, the *Colorado* and *Maryland* were, in effect, too valuable to refit. The stump towers that had been fabricated to replace their mainmasts remained in storage until the spring of 1944. Early in 1942, the ships' companies cut down their cage mainmasts roughly to the searchlight platform level, mounting several light machine guns on top. For a time the removal of the entire 5in/51 battery was planned, but it was November 1943 before even one was removed on each side. Through 1942 both ships mounted four quadruple 1.1-inch guns, eight 5in/25, and an almost constantly varying number of 20mm. For example, the *Colorado* had fourteen (and eight 0.50-calibre guns) in June 1942 and twenty-two in November (with thirty-six "temporarily approved" for later installation). The following February, the *Maryland* was fitted with another pair of quadruple 1.1s, and she had forty-eight Oerlikons. By March 1943 she also had ten 0.50s. Her sister was similarly armed.

In November 1943, two 5in/51 (out of ten) and all of the 1.1s were removed. Bofors production now sufficed for six quadruple and four twin mounts per ship. The 0.50s were landed, and the 20mm batteries slightly reduced to, respectively, forty-two and forty. These latter numbers, however, fluctuated constantly. In the *Maryland*, for example, six guns were added, then four more, then two were removed.

Neither ship was available for a major yard refit until early 1944, when the cage mainmasts were finally removed. At this time two twin 40mm were replaced by quadruples, for a total of thirty-six 40mm guns. Each ship was fitted with one quadruple 20mm gun. By the end of 1944 each ship also had thirty-nine or forty single 20mm. The new stump tower had provision for the cupola director (Mk 11) formerly mounted on the maintop, and it was expected that ultimately it would be replaced by a modern Mark 34 surmounted by a Mark 8 radar. The *Colorado* was so fitted during a Puget Sound overhaul, between 21 August and 9 October 1944.

A larger refit was planned. On 16 February 1944 Admiral King asked for estimates of time and cost for installation of eight twin 5in/38 (directed by four Mark 37), two Mark 34s and remote control for the main battery, and additional second (protective) deck plating. BuShips proposed that the conning tower and tube, uptake armor, main battery ammunition above 100 rounds per gun, and some stores be removed as compensation for 80-pound deck plating and the new guns. The bureau suggested that a much more limited arrangement, perhaps similar to that in the *Idaho*, would be more sensible.

As of January 1945, it appeared that complete reconstruction would take seven to eight months, or four to five months for the *Idaho*-type alternative. In

In February 1944, Admiral King asked BuShips to consider reconstruction of the *New Mexico*s. They would be fitted with eight twin 5in/38. By this time the ships were so overweight that, even without any addition to deck armor, they would require 114 foot blisters. They in turn would take about eight months to fit, and the *Idaho* refit, which could be completed in about three months, seemed a useful compromise. By early 1945 plans called for similar alterations to the other two ships, the *Mississippi* and *New Mexico*. In fact, as noted above, the *Mississippi* was refitted very differently at Pearl Harbor.

The *Idaho* as refitted with single 5in/38 guns, 2 January 1945 off Puget Sound.

The *New Mexico* (uncamouflaged, on 6 October 1943) and *Mississippi* (camouflaged, 13 July 1944) illustrate the main wartime configuration of the *New Mexico* class, heavily laden with 40mm guns, with funnel searchlights brought well down from their former positions, and with the catapult removed from No. 3 turret. Only six of the former ten main deck 5in/51 guns remained, in the three forward positions on each side.

Little damaged at Pearl Harbor, the *Maryland* still retained her prewar appearance through early 1942. She is shown at Puget Sound, 9 February 1942, when all the operational battleships were being kept at short steaming notice in view of fears of invasion. Note the enclosed 5-inch antiaircraft directors, the splinter bulwarks, and the splinter shields on her 5in/25 guns.

The *Maryland* soon had her mainmast cut down; 20mm gun galleries were built abeam her funnels. She is shown at Hauannah Bay in the New Hebrides in 1943, little changed since late 1942.

The *Colorado* was finally refitted with a stump mainmast only in 1944. She is shown running post-refit trials in Puget Sound (at 19.2 knots) on 3 October 1944. Note the installation of a Mark 34 director atop the tower, supplementing the old main battery director atop her foremast. She was also fitted with Mark 33, 5-inch directors at this time.

each case massive electrical work would be necessary. There matters would have stood, except that the *Maryland* was damaged by a kamikaze and had to be repaired. Although she was fitted with a new secondary battery (eight twin 5in/38), no additional armor was applied to her protective deck. Her conning tower was replaced by a 50-pound STS structure as weight compensation.

The *Nevada* was the first of the severely damaged battleships to be refitted, and in some ways she was the prototype for five wartime reconstructions. She was also the oldest ship rebuilt. Refloated on 12 February 1942, she departed from Pearl Harbor on 22 April and emerged from Puget Sound in December 1942. Planning had begun even before she had been raised. As of 2 February, BuShips expected to try to achieve the ultimate battery, approved by the CNO

on 20 August 1941, of eight twin 5in/38, four quadruple Bofors, and sixteen Oerlikons.* They would add 700 tons, increasing full load displacement to 35,400 tons. The CNO directed that the mainmast be replaced by a stump carrying main and secondary directors and that the boat cranes be removed, leaving the turret and quarterdeck catapults. Weight compensation would include removal of the conning tower and tube and also of some portion of the main battery ammunition. For example, thirty rounds per gun would amount to 300 tons.

* At first, in view of the ship's age and the subsidiary duties she was expected to perform, BuShips proposed restricting her reconstruction to approximately her condition as of 6 December 1941, adding only a 20mm battery and remote control for her 5in/25 antiaircraft battery. The decision for a more complete reconstruction was made at the CNO level.

Severely damaged at Pearl Harbor, the *Nevada* was rebuilt at minimum cost. Her main battery directors were not replaced, but she was fitted with new Mark 37s to control her 5-inch battery. These 23 August 1943 photographs show her after a Norfolk refit, when she was fitted with a big new SK air-search radar on a lattice topmast. Remarkably, she retained her earlier SC air-search set on a mainmast. During a later refit (November 1944), the lattice was replaced by a simple pole, and the SC removed. The main-topmast was replaced by a tall pole carrying a surface-search set. Note her unusual tall sloping funnel.

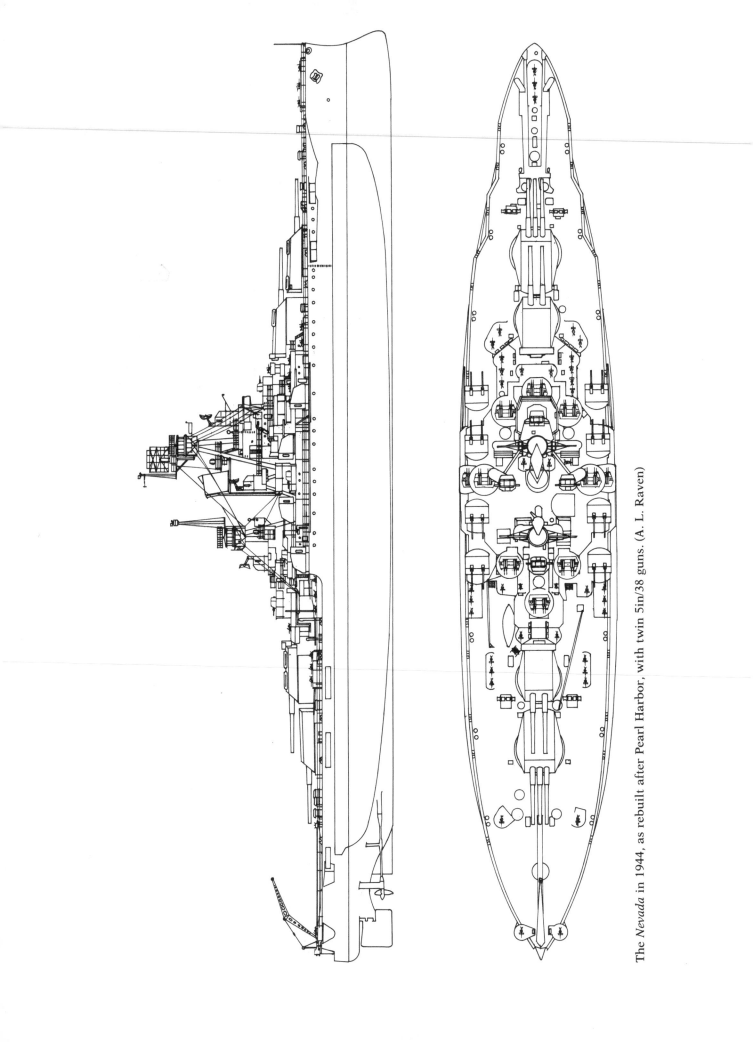

The *Nevada* in 1944, as rebuilt after Pearl Harbor, with twin 5in/38 guns. (A. L. Raven)

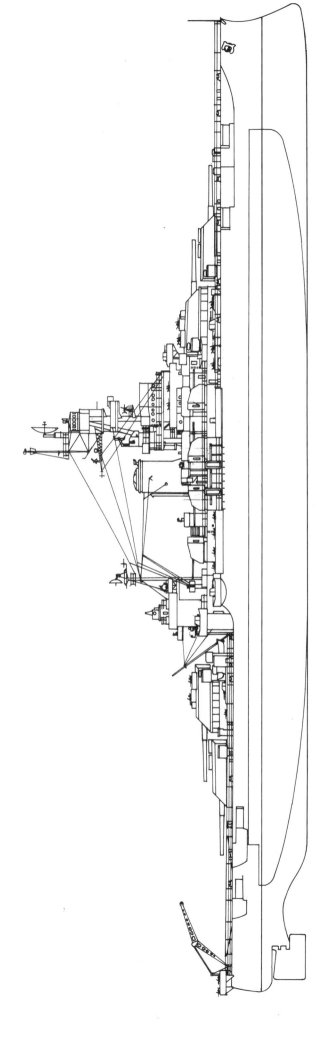
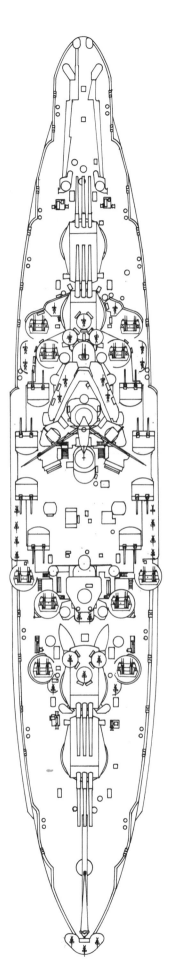

The *Pennsylvania* in July 1945, as rebuilt, with twin 5in/38 guns. (A. L. Raven)

The *Pennsylvania* was rebuilt. She is shown near Puget Sound on 1 August 1943. Note that she retained her old main battery directors fore and aft but that the secondary battery directors had been replaced by Mark 37s. Her conning tower was removed.

battery ammunition. For example, thirty rounds per gun would amount to 300 tons.

Detailed plans were available by April. The existing structure was retained wherever possible, but much new structure was needed. As in contemporary cruisers, the ship was fitted with an open bridge, an enclosed primary steering station, a secondary conning station, radar plot, radar control, a main battery fire control station that replaced the fire control tower removed as part of the old conning tower, and forward and after air defense stations. The new forward main battery director was lowered to the level of that in the *New Mexico*. The 20-foot coincidence range-finder of No. 2 turret was replaced by a 26.5-foot stereo unit similar to that already installed in No. 1. Not until well into the refit was it decided that the catapult atop No. 3 turret should be removed.

Weight compensation included a reduction of 300 tons in fuel oil, of 200 in reserve feed water, and in main battery ammunition to ninety rounds per gun.

The *Nevada* emerged in December 1942 with eight quadruple Bofors and forty-one Oerlikons. Although she had four new Mk 37 directors for her new 5in/38 battery, she retained her original pair of Mk 20 main battery directors, in new cylindrical fire control tops, atop new stub tripods. A sharply raked extension was added to her original smokepipe to keep the new bridgework clear of smoke.

Although the *Pennsylvania* operated at first in much her original configuration, she was rebuilt at Mare Island between 4 October 1942 and 5 February 1943. The result was intermediate between that achieved in the *Nevada* and the *Maryland*. Her conning tower was removed (and for a time a long-base range-finder

mounted in its place) and a new deckhouse built as a base for eight twin 5in/38. A new deckhouse replaced her mainmast, the after director cupola being relocated to its top. On the other hand, provision for dual-purpose fire control was limited to replacement of the two Mk 33 by two new Mk 37, with their associated radars. The bridgework was simplified, mainly by the elimination of the previous outside platforms, and the turret-top catapult and boat cranes were removed. Ten quadruple Bofors and fifty-one Oerlikons were mounted. In May 1943, the ships still had eight 0.50-calibre machine guns as well.

The *Pennsylvania* was again refitted at Hunters Point (13 March through early July 1945), following kamikaze damage. Her after cupola director was replaced by a modern Mark 34.

The "Big Five" were the prime candidates for major reconstruction. The modest blistering applied to the *Maryland* and *Colorado* did not solve their problems, since their 3.5-inch decks would barely defeat a 1,600-pound armor-piercing bomb dropped from 3,000 feet. Thus the major requirement was to provide an extra 120 pounds (3 inches) of STS over magazines and 80 pounds elsewhere over the protective deck. With these improvements the deck could defeat a similar bomb dropped from, respectively, 8,000 or 6,000 feet. In addition turret tops were replaced to achieve greater protection. This extra deck armor alone would weigh 1,319 tons.

To keep the armored deck above the waterline, the ships were fitted with a double-layer blister which increased their beam to 114 feet. The ships could, therefore, no longer transit the Panama Canal. The combination of beam and extra displacement cost about a knot in speed.

The *Pennsylvania* is shown on 28 June 1945, soon after her last wartime refit. She now had such advances as an SP radar on her mainmast and a twin 40mm mount superfiring over No. 2 turret, replacing the long-base range-finder formerly mounted there. A TDY radar jammer is visible under the foremast antiaircraft platform. Two others were mounted on the other mast legs. Experience at Surigao Strait showed that the ship's elderly main battery fire control system was relatively inefficient, and she was fitted with a new Mark 34 carrying the standard Mark 8 radar aft.

Torpedoed aft by a Japanese airplane on 12 August 1945, the *Pennsylvania* was never completely repaired. Instead, she was stripped for the bikini nuclear test. She is shown leaving Puget Sound, 15 March 1946. Note that two of her four portside 5-inch mounts have been removed.

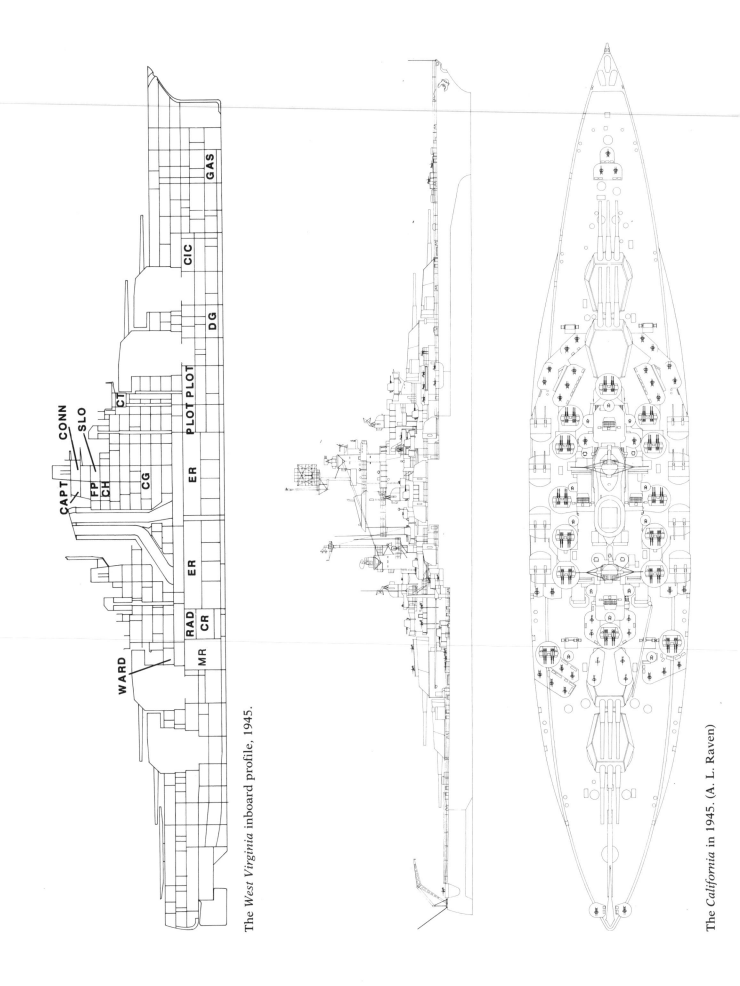

The *West Virginia* inboard profile, 1945.

The *California* in 1945. (A. L. Raven)

Labels on *West Virginia* inboard profile: WARD, MR, RAD, CR, ER, ER, CG, CH, FP, CAPT, CONN, SLO, CT, PLOT, PLOT, DG, CIC, GAS

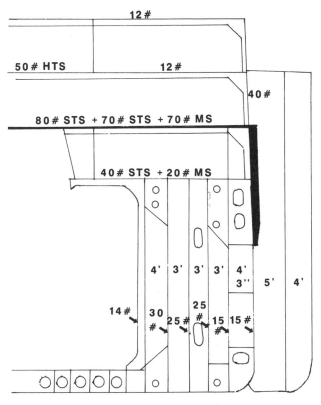

Cross section of the *California* as rebuilt.

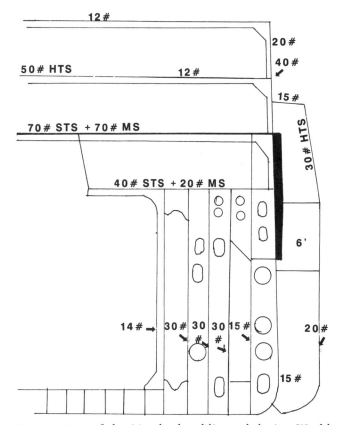

Cross section of the *Maryland* as blistered during World War Two.

Much of the reconstruction design followed that of the *Nevada*: the two-level secondary battery controlled by four Mark 37 directors; and the same light battery of four quadruple Bofors and sixteen Oerlikons. With greater beam, however, the antiaircraft battery could be arranged better, and the planned battery grew. By March 1943 ten quadruple Bofors and forty to forty-five Oerlikons were planned; forty-three of the latter were actually aboard the *Tennessee* when she was completed. In two ways the example of the *Nevada* was not followed. The original conning tower (which, with its tube and foundation, weighed 765 tons)* was replaced by one taken from a *Brooklyn*-class light cruiser, a 5-inch structure with a 9-foot internal diameter, weighing less than 10 percent as much. In addition, the heavy gun turrets were modified for automatic control, and cruiser-type Mark 34 directors, originally ordered for light cruisers completed as carriers, were installed. Similar units were later fitted to the *Pennsylvania*, *Colorado*, and *Maryland*.

Two factors were important in determining bridge arrangements: the waveguide problems of the SG surface-search radar; and the need for clear sky arcs for the primary conning position. Radar plot had in any case to be near the primary ship control position. The solution adopted was to place the primary conn in the main battery control tower, with leads to the central station passing through the main battery director tube. Again, unlike the *Nevada*, these ships had solid towers rather than stub tripods.† The fire control station formerly located in the after part of the conning tower was now replaced by a fire control station directly above the primary conn.

Work on this project began soon after Pearl Harbor, and it was approved by the secretary of the navy in May 1942. The *Tennessee* was the first, begun in September, and completed in May 1943. She was followed by the *California* (7 June 1942 to 31 January 1944) and then by the *West Virginia* (completed in September 1944). These large refits suffered from low priorities and from the enormous mass of work pouring into the West Coast yards. Thus actual costs in time and money are deceptive. Even so, they give some idea of the magnitude of the work, compared with prewar estimates. For example, through 17 April 1943 the *Tennessee* reconstruction cost a total of

---

* This figure refers to the *California*. The flag portion of the tower weighed 220 tons. Heavy uptake armor and gratings accounted for another 460 tons. This plating would be replaced by armor gratings on the second deck and by splinter protection around the uptakes.

† The original sketch design for reconstruction did, however, show tripod masts.

The *Arkansas* (*above and facing*) was rebuilt in 1942, with a tripod foremast and the new open bridge. Note the big range-finder on her No. 2 turret, which had never been fitted with a fixed long-base instrument, and the paravane fixed to the barbette. The structure on the open navigating bridge was a pilot house, with the auxiliary CIC abaft it. Below it was the chart house. Although the ship's appearance changed radically, the conversion was effectively limited to the former bridge structure. The two close-ups were taken at Norfolk late in June 1942. The overall photograph was taken after minor improvements at New York on 23 September 1942.

$20,250,292, of which 64 percent was the cost of material.

The less modern ships received attention as well. The ex-coal burners were refitted, but the most extreme suggestion, that the amidships turrets be removed, seems not to have been pursued very seriously. On the other hand, the *Arkansas* was extensively refitted at Norfolk between 6 March and 26 July 1942. All four remaining gun deck 5in/51 were removed and their ports plated over; the two open mounts in the superstructure were removed. The bridgework was rebuilt, a tripod foremast somewhat similar to that of the *Texas* being installed. In September two quadruple 1.1-inch guns were added to the four already in place, and another two appeared in December. By that time she had thirty Oerlikons and six 5in/51, the eight 0.50-calibre guns having been landed

only in November. The next April and May first six and then the last two 1.1-inch weapons were replaced by quadruple Bofors. In May 1944 four 20mm were replaced by two quadruple 20mm. The *Arkansas* was again refitted at Boston, 14 September through 7 November 1944, as she was prepared for Pacific service. Her bridgework was again greatly extended, the former stump superstructure abaft the funnel reduced, and the secondary and light batteries altered: two 3 inchers and a quadruple 40mm on the fantail were added. The next year a director replaced the mainmast radar antenna. As of December 1944, she was armed with twenty-eight single and two quadruple 20mm.

The *New York* and *Texas* were much less altered. In both the gun deck 5in/51 were plated over, leaving only six such weapons in the amidships casemate.

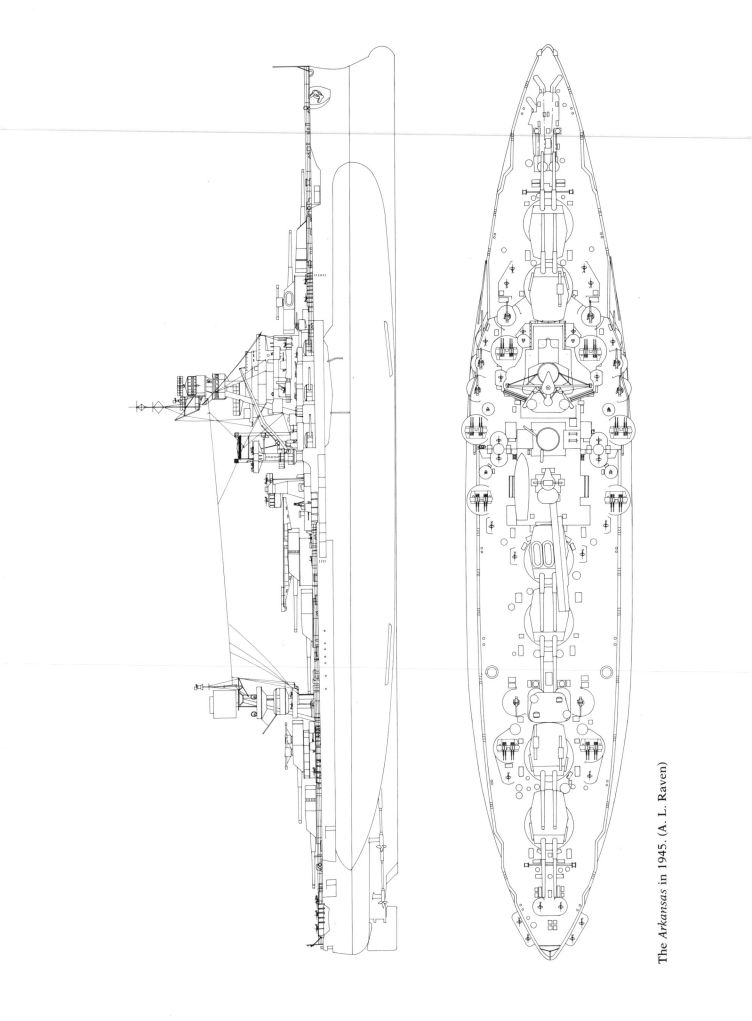

The *Arkansas* in 1945. (A. L. Raven)

The *Texas* was little changed in wartime. She is shown on 1 April 1944, liberally covered in light antiaircraft guns.

During August 1942, the *New York* was fitted with four more quadruple 1.1-inch guns, and her 20mm battery increased to forty-two. During 1943 and 1944 the 1.1s were gradually replaced by Bofors guns. For example, in November 1943 she had four of each. Two more quadruple 40mm were soon added, for a total of ten multiple machine cannon. The 1.1-inch guns were not completely eliminated until October 1944. By the end of 1944, each ship had ten 3 inchers, ten 40mm mounts, and forty-eight and forty-four Oerlikons, respectively.

Table 16-1 shows the improvements planned for the old battleships as of the end of the war, with notes on their actual batteries at that time. The *Pennsylvania* had just completed a major refit, and the *Maryland* was being refitted. Note the rather ambitious plans for the oldest ships. It is not clear whether designs for these large refits had been worked out in detail, as no drawings appear to have survived.

There were also two former battleships, the target ship *Utah* and the training ship *Wyoming*. Both had been demilitarized under the terms of the London Treaty of 1930.

The *Utah* had been stripped of her guns and converted to radio control. She retained the appearance of a battleship, in that her empty turrets remained in place and her casemates were merely covered over. She even retained her cage foremast and pole mainmast. However, in accordance with the treaty she was entirely disarmed.

By the late 1930s, the battle fleet needed antiaircraft training far more than target practice against ship targets. During 1935 the *Utah* was converted into a "fleet machine gun school": the C-in-C U.S. Fleet, in his FY36 *Annual Report*, considered her superior to a school ashore because she better duplicated shipboard conditions. She could also follow the fleet as it changed operating areas, and it was simple to transfer men to her, as her berthing and messing facilities could serve far more than her limited crew. Moreover, she retained her target-ship capability and often served as a bombing target. "Under her present employment, she is one of the most useful vessels in the fleet."

During a summer 1939 Puget Sound refit four 5in/25 guns and two quadruple 1.1-inch machine cannon

The *New York* is shown on 8 June 1944. She differed from *Texas* in her bridge structure. For example, unlike her sister, she carried two 20mm guns on her pilot house level, forward of her bridge.

were added, and the *Utah* became a general-purpose training ship. Two of the the 5-inch guns were mounted atop No. 2 barbette, which was cleared and extended over the former No. 1 turret for this purpose. The other two were alongside the superstructure. During a second refit at Puget Sound (31 May to 26 August 1941) the *Utah* was again rearmed. This time four 5in/38 were added, the total battery as of June 1941 comprising eight 5 inchers, two quadruple 1.1-inch, and sixteen 0.50-calibre machine guns, at least some

Table 16-1. Radar and Antiaircraft Improvements Planned for the Old Battleships, Summer 1945 (A BuShips Table)

	Air Search	Heavy AA	40mm	20mm
Arkansas	AB	CDEF	GHI	J
Texas	AB	CDEF	HIK	J
New York	AB	CDEF	HIK	J
Colorado	AB	CEDL	IM	J
New Mexico	AB	CDEL	HIK	J
Idaho	AB	CDN	HIK	J
Mississippi	AB	CDL	HIO	P
West Virginia	AB	D	KQ	J
Pennsylvania	B	R	HIS	T
Nevada	AB	D	HIK	T
Tennessee	B	D	KQ	J
California	B	D	U	T
Maryland	BV	V	V	V

Key:

A—Install one SP primarily for coaching AA-fire control radar onto the target.

B—Install one SCR 720 for zenith search.

C—Install eight 5in/38 twin mounts controlled by four Mk 37 directors, with Mk 12/22 radars.

D—Install four GFCS Mk 57.

E—Remove 5in/51 battery.

F—Remove 3in/50 battery.

G—Add five quadruple, two twin 40mm mounts. (In August 1945, the *Arkansas* actually mounted nine quadruple 40mm.)

H—Install six Mk 57 (if not possible, install as less desirable four Mk 63).

I—Add Mk 51 directors so that each mount can be individually controlled.

J—Install twin 20mm in remaining space for a total (minimum) of forty 20mm guns. (In August 1945, the *Arkansas* actually mounted two quadruple and twenty-eight single 20mm guns; *Texas*, forty-four single; *New York*, forty-four single and two twin; *Colorado*, thirty-nine single and one quadruple; *New Mexico*, forty single; *Idaho*, forty single; *West Virginia*, fifty-eight single, 1 twin, and 1 quadruple; and *Tennessee*, forty-three single 20mm.)

K—Add four quadruple, two twin 40mm mounts. (In August 1945, *New York*, *Texas*, *New Mexico*, *Idaho*, *West Virginia*, and *Nevada* all had ten quadruple 40mm.)

L—Remove 5in/25 battery.

M—Add six quadruple 40mm mounts, six Mk 57 directors. (In August 1945, *Colorado* actually had eight quadruple and two twin 40mm guns aboard.)

N—Remove 5in/38 single mounts.

O—Add two quadruple, two twin 40mm mounts. (In August 1945 *Mississippi* had twelve quadruple 40mm guns.)

P—Present battery acceptable, though at least three more twin mounts should be installed. (In August 1945, *Mississippi* actually mounted seventeen twin 20mm.)

Q—Install six Mk 57 directors.

R—Add two Mk 37 directors with Mk 12/22 radars and two Mk 57 directors.

S—Add four quadruple and one twin 40mm mounts; four Mk 63 directors are already installed. (In August 1945, *Pennsylvania* had ten quadruple and one twin 40mm mount aboard.)

T—Satisfactory. (In August 1945, *Pennsylvania* mounted twenty-seven single and twenty-two twin 20mm plus six 0.50-calibre machine guns; *Nevada*, five single and twenty twin 20mm; and *California*, forty *twin* 20mm.)

U—Add two twin 40mm mounts, two Mk 57 directors. (In August 1945, *California* had fourteen quadruple 40mm mounts aboard.)

V—Now under major overhaul, will emerge with not less than one SK, one SP; eight twin 5in/38; four Mk 37 directors with Mk 12/22 radar; four Mk 57 directors; fourteen quadruple and two twin 40mm mounts; six Mk 57, ten Mk 51; twenty twin 20mm. *Maryland* actually had two twin and eleven quadruple 40mm mounts, twenty twin and one quadruple 20mm. She emerged from refit with two Mark 57 directors, but as of November 1945 had four Mark 57 and four Mark 63 (but only seventeen twin 20mm).

of which had first been added during the conversion to machine gun school in August 1935. The 5-inch guns were rearranged, with 5in/38 to port, 5in/25 to starboard.

As of June 1941 the *assigned* battery was the eight 5 inchers, four 3in/50, one quadruple and one twin Bofors (40mm), the two quadruple 1.1s, four 20mm and eight 0.50-calibre machine guns. At the time of her loss that December, the *Utah* had aboard one

quadruple 1.1 and fifteen 0.50s. Just what had become of the other 1.1 is not clear.

As a demilitarized training ship, the *Wyoming* corresponded to the British *Iron Duke* and the Japanese *Hiei*. In accordance with the treaty requirements, her side armor and her blisters were removed, reducing her beam to 93 feet. Turrets 3, 4, and 5 were landed, but their barbettes remained, as did the entire secondary battery and the full fire control system. Her

Serving as a combination target ship and antiaircraft gunnery training ship, the *Utah* is painted dark gray at Puget Sound, 18 August 1941. She was armed with two 5in/25 forward, two 5in/38 (open mounts) to port on her forecastle, two 5in/25 (as shown) to starboard on her forecastle, and two enclosed 5in/38 aft. The 01 level abeam the bridge carried two 3in/50 antiaircraft guns to port and a quadruple 1.1-inch gun to starboard (with two 0.50-calibre machine guns abaft it). All of these weapons, and their directors, had to be covered over when she served in her alternate role as a target ship. The accompanying sketch shows the covers planned.

machinery was gutted (one boiler removed) to reduce power to 20,000SHP and speed to 18 knots. Standard displacement fell to 19,700 tons.

As befitted a training ship, the *Wyoming* spent most of her prewar service cruising. She also participated in several amphibious exercises, and that experience suggested to some that she might be usefully employed in future as a specialized assault ship.

That would require additional antiaircraft weapons. In July 1940, the General Board proposed that two 5in/51 (numbers 15 and 16 on the bridge wings) be removed, and that eight 3in/50 AA guns be added: two replacing the two 5in/51; two each in gun tubs built atop Nos. 3, 4, and 5 barbettes. These weapons would be replaced by a total of six quadruple 1.1-

inch machine cannon when the latter became available. The exisiting 3-inch antiaircraft battery would receive splinter protection in the form of 25-pound STS bulkheads. The (removed) side belt might be replaced by 2 inch to 4 inch STS; 3.5 inchers would resist conventional field artillery. The existing 5in/51 secondary gun was lauded at a General Board hearing as "the most effective. . . for supporting a landing."

In this form the ship would be useful as a transport or as an escort or as a fire support unit. She foreshadowed the "commando ship" proposal for *Iowa*-class conversion.

Fleet Training wanted instead to use the ship as "another *Utah*." New guns would be needed, but their

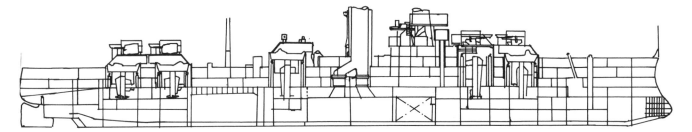

The *Utah* as a target/training ship (AG 16), 1941, inboard profile.

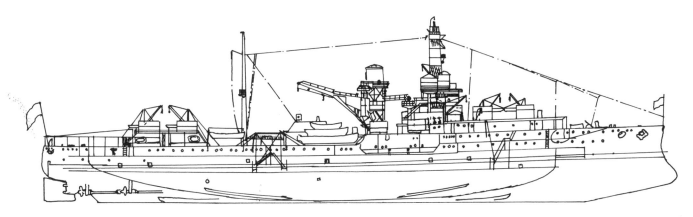

The *Utah* as a target/training ship (AG 16), 1941, outboard profile. Note the protective covers over her 5-inch guns and her directors, each with a small crane to uncover it. Because the booklet of plans on which this drawing is based does not perfectly match the 1941 photograph of the ship, it is not certain that all of the planned directors were fitted. They would have composed 1.1-inch directors on the lookout level, and, below them, a 5in/38 director to port and a 5in/25 director to starboard. The object atop her pilot house in the photograph is presumably an antiaircraft range-finder.

numbers would have to be limited, because the ship would be covered over from time to time as a target. There would have to be at least four 5in/25 (5in/38 if possible) on one side.

In August, the General Board ruled in favor of the training/target role. For example, the services of the *Wyoming* as a transport for Marines would soon be provided by four ships just acquired and then under conversion. Fire support and reserve training would be provided by existing ships. Conversion was scheduled for the next overhaul period, to begin in October 1940. All 5in/51 would be removed, but the mounts would remain and the guns would be held in reserve for possible reinstallation. Four 3in/50 AA on one side would be replaced by 5in/38, controlled by a Mark 33 or Mark 37 director. There would also be two quadruple 1.1-inch machine cannon, firing on the same side, and eight 0.50-calibre machine guns. There would be special bomb protection, and 70-pound STS would cover ship control positions. The full planned battery was aboard by July 1941. In November, the *Wyoming*, which had been flagship of the training patrol force since 2 January, became an antiaircraft training ship in the Chesapeake Bay. As of mid-1941 her *assigned* battery included one quadruple and one

twin Bofors and four 20mm guns, that is, her battery matched that of the *Utah* except that she had four 3in/50 where the older ship had 5in/25s. As of late 1941 the *Wyoming* retained all six 12-inch guns and ten of her 5in/51, and as late as June 1942 her only automatic AA guns were her 20mm and 0.50-calibre pieces.

The surviving single-purpose secondary guns were removed in July 1942 and in September the 0.50s were deleted from her "ultimate approved" battery, replaced by four more 20mm. A quadruple 40mm mount was finally fitted early in the fall, and in November 1942 further changes brought aboard a twin 40mm at the expense of four of the eight 0.50s. In June 1943, she carried six single and one twin 5in/38, four 3in/50, one quadruple and one twin 40mm, two quadruple 1.1-inch, eight Oerlikons, and four 0.50s. Antiaircraft guns were mounted atop all three empty barbettes. The weapons atop Nos. 4 and 5 appear to have been open single 5in/38s. The 3in/50 were lined up on the main deck (starboard side) abaft the deckhouse, on which were mounted four single 5in/38, two on each side; the two to starboard were enclosed mounts. The twin 5in/38 was on a pedestal just abaft the deckhouse on the starboard side. The

The ex-battleship *Wyoming* served as a training ship. She is shown in her prewar configuration, armed with six 12-inch guns. Note the antiaircraft range-finders atop her torpedo-defense platform. In 1940 it was proposed that she be rebuilt as a target ship similar to the *Utah*, but nothing was done.

Serving as a gunnery training ship during World War Two, *Wyoming* (*above and opposite, top*) was fitted with the full range of antiaircraft guns and directors. Two photographs are needed to capture her asymmetrical arrangement. The port view was taken on 17 June 1943, but the starboard view is undated.

The *Wyoming* was rebuilt in 1945, her 12-inch guns removed and additional antiaircraft weapons fitted. She is shown as she emerged from Norfolk Navy Yard, 31 March 1945. A few months later she was detached to the new Operational Development Force in Casco Bay. She was succeeded postwar in this role by the *Mississippi*.

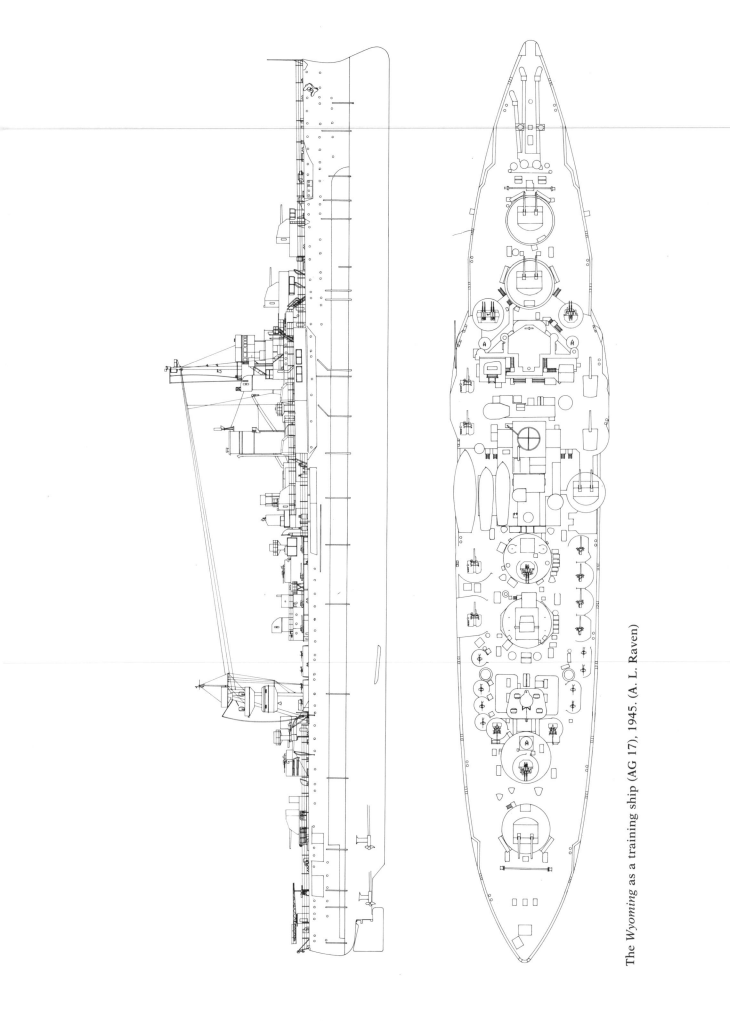

The *Wyoming* as a training ship (AG 17), 1945. (A. L. Raven)

twin Bofors was located to starboard on the forward end of the 01 level, the quadruple mount to port. The bridge carried two directors, a Mark 37 for the enclosed guns to starboard; and a Mark 33 for the open mounts to port.

As an antiaircraft training ship, the *Wyoming* had no need for her three twin 12-inch turrets, which merely occupied space better devoted to additional antiaircraft weapons. Admiral King approved the ultimate removal of all three turrets, as well as of the surviving 0.50-calibre machine guns, in January 1944. During a large refit at Norfolk (12 January to 3 April 1944) each turret was replaced by a twin 5in/38 and a second Mark 37 director was installed abaft the funnel atop No. 4 barbette. The former after main battery control position was replaced by a Mark 50 director for 3in/50 control. That made a total of fourteen 5in/38, eight in twin and six in single mounts. By the end of 1944 there were also the four 3in/50, one quadruple and two twin Bofors, one single Army-type Bofors, one quadruple 1.1-inch machine cannon, and nine 20mm.

By 1945 there was an urgent need for new antiaircraft measures to counter the kamikazes. The *Wyoming* was refitted at New York from 30 June through 13 July 1945 as flagship of Task Force 69, assembled at Casco Bay for antiaircraft research under the command of Rear Admiral W. A. Lee. This organization later became the Operational Development Force, operating out of Norfolk. As a unit of the latter, the *Wyoming* remained operational until 1 August 1947.

The main alteration at this time appears to have been the installation of newer fire controls. Early in 1945 the cage foremast, now useless since it carried only 12-inch and 5in/51 controls, was finally removed. By this time the 1.1-inch mount was gone, and there were two more twin Bofors, in Nos. 3 and 5 barbettes.

In November 1945 the single Bofors was finally gone, but there were one quadruple and two twin 20mm, as well as three surviving single mounts. The ship carried the latest light AA directors: two Mark 57 and Mark 53. She was scheduled to receive the new Marks 56 and 61 when they became available.

17

Postwar

After 1945 the battle fleet no longer had any capital ships to fight. The only potential opponent, the Soviet Navy, was (and for that matter remains) primarily a submarine and land-based bomber force. Stalin did lay down at least one battle cruiser, the *Stalingrad*, in 1949, but his substantial postwar capital ship program was cancelled upon his death.* The very large surviving U.S. battle fleet, ten new ships, five old but modernized ones, and one incomplete hull (the *Kentucky*), was therefore reduced to what, before 1941, had been subsidiary tasks: fire support, carrier escort, fleet flagship duty, ordnance experimentation. As this is written, however, two *Iowa*s have been recommissioned for duty with surface action groups, their 16-inch guns supplemented by long-range land-attack cruise missiles. The other two will follow within a few years. They are, then, performing a new and distinctive mission, only dimly perceived before about 1975.

Initial plans for a postwar fleet envisaged maintaining the *Iowa*s in commission, with the earlier modern battleships in semiactive ("ready reserve") status. Given the shortage of funds, however, this was impossible. The *South Dakota*s were rapidly mothballed, although the *Massachusetts* and *Indiana* were refitted late in 1945, apparently for further service. The *Washington* was fitted with bunks and employed briefly to bring U.S. troops home from overseas, but she then went into reserve as well. The *North Carolina*, on the other hand, was refitted at the Brooklyn Navy Yard early in 1946 and then employed briefly

for training, including a Naval Academy cruise to the Caribbean. By the end of 1946 she, too, had been reduced to the inactive reserve. The *North Carolina*s may have survived longer in service because they were more comfortable than the *South Dakota*s.

Four of the older battleships, the *Arkansas*, *New York*, *Nevada*, and *Pennsylvania*, were exposed to the two atomic bombs at Bikini in 1946. The *Arkansas*, almost directly above the underwater bomb, was lifted up vertically by the column of water it created, and then dropped back into the sea; she sank. The other three survived as hulks, to be sunk up to two years later by conventional weapons. The test results suggest that the protective material worked into old-fashioned capital ships could be effective against nuclear weapons as well.

The *Texas* became a war memorial in 1948. The *Idaho* and *New Mexico* were decommissioned in July 1946. They were initially to have been retained in the postwar fleet, but instead they were stricken in 1947. Their sister ship, the *Mississippi*, was converted into an experimental gunnery ship, replacing the old *Wyoming*; she lasted another decade.

The "Big Five" were retained. The three fully reconstructed units were often described as equivalent to modern battleships in everything but speed. It might be supposed that a ship like the *West Virginia* would be far more economical than an *Iowa* in shore bombardment. As the least modern of the lot, the *Colorado* was to have been rebuilt as a radio-controlled test ship for antiship guided missiles, a modern counterpart of the old *Utah*. This project fell victim to the general postwar shortage of funds and particularly to the emphasis on fleet air defense rather than antiship missiles.

Two more battleships, the last two *Iowa*s, were still under construction at the end of the war. The

---

* In 1945, the Soviets also had the remains of a large prewar capital ship program, including two battleships at Severodvinsk, a battleship and a battle cruiser at Leningrad, and a battleship and battle cruiser at Nikolaev. All had been broken up by 1950, but in 1945 it seemed likely that some, at least, would be completed.

Born for a third time, the *New Jersey* steams on post-refit trials, September 1982. Note the large booms for more efficient fueling at sea, the new heavy mast, and the enlarged ECM "box" atop her fire control tower. Her helicopter control station can be seen below her after 5-inch director. Missiles have not yet been mounted.

Illinois (BB 65), under construction at Philadelphia, was cancelled on 11 August 1945, but material already in place was not immediately disposed of. On 13 September, Admiral King proposed that the *Illinois*, the incomplete carrier *Reprisal* (CV 35), one light cruiser, and one submarine be held "in current status" as potential nuclear targets. It would cost $25 to $30 million to bring the battleship to the launching stage, which the General Board considered excessive. The hull was ultimately broken up in place.

As for the *Kentucky* (BB 66), in December 1945 Secretary of the Navy Forrestal announced that she would be suspended and completed to a new design as a prototype antiaircraft battleship, or BB (AA); the Ship Characteristics Board designation SCB 19 was assigned. Work was suspended in August 1946 and then resumed in August 1948 only to clear the building dock. She was floated out, completed to the second deck, on 20 January 1950. It appears that the original battleship plans, rather than any radical alternative, had been followed. Although completion as a missile battleship was proposed several times, no further work was ever done, and the *Kentucky* hulk was broken up in 1958. Her machinery, which had been installed, was used in two fast underway replenishment ships (AOE). Her bow had already been used to repair that of the *Wisconsin*, damaged in a collision with the destroyer *Eaton* in 1956.

Only the *Iowa*s were really compatible with fast carriers, and only they remained in commission for very long. By the beginning of 1950, however, only the *Missouri*, flagship of Fleet Training Command, Atlantic, remained, and even she was in limited commission. Then the Korean War began, and heavy ships were badly needed for fire support. All four *Iowa*s were back in service by August 1951 and all operated off Korea, generally as flagship of Task Force 77. Postwar employment included fleet flagship duty in the Mediterranean, and perhaps only once were all four together at one time. Beginning with the *Missouri* in 1955, they began to return to reserve. The last to go was the *Wisconsin*, deactivated 8 March 1958.

Again, only the *Iowa*s remained active long enough after 1945 to experience extensive refits. From 1952 onwards, however, class improvement plans (CIPs) were maintained for all of the battleships, to be implemented in the event of reactivation. The planned changes fall into three categories:

—Reduction of the wartime light antiaircraft battery to reduce the burden of maintaining mounts often subject to weather damage.
—Modernization of radars.
—Replacement of 40mm guns by the new 3in/50.

Aircraft and catapults were replaced by helicopters. The *Missouri* was the last U.S. battleship to operate fixed-wing aircraft, a pair of SC-1s carried during her 1948 Mediterranean cruise. The other *Iowa*s had their catapults (but not their cranes) removed during Korean War reactivation refits. Unlike the Royal Navy, the U.S. Navy had been unwilling to replace catapult aircraft with carrier aircraft. The U.S. catapult aircraft were spotters, not scouts, and helicopters performed the same function.

In June 1946 the new Ship Characteristics Board approved removal of four main deck quadruple Bofors guns from each of the two *North Carolina*s and the four *Iowa*s, leaving, respectively, eleven and sixteen (fifteen in *Iowa*) mounts. They were those abeam Nos. 2 and 3 turrets in the former class and those forward of No. 1 turret and just forward of No. 3 in the latter. In each case, wiring and foundations were to be retained, so that guns could be reinstalled. The *North Carolina*s actually lost only the two forward mounts on the main deck, but the *Iowa*s lost all four. By this time the *Massachusetts* had already been modified; her two sisters had never had the full complement of main deck guns. All of the removed weapons were reinstalled aboard the *Iowa*s for the Korean War.

At the same time 20mm batteries were sharply reduced, although (at least at first) these free-swinging weapons were not eliminated altogether. Instead, pairs of single mounts were replaced by twins to save weight, space, and manpower. Thus the ultimate authorized battery, late in 1945, was eight twin mounts and thirty-two single mounts. Battleships went into reserve with only the twins, sixteen in the *North Carolina*s and in the *South Dakota*, none in the latter's three half-sisters. In 1951 each *Iowa* was assigned a total of thirty-two twin mounts. The name ship carried none, the *Missouri* had all of them, and the other two had sixteen each. By October, the ultimate battery included no 20mm guns, and within a year all of them were gone.

The primary postwar change in fleet light antiaircraft batteries was the replacement of 40mm quadruple mounts by twin 3in/50. Detailed plans for the *Iowa*s were not drawn until 1955. They called for a total of sixteen mounts, none on the turret tops, and no high guns abeam the second funnel. The latter were eliminated as weight compensation for the new Mark 56 directors nearby. In peacetime the two main deck mounts near No. 3 turret would be landed but their wiring and foundations retained. Although this conversion proceeded far enough into the budget process to receive a Ship Characteristics Board designation (SCB-74E), it was never funded, and the ships went into reserve with their 40mm guns still aboard. However, Mark 56 directors were fitted to the *Iowa* and *New Jersey*.

The May 1954 class improvement plans for the other modern battleships showed twelve twin 3in/50 aboard each *North Carolina* (controlled by six Mark

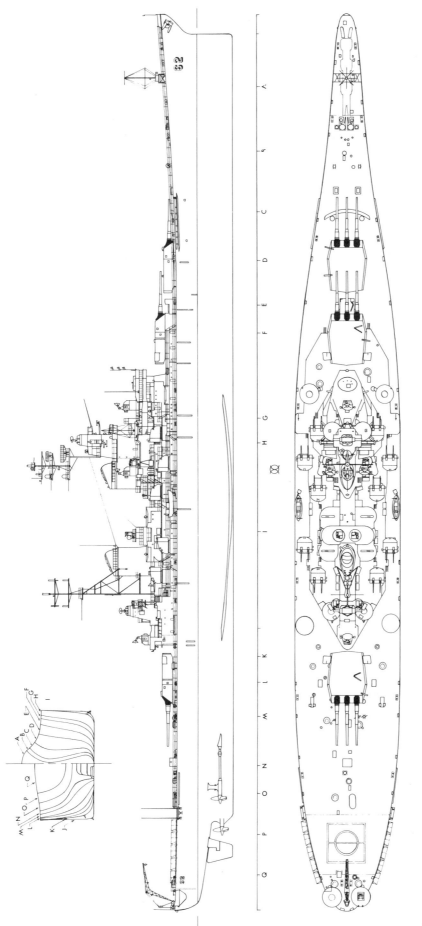

The *New Jersey* as recommissioned, 1969. (A. D. Baker III)

56) and the *South Dakota* and ten twin 3in/50 aboard her three half-sisters.

The new 3-inch battery of the *Iowa* was to have been controlled by six Mark 56 (two on short towers abeam the funnels, two abeam the after fire control tower, two forward of and abeam the forward pair of Mark 37 directors) and by three Mark 63 (one each for the two right aft, and one for the two mounts replacing the two Bofors right forward). Since Mark 56 could also control the 5-inch battery, in effect there would be one director per 5-inch gunhouse.

Only the *Iowa* and *New Jersey* were fitted with the new fire controls, except, they had no Mark 63 right forward. As a consequence they had the high pair of quadruple 40mm abeam the second funnel removed. This last alteration was approved in October 1955, in connection with installation of a new duopod mainmast. Two more mounts were to be removed for boat stowage. The *Missouri*, already in reserve, was not modified and retained all twenty 40mm mounts. The *New Jersey* entered reserve with eighteen mounts and without a duopod. The *Wisconsin* lost her two after main deck mounts when she was fitted with a new mainmast carrying an SPS-8 height-finding radar. She lost her two forward ones on her final refit in 1955-56. The *Iowa* lost her after main deck mounts when she was fitted with the duopod and her high pair abeam the second funnel as well. She alone received the full treatment.

At the same time another modification was planned. Two large kingposts were to be stepped just abaft the after funnel, to support big cranes for heavy-weather fueling at sea and for boats. They would also become a new supporting structure for the mainmast. Pump capacity was also increased. This modification required weight compensation, as the ships were already seriously overweight. Of the 100 tons required, it was estimated that 27 could be gained by removal of the range-finders of Nos. 2 and 3 turrets (that of No. 1 had already been removed in December 1947). Of the four ships, the *Missouri* was not modified, as she was already in reserve. The *Iowa* and *Wisconsin* received the kingposts, but the *New Jersey* did not.

About 1956 the three *Iowa*s still in active service were modified to carry, assemble, and fire the new KATIE (Mark 23) nuclear 16-inch shell. All projectiles were stowed in No. 2 turret, the planned allowance being nine nuclear shells plus nine spotting rounds, but more could be carried. Shells could be moved by monorail along the third deck to No. 1 or No. 3 magazines, and there were assembly stands in Nos. 1 and 3 turrets. It is not clear which ships, if any, actually carried these weapons at sea.*

Other CIP modifications included new radars (SPS-12 and -8), TACAN, airborne early-warning receiving equipment, infrared signaling beacons, a bombardment computer Mark 48 to replace the existing Dead Reckoning Tracer, and increased underway replenishment capacity (700 gallons/minute rather than 250, four port and four starboard housefall receiving stations).

By the time the ships had been laid up, none had served actively for much more than a decade. Their hulls were, therefore, still in excellent condition, and a variety of proposals were made for alternative uses, including missile conversions and an amphibious support ship. None was accepted. Although the surviving documents do not say as much, it appears that they were preserved specifically as fire support ships. Their potential value in this role increased as the number of active gun-armed cruisers declined during the late 1950s and early 1960s. Even so, all of the older battleships were discarded. The "Big Five" were stricken on 1 March 1959, the *North Carolina*s on 1 June 1960 and the *South Dakota*s on 1 June 1962, in each case about twenty years after launch. The *North Carolina*, *Alabama*, and *Massachusetts* have all been preserved as memorials. Although the active service of the 35,000-ton battleships ended in 1946, plans for their reactivation were kept up to date through the 1950s, as were projects for more radical alterations.

As the war in Vietnam intensified from 1964 onwards, the Marines' demands for heavy-ship fire support began to gain force. Airplanes, which were now relatively expensive, were being lost in large numbers in missions which a battleship could execute at least as well. By 1966 the Department of Defense was considering recommissioning either one battleship or two heavy cruisers. Senator Richard B. Russell was a strong advocate of the battleship. However, the then-chief of naval operations, Admiral David L. MacDonald, strongly opposed it, and the decision to recommission the *New Jersey* was not announced until the day after he left office, 1 August 1967. She was recommissioned at Philadelphia on 6 April 1968 after an extensive overhaul. The *New Jersey* began conducting fire support off Vietnam the following 30 September.

Modernization was purposely made extremely austere, to avoid criticism that the ship was intended more as an admiral's flagship than for shore-bombardment. For example, although the ship had served

---

* At this time the U.S. Navy appears to have expected to use nuclear weapons relatively freely, for example, for tactical fire

support. For example, when double-ended Terrier missile frigates were proposed, objections to the absence of guns (for bombardment) were met by the argument that the nuclear version of the antiaircraft missile would do as well. As late as 1961 standard doctrine was to bombard a beach with nuclear weapons prior to H-hour. At that time Admiral McCain argued for the 16-inch gun as a superior close-support weapon because tests had shown that tanks could operate within a few hundred yards of a nuclear detonation.

Recommissioned for Vietnam, the *New Jersey* was little modified. She is shown in September 1968. Although she appears festooned with radio antennas, in fact her communication suit was extremely austere. It symbolized a key problem of the reserve fleet. Communications equipment changes relatively rapidly. Ships otherwise quite usable may be entirely unable to communicate with more modern craft unless they are given entirely new radio systems. The other major modification was for self-defense: an early version of SHORTSTOP, a combination jammer and chaff-launcher. The ULQ-6B jammer was located in the box atop her foremast, its antennas projecting out on both sides. When the *New Jersey* was refitted again in 1981–82, the box was retained as a base for a new SLQ-32 system. It was not particularly convenient, and the other refitted battleships have a more streamlined ECM housing. The *New Jersey* had been laid up with her 40mm mounts in place. All were removed when she was recommissioned, but the forward gun tubs (on the 01 level), painted white, were used by the crew as swimming pools. Note that the ship retained her old (and quite obsolescent) SPS-12 air-search radar.

as a flagship in the past, her admiral's quarters were deliberately not reactivated. It was claimed at the time that 80 percent of all naval targets in Vietnam were within 16-inch range of the coast, and during her brief deployment the *New Jersey* fired 5,688 16-inch shells, compared with 771 during the whole of World War Two.

The *New Jersey* was chosen because she was in the best material condition. The *Wisconsin*, which had suffered a minor electrical fire after deactivation, was in the worst shape. The ten month "austere" refit at Philadelphia cost $22.2 million, of which $13.6 million went for basic activation and repair, $3.6 million for outfitting, and only $6.0 million for alterations and new equipment. There were severe problems: equipment history cards, change cards, in fact all documentation, were incomplete. Ammunition had not been manufactured for over a decade, and at first it ap-

peared that there would not be enough barrel liners for the main armament. A factory had to be reactivated. Much of the ship's equipment was obsolete, and spares were not available, since the equipment in question was not used aboard active ships.

Of the battery, all of the Bofors guns were removed but the six Mark 56 directors were retained. Only the two amidships were reactivated, the other four remaining under covers and lacking their radar dishes. The entire main and secondary batteries were activated, along with all the relevant directors. In addition, two Mark 48 computers and a target-designation system were added for the main battery.

The major obvious external change in the ship was in electronics. Her heavy mainmast was fitted with extensive communications arrays in place of the previous radar, and a large radio mast appeared forward of the two gun tubs on the forecastle. Aft, whips ex-

Amidships *New Jersey* seemed almost unchanged in her Vietnam configuration. Note, however, the canvas-covered rocket launchers in her old 40mm gun tubs. They fired chaff rockets, which at this early stage were modified versions of the standard air-launched Zuni, fired from aircraft-type four-round launchers. The tripod abaft the after 5-inch mount was for replenishment at sea.

tended outboard from the fantail, on which a helicopter pad was painted. Some new communications systems were associated with SNOOPY DASH, a spotting system using a TV-equipped DASH remote-controlled helicopter. Reportedly, the ship was also assisted by a Marine A-4 Skyhawk spotter.

Although no light weapons were fitted for self-defense, the *New Jersey* did receive a prototype SHORTSTOP antimissile ECM system incorporating a ULQ-6B deception jammer in a large box on her foremast, with electronic arrays protruding from either side. SHORTSTOP was intended to detect incoming SS-N-2 (Styx) missiles, some of which the Soviets had supplied to the North Vietnamese. It would deceive their radar seekers, deflecting them into a chaff cloud projected by rockets; four converted Zuni chaff aircraft rocket launchers replaced the quadruple Bofors abeam the second stack.

The decision to recommission the battleship was very controversial. Among its severest critics was Congressman Melvin Laird, who became secretary of defense in January 1969. He began to consider deactivation that June, as the ship prepared for a second deployment to Southeast Asia. Her inactivation was announced on 21 August 1969, and she was laid up at Bremerton.

Confusion over the ship's mission may have been a factor in this decision. The secretary of defense saw her as an interdictor of the Ho Chi Minh Trail, and thus as a means of reducing aircraft losses to ground fire. That entailed night fire, but her captain, J. E. Snyder, Jr., thought his ship would spend two-thirds of her time supporting the Marines in a more traditional role. He minimized night fire to avoid wasting ammunition. Snyder felt that the ship's deactivation reflected his failure to convince his superiors of her value in fire support. The Marines themselves argued that the presence of a battleship off the DMZ discouraged enemy attacks and hindered infiltration. It was later reported that they had initially asked for the ship (in 1967) as standby support in the event they had to make an amphibious assault in North Vietnam.

In fact the ship spent only twenty days firing at North Vietnam, since President Johnson ended the bombardment of the North as a deescalatory gesture. She spent the remainder of her 120-day deployment off South Vietnam.

That did not end the story. Action to dispose of the *Iowa* and *Wisconsin* reportedly was begun on 6 June 1973 but then cancelled on 11 September of that year. The Navy later rejected an attempt by the

State of New Jersey to obtain the *New Jersey* as a memorial; she was still seen as a national resource. Less than a decade later the ships were once again being reactivated. As of 1977, the Board of Inspection and Survey estimated that each had at least fifteen remaining years of active service life.

It is difficult to trace the precise origins of the decision to modernize and recommission the battleships. As early as 1974, for example, an analyst at the Center for Naval Analyses suggested that battleships might replace carriers in forward areas in time of crisis. They would be better able to survive an initial Soviet surprise attack, even though they would have nothing like the firepower of a carrier. They might, moreover, be able to engage Soviet ships at considerable distances, using future guided and rocket-assisted shells.

By about 1977 there was some Navy interest in recommissioning. The Board of Inspection and Survey examined all four ships and found them fundamentally sound. Two years later a proposal to recommission the *New Jersey* figured in studies of quick improvements to U.S. naval power, in response to mounting crises such as Iran and Afghanistan. Early in 1980 the Senate Armed Services Committee considered recommissioning the ship as part of the FY81 (Carter) program, but it was deleted. At this time it was estimated that an austere refit, incorporating NATO Sea Sparrow for self-defense, would have cost $255 million in FY80 dollars, or $270 million in FY81 funds. Modernization would take twelve to fifteen months.

A retired Air Force fighter pilot and Washington defense consultant, Charles E. Myers, is credited with publicizing the merits of a battleship under the designation "interdiction assault ship." He was particularly interested the all-weather capability inherent in 16-inch guns. It is not clear at this remove whether Myers originated the idea or whether he was an early proponent of an idea originated by the Marines, who certainly wanted the ship. The battleship was part of the official Navy budget request by February 1980. It did not survive the process of budget-cutting, but funds for the *New Jersey* were included in the Reagan Administration's FY81 supplemental budget. The reactivation of the *Iowa* was included in the FY82 program. The *Missouri* is being reactivated using reprogrammed funds, money made available by savings achieved in the FY81–FY84 budgets. The reactivation of the fourth ship, the *Wisconsin*, has been requested under the FY86 program.

The battleships will be deployed with air-defense escorts in surface action groups and should be able to survive considerable air attack yet deliver substantial blows (via cruise missiles and guns) against land targets. The key offensive weapons of such a group would be Tomahawk land-attack cruise missiles aboard the battleship. Although a surface action group clearly cannot match aircraft carrier capability, it can make up for the severe limitation in the total number of deployed carrier battle groups.

Moreover, under some circumstances long-range gun strikes may be preferable to carrier air attacks. They do not, for example, risk the loss of valuable pilots. We saw such a use in Lebanon. Some would suggest that it is peculiarly disheartening to the victims of shelling that they cannot hope to do anything about the attack. They can at least shoot back at aircraft. This is hardly to suggest that the gun can somehow be revived in such a way as to supplant aircraft, but only that, within its niche, the gun remains valuable.

The battleships are also potentially valuable as fleet flagships, replacing the missile cruisers of the 1960s and 1970s, the last of which, the *Oklahoma City*, was retired in 1979. Such a configuration was studied in 1981, but rejected for the time being as too expensive. However, a flagship conversion would be a viable possibility for a future large battleship refit.*

Battleship survivability is an important consideration in the reactivation. Antiship missiles, such as Exocet, are now the common coin of Third World navies. Although a fleet at sea should be able to deal relatively easily with the platforms carrying such weapons, the prospect of surprise attack remains sobering. Carriers, with their masses of explosives and jet fuel, have always been vulnerable. A battleship is different. Most of her limited volume of explosives is underwater. The new missile installations are above deck but they are not connected to magazines or other explosive concentrations below. A small missile would be unlikely, then, to do very much damage. Even the big Soviet armor-piercing missiles would generally hit well above the waterline, where they would be unlikely to strike the ship's magazines. Apart from the Soviet weapons, there are few armor-piercing weapons left in the world's inventories, simply because there are so very few armored warships left. In this sense, the gross obsolescence of the battleship is a major asset. This is not to say that a ship like the *New Jersey* cannot be sunk, only that sinking it is no easy matter.

Out of a total cost of about $326 million, $170 million went for rehabilitation. The rest bought a variety of new systems: eight quadruple armored box launchers for Tomahawk land-attack and long-range antiship missiles; four quadruple launchers for Harpoon antiship missiles; four Phalanx close-in defen-

---

* No such refit is currently planned, and command and control facilities aboard the battleships are spartan at best. At this writing the missile cruiser *Belknap* (CG-26) is refitting as Sixth Fleet Flagship, for completion in July 1985. However, improvements to battleship command and control are currently planned.

The *New Jersey* was much more extensively modified in 1981–82. Her foremast shows not only a new SPS-49 air-search radar, but also a TACAN and LAMPS data link electronics for over-the-horizon targeting. Phalanx close-in defensive weapons (indicated by their white radomes) have been added, and Harpoon and Tomahawk offensive missiles replace four twin 5in/38. However, a much-discussed (and extremely expensive) Phase II reconstruction, adding more missiles and VSTOL aircraft, will not be carried out. The overhead view shows the eight large armored box launchers for Tomahawks, and two of the four Harpoon launchers abeam the second funnel. Future improvements may include more capable communications facilities and perhaps the replacement of some or all of the old 5in/38s with unmanned lightweight 5in 54s or with small defensive missiles. In any case they are unlikely to change the classic profiles of these elegant ships.

sive guns; improved communications (to cruiser standard); SLQ-32 defensive ECM gear; and a new SPS-49 air-search radar. In all but the *New Jersey*, an SPS-67 replaces the SPS-10F surface-search radar. The stern was cleared and raised about 2 feet to provide one operating helicopter spot and three parking spots. Four twin 5in/38 guns were landed to make space for some Tomahawk launchers. The ship was converted to use Navy distillate fuel, not black oil, and her fire-fighting facilities were improved.

Once the project had been approved, it moved very rapidly. The design team was assembled aboard the ship at Long Beach and given a very short time to complete work. Time pressure was also used to force the hands of the many offices within the Office of the Chief of Naval Operations. In other cases, each branch might have many chances ("chops") to review a given project, each "chop" adding delay. In this case, everyone was allowed only a single "chop." As a result, the *New Jersey* was completed on time and within cost limits, a salutary example for other shipbuilding projects.

The austerity of the conversion was justified, at the time, by the urgent need to add to U.S. naval force projection capabilities, and by the expectation that more might be accomplished in a future Phase II or III. After all, a battleship is an enormous platform, and its sheer size invites proposals for installations such as Aegis and a flight deck aft. More recently the Phase II plan has been abandoned, although the ships will receive command and control upgrades. The deterrent is the sheer cost of such radical alterations as the removal of No. 3 turret. Moreover, removal of this heavy weight would have placed the ship dangerously out of trim, even with the planned flight deck and hangar.

The *New Jersey* was funded under the FY81 and FY82 budgets, the latter providing long-lead funds for the *Iowa*. The *Iowa* was fully funded under FY83 and was recommissioned on 28 April 1984, well ahead of the originally planned date of January 1985. Preliminary work began in October 1982. In theory, two battleships provide a minimum force sufficient to support simultaneous Marine operations in both oceans. But because at least one ship will always have to be refitting or working up, three is a more realistic figure. In 1984 work began on the *Missouri*, financed out of savings achieved in earlier shipbuilding budgets.

The *New Jersey* has now proved her value in each of the numbered fleets and has fired her guns in anger for the first time in over a decade off Lebanon. There, the loss of U.S. carrier attack aircraft proved Meyers's point: no one can shoot down or capture a 16-inch shell. She is probably good for at least another fifteen years of service, which should bring her nearly to the year 2000.

There were several more or less exotic proposals for battleship modernization or reconstruction. In July 1954, the SCB chairman wrote that the 35,000-ton battleships seemed ideal for task force duty, except that they were too slow. BuShips was, therefore, to study a conversion which would provide them with a speed of 31 knots. Since "preliminary considerations indicate that the main batteries of these ships are considerably in excess of that required at the present time . . . one turret might be removed in order to provide weight compensation for additional machinery and to lighten the ship."

Just such an improvement of the original *South Dakota* had led to the *Iowa* class; clearly the project would be far from trivial. BuShips reported in mid-September that a *North Carolina* hull would require 240,000SHP, and a *South Dakota* 256,000SHP to achieve 31 knots. This kind of power in turn would require extremely large steam plants, far larger than could be accommodated in the space that would be made available by the removal of (say) No. 3 turret and barbette. Even if the entire external belt of a *North Carolina* were removed, 216,000SHP would still be required. Moreover, the stern would have to be modified to clear the much larger propellers needed to transmit this much power. Shaft lines would have to be changed, and the entire hull form aft modified. The best the bureau could suggest was a gas turbine boost plant (COSAG) or some new high-pressure steam boost plant. Total cost, exclusive of activation, armament, electronic, and other modernization, was estimated at $40 million per ship, which killed the project.

Work sheets show that the full-load displacement of the *North Carolina* could have been reduced from 44,377 to about 40,541 tons and that trial displacement would have been about 38,400 (rather than 42,236). Thus, 210,000SHP would yield the 31 knots. Even these figures included considerable margins. For example, a curve dated 14 August 1954 shows 186,000SHP for 31 knots at 38,400 tons; total power would be 195,000SHP. The 210,000SHP figure was for a *sustained* speed of 31 knots, and it included a service factor of 12.5 percent for fouling and weather. On 42,000 tons the comparable figures would be 204,000, 215,000, and finally 233,000SHP.

There was sufficient weight but *not* sufficient volume for the *Iowa* plant to replace the *North Carolina* plant. That is, No. 3 turret and barbette (including ammunition) came to 2,650.5 tons; removable side armor, another 3,000. Against this, the existing machinery plant weighed 3,286.4 tons plus 290 of foundations, compared with 4,797 and 390 for the 212,000SHP *Iowa* plant. However, The *North Carolina* machinery box measured 176 × 70 × 24 feet, whereas the *Iowa* box measured 256 × 72 × 26 feet. The *Iowa* propellers were 19 feet in diameter, compared with 17 for the *North Carolina*. It was, then, barely conceivable that 31 knots would be achieved, but 35 knots would have required 470,000SHP and the removal of all three turrets.

Possibly the most interesting of the postwar conversion concepts were those connected with guided missiles. Plans to convert the large cruiser *Hawaii* are described in the companion volume on cruisers. The suspended *Iowa*-class battleship *Kentucky* was the subject of similar studies. As early as June 1946 BuOrd suggested that the newly converted gunnery experimental ship *Mississippi* and the suspended battleship *Kentucky* were most suitable for design studies of a turret-type launcher for jet-propelled missiles. An antiaircraft conversion of the *Kentucky* was designated SCB 19, but it appears that only limited design work was undertaken. The only surviving reference mentions design sketches showing new triple or quadruple 8in/55 antiaircraft turrets. Copies, however, have not come to light.

In March 1955, Rear Admiral W. K. Mendenhall, Jr., the chairman of the SCB urged that the *Kentucky* be completed as a missile battleship (BBG), a type incorporated in the early reports of the new Long-Range Objectives Group. He was particularly impressed by the advent of nuclear shells. It was no longer necessary to mount nine 16-inch guns, since "an adequate number of targets simply could not exist within the range of the guns from one position." Firepower would be multiplied fiftyfold by installation of Regulus missiles. Admiral Mendenhall wanted two 16-inch turrets retained (weight might require the removal of one gun from each), six single 5in/54 (twin 5in/38 if the latter had already been procured for the ship), and ten twin 3in/50. The missile battery would consist of two launchers for either Terrier or Talos (or one Talos and one Tartar if the latter were available in time) and one for Regulus (with not fewer than eight Regulus II missiles). Conversion would cost $123 to $130 million.

Admiral Mendenhall thought of her as a one-ship task force, capable of escorting a fast carrier task force or of raiding enemy shore targets at long range, using a submarine to assist in terminal Regulus guidance. She would retain 16-inch guns for shore bombardment and would be able to defend herself against air attack. Speed and torpedo defense would protect her against submarine attack. In July 1955, the cost of completing the *Kentucky* as a BBG was given as $115 million. The strike cruiser (CSGN) of the mid 1970s was similar in concept.

The Long-Range Objectives Group was formed with Opnav in 1954 to develop concepts for using the emerging naval technologies. Its first report (December 1955) described naval forces for the 1960–70 era. The group envisaged a BBG as an important element of an integrated fleet. It called for the formation of five striking forces, each consisting of three attack carriers, one support carrier (CVS), one BBG, four missile cruisers (CAG), three missile frigates (DLG; they would now be classified as cruisers), six missile destroyers (DDG), and two radar picket submarines (SSR). Each BBG would be armed with two Talos long-range antiaircraft missile launchers and with one launcher for the new supersonic Regulus II or Triton missile. It would carry the very long-range (1,000nm) striking power of the fleet. The carriers would be responsible primarily for tactical air support, for ASW, and for a proportion of fleet air defense. The battleship and cruisers would share responsibility for controlling fleet aircraft, and they would have primary responsibility for inner-zone air defense against high-altitude attackers. Ultimately, too, both classes would operate a combination of VTOL fighters and radar early-warning (and, in the case of the cruisers, antisubmarine) helicopters. The DLGs were envisaged as a last-resort missile-defense screen, and they would share ASW responsibility with the destroyers.

The Long-Range Objectives Group expected each battleship conversion to cost about $160 million; the *Kentucky* would be completed as the fifth BBG. Work on a BBG design for the FY58 program began in the spring of 1956. Preliminary studies showed, instead of the air-breathing Regulus II or Triton, two ballistic missile (Polaris) launchers (sixteen missiles stowed horizontally). The ship would also accommodate four Talos launchers (eighty missiles each, three hundred twenty altogether); and twelve Tartar launchers (forty-two missiles each, five hundred four altogether). Special equipment for Polaris would include the new inertial navigational system (SINS), a Doppler sonar for precision measurement of ship speed over the ground, antipitch fins and roll stabilizers. An account of a design meeting in mid-1956 mentions a "citadel" type radar antenna array, presumably the SPS-32/33 combination then being designed for the *Enterprise* and the cruiser *Long Beach*. Conversion would cost $252 million and would require about forty-two months, including thirty-one for construction proper. As of July 1956 BuShips expected to complete the *Kentucky* to this new design (under the FY58 program) about 31 July 1961.

The figures for the missile battery were based on the sheer size of the hull. They did not take into account the problem of interference between the twenty guidance radars involved. All of the Talos and Tartar missiles would require continual guidance from launch to engagement. By late 1956, therefore, the proposed missile battery had been reduced to two Talos and four Tartar, plus fourteen to sixteen IRBM. Such a conversion would cost about $181 million and would require about forty months. This was not particularly attractive; it was little better than the con-

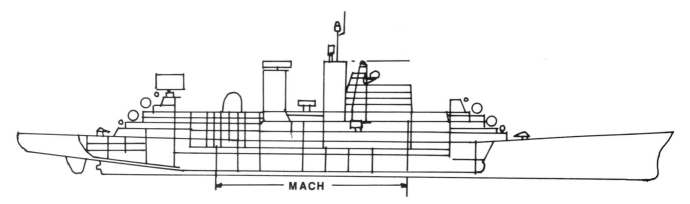

Scheme II for a missile-armed battleship, 9 February 1959. The missiles shown are Talos, fore and aft, with an ASROC box amidships, and they are controlled by SPG-56, at that time the planned replacement for the earlier SPG-49. The big radar aft is a multibeam (three-dimensional) SPS-34, with a two-dimensional SPS-37 atop the after mack. The dome between the after missiles and the mack houses a radio star tracker for precision navigation; another navigational aid (required for successful Polaris firing) was a doppler sonar in the bow (which also housed an SQS-26 long-range sonar). The foremast carried a TACAN and a hemispheric search radar; the horizontal line in the drawing indicates the limit of clearance under the Brooklyn Bridge, for access to the New York Naval Shipyard. The pylon forward of the bridge would have carried surface search radar. An alternative Scheme I would have retained the two forward 16-inch turrets; both would have retained the two forward 5in/38 twin gunhouses.

temporary *Albany*-class missile cruiser. A dedicated Polaris cruiser then in the design stage (and described in *U.S. Cruisers: An Illustrated Design History*) would carry the same Talos and Polaris batteries on a displacement of only 10,000 tons and at a cost of about $130 million.

By this time, too, cost overruns in existing programs were squeezing the shipbuilding budget. The BBG conversion was abandoned late in 1956. No BBG was included in the 1956 Long-Range Objectives Group report. Testimony prepared for the CNO, Admiral Arleigh Burke, to submit to Congress in January 1957 emphasized the cost of completing the battleship for a task for which she had not been designed. At this time the *Kentucky* was structurally complete to the third deck, with some work accomplished up to the to second deck. Her main machinery had been installed, but her piping and wiring were incomplete. It would take about thirty months to complete her as a battleship. Even at this stage of completion, however, her hull compartmentation and distribution of armor were clearly tailored for battleship rather than for guided missile use. Rip-out costs would be high, and there was little hope of making full use of the *volume* of the hull. The cost and effort involved might well approach those required for a new ship.

Even so, interest in missile conversions remained. In 1957, preliminary estimates were made for both *South Dakota* and *Iowa* conversions. All main battery guns would have been removed from the *South Dakota*. She would have had one twin Talos forward and two Tartar aft, ASROC and the new lightweight Mark 32 tubes for ASW, fleet flagship facilities, in-

creased oil fuel supply, and helicopter capacity. Total cost would be $125 million. A similar *Iowa* conversion would cost $150 million. An *Iowa* retaining the two forward turrets and their director, with Tartar amidships and Talos aft, would cost $110 million ($95 million without Tartar).

The chairman of the SCB, Rear Admiral Denys W. Knoll, formally requested a new BBG study early in May 1958. It would be a combination air-defense ship and fleet oiler (see below for oiler studies); BuShips added fleet flagship facilities on the basis of CNO action on a recent proposal to use the battleships as combat oilers. Armament would match that of the new *Albany*-class converted missile cruisers (two Talos, two Tartar, ASROC, Regulus II with four missiles), and flagship facilities would match those of the newly converted *Cleveland*-class missile cruisers. The ship would be fitted with the massive new SQS-26 sonar and would carry two ASW helicopters. Preliminary Design found that it could carry 8,600 tons extra fuel, for a total of about 16,500, which compared with 14,600 for the oiler *Cimarron* and 21,500 for the larger *Neosho* (AO 143). Cost was estimated at $178 million, of which $5 million was attributable to fleet flagship facilities. Preliminary Design also estimated that the addition of two more Tartar launchers, for a total of four, would add about $15 million. A similar study was done of a missile conversion of the large cruiser *Alaska*.

In September the SCB asked for a single-ended BBG, to be armed with one twin Talos (56 missiles), one ASROC, and two Regulus II launchers with six missiles. Early versions included a single Tartar. All existing armament was to be removed except the two forward turrets and the two forward 5-inch mounts. The ship would be fitted with the new SQS-26 sonar (and the associated 600 kW 400-cycle generator) and would carry two ASW helicopters. Her electronics would match those of the new missile cruiser *Albany*, and her superstructure would have to be redesigned to match, with integrated mast-stacks (macks). To meet the new electrical load, the two existing 300 kW emergency diesel generators would have to be replaced by 1,000 kW units. Conversion would add about 4,100 tons of fuel oil, for a total of about 11,800T. Complement would be 118 officers, 74 CPOs, and 1,938 other enlisted men, compared with a typical World War Two complement of 127 officers and 2,337 enlisted men, with accommodation for 159 to 180 officers and 2,312 to 2,574 enlisted men. Cost of conversion was estimated at $84 million for the lead ship and $79 million for later units.

Early in 1959 this design was revised, with sixteen Polaris ballistic missiles added in tubes abaft the second funnel. It was estimated that such a conversion would take two and a half years (that is, July 1960 through January 1963) and would cost $115 million, $35 million of which would be attributable to Polaris. It appears that there was also an alternative with six 5in/38 and Regulus, without Tartar, priced at about $82 million in October 1958.

At this time Preliminary Design also developed a new double-ended BBG conversion scheme, with Talos fore and aft, with Tartar to port and starboard abaft the two remaining 5in/38 gunhouses. There would also be 4-missile Regulus and flag facilities. To retain sufficient stability, the ship would have to be loaded with an additional 8,600 tons of oil, which would give her a total capacity of about 16,000 tons. The February 1959 Polaris version called for sixteen tubes abaft amidships, at a total cost of $210 million ($36 million specifically for Polaris). It would require about three and a third years (for example, from September 1960 through January 1964). A version of Scheme II without any strategic missiles was priced at $160 million in October 1958.

In both cases estimates were made to see just how quickly surface Polaris systems could be made operational. Contemporary studies covered most other classes of surface ships. By this time the *Kentucky* was already gone, and the four completed ships would have been completed.

The BBG was included in the tentative FY58 program as of April 1956, but was deleted from both FY58 and FY59 programs. However, in November 1958 the director of the Long-Range Objectives Group indicated that he favored conversion (for Talos) in FY61–62 or, for Typhon, in FY62–63, as long as manning could be held down and costs kept below those of a nuclear missile cruiser. A 27 October 1958 table of "Additional Ships That Have Been Recommended

For FY 61 or Later Shipbuilding and Conversion Programs" included a Heavy Missile Ship, BG, converted from an *Iowa*-class battleship, at a cost of $160 million. There was serious interest in this idea as late as 1960.

One other missile conversion study deserves brief mention: a specialized satellite-launch ship, which was needed to launch satellites into particularly favorable (presumably polar or equatorial) orbits. A March 1960 list of FY62 projects not yet worked out in detail shows a battleship or AVT (ex-carrier) conversion, which BuShips priced at $100 million. Characteristics were as yet entirely unformulated. Later such a ship, designated AGSL, appeared in early versions of the FY65 budget as SCB 900.65. Details have never been found; sketches in early booklets describing the FY65 program suggest that by that time a former seaplane tender was the preferred platform.

The fast carrier task force was the operational focus of the postwar Navy. It required not only combatant ships like the BBG but also fast support ships. Protracted strike operations required resupply in minimum time, and by 1955 the one-stop replenishment concept (which later resulted in the AOE and AOR) had been accepted, based on experiments with USS *Conecuh* (AOR 110), formerly the German *Dithmarschen*. Opnav requested studies of battleship and axial-deck carrier conversions in August 1957. BuShips chose the *South Dakota* class. The *North Carolina* was studied but proved less attractive. All three 16-inch turrets and all other guns except four twin 5in/38 would be removed, together with the entire superstructure except for the smoke pipe and the 5in/38 handling rooms. A shelter deck would be added for underway replenishment fore and aft, together with cargo spaces for dry and refrigerated provisions and ammunition in way of the removed barbettes on the second and third decks, served by cargo elevators. Cruising radius would be reduced from 12,000 to 8,000nm and tankage gained by filling the voids of the torpedo-protection spaces, the upper bottom, and the bottoms of the barbettes with cargo oil, for a total of 10,700 tons of cargo oil and 2,600 tons of bulk cargo, a proportion matching that of the successful *Conecuh*, with draft limited to 36 feet for operational reasons. In the end, the ship would carry about half as much oil as the largest fleet tanker, and about a seventh of the stores and ammunition carried by standard store ships and ammunition ships. BuShips argued that she would be extremely inefficient, with too large a crew and with too little space for essential helicopter resupply of carriers. Conversion would have cost about $25 million.

The concept of a fast and well-protected resupply ship remained attractive. In January 1958, Opnav asked for a study of a minimum conversion of an *Iowa*-class battleship. BuShips considered the *Iowa*

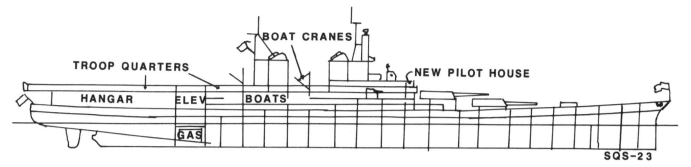

Proposed commando ship (CS) conversion of an *Iowa*-class battleship, as envisaged by BuShips, April 1962. A hangar would have been installed aft, with an elevator forward of it, and boat stowage (with cranes above) between the elevator and the two surviving twin 5in/38 guns. A new pilot house would have been installed, and an ASROC box launcher fitted forward of No. 1 turret. The hangar would have accommodated ten helicopters and four vehicles, with ten more helicopters on the flight deck, and the ship would have carried six LCM-6 Mod 1 landing craft on the 2nd superstructure deck and eight more on the main deck. The landing deck would have been 200 × 108 feet, with a 25-foot wide and 50-foot long elevator. Loads would have included 8,000 tons of fuel oil, plus 100 tons of aviation gasoline (in the gas tank under the elevator, aft), 25 tons of motor gasoline, and 675 tons of JP-5, at a full-load displacement of 57,100 tons. An SQS-23 sonar would have been installed in the forefoot.

and *Wisconsin*, which had been modified for heavy-weather fueling and supplied with additional pumping capacity as suitable interim combat oilers. For about $1,850,000 they could be activated and two propellers and their tail shafts removed. Half the machinery plant would drive them at about 26 knots. They typically carried 7,900 tons of oil. Filling the existing torpedo-protection voids would add about 2,600 more. They needed only 4,000, however, to match the steaming radius of the standard existing tanker, the *Neosho*. That would leave up to 6,500 tons of cargo fuel, without any major modification. The result would, however, be extremely inefficient, with a low pumping rate and inferior performance in bad weather, since the tanker had superior constant-tensioning gear. Its only advantage would have been higher speed. The project was dropped, although a month later Second Fleet pressed for conversion of an *Iowa* to a combination fleet flagship and combat oiler.

High speed and one-stop replenishment remained important, and within a few years the U.S. Navy built four AOEs, with hull forms based on the *Iowa* and propelled by half-*Iowa* machinery.

The other major area of postwar surface fleet development was the amphibious force. Records of the design of the helicopter carrier (LPH) include a brief description of a possible *North Carolina* conversion, at a cost of $30,790,000. She would have carried twenty-eight helicopters and 1,880 troops as well as 530 tons of troop cargo and 200,000 gallons of gasoline. Armament would have been reduced to eight twin 3in/50; the No. 1 16-inch turret would be retained "for trim," that is, to balance weights added aft. Light displacement would be 32,390 tons, full load 41,930. Speed would remain constant at 28 knots. It was estimated that such a ship would have a re-

maining service life of fifteen to twenty years and that she would cost about $440,000 a year to maintain. As in the case of the AOE, a specially built ship was much more efficient.

The LPH was envisaged as part of a substantial amphibious task force, which would land a large Marine force. By 1961, however, there was increasing interest in small operations, and in more flexible means of employing sea power. Admiral John S. McCain, Jr., chairman of the Amphibious Warfare Evaluation Board argued that August for a single-package amphibious force which could promptly be sent to a trouble spot. Greater dispersion of amphibious forces would also reduce their vulnerability to nuclear attack. Finally, he decried the rapid decline in naval gunfire support. In November, he reported studies of an *Iowa*-class battleship converted to a "commando ship" (CS) with a secondary underway replenishment capability.

Admiral McCain argued that naval gunfire support continued to be vital. Troops badly needed air and surface support as they landed, and they might easily be denied air support by weather conditions. Moreover, there were fewer and fewer guns afloat capable of breaching such hard targets as field fortifications. For example, the caves and the Shuri Castle on Okinawa had resisted everything short of 12-inch fire. Nonnuclear war seemed more and more likely, and surely any future enemy would take full advantage of existing natural and manmade obstacles. Only the 16in/50 could penetrate up to 31.5 feet of concrete. Of the other heavy guns afloat, those aboard missile cruisers would probably not be available, since their missile batteries would be required for fleet air defense.

In the proposed conversion, troops and a helicopter deck would have replaced the after triple 16in/

50 turret and all of the light AA guns, as well as all but the two forward twin 5in/38 mounts around the bridge structure. One of the remaining 16-inch guns would be converted to fire the Mark 23 nuclear round, and the ship would ultimately fire a combination of Tartar, rocket-assisted shells (apparently from the lightweight 5in/54 already under development), and a projected surface-to-surface missile. Initial estimates showed a troop capacity of 1,800 men, and the ship would carry eighteen LCM-6 or six LCM-6 and six LCM-8 landing craft, as well as thirty-two HUS helicopters. By way of comparison, the specially built helicopter carrier *Iwo Jima* carried 1,500 troops and thirty HUS (CH-46) helicopters, but no landing craft, and consequently could not operate in bad weather. Even a converted *Essex*-class carrier would accommodate only 1,650 Marines.

Within three months the CS had been renamed the Heavy Assault Ship. It was strongly supported by the commander of the Atlantic Fleet, Admiral R. L. Dennison, as a means of bridging the gap in capability expected when the many World War Two-built amphibious ships were discarded, probably about 1969–72. His staff compared the current PHIBRON, consisting of one command ship (AGC), one transport (APA), two LSDs, two LST, and one cargo ship (AKA), which might be accompanied by a heavy cruiser for fire support, with an amphibious striking unit consisting of one commando ship and three LSD. The total PHIBRON operating cost was $12,930 million; the striking unit's, $13,965 million; a heavy cruiser cost $5,652 million per year to run. Both had similar capabilities, and the striking unit actually cost less.

In June, BuShips reported a feasibility study. A raised flight deck aft covered a hangar accommodating vehicles, 1,800 troops (on a gallery deck), and twenty helicopters. The other ten would have to be stowed topside; three helicopters could operate simultaneously. Fourteen LCM-6 landing craft would be stowed in cradles on the main deck and 02 levels, handled by four 35-ton cranes. A saddle tank would accommodate 100 tons of aviation gasoline, and 675 tons of JP-5 jet fuel could be carried. Stowage would amount to 7,000 square feet of vehicles (about 250 tons) and 100,000 cubic feet (about 1,600 tons) of ammunition and cargo. Self-defense of a solitary unit might require an SQS-23 sonar in the forefoot and the associated ASROC antisubmarine rocket.

Conversion in the FY64 program would cost $65 million, compared with $61 million for a helicopter carrier or $47 million for an LPD. BuShips noted that, although this might seem high, one CS could carry as much bulk cargo and ammunition as an LPD and a helicopter carrier, or 64 percent of the troops, or all of the helicopters. Also, the CS would be nearly 50 percent faster, with a sustained speed of 29.6 knots.

Money was, however, very tight, with a large ongoing fleet ballistic-missile program. ASW modernization, and new amphibious construction all competing for limited funds. In June 1962, Op-09 (Admiral Claude Ricketts) ruled that the first conversion should not be earlier than FY64 and that it could not represent a net addition to the shipbuilding budget; compensation would be required. The CS was attractive, but not attractive enough, and the project died.

Two subsidiary battleship roles complete this chapter: the experimental ship *Mississippi* and the abortive target ship *Colorado*. Both were part of a larger post-1945 program of missile test ships. In the fall of 1945 it was decided to convert a *New Mexico*-class battleship into a replacement for the elderly *Wyoming*, a combination training and experimental ship. Although the CNO decision was dated 10 December, as early as 5 November BuShips sent the commandant of Norfolk Navy Yard a set of plans for conversion of the *Mississippi*.

Only No. 4 turret would be retained. No. 1 would be replaced by a twin 6in/47 DP turret. No. 2 would be removed, leaving in place its foundation, covered by a flat blastproof structure on which instruments might be mounted. No. 3 would be replaced by a triple rapid-fire 8in/55 turret of the type later mounted aboard *Des Moines*-class cruisers. In addition, there would be two single and two twin 5in/54, four twin 5in/38, two twin 3in/70 (quadruple 40mm as interim), two twin 3in/50, four quadruple 40mm, one quadruple 20mm, four twin Oerlikon, and two single Oerlikon. These secondary weapons were mounted mainly on the 01 level, which was built out, as in the *Maryland*. On the other hand, light gun mounts on the 02 and 03 levels were to be removed, and these levels reduced to allow for sky arcs for the antiaircraft battery. The quadruple Bofors at the break of the forecastle would be retained, and the new 20mm battery installed aft to port.

Of these weapons, the twin 5in/54 never entered service. The single 5in/54 actually installed were the semiautomatic type mounted in the *Midway*-class carriers, not the automatic weapon which later appeared in many U.S. warships. The inclusion of 3in/70s shows the optimism of 1945. This weapon did not enter service for another eleven years.

The proposed director installation was ambitious: one Mark 54 (successor to the wartime Mark 34), two Mark 37, three Mark 56, and then the lighter types: two Mark 51, five Mark 57, three Mark 61, three Mark 63. Three CICs were to be installed—a destroyer type in the forward superstructure, and battleship and cruiser types on the second deck. A big tripod mainmast carried the new SX search/height-finding radar.

The ship entered Norfolk on 27 November 1945, and the following 15 February was reclassified EAG 128, an experimental auxiliary. While in the yard she became flagship of the operational development

As the postwar ordnance test ship, the *Mississippi* was the first combatant ship to fire the Terrier antiaircraft missile. She is shown carrying it, in February 1955. A 1948 photograph shows her, newly converted, still retaining both No. 4 14-inch turret and her quarterdeck catapult. Her foremast radar is the relatively unsuccessful SR-3.

force (18 March–15 May 1947) and of Battleships–Cruisers Atlantic Fleet (11 June–14 July 1947). During July the old *Wyoming* tied up across a pier and her crew transferred to the new ship, carrying considerable material with them. The *Mississippi* re-entered service as an EAG in April 1948.

At the time, beside the remaining 14-inch turret, she actually mounted two single 5in/54 (one on forecastle and one on 01 level to port), three twin 5in/38 (all on the 01 level to starboard), two twin 3in/50, and two quadruple Bofors. By April of the next year a twin 6-inch turret occupied No. 1 barbette, but the triple 8 inch was never fitted.

Meanwhile the ship was designated to test the new Terrier antiaircraft missile, two Mark 1 launchers for which would be installed aft in place of Nos. 3 and 4 turrets. These weapons were first test-fired off the Virginia Capes on 28–29 January 1953. The *Mississippi* was also employed in tests of the Petrel air-to-surface missile (February 1956). By this time the Bofors were gone.

The *Mississippi* was decommissioned on 17 Sep-

tember 1956, having entered Norfolk for deactivation overall on 26 May. She was sold to Bethlehem Steel and towed away for breaking up on 7 December 1956, after a career of nearly thirty-nine years.

The other experimental conversion was SCB 38, a FY50 project for a radio-controlled target ship to test antiship missiles. Some members of the General Board considered it even more important than the new missile cruiser (CAG) in view of the need to test missiles. On the other hand, the weapons in question would have been the least important of the new generation: antiaircraft weapons had priority. SCB 38 would have been a new *Utah*, retaining all of her belt armor. In addition, 4-inch STS would cover everything else except for nonvital upper works. The existing bridge, turrets, guns, and equipment would be removed and new bridgework built up. The complement would be reduced to 25 officers and 215 enlisted men, and the ship would have a six-hour radio-controlled (unmanned) endurance at 15 knots. SCB 38 died of postwar fiscal stringency, which killed off several other missile-related projects.

A

The Monitors

The monitors of the Civil War were among the first modern armored ships. They were unique, for their time, in concentrating two or four very powerful guns on a relatively small, shallow-draft hull. Nearly all, moreover, were suitable only for coastal or even for riverine warfare. Thus a recent list of the monitors breaks them down into coastal and river classes, the former including the only types even nominally capable of ocean work. The coastal series comprised two types, single- and double-turreted. The former comprised the *Monitor* herself; the *Passaic* class (ten units, enlarged versions of the prototype ship); the *Canonicus* class (nine ships of improved design, only five of which saw war service; three were completed without being commissioned at all and two were sold to Peru); and the unsuccessful shallow-draft *Casco* class (twenty units, eight of which were completed during the war, although none was in combat). The twin-turret classes were the single *Onondaga* and the four *Miantonomahs*. The former was sold to France in 1867 as a coast-defense ship. The latter were sometimes described as seagoing. The *Miantonomah* was sent to Europe in 1866, albeit part way under tow, and the *Monadnock*, transferred to the Pacific, succeeded in rounding Cape Horn under her own power. However, none could reasonably be considered effective in a seaway. There was also the *Roanoke*, a pre–Civil War steam frigate cut down, armored, and equipped with three turrets.

The *Dictator* and *Puritan* were conceived as ocean-going monitors, more than 300-feet long (compared with 200 feet for the *Passaic* type). They were, in effect, competitive designs, only the *Dictator* being completed. She was unsuccessful because of machinery trouble and could not take part in any action. In addition, four even larger *Kalamazoos* were ordered. Incomplete and unlaunched in 1865, they were ultimately broken up on their slips. Finally, there were riverine monitors of very different design, intended for the Mississippi.

Of the twenty successful single-turret coastal units, the *Monitor* herself and the *Weehawken* foundered; the *Patapsco* and *Tecumseh* were mined. With two of the best class (*Canonicus*) sold to Peru in 1868, that left twelve ships, plus the four *Miantonomahs*, the *Dictator*, and the *Roanoke*. All units surviving the sales of the 1867–68 remained in existence until 1874, when the twenty *Cascos* were sold or broken up. At that time, too, one of the *Kalamazoos*, at the Philadelphia Navy Yard, was broken up. The three surviving *Milwaukee*-class riverine monitors were sold, one other (the name ship) having been mined.* The large *Puritan* had been launched in 1864 but was laid up incomplete; it survived the scrappings.

Useless for the major peacetime role of the Navy—naval presence abroad (showing the flag and, at this time, opening markets such as Korea)—most of the surviving monitors were laid up. A few served as receiving ships or, later, as drill ships for state militia. The *Catskill, Lehigh, Nahant, Nantucket, Passaic, Sangamon*, and *Wyandotte* (ex-*Tippecanoe*) were recommissioned briefly for defensive service during the Spanish-American War. By that time their main virtue was that, by reassuring urban U.S. populations, they allowed the Navy to concentrate its modern ships at sea, to deal with the Spanish fleet.

---

* This wholesale scrapping was necessary to make up for unexpected costs incurred in 1873, when it appeared that the United States might have to fight Spain. The major shipyards were offered scrap because the Navy Department had no cash with which to settle their accounts. Further scrappings were sanctioned to pay for the new ("rebuilt") monitors. Robeson was sharply criticized for this practice. At the very end of his administration he authorized Roach to break up the *Roanoke*; this order was cancelled by his successor, the ship lying at the Roach yard from 1876 through 1883 (after having been stricken in 1882).

The *Wisconsin* is shown at the International Naval Review, Hampton Roads, 12 June 1957. Note the heavy-weather fueling at sea king posts.

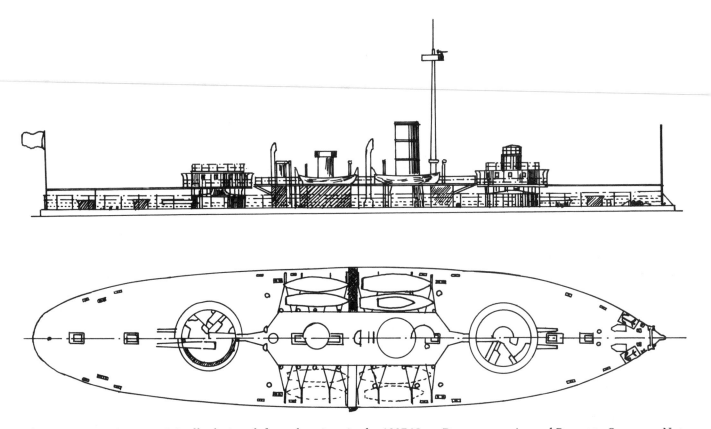

The monitor *Puritan* as originally designed, from drawings in the 1887 Navy Department *Annual Report* to Congress. Note her similarity to Civil War *Monitors*, except for cabin structures built atop her two turrets. The forward structure carries her chart room, with her pilot house atop it. The deck view shows internal details of these structures and also the massive armored ventilator abaft her funnel. Her smoke pipe was also to have been armored. The rectangular structures in her main deck were all companionways. At this stage her main battery had been fixed at four 10-inch breech-loading rifles. The objects at the ends of her flying bridges are running lights. The fighting top carried a 37mm revolver cannon.

Although naval ordnance and armor technology were changing rapidly, many in Congress preferred to imagine that ships which had been revolutionary a decade before were still modern. Their inadequacy was made painfully clear by the *Virginius* incident. On 31 October 1873, a Spanish gunboat captured a U.S. merchant ship, the *Virginius*, which was running arms to Cuban rebels. About half the passengers and crew were executed, and war feeling ran high in the United States. An examination of existing resources was depressing, however. A Spanish ironclad, clearly superior to any U.S. warship, was actually visiting New York at this time, and her presence alone was sobering. Secretary of the Navy George M. Robeson decided that his primary duty was to provide sufficient modern ironclads to protect U.S. coasts and harbors.

Congress was unwilling to build new ships, but it did provide money to "reconstruct" existing ones, using funds appropriated for operations and maintenance. Robeson chose the five largest: the incomplete *Puritan* and the four *Miantonomah*s. The smaller single-turret craft remained in reserve. They were distributed among the major yards. The *Monadnock*, on the West Coast, was assigned to Phineas Burgess of Vallejo. On the East Coast, the *Puritan* and *Miantonomah* went to Roach, the *Terror* to Cramp, and the *Amphitrite* to Harlan and Hollingsworth. In each case, the scrap value of the existing ship was used to pay part of the cost of the new one, and existing ships were also sent to be broken up to pay even more of the cost.

Work began in 1874, but (except for the almost-complete *Miantonomah*, launched 5 December 1876) it was suspended in 1876, Robeson failing to obtain $2.3 million to complete the ships. Roach in particular was charged with corruption, and in 1877 a special board examined his *Puritan*. It discovered that, although the workmanship was excellent, the ship was so badly overweight (at about 7,200 tons) that it would not float. It would be necessary to reduce weight by about 1,000 tons. The problem was the existing bureau system: C&R had designed the hull without reference to BuEng or to BuOrd.

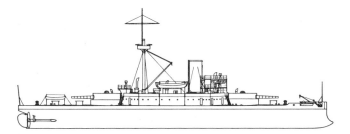

The *Puritan* as completed. (A. D. Baker III)

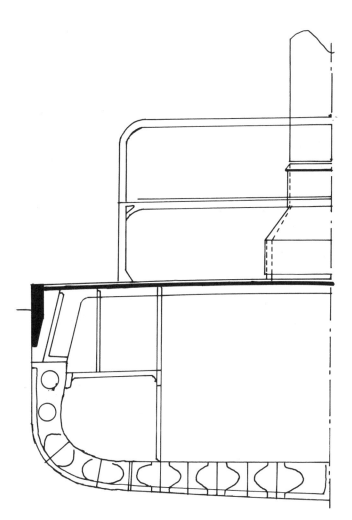

Cross section of *Puritan*.

Robeson's public description of an ironclad fleet in fairly good health contrasts with what must have been his private fear of the consequences of going to war. In his 1875 *Annual Report* to the Congress, he listed a total of twenty-one monitors, including the five under reconstruction (which he claimed could be ready in four to six months if pushed), the *Roanoke*, and fifteen single-turret craft. The three surviving *Kalamazoo*s were already too badly deteriorated to list, although their armor and their incomplete machinery were still held by the navy yards.

Thus, in 1883, at the beginning of the New Navy, the five new monitors, the only ironclads laid down in the United States after the Civil War, were still suspended. The 1883 act that authorized the construction of the first four New Navy cruisers also approved funds to complete these ships. Work, suspended for some years was resumed only in 1887, after which the designs were largely recast. In the case of the *Puritan*, suspended in 1876, the Congressional Act of 5 August 1882 authorized her launch (6 December 1882) and directed the new Naval Advisory Board to report on the wisdom of completing her. The act of the following year required the board to pass on her machinery contract. Her estimated machinery weight (including water) had been 1,016 tons, but the actual weight was 1,241, 225 tons overweight, which had to be balanced by reductions elsewhere in the ship. In 1886 a board under Naval Constructor George W. Much was appointed. It determined that she could not carry her designed weights, and the bureaus were ordered to readjust their plans. It was then recommended that her turrets be replaced by those designed for the *Terror*, her 10.5-inch guns replaced by new 10-inch weapons.

Revised plans for the *Puritan* were approved by the Board on Construction in June 1889. They envisaged considerable increases in armament and in protection. Crew quarters would be roomier as well. The previously planned four 10-inch guns in roller-base turrets would be replaced by four 12-inch in barbettes. The simple hurricane deck between the turrets would be replaced by a conventional superstructure carrying two 6-inch (later six 4-inch) guns. Barbettes were lighter than turrets, and guns in them were much higher above the waterline, 10feet 6inches in this case, so they could be fought in heavier weather. As weight compensation, two of the ten planned boilers were removed (saving 85 tons), the rest being given forced draft (3,000IHP with natural draft, 4,000 forced was expected to give 12 to 13 knots). In addition, the depth of the belt was reduced by 18 inches and its thickness increased from 12 to 14 inches amidships.

The *Amphitrite* was to be completed along similar lines. The four smaller double-turret monitors fell into two subgroups: the *Miantonomah* and *Terror* with 7-inch side armor; and the *Amphitrite* and *Monadnock* with 9-inch. Only the latter two ships had two 4-inch guns each, the first pair, had none. The latter pair also had barbettes rather than roller-base turrets. The *Terror* was unique in having pneumatically powered gun turrets.

For the two post–Civil War decades the force of surviving war-built monitors was also a primary congressional excuse for avoiding the construction of modern capital ships. As coast-defense ships, moreover, they could not contribute to the kind of

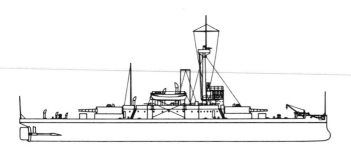

The *Amphitrite* as completed. (A. D. Baker III)

oceanic sea power desired by Secretary of the Navy Benjamin Tracy and his successors. Although Tracy advocated a few powerful coast-defense ships in his last annual report to the Congress, it seems likely that this was no more than a sop thrown to critics of his strategy.*

Thus the five monitors ordered after 1883 were all anomalies. They are included here because they were often so thought of as alternatives to modern armored ships.

In 1885, the congressional appropriation for coast defenses included a provision setting up an Army–Navy Board on "fortifications and other defenses." The latter included "floating batteries," that is, monitors. Commander W. T. Sampson, later chief of BuOrd and then senior afloat commander in the Spanish-American War, wrote the report on floating batteries, which were designed by Assistant Naval Constructor Richard Gatewood.

The board distinguished such vessels from future battleships, which it assumed would act offensively. The batteries would trade speed and endurance for very heavy armor and for extremely powerful guns on a light draft. BuOrd promised new 10-, 12-, 14-, and 16-inch weapons. Small size and twin screws would guarantee great maneuverability. Sampson argued further that light draft would be a positive advantage in defending the Atlantic coast, whose ports had relatively shallow mouths. Conventional capital ships would draw too much water to maneuver freely and might prove inferior to his batteries.

Sampson envisaged four types: a 7,000 tonner to act as primary defense for the mouth of the Mississippi; a 6,500 tonner designed specially for the Chesapeake; a 4,000 tonner; and a 300-ton gunboat. The first would be armed with 16-inch guns equalled by only three battleships in the world, although several others of such power were then under construction. The second was somewhat inferior but could operate in shallower water. Both would, however, be limited to only two dry docks on the Atlantic coast and two at San Francisco. Hence the design of the smaller unit. Sampson recommended two 7,000 tonners for the mouth of the Mississippi, three 6,500 tonners for San Francisco, and two each of the 6,500- and 4,000-ton classes for Long Island Sound and Hampton Roads, for a total of two 7,000-ton, seven 6,500-ton, and four 4,000-ton ships. San Francisco was a special case in that the batteries would have to sortie to meet their enemy outside the port. The 300-ton gunboat was designed for harbor defense, and there was also a 128-ton gunboat (with one or two 5-inch guns) intended specifically to pass through the Erie Canal, to defend the Great Lakes.

All three of the heavily armored floating batteries were similar in configuration, with a wall-sided circular turret forward and an open barbette, that is, a gun in a heavily protected gun tub, aft. In theory the advantage of the barbette was that, because the heavy armor was fixed, the gun on its pivot could be maneuvered rapidly by hand in the event of damage to the machinery. On the other hand, the crew of a barbette gun could be killed off by an enemy's light rapid-fire weapons.

The board recommended that $2 million a year be appropriated for coast-defense vessels, apart from the usual naval appropriation. In 1886 this money was spent on a torpedo boat. The following year Secretary of the Navy Whitney argued that such craft were too weak to be effective, and he spent his money on a monitor, for West Coast defense. The *Monterey's* design followed that proposed for the 4,000-ton ship, but only in outline. It is described in Table A-1.

Even Whitney was unenthusiastic. In his *Annual Report* to Congress, he remarked that the coast defense money was unique among his funds in that it had not been requested for any specific ship. The only other ship bought under the Endicott program was the "harbor defense ram" *Katahdin*.

As for the *Monterey,* her ambitious design was reviewed by the Board on Construction in November 1889. The design was recast to better protect her battery, on the theory that she would be engaging battleships at close range. The 110-ton, 16-inch gun was abandoned because it was expected to fire too slowly. (It did not yet, in fact, exist.) The dynamite gun was also abandoned, and the side armor was reduced from 16- to 13-inch thickness. The planned 4-inch secondary weapons and their armored towers were also abandoned. Their weight was equivalent to that of a 12-inch gun, the then-secretary of the navy, Benjamin Tracy, remarking that, as the ship would have to face battleships at short range, a powerful main battery was the most important requirement. It was changed to two 12-inch (46.5-ton) guns forward and two 10-inch guns aft, with more am-

* He called for a few enlarged *Puritan*s, each armed with eight 13-inch guns and protected by 20-inch armor, with a draft of only 14 to 16 feet, for smooth-water service. Tracy described them as strong points for the defense of key ports. The figures he gave suggest that they were not serious proposals.

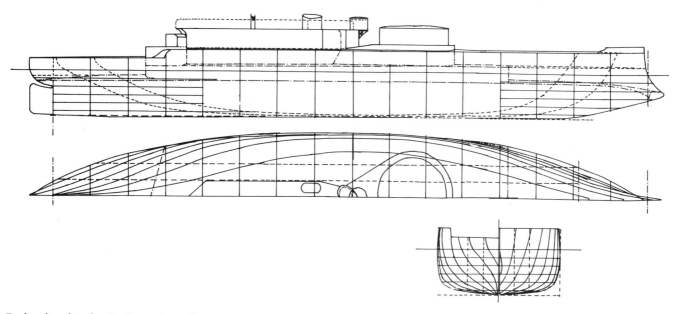

Body plan for the Endicott Board's 7,000-ton coast defense ship. Note her similarity to contemporary British battleship designs.

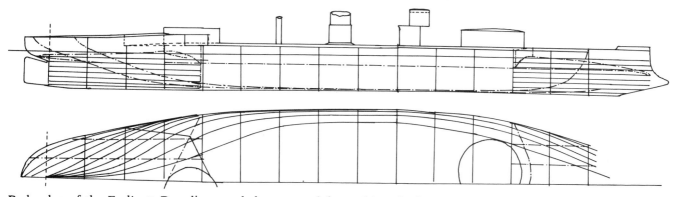

Body plan of the Endicott Board's second-class coast defense ship, which may have formed the basis of the *Monterey*. Note that the turret and barbette are both off center.

munition than had originally been provided: 30 rounds per 12-inch, 40 per 10-inch, versus 25 per 16-inch and 20 per 12-inch in the original design. The forward guns were mounted in a 14-inch barbette with an 8-inch rotating shield, as in the *Puritan*; the after guns, in an 11.5-inch barbette, with a 7.5-inch shield. At this time, too, 1 inch was added to the deck armor forward of the forward barbette, and 1/2 inch to the deck armor under the superstructure, for a uniform 3 inches back to abaft the after barbette, and 2 inches abaft that to the stern.

The unbalanced battery (fore and aft) was unusual, but explainable. Without the dynamite gun forward, the ship might have trimmed by the bow; hence the greater weight of guns forward. The board would have preferred a uniform battery, but had no real choice. Secretary Tracy approved the revised design in March 1890.

U.S. monitor construction was briefly revived by the public clamor for coast defense during the Spanish-American War. The Navy had to go so far as to recommission entirely obsolete Civil War monitors for coast defense, and Congress authorized four new ships, which became the *Arkansas* class. A sketch design approved by the Board on Construction in May 1898 showed two 12-inch guns in one turret forward, and four 4-inch guns, on a length of 210 feet. Chief Constructor Hichborn maintained that, on the displacement he thought the appropriation would buy, he could not accommodate a more balanced battery like four 10-inch guns (in two turrets).

To the intense surprise of Secretary of the Navy Long and of the Board of Construction, all the bids for construction were well below the sum appropriated. Now the Board on Construction could seek major improvements, such as a new battery of four 10-inch guns. Admiral Melville of BuEng sought to double the coal supply to 400 tons, on the ground that even a coast-defense ship would have to be able to steam along the U.S. coast. He also asked about the possibilities of accommodating four *12-inch* guns. BuOrd supported the 10 inch, a new weapon.

Table A-1. Endicott Board Ships

Scheme	1st Class	1st Class	2nd Class	Monterey
LWL(Ft)	303-0	310-0	260-0	256-0
LOA(Ft)	323-4.5	330-5		260-11
Beam(Ft)	63-7	63-0	57-6	59-0
Draft(Ft)	22-4	19-0	14-6	14-6
Depth(Mld, Ft)	33-7	29-10	18-3	
Displacement(Tons)	7028	6500	4018	4003
IHP(ND)	5000	4650	2500	
IHP(FD)	7000	6500	3300	5400
Speed(Kts)	15.5	15.25	13	16
Radius(10 Kts)	1900	1750	1300	2173
Coal	300/600	270/550	200/330	200
Main Battery				
Turret	2-16in	2-14in	2-12in	1-16
Barbette	1-10in	2-10in	2-10in	1-12
Dynamite Gun				1-15
4in Guns				6
9 PDR RF				3
57mm Guns	4	4	2	2
47mm R.C.	3	3	2	4
Gatlings	4	4	3	---
Torpedo Tubes	5(10)	5(10)	3(6)	---
Belt	18	16	12	16
Deck(Ends/Amids)	3.25/2.75	3/2.75	4/2.5	2/3
Turret	15	16	16	8

NOTE: Data for the *Monterey* describe her original design, as in the 1889 Navy Department *Annual Report* to the Congress. In all of the earlier designs, the after guns were in an open barbette.

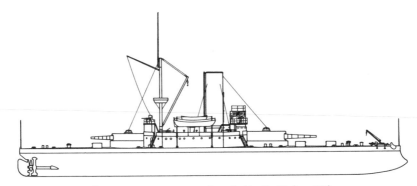

The *Monterey* as completed. (A. D. Baker III)

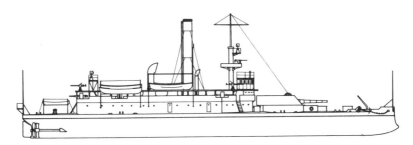

The *Arkansas* (monitor) as completed. (A. D. Baker III)

Table A-2. 1917 *Monitor* Designs

Scheme	1	2	3	4	5	6
Length	600	650	650	750	450	450
Beam	108	130	108	130	108	108
Draft	13.5	15.0	14.5	17.0	22.75	16.5
Depth(To Str. Dk)	19.0	20.0	20.0	22.0	27.75	21.5
Freeboard(Fwd)	2.5	2.5	2.5	2.5	2.5	2.5
Displacement(Nor)	20,500	33,000	26,000	43,000	22,750	16,800
Cruising Radius	5000	---	5500	4350	6000	5000
Belt Width	8.0	---	8.0		8.0	8.0
Belt Below Wl	5.5	---	5.5		5.5	5.5
Thickness(In.)	18	---	18		18	18
Deck(In.)	5-4.5-4	5-3.125	5-4.5-4	5-3.125	5	5
Main Battery	4-16/50	4-16/50	8-16/50	8-16/50	8-16/50	2-16/50
Weights(Tons):						
Hull	11,200		13,000	16,300	10,540	9000
Hull Fittings	1000		1050	1275	1000	900
Machinery	240		300	450	615	450
Res. Feed(2/3)	15		16	25	35	25
Battery	850		1600	1600	1600	475
Ammunition	944		1770	1770	1770	531
Protection	4770		6200	19,350*	5170	3555
Eq.,Outfit,2/3 Stores	780		780	935	780	650
Fuel Oil	650		1200	1000	1000	850
Margin	51		84	295	240	64
Displacement	20,500	33,000	26,000	43,000	22,750	16,500
Max EHP	1000		1250	1800	2450	1800
Max Speed(Kts)	6	6	6	6	12	12

NOTE: This table was dated 7 July 1917. The starred figure for protection includes 15,600 tons of concrete and 1,150 tons of tin cans (for crushable antitorpedo protection).

The ultimate result was disappointing. Although the bids had been low, they had not been low enough to leave sufficient surplus for major changes to the design and not nearly low enough to leave a surplus for an extra turret. Secretary of the Navy Long had just circulated a memorandum reemphasizing the need to remain within the appropriated sums for ships. The builders were called in, and the board asked what they could do. Neither they nor the members of the board were willing to approach Congress for more money, and in the end all that the board could get was a longer hull and more coal.

Since the monitors had little relevance to the developing U.S. naval strategy, they were soon relegated to secondary roles. They were given city names as the new dreadnoughts took their state names, and they were used for experiments, such as the tests with the cage mast and with the superfiring gun described in Chapter 2.

The United States was the last major sea power to build coast-defense ships, and the monitor as a type died out in the major navies. It was revived during World War One for a very different role: coastal *attack*. The British discovered that by mounting battleship guns aboard simple, shallow-draft craft they could gain capital ship firepower in coastal bombardment without risking valuable ships in extremely hazardous waters. The Italian Navy built somewhat similar (and even simpler) craft.

During 1917 Preliminary Design developed its own version of the monitor concept. No documentation beyond the characteristics of the designs (see Table A-2) appears to have survived, so it is impossible to say how serious the project was. In the event, the only U.S. contribution to monitor construction during World War One was the provision of Bethlehem 14-inch guns for some of the earliest British monitors, well before 1917.

The offensive monitor concept was revived about half a century later, however, for Vietnam. In 1965 the U.S. Navy, which had discarded many of its heavy-gun warships, suddenly found itself fighting a war that demanded shore bombardment. Work began on a specialized bombardment ship, the LFS. One early

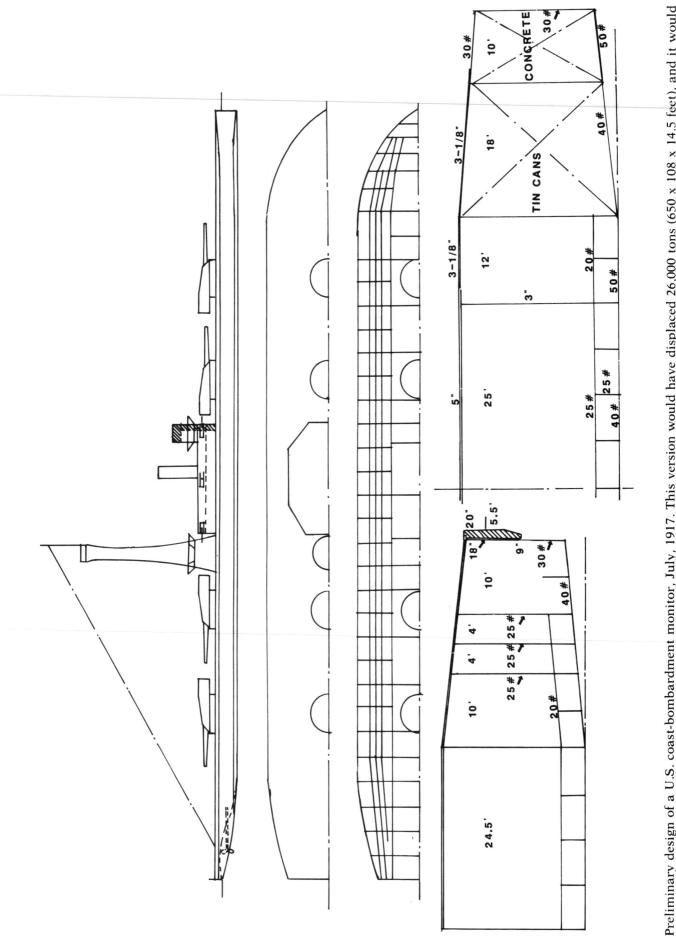

Preliminary design of a U.S. coast-bombardment monitor, July, 1917. This version would have displaced 26,000 tons (650 x 108 x 14.5 feet), and it would have been armed with eight 16in/50 guns in battleship-type turrets, plus six 5-inch RF and several machine guns on turret tops and in the superstructure. Reciprocating machinery would have driven it at 6 knots. An alternative version, protected by concrete rather than conventional armor, would have displaced 42,500 tons. It is represented by the cross section at left. There was also a smaller two-turret version, very similar in configuration. Note the tunnel stern.

proposal was to mount turrets, taken from existing or recently stricken heavy ships in austere hulls. No design figures have survived, and the rough sketches produced at the time were all marked to show that calculations had not yet been carried out. The LFS design actually proposed was quite different, mounting a combination of lightweight 5- and 8-inch guns. As for heavy guns, it seemed simpler to recommission one of the existing four battleships—which had been retained with exactly that application in mind.

B

Damage At Pearl Harbor

The Japanese attack at Pearl Harbor was the great test of the reconstructed battleships. Of eight ships present, the *Oklahoma* capsized after being torpedoed. The *Arizona* was destroyed by internal (magazine) explosion. Both losses could be described as design failures, in that a properly designed ship should sink by flooding rather than by capsizing, that is, it should sink on an even keel, and in that the *Arizona* should have been safe from a magazine explosion because the Japanese bombs (converted 16-inch shells) used at Pearl Harbor should not have penetrated existing U.S. deck armor. The *Nevada* was an intermediate case: she survived but should have suffered less damage. The other badly damaged ships, the *California* and *West Virginia*, performed as might have been expected.

The Japanese torpedoes were little more powerful than the standard charge which the ships had been designed to resist, 400 pounds of TNT. At the time of the attack, the latest Japanese torpedo had a charge of 450 pounds. Earlier torpedoes, which may have been used by some of the aircraft, had a 330-pound charge. Both the *Nevada* and *California* successfully resisted these charges; their inner torpedo bulkheads were not penetrated.

The case of the *Arizona* illustrates a general truth of war damage, that ships were often lost, not to the types of damage envisaged when they were designed, but rather to factors quite outside the normal purview of the designer. As a consequence, conventional survivability analysis may not always be relevant. Perhaps the most spectacular World War Two cases were the effect of a bent propeller shaft, which opened up the hull of the *Prince of Wales*, and the ventilation operating error, which doomed the Japanese carrier *Taiho* by filling her with explosive fumes. The key factor in the *Arizona* appears to have been a small magazine holding the black powder charges for her turret catapult. Much more explosive than the 14-inch powder magazines nearby, its detonation set them off and thus led to the destruction of the forward part of the ship. This magazine in turn appears to have been set off by an oil fire in the ship. Thus, although *in theory* the magazines were protected by sufficient thicknesses of deck armor, a Japanese bomb that failed to penetrate the armor was able to start a fire which caused the fatal damage.

A movie of the attack showed a large fire, clearly involving oil, engulfing the forward part of the ship, followed only seven seconds later by a magazine explosion. Army experiments had shown that smokeless (propellant) powder in magazines was unlikely to explode if it burned. According to an Army manual, however, black powder was considered "one of the worst known explosive hazards. . . . It can be ignited easily by very small sparks, heat, and friction." Aboard the *Arizona*, the black powder magazine, containing 1,075 pounds of the substance, was surrounded by large smokeless powder magazines serving the two forward turrets.

A BuShips analysis, dated 31 October 1944, noted that war experience suggested that, although fire could detonate a magazine, it generally required much more than seven seconds. A bomb in the magazines might also detonate them, "although smokeless powder as such is not an unusually severe hazard." Of five hatches in the protective deck near the two forward barbettes (all of which were probably open at the time of the attack), one was almost directly over the black powder magazine. BuShips considered it the culprit: the black powder could have detonated either as the result of a bomb explosion above it or, more likely, of a fire above the protective deck passing through the open hatch. As for a bomb (such as the converted 16-inch shell the Japanese were using), it had a relatively small explosive charge, less than 70 pounds of TNT. Moreover, the movie definitely showed the massive fire well above the waterline at first.

The *North Carolina*, April 1942.

In the case of *Oklahoma*, the key factor appears to have been the very short interval between the torpedo hits. She was struck by five torpedoes, all within only one minute and ten seconds. She therefore began listing rapidly, so much so that the last one or perhaps two torpedoes hit above the belt, opening the main, second, and third decks on the port side. One torpedo probably hit the belt itself. There had been little time to close up the ship (set condition Z), so each successive hit added to flooding through hatches, ventilation ducts, and pipe lines. Nor was there any hope of counterflooding in time.

Stability against battle damage was calculated on the basis of allowing the water from any one hit to spread evenly before the next hit. The *Oklahoma* capsized because everything happened so quickly. Hence, although capsizing had to disappoint BuShips, it could not really be traced to a design flaw. Note that the single torpedo hit to *Nevada*, *Oklahoma's* sister ship, did not cause disproportionate listing.

The *West Virginia* was struck by seven torpedoes, six of them running quite shallow (the deepest only 11 feet below the surface); a seventh, 19 feet down, struck her aft, nearly destroying her steering gear. The shallow-runners struck on or even above her belt armor. As a result, they were relatively ineffective, since the armor limited damage. Even so, the side of the ship below the belt was pushed in so far that it split. Even the inner torpedo bulkhead was dished in, and (as in the case of the *Nevada*) it was torn loose at its lower edge, allowing water to flood the fire rooms. As a result, the ship listed. That in turn caused two torpedoes to strike the upper part of the side of the ship, leading to the extensive flooding across and down through the second and third decks, which sank her. This was much the same sort of damage that actually sank the *Oklahoma*, the torpedoes striking so close together that she took on a considerable list before counterflooding could take effect. She was counterflooded, however, and that probably saved her from capsizing.

The *Nevada* was the only battleship to get under way during the Pearl Harbor attack. Striking between the two forward turrets, about 14 feet above the ship's keel, a torpedo blew holes in the blister, shell, and inner bottom. As the designers had expected, the inner (holding) bulkhead was dished in rather than opened. Its seams and butts opened 2 to 4 inches, however, and the ship began to flood below her first platform deck. She listed four or five degrees, but counterflooding restored her to an even keel. The hole in the blister was about 16-feet long and 27-feet high.

Five bombs struck after the ship had anchored in the channel. One penetrated her forecastle and exploded between her gasoline tank and her outer side. Other bombs wrecked the anchor gear, and the ship was beached so as not to block the channel. Two large

fires broke out, and there was not enough fire main pressure to fight them. Meanwhile, the ship began to flood slowly, and the forward magazines, whose bulkheads were already hot, were flooded. The after magazines had already been flooded (by mistake).

When the ship grounded, her stern hung on a coral ledge, her bow afloat but gradually sinking as it flooded. Ultimately water spread aft over the second deck (above the armor deck) and flooded down through ventilators. As the ship settled by the bow, water reached the "bull ring," the air intake and blower room surrounding the uptakes on the second deck (and the source of air for the fire rooms and for the forward part of the ship) and put the boilers out of action. Finally the stern slipped off the coral ledge, and the ship settled onto the harbor bottom, which was only about 40 feet deep.

Of the fires, one burned out the forward superstructure, fed largely by papers in the captain's office and aggravated by drafts caused by the stack and the fire room blowers. It exploded ready service ammunition. The other major fire, forward, caused gasoline vapor (due to the bomb hit forward), to explode on the afternoon following the attack, causing further structural damage.

BuShips concluded that the ship had succumbed to relatively superficial damage; her main machinery and her main battery were not affected. The problem was a lack of watertight integrity. There were no watertight bulkheads on the second deck, and boundaries and fittings elsewhere which should have been watertight, were not.

Using the ship's damage control book, BuShips analysts tried to discover the cause of her flooding. Before being hit, she drew 30 feet 6 inches forward and 31 feet 3 inches aft. The torpedo hit and counterflooding would have changed these figures to only 33 feet 8 inches forward and 31 feet 2 inches aft; flooding the after magazine (in error) would have brought her to 34 feet 11 inches forward and 34 feet 5 inches aft. At this point the second deck, in theory the highest watertight deck in the ship, would still have been nearly 3 feet above water. However, flooding the forward magazine would then have brought the ship to 40 feet 8 inches forward and 32 feet 6 inches aft. This would have brought the waterline to between the second and main decks and would have placed a bomb hole forward below water, where it could flood the second deck. Despite this calculation, the BuShips war damage report suggested that the ship would have flooded even had the magazines *not* been flooded, as the draft forward would have reached nearly 37 feet, presumably caused by flooding through bomb holes.

The primary conclusion was that detail failures, in this case in watertightness, had been responsible for the loss of the ship. Not only were there no watertight bulkheads above the second (main armored) deck, but the deck itself, consisting of four separate layers of plating, was not watertight. Finally, the centralized heavily armored air intake, a major feature of the modernized battleships and of the "Big Five," was seen as a major design flaw, since its flooding could put all machinery out of action and could also flood the entire forward portion of the ship. BuShips claimed that this danger had been known for some years and that ships designed in recent years (including the new battleships) had a very different system, vertically segregated. Ventilation was divided into a number of separate systems, each bounded by two transverse watertight bulkheads. Ducts serving compartments below the watertight (damage control) deck were carried up to this deck before running horizontally, and watertight closures were required in the duct at the boundary of the compartment served.

From a BuShips point of view, the *California* was probably the most satisfactory case. She was struck by two torpedoes (one forward and one aft) and by one bomb, which ricocheted off her second (armored) deck and blew a large hole in her main deck, starting a major fire. Neither torpedo was particularly effective. In each case, not only did the inner (holding) bulkhead remain intact, but also the two bulkheads outboard of it. Before counterflooding, these hits gave her a 5 or 6 degree list. Finally, a near-miss bomb forward opened a hole in her port bow, and flooded her down to about 3 1/2 feet down by the head.

None of this damage was particularly severe, and the ship was ready to sortie when ordered to do so. Even so, she sank. When attacked by surprise, she had had many manholes open for inspection, and many others were only loosely closed. Water rose over the third deck on her port side and slowly flooded the ship. This was not particularly surprising or alarming; had she been at sea, these covers would have been fastened down.

There were only two other cases of torpedo damage to the older battleships. The *Maryland* was torpedoed in her bow while at anchor off Saipan shortly after dusk on 22 June 1944. Her watertight doors were closed and she was ready to get under way, which she actually did fifteen minutes later, as soon as it was clear that her anchor gear could be operated. The torpedo punched holes through both sides of her bow, breaking open the aviation gasoline tank forward. However, the 3,750 gallons aboard did not burn or explode. Damage was confined to the area forward of her collision bulkhead, and she was able to steam at 10.5 knots.

There was no question but that the torpedo had exploded; it made a hole about 25 feet in diameter and caused the ship to flex along its length. It caused no shock damage, however. Presumably its force was vented through the entire (narrow) beam of the ship, about Frame 8; flooding was confined to the area forward of Frame 18, and plating was torn only below the second deck. All told, damage was quite minor.

By way of contrast, the *Pennsylvania*, also at anchor, was hit aft, on 12 August 1945 at Buckner Bay, Okinawa. The torpedo struck her outboard starboard propeller shaft, and the resulting noncontact explosion blew a hole 32 feet long and 30 feet high in her stern, at about the position of her steering engine. The outboard propeller shaft was blown off, and the inboard starboard shaft (No. 2) had to be cut off, as its strut was broken. The ship's keel and her entire stern were badly twisted. As a result, the inboard port shaft was thrown out of alignment (about 5.5 inches vertically, and about 2.5 inches horizontally). Although all watertight doors aft were closed, the ship flooded through the large hole and also through her ventilators and through exhaust vents near the overheads of flooded spaces. She took on about 3,400 tons of water and trimmed about 6 feet by her stern. The combination of twisting and damage aft made her yaw back and forth during a lengthy tow to Guam for temporary repairs. These consisted of a steel patch over her hole, realignment of No. 3 shaft, and restoration of her rudder.

Probably the main surprise was the extent to which the ship flooded, even after wartime efforts to ensure battle watertightness. Her captain recommended that ships be fitted with at least one trunked-in access from the weather decks to spaces below, between consecutive watertight bulkheads. If the ship had been so fitted, considerable time might have been saved in freeing lower compartments of water. Her flooding at the stern was uncontrollable because access to the compartments involved was blocked from above. Similarly, he suggested that ventilation trunks be fitted with watertight closures on each side of a bulkhead or deck. This echoes similar recommendations made in view of experience at Pearl Harbor.

In each case, the torpedo exploded well beyond fore-and-aft limits of the antitorpedo armor. Even so, in the case of the *Pennsylvania*, it was able to do very serious damage; it took just over two hours to control the flooding. Had the ship been under way, she might have been damaged further by the rotation of the bent propeller shafts, as was the case with the *Prince of Wales*. As it was, repairs at Guam were only temporary, for the ship was scheduled for decommissioning and scrapping. On passage to Puget Sound in October 1945, No. 3 shaft suddenly carried away in its stern tube, and it and its propeller had to be cut away. The *Pennsylvania* entered Puget Sound shipping water, with only one shaft turning.

Ironically, slow flooding due to the damage aft was considered a more serious threat than the topside damage she suffered during two nuclear tests at Bikini. It, rather than the nuclear damage, justified her scuttling two years later, in 1948.

C

List of U.S. Battleships

In the list, the first column gives dates of keel-laying and launching. The second gives dates of commissioning and recommissioning. Note that the date of commissioning may *not* be the actual date of completion, particularly if the ship was built in a private yard; she would be commissioned at a navy yard, then fitted out. The last column gives dates of decommissioning.

KEY TO BUILDERS

BATH	Bath Iron Works
BETHQ	Bethlehem Quincy (formerly Fore River)
BOSNY	Boston Navy Yard
CIW	Continental Iron Works, Vallejo, Cal.
CRAMP	Wm. Cramp and Sons, Philadelphia
FORE	Fore River SB Co., Quincy, Mass.
MORAN	Moran Co., Seattle

MINY	Mare Island Navy Yard
NIXON	Lewis Nixon
NN	Newport News
NORNY	Norfolk Navy Yard
NYNY	New York Navy Yard
NYSB	New York Shipbuilding Corp., Camden, N.J.
PHNY	Philadelphia Navy Yard
PSNY	Puget Sound Navy Yard
ROACH	John Roach & Son, Chester, Pa.
UIW	Union Iron Works

ABBREVIATIONS

BU	Broken up
Str	Stricken (from Navy List)
WL(B)	War loss (bombing)
WL(E)	War loss (internal explosion)
WL(T)	War loss (torpedoing)

	LD/Launch	Comm	Decomm	Fate
Maine NYNY	17 Oct 88 18 Nov 90	17 Sep 95 WL(E)	15 Feb 98	Floated 13 Feb 12; scuttled 16 Mar 12
Texas NORNY	1 Jun 89 28 Jun 92	15 Aug 95 20 Jul 96 3 Nov 02 1 Sep 08	27 Jan 96 3 Nov 00 11 Jan 08 1 Feb 11	Renamed *San Marcos* 16 Feb 11; sunk as target 21-22 Mar 11; str 11 Oct 11
1 *Indiana* CRAMP	7 May 91 28 Feb 93	20 Nov 95 9 Jan 06 24 May 17	29 Dec 03 23 May 14 31 May 19	Renamed *Coast Battleship No. 1*; 29 Mar 19. Sunk as target 1 Nov 20; sold 19 Mar 24
2 *Massachusetts* CRAMP	25 Jun 91 10 Jun 93	10 Jun 96 2 May 10 9 Jun 17	8 Jan 06 23 May 14 No. 2 31 Mar 19	Renamed *Coast Battleship No. 2*; str 22 Nov 20; sunk as army artillery target, Pensacola, Fla., Jan 21
3 *Oregon* UIW	19 Nov 91 26 Oct 93	15 Jul 96 29 Aug 11 21 Aug 19	27 Apr 06 12 Jun 19 4 Oct 19	To state of Oregon as museum, 25 June 25; became IX-22 17 Feb 41; str 2 Nov 42; sold for scrap 7 Dec 42, but stripped hulk returned to Navy Sep 43 as IX-22 for use as ammunition hulk; sold for scrap 15 Mar 56
4 *Iowa* CRAMP	5 Aug 93 28 Mar 96	16 Jun 97 23 Dec 03 2 May 10 23 Apr 17	30 Jun 03 23 Jul 08 23 May 14 31 Mar 19	Renamed *Coast Defense Battleship No. 4*; 2 Sep 19; str 4 Feb 20, but order revoked and became unnamed radio-controlled Mobile Target (IX-6); sunk as target in Gulf of Panama 23 Mar 23; str 27 Mar 23

	LD/Launch	Comm	Decomm	Fate
5 *Kearsage* NN	30 Jun 96 24 Mar 98	20 Feb 00 17 Jun 12	4 Sep 09 18 May 20	Converted to crane ship (AB-1) at PHNY; re-designated 5 Aug 20; name changed to *Crane Ship No. 1*; 6 Nov 41; str 22 Jun 55; sold 9 Aug 55.
6 *Kentucky* NN	30 Jun 96 24 Mar 98	15 May 00 4 Jun 12	28 Aug 09 29 Mar 20	Str 27 May 22; sold 24 Mar 23
7 *Illinois* NN	10 Feb 97 4 Oct 98	16 Sep 01 15 Apr 12	4 Aug 09 15 May 20	To New York State naval militia 25 Oct 21; renamed *Prairie State* (IX-15) 23 Jan 41; was decked-over as drill ship; str 26 Mar 56; sold 18 May 56
8 *Alabama* CRAMP	2 Dec 96 18 May 98	16 Oct 00 1 Jul 12 5 Apr 17	17 Aug 09 1 Jul 14 7 May 20	To War Department as bombing target 15 Sep 21; hulk sold 19 Mar 24
9 *Wisconsin* UIW	9 Feb 97 26 Nov 98	4 Feb 01 1 Apr 08	15 Nov 06 15 May 20	Sold 26 Jan 22
10 *Maine* CRAMP	15 Feb 99 27 Jul 01	29 Dec 02 15 Jun 11	31 Aug 09 15 May 20	On sale list 1 Jul 21; sold 26 Jan 22
11 *Missouri* NN	7 Feb 00 28 Dec 01	12 Jan 03	8 Sep 19	On sale list 1 Jul 21; sold 26 Jan 22
12 *Ohio* UIW	22 Apr 99 18 May 01	4 Oct 04 1 Jun 11	20 Dec 09 31 May 22	Str 14 Aug 22; sold 24 Mar 23
13 *Virginia* NN	21 May 02 5 Apr 04	7 May 06	13 Aug 20	Str 12 Jul 22; transferred to Army; sunk by bombing off Diamond Shoals, N.C., 5 Sep 23
14 *Nebraska* MORAN	4 Jul 02 7 Oct 04	1 Jul 07	2 Jul 20	Str 12 Jul 22; sold 30 Nov 23
15 *Georgia* BATH	31 Aug 01 11 Oct 04	24 Sep 06	15 Jul 20	Str 12 Jul 22; sold 1 Nov 23
16 *New Jersey* FORE	2 Apr 02 10 Nov 04	12 May 06	6 Aug 20	Str 12 Jul 22; to Army; sunk by bombing Diamond Shoals, N.C., 5 Sep 23
17 *Rhode Island* FORE	1 May 02 17 May 04	19 Feb 06	30 Jun 20	Str 12 Jul 22; sold 1 Nov 23
18 *Connecticut* NYNY	10 Mar 03 29 Sep 04	29 Sep 06	1 Mar 23	Sold 1 Nov 23
19 *Louisiana* NN	7 Feb 03 27 Aug 04	2 Jun 06	20 Oct 20	Sold 1 Nov 23; str 10 Nov 23
20 *Vermont* FORE	21 May 04 31 Aug 05	4 Mar 07	30 Jun 20	Str 10 Nov 23; sold 30 Nov 23
21 *Kansas* NYSB	10 Feb 04 12 Aug 05	18 Apr 07	16 Dec 21	Str 10 Nov 23; BU PHNY
22 *Minnesota* NN	27 Oct 03 8 Apr 05	9 Mar 07	1 Dec 21	Str 10 Nov 23; BU PHNY
23 *Mississippi* CRAMP	12 May 04 30 Sep 05	1 Feb 08	21 Jul 14	Str 21 Jul 14; sold to Greece (*Kilkis*); WL(B) 10 Apr 41
24 *IDAHO* CRAMP	12 May 04 9 Dec 05	1 Apr 08	30 Jul 14	Str 30 Jul 14; sold to Greece (*Lemnos*); WL(B) 10 Apr 41
25 *New Hampshire* NYSB	1 May 05 30 Jun 06	19 Mar 08	21 May 21	Sold 1 Nov 23; str 10 Nov 23
26 *South Carolina* CRAMP	18 Dec 06 25 Jul 08	1 Mar 10	15 Dec 21	Str 10 Nov 23; sold 24 Apr 24
27 *Michigan* NYSB	17 Dec 06 11 Jul 08	4 Jan 10		Str 24 Aug 23; sold 23 Jan 24
28 *Delaware* NN	11 Nov 07 6 Feb 09	4 Apr 10	10 Nov 23	Sold 5 Feb 24
29 *North Dakota* FORE	16 Dec 07 10 Nov 08	11 Apr 10	22 Nov 23	Target 1923-31; str 7 Jan 31; sold 16 Mar 31
30 *Florida* NYNY	9 Mar 09 12 May 10	15 Sep 11	16 Feb 31	Str 6 Apr 31; scrapping completed 30 Sep 32; had been rebuilt BOSNY 1 Apr 25–1 Nov 26 (laid up Jun 24)
31 *Utah* NYSB	15 Mar 09 23 Dec 09	31 Aug 11		Rebuilt BOSNY Aug 26–28 Oct 27; rebuilt as target ship (AG16) 1930–32; recommissioned 1 Apr 32 (controlled by destroyers *Hovey* and *Talbot*); Machine Gun School Aug 35; refitted PSNY summer 1939, 4–5in/25 and several 1.1in added; refitted PSNY 31 May-26 Aug 41, 5in/38 added; WL(T) 7 Dec 41; str 13 Nov 44

	LD/Launch	Comm	Decomm	Fate
32 *Wyoming* CRAMP	9 Feb 10 25 May 11	25 Sep 12 1 Jul 31	21 May 30 1 Aug 47	Rebuilt PHNY 1926–2 Nov 27; to training ship (AG 17) and rebuilt at NORNY 1930–31; Large refit NORNY 21 Jan–3 Apr 45, when her remaining 12in guns were removed; stricken 16 Sep 47; sold 30 Oct 47; scrapped Newark 1948
33 *Arkansas* NYSB	25 Jan 10 14 Jan 11	17 Sep 12		Rebuilt PHNY 1 Sep 25–21 Nov 26; Sunk in second (underwater) nuclear test at Bikini 25 Jul 46; had been extensively refitted (NORNY) 6 Mar–26 Jul 42
34 *New York* NYNY	11 Sep 11 30 Oct 12	15 Apr 14	29 Aug 46	Rebuilt NORNY 1926–10 Oct 27; flagship of 6th Battle Squadron, Grand Fleet, 1917–18; at Bikini nuclear tests, towed to Kwajalein and decommissioned there; then towed to Pearl Harbor, but too radioactive for her fittings to be removed; sunk as target 8 Jul 48
35 *Texas* NN	17 Apr 11 18 May 12	12 Mar 14	21 Apr 48	Rebuilt NORNY 1 Aug 25–23 Nov 26; str 30 Apr 48; war memorial
36 *Nevada* FORE	4 Nov 12 11 Jul 14	11 Mar 16	29 Aug 46	Rebuilt NORNY 27 Sep 27–26 Nov 29; turbines replaced by units from scrapped *North Dakota*; rebuilt PSNY (completed Oct 42) after damage at Pearl Harbor; survived both Bikini explosions; sunk as target 31 Jul 48
37 *Oklahoma* NYSB	26 Oct 12 23 Mar 14	2 May 16		Rebuilt PHNY 16 Sep 27–15 Jul 29. WL(T) 7 Dec 41; raised and drydocked 28 Dec 43 but str 1 Sep 44 and sold for scrap 5 Dec 46; sank under tow, 540 miles NE Pearl Harbor 17 May 47
38 *Pennsylvania* NN	27 Oct 13 16 Apr 15	12 Jun 16	29 Aug 46	Rebuilt PHNY 1 Jun 29–8 May 31, using turbines intended for *Washington*; again rebuilt MINY 4 Oct 42–5 Feb 43; survived both Bikini bombs; scuttled 10 Feb 48
39 *Arizona* NYNY	16 Mar 14 19 Jun 15	17 Oct 16		WL(B) 7 Dec 41; str 1 Dec 42; later recommissioned as a war memorial at Pearl Harbor
40 *New Mexico* NYNY	14 Oct 15 23 Apr 17	20 May 18	19 Jul 46	Rebuilt PHNY 5 Mar 31–22 Jan 33; str 25 Feb 47; sold 9 Nov 47
41 *Mississippi* NN	5 Apr 15 25 Jan 17	18 Dec 17	17 Sep 56	Rebuilt NORNY 30 Jan 31–31 Aug 32; rebuilt NORNY Nov 45–Jul 47 as test and training ship (AG-128); Terrier missile system installed 1952 and test fired for first time 28–29 Jan 53; sold 29 Nov 56; towed away for scrapping 7 Dec 56
42 *Idaho* NYSB	20 Jan 15 30 Jun 17	24 Mar 19	3 Jul 46	Rebuilt NORNY 30 Sep 33–9 Oct 34; rebuilt again at PSNY 22 Oct 44–1 Jan 45; str 16 Sep 47; sold 24 Nov 47
43 *Tennessee* NYNY	14 May 17 30 Apr 19	3 Jun 20	14 Feb 47	Rebuilt PSNY Sep 42–May 43; note that she was assigned to the inactive fleet 8 Dec 45; Str 1 Mar 59; sold Jul 59
44 *California* MINY	25 Oct 16 20 Nov 19	10 Aug 21	14 Feb 47	Rebuilt PSNY 7 Jun 42–31 Jan 44 str; sold 10 Jul 59
45 *Colorado* NYSB	29 May 19 22 Mar 21	30 Aug 23	7 Jan 47	Sold 23 Jul 59
46 *Maryland* NN	24 Apr 17 20 Feb 20	21 Jul 21	3 Apr 47	Str 1 Mar 59; sold 8 Jul 59
47 *Washington* NYSB	30 Jun 19 1 Sep 21			Cancelled 8 Feb 22 when 75.9 percent completed (up to boilering and armoring stage); bombed off the Virginia Capes and sunk 25 Nov 24
48 *West Virginia* NN	12 Apr 20 19 Nov 21	1 Dec 23	9 Jan 47	Rebuilt PSNY 1942–Sep 44; arrived PSNY to deactivate 20 Dec 45; str 1959; sold 15 Sep 59
49 *South Dakota* NYNY	15 Mar 20			Cancelled 8 Feb 22; was 38.5 percent complete; str 25 Oct 23
50 *Indiana* NYNY	1 Nov 20			Cancelled 8 Feb 22; was 34.7 percent complete; str 25 Oct 23

	LD/Launch	Comm	Decomm	Fate
51 *Montana* MINY	1 Sep 20			Cancelled 8 Feb 22; was 27.6 percent complete; str 25 Oct 23
52 *North Carolina* NORNY	12 Jan 20			Cancelled 8 Feb 22; was 36.7 percent complete; str 25 Oct 23
53 *Iowa* NN	17 May 20			Cancelled 8 Feb 22; was 31.8 percent complete; str 8 Nov 23
54 *Massachusetts* BETHQ	4 Apr 21			Cancelled 8 Feb 22; was 11 percent complete; str 8 Nov 23
55 *North Carolina* NYNY	27 Oct 37 13 Jun 40	9 Apr 41	27 Jun 47	Str 1 Jun 60; war memorial 29 Apr 62; note that Apr 41 was commissioning, *not* completion, date; completed August 1941
56 *Washington* PHNY	14 Jun 38 1 Jun 40	15 May 41	27 Jun 47	Str 60; sold 24 May 61; Note that actually completed March 1942
57 *South Dakota* NYSB	5 Jul 39 7 Jun 41	20 Mar 42	31 Jan 47	Str 1 Jun 62; sold 25 Oct 62; actually completed 16 Aug 42
58 *Indiana* NN	20 Nov 39 21 Nov 41	30 Apr 42	11 Sep 47	Str 1 Jun 62; sold 6 Sep 63; completed Oct 42
59 *Massachusetts* BETHQ	20 Jul 39 23 Sep 41	12 May 42	27 Mar 47	Str 1 Jun 62; war memorial at Fall River 14 Aug 65; completed Sep 42
60 *Alabama* NORNY	1 Feb 40 16 Feb 42	16 Aug 42	9 Jan 47	Str 1 Jun 62; war memorial 9 Jan 65; Completed Nov 42
61 *Iowa* NYNY	27 Jun 40 27 Aug 42	22 Feb 43 25 Aug 51 28 Apr 84	24 Mar 49 24 Feb 58	
62 *New Jersey* PHNY	16 Sep 40 7 Dec 42	23 May 43 21 Nov 50 6 Apr 68 28 Dec 82	30 Jun 48 21 Aug 57 17 Dec 69	
63 *Missouri* NYNY	6 Jan 41 29 Jan 44	11 Jun 44	26 Feb 55	
64 *Wisconsin* PHNY	25 Jan 41 27 Dec 43	16 Apr 44 3 Mar 51	1 Jul 48 8 Mar 58	
65 *Illinois* PHNY	15 Jan 44			Cancelled 12 Aug 45 when about 22 percent complete; she was originally to have been laid down in 1941 or 1942 but was delayed to make way for more urgent construction; BU from Sep 58 onwards
66 *Kentucky* NORNY	6 Dec 44 20 Jan 50			Suspended Aug 46, resumed 17 Aug 48; when launched she was 73 percent complete; when stricken 9 Jun 58 she was described as "no longer a battleship, merely an empty hull," 69.2 percent complete (up to second deck). Her bow was used to repair *Wisconsin* after a collision, 6 May 56; her turbines were used in the fast replenishment ships *Sacramento* and *Camden*. Originally laid down 7 Mar 42, but her keel was scrapped to make way for the carrier *Lake Champlain*. Sold Sep 58; towed away for BU Feb 59
67 *Montana* PHNY				Never laid down; scheduled for 25 Jan 41; Stopped Jun 42; cancelled 21 Jul 43
68 *Ohio* PHNY				As BB 67
69 *Maine* NYNY				Never built; cancelled 21 Jul 43
70 *New Hampshire* NYNY				Never built; cancelled 21 Jul 43
71 *Louisiana* NORNY				Never built; cancelled 21 Jul 43

MONITORS (BM)

	LD/Launch	Comm	Decomm	Fate
1 *Puritan* ROACH	75 6 Dec 82	10 Dec 96 3 Jun 03	16 Apr 03 23 Apr 10	Completed at NYNY; Naval Academy practice ship 1899–1902; receiving ship League Island 1903; DC Naval Militia 1904–09; str 27 Feb 18; sold 26 Jan 22; target ship (*Target B*) 1910–17
2 *Amphitrite* H&H	74 7 June 83	23 Apr 95 1 Dec 02 1 Jun 10	30 Nov 01 3 Aug 07 31 May 19	Training ship with state naval militias 1910–17; then guard ship at New York; sold 3 Jan 20
3 *Monadnock* CIW	15 Jan 75 19 Sep 83	20 Feb 96 20 Apr 11	10 Mar 09 24 Mar 19	Completed at MINY; to Philippines 1898; considerable China duty, mainly at Shanghai; submarine tender, target tower in Philippine waters 1912–19; str 2 Feb 23; sold 24 Aug 23; reclassified IX-17 1 Jul 21
4 *Terror* CRAMP	74 24 Mar 83	15 Apr 96 01	25 Feb 99 8 May 06	Suspended 1877–83; delivered incomplete 1887; completed NYNY; Naval Academy practice ship 1901–05; str 31 Dec 15; target hulk at Indian Head, Md (Naval Proving Ground); sale list Jun 20; sold 10 Mar 21; sank off Shooter's Island, N.Y.; raised and BU 1930; designated *Target D* as hulk.
5 *Mianonomoh* ROACH	74 5 Dec 76	27 Oct 91 10 Mar 98 9 Apr 07	20 Nov 95 8 Mar 99 21 Dec 07	Originally commissioned incomplete 6 Oct 82; steamed to NYNY and decommissioned 13 Mar 83; completed at NYNY 1883–91; Maryland Naval Militia 1906–07; str 31 Dec 15 for use as target; sold 26 Jan 22; designated *Target C* as hulk
6 *Monterey* UIW	20 Dec 89 28 Apr 91	13 Feb 93 28 Sep 07	15 Dec 04 27 Aug 21	To Philippines 1898 as major-calibre support for Dewey's cruiser squadron, remaining in the Far East until Nov 17; although in commission, she spent 1907–11, 1913–14 in reserve; station ship Pearl Harbor 1917–21, including submarine base service; towed to California 1921 for BU
7 *Arkansas* NN	14 Nov 99 10 Nov 00	28 Oct 02	20 Aug 19	Renamed *Ozark* 2 Mar 09; D.C. Naval Militia 1910–13; converted to submarine tender 1913; sold 26 Jan 22
8 *Nevada* BATH	17 Apr 99 24 Nov 00	5 Mar 03	Jan 19	Renamed *Tonopah* 2 Mar 09; Converted to submarine tender; supported U.S. submarines in the Azores, Jan–Dec 18; Sold 26 Jan 22
9 *Florida* NIXON	23 Jan 99 30 Nov 01	18 Jun 03 1 Aug 10 3 Aug 20	19 Jun 08 24 Mar 19 24 Mar 22	Renamed *Tallahassee* 20 Jun 08; used for armament tests; superfiring gun (March 1907); survey of gunnery test area; tests against *San Marcos* (with HE shells) June 1911; spotting for shelling by *Arkansas* late 1912; converted to submarine tender Sep-Nov 14 NORNY; redesignated IX-16 20 Jul 21; sold 25 Jul 22
10 *Wyoming* UIW	11 Apr 99 8 Sep 00	8 Dec 02 8 Oct 08 11 Jul 10 20 Aug 13 22 Sep 20	29 Aug 05 13 Nov 09 Feb 13 23 Oct 19 1 Jun 26	Renamed *Cheyenne* 1 Jan 09; used to test oil fuel 1908–10; converted to submarine tender PSNY 1913; had trained Washington State Naval Militia 1910–13; station ship at Baltimore 1920–26; sold 20 Apr 39; redesignated IX-14 1 Jul 21

D

Battleship Data List

NOTES TO TABLES

The following data tables give *representative* data for each class as built and, where possible, as subject to typical modifications. Displacement and loading data have been taken from inclining experiment (IX) reports, and the names and dates refer to those reports.

Dimensions are given in feet and inches; for example, 83-10 is 83 feet 10 inches. Fractions of feet and inches are used only when the original source material was given in that form.

Under protection, deck thicknesses are sometimes given in pounds (lb) of plating, where 40 lb is approximately one inch; STS is special treatment steel, NS is nickel steel (the predecessor to STS), and MS is mild steel. Where no designation is given for a thickness in pounds, it is mild or structural steel. Turret armor is given as face plate/roof/side/rear; side and rear are not separated if they are equal in thickness. Note that thicknesses are sometimes compound, as in 4 + 4 inches. That indicates a thickness built up from two layers, which was less effective ballistically than a single 8-inch thickness.

Generator capacity is given in kilowatts (kW). Steam conditions are in pounds per square inch (psi). In a few cases superheat temperature (in degrees F) is also given. Note that SSG is a Ship Service Generator (reciprocating); SSTG is a turbogenerator.

Under armament, SA are semi-automatic guns and MG are machine guns.

Under complement, the figures are officers/enlisted, the latter including CPOs.

Partial weight data in parentheses are designed as opposed to returned (actual) weights. In many cases the returned weights of the ship in light condition do not match the light ship displacement deduced from the inclining experiment, and the figure in parentheses *below* the light ship weight is that found upon inclining. The same convention applies

when the light ship weight breakdown refers to a sister ship of the one inclined; such instances are noted.

Among the weights, the margin is a designer's figure. Machinery liquids include lubricating oil and fuel oil "in the system," i.e., not in storage tanks.

Note that prewar standard displacements were computed on the basis of a "normal" or design condition, with two-thirds of stores and other loads (except ammunition) aboard. However, at the end of the treaty period, this allowance was modified to reflect half stores and only five gallons per man of potable water, the latter on the theory that in practice the ship's evaporators could make up the difference. Since potable water might amount to as much as half the total of stores and water, this was a very significant change.

Standard displacements have been computed for all battleships in the tables, to give the reader a feeling for the impact of the Washington Treaty. Given the changes introduced late in the 1930s, the standard displacements for the later U.S. battleships have been somewhat overstated. Note, however, weight growth between design and returned weights for these classes.

Note that the weight of *protection* includes only vertical armor, although decks were a substantial fraction of total *hull* weight. Some other navies included deck armor in their definition of protection; others counted turret armor under the armament group.

All weights are given in long tons of 2240 pounds.

Stability data refer to the loading noted. GM is the metacentric height. GZ is the maximum righting arm at an angle indicated below it; the range is the range of angles at which the ship would retain positive stability.

Name *Maine*
Date 1895
Design Displacement 6650
LOA 324 - 4½
LWL 318-3
Beam (wl) 57-2½
Hull Depth 30-2¹³⁄₁₆
CB 0.669
CM 0.878
Boilers 8 (135 PSI)
SSG 2 - 32
IHP (trial) 9171
Speed (trial) 17.45
AT (disp't) 5500
Endurance (service)
Tactical Diameter (yds/kts) 480/12 (stbd), 450/12 (port)
IHP (design) 8750

Speed (design) 17.0
Fuel Capacity (design) 400/896
Endurance (design) 4250/10
Main Battery 4 - 10in (90)
Complement
Secondary Battery 6 - 6in BL (100), 7 - 6pdr Driggs - Schroeder, 4 - 1pdr Driggs - Schroeder, 4 Gatling
Torpedo Tubes 6 - 18in (above water)
Protection:
Belt 12 - 7in (3ft above, 4ft below design waterline of 21ft6in, over 180ft of length; taper begins 4ft below top of belt)
Bulkheads 6in
Armor Deck 1 + 1in/3in sloped deck at ends
Barbettes 12in
Turrets 8in
Secondary Battery none
Conning Tower 10in (4.5in tube)

WEIGHTS

	Normal	Full Load
Hull & Fittings	3002	(2630.8)*
Protection	1059(†)	(1691.0)
Machinery	733	(912.9)
Armament	279	(527.1)
Equipment & Outfit	208	(171.0)
Light Ship	5281	(5932.8)
	(5378)	
Ammunition	212	
Machinery Liquids	180	
Complement	60	
Stores & PW	190	
Std. Disp.	6020	
Coal	823	
Displacement	6843	
Draft	21-11½	
GM	3.43	
GZ	2.2	
Angle	36	
Range	84.5	

* Design data as in October 1887. In 1890 the barbettes were raised to heighten the axes of the guns, and turret weights were reduced to compensate. Ultimately, the 124.6 tons saved on the turrets were applied to the belt, which increased to 12 inches, and to the barbettes, which increased from 10.5 to 12 inches. At this time inclined turret armor was planned.
† Side armor 526 tons, turrets and breastworks 533 tons.

Name *Texas*
Date May 1895
Design Displacement 6315
LOA 308-10
LWL 301-4
Beam (wl) 64-1
Hull Depth 39-8
CB 0.555
CM 0.906
Boilers 4 Double-ended(150 PSI)
SSG 4-24
IHP (trial)
Speed (trial)
AT (disp't)
Endurance (service) 3125/10
Tactical Diameter (yds/kts) 540/11.5
IHP (design) 8600

Speed (design) 17
Fuel Capacity (design) 500/850
Endurance (design) 6000/11.8
Main Battery 2 - 12in/35 (80)
Complement 30/362
Secondary Battery 2 - 6in/35(100), 4 - 6in30(100), 12 - 6pdr, 6-1pdr, 4-37mm
Torpedo Tubes 4 - 14in (above water)
Protection:
Belt 12in (2ft above, 4.5ft below waterline, 118ft long; taper began 1ft below waterline)
Bulkheads 6in
Armor Deck 2in/3in*
Barbettes 12in diagonal armored redoubt
Turrets 12in/1in/3in sighting hoods
Secondary Battery
Conning Tower 12in/1.5in

WEIGHTS†

	Normal	Full Load
Hull		(2279.3)
Hull Fittings		(699.0)
Protection		(1094.4)‡
Machinery (wet)		(816.0)
Armament		(217.6)
Equipment & Outfit		(163.0)
Margin		(103.2)
Light Ship		(5372.5)
Ammunition		(262.2)
Complement		(35.0)
Stores & PW		(105.0)
Std. Disp.		(5774.7)
Coal		500.0
Displacement	6315§	(6314.5)
Draft	24-6	22-6
GM §	2.54	3.1
GZ		
Angle	42-30	
Range	75	

* This deck covered the belt. There was also a 2in flat deck atop the diagonal redoubt connecting the two turrets, and a 1in deck around the casemates for the 6in guns.

† These are estimated weights prepared at Norfolk in December 1888 in answer to congressional questions concerning the *Texas* design. The stability figures are those given in the 1887 *Annual Report* of the secretary of the navy.

‡ This figure does not include the protective deck, 483.2 tons of armor, or the side plating over the secondary battery, 57.2 tons, or the top of the redoubt, 62.5 tons.

§ Stability data from J. C. Reilly, Jr., and R. L. Scheina, *American Battleships 1886–1923* (U.S. Naval Institute, 1980).

Name *Indiana*
Date
Design Displacement 10,225
LOA 350-11
LWL 348-0
Beam (wl) 69-3
Hull Depth 32-0
CB 0.622
CM 0.931
Boilers 4 (160 PSI)
SSG 3 - 24*
IHP (trial) 9498
Speed (trial) 15.55
AT (disp't) 10,225
Endurance (service) 5640/10
Tactical Diameter (yds/kts) 585/12(to port), 425/12(to starboard)
IHP (design) 9000
Speed (design) 15

Fuel Capacity (design) 1500
Endurance (design)
Main Battery 4 - 13in/35(60), 8 - 8in/35(75)
Secondary Battery 4 - 6in/40(100), 20 - 6pdr Hotchkiss, 6 - 1pdr Hotchkiss, 4 machine guns (in tops)
Torpedo Tubes 6 (above water) (16)
Complement 32/441
Protection:
Belt 18in - 8in (3 ft above, 4ft6in below waterline, tapered from 4ft below top of belt); 4in - 2.5in at ends
Casemate 5in
Bulkheads 14in
Armor Deck 2.75in (3in ends)
Barbettes 17in (8in for 8in guns, with 6in inboard sides)
Turrets 17in/2in (6in/2in for 8in guns)
Secondary Battery 5in (2in for 6pdr and 1pdr guns)
Conning Tower 10in (7in tube)

WEIGHTS

	Normal	Full Load	(*Oregon*, 16 Aug 11) Normal	Full Load
Hull	4688†	(3149.5)		
Hull Fittings		(513.9)		
Protection	2927	(2997.6)‡		
Machinery (wet)	1029	(890.3)		
Armament	858	(637.2)		
Equipment & Outfit	330	(444.2)§		
Light Ship	9832	(8632.7)	9692.1	
Ammunition		(459.6)	232.1	348.1
Machinery Liquids		(188.1)	167.0	
Complement		(57.0)	77.0	
Stores & PW		(119.4)	201.0	300.5
Std. Disp.			10,369.2	

RFW			75.7	113.5
Coal		(400.0)	950.2	1425.4
Displacement	10,524‖	(10,025.8)	11,305.0	12,034.6
Draft	24-6		25-11¼	27-4¼
GM	3.5		3.48	3.53
GZ	1.6		1.51	1.34
Angle	33		30-42	29-48
Range	57		56-30	54-30

* Replaced about 1908 with 3 - 100 kW units.

† Returned weight data for *Massachusetts*, as compiled in 1907 for the General Board. Thus hull and hull fittings are taken together, and machinery weight includes liquids *and generators*, which at this time still came under the Bureau of Equipment. Armament weight includes ammunition. The figure for equipment and outfit includes complement and stores.

‡ This figure includes 533.6 tons of deck armor, *not* including supporting structure.

§ This design figure includes stores and complement (normal condition).

‖ Stability data taken from W. Hovgaard, *General Design of Warships* (London: E. & F. Spon, 1920)

Name *Iowa* (BB 4)
Date 1897
Design Displacement 11,410
LOA 362-5
LWL 360-0
Beam (wl) 72-3
Hull Depth
CB 0.637
CM 0.944
Boilers (160 PSI)
SSG 4 - 24
IHP (trial) 11,834
Speed (trial) 17.09
AT (disp't) 11,363
Endurance (service) 5140/10
Tactical Diameter (yds/kts) 390/14, 550/10
IHP (design) 11,000

Speed (design) 16
Fuel Capacity 1650
Endurance (design)
Main Battery 4 - 12in/35, 8 - 8in /35
Secondary Battery 6 - 4in/40, 20 - 6pdr, 4 - 1pdr, 4 - 0.30 MG
Torpedo Tubes 4 - 14in (above water)
Complement 36/450
Protection:
Belt 14in - 7in (3ft above, 4ft6in below 24ft-6in waterline; taper begins 4ft below top of belt)
Casemate 5in
Bulkheads 12in
Armor Deck 2.75in (3in curved deck at ends)
Barbettes 15in (for 8in guns: 8in, 6in inboard)
Turrets 15in/2in crowns (for 8in guns: 6in/2in)
Secondary Battery 5in over 4in guns, 2in over 6pdr and 1pdr
Conning Tower 10in

WEIGHTS

	Normal	Full Load
Hull	3677.8	
Hull Fittings	596.0	
Protection	2831.7*	
Machinery (wet)	984.8	
Armament	515.6	
Equipment & Outfit	209.5	
Light Ship	9025.4	
Ammunition	340.0	509.9
Machinery Liquids	123.5	
Complement	65.0	
Stores & PW	143.3	215.0
Std. Disp.	9697.2	
RFW		
Coal	1196.6	1795.0
Displacement	11,340†	
Draft		
GM	4.01	
GZ	2.23	
Angle	35-23	
Range	61.35	

* This figure does not include 962.1 tons of protective deck, including both protective material and structural material.

† Stability data from J. C. Reilly, Jr., and R. L. Scheina, *American Battleships 1886–1923* (U.S. Naval Institute, 1980).

Name *Kearsage*
Date
Design Displacement 11,540
LOA 375-4
LWL 368-0
Beam (wl) 72-3
Hull Depth
CB 0.646
CM 0.957
Boilers
SSG 7 - 50
IHP (trial) 11,788
Speed (trial) 16.82
AT (disp't) 11,550
Endurance (service) 5070/10
Tactical Diameter (yds/kts) 475/12 (port), 455/12 (starboard)*
IHP (design) 10,000
Speed (design) 16.0
Fuel Capacity (design) 1500

Endurance (design)
Main Battery 4 - 13in/35(60), 4 - 8in/35(125)
Secondary Battery 14 -5in/40 (256), 20 - 6pdr, 19 - 1pdr, 2 - 6mm MG
Torpedo Tubes 4 - 18in (above water) (6)
Complement 40/513
Protection:
Belt 16.5in - 9.5in (uniformly tapered); reduced to 10.5in - 9.5 in at No. 1 turret, then to 4in at bow.
Lower Casemate 5in
Upper Casemate 6in
Bulkheads 10in forward, 12in aft (between top of belt and deck slopes)
Armor Deck 2.75in; forward, 2.75in/3in; aft, 2.75in/5in
Barbettes 15in (12.5in rear)
Turrets 17in/3.5in/25in (for 8in: 11in/3.5in/9in)
Secondary Battery Upper casemate, plus 2in splinter bulkheads between guns
Conning Tower 10in/2in

WEIGHTS

	Normal	Full Load
Hull	4792.5	
Hull Fittings	756.3	
Protection	3020.1†	
Machinery (dry)	1209.4	
Armament	626.8	
Equipment & Outfit	259.7	
Light Ship	10,664.8	
Ammunition		626.8
Complement		76.1
Stores & PW		235.5
Std. Disp.		
RFW		
Coal		1591.0
Displacement	12,905‡	13,100.5
Draft	25-9	
GM	4.5	
GZ	2.3	
Angle	34	
Range	63	

	Normal	Full Load	Normal	Full Load
	29 May 1912		3 October 1918	
Light Ship	10,085.2		10,547	
Ammunition	332.6	498.8	378	
Machinery Liquids	85.6		85	
Complement	60.3		119	
Stores & PW	135.2	171.5	136	217
Std. Disp.	10,698.9		11,265	
RFW	148.9	223.4	128	191
Coal	1093.9	1640.8	1120	1679
Displacement	11,941.7	12,797.0	12,523	13,217
Draft	24-2½	25-8	25-2	26-4½
GM	5.29	5.10	4.31	4.20
GZ	2.17	1.82	1.48	1.20
Angle	29.7	27.4	26-20	21-40
Range	55.6	52.0	47-30	43-40

* Corresponding figures for *Kentucky* were 393/10 and 430/10, respectively.

† This figure does not include the protective deck, 994.3 tons, which latter included both structural and protective material.

‡ Stability data for *Kearsage* as completed are taken from W. Hovgaard, *General Design of Warships* (London: E. & F. Spon, 1920).

Name *Illinois*
Date
Design Displacement 11,565
LOA 375-4
LWL 368-0
Beam (wl) 72-3
Hull Depth 34-6
CB 0.644
CM 0.957
Boilers 8
SSG 8 - 32
IHP (trial) 12,757
Speed (trial) 17.45
AT (disp't) 11,540
Endurance (service) 4190/10
Tactical Diameter (yds/kts) 362/12
IHP (design) 10,000
Speed (design) 16.0
Fuel Capacity (design) 800/1270

Endurance (design)
Main Battery 4 - 13in/35(54)
Complement 40/496
Secondary Battery 14 - 6in/40 (Total 2760), 16 - 6pdr, 7 - 1pdr, 4 - 0.30 MG
Torpedo Tubes 4 - 18in (above water) (8)
Protection:
Belt 16.5in - 9.5in (3.5ft above, 4ft below designed waterline; uniform taper top to bottom), tapering to 4in (at the bow) from just forward of the boiler spaces.
Lower Casemate 5.5in (partly coal-backed)
Upper Casemate 5.5in
Bulkheads 12in
Armor Deck 2.75in (flat); 2.75in/3in forward, 2.75in/5in aft
Barbettes 15in (10in rear)
Turrets 14in/3in top
Secondary Battery Upper casemate; also 1.5in splinter bulkheads between guns
Conning Tower 10in/2in

WEIGHTS

	Normal	Full Load
Hull	5338.3	(4625.5)
Hull Fittings	744.9	(498.3)
Protection	2826.3*	(2855.8)
Machinery (wet)	1278.8	(1128.3)
Armament	622.6	(568.3)
Equipment & Outfit	258.8	(398.0)
Light Ship	11,069.7	
Ammunition		454.1
Complement	86.9	
Stores & PW		263.5
Std. Disp.	11,635.0	
RFW		
Coal	800	1270.0
Displacement	11,653†	12,719.8
Draft	23 - 8	
GM	4.0	
GZ	2.7	
Angle	39	
Range	66	

* This figure does not include the protective deck, 983.2 tons, which includes both structural and protective plating.
† Stability data are for *Wisconsin*, as given by W. Hovgaard, in *General Design of Warships* (London: E. & F. Spon, 1920).

Name *Missouri*
Date 27 November 1903
Design Displacement 12,846
LOA 393-11
LWL 388-0
Beam (wl) 72-3
Hull Depth 34-6
CB 0.654
CM 0.946
Boilers 12
SSG 4 - 50, 4 - 32
IHP (trial) 15,845
Speed (trial) 18.15
AT (disp't) 12,300
Endurance (service) 5660/10 (*Ohio*: 6560/10)
Tactical Diameter (yds/kts) 350/10
IHP (design) 16,000
Speed (design) 18.0
Fuel Capacity (design) 1000/1887 (*Ohio*: 2215)

Endurance (design) 4900/10
Main Battery 4 - 12in/40(60)
Complement 40/521
Secondary Battery 16 - 6in/50(200), 6 - 3in/50, 8 - 3pdr
Torpedo Tubes 2 - 18in (submerged)(6)
Protection:
Belt 11in - 7.5in (3ft above, 4ft6in below design waterline, tapering from 1ft below the design waterline at 23ft10.5in); 8.5in/5.875in at No. 1 barbette, then tapering to 4in at bow.
Lower Casemate 6in
Upper Casemate 6in
Bulkheads 9in
Armor Deck 1 in MS + 62.5 lbs NS (2.5in) (flat); forward, 2.5in/2.75in; aft, 2.75in/4in
Barbettes 12in (8in rear)
Turrets 12in/-/8in
Secondary Battery 6in
Conning Tower 10in/2in

WEIGHTS*

	Normal	Full Load
Hull	5097.7	
Hull Fittings	780.1	
Protection	2705.4	
Machinery (dry)	1610.8	
Armament	691.6	
Equipment & Outfit	278.7	
Light Ship	11,164.3	
	(10,668.0)	
Ammunition	306.8	460.2
Machinery Liquids	80.0	
Displacement	83.5	
Stores & PW	169.6	254.4
Std. Disp.	11,307.9	
RFW	142.1	
Coal	1000.0	1836.2
Displacement	13,443.3	
Draft	25-6¼	
GM	3.77	
GZ	2.36	
Angle	37-0	
Range	64-30	

* Weights refer to the battleship *Maine* (BB 10), as completed. When *Missouri* was inclined late in her career, her metacentric height was only 3.6ft in the fully loaded condition, and 3.88 ft in the normal condition; range of stability, fully loaded, was 63 degrees 6 minutes (60 degrees in normal condition). These figures are from C&R Miscellaneous files, and neither date nor displacement is given.

Name *New Jersey*
Date 28 April 1906
Design Displacement 14,948
LOA 441-3
LWL 435-0
Beam (wl) 76-3
Hull Depth 42-3
CB 0.656
CM 0.906
Boilers 12
SSTG 2 - 100, 6 - 50
IHP (trial) 23,089
Speed (trial) 19.18
AT (disp't) 14,930
Endurance (service) 4860/10 (*Nebraska*: 5950/10)
Tactical Diameter (yds/kts) 478/12 (starboard), 455/12 (port)
IHP (design) 19,000
Speed (design) 19.0
Fuel Capacity (design) 1955

Endurance (design) 3825/10
Main Battery 4 - 12in/40(60), 8 - 8in(125)
Secondary Battery 12 - 6in/50(200), 12 - 3in/50, 12 - 3pdr, 2 - 1pdr, 4 - 0.30 MG
Torpedo Tubes 4 - 21in (submerged)(12 to 16)
Complement 40/772
Protection:
Belt 11in - 8in (3ft above and 5ft below water; 192ft long); end belts fore and aft.
Casemate 6in (245ft long)
Bulkheads
Armor Deck 1.5in/3in (slope met bottom of belt); forward, 3in; aft, 3in
Barbettes 10in (7.5in rear) (for 8in: 6in, 4in rear)
Turrets 12in/2in/8in/6in; 8in wing turrets: 6.5in/2in/6in
Secondary Battery Casemate, with 2.5in bulkheads; 2in for 3in guns
Conning Tower 9in/2in

WEIGHTS*

	Normal	Full Load	(Virginia, 14 September 1912) Normal	Full Load
Hull	6095.7			
Hull Fittings	953.1			
Protection	3730.9†			
Machinery (dry)	2006.9			
Armament	918.2			
Equipment & Outfit	305.9			
Light Ship	13,373.9	13,736.3		
Ammunition	398.0	597.1	398.0	597.1
Machinery Liquids	156.1		146.4	
Complement	104.5		89.7	
Stores & PW	236.9	349.0	253.2	379.8
Std. Disp.	14,269.4		14,623.6	

RFW	66.0	121.5	66.0	100.0
Coal	900.0	1994.9	900.0	1924.2
Displacement	15,235.4	16,696.9	15,589.6	16,973.4
Draft	24-2¾	26-2½	24-7	26-5
GM	5.15	5.21	4.91	5.03
GZ	3.31	3.05	2.95	2.79
Angle	38-15	37-10	37-4	35-40
Range	66-40	67-5	64-12	66-0

* Weight data refer to *Virginia*, as built.

† This figure does not include the protective deck, 1015.2 tons, which includes both structural and protective material.

Name *Louisiana*
Date 4 May 1906
Design Displacement 16,000
Design Full Load 17,700
LOA 456-4
LWL 450-0
Beam (wl) 76-10
Hull Depth 43-01⅜
CB 0.660
CM 0.961
Boilers 12 (250 PSI)
SSG 8 - 100*
IHP (trial) 20,748
Speed (trial) 18.82
AT (disp't) 16,000
Endurance (service) 6620/10 (*New Hampshire*: 7590/10)
Tactical Diameter (yds/kts) 620/12
IHP (design) 16,500
Speed (design) 18.0
Fuel Capacity (design) 900/2200
Endurance (design) 5275/10

Main Battery 4 - 12in/40 (60), 8 - 8in/45 (100)
Secondary Battery 12 - 7in/45(100), 20 - 3in/50(300), 12-3pdr(600)
  SA, 6 - 1pdr automatic (960), 2 - 1pdr SA, 2 - 0.30 MG
Torpedo Tubes 4 - 21in (submerged) (16)
Complement 42/785
Protection: †
Belt 11in - 9in (9ft3in wide, 200ft long amidships); 9in forward
  and aft to main barbettes, tapering to 7in, 5in, then 4in at bow
  and stern
Lower Casemate 6in (to lower edge of 7in gun ports, between
  main barbettes)
Upper Casemate 7in with 1.5 - 2.5in transverse splinter bulkheads
  between 7in guns
Bulkheads 6in (to lower casemate)
Armor Deck 1.5in/3in (meets lower edge of belt); 3in/3in fore and
  aft
Barbettes 10in (6in inside casemates)(for 8in guns: 6in, 4in in-
  board)
Turrets 11in/2.5in/9in (8in guns: 6.5in/2in/6in)
Secondary Battery 7in around 7in guns, 2in around 3in guns
Conning Tower 9in/2in

WEIGHTS:‡

	Normal	Full Load
Hull	6691.6	
Hull Fittings	1071.7	
Protection	3997.7§	
Machinery (dry)	1492.5	
Armament	1143.0	
Equipment & Outfit	436.7	
Light Ship	14,833.2	
	(14,506.9)	
Ammunition	405.0	579.7
Machinery Liquids	134.7	
Complement	112.2	
Stores & PW	225.3	337.9
Std. Disp.	15,271.9	
RFW	74.0	110.9
Coal	1602.6	2403.9
Displacement	17,070.7	18,186.3
Draft	25-11½	27-5
GM	4.62	5.10
GZ	3.11	3.08
Range	39-0	38-12
Draft	66-48	67-24

* However, *New Hampshire* had 4 - 100 kW units and 2 - 200 kW *turbo*generators.

† These figures apply only to *Connecticut* and *Louisiana*. The other four ships of the class had 9in belts, tapering to 7in-5in-4in at the ends. *New Hampshire* had 7in bulkheads and 7in casemates; the others had 6in bulkheads and 7in casemates. *New Hampshire* was unique in having 11in barbettes (7.5in rear).

‡ Weight data refer to *Connecticut*, as built.

§ This figure does not include the protective deck, 1017.4 tons, of which 591.4 tons was protective plating and 63.2 tons was protective grating and covers.

Name *Mississippi* (BB 23)
Date 2 November 1907
Design Displacement 13,000
LOA 382-0
LWL 375-0
Beam (wl) 77-0
Hull Depth
CB 0.670
CM 0.974
Boilers 8(250 psi)
SSG 8 - 100
IHP (trial) 13,607
Speed (trial) 17.11
AT (disp't) 13,000
Endurance (service) 5800/10
Tactical Diameter (yds/kts) 410/15.3
IHP (design) 10,000
Speed (design) 17.0
Fuel Capacity (design) 600/1750

Endurance (design) 5775/10
Main Battery 4 - 12in/40(71)
     8 - 8in/45(111)
Complement 34/710
Secondary Battery 8 - 7in/45(111), 12 - 3in/50(250) 6 - 3pdr SA,
 2 - 1pdr automatic, 2 - 1pdr RF
Torpedo Tubes 2 - 21in (submerged)(13)
Protection:
Belt 9in (244 ft × 9ft3in wide); tapered to 4in at ends
Lower Casemate 7in
Upper Casemate 7in
Bulkheads 7in
Armor Deck 40 lbs NS flat/100 lbs NS sloped, both on 20 lbs steel
Barbettes 10in (7.5in rear)(6in between main and armor decks)
 (barbettes for 8in guns: 6in, 4in rear)
Turrets 12/2.5/8 in (for 8in guns: 6.5/2/6 in)
Secondary Battery 7in over 7in guns, 2in over 3in guns
Conning Tower 9in

WEIGHTS*

	Normal	Full Load
Hull	4954.7	5292.3
Hull Fittings	799.3	661.1
Protection	3238.1†	3323.0
Machinery (dry)	914.1	932.5
Armament	944.8	849.3
Equipment & Outfit	329.0	395.6
Margin		
Light Ship	11,180.1	
	(11,176.2)	
Ammunition	342.2	513.3
Machinery Liquids	82.0	
Complement	95.4	
Stores & PW	248.6	352.7
Std. Disp.	11,944.4	
RFW	40.0	80.0
Coal	600.0	1750.0
Displacement	12,584.4	14,049.5
Draft	24-0³⁄₁₆	26-4¾
GM	4.34	4.83
GZ	2.78	2.68
Range	35-39	34-36
Range	62-12	63-33

* Returned weights are for *Idaho*.
† Excluding protective deck, 819.6 tons, of which 507.9 tons were armor, and 46.9 tons were protective gratings and so forth.

Name *Michigan*
Date 28 August 1909
Design Displacement 16,000
LOA 452-9
LWL 450-0
Beam (wl) 80-2½
Hull Depth 34-6³⁄₈
CB 0.637
CM 0.943
Boilers 12 B&W
SSTG 4 - 200
IHP (trial) 16,313
Speed (trial) 18.79
AT (disp't) 16,064
Endurance (service) 6950/10
Tactical Diameter (yds/kts)
IHP (design) 16,500
Speed (design) 18.0

Fuel Capacity (design) 900/2200 coal
Endurance (design) 5000/10
Main Battery 8 - 12in/45(100)
Complement 51/818
Secondary Battery 22 - 3in/50(300)
Torpedo Tubes 2 - 21in (submerged)
Tactical Diameter (yds/kts)
Protection:
Belt 11in - 9in over machinery and 12in - 10in over magazines
 (both 8ft wide, both tapered uniformly top to bottom); 10in -
 8in belt forward of forward magazines; 60 lb NS from belt
 forward (Frame 17 to Frame 8) and abaft belt to stern (Frame
 81 aft)
Casemate 8in - 10in
Armor Deck 50 lb NS + 30 lb over magazines, 30 lb structural
 + 30 lb structural over machinery; 70 lb NS + 30 lb forward
 of forward magazines (over forward belt); 40 lb NS + 20 lb to

bow; 80 lb NS + 30 lb abaft belt; 100 lb NS + 20 lb sloping
to stern
Bulkheads
Uptake Protection 40 lbs over 20 lbs NS; 40 lbs NS sides

Barbettes 10in - 8in
Turrets 12in/2.5in NS/8in
Secondary Battery
Conning Tower 12in/2in

WEIGHTS*

	Normal	Full Load
Hull Hull	6571.6	(6617.7)
Hull Fittings	861.3	(753.8)
Protection	3963.3†	(4052.8)
Machinery (dry)	1539.9	(1550.0)
Armament	872.6	(831.8)
Equipment & Outfit	341.2	(820.3)‡
Margin		(120.7)
Light Ship	14,149.9	
	14,038.5	
Ammunition	402.1	603.2
Machinery Liquids	111.2	
Complement	112.5	
Stores & PW	226.9	343.3
Std. Disp.	14,891.2	
RFW	84.4	126.6
Coal	900.0	2374.2
Displacement	15,875.6	17,709.5
Draft	24-4⅛	26-8½
GM	6.90	6.30
GZ	3.58	2.84
Angle	34-30	32-35
Range	64-30	61-8

* Weight data refer to *South Carolina*, as built.
† This figure does not include protective deck, 928.55 tons (including both structural and protective material).
‡ This design figure includes both equipment (347.3 tons) and outfit and 2/3 stores.

Name *North Dakota*
Date 20 February 1910
Design Displacement 20,000
LOA 518-9
LWL 510-0
Beam (wl) 85-2½
Hull Depth 45-6
CB 0.600
CM 0.978
Boilers 14 (265 PSI)
SSTG 4 - 300
SHP (trial) 31,635
SHP (design) 25,000
Speed (trial) 21.01
AT (disp't) 20,020
Endurance (service) 6560/10 (*Delaware*: 9750/10)
Tactical Diameter (yds/kts) 640/19
Speed (design) 21.0

Fuel Capacity (design) 1000/2500 coal
Endurance (design)
Main Battery 10 - 12in/45(100)
Complement 55/878
Secondary Battery 14-5in/50(240)
Torpedo Tubes 2 - 21in (submerged) (12)
Protection:
Belt 11in - 9in (8ft wide, uniformly tapered top to bottom)
Lower Casemate 8in - 10in (7ft3in wide amidships)
Upper Casemate 5in
Armor Deck magazines: 50 lb NS + 30 lb; machinery and boiler
spaces: 30 lb + 30 lb; forward of forward magazine (behind
armor) 70 lb NS + 30 lb; to bow, 40 lb NS + 20 lb; abaft belt
100 lb NS + 20 lb
Bulkheads 10in
Barbettes 10in - 4in
Turrets 12in/3in NS/8in
Conning Tower 11.5in/2in

WEIGHTS

	Normal	Full Load
Hull	7962.2	(8186.9)
Hull Fittings	1143.2	(919.9)
Protection	4992.0*	(4980.6)
Machinery (dry)	2011.0	(1947.0)
Armament	1168.5	(1660.2)†
Equipment & Outfit	382.4	(872.0)
Light Ship	17,659.3	
	(17,264.6)	

Ammunition	547.6	821.3
Machinery Liquids	136.9	
Complement	120.8	
Stores & PW	303.7	455.7
Std. Disp.	18,373.6	

RFW	66.0	200.0
Coal	1000.0	2500.0
Fuel Oil	380.0	380.0
Displacement	19,819.5	21,879.3
Draft	26-8½	29-1½
GM	3.78	4.24
GZ	2.52	2.32
Angle	35-0	34-30
Range	58-15	59-0

* This weight does not include the armor deck, 1048.39 tons (including both structural and protective material).

† This design figure includes both armament and ammunition. The design figure for equipment and outfit includes 2/3 stores; equipment was listed as 355.2 tons.

Name *Utah*
Date as built
Design Displacement 21,825
Design Full Load 23,033
LOA 521-6
LWL 510-0
Beam (wl) 88-2½
Hull Depth 45 - 7⅞
CB 0.584
CM 0.979
Boilers 12 (200 PSI)
SSTG 4-300
SHP (trial) 27,445
Speed (trial) 21.04
AT (disp't) 21,282
Endurance (service) 5776/10, 2760/20 (clean: 7220/12, 3450/20)
Tactical Diameter (yds/kts) 440/14, 427(18) (*Florida*); 640/21 (*Utah*)
SHP (design) 28,000

Speed (design) 20.75
Fuel Capacity (design) 2500
Endurance (design) 6860/10
Main Battery 10 - 12in/45(100)
Complement 60/941
Secondary Battery 16 - 5in/51(240)
Torpedo Tubes 2 - 21in (submerged)(8)
Protection:
Belt 11in - 9in (8ft wide, uniformly tapered)
Lower Casemate 8in - 10in (7ft3in wide)
Upper Casemate 6.5in
Armor Deck 60 lb STS + 20 lb over magazines; 40 lb STS + 20 lb over machinery; 100 lb STS + 20 lb sloping from belt to stern; 80 lb STS + 20 lb forward end of belt; 40 lb STS + 20 lb watertight deck (at upper platform level) to bow
Barbettes 10in - 4in
Turrets 12in/3in STS + 1in STS/8in
Conning Tower 11.5in/4in STS

WEIGHTS

	Normal	Full Load
Hull	7774.1	(8353.0)
Hull Fittings	1223.2	(1030.3)
Protection	5067.7	(5139.5)*
Machinery	2110.9	(2074.9)
Armament	1268.1	(1194.7)
Equipment & Outfit	401.6	(415.7)
Light Ship	17,845.6	(18,212.5)

Margin	(17,642)	(14.4)
Ammunition	565.6	844.9
Complement	112.2	
Stores & PW	513.9	730.6
Std. Disp.	18,833.7	

RFW	66	296.6
Fuel Oil	381.4	466.4
Coal	1000.0	2520.4
Displacement	21,230	22,439†
Draft		
GM	4.01	3.37
GZ		
Angle		
Range		

* This figure excludes splinter protection, such as the armor deck (1046.96 tons, including both structural and protective material). Note, too, that the enlarged conning tower weighed about twice as much as that of the earlier class (216.94 tons of armor compared with 102.75 tons for *North Dakota* and 95.7 tons for *Delaware*.

† For *Florida*, inclining experiment results showed 21,750.2 tons normal load (1673.1 tons of coal and 361.2 tons of oil), for a draft of 28-4⅛, GM 4.56ft; deep load (2509.7 tons coal, 541.8 tons oil) gave a displacement of 23,074.0 tons (draft 29-10 3/4, GM 5.09ft).

Name *Florida* (BB 30) (Rebuilt)
Date August 1926
Design Displacement 23,700
Design Full Load 24,800
Boilers 4 White-Foster
SSTG 4 - 400
Beam (wl) 106-0
CB
GM
SHP (trial) 47,376
Speed (trial) 22.16
AT (disp't) 24,666
Endurance (service)
Tactical Diameter (yds/kts)
SHP (design)
Speed (design)

Fuel Capacity (design)
Endurance (design) 16,500/10 (using emergency fuel oil)
Main Battery 10 - 12in/45
Complement 81/1090
Secondary Battery 12 - 5in/51
AA Battery 8 - 3in/50
Protection: (Changes)
Second Deck (former berth deck) 70 lb STS + 70 lb STS over existing 20 lb MS + 20 lb MS over magazines between end barbettes; 70 lb STS + 70 lb NS over existing 12 lb MS outboard of boilers; 50 lb STS + 70 lb STS + 70 lb NS over boilers; 30 lb over engines.
Armor Deck Add 70 lb STS to existing 12 lb MS over steering gear
Turrets Add 70 lb STS to turret and conning tower tops

WEIGHT CHANGES DUE TO RECONSTRUCTION (WEIGHTS IN PARENTHESES ARE BUREAU ESTIMATES OF CHANGES):

CHANGES DUE TO CONVERSION TO OIL	
BURNING	−260 (249)
ADDED PROTECTION	+2750 (2705)
BLISTER	825*
DECK PROTECTION	1753
MISCELLANEOUS SAVINGS	−20 (10)
NET CHANGE	+2470 (2446)
LIGHT SHIP (1924)	18,517
ESTIMATED LIGHT SHIP AS REBUILT	20,987 (20,963)

	Normal	Full Load
Light Ship	20,226	
Ammunition	962	
Machinery Liquids	116	
Complement	147	
Stores & PW	544	814
Std. Disp.	21,995	
RFW	315	472
Fuel Oil	2434	4999†
Displacement	24,744	27,726
Draft	28-6	31-7 ½
GM	9.12	8.17
GZ		
Range		

* These figures are not consistent with the others; they were developed by C&R in June 1925.
† There was also an optimum battle condition, in which the ship carried her normal liquid loads, except for full-load potable water (229 rather than 152 tons), 2581 tons of oil fuel, and 140 tons of water in a floodable space. GM was 9.18 ft, draft 28-9 ¾.

Name *Arkansas*
Date 24 August 1912
Design Displacement 26,000
LOA 562-0
LWL 554-0
Beam (wl) 93-2 ½
Hull Depth 48-8 ¼
CB 0.622
CM 0.985
Boilers 12
SSTG 4-300
SHP (trial) 28,787
Speed (trial) 21.22
AT (disp't) 25,546
Endurance (service) 5190/12, 2655/20 (clean: 6488/12, 3319/20)
Tactical Diameter (yds/kts) 520/18 (port), 580/18 (starboard) (*Wyoming*: 710/10, 605 left/16, 680 right/16)
SHP (design) 28,000

Speed (design) 20.5
Fuel Capacity (design) 1667 Coal, 266 Oil
Endurance (design) 6860/10
Main Battery 12-12in/50
Complement 58/1005
Secondary Battery 21 - 5in/51
Torpedo Tubes 2 - 21in (submerged)
Protection:
Belt 11in - 9in
Lower Casemate 11in - 9in
Upper Casemate 6.5in
Bulkheads
Armor Deck 100 lb STS + 20 lb − 68 lb STS + 20 lb − 40 lb STS + 20 lb
Barbettes 11in - 4.5in
Turrets 12in/3in STS/8in/12in
Secondary Battery
Conning Tower 11.5in/3in STS

WEIGHTS

	Normal	Full Load
Hull	9329.0	(9924.6)
Hull Fittings	1428.3	(1123.8)
Protection	6935.0*	(6859.9)
Machinery (dry)	2012.9	(2071.0)(wet)
Armament	1528.8	(1558.8)
Equipment & Outfit	442.3	
Margin		(248.7)
Light Ship	21,676.3	
	(21,671.8)	
Ammunition	1009.3	
Machinery Liquids	165.2	
Complement	145.6	
Stores & PW	336.2	504.4
Std. Disp.	23,328.1	
RFW	194.3	291.4
Coal	1799.2	2698.8
Oil Fuel	305.3	458.0
Displacement	25,627.0	26,944.6
Draft	28-0 ¼	27 - 3 ¾
GM	5.40	5.49
GZ	3.34	3.23
Angle	35-48	35-48
Range	61-24	61-48

*This figure does not include the protective deck, 1215.9 tons, of which 685.0 tons was splinter armor (STS).

Name *Arkansas* (rebuilt)
Date 24 June 1927
Design Displacement 27,900
Design Full Load 29,000
Boilers 4 White-Foster
SSTG 4 - 400
Beam (wl) 106-0
CB
CM
SHP (trial) 43,187
Speed (trial) 21.41
AT (disp't) 29,068
Endurance (service) 14,000/10, 7000/18 (emergency tankage)
Tactical Diameter (yds/kts) 630/12, 605/15
SHP (design) 28,000
Speed (design) 21.0
Fuel Capacity (design) 3786/5543 (emergency)

WEIGHT CHANGES DUE TO MODERNIZATION (BUREAU ESTIMATES IN PARENTHESES):

CONVERSION TO OIL BURNING	− 224 (209)
ADDED PROTECTION	+2775(3011)
MISCELLANEOUS DEDUCTIONS	−45(25)
NET CHANGE	+2506(2777)
LIGHT SHIP (1925)	22,257
PREDICTED NEW DISPLACEMENT	24,763 (25,034)

Endurance (design) 11,000/10 (using emergency oil)
Main Battery 12 - 12in/50
Complement 65/1177
Secondary Battery 16 - 5in/51
AA Battery 8 - 3in/50
Protection: (changes)
Second Deck (former berth deck) Add 70 lb STS + 70 lb STS over magazines to existing 20 lb STS + 20 lb STS between barbettes 2 and 6 (over existing 12 lb MS outboard of boiler rooms); 50 lb STS + 70 lb STS over existing 70 lb NS over boiler rooms; 30 lb STS + 70 lb STS + 70 lb STS over existing 12 lb MS over engines (between Nos. 4 and 5 barbettes)
Half Deck 70 lb STS + 70 lb STS over existing 20 lb STS + 20 lb MS to forward limit of lower belt armor
Armor Deck 70 lb STS added over existing 12 lb MS over steering gear spaces
Turrets 70 lb STS added to turret and conning tower tops

(*Wyoming* as AG 17, 11 MAY 1931)

	Normal		Full Load	
Light Ship	24,341.3		19,163	
Ammunition	1007.2		65.5	
Machinery Liquids	102.9		90.3	
Complement	168.8		113.7	
Stores & PW	446.9	670.3	301.0	451.5
Lube Oil				
Std. Disp.	26,067.1		19,733.5	

RFW	182.8	274.2	182.8	274.2
Fuel Oil	2705.6	4045.4	1666.1	2502.7*
Gasoline			8.1	12.1
Displacement	28,955.5	30,610.2	21,591	22,673
Draft	28-6	29-11 ¾	24-3	25-3 ½
GM	8.15	7.70	6.47	6.16
GZ				
Angle				
Range				

* Full fuel capacity is 5278.3 tons, and full RFW capacity 539.3 tons, for an emergency displacement of 25,714 tons (GM 6.59ft, draft 28ft3in).

Name *Texas*
Date 21 February 1914
Design Displacement 27,000
LOA 573-0
LWL 565-0
Beam (wl) 95-3
Hull Depth 48 - 8¼
CB 0.616
CM 0.977
Boilers 14 B&W(8 Superheated) (295 PSI)
SSTG 4 - 300
SHP (trial) 28,850
Speed (trial) 21.13
AT (disp't) 26,132
Endurance (service) 7684/12, 2932/20 (clean: 9605/12, 3665/20)
Tactical Diameter (yds/kts) 1000/19 (*New York*: 689/10, 725/16, 800/19)
IHP (design) 28,100
Speed (design) 21.0

Fuel Capacity (design) 1900 Coal 267 Oil
Endurance (design) 7060/10
Main Battery 10 - 14in/45 (100)
Complement 58/994
Secondary Battery 21 - 5in/51 (230)
Torpedo Tubes 4 - 21in (submerged)(12)*
Protection:
Belt 12in - 10in (7ft11.5in wide, top 23.5in above designed waterline of 28ft6in); 6in belt aft
Lower Casemate 9in - 11in
Upper Casemate 6.5in
Bulkheads 10in and 11in(9in abaft lower belt aft)
Armor Deck 100 lb STS + 20 lb aft; 60 lb STS + 20 lb amidships; 40 lb STS + 20 lb forward of belt
Barbettes 12in - 5in
Turrets 14in/4in STS/8in
Secondary Battery 40lb STS transverse splinter bulkheads, 60lb longitudinal splinter bulkheads
Conning Tower 12in/4in STS

WEIGHTS

	Normal	Full Load
Hull	9681.9	(9898.3)
Hull Fittings	1552.8	(1164.5)
Protection	7030.7†	(7120.8)
Machinery (dry)	2311.3	(2390.0)(wet)
Armament	1449.4	(1377.7)
Equipment & Outfit	444.4	
Light Ship	22,470.5‡	
	(22,082.9)	
Ammunition	1136.5	
Machinery Liquids	140.8	
Complement	138.7	
Stores & PW	459.0	688.5
Std. Disp.	23,957.9	
RFW	214.8	322.5
Coal	1973.6	2960.4
Fuel Oil	309.4	463.5
Displacement	26,455.6	27,933.8
Draft	27-10½	29-3¼
GM	6.53	6.86
GZ	4.16	4.14
Angle	35-24	35-24
Range	63-28	65-6

* Four torpedoes in reserve. This magazine also held twelve naval defense mines, to protect an advanced fleet anchorage against surprise attack.
† This figure does not include the protective deck, 1337.6 tons (including 770.1 tons of STS).
‡ *New York* as inclined at Puget Sound 14 April 1920 displaced 21,977.7 tons (light) and showed a loss of 1.15 feet of GM (as compared with her condition in 1914), because of reconstruction of her bridge and torpedo defense positions, reinforcement of her cage masts, and removal of four 5in guns.

Name *Texas* (BB 35)(Rebuilt)
Date 26 September 1928
Design Displacement 28,700
Design Full Load 30,000
Boilers 6 Bureau Express
SSTG 4 - 400
Beam (wl) 106-0
CB
CM
IHP (trial) 25,402
Speed (trial) 19.72
AT (disp't) 29,589
Endurance (service) 15, 400/10, 6500/18 (emergency tankage)
Tactical Diameter (yds/kts)
IHP (design) 28,100
Speed (design)
Fuel Capacity (design) 2810/4600 (emergency)

Endurance (design) 15,000/10 (using emergency oil)
Main Battery 10 - 14in/45
Complement 87/1208
Secondary Battery 16 - 5in/51
AA Battery 8 - 3in/50
Protection: (Changes)
Second Deck (formerly berth deck) 70 lb STS + 70 lb NS added to existing 20 lb STS + 20 lb STS over magazines between Nos. 2 and 5 barbettes; 70 lb STS + 70 lb NS added over engines to existing 28 lb STS + 12 lb MS; 70 lb STS + 70 lb NS added to existing 12 lb MS over boilers amidships*
Half Deck 70 lb STS + 70 lb NS from aft side of No. 2 barbette to forward limit of lower belt armor
Armor Deck 70 lb NS added to existing 12 lb MS from No. 5 barbette to stern (over steering gear)
Turrets 70 lb added to turret tops

WEIGHT CHANGES DUE TO MODERNIZATION:
CONVERSION TO OIL BURNING   − 564 (187)
ADDED PROTECTION   +2976 (2911)
MISCELLANEOUS REMOVALS   − 27 (80)
NET CHANGE (NORFOLK NAVY YARD ESTIMATE)   2385
                                     TONS (ADDED)
        BUREAU ESTIMATE   (2644 TONS)

	Normal	Full Load
Light Ship (1925)		22,676
Estimate Post-Refit		25,061
Light Ship	24,863.0	(as actually inclined)
Ammunition	1391.0	
Machinery Liquids	70.5	
Complement	150.8	
Stores & PW	429.0	796.6
Lube Oil	9.6	14.3
Std. Disp.	26,913.9	
RFW	267.4	401.2
Fuel Oil	2824.6	4236.9†
Displacement	30,118.6	31,924.2
Draft	28-7⅜	30-2⅜
GM	10.38	10.27
GZ	5.65	5.64
Angle	35-30	36-0
Range	68-45	71-0

* The 50 lb STS over the boiler rooms in the other two conversions had to be omitted in this one to remain within the Washington Treaty limit of 3000 tons of additions for protection against air and submarine attack.
† Full fuel tank capacity was 5192.59 tons; full RFW capacity was 782.57 tons. Emergency displacement, then, was 33,261.3 tons (GM 10.8ft, draft 31-3½)

Name *Nevada* (BB 36)
Date 27 February 1916
Design Displacement 27,500
Design Full Load 28,400
LOA 583-0
LWL 575-0
Beam (wl) 95 - 2½
Hull Depth
CB 0.617
CM 0.984
Boilers 12 Yarrow(295 PSI)
SSTG 4 - 300
IHP (trial) 26,291
Speed (trial) 20.90
AT (disp't) 27,222
Endurance (service) 5195/12, 1980/20 (clean: 6494/12, 2475/20)
Tactical Diameter (yds/kts) 825/15, 580/19 (*Oklahoma* 625/20)
IHP (trial) 26,500

Speed (design) 20.5
Fuel Capacity (design) 1333/2000 oil
Endurance (design) 8000/10
Main Battery 10 - 14in/45
Complement 55/809
Secondary Battery 21 - 5in/51
Torpedo Tubes 2 - 21in (submerged)
Protection:
Belt 13.5in - 8in (17ft4⅝in wide, 8ft6in below water)
Armor Deck 50 lb STS + 50 lb STS + 20 lb; aft 180 lb STS + 70 lb
Splinter Deck 40 lb NS + 20 lb/60 lb NS + 20 lb STS + 20 lb/ 60 lb STS + 20 lb
Bulkheads 13in - 8in
Barbettes 13in
Turrets 18in and 16in/5in STS/10in - 9in/9in
Conning Tower 16in + 50 lb STS/5in STS
Uptake Protection 13in

WEIGHTS*

	Normal	Full Load
Hull	11,348.3	(11,300)
Hull Fittings	1 600.3	(1117)
Protection	7 835. 3	(7981)†
Machinery (dry)	1 822.4	(1900)
Armament	1 383.5	(1347)
Equipment & Outfit	425.4	
Margin		(77)
Light Ship	24,467.2	
	(24,166.9)	
Ammunition	1389.4	
Machinery Liquids	148.3	
Complement	112.1	
Stores & PW	303.68	455.0
Std. Disp.	26,115.4	
RFW	181.3	271.9
Fuel Oil	1362.7	2042.8
Displacement	27,663.8	28,581.4
Draft	27-7⅝	29-6¹/₁₆
GM	5.95	6.78
GZ	3.51	3.85
Angle	35-0	36-0
Range		

* Returned weights refer to *Oklahoma*.
† This figure does not include the protective deck, 2000.1 tons, or the splinter deck, 1155.9 tons.

Name *Nevada* (rebuilt)
Design Displacement 30,500
Design Emergency Displacement 33,901
Boilers 6 Bureau Express (300 PSI)
SSTG 4 - 400*
Beam (wl) 107 - 11
CB 0.606
CM 0.980
SHP (trial) 31,214†
Speed (trial) 20.22
AT (disp't) 32,075
Endurance (service) 15,700/10, 6090/18 (emergency tankage)
Tactical Diameter (yds/kts) 750/10, 755/15‡
SHP (design) 25,000

Speed (design) 20.5
Fuel Capacity (design) 3148/6274
Endurance (design)
Main Battery 10 - 14in/45
Complement
Secondary Battery 12 - 5in/51
AA Battery 8 - 5in/25, 8 - 0.50 MG
Protection: (changes)§
Armor Deck 80 lb STS added
Torpedo Bulkhead 15 lb cofferdam bulkhead added through boiler spaces; 30 lb torpedo bulkhead added outboard of existing torpedo bulkhead; additional skin (for a total of three) added under boiler rooms

ESTIMATED WEIGHT CHANGES DUE TO RECONSTRUCTION
(*Oklahoma*, December, 1928):
(Weight groups divided for costing)

I. Addition of deck armor	930
Torpedo bulkheads	156
Blister	800
II. Rebuilt turbines, etc.	−121 (*Nevada* −263)‖
III. Increased turret gun elevation	13
IV. New masts	79
V. Catapults	24
VI. 5in AA guns (including ammunition)	191
VII. Raising secondary battery	149
VIII. Miscellaneous alterations	50
TOTAL	2279
Oklahoma AS INCLINED 1916	24,305
ESTIMATE OF FLIGHT SHIP AS MODERNIZED	26,584

WEIGHTS

	(*Oklahoma*, 11 July 1929)		(27 November 1942)	
	Normal	*Full Load*	*Normal*	*Full Load*
Light Ship	27,051		25,944.8	
Ammunition	1385.7		1493.8	
Machinery Liquids	132.9		148.4	
Complement	140.8		226.8	
Stores & PW	354.5	533.7	623.5	900.4
Lube Oil			7.8	7.8
Std. Disp.	29,064.9		28,445.1	
RFW	165.4	248.0	299.7	449.6
Fuel Oil	1466.1	2199.2#	3197.5	4541.0
Gasoline	10.0	14.9	12.3	12.3
Displacement	30,708	31,706	31,864.8	33,747.0
Draft	28-9½	29-7½	29-9¾	31-5¼
GM	6.98	6.47	7.06	7.70
GZ	3.75	3.35	3.63	3.31
Angle	30-15	29-36	30	30
Range	54-10	52-54	56	56.5

* Two 750 kW turbogenerators and two 100 kW diesel emergency generators added during reconstruction, 1942. At this time, too, a seawater ballast system was installed to facilitate damage control, the conning tower was removed, and boat complement reduced to two 26 ft motor whaleboats.

† Corresponding figures for *Oklahoma* as reconstructed: 19.68 kts on 23,599 IHP at 32,338 tons.

‡ Modernization changed her turning characteristics—before, she had started slowly; after, she began to turn quickly, the turn being regular and much slower than before. Twenty degrees of helm was needed where eight had sufficed before.

§ As reconstructed in 1942, she had twin 5in/38 added, in 30 lb STS shields, atop armored-box handling rooms (25 and 30 lb STS bulkheads). Her directors were protected by 40 lb STS, and her main battery fire control position by 50 lb STS. Her conning tower was removed.

‖ There was also an emergency condition, in which the ship carried 5013.4 tons of oil fuel, 658.1 tons of RFW, and 424.7 (rather than 200.4, as fully loaded) tons of fresh water; displacement was 35,155 tons (draft 32ft 6¾in, GM 7.7 ft).

Oklahoma showed less weight saving because her reciprocating engines were not replaced during reconstruction. Both ships saved weight on boilers, their original units (respectively, 336.6 and 531.7 tons) being replaced by 245.0 ton boilers.

Name *Pennsylvania* (BB 38)
Date 26 October 1916
Design Displacement 31,400
Design Full Load 32,440
LOA 608-0
LWL 600-0
Beam (wl) 97-0½
Hull Depth 46-0
CB 0.650
CM 0.976
Boilers 12 B&W
SSTG 4 - 300
SHP (trial) 29,366
Speed (trial) 21.05
AT (disp't) 30,812
Endurance (service) 6070/12, 2652/20 (clean: 7585/12, 3315/20)
Tactical Diameter (yds/kts) 550/20 (*Arizona*: 525/16.5, 650/19)
SHP (design) 31,500
Speed (design) 21.0

Fuel Capacity (design) 1548/2322 oil
Endurance (design) 8000/10
Main Battery 12 - 14in/45 (100)
Complement 55/860
Secondary Battery 22 - 5in/51 (230)
AA Battery 4 - 3in/50
Torpedo Tubes 2 - 21in(24)
Protection:
Belt 13.5 in - 8in (17 - 6 wide, 8 - 9 3/4 below waterline; taper
    begins 2ft4in below waterline)
Bulkheads 13in - 8in
Armor Deck 50 lb STS + 50 lb STS + 20 lb; aft over steering,
    180 lb STS + 70 lb
Splinter Deck 40 lb STS/60 lb STS + 20 lb
Barbettes 13in - 4.5in
Turrets 18in/5in/9in
Conning Tower 16in/14in + 4in(equivalent to 6.8in)
Uptake Armor 13in
Torpedo Bulkheads (outer) 60 + 60 lb STS

WEIGHTS

	Normal	Full Load
Hull		(13,483)
Hull Fittings		(1295)
Protection		(8422)
Machinery		(2399)
Armament		(1658)
Equipment & Outfit		(1073)
Margin		(3)
Light Ship	27,224.2	(28,231)
Ammunition	1343.8	
Machinery Liquids	152.7	
Complement	130.9	
Stores & PW	306.2	459.4
Std. Disp.	29,157.8	
RFW	206	308.8
Fuel Oil	1537	2305.5
Gasoline	1.1	1.7
Displacement	30,891.9	31,916.9
Draft	28-4⅝	29-2⅝
GM	7.46	7.82
GZ	4.86	5.04
Angle	38-30	38-36
Range	68-10	70-24

Name *Pennsylvania* (BB 38) (as reconstructed)
Date 10 June 1931
Design Displacement 34,400
Design Emergency Displacement 39,224
Boilers 6 Bureau Express (300 PSI)
SSTG 4 - 400*
Beam (wl) 106 - 2¾
CB 0.652
CM 0.984
SHP (trial) 35,207
Speed (trial) 21.04
AT (disp't) 37,459
Endurance (service) 19,900/10, 7310/18

Tactical Diameter (yds/kts)
SHP (design) 32,000
Speed (design) 21.0
Fuel Capacity (design) 3778/6083 (emergency)
Endurance (design)
Main Battery 12 - 14in/45
Complement
Secondary Battery 12 - 5in/51
AA Battery 8 - 5in/25, 8 - 0.50 MG
Protection: (changes)
Armor Deck 70 lb STS added
Torpedo Bulkhead One 30 lb bulkhead added outboard each side

ESTIMATED WEIGHT CHANGES DUE TO RECONSTRUCTION
(*Pennsylvania*, December 1928):
(Weight groups divided for costing)

I. Addition of deck armor		1073
Torpedo bulkheads		494
Blister		894
II. Rebuilt turbines, etc†	−103 (*Arizona*: −88)	
III. Increased turret gun elevation		11
IV. New masts		76
V. Catapults		27
VI. 5in AA guns (including ammunition)		191
VII. Raising secondary battery		125
VIII. Miscellaneous alterations		50
IX. Protected flag conning tower		263
TOTAL		3101
Pennsylvania AS INCLINED, 1916		27,224
ESTIMATE OF LIGHT SHIP AS MODERNIZED		30,525

(10 January 1943)

WEIGHTS

	Normal	Full Load	Normal	Full Load
Light Ship	30,912		30,265	
Ammunition	1434.9		1895	
Machinery Liquids	132.1		130	
Complement	155.2		247	
Stores & PW	490.6	735.9	673	858
Lube Oil			12	14
Std. Disp.	33,124.8		33,222	
RFW	216.7	325.1	217	325
Fuel Oil	1472.3	2220.2‡	3499	4836§
Diesel Oil			51	76
Gasoline	8.7	13.1	14	13
Displacement	34,823	35,929	37,003	38,659
Draft	29-3½	30-1¾	31-0¼	32-4⅛
GM	5.84	6.02	7.09	7.53
GZ	3.38	3.45	4.00	4.03
Angle	32.66	33.5	35.0	35.85
Range	58.75	60.25	69.2	65.75

* Two 750 kW SSTG and two 100 kW diesel emergency generators added during reconstruction, 1942.

† Reconstruction of *Arizona* involved installation of Westinghouse geared (3600 RPM) HP turbines; the direct-drive (226 RPM) LP turbines were not replaced.

‡ Maximum tank capacities: 5724.7 tons of fuel oil, 715.8 tons of reserve feed water; when these are filled, displacement is 39,824 tons and draft is 33ft3in. There is also an optimum battle condition, identical to normal condition except that 2198.1 tons of oil fuel is carried, for a displacement of 35,548 tons (GM 5.9 ft).

§ Maximum tank capacities: 5745 tons of fuel oil, 715 of reserve feed water; when these are filled, displacement is 40,605 tons (with 2136 tons of ammunition): GM is 8.15 feet, draft is 33ft10⅞in. Reconstruction involved removal of the conning tower and the after tripod; only two 26ft motor whale boats were retained.

Name *New Mexico* (BB 40)
Date 18 May 1918
Design Displacement 32,000
Design Full Load 33,000
LOA 624-6
LWL 600-0
Beam (wl) 97-4½
Hull Depth 46 - 3¹/₁₆(mld)
CB 0.638
CM 0.979
Boilers 9 B&W (280 PSI)
SSTG 4 - 300
SHP (trial) 31,197
Speed (trial) 21.08
AT (disp't) 32,000
Endurance (service) 5120/12, 1931/20 (clean: 6400/12, 2414/20)
Tactical Diameter (yds/kts) 690/21
SHP (design) 27,500*

Speed (design) 21
Fuel Capacity (design) 1467/2200 oil
Endurance (design) 8000/10†
Main Battery 12 - 14in/50
Complement 58/1026
Secondary Battery 22 - 5in/51‡
AA Battery 4 - 3in/50
Torpedo Tubes 2 - 21in
Protection:
Belt 13.5in - 8in
Bulkheads 13.5in - 8in
Armor Deck 70 lb STS + 70 lb NS; aft over steering, 180 lb STS + 70 lb
Splinter Deck 40 lb STS + 20 lb/60 lb STS + 20 lb
Barbettes 13in - 4.5in
Turrets 18/5 STS/10-9/9
Conning Tower 16in/4in + 4in STS
Uptake Protection 9in

WEIGHTS§

	Normal	Full Load
Hull	13,769.4	(13,577)
Hull Fittings	1480.3	(1379)
Protection	8497.5‖	(8489)
Machinery (dry)	2435.4	(2408)
Armament	1859.3	(1900)
Equipment & Outfit	404.0	
Light Ship	28,445.9	
	(27,891.8)	
Ammunition	1343.7	
Machinery Liquids	153.0	
Complement	119.7	
Stores & PW	445.1	667.6
Std. Disp.	29,953.3	
RFW	225.2	337.8
Fuel Oil	1481.8	2222.7
Displacement	31,660.3	32,736.3
Draft	29-8¼	30-7
GM	4.52	5.07
GZ	2.86	3.06
Angle	36-0	36-0
Range	60-12	60-30

* The other two ships in this class were designed for 32,000 SHP; *New Mexico* had the prototype turboelectric power plant.

† As a measure of relative steaming efficiency, fuel loads required to make 8000nm at 10 kts were: *New Mexico*, 2055 tons; *Mississippi*, 2790; *Idaho*, 2850. In 1922, *Mississippi* was credited with an endurance of 7020/12 or 3036/20 with a foul bottom; 8770/12 or 3976/20 with a clean bottom.

‡ The third ship in the class, *Idaho*, was completed with 14 - 5in/51 guns and 4 - 3in/50; the other two ships were modified soon after completion.

§ Weights given are for *Mississippi* as completed.

‖ This weight group does not include protective deck, 2446.6 tons, or splinter deck, 1237.5 tons. In each case much of the weight was structural and so may not properly be considered protective; note the proportion of nickel steel in both decks (above). Total of decks structures including STS was 3684.1 tons; of STS, 1962.0 tons. There were also torpedo bulkheads; the weight breakdown gives 1339.6 tons of such bulkheads below the protective deck, but provides no breakdown into nickel steel and STS.

Name *New Mexico* (BB 40) (rebuilt)
Date 26 October 1933
Design Displacement 35,000
Design Emergency Displacement 40,000
Boilers 4 White-Foster(300, 472F)*
SSTG 4 - 400
Beam (wl) 106-2
CB 0.638
CM 0.991
SHP (trial) 44,044
Speed (trial) 21.80
AT (disp't) 36,985
Endurance (service) 23,400/9†, 12,750/18
Tactical Diameter (yds/kts) 560/15 (port), 650/15 (starboard) (*New Mexico*)

SHP (design) 40,000
Speed (design) 21.0
Fuel Capacity (design) 3795/7053 (emergency)
Endurance (design)
Main Battery 12 - 14in/50
Complement
Secondary Battery 12 - 5in/51
AA Battery 8 - 5in/25, 8 - 0.50 cal MG
Protection: (changes)
Second Deck 80 lb STS added
Third Deck 50 lb STS added over boiler spaces
Torpedo Bulkhead 30 lb STS added outboard of original bulkhead

WEIGHTS

	Normal	Full Load	
Light Ship	31,275		
Ammunition	1457.9		
Machinery Liquids	119.6		
Complement	160.9		
Stores & PW	390.0	583.0	
Std. Disp.	33,353		
RFW	213.3	320.0	
Fuel Oil	1467.1	2212.6‡	
Diesel Oil		-	
Gasoline	31.3	27.6	
Displacement	35,114	36,157	
Draft	30-2½	31-0¼	
GM	6.65	6.76	
GZ	3.40	3.43	
Angle	32-57	34-78	
Range	56-42	58	

* The other two ships were each fitted with 6 Bureau Express boilers (300, 422F).
† Cruising radius using emergency fuel oil capacity of 5409 tons. Corresponding figures for *Mississippi*, which had an emergency capacity of 5165 tons, were 22,400nm at 9kts and 12,750/18 kts. Naval War College average figures: 26,200/10, 12,450/18 for *Idaho*.
‡ Maximum fuel tank capacity was 5401.6 tons; maximum RFW, 710.8 tons, and maximum freshwater tankage 622.4 tons (compared with the figure of 228 tons used for full-load displacement); with tanks thus filled, displacement was 40,131 tons. There was also a battle condition, corresponding to normal displacement except for 1870.3 tons of fuel; displacement was 35,518 tons and GM 6.67ft.

Name *Tennessee* (BB 43)
Date 7 April 1921
Design Displacement 32,300 tons
Design Full Load 33,190 tons
LOA 624-0
LWL 600-0
Beam (wl) 97-5 3/4
Hull Depth 46-3
CB 0.635
CM 0.977
Boilers 8 B&W (280 PSI)
SSTG 6 - 300
SHP (trial) 29,609
Speed (trial) 21.378
AT (disp't) 32,300
Endurance (service) 20,500/10, 9700/18 (emergency tankage)*; 5240/12, 2500/20 (normal tankage, foul; clean: 6550/12, 3123/20)
Tactical Diameter (yds/kts) 670/10, 643/15

SHP (design) 21.0
Speed (design) 28,600
Fuel Capacity (design) 1267/1900 oil (4656 emergency)
Main Battery 12 - 14in/50
Complement 57/1026
Secondary Battery 14 - 5in/51
AA Battery 4 - 3in/50
Torpedo Tubes 2 - 21in (submerged)
Protection:
Belt 13.5in - 8in
Bulkheads 13.5in
Armor Deck 70 lb STS + 70 lb NS; aft over steering, 180 lb STS + 70 lb
Splinter Deck 40 lb STS + 20 lb
Barbettes 13in
Turrets 18in/5in/10in/9in
Conning Tower 16in/6in
Uptakes 9in

WEIGHTS

	Normal	Full Load
Hull	15,321.9	(14,885)
Hull Fittings	2069.8	(1380)
Protection	8610.3	(8383)†
Machinery (dry)	1862.3	(1805)
Armament	1886.3	(1887)
Equipment & Outfit	524.0	
Light Ship	30,274.6	
	(30,029.8)	
Ammunition	1297.1	
Machinery Liquids	132.8	
Complement	180.1	
Stores & PW	499.9	747.0
Std. Disp.	32,139.7	
RFW	180.0	270.0
Fuel Oil	1269.3	1903.9‡
Displacement	33,588.9	34,560.6
Draft	31-3¼	32-1³⁄₁₆
GM	3.88	4.3

* As a measure of relative steaming efficiency, *Tennessee* required 2100 tons for 8000 nm at 10 kts; *California*, 1740 tons.
† This figure does not include substantial protective material worked into the hull: a main armor deck (2436.2 tons, including 1116.5 tons of STS and 1121.9 tons of NS), a splinter deck (1031.0 tons, including 595.3 tons of STS), and torpedo bulkheads (2464.3 tons of longitudinal bulkheads below the third deck, including 184 tons of STS).
‡ There was also an emergency condition, in which the ship carried 4656.4 tons of oil fuel, 587.5 tons of RFW, and 1614.0 tons of ammunition, displacing 37,947.5 tons (draft 34ft9 7/8in, GM 5. 46ft)

Name *Tennessee* (BB 43) (rebuilt)*
Date 25 April 1943
Design Maximum Load 40,950
SSTG 2 - 750 installed; 4 - 400
Diesel Generators 1 - 100 (emergency)
Beam (wl) 114-0
CB
CM
SHP (trial) 32,500†
Speed (trial) 20.6
AT (disp't) 39,500

Endurance (service)
Tactical Diameter (yds/kts) 610/20
Main Battery 12 - 14in/50‡
Complement 114/2129
Secondary Battery 16 - 5in/38 (DP)
AA Battery 10 quad 40mm
Protection: (changes)
Armor Deck 80 lb added (120 lb over magazines)§
Turrets tops replaced by 7.25in or 7in
Secondary Battery
Conning Tower 5in

WEIGHT ESTIMATES FOR MODERNIZATION (*California*, May 1942):

	Existing Ship	As Modernized
AA Battery, Topside		
Arrangements	718	1309
Ammunition	1600	1700
CT, Tube, etc.	765	0
Uptake Armor	460	147
Added Deck Armor		1362
Stores	500	435
Potable Water	450	450
RFW	560	450
Fuel Oil	5035	4659
Net Change		424‖

WEIGHTS

	Normal	Full Load
Light Ship	32,033.7	
Ammunition	1820.5	
Machinery Liquids	153.5	
Complement	233.6	
Stores & PW	610.0	889.0
Lube Oil	7.4	11.2
Std. Disp.	34,858.7	

RFW	280.0	446.0
Fuel Oil	4353.0	4700.0
Diesel Oil	36.0	54.0
Gasoline	12.7	12.7
Displacement	39,540	40,354
Draft	32-6	33-1
GM	11.45	11.55
GZ	5.32	5.26
Angle	32	32
Range	64	65

* A cruiser conning tower was installed, and second deck armor increased from 5 to 7 inches; new plates were installed to increase turret roof armor from 5 to 7 inches. Note that *West Virginia* was fitted with turret top armor originally made for *Iowa*, 7.25 inches thick. The uptake armor was removed. The generators listed above were installed and the former battery emergency power supply removed. The central and steering gear room were air conditioned. Permanent degaussing replaced the former temporary system. Finally, longitudinal and transverse watertight bulkheads were installed on the second and main decks.

† *Tennessee* trial, 10 May 1943, fifty days out of dock. It was estimated that she would require 34,400 SHP to make 21 knots. By way of contrast, *Maryland*, with a 108ft blister, would have required 32,150 SHP for this speed (according to model tests) at a displacement of 39,200 tons with a clean bottom.

‡ Main gun ammunition reduced from 100 to 90 rounds per gun to compensate for extra protection and the weight of light automatic weapons.

§ The new deck plating could resist a 1600 lb AP bomb dropped from, respectively, 6000 and 8000 ft (80, 120 lb STS), compared with 3000ft for the original deck armor.

‖ At this time BuShips estimated that, with the new blister, the ship would displace 40,950 tons with maximum load, compared with 39,650 in the fall of 1941; the blister presumably was expected to weigh about 875 tons.

Name *West Virginia* (BB 48)
Date 4 January 1926
Design Displacement 32,693 tons
Design Full Load 33,590 tons
LOA 624-0
LWL 600-0
Beam (wl) 97-6
Hull Depth 46-3(edge; 47-3 at centerline)
CB 0.640
CM 0.977
Boilers 8 B&W (285 PSI)
SSTG 6 - 300*
Diesel Generators 2 - 400†
SHP (trial) 31,268
Speed (trial) 21.09
AT (disp't) 33,287
Endurance (service) 21,100/10, 9900/18 (emergency tankage)‡; normal tankage: 5130/12, 2400/20 (foul; clean: 6410/12, 3000/20)
Tactical Diameter (yds/kts) 680/10 (left), 635/10 (right), 695/15 (left), 630/15 (right), 690/20.7 (left), 705/20.7 (right)§
SHP (design) 28,900

Speed (design) 21.0
Fuel Capacity (design) 1267/1900 oil (4794 emergency; 4656 emergency in *Colorado*)
Endurance (design) 8000/10
Main Battery 8 - 16in/45
Complement 64/1241
Secondary Battery 12 - 5in/51‖
AA Battery 8 - 3in/50
Torpedo Tubes 2 - 21in
Protection:
Belt 13.5in - 8in
Armor Deck 70 lb STS + 70 lb NS; aft over steering, 180 lb STS + 70 lb
Splinter Deck 40 lb STS + 20 lb STS
Bulkheads 13.5in
Barbettes 13in - 4.5in
Turrets 18in/5in/10in/9in
Conning Tower 16in/4in + 4in
IZ(kyds) 25.7 - 25.8
VS 16in/2240 lbs/2540 ft/sec
VS 1600 lb AP bomb below 2600 ft

WEIGHTS:#

	Normal	Full Load	(BB 45, 24 April 1944) Normal	Full Load
Hull	15,405	(14,967)		
Hull Fittings	1729	(1866)		
Protection	8694	(8433)**		
Machinery (dry)	2732	(1867)		
Armament	1624	(1670)		
Equipment & Outfit	474	(560)		
Light Ship	30,658 (30,298.4)	(29,363)	31,116.3	

Ammunition	1452.1(1361)	
Machinery Liquids	134.9	
Complement	157.0	
Stores & PW	394.3 591.6	
Std. Disp.	32,436.7	

RFW	185.7	313.1		
Fuel Oil	1333.6	1999.3††		
Displacement	33,956.0	34,946.4	39,026.7	40,396.5
Draft	31-8	32-5¾	33-4½	34-3½
GM	3.77	4.25	8.62	8.59
GZ			4.85	4.69
Angle			36	36
Range			71	71

* In 1945, *Maryland* and *Colorado* each had 4 - 400 kW SSTG.

† For port use.

‡ As a measure of relative steaming efficiency, *Colorado* required 2100 tons of oil for 8000nm at 10 kts; the others, 1905 tons.

§ These ships could turn more tightly by backing at full power on one shaft. For example, *Maryland* was credited with 750/12 (both ahead) but could achieve 610/12 (one astern), thanks to her turboelectric power plant.

‖ *Maryland* was completed with 14 - 5in/51 and 4 - 3in/50.

Returned weight data refer to *Colorado* (BB 45).

** This figure does not include deck and underwater protection.

†† There was also an emergency condition, in which the ship could carry 4809.1 tons of fuel oil, 1577. 8 tons of ammunition, and 594.9 tons of RFW; she then displaced 38,143.1 tons (GM 5.15ft, draft 35-1¼ft).

Name *South Dakota* (BB 49)
Design Displacement 43,200
Design Full Load
LOA 684-0
LWL 660-0
Beam (wl) 106-0
Hull Depth
CB 0.662
CM 1.005
Boilers 12 (285 PSI)
SSTG 8 - 500
SHP (design) 60,000
Speed (design) 23.0
Fuel Capacity (design) 1400/2100 (emergency: 6600 tons)
Endurance (design) 8000/10
Tactical Diameter (yds/kts)
Main Battery 12 - 16in/50

Complement 62/1129
Secondary Battery 15 - 6in/53
AA Battery 8 - 3in/50
Torpedo Tubes 2 - 21in
Protection:
Belt 13.5in - 8in
Bulkheads 13.5in - 8in
Armor Deck 70 lb STS + 70 lb NS; forward of belt 5in STS + 40 lb NS; aft over steering gear (sloping 45 degrees) 5in STS + 40 lb NS
Splinter Deck 50 lb STS
Uptakes 9in - 13.5in
Barbettes 13.5in - 4.5in
Gunhouses 18in/5in/10in - 9in
Secondary Battery None
Conning Tower 16in/8in

WEIGHTS

	Normal	Full Load
Hull	19,780	
Hull Fittings	1673	
Protection	10,036	
Machinery (dry)	2698	
Armament	2750	
Equipment & Outfit	1132	
Margin	603	
Light Ship	38,672	
Ammunition	2088	
Machinery Liquids	189	
Complement	451	
Std. Disp.	41,400	
RFW	400	
Fuel Oil	1400	
Displacement	43,200	
Draft	33-0	
GM	3.47	
GZ		
Angle		
Range	52-20	

Name *Washington* (BB 56)
Date 24 August 1941
Design Displacement 42,279
Design Std. Displacement 35,000
Design Full Load 44, 800
LOA 728-11
LWL 713-8
Beam (wl) 108-4
Hull Depth 49-2
CB 0.622
CM 1.002
Boilers 8 B&W (575 PSI, 850F)
SSTG 4 - 1250
Diesel Generators 4 - 850, 2 - 200 (emergency)
SHP (trial) 199.1 RPM (full power)
Speed (trial) 26.15
AT (disp't) 43,166
Endurance (service) 13,500/15, 9060/20
Tactical Diameter (yds/kts) 759/27.5 (model), 683/27.5 (trials); 620/20 (model)
SHP (design) 121,000
Speed (design) 27.0

Fuel Capacity (design) 6959
Endurance (design) 15,000/15
Main Battery 9 - 16in/45 (100)
Complement 99/2035
Secondary Battery 20 - 5in/38 (340)
AA Battery 4 Quad 1.1in, 18 - 0.50
Protection:
Belt 12in - 6in on 30 lb STS (sloped 15 degrees) 3.75in-2.2in internal over magazines
Bulkheads 11.1in - 1.9in
Bomb Deck 58 lb
Armor Deck 4.1 - 3.6 on 56 lb
Splinter Deck 30 - 25 lb
Barbettes 16in -14.7in
Gunhouses 16in - 9.8in
Secondary Battery 78 lb STS
Conning Tower 16in-14.7in/7in
IZ(kyd)
VS 14in (1500 lbs), 20 - 30.8 (to 33.0 over magazines; 19.0 inner limit for barbettes)
VS 16in (2240 lbs) at 2520 ft/sec, 21.3 - 32
VS 1600 lb AP bomb: below 8750 ft

WEIGHTS:

	Opt Battle	Full Load
Hull	18,992.5	(17,607)
Hull Fittings	1725.7	(1383)
Protection	8121.1	(8161)*
Machinery (dry)	3181.6	(2863)
Armament	2548.5	(2589)
Equipment & Outfit	418.3	(440)
Aeronautics	52.5	(54)
Light Ship	35,040.2 (34,708.0)	(33,098)
Ammunition	1845.5	(2235)
Machinery Liquids	144.6	
Complement	194.4	
Stores & PW	579.4	869.0
Lube Oil	13.7	13.7
Std. Disp.	37,485.6	
RFW	229.0	343.5
Fuel Oil	5086.9	5540.4†
Diesel Oil	463.1	694.6
Gasoline	24.9	24.9
Displacement	43,288	44,377
Draft	32-3¾	32-11½
GM	8.06	8.58
GZ	4.28	4.23
Angle	32.5	32.5
Range	64.6	65.4

* This figure for protection does not include deck armor or torpedo bulkheads. Some STS and armor weight was structural, so the following figures probably overstate armor weight: bomb deck STS plating, 1179.4 tons plus 50.7 tons of gratings and hatch covering; second deck STS, 3671.8 tons plus 154.3 tons of gratings and hatch covers; third (splinter) deck STS, 1102.7 tons plus 34.5 tons of gratings and hatch covers; longitudinal bulkheads, 1237.9 tons (STS only). There was also other STS worked into the ship (e.g., 469.6 tons out of a total of 1642.8 tons of outside plating), but the total of these figures alone was 7431.3 tons.
† Maximum fuel tank capacity was 6859.7 tons; maximum fresh water, 608.5 tons rather than the 409.7-ton figure incorporated in total stores and potable water; maximum ammunition capacity was 2746.8 tons. Loaded to emergency capacity, then, *Washington* displaced 46,796 tons. When inclined, she had four quadruple 1.1in guns and twelve 0.50 calibre guns on board, as well as a full boat outfit: three 50ft motor launches, two 40ft motor launches, three 40ft motor boats, one 35ft motor boat, two 30ft sail whaleboats, two 26ft motor whaleboats, and two 14ft punts, as well as twelve 60-man, twelve 40-man, and twelve 25-man rafts.

Name *South Dakota* (BB 57)
Date 15 March 1942
Design Displacement 42,500
Design Std. Displacement 35,412
Design Full Load 42,782
LOA 680-0
LWL 666-0
Beam (wl) 108-2
Hull Depth 52-0
CB 0.613
CM 0.994
Boilers 8 B&W (570 PSI, 850F)
SSTG 7 - 1000
Diesel Generators 2 - 200 (emergency)
SHP (trial) 133,070 (*Alabama*)
Speed (trial) 27.08
AT (disp't) 42,740
Endurance (service) 15,020/15
　　　　　　　　　　　10,610/20
Tactical Diameter (yds/kts) 733/26.5 (model), 700/16 (model)
SHP (design) 130,000

Speed (design) 27.5
Fuel Capacity (design)
Endurance (design) 15,000/15
Main Battery 9 - 16in/45*
Complement 145/2112
Secondary Battery 16 - 5in/38 (BB 58-60, 114/2240)
AA Battery 3 Quad 1.1in, 12 - 0.50 (as designed) (20 - 5in/38 in BB 58-60)
Protection:
Belt 12.2in on 30 lb (sloped 19 deg)
Bulkheads 13.4in
Bomb Deck 60 lb
Armor Deck 5.3in-5.0in on 30 lb
Splinter Deck 25 lb
Barbettes 17.3in-14.8in-11.5in
Turrets 18in - 9.5in on 30 lb
Secondary Battery 80 lb STS
Conning Tower 15in/7.25in
IZ(kyds) 17.7 - 30.9
VS 16in (2240 lbs) at 2520 ft/sec
VS 1600 lb AP bomb below 11,800 ft

WEIGHTS			(BB 58, 18 April 1942)	
	Normal	*Full Load*	*Normal*	*Full Load*
Hull	18,509.4	(17,737)		
Hull Fittings	1759.2	(1387)		
Protection	8198.0	(8255)†		
Machinery (dry)	3236.3	(3042)		
Armament	2479.9	(2458)		
Equipment & Outfit	338.0	(454)		
Aeronautics	53.9	(54)		
Light Ship	34,574.7	(33,387)		
	(34,526.5)		(34,044.2)	
Ammunition	2230.6		2482.4	
Machinery Liquids	205.4		279.6	
Complement	194.5		222.3	
Stores & PW	603.3	904.9	641.6	923.2
Lube Oil	23.9		11.8	17.7
Std. Disp.	37,375.4		37,681.9	
RFW	250.0	374.8	272.0	341.1
Fuel Oil	5011.7	5872.4‡	4948.2	5849.4§
Diesel Oil	107.5	161.2	126.8	190.2
Gasoline	25.0		24.1	
Displacement	43,178	44,519	43,052.9	44,374.1
Draft	34-1¾	35-0¾	34-0½	34-11½
GM	8.94	9.51	8.84	9.36
GZ	5.03	5.06	4.95	4.95
Angle	34-12	34-12	33.7	33.7
Range	67-0	68-48	66.2	67.7

* These ships were designed with a total 16in ammunition capacity of 1280 rounds, comprising 675 counted for calculation of standard displacement, and 495 for "mobilization." Similarly, 5in capacity was 6000 rounds (4800 in *South Dakota*) plus 800 plus 2800, a total of 9600 rounds, or 480 per gun.

† This weight group does not include deck or underwater (torpedo bulkhead) armor, most of it STS (Special Treatment Steel). Figures from weight estimate of March 1940: longitudinal bulkheads below third deck: 1754.3 tons; armor deck: 3653.7 tons, including 3337.0 tons of STS; splinter deck and third deck: 1290.5 tons, including 972.8 tons of STS.

‡ Full fuel-tank capacity was 7126.6 tons; full ammunition, 2643.6 tons; full RFW, 452.0 tons.

§ Full fuel-tank capacity was 6673.2 tons. BB 57 was inclined carrying seven quadruple 1.1 inch guns, 16 20mm, and 8 0.50 calibre machine guns; another 18 20mm were added at the outfitting yard, and their weight is included in the weights above. BB 58 was inclined carrying six quadruple 40mm and 35 20mm guns, including 3 20mm atop Nos. 2 and 3 turrets.

Name *Iowa* (BB 61)
Date 28 March 1943
Design Displacement 53,900
Design Std. Displacement 45,000
Design Full Load 56,270
LOA 887-3
LWL 860-0
Beam (wl) 108-2
Hull Depth
CB 0.593
CM 0.996
Boilers 8 B&W (600 PSI, 850F)
SSTG 8 - 1250
Diesel Generators 2 - 250 (emergency)
SHP (trial)*
Speed (trial)
AT (disp't)
Endurance (service) 14,890/15
11,700/20
Tactical Diameter (yds/kts) 1430/33 (model); 814/30(trials);
760/20(model)

SHP (design) 212,000
Speed (design) 32.5
Fuel Capacity (design)
Endurance (design) 15,000/15
Main Battery 9 - 16in/50
Complement 117/1804
Secondary Battery 20 - 5in/38
AA Battery 19 Quad 40mm, 52 - 20mm
Protection:
Belt 12.2in (sloped 19 degrees)
Bulkheads 11.2in
Bomb Deck 60 lbs
Armor Deck 5.0in - 4.75in on 50 lbs
Splinter Deck 25 lbs
Barbettes 17.3in-14.8in-11.6in
Gunhouses 17in/2.5in
Secondary Battery 100 lb STS
Conning Tower 17.3in
IZ (kyds) 17.6 - 31.2
VS 16in (2240 lbs) at 2520 ft/sec
VS 1600 lb AP bomb below 12,200 ft

WEIGHTS:

	Normal	Full Load	Emergency
Hull	23,680.0	(23,221)	
Hull Fittings	1908.5	(1786)	
Protection	10,175.3	(10,163)	†
Machinery (dry)	4443.8	(4265)	
Armament	3337.9	(3042)	
Equipment & Outfit	346.5	(501)	
Aeronautics	51.7	(54)	
Light Ship	43,943.7	(43,032)‡	
	(43,875)		
Ammunition	2557	2887	3068
Machinery Liquids	392		
Complement	284		
Stores & PW	990	1485	
Lube Oil	11	17	28
Std. Disp.	47,825		
RFW	327	421	777
Fuel Oil	6835	7892	9320
Diesel Oil	128	192	192
Gasoline	25		
Displacement	55,425	57,540	59,331
Draft	35-0¾	36-2¼	37-2
GM	7.68	8.4	8.68
GZ	4.38	4.48	4.36
Angle	32.2	32.1	31.5
Range	64.3	66.4	66.5

* Full power trials were never run, at least not before the ships were reactivated from 1982 onwards. As an indication of performance, BuShips estimated that *Missouri* would require 197,000 SHP to make 32 knots, and 219,000 to make 33, with new larger-diameter propellers (October 1951). They required somewhat more power than her original type, and these figures presumably referred to full-load condition. *New Jersey* was run at 220,982 SHP on standardization trials in October 1943, but no speed was taken.

† This figure excludes STS (Special Treatment Steel) in deck and underwater armor. For example, the full belt of these ships was 38ft6in wide, but only the upper 10ft6in was Class A armor. The following figures somewhat overstate armor weight, because they include STS required for structural strength: bomb deck STS, 1447.3 tons; second (protective) deck, 4189.0 tons plus 112.4 tons of gratings and covers; third (splinter) deck, 1245.2 tons; longitudinal bulkheads, 1 044.7 tons; total, 7998.6 tons.

‡ However, a final weight report of February 1945 showed a hull weight of 24,511 tons, fittings 1959 tons, equipment and outfit 375 tons, for a total light ship weight of 44,854 tons, an overweight (compared with the design figure) of 1062 tons.

Name *Montana* (BB 67)
Design Displacement 68,317 (trial)
Design Std. Displacement 60,500
Design Full Load 70,965
LOA 921-3
LWL 890-0
Beam (wl) 115-0 (121-2 max)
Hull Depth 54-6
CB 0.665
CM 1.008
Boilers 8(615 PSI, 850F)
SSTG 10 - 1250
Diesel Generators 2 - 500
SHP (design) 172,000
Speed (design) 28
Fuel Capacity (design) 7500
Endurance (design) 15,000/15
Main Battery 12 -16in/50

Complement 115/2240 (189/2789 flag)
Secondary Battery 20 - 5in/54
AA Battery 10 Quad 40mm, 56 - 20mm
Protection:
Belt 16.1in + 40 lb - 10.2in (sloped 19 degrees); 8.5in - 2.75in - 1.5 internal belt on 30 lb STS
Bulkheads 18in fwd, 15.25in aft
Bomb Deck 2in STS
Armor Deck 6.2in + 50 lb; 7.4in over steering gear aft
Splinter Deck 25 lb
Barbettes 21.3in(18in rear) - 7.75in
Turrets 18in on 4.5in/7.75in/10in/12in
Secondary Battery 100 lb STS
Conning Tower 18in/7.4in
IZ(kyd) 18 - 32 vs 16in 2700
VS 16in (2240 lb) at 2520 ft/sec: 16.5 - 34.5
VS 1600 lb AP bomb below 18,000 ft

WEIGHTS:

	Trial	Full Load	Maximum
Hull	29,789		
Hull Fittings	2152		
Protection	15,538*		
Machinery	4738		
Armament	4018		
Equipment & Outfit	991		
Aeronautics			
Light Ship	57,414		
Ammunition	2700		
Stores & PW	991		
Std. Disp.	60,957		
RFW	450		
Fuel Oil	7500		
Diesel Oil	200		
Displacement †	68,135	70,783	71,762
Draft	35-0⅜	36-3¾	36-9³⁄₁₆
GM	8.20	9.33	9.63
GZ	5.37	5.37	5.23
Angle	32	32	32
Range	62-30	74-15	64-30

* This figure does not include large amounts of deck and underwater bulkhead protection. Final figures were not available, but the following are taken from detailed estimates prepared for design BB 67-3 in January 1941: main (bomb) deck, 708.8 tons of structural steel (MS, or mild steel) and 2593.0 tons of STS; second (protective) deck, 392.3 tons of MS and 7352.7 tons of STS; third deck, 447.0 tons of MS and 708.2 tons of STS; splinter flat, 255.0 tons total (MS and STS); transverse, longitudinal, and torpedo bulkheads, 4749.7 tons total.

† Stability data from estimates of May 1942. BB 69 differed slightly from the others.

MONITORS

Name *Miantonomoh*
Design Displacement 3815
LOA 262-0
LWL 259-0
Beam (wl) 55-6
Hull Depth 14-0
CB
CM 0.913
Boilers 6 S.E.
SSG 2 - 16
IHP (trial) 1426
Speed (trial) 10.5
AT (disp't) 3900

Endurance (service) 1090/10
Tactical Diameter (yds/kts) 502/6 (starboard), 399/6 (port) (*Amphitrite*)
IHP (design)
Speed (design) 250
Fuel Capacity (design) 250
Endurance (design)
Main Battery 4 - 10in/30
Complement 19/164
Secondary Battery 4 - 6pdr
Protection (iron):
Belt 7in (5in ends) (about 4ft below and 25in above waterline)
Bulkheads

Armor Deck 1.75in
Barbettes none
Turrets 11.5in (roller-base type)
Uptakes 10.5in; Ventilator 9in

Conning Tower 9in
Displacement 3815
Draft 14.14
GM 7.96

Name *Puritan*
Design Displacement 6000
LOA 295-8 ½
LWL 291-0
Beam (wl) 60-1 ½
Hull Depth 20-9
CB
CM 0.943
Boilers 8 S.E.
SSG 2 - 32
IHP (trial) 3700
Speed (trial) 12.4
AT (disp't) 6060
Endurance (service)
Tactical Diameter (yds/kts)
IHP (design) 3600

Speed (design) 13
Fuel Capacity (design) 400
Endurance (design)
Main Battery 4 - 12in/35
Complement 19/210
Secondary Battery 6 - 4in/40, 6 - 6pdr RF
Protection:
Belt 14in - 6in
Bulkheads
Armor Deck 2in
Barbettes 14in
Turrets 8in
Conning Tower
Displacement 6060
Draft 18-0
GM 10.2

Name *Monterey*
Design Displacement 4084
LOA 260-11
LWL 256 - 0
Beam (wl) 56-0
Hull Depth 17-4 ½
CB
CM
Boilers 4 B&W
SSG 3 - 16
IHP (trial) 5104
Speed (trial) 13.6
AT (disp't) 4084
Endurance (service) 1100/10
Tactical Diameter (yds/kts) 300/full speed

IHP (design)
Speed (design)
Fuel Capacity (design) 206
Endurance (design)
Main Battery 2-12in/35, 2-10in/30
Complement 21/172
Secondary Battery 6 - 6pdr Hotchkiss, 4 - 1pdr Hotchkiss
Protection:
Belt 13in - 5in
Bulkheads
Armor Deck 2.5in
Barbettes 13in (for 10in guns, 11.5in)
Turret 8in (for 10in guns, 7.5in)
Conning Tower

WEIGHTS

	Normal	Full Load
Hull		(1664.1)
Hull Fittings		(198.8)
Protection		(773.8)
Machinery (wet)	356*	(468.4)
Armament & Ammunition	257†	(142.6)
Equipment & Outfit		(289.2)
Stores, Complement, Etc.		
Margin		(97.1)
Coal		(236.0)
Displacement		(3870.0)
Draft	14-0 ¼	

* Actual weight of machinery (dry); 35 tons of water in boilers, 12 tons in condensers, 8 tons in tanks, as well as 16 tons of fresh water. Design figures reflect the original design with 16in gun and 16in armor.
† Battery weight: 189 tons; 68 tons of ammunition.

Name *Arkansas*
Design Displacement 3225
LOA 255-1
LWL 252-0
Beam (wl) 50-0
Hull Depth
CB 0.711
CM 0.960
Boilers 4 Thornycroft
SSG 4 - 32
IHP (trial) 1739
Speed (trial) 12.03
AT (disp't) 3215
Endurance (service) 2360/10
Tactical Diameter (yds/kts) 320/12

IHP (design) 1830
Speed (design)
Fuel Capacity (design) 344
Endurance (design)
Main Battery 2 - 12in/40
Complement 13/209
Secondary Battery 4 - 4in/50, 3 - 6pdr RF
Protection:
Belt 11in - 5in
Armor Deck 1.5in
Bulkheads
Barbettes 11in - 9in
Turrets 10in - 9in
Conning Tower

WEIGHTS

	Normal	Full Load
Hull		(1498.0)
Hull Fittings		(176.2)
Protection		(568.6)
Machinery		(225.4)
Armament		(196.3)
Equipment & Outfit		(73.0)
Light Ship		(2810.5)
Ammunition		196.3
Complement		16.9
Stores & PW		45.5
Std. Disp.		(3069.2)
RFW		10
Coal		400
Displacement	3011*	(3114.7)(with margin, 3213.8)
Draft	11-9	
GM	11.2	
GZ	2.9	
Angle	32	
Range	65	

* Stability data from W. Hovgaard, *General Design of Warships* (London: E. & F. Spon, 1920).

Notes on Sources

This book is based primarily on navy internal papers held by the National Archives, the Federal Record Center (FRC) at Suitland, Maryland, the Naval Historical Center (NHC) at the Washington Navy Yard, and the Naval War College (NWC) at Newport, Rhode Island.

The primary sources were the records of C&R and BuShips; of the Office of Secretary of the Navy (SecNav); of the Board on Construction; of the General Board; and of the Naval Ship Engineering Center (NavSEC). The wartime OpNav (CominCh/CNO) files include the VCNO files, which reveal most wartime ship production and modification decisions.

These records reflect three distinct periods. Prior to 1900, the only central authority was the secretary of the navy. Where design was coordinated at all, it was a function of the Board on Construction, which came into existence only in 1889. Moreover, the early correspondence records of the secretary himself were not well indexed. Therefore the primary source for the period before 1889 is the series of *Annual Reports* issued by successive secretaries of the navy. The only easily accessible C&R material is a series of books of calculations, which are limited to some of the ships. However, the National Archives also possesses the bulk of the C&R plan files for the period up to about 1920. They include many, but not nearly all, sketch designs. Unfortunately, many of the plans included in the card index have been lost or misfiled.

From 1889 on, the files of the Board on Construction supplement the *Annual Reports*. They comprise minutes of board meetings as well as letter books and are held by NNMO(RG 80). The Board of Construction was abolished in 1909, when the General Board took over the coordination of design.

General Board records indicate central naval policy for 1900 through 1950, and specific design policy for 1908 to 1950. In some cases the board's files include copies of C&R or BuShips design proposals, although this series is by no means complete. The most important supplements to the General Board files are the pre-1914 NWC files and the correspondence of the secretary of the navy, particularly after 1933, when the CNO was frequently acting secretary of the navy.

Finally, for the years after 1950, there is no central policy source; material has been taken from retired BuShips files, from retired files of the SCB, and from some surviving active files in the possession of the Preliminary Design group of the Naval Sea Systems Command.

The pre-1941 SecNav, OpNav, and bureau files are all held by the Navy and Old Army Branch (NNMO) of the National Archives. Wartime BuShips files are held by FRC. Recently the wartime SecNav and OpNav files were transferred from NHC to NNMO. NHC still holds the General Board records and a variety of miscellaneous files, such as those of the prewar OpNav War Plans division. FRC holds the SCB files, as well as many prewar, wartime, and postwar C&R/BuShips files, such as those of the Preliminary (Code 420) and Contract (Code 440) Design divisions.

The archives of the NWC hold the annual reports of the summer conferences, at which members of the General Board met with students and faculty members to discuss the results of the year's war gaming. These meetings continued through about 1914. In a few cases, post-World War One NWC lectures provided valuable information on the then-current state of warship design, protection, and armament.

From a policy point of view, the primary papers on battleship design from 1910 through 1945 are those of the General Board: series 420 (construction program), 420-2 (building programs on an annual basis), 420-6 (battleships), and 430 (naval ordnance). These papers were supplemented by the transcripts of the General Board Hearings, which are held by NHC. During World War Two, however, the ship modification role of the General Board was largely taken over by the VCNO.

The General Board did not, particularly in the 1930s, have quite the decisive power over ship characteristics that its files might suggest. It derives much of the *appearance* of full control from the completeness of the records that it has left.

Ship design files in the C&R/BuShips series are BB/S1-1 and and BB/L9-3 (modifications). There were also Preliminary and Contract Design files (design books and flat files, respectively), collections of relevant correspondence and, sometimes, notes of actual design decisions. NNMO holds design books for between 1910 and 1922; later material is in FRC (RG 19, particularly Entry 6114). NNMO also holds flat files for approximately 1920–40, as well as General Information Books for that period. Finally, NNMO holds a series of "research memoranda" compiled by Preliminary Design.

FRC holds later design files. For battleships, the major file was RG 19 Entry 6114, covering the period from 1924 onwards.

Two special BuShips files deserve mention. In 1945 the Preliminary Design group compiled a series of special design histories, which are held in FRC entry 344-74-564. They include a general account of U.S. battleship design between 1935 and 1941, concentrating on a few details of each design rather than on overall considerations. However, the same record group includes a collection of chronological notes and battleship data. The other special file is RG 19 entry 1036 in FRC, which contains the inclining experiments of most U.S. warships from about 1914 through 1945; it is the source for most of the breakdowns of loads in the data tables. In many cases, too, inclining experiment booklets included notes on the refits carried out prior to inclining. Preliminary Design also compiled extensive reports on war damage, from which some of the details in Chapters 12 and 13 and in Appendix B have been taken. A full set is held by NHC.

These files generally consist of masses of correspondence often duplicated in other files, so that a citation from one source does not indicate the absence of a document from others. Policy papers were generally found in SecNav and General Board files. The SCB correspondence reflects policy choices, but on a much narrower basis. It provided data on the postwar Class Improvement Programs. Similarly, the post-1950 BuShips records sometimes include policy documents prepared by OpNav.

For detailed technical data on prewar dreadnought battleships, I have relied on the general information books (ship information books) held by NNMO. They include hull and, in most cases, armament and armor data. They do not include details of machinery. There were also the volumes of *Ships Data, U.S. Naval Vessels*, which were regularly published from 1912 through 1952 and which include accurate dimensions as well as details of electrical generators and weapons of 40mm and larger calibre. Prior to 1912, similar data were printed in the *Annual Report* of the Navy Department. Through about 1908, annual reports also included details of designs of ships that had been authorized by Congress. These printed sources were supplemented by a compilation of pre-World War II ship design data compiled by Preliminary Design, which included hull characteristics and protection as well as designed weights and designed steaming endurance. Other endurance data were taken from the compilation of ship endurance prepared in 1945 as a fleet tactical publication (FTP 218). Plans came from the records of BuShips, including microfilms of the older C&R plans formerly held by NavSea at the Washington Navy Yard.

Until about 1906 the *Annual Report* of the Navy Department included details of ships for which contracts were to be let, sometimes including sketches as well. In a few cases, too (most notably those of the *Pennsylvania* and of "Ironsides"), RG 19 Entry 152, which is nominally a compilation of ships' weights, includes design books.

Besides manuscript files including correspondence, there are official handbooks. Especially important was BuOrd's *Armament Summary*, updated on a biweekly basis during World War II and issued annually since.

In general, published accounts were used to organize the material taken from the primary sources. In a number of cases the major value of the published works turned out to be the photographs they contained, which drew attention to the significance of items in official correspondence. However, for the politics of the Navy prior to the Washington Conference I have drawn on several published works, most notably G. T. Davis, *A Navy Second to None* (New York: Harcourt, Brace, 1940) and H. and M. Sprout, *The Rise of American Naval Power, 1776–1918* (Princeton University Press, 1939).

Chapter 1

The material in this chapter is based largely on the annual reports of the secretary of the navy, supplemented by the records of the Board on Construction, for 1889 onwards. NARS also holds books of calculations and returned weights for some of the New Navy battleships (RG 19 entry 147). The report of the Policy Board was published in the Proceedings of the U.S. Naval Institute for 1890. The account of the *Kearsage* design is based on a series of papers in the secretary of the navy's correspondence (1263–95); that of the *Illinois*, on the report of the Walker Board; that of the *Maine*(ii) class, largely on the relevant correspondence file (C&R correspondence series, 6093E) and on the files of the Board on Construction. The *Idaho*-class alternatives are described in a Preliminary Design Research Memorandum. In addition, at least one of the unsuccessful sketch designs for the *Kearsage* (with superfiring rather than superimposed guns) is in RG 19 Entry 152. The drawings of the original design of the *Maine*, of the armored cruiser of 1885, and of the proposed battleship with single turrets were all taken from the plans collection of the National Archives. No drawing of the proposed 1885 battleship could be located. Details of both the battleship and the armored cruiser were taken from the *Annual Report* of the secretary of the navy to Congress, November 1884. Much of the material on Secretary Tracy and the politics of the Policy Board is based on his biography, by B. F. Cooling, *Benjamin Franklin Tracy: Father of the Modern American Fighting Navy* (Hamden, Conn.: Archon Books, 1973).

Chapter 2

This chapter is based largely on the papers (minutes of meetings and correspondence) of the Board on Construction, supplemented by the correspondence files of the Bureau of Construction and Repair (17221E and 19421E) and of the General Board. The Poundstone papers, which include sketches of the three alternative designs, are held by the U.S. Naval Academy and were kindly made available to the author. Additional material on Poundstone's significance came from E. E. Morison's biography of Sims, *Admiral Sims and the Modern American Navy* (Cambridge, Mass.: Harvard University Press, 1942). Morison's account of Sims is relatively uncritical; as an ardent naval reformer, Sims himself was an effective politician and thus probably somewhat exaggerated his role (and, by extension, Poundstone's). For example, he badly wanted to show that the technical bureaus had tried to prevent the most important naval reform of all, the all-big-gun battleship. Note, however, that the Newport material came from the historical archives of the Naval War College, which include the reports of the annual conferences. It makes no reference to Sims or to Poundstone, but that does not affect the claim that Poundstone's work had motivated the Naval War College. Nor is it clear from Poundstone's papers whether Sims was urging him to join an existing movement forward or to claim proper credit for a movement he had (albeit very quietly) set in motion. Although the card file of C&R plans held by the National Archives included a set of preliminary designs for the *Michigan*, these drawings were missing from the appropriate drawers. Lieutenant Commander McCully's report was published by the U.S. Naval Institute in 1977 as *The McCully Report: The Russo–Japanese War, 1904–05*; it was edited by Richard von Doenhoff of the National Archives. McCully himself helped evacuate Russians from the Crimea in 1920, as a rear admiral. The report of the Newberry Board was taken from NNMO files.

Chapter 3

The report of the Newport Conference is held by NNMO. Reports of the congressional hearings were printed; I used copies in the collection of the New York Public Library. The reports of seagoing experience cited in this chapter were published in various journals, including *Engineering*, in 1907; more detailed papers were found in RG 19 15272A. The cage mast story was taken largely from Research Memoranda in NNMO RG 19.

Chapter 4

The *New York* C&R design correspondence file is 25536E; it includes detailed descriptions of Designs 506 and 602. British comments on the *New York* have been taken from a Foreign Warship Cover in NMM. Secretary Meyer's comments on economy are taken from his biography, M. A. DeWolfe Howe, *George von Lengerke Meyer: His Life and Public Services* (New York: Dodd, Mead, 1920).

Chapter 5

The background of the *Nevada* design is taken largely from General Board (420-6) records; the principal design alternatives are given in her C&R correspondence file (series 26162E). The May 1910 design, however, is taken from C&R 17622E. The various proposals for the *Pennsylvania* design are listed in her design book, in RG 129 Entry 152 (which otherwise contains weight books). Other material on this class was taken from RG 19 correspondence (2182 A) and from RG 80 correspondence (8557-75). For later classes through 1916, the primary sources were C&R correspondence (15272A series and 22-B series).

Chapter 6

The account of "Ironsides" is based on a research memorandum; weight data and the cross-section in the text were taken from RG Entry 152. Material on the torpedo battleship was taken from RG 19 Entry 449 and from the NWC Archives. The Tillman material was taken from C&R correspondence (15272A), from RG 19 Entry 449, and from General Board correspondence (420-6).

Chapter 7

This chapter is based on the Preliminary Design book of the *South Dakota* class, on General Board papers (420-6), and on the C&R battleship design correspondence (series 22-B). The small battleship of 1919 is taken entirely from the Preliminary Design file.

Chapter 8

U.S. wartime reactions to the Grand Fleet have been taken from General Board Hearings. British comments have been drawn from a Foreign Warships (Battleships) Cover in NMM. Goodall published many of his comments in a lecture before the Portsmouth Engineering Society, 31 January 1922 (and published in the British journal, *Engineering*, for 17 and 24 March 1922). McBride's comments and the C&R wartime lessons were found in the C&R miscellaneous ("envelope") files, RG 19 Entry 1252.

Chapter 9

Material on the treaty itself was taken from standard published sources, including (for the British strategy) S. Roskill, *Naval Policy Between the Wars*, Volume I (London: Collins, 1968). The traditional British view, that the United States pressed for the Washington Conference because its ships would have been outclassed by the new British and Japanese types, is best expressed by O. Parkes, *British Battleships* (London: Seeley, Service, 1957). I have rejected it in view of the lack of information on Japanese and British designs reflected in contemporary C&R and General Board material; for example, the high speed of the *Nagato* was not known for fifteen more years. Nor do surviving General Board proposals for U.S. policy at the conference appear to have been followed.

Chapter 10

For basic reconstruction policy, see General Board Hearings for the period, as well as General Board file 420-11. For the 1922–23 reconstruction studies, see C&R preliminary design (Entry 449) and flat files (Entry 448); the latter include the design of the *South Carolina* blister. The flat files also include details of the later reconstructions. NNMO RG 80 includes some information on the planned reconstruction of the "Big Five," but little detail. Moreover, the design books on the reconstruction were listed as part of, but not included in, FRC RG 19 Entry 6114, when the latter was examined. It appears that Entry 6114 was later destroyed; it is not clear whether the missing book or books were ever reunited with it. Finally, some details of reconstruction were taken from the series of General Information Books on individual ships, such as the *Arizona*. The detailed cross-sections of ships as reconstructed are based on drawings filed with the battleship history in FRC; the exception is the *Utah*, based on a drawing in her booklet of general plans.

Chapter 11

This chapter was based on design books in FRC RG 19 Entry 6114, including one on the U.S. evaluation of the *Nelson* design. The first attempts at developing a treaty battleship based on the *South Dakota* were taken from design books in NNMO RG 19 Entry 449, however. The basic 1928 and 1931 Characteristics were taken from General Board Hearings, and some material was included in NHC 420-6. The Preliminary Design compilation of designs included some of the summary charts of alternatives produced during this period. NNMO RG 80 included the gun evaluation of 1926; some similar data was to be found in NHC 430. Finally, the sketch of the 1933 battle cruiser design was taken from RG 19 Entry 8995.

Chapter 12

Sketches of the alternative designs leading to the *North Carolina* were taken from 420-6 papers in NHC. The Battleship Board papers are in RG 80 General Correspondence files, BB 55&56/S1-4. Material on vibration problems was taken from RG 80 correspondence and from material held with the design history at FRC. The British evaluation of the *North Carolina* design was taken from a DNC Department paper on U.S. Warship design, ADM 1/15578, in the Public Record Office, Kew. Basic material on the *North Carolina* design was found in FRC RG 19 Entry 6114. As for the *Kongos*, as late as 1944-45 the standard U.S. reference manual on Japanese warships, ONI 222-J, listed their speed as 27 knots, with a note that it might be 30 knots with a radius of 9,000nm (which were the correct figures).

Chapter 13

This chapter is based on General Board hearings, primarily for 1937, on NHC 420-6 papers (which include the sketch design and the cross-section of the original design), and on the design book, in FRC RG 19 Entry 6114. Except for the *Montana*, the comparative structural cross-sections in this chapter are based on drawings provided to the author by NavSea in November 1974. They appear to have been consecutive pages in a book of structural cross-sections showing all U.S. warships of the World War Two or early postwar period. The *Montana* cross-section is based on her contract plans. The information on the speed of the Japanese battleship *Nagato* was taken from a 1952 oral history of the U.S. prewar naval signals intelligence program, by Captain W. P. Safford, now declassified and held by the Modern Military division of the National Archives (NNMM).

Chapter 14

The design book of the *Iowa* class, in FRC RG 19 Entry 6114, was the basis of this chapter, supplemented by General Board Hearings (particularly for 1938), and by the general correspondence of C&R and of the secretary of the navy for the period before 1941. Wartime changes were taken from a variety of sources, including the reports of changes to the BuOrd Armament Summary. The evaluation of the *Iowa* design was taken from the report of the Comstock Board, November 1945, held by NHC. For pre-1945 information on the *Yamatos*, I relied on ONI 222-J, the reference manual on the Japanese Navy, for 1942, 1944, and 1945; it was supplemented by a British analysis of Japanese naval shipbuilding compiled in 1938–40 and held by PRO (ADM 116/5757).

Chapter 15

This chapter is based, first, on design books in FRC RG19 Entry 6114, on the FRC battleship design history, and also on General Board hearings and on the General Board 420-6 files for 1940-42. Data on the British 1945 battleship design were taken from the report of the committee considering the design of the proposed post-World War II British battleship, ADM 1/17251, in the Public Record Office, Kew. Further details of the ship are contained in a "cover" which has not yet been released, but which should ultimately be held by NMM.

Chapter 16

The account of *Idaho's* "firing to exhaustion" is taken from a BuShips report by P. W. Snyder, in current Preliminary Design files; it was made available by P. J. Sims. Most of this chapter is based on BB/L9-3 (modification) files in the wartime BuShips correspondence files, supplemented by the CominCh/CNO files and, to a lesser extent, the General Board (NHC) 420-6 files. NHC held a sketch of the original reconstruction plan of the *California*, with tripod masts, but it could not be found at the time drawings for this book had to be executed.

Chapter 17

The account of early reconstruction plans is based on material in General Board files. Accounts of later planned reconstructions were taken from Code 440 files and from Preliminary Design files. For a very full account of the latest modernization of the *New Jersey*, see P. J. Sims, J. F. Edwards, Sr., LCdr. R. L. Dickey, and H. S. Shull, "Design of Modernized Battleships and Cruisers," in *Naval Engineers Journal*, May 1984, pp. 25 ff. Although several postwar BuShips files listed BBG designs among their contents, no such design calculations were found.

Appendix A

The material on the planned coast defense craft of 1885 is taken from the Endicott Report itself, a copy of which has survived in the Army Library in Washington. It includes body plans of some of the proposed craft. For the political background to the monitor "reconstructions," I have used Leonard A. Swann, Jr., *John Roach, Maritime Entrepreneur: The Years as Naval Constructor, 1862–1886* (Annapolis, Md.: U.S. Naval Institute, 1965). Actual data, however, have been taken from notebooks in RG 19 Entry 447 and from the annual reports of the secretary of the navy. The modifications to the 1898 monitor design were taken from the records of the Board on Construction, and the 1917 designs from the Preliminary Design files, RG 19 Entry 449. Notes on the Civil War monitors were taken from standard published sources, most notably the official *Dictionary of U.S. Naval Fighting Ships*.

Appendix B

This appendix is based on a combination of official reports filed soon after the Pearl Harbor attack, on the BuShips

War Damage Reports for the *California* and *Nevada*, and on the 31 October 1944 report on the *Arizona* written by Code 524. It appears that no overall report on damage at Pearl Harbor was written; at least, no such report has come to light. No formal War Damage Reports were submitted for the *Arizona*, *Oklahoma*, or *West Virginia*. This material is all held by NHC; I am grateful to Dr. Thomas Hone, now of the National War College, for having made copies available to me. Accounts of damage to the *Maryland* and *Pennsylvania* in 1944 and 1945 are taken from the war damage reports submitted by those ships, both at the time of damage and after they had been inspected in drydock. In neither case was a formal BuShips War Damage Report written.

Index

NOTE: design history for a *class* is generally given under the entry for the *name ship* of the class, for example, the entries for *Indiana* (BB 1) include entries for the class of that name.

The Naval Institute Press is the book-publishing arm of the U.S. Naval Institute, a private, nonprofit professional society for members of the sea services and civilians who share an interest in naval and maritime affairs. Established in 1873 at the U.S. Naval Academy in Annapolis, Maryland, where its offices remain today, the Naval Institute has more than 100,000 members worldwide.

Members of the Naval Institute receive the influential monthly naval magazine *Proceedings* and substantial discounts on fine nautical prints, ship and aircraft photos, and subscriptions to the Institute's recently inaugurated quarterly, *Naval History*. They also have access to the transcripts of the Institute's Oral History Program and may attend any of the Institute-sponsored seminars regularly offered around the country.

The book-publishing program, begun in 1898 with basic guides to naval practices, has broadened its scope in recent years to include books of more general interest. Now the Naval Institute Press publishes more than forty new titles each year, ranging from how-to books on boating and navigation to battle histories, biographies, ship guides, and novels. Institute members receive discounts on the Press's more than 300 books.

For a free catalog describing books currently available and for further information about U.S. Naval Institute membership, please write to:

Membership Department
U.S. Naval Institute
Annapolis, Maryland 21402

or call, toll-free, 800-233-USNI.